D-DAY
THEN AND NOW

Volume 2

People of Western Europe. A landing was made this morning on the coast of France by troops of the Allied Expeditionary Force. This landing is part of the concerted United Nations plan for the liberation of Europe, made in conjunction with our great Russian Allies.

GENERAL DWIGHT D. EISENHOWER
Supreme Commander,
Allied Expeditionary Force

LCIL 299

D-DAY

THEN AND NOW

Volume 2

Credits

© *After The Battle* 1995
ISBN: 0 900913 89 4
Printed in Great Britain
Edited and designed by Winston G. Ramsey

PUBLISHERS
Battle of Britain Prints International Ltd,
Church House, Church Street, London E15 3JA
An *After the Battle* publication

PRINTERS
Plaistow Press Limited,
Church House, Church Street, London E15 3JA

FRONT COVER
The scene at 8.45 a.m. on the morning of D-Day at the junction of White and Red Beaches in Queen Sector with Jimmy Leask of No. 84 Field Squadron, Royal Engineers, in the foreground (see page 525). From a painting by George A. Campbell.

REAR COVER
Arromanches after the battle. Supplies for the battle to liberate Europe are unloaded on the beach as French children resume their playful activities. (Imperial War Museum)

FRONTISPIECE
The Stormont, Dundas and Glengarry Highlanders come ashore on White Beach, Nan Sector at Bernières-sur-Mer. Although this shot is often used to illustrate the assault, Gilbert Milne's picture shows the reserve 9th Brigade landing on the afternoon of D-Day. (Canadian National Archives)

FRONT ENDPAPER
'The invasion has begun.' The panorama of awesome seaborne might viewed from a German artillery position on Omaha. (US Signal Corps)

REAR ENDPAPER
Crossed rifles in the sand — a soldier's tribute to a fallen comrade. The German defences were breached, and a foothold established in France, but of the estimated 2,500 killed on D-Day, nearly half were suffered on Omaha. (US Signal Corps)

EXTRACTS
Acknowledgement is given to the following authors and their publishers for permission to quote from published works:

'DIE INVASION HAT BEGONNEN' from *The Fatal Decisions* published by Michael Joseph, London, 1956.
OMAHA AND UTAH AREAS from *A Soldier's Story* by Omar Bradley published by Henry Holt, 1951, reprinted by permission of the William Morris Agency Inc. on behalf of the author.
GOLD AREA from *Call to Arms* by General Sir Harold Pyman published by Leo Cooper Ltd, 1971.
JUNO AREA from *The Victory Campaign*, Volume III of the Official History of the Canadian Army in the Second World War published by The Queen's Printer and Controller of Stationery, Ottawa, 1960, extracted by permission of Canada Communications Group Publications, Ottawa.
SWORD AREA from *Victory in Normandy* by Major-General David Belchem published by Chatto & Windus, 1981, and *All in the Day's March* by the same author published by Harper Collins, 1978.
GOOSEBERRY AND MULBERRY from the War Office monograph *The Story of the Mulberries* by Rear-Admiral H. Hickling, 1947.
AIRFIELD CONSTRUCTION from the Fourth Supplement to *The London Gazette* published by HMSO on December 31, 1946.
The Editor is indebted to Major-General C. A. Ramsay, CB, OBE, for granting permission to include extracts from his father's diary for 1944 published as *The Year of D-Day* by the University of Hull Press, 1994. Also to Brigadier General S. L. A. Marshall and his publishers Little, Brown & Co. for the extract from *Night Drop* on pages 344-349.

ACKNOWLEDGEMENTS
The Editor is indebted to many individuals and organisations for their assistance:

Paul Almasy; R. R. Aspinall, The Museum of London; P. Aufenast, University of London; Roger Bell; Pam Bendall, College Librarian, Staff College, Camberley; Maria Blyzinsky, National Maritime Museum; Colonel J. B. Boileau, Canadian Defence Liaison Staff; Phillip N. Bradley; David Buxton; Steve Casely; Peter Chamberlain; Terry Charman, Imperial War Museum; Lieutenant-Colonel M-J. P. Chilcott; M. M. Chrimes, Librarian, The Institution of Civil Engineers; Fabrice Corbin, Musée du Mur de l'Atlantiqe, Ouistreham; John Cortvriendt; Major R. K. Cross; Patrick Cully, US Defense Enquiry Office; S/Sgt. Anthony S. Davis, USAF; Brian L. Davis; S. Dawson, Royal Engineers Library; Stephen F. Dent; Gerard M. Devlin; Harrie Dijkhuizen; Thomas Dunstall; James W. Eikner; Andy Flanagan; David Fletcher, The Tank Museum, Bovington; Dick Foreman; Roger Freeman; Ray Funnel, RAF Museum, Hendon; Frank Gillard; Michael Ginns; Cathy Goodwin, Clifton College, Bristol; David Green; Squadron Leader A. I. Le Gresley; A. G. Gueymard; David O. Hale; T. M. Hancock; Douglas Harper; Guy Hartcup; Max Hastings, *The Daily Telegraph*; Robin Hastings; Major Winfried Heinemann, Militärgeschichtliches Forschungsamt, Freiburg; Jan Heitmann; Jan Hey; Hans Houterman; Gillian Hughes; Ken Johnson; Seimon Pugh Jones; Paul Kemp, Imperial War Museum; Bill King; Brad King, Imperial War Museum; Norman Kirby; Lyn Kukral, United States Navy and Marine Corps WWII Commemorative Committee; the late Mari Laurent; George Laws; D. Leavy; Peter G. de Lotz; Lieutenant-Colonel E. T. Lummis; Herr von Lutzau, Volksbund Deutsche Kriegsgräberfürsorge; D. McCabe, Ohio University; Lieutenant-Colonel N. D. McIntosh; Alistair Macdonald; John Major, The University of Hull; Armand Martin, Musée de la Guerre des Ondes, Tourcoing; Herr Meyer, Bundesarchiv, Freiburg; Hubert Meyer; Lieutenant-Colonel Terence Miller; J. P. A. Mullinger; Barry Murphy, Commonwealth War Graves Commission; Gabrielle Nishiguchi, Directorate of History, Ottawa; Michael Ockenden; Bernard Paich, Heimdal; Flying Officer R. Patounas, RAF; Rear Admiral Thomas J. Patterson; Richard Ponman, Cabinet Office, Historical Section; Alan Potts; Philip Powell, Imperial War Museum; Brana Radovic; Clive Richards, RAF Museum; Professor R. H. Roy, University of Victoria, Canada; Margaret Rudder; William E. Ryan, The American Battle Monuments Commission; Hans Sakkers; P. A. Sanderson Esq, EODTIC; Derek R. Sansom, Ford Motor Company; Andy Saunders; Lieutenant-Colonel Chris Sexton; Lieutenant Ike Skelton, US Navy; Don Skinner; Neil Somerville, BBC Written Archives Centre; Mark Smith; Neil Stevens, Wilts & Berks ETO Research Group; Kathleen A. Struss, Dwight D. Eisenhower Library; Denis Sweeting; Stephen Sykes; Michael J. Teevens; R. D. Tennant; Peter Thompson; Father Gerard Thuring, Groesbeek Liberation Museum; Alan Tomkins; Michel De Trez; Bart Vanderveeen; Jean-Bernard Valognes; Henri Vasselin; Robert Voskuil; Bill Walker, *Stars & Stripes*; Trevor White, BBC Written Archives Centre; Henry Wills; Michael J. Winey, US Army Military History Institute; Marion Wollaston, Port of Tilbury Ltd.

PHOTOGRAPHS
Copyright is indicated for all original illustrations where known. Present-day photographs are the copyright of *After the Battle* magazine unless otherwise stated.

Agence France Presse: 640.
Paul Almasy: 687 top, 688 bottom right, 696 top.
Apex Photo Agency: 647 bottom right.
Associated News: 617 top left.
Associated Press: 624 bottom right, 645 bottom right, 672 top left, 675 top left, 679 bottom right.
Major General R. O. Barton: 382 middle left.
BBC: 569 bottom right, 637 middle.
Bundesarchiv: 318 top left, 459 middle, 460 top, middle right, 498 top left, 551 top right, 558 top, 570 top left and right, 574 bottom, 575 top left, top right.
Dave Burges: 654 top.
Canadian Defence Liaison Staff: 657 top, bottom left, bottom right.
Canadian Historical Research Section: 453 top.
Canadian National Archives: 452 top right, bottom left, 469 top left, 472 top left, 475 top left, top right, 479 top left, middle right, 481 top left, middle left, 485 middle right, 486 top right, middle, 487 top, middle right, 489 middle right, 490 top left, bottom right, 491 top, bottom, 492 top left, middle right, 493 top, middle right, 496 middle, 497 top left, bottom, 564 bottom, 566 bottom right, 567 middle left, 571 top, 603 bottom right, 629 middle, 692 top.
***Collier's*:** 333 bottom left, middle right, 334 top left.
Commonwealth War Graves Commission: 693 top left, top right.
John A. Cook: 700 top right, middle, bottom left, bottom right.
Cornelius Ryan Collection, Alden Library, Ohio University, Athens, Ohio: 350, 351, 628 below left and right.
CS (Photography): 638 bottom, 639 bottom, 641 middle, 642 top right, 659 top, middle left, bottom, 660 top, middle left, middle right, bottom, 662 top, bottom, 664 middle, 666 top, middle, bottom, 669 bottom left, bottom right, 671 top right, 672 bottom left, 673 top right, middle, bottom right, 676 top, middle right, bottom right, 677 top, middle right, bottom left, 678 top left, top right, middle, bottom left, bottom right, 684 top, middle, bottom left, bottom right, 685 middle, bottom.
Daily Express: 672 bottom right.
Daily Telegraph: 416 top.
Roger Day: 648 top right.
John Dibbs: 669 top.
Dorset News Agency: 653 middle, bottom.
Dwight D. Eisenhower Library: 622 top, bottom, 623 top left, middle, bottom right, 703 bottom, 705.
ECP Armées, Paris: 397 top left, 399 bottom left, 415 top, 456 left, 457 left, 458 top, 584 bottom right, 625 top, 638 top, 639 top, 685 top.
Editions Heimdal (*39-45 Magazine*): 563 right.
Elsevers Magazine: 689 top.
***Evening Gazette,* Middlesborough:** 450 bottom right.
Richard Foreman: 670 top.
Tonie and Valmai Holt: 686 bottom right, 687 bottom right, 699 top right, middle left.
HQ 1st Division, BAOR: 466 middle.
IGN, Paris: 338 bottom right, 339 bottom, 340 bottom, 378 bottom, 402 top right, 403 top left, 420 bottom, 427 middle, 463 top, 474 bottom left, 482 bottom, 522 bottom, 523 bottom, 555 bottom, 562 bottom right, 573 bottom left, 636 bottom.
Imperial War Museum: 404 top, middle right, 405 top, bottom left, 412 top, 414 top left, 417 top right, 418 top right, bottom left, bottom right, 423 top, 432 bottom right, 435 top, 441 bottom left, 442 top left, top right, 446 top, 447 top, 448 top right, 451 top right, bottom left, 467 top, 470 top, middle right, 471 top left, top right, 472 middle, 480 top left, middle right, 481 bottom left, 489 top, 504 top, 505 top left, top right, middle right, 507 bottom, 508 top, 509 top right, middle, 510 top, 511 top right, 512 top left, bottom, 513 top left, top right, 514 top left, middle right, 515 top, 516 top, 519 bottom left, 521 top, bottom, 524 top, middle right, 525 top, 526 bottom, 527 top, middle right, 528 top, bottom, 530 top, middle left, 531 top left, 532 top, 534 top right, middle, bottom left, 535 top left, middle left, bottom left, 536 top, bottom left, 537 bottom right, 538 top, 539 bottom, 540 middle, 541 top right, 542 middle, bottom left, 543 top right, middle, 544 top left, middle, 545 top left, middle left, bottom left, 548 top left, 552 top right, 553 top left, bottom left, 556 top left, middle right, 557 top left, middle left, 559 top left, middle right, bottom right, 560 top right, middle, 561 top left, 566 top right, 571 bottom left, 576 bottom left, 577 bottom right, 578 top left, top right, bottom right, 582 bottom, 587 top, bottom, 588 top, 589 bottom, 590 top, bottom right, 591 top, bottom, 595 middle right, 596 top left, middle, bottom left, 597 top left, middle right, bottom left, 601 top, 602 top, bottom left, 603 top left, bottom left, 604 top right, 605 top, 632 top right, 688 top.
J. H. Jellett: 594 top, bottom, 595 top.
Jersey Evening Post: 631 top right.
Seimon Pugh Jones: 681 all, 682 all, 683 all.
Keele University: 440 middle, 551 bottom, 448 middle.
Squadron Leader P. Lamboit: 436 middle.
George Laws: 629 bottom.
Squadron Leader A. I. Le Gresley: 680 middle left, middle right, bottom.
Eric Lummis: 680 top right.
Mail on Sunday: 667 top.
J. P. A. Mullinger: 673 top left.
Musée du Mur de l'Atlantique: 546 top, centre.
National Maritime Museum: 570 bottom right.
National Trust for Scotland: 404 bottom right.
Ordnance Survey: 659 right.
M. Parsons: 624 top left.
Planet News: 346 top, bottom.
Planwork Ltd: 650 top left, top right.
Portsmouth City Council: 661 top left, top right, bottom.
Press Association: 645 top, 671 bottom.
Public Record Office: 325 bottom, 436 top.
RAF Chivenor: 667 bottom.
Robert Rieske: 350 middle and bottom, 351 top.
Royal Navy Submarine Museum: 462 bottom.
Service Historique de la Marine: 402 bottom left.
79th Armoured Division History: 423 bottom left, 424 top right, middle, 426 top right, bottom left, 434 top, 468 top, 492 bottom left, 503 top, 567 top right.
Brian Smith: 646 top left.
Mark Smith: 689 bottom left.
Southampton Docks Board Collection: 618 top.
Stars & Stripes: 334 bottom, 672 top right, 675 top right, bottom right.
Dennis Sweeting: 613 middle right, bottom left and right.
Stephen Sykes: 517 top, 529 top right, middle, bottom right, 547 top right, middle left, bottom left, 572 top, bottom.
Airman First Class Kevin Thomsen: 658 top left, top right, 670 middle, bottom.
US Air Force: 326 top, 327 top left. top right, bottom right, 337 bottom left, 342 top, 355 bottom, 381 middle right, 430 top, bottom, 431 middle, 433 top, bottom right, 436 bottom right, 467 bottom right, 468 bottom, 469 bottom, 484 top, 485 top, 532 bottom, 537 top, 580 top, 585 bottom.
US Army: 387 top right, 579 top right, 612 top left, bottom right.
US Army Military History Institute: 378 top right.
US Coast Guard: 322 bottom, 323 bottom left, bottom right, 343 top, 361 top right, 375 middle right, 401 top right.
US Navy: 321 top, bottom right, 322 top left, 331 top right. middle left, middle right, 336 top left, middle left, 350 top right, bottom, 351 top, middle right, 355 top, 357 top left, 358 bottom, 360 top left, 362 top, 363 top, bottom left, 371 top left, 373 bottom left, 383 top, bottom left, 385 top, 386 top left, top right, bottom right, 387 bottom right, 388 middle right, 389 top, middle right, 390 bottom left, 392 bottom left, 569 top, 598 bottom, 608 top.
US Signal Corps: 316 bottom right, 319 bottom, 320 top, bottom left, 328 top, 329 top left, 330 top left, top right, 332 top right, 333 top left, 335 top, 337 top left, 338 top right, middle left, 339 middle left, 347 top left, top right, bottom left, bottom right, 348 top, 349 middle, 354 top, bottom, 359 top, 361 middle, 363 middle right, 364 bottom, 366 top right, bottom left, 367 top, 368 top, bottom left, 369 top, 370 top, 372 bottom left, 373 middle left, 374 top, 375 top, 377 middle right, 380 top, 382 top, 384 top left, middle, bottom right, 387 middle, 388 top, 389 bottom left, 390 top left, 393 top, bottom left, 394 top left, middle, 395 top, 396 top, 397 top right, bottom left, 400 top left, 404 bottom left, 406 middle right, 407 top, 408 top right, middle, 592 top, bottom, 593 top, 598 top, 599 top right, middle right, bottom, 600 top, 609 middle right, 611 top, bottom, 616 top, bottom 629 top left, 630 top, bottom left, bottom right, 675 bottom left, 690 top, bottom right, 691 top, middle, 694 bottom right.
USS *George Washington*: 668 top, bottom right, 674 middle, bottom.
US War Department: 330 bottom right, 340 top, 343 bottom, 357 middle left, bottom left, bottom right, 358 top, middle right, 360 middle, 364 top right, 366 top left, 367 middle, 369 middle, 370 bottom left, 371 middle, 372 top, 375 bottom, 376 bottom right, 381 top, bottom, 390 top right, 399 top, 400 bottom, 401 bottom, 403 bottom right, 406 top.
Volksbund Deutsche Kriegsgräberfürsorge: 695 top right, bottom.
Henry Wills: 648 bottom, 650 middle, bottom right, 651 top left, top right.

Contents

Volume 1

Volume 2

'Die Invasion hat begonnen!'

By Oberst Bodo Zimmermann
ERSTER STABSOFFIZIER, OBERBEFEHLSHABER WEST

At about a quarter-past nine in the evening of June 5, I was in our officers' mess at St Germain when the chief intelligence officer on the staff of OB West came to look for me. He was in a state of high excitement, for his people had just decoded a British wireless message. It was the habit of the Allies to communicate with their many agents in the West by radio, and, not infrequently, our experts succeeded in decoding these apparently harmless signals. This, however, was a signal of a very different type, for it ordered the mobilisation of the entire French resistance movement for the coming night. This could have only one meaning: the invasion was about to begin.

Needless to say we had made detailed arrangements, which were immediately and automatically put into force. Von Rundstedt and his Chief-of-Staff, Generalleutnant Günther Blumentritt, were informed, as was Rommel's headquarters. Rommel himself was on his way back from Germany [he had an appointment to see Hitler], and was not expected to arrive before the following afternoon. The orders for a general alert were sent out, though many of the senior officers of the 7. Armee could not be reached personally, since they were in their cars returning from Rennes to their respective units. OKW in Germany was informed of the decoded signal and of the measures taken.

All this was done quite quickly. And then, for a time, nothing more happened. Midnight passed, one o'clock, and still no further messages reached St Germain. At about two o'clock we were ready to believe that it was just another false alarm when Heeresgruppe B rang through, reporting parachute landings in Normandy shortly after midnight. These parachutists were being supported by glider-borne troops and it became apparent almost at once that there were three large-scale landings taking place: two on the Cotentin peninsula, northwest and west of Carentan, the third just east of the Orne. Heeresgruppe B informed us that the necessary countermeasures were being taken and that

Top: **June 6, 1940 — Hitler plans the next move in his campaign on the Western Front with Generaloberst von Brauchitsch, chief of the OKH, at Führerhauptquartier 'Wolfsschlucht' in southern Belgium. Four years later, Hitler was caught napping — literally — when the invasion of France took place as he slept in his bedroom *(left)* at the Berghof on Obersalzberg. However, contrary to some popular accounts, Hitler was up at 9 a.m. — early for him — as he had to attend a conference at Klessheim castle near Salzburg, an hour's drive away. *Right:* It was ironic that the first American unit to land in France — the 101st Airborne — was also the one to capture Hitler's mountain retreat eleven months later. These Screaming Eagles are passing the ruins of the telephone exchange through which the first news of the invasion would have reached the Berghof.**

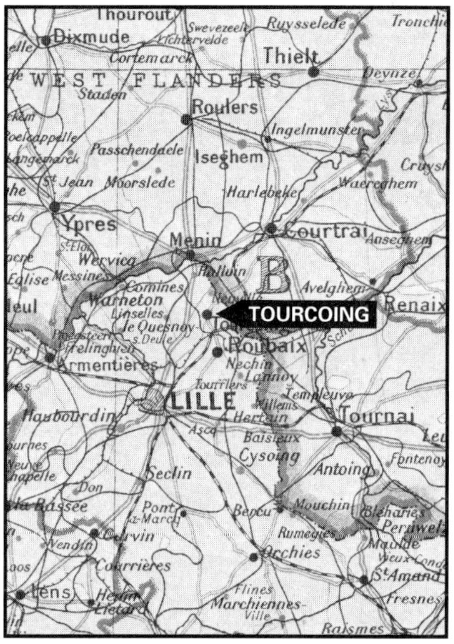

An important part of the SHAEF invasion plan was to call the French resistance into action on the night before D-Day to cut telephone wires, disrupt communications, and carry out general guerrilla sabotage. The innocent-sounding messages to each Maquis 'circuit' were to be transmitted by the BBC, the first part of each message warning the groups to stand by being put out on June 1, to be followed by a second part triggering action. However, several months earlier, the Germans had arrested the wireless operator for the 'Butler' circuit, putting in place their own operator to maintain contact with London. One particular pair of messages that the Germans either discovered or were sent by SOE comprised two halves of the first verse of *Chanson d'Automne* by Paul Verlaine. The Germans misunderstood their true meaning and thought that when they were broadcast they would signal a general call to railway resistance forces all over France. In fact, the message had been transferred by SOE to action the railway cutting teams of the 'Ventriloquist' circuit but, either way, the effect was the same. The intelligence section of 15. Armee under Oberstleutnant Hellmuth Meyer had its radio interception centre in Tourcoing in northern France. Originally, it was at Nos. 37-39 Avenue de la Marne where the intercept operators had recorded many messages sent by the BBC to the resistance.

heavy fighting was already developing. Incidentally, though Heeresgruppe B did not know this at the time, the unsuspecting commander of our 91. Luftlande-Division, Generalleutnant Wilhelm Falley, returning from Rennes, had driven straight into one of these air landing areas and was killed instantly. During the course of the night, the troops were identified. They were the American 82nd and 101st and the British 6th Airborne Divisions.

VON RUNDSTEDT'S FIRST REACTION

Though it was quite impossible at this early stage to say whether or not the Allies intended also to attack elsewhere, it was obvious that they must support their airborne divisions by seaborne landings almost immediately, since otherwise their most valuable parachute and glider troops would

CHANSON D'AUTOMNE

Les sanglots longs
Des violons
De l'automne
Blessent mon cœur
D'une langueur
Monotone.

Tout suffoquant
Et blême quand
Sonne l'heure,
Je me souviens
Des jours anciens
Et je pleure;

Et je m'en vais
Au vent mauvais
Qui m'emporte,
De çà, de là,
Pareil à la
Feuille morte.

Paul Verlaine
1844-1896

By June 1944, the interception centre had moved to Generaloberst von Salmuth's new HQ bunker further along the street. In September 1991 it was opened as a museum.

Having already intercepted the first three lines of the poem: 'Les sanglots longs des violons de l'automne' (The long sobs of the violins of autumn), the second, slightly misquoted, part 'Blessent mon cœur d'une longs monotone' (Soothe my heart with monotonous languor) was picked up at 9.15 p.m. on June 5. Information collected by them had led the Intelligence Section to accept this message as meaning that the invasion would begin within the next 48 hours. Von Salmuth *(left)* accepted the evidence and, at 10.33 p.m., 15. Armee transmitted the code-word for the pre-alert stage to all units under its command. *Right:* The General's office preserved today.

inevitably be cut to pieces. We could therefore expect the seaborne landings at first light and, to judge by the dropping areas of the airborne divisions, the assault was likely to come between the Orne and St Vaast-la-Hougue.

Whether this was the main operation or only a preliminary to another landing elsewhere along the coast could not, of course, be known at this stage. Von Rundstedt, however, was of the opinion that if the Allies succeeded in establishing a firm beach-head, they would make this their point of main effort. It was therefore essential that their invading troops be defeated while there was yet time.

There were two panzer divisions in the West which were technically under command of the OKW, not of OB West, and were officially described as OKW reserve. These were the 12. SS-Panzer-Division 'Hitlerjugend', in western France, and the formidable Panzer-Lehr-Division, stationed southwest of Paris. Without waiting for the approval of the OKW, von Rundstedt now put these two divisions under command of Heeresgruppe B and ordered them to march towards Caen. He also activated the headquarters called Panzergruppe West, commanded by General Leo Freiherr Geyr von Schweppenburg, which was the staff intended to fight the armoured battle which, it was hoped, would result in the expulsion of the British and American forces from the Continent as soon as they had landed.

EARLY HOURS

Towards six o'clock on the morning of June 6, the OB West received two important messages. The first was from the front. Under very heavy artillery and air cover, large Allied forces were attempting to land between the mouths of the Rivers Orne and Vire and also farther to the north, on the base of the Cotentin. The second, which came in a few minutes later, was from the OKW. In violent terms, von Rundstedt was upbraided for his orders to the two panzer divisions which, we were informed, should not have been moved

The message was passed to OB West at St Germain and to Heeresgruppe B at La Roche-Guyon, but the latter's commander was not even in France. Seizing the opportunity of the period of bad weather, when German forecasters felt that there was no immediate risk of invasion, Generalfeldmarschall Rommel had decided to make a quick trip to Germany. First, he planned to visit his home in Bavaria to celebrate his wife's 50th birthday which fell on Tuesday (June 6). Then, he planned to seek an audience with Hitler at the Berghof to try to persuade him to release to him some additional forces for Normandy.

Having stopped in Paris to buy a birthday present, Rommel left France on Sunday for Herrlingen, a small village just off the Stuttgart–Munich autobahn five miles west of Ulm. *Left:* Here Rommel and his wife Lucie (in the spotted dress) have been joined for a birthday photograph on the terrace overlooking the garden by their 15-year-old son Manfred (right), on temporary leave from his Flak unit, Rommel's sister Helene (far left), and a family friend, Hildegard Kirchheim. *Right:* Rommel's house still stands on Wippinger-Steige, having been purchased by the present owner, Dieter Keppler, in 1984.

Back at La Roche-Guyon on the evening of June 5, Rommel's Chief-of-Staff, Generalleutnant Speidel *(left)* had taken the opportunity of the absence of his boss to hold an informal drinks party for members of the anti-Hitler movement in the Paris area. This was still going on when the intelligence officer, Oberst Anton Staubwasser, rang some time after ten o'clock, reporting that he had received a call from Tourcoing to say that the second part of the code-poem had been received. Speidel advised Staubwasser to telephone von Rundstedt's HQ for advice and, although there is no written evidence or telephone log to confirm it, OB West is said to have rung back to say that Dollmann's 7. Armee was not to be alerted. Speidel's guests departed about midnight, and around 1 a.m. he went to bed. When, following reports of airborne landings, the 716. Infanterie-Division finally went on the alert at 1.10 a.m., 7. Armee was informed, and Generalmajor Max Pemsel, its Chief-of-Staff, telephoned Rommel's headquarters at 1.35 a.m. to awake Speidel and then put the army on alert at 1.40 a.m. At this point, a report came in from the 15. Armee sector of airborne landings further up the coast, and that dummy parachutists had been found. From then on, the night developed into a farce as Pemsel tried to convince Speidel that a major operation had been launched, but with Rommel's Chief-of-Staff maintaining in his calls to 7. Armee and OB West that it was a 'local attack' and that 'people are taking baled-out aircrews for paratroops'. By 3.50 a.m., General Blumentritt in Paris was acceding to Pemsel's view that 'the width of the sector under attack shows that this is no operation of purely local significance', and at 4.30 a.m. the 7. Armee Chief-of-Staff reported that his army's artillery had started shelling enemy warships. But still Speidel refused to act. 'Have any troops actually landed from the sea?' he asked Pemsel. At 6.15 a.m., Pemsel reported that naval bombardment of the shore had begun, yet, it was not until 7.30 a.m. that Speidel first telephoned Rommel to inform him, whereupon the latter cancelled his visit to see Hitler and began the long drive back to Normandy. He arrived back at La Roche-Guyon just after 9.30 p.m.

without the prior approval of the OKW: 'one cannot yet say for sure where the main invasion will come and, besides, Hitler has not yet decided'. Despite von Rundstedt's insistence that the landing was in full progress, the OKW remained adamant. The two panzer divisions were therefore halted.

Throughout the morning and early afternoon, I, the Chief-of-Staff, General Blumentritt, and von Rundstedt personally, repeatedly telephoned the OKW in order to find out what Hitler had decided in the matter of these two divisions. Apparently the Führer was asleep and no one dared wake him. It was not until his usual conference, between three and four o'clock that afternoon, that Hitler decided to allow the commitment of the divisions. They were immediately ordered to resume their advance.

By noon on June 6, it was clear that the enemy, making full use of his technical superiority, had succeeded in carrying out small landings — at ebb-tide, on account of our underwater obstacles — north of Caen, in the Bayeux area and apparently also in the neighbourhood of the Vire estuary. Farther to the north, in the area of Ste Mère-Eglise, other assaults were in progress but these had not yet gained a firm foothold on shore.

Our battle against the airborne forces which had landed inside the Cotentin seemed to be developing favourably, and the British 6th Airborne Division, east of the Orne, was keeping relatively quiet. The 21. Panzer-Division, Rommel's mobile reserve, should have attacked here at once, on its own initiative, but instead it awaited orders. When the division was at last sent in, in the course of the morning, it seemed more important to 7. Armee that it be used to clear up the beach-head north of Caen and to relieve our encircled strong points in that area, rather than to attack the 6th Airborne. This involved a crossing of the Orne which of course took time.

In the late afternoon, when the 21. Panzer-Division attacked the beach-head, its advance guard did, in fact, reach the coast and a few of our strong points were relieved. But at this moment, fresh British airborne forces landed immediately behind the attacking division, which therefore turned about and withdrew. It is fruitless to criticise this decision by the divisional commander: he was on the spot and had no choice but to follow his own judgement.

Omaha and Utah Areas

By Lieutenant General Omar N. Bradley

COMMANDING GENERAL, US FIRST ARMY

On December 23, 1943, Eisenhower radioed General Marshall from the Mediterranean recommending that I be named field commander on the 'Overlord' invasion and that Lieutenant General Jacob L. Devers, commander of the European Theater of Operations since May 1943, be sent south as second in command to General Sir Henry Maitland 'Jumbo' Wilson, Eisenhower's successor as Allied commander-in-chief in the Mediterranean. Eisenhower had presumably picked me for commander of the US army group primarily because he valued combat experience on so sensitive a high level of planning. The recommendation meant that I was not only to command the US 1st Army Group 'for planning purposes', but that I would also head it when Army Group eventually entered the line-up in France.

Command of the army group, however, was not to preclude my command of First Army in the Channel assault. Instead, I was to take First Army ashore as First Army commander and build it up on the beach-head. Once our US build-up had been expanded to a force the size of two armies, I was to relinquish command of the First and step up to Group in command of them both. Until then, I would wear two hats, one as commander of US First Army, the other as commander of US 1st Army Group.

In practice, this dual command was not as complex as it may sound, for neither headquarters overlapped the other. For one thing, First Army in Bristol and Army Group headquarters in London functioned as entirely separate establishments more than 100 miles apart. Furthermore, the command of all US invasion troops had been centered in First Army. At that time, Army Group existed simply as a planning headquarters. Despite the confusion it may have caused, there were many advantages to this dual system of command; it permitted excellent continuity between the Army and Army Group. First Army was to schedule its build-up for the first 14 days ashore; thereafter Army Group would phase in the reinforcements. And since Group would pick up where Army left off, it was evident that, with one man commanding them both, they could be linked together more securely.

Top: **US First Army headquarters was located in Bristol at Clifton College, one of Britain's renowned public schools.** *Centre:* **It was a fitting location to plan a military operation as one of its former pupils had been Douglas Haig — better known as Field-Marshal Earl Haig. His statue stood on the terrace overlooked by General Bradley's office in School House.** *Left:* **The Council Room: then staffed by First Army; now the Governors' meeting room** *(right).*

Left: **For June 6, General Bradley's headquarters was located aboard Admiral Kirk's flagship, the USS *Augusta* (see page 175) and this picture of the Admiral (left), his Chief-of-Staff, Rear Admiral Struble, and General Bradley on the bridge is said to have been taken on D-Day. However, for reasons that General Bradley explains, that is doubtful. 'As in the Sicily invasion, I was beset by a small but painful physical problem, this time in a different location. A monstrous boil arose on my nose. It was so painful I had to have it lanced in the infirmary. The Navy medic insisted that to prevent further infection I must wear a bandage for several days. I complied, lest this minor problem grow into a serious one that might incapacitate me. But I felt ridiculous with that big bandage on my nose — and told Chet Hansen to ban all photographers from taking my picture.'** *Right:* **Undoubtedly D-Day, this cine clip shows the General sporting both plaster and stars.**

It was 7.15 a.m. when I went down to breakfast at my quarters in Bristol on the morning of June 3. We had loitered late over dinner the night before, our last evening together in England. Today, we were to board Admiral Kirk's flagship for the invasion. D-Day had been set for June 5 and the warm summer sun that poured through the leaded-glass windows of the Holmes cheered us with the promise of good weather. Tubby Thorson, my G-3, was downing his third cup of coffee. 'Morning, General,' he called, 'how did you sleep with all that brand-new rank you've got?' Bob Wilson, my G-4, chuckled.

The day before I had been notified of my promotion to a brigadier general on the permanent list. The commission had been predated to September 1, 1943. Because my rank as a permanent colonel dated from October 1 of the same year, we were not yet certain as to whether I was going ahead or backward. Until the day before I had been a Sears Roebuck general; all three stars were temporary, good for 'the duration and six months'. Now, I was assured at least one permanent one in Arlington.

Most of the First Army headquarters had been evacuated from Bristol several days before to board the army command ship and two additional LSTs on the hards at Portland. The rear echelon was to remain in England until priorities slackened on lift. Because space was cramped aboard the *Augusta*, my command group had been trimmed to fit the bunk space allotted us. Besides Bill Kean, my Chief-of-Staff, it included 'Monk' Dickson, my G-2; Thorson; Wilson; a fifth officer from signals; five journal clerks and draftsmen. Courtney Hodges was to sail as deputy on the army command ship, *Achernar*. While Chester Hansen sailed with us aboard the *Augusta*, Lew Bridge, my other aide, was to remain in London and there frequent the nightspots. His disappearance from London, we feared, might alert the enemy agents.

We knew there were agents in London. In fact, several were permitted to operate under secret surveillance by the British, for they could be useful in sending deliberately-misleading reports to Berlin. Except for those under surveillance, however, few enemy agents were able to penetrate the security net that had been tightened around England in the spring of 1944. As D-Day approached, the net was pulled tighter and traffic was even halted to Ireland.

Shortly after 8 a.m., we turned south from Bristol across the Avon on the road to Plymouth where we were to rendezvous with Joe Collins of VII Corps. Hansen rode with an aluminum tube of Top Secret invasion maps between his knees. Kean and Dickson, Thorson and Wilson followed in a second sedan. It was a Saturday morning and we slowed down through the market at Taunton where British housewives had already formed their patient queues before the shops. Although the forward troop concentration areas (which, because of their peculiar oval shape on our maps, we referred to as 'sausages') were now packed with invasion troops, so quietly had the D-Day force been assembled that Taunton, like those other southern tier towns, remained blissfully unaware that 'The Day' was at hand.

This picture shows the scene on June 6 from the *Augusta* as she lay off the US beaches (see pages 112-113).

It is not generally appreciated that the US Coast Guard played an important part in the manning and operation of vessels for the invasion. Captain Alfred C. Richmond (extreme right) was the senior USCG officer in the European Theater, with offices alongside the US Navy in Grosvenor Square. This photo shows one of Richmond's publicity exercises when he brought to England the former heavyweight boxing champion, Jack Dempsey, who was a commander in the Coast Guard Reserve.

Collins was waiting at a road junction north of Plymouth. He sped us through the MP checkpoints to the quay where a barge from the *Augusta* was standing by. For the first time since Sicily, I buckled on a pistol and bent my neck under the weight of a steel helmet. I tossed my field pack with its greasy gas-protective coveralls to the deck and jumped aboard.

The *Augusta* waited offshore, a rakish beauty among the snub-nosed LSTs. Its curved yacht-like bow and 8-inch turrets pointed toward the Channel. Rear Admiral Alan G. Kirk, commander of the Western Naval Task Force, had gone ashore, but Rear Admiral A. D. Struble, his Chief-of-Staff, welcomed us aboard. I was assigned the skipper's cabin, the one occupied by President Roosevelt in 1941 when he joined Churchill off the Newfoundland shore to draft the Atlantic Charter.

The army war room had been constructed on the after-deck ordinarily used by the cruiser's spotter aircraft. It consisted of a temporary shed 10 feet by 20 feet whose sheet-metal walls were to pucker whenever the AA mount above it fired. The three overhead lights were caged and the face of the clock on the wall had been taped against concussion. The outer wall had been papered with a Michelin motoring map of France. Next to it hung a terrain study of the assault beaches, neatly bracketed into letter and color designations. Between them, a pretty pin-up girl lounged on a far more alluring beach. On the near wall, a detailed map of Normandy described in concentric arcs the ranges of enemy coastal guns. Still another charted the disposition of enemy divisions in blurred red markings. A long plotting table filled the center of the room. There, a naval lieutenant traced an overlay of the beach defenses. And on a waist-high shelf the length of the seaward wall stood a row of typewriters for the journal clerks.

Kirk and I had worked together once before on the Sicilian assault. As naval commander of the Western Task Force, he was again my opposite number. But my directives came from Montgomery, while his originated with Ramsay, the Allied naval commander-in-chief.

Kirk's fleet was divided into three forces. The first, Force 'O' for Omaha, was commanded by Rear Admiral John L. Hall, Jr, another old friend from the Sicilian invasion. The second, Force 'U' for Utah, sailed under the flag of Rear Admiral Don P. Moon. Hall was paired with Major General Leonard T. 'Gee' Gerow, commander of our V Corps, aboard the *Ancon*, command ship for V Corps; Moon shared the *Bayfield* with Collins' VII Corps. The third mounted a follow-up force, combat-loaded from the Bristol Channel. It contained the 2nd Division bound for Omaha Beach and the 90th Division for Utah.

During spring planning, Kirk and I had battled side by side in a strenuous effort to coax additional naval gun-fire support from Naval Operations in Washington, for originally the bombardment fleet assigned to the invasion looked woefully inadequate for its task. As late as April 1944, the US Navy could spare only two battleships, four cruisers, 12 destroyers, and a variety of small craft to support the American landing. We anticipated little resistance from the hit-and-run German Navy, but we were apprehensive over the coastal guns. Against those fixed shore batteries, I would gladly have swapped a

It was the USCG's pre-eminence for saving lives at sea that led to the establishment, just a few weeks before the invasion, of the Coast Guard Rescue Flotilla. Sixty of the service's 83-foot cutters, normally based on the Atlantic seaboard, were shipped to England on the decks of LSTs. Based at Poole in Dorset, the Flotilla (numbered USCG 1–60) was allocated fifty-fifty between the British and American beaches, and on D-Day alone effected 1,438 rescues.

dozen B-17s for each 12-inch gun I could wrangle. As in Sicily, the American deficit in naval support was to be made up by the British, but, because an American destroyer packed almost the fire-power of a British cruiser, while the American cruiser outgunned her British counterpart, I was anxious that our allotment in naval support be tallied in US ships.

Even at the risk of slowing down its timetable in the Pacific war, I begged the Navy to stack the odds more heavily on our side. Eventually, Washington agreed and Kirk's bombardment fleet was enlarged to four battleships (two of which were hold-overs from World War I), four cruisers, and 26 destroyers. It could not be called a formidable force in terms of Pacific naval campaigns, but at least our pinchpenny days were ended.

On the morning of June 6, we could be thankful that they were. Our forces on Omaha Beach *might* have held even without this additional fire support. But the first message to reach me from V Corps read: 'Thank God for the US Navy!'

Later that afternoon, I boarded a barge to visit Hodges and the First Army staff. They were headquartered aboard the *Achernar*, a converted cargo ship now draped with the antennae and radio mounts of a command ship.

Strings of LCTs were already chugging toward the outer harbor, dragging their barrage balloons behind them. In contrast to the somber, gray LSTs, the smaller craft had been daubed in spectacular camouflage paints. Now sealed aboard their cramped craft for the second day, the troops had wearily reconciled themselves to the ordeal of waiting. They stretched atop their heavily-laden trucks, to write letters, read, or simply doze in the afternoon sun that still brightened the windy harbor. Aboard a nearby LCT, the assault ramp had been lowered to the water's edge, and a dozen hardy soldiers were using it as a diving platform. On still another, the troops had relieved the monotony of waiting by washing. GI laundry hung from a line that had been strung between the aerials of two Sherman tanks.

That evening, Kirk asked if I would brief the correspondents aboard the *Augusta* on First Army's assault plans. Only three of them had been accredited to Kirk's staff. I first outlined the missions of the airborne and seaborne troops.

The Coast Guard also manned ten LSTs and 24 LCI(L)s, and had their own photographers aboard on D-Day.

These pictures were taken aboard 'Elsie' (as the LCIs were nicknamed) 326 of the Coast Guard LCI(L) Flotilla commanded by Captain Miles H. Imlay. Altogether, the USCG manned 97 vessels, not counting smaller craft carried aboard transports.

SECRET

The following message from the Supreme Commander will be read to troops by an officer after embarkation, if prior to 0001 hrs. D + 1, and only when no postponement of the operation is likely; alternatively, when briefing prior to embarkation after 0001 hrs. D + 1.

" You are soon to be engaged in a great undertaking—the invasion of Europe. Our purpose is to bring about, in company with our Allies, and our comrades on other fronts, the total defeat of Germany Only by such a complete victory can we free ourselves and our homelands from the fear and threat of the Nazi tyranny.

" A further element of our mission is the liberation of those people of Western Europe now suffering under German oppression.

" Before embarking on this operation, I have a personal message for you as to your own individual responsibility, in relation to the inhabitants of our Allied countries.

" As a representative of your country, you will be welcomed with deep gratitude by the liberated peoples, who for years have longed for this deliverance. It is of the utmost importance that this feeling of friendliness and goodwill be in no way impaired by careless or indifferent behaviour on your part. By a courteous and considerate demeanour, you can on the other hand do much to strengthen that feeling.

" The inhabitants of Nazi-occupied Europe have suffered great privations, and you will find that many of them lack even the barest necessities. You, on the other hand, have been, and will continue to be, provided adequate food, clothing and other necessities. You must not deplete the already meagre local stocks of food and other supplies by indiscriminate buying, thereby fostering the 'Black Market,' which can only increase the hardship of the inhabitants.

" The rights of individuals, as to their persons and property, must be scrupulously respected, as though in your own country. You must remember, always, that these people are our friends and Allies.

" I urge each of you to bear constantly in mind that by your actions not only you as an individual, but your country as well, will be judged. By establishing a relationship with the liberated peoples, based on mutual understanding and respect, we shall enlist their wholehearted assistance in the defeat of our common enemy. Thus shall we lay the foundations for a lasting peace, without which our great effort will have been in vain."

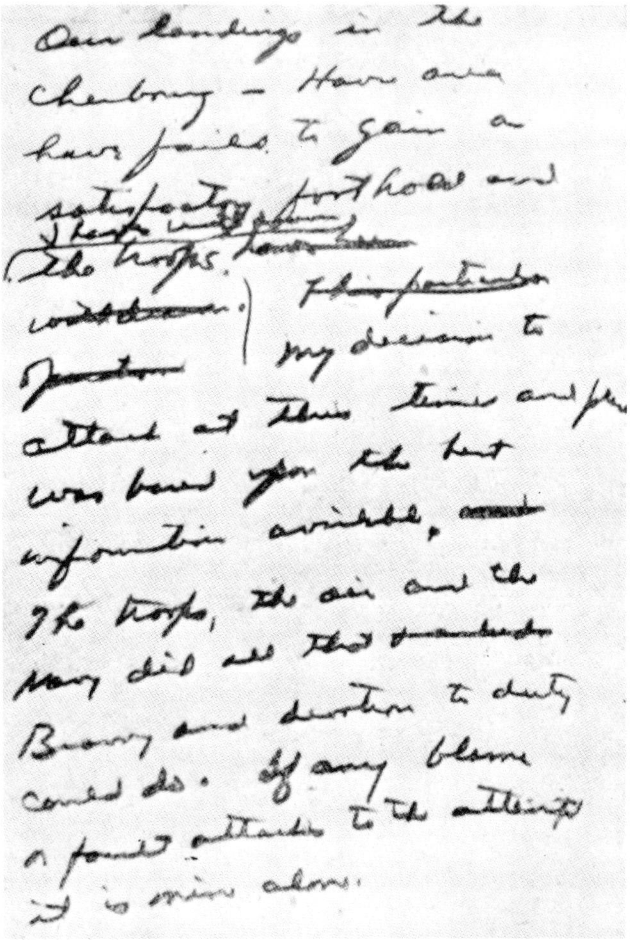

While General Bradley was briefing journalists aboard the *Augusta* on Saturday evening, Eisenhower was debating the worsening weather situation at Southwick (see page 162). His official briefing *(left)* had already been distributed to all commanding officers to be read out to all troops; privately, however, Eisenhower prepared for the worst eventuality that the landings might not succeed and he roughed out a communiqué accepting full responsibility for the failure *(right)*. He kept the draft in his wallet and forgot about it until he found it several weeks later and gave it to Commander Butcher.

'To help the amphibious get elements ashore,' I said, 'we're going to soften up each of the beaches with an 800-ton carpet bombing. Ten minutes before the first wave touches down, we'll drench Omaha with 8,000 rockets, put another 5,000 on Utah. These rockets should tear up his wire, detonate his mines, and drive him under cover the instant before we land.' I pointed to the detailed beach map. 'Then promptly at H-Hour we'll swim 64 tanks ashore . . . '

'Swim them ashore?' someone asked.

'They're DD tanks', I explained, forgetting for the moment how closely we had guarded this secret.

One of Kirk's correspondents nodded toward the map where the words *Festung Cherbourg* had been heavily ringed by a red crayon.

'How soon do you expect to take Cherbourg?' he asked.

'I'm going to have to stick my neck out', I told him. 'But as of this moment, I'd gladly sell out for D+15 — yes, or even D+20. The D+8 estimate you see here on the map is probably much better than we can do.'

I pointed toward a map on the wall. 'You've got to remember that just as soon as we land, this business becomes primarily a business of build-up. For you can almost always force an invasion — but you can't always make it stick.

'We're going to face three critical periods in this invasion. The first will come in getting ashore. It'll be difficult — but we're not especially worried about that part of it. The second may come on the sixth or seventh day when the other fellow gets together enough reinforcements for a counter-offensive. This counter-attack will probably give us our greatest trouble. Then, once we hurdle the counter-attack, our third critical period will come when we go to break out of the beach-head.'

It was a bright moonlit night and the harbor waters of Plymouth were almost iridescent. Our first day aboard ship had gone by with few passes from enemy air. Several recce ships had poked toward the harbor but they were chased off by shore-based AA. The watch rang four bells. Naval elements in northern ports had already set sail to rendezvous with Kirk's main force.

'Overlord' had already gotten under way for D-Day on the morning of June 5. Either Eisenhower would halt it early this morning of June 4 or the invasion would have gone too far to be called back.

At midnight, I turned in and fell asleep. It was almost 6 a.m. when I was awakened on Sunday, June 4. The weather in Plymouth harbor was soupy and wet; visibility was down and I shivered as I dressed. Kean came in with a copy of the Admiralty radio to Kirk.

'Postponed?' I asked.

'Twenty-four hours.'

Just as soon as Eisenhower had reached his decision, the Navy rushed fast destroyers to head off the units that had put to sea and shepherd them back to ports. Now, the sharp edge of those troops would be dulled and seasickness would take its toll in another day on the choppy Channel. We checked the weather forecast that had been posted on our journal. It was even less promising that the one on June 3: five-foot waves in the Channel and no sign of a break in the overcast until June 7 or 8.

But unless we adjusted the H-Hour, tidal conditions on June 8 would rule out that long a postponement. The rising tide would not reach its halfway high-water mark until long after daylight that morning. And while we had planned a daylight invasion at dawn, we backed off at the thought of a late mid-morning attack that would enable the enemy to regain his wits after the heavy night bombing.

Thorson ordered his working staff on the *Achernar* to notify all First Army units of the postponements. The staff there had already been tipped off in a message from Montgomery's headquarters at 5.15 a.m. that morning. G-3 had devised a pre-arranged signal to circulate news of a postponement. The code-words went out: 'Hornpipe' to indicate 'Overlord', 'Bowsprit' for the one-day delay.

On that Sunday afternoon, June 4, I was to go ashore with Kirk to agree on our recommendations in the event of a second postponement. Meanwhile, I shuffled impatiently about my cabin. First I sat down with a copy of *A Bell for Adano*. But I was too restless to read it and exchanged it for the previous day's *Stars and Stripes*. Detroit had won a 16-inning game from New York. I tossed the paper aside and went back up to the bridge. A batch of recce photos had just come in. They showed where a battery of six enemy 155mm guns had been smothered by air bombing. G-2 reported them abandoned.

Before going ashore, I crossed over once more to the *Achernar* for one last session with the Army staff. For a conference table we used the air filter room where A-2 would track enemy air attacks during our crossing of the Channel. The huge plotting board was painted with naval force channels from the English coast to France. These channels ran from the British ports in the east of England and the American ports in the west to converge in an assembly area off the Isle of Wight. From there, they paralleled each other for 50 miles toward the Normandy coast. Within 30 miles of the shoreline they fanned out again toward the five invasion beaches.

Aboard the *Augusta*, we awaited a postponement signal. But none came and by midnight we heard that Eisenhower had chosen to go. 'Overlord' was under way; 'The Plan' had taken over. For the next 24 hours, the fate of the war in Europe was to ride not in the big-hulled command ships but in the wet, flat-bottomed craft where many GIs were to be seasick on the slippery steel floors as they groaned through the choppy Channel.

'Ike has the forecasters and he undoubtedly knows what he's doing,' I confided to Kean, 'but by golly, the weather certainly looks lousy here.'

The decks were wet from the drizzle, a wind lashed at the canvas curtain to our war room. And the radar antenna on the tip of our foremast washed in and out of the overcast that hung low in the dark sky.

That evening as I fell into bed worrying about the weather, I was quite uneasy on three counts:

1. Unless the wind and surf abated, they might swamp our DD tanks in their unsheltered run to Omaha Beach. We had bargained on the shock effect of those tanks. It would hurt badly to lose them.

2. If the overcast were to prevent spotter aircraft from directing naval gun-fire, we might lose the effectiveness of our principal weapon in the initial assault. With but slight superiority in ground forces, we had banked heavily on this fire support to help break through the water's-edge defenses. Fear of losing the naval gun-fire worried me more than the likelihood of a wash-out in heavy-bomber missions.

3. The Channel could be distressingly cruel to GI stomachs. A heavy surf might defeat our troops with seasickness before they landed.

But these hazards, I reasoned, must have been equally apparent to Ike. He clearly must have had more pertinent weather forecasts than those available to us. Trusting to Ike's judgment, I went to sleep.

Confirmation came at dawn the following morning when a courier arrived from the *Achernar* with a teletype message from Portsmouth: 'D-Day stands as is, Tuesday, June 6th'. Soon, the waters of Plymouth harbor churned in a tangle of wakes as hundreds of ships turned obediently into line. As the columns uncoiled toward the Channel, the *Augusta* put to sea, rapidly overtaking the awkward, slow-moving craft.

At an easy 15 knots, the *Augusta* flanked the Utah-bound column out of Plymouth harbor and headed for the Isle of Wight. From the 'Yoke' assembly point there, she would head with the Omaha forces through a mine-swept Channel to the Normandy coast. There she was to fire in support of the initial landing. As far as we could see both fore and aft, ships crowded the British coast line. Overhead, their barrage balloons bucked in the wind. Fast destroyers screened us seaward.

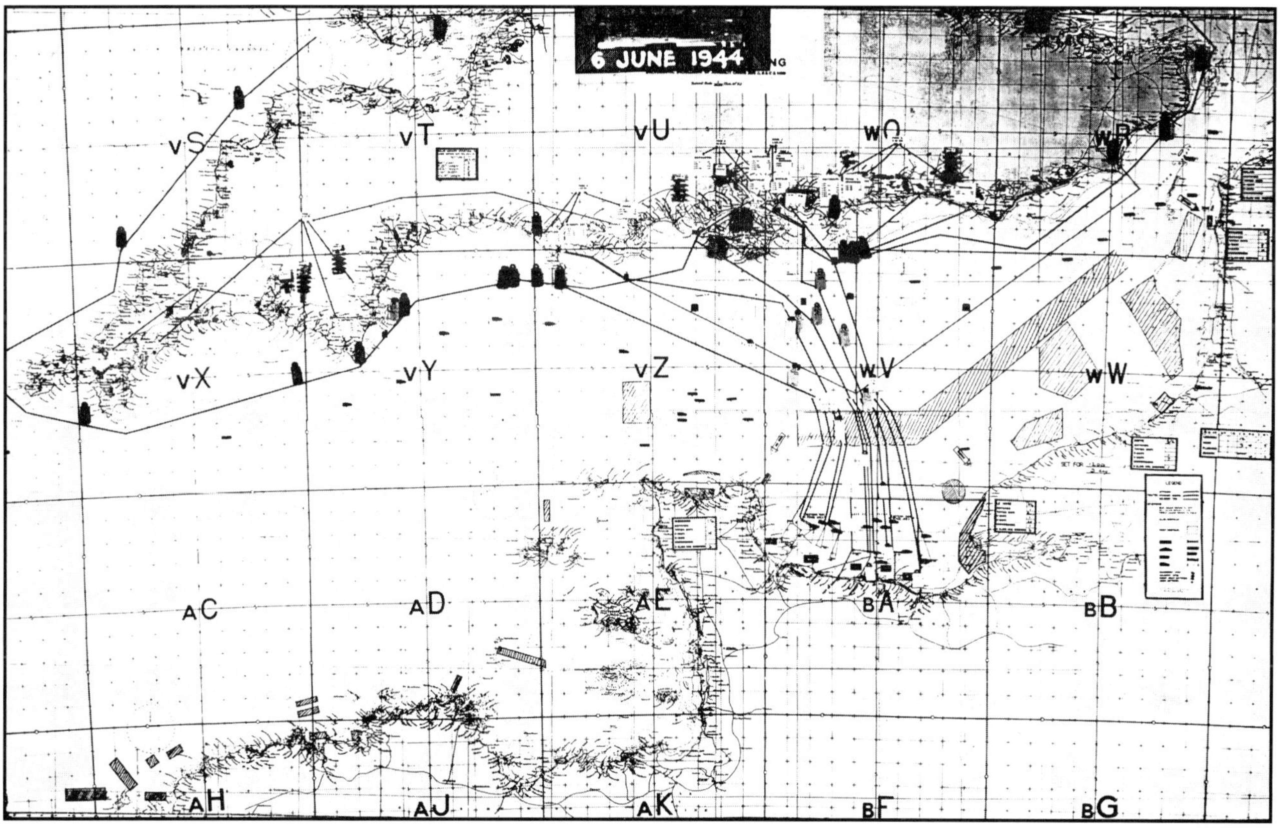

To a supreme commander, or the top commanders of the army, navy and air force, a battle unfolds on their maps, charts and plotting tables, each with its continually changing lines and symbols. Yet it is one aspect of an operation which is immediately lost to history as the fighting — or in the case of 'Neptune', the landing — progresses. General Bradley describes the scene on the First Army plot on Sunday afternoon, but SHAEF went one better. Every day, the main operations board was photographed to provide a lasting record — now preserved in War Office file 219/2936.

On those maps and plans, every enemy installation had been allocated a reference number, some 300 being listed in the First Army sector from the beaches to Cherbourg. Target No. 1 was the battery on the cliff-top at Pointe du Hoc (miss-spelt in many original documents including the First Army list and this 'Neptune' plan, *below*, as Hoe). With a range of over 20,000 yards, the battery's six guns were a threat to both the V Corps beach at Omaha to the east and Utah of VII Corps to the west. Near-vertical cliffs, 100 feet high, guarded it from an assault from the sea, while the landward side was protected by minefields and wire. This picture was taken in 1943 before the cliffs were broken by the preliminary aerial bombardment.

All afternoon on Monday, June 5, the *Augusta* scudded past the Utah-bound convoys, heading for her rendezvous with the Omaha force. High above the cruiser's bridge, a radar antenna rotated monotonously under the woolly sky. In the plotting room below, an officer bent before the radar screen searching for the tell-tale pips that would signify enemy air. But day passed and evening came without a bogey report.

At 11 p.m. that evening, I went below, unbuckled my Mae West, and fell into bed with my shoes on. Kirk remained on the bridge, buttoned up in his foul-weather gear, as the *Augusta* slipped quietly past the buoys that marked the mine-swept channel. Only the lonely wind in the rigging and the wash of water past our sides broke the silence of the night. It was 3.35 a.m. when the clanking bell outside my cabin called the crew to battle stations. I reached for my helmet, scrambled into a Mae West, and hurried to Kirk's bridge. The moon hung misted in an overcast sky and the wind still lashed the Channel. According to the log, the breeze had slackened but the change was not yet evident in the seas that washed by the *Augusta*. Off in the Cotentin peninsula, almost 30 miles to the west, both airborne divisions had already been dropped.

A far-away roar echoed across the Channel and off our starboard bow orange fires ignited the sky as more than 1,300 RAF bombers swarmed over the French coast line from the Seine to

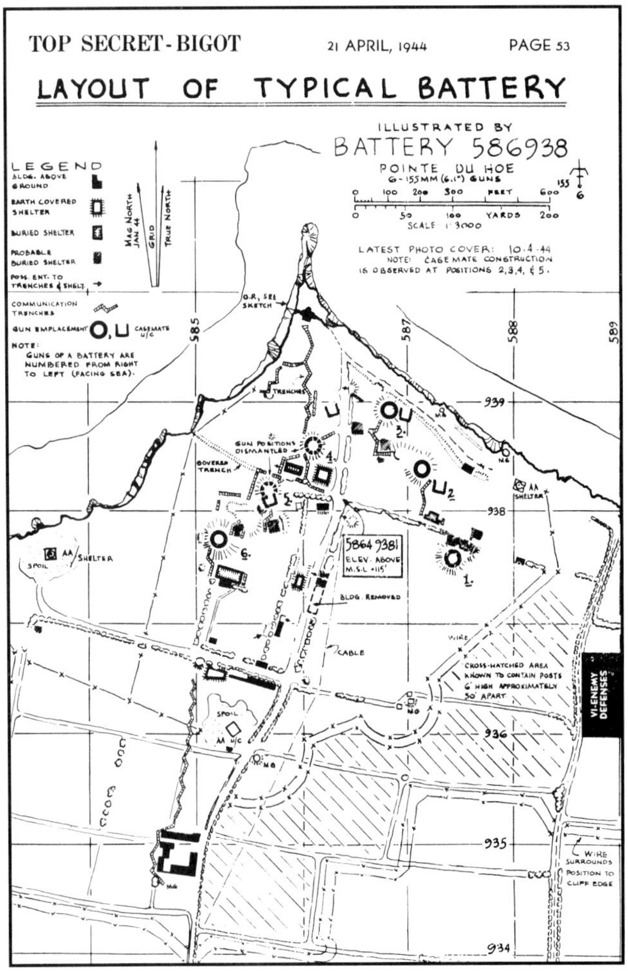

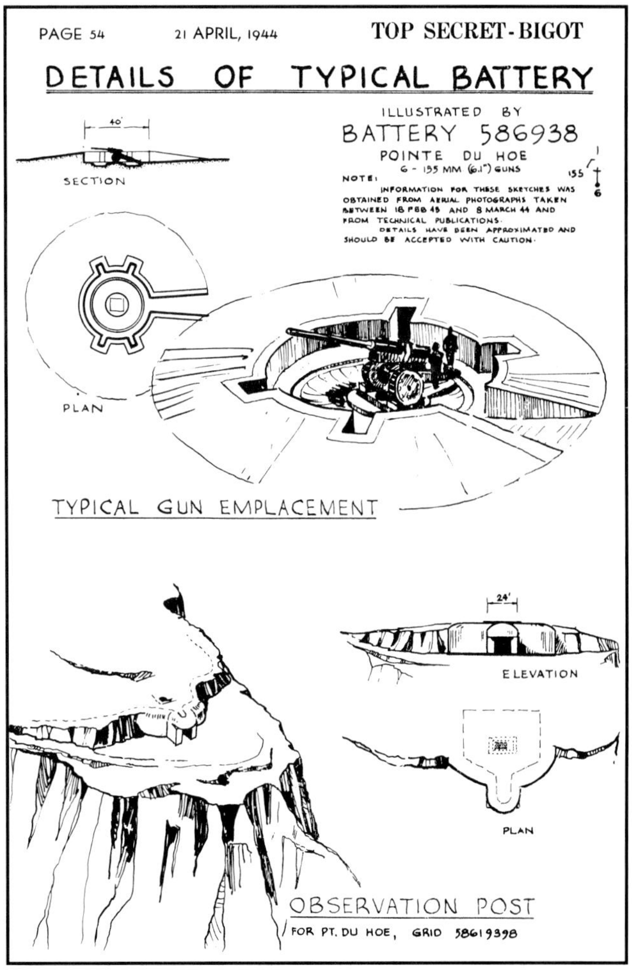

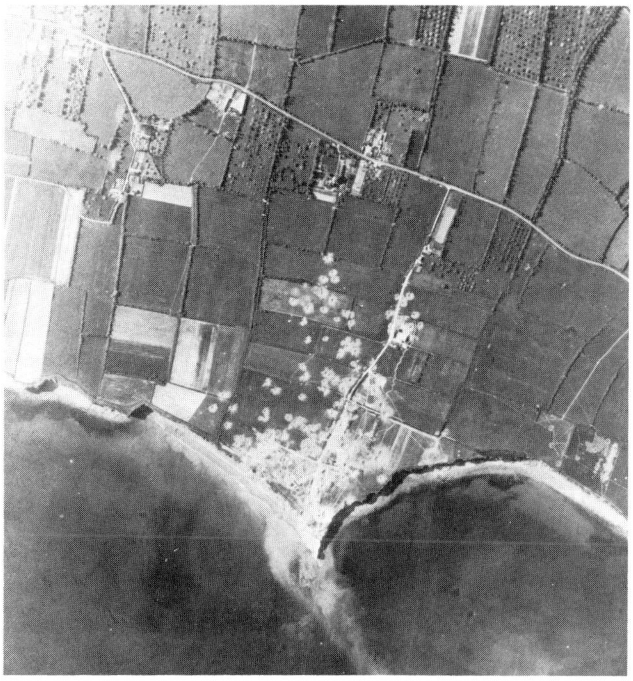

A close watch had been kept on the position and it was singled out for special treatment in the preliminary air bombardment plan (see page 149). Further construction work was spotted by aerial reconnaissance in April 1944, and the Ninth Air Force carried out an attack on the 15th to slow the work down. However, Pointe du Hoc could not be singled out too often lest the invasion area be compromised, and it was not bombed again until May 22, this picture being taken by the 10th Photographic Reconnaissance Group nine days later.

The Ninth struck again on June 4, and RAF Bomber Command on the following night when nearly 1,000 aircraft dropped 5,000 tons of bombs on ten different batteries along the Normandy coast, to date, the heaviest tonnage dropped by the RAF on any single night during the war. Naval bombardment from the 14-inch guns of the *Texas* began at 0550 on June 6, and a last-minute strike by 18 medium bombers of the Ninth took place at 0610. This picture, also taken by the 10th PRG, shows the Pointe on June 8.

Cherbourg. An enemy AA battery stabbed blindly through the night. A shower of sparks splintered the darkness and a ribbon of fire peeled out of the sky as a stricken bomber plunged toward the *Augusta*. It levelled off, banked around our stern, and exploded into the Channel. By 5.30 a.m., first light had diluted the darkness and three Spits whistled by overhead, the first sign of our air umbrella. High above the overcast, relays of American fighters formed a second layer of air cover.

The *Augusta* closed in at five knots to its firing position offshore. High up on the cruiser's open bridge, I squinted toward the shore where it lay blurred in the morning mist. Zero hour had come for the DD tanks on Omaha Beach. They were to be launched from their mother craft at H–50 minutes and make their way ashore through paths cleared by demolition teams through the obstacle line. The infantry would swarm ashore on the heels of these DD tanks and push on inland under the cover of their fire.

Thorson stared at the heaving, black Channel and shook his head. 'I don't like it, General. The DDs are going to have one helluva time in getting through this sea.'

'Yes, Tubby, I'm afraid you're right. But at this point there's nothing we can do.'

'Any sign of a let-up in the surf?'

'Not yet. Kirk tells me the DDs may be swamped in these seas if they're launched from the LCTs. Either the LCTs cart them ashore — or we'll have to count on getting along without them.'

The decision as to whether those tanks would swim or be carted ashore could not be made aboard the *Augusta*. It fell to the commanders of those tank detachments. By now, 'Overlord' had run beyond the reach of its admirals and generals. For the next few tortured hours, we could do little but pace our decks and trust the men to whom 'The Plan' had been given for execution.

A striking picture of the June 4 attack by Douglas A-20 Havocs of the 416th Bomb Group based at Wethersfield.

However impressive the destruction might appear from the air, General Bradley had to be certain that the battery would be unable to harass the invasion force. So, noting that the Rangers (the American counterpart of the British commandos) had two battalions in England, he put the problem to the senior commander, Lieutenant Colonel James E. Rudder of the 2nd Battalion. Here, Rudder (on the right) with his Intelligence Officer, Captain Harvey J. Cook (left), and his Communications Officer, 1st Lieutenant James W. Eikner (second left), leads Company A of the 2nd Battalion along the Esplanade at Weymouth on June 1. Marching to the right of the column is platoon leader 1st Lieutenant Robert T. Edlin, who was later officially credited as being the first American soldier to board a landing craft for the invasion.

At 5.47 a.m., a message appeared on the G-2 journal. Fifteen German E-Boats had left the harbor at Cherbourg to engage our fleet. Kean smiled and chewed on a piece of gum. Fifteen E-Boats against our armada.

The *Augusta*'s 8-inch turrets were turned toward the shore. We plugged our ears with cotton. At 5.50 a.m., the ship shuddered as it opened fire upon its predesignated targets among the beach defenses. The salvo coasted over the armada and we followed the pinpoints of fire as they plunged down toward the shore. The targets had been painstakingly picked from thousands of aerial photos, by which each gun, trench, and pillbox was sited on a detailed map.

At 6.15 a.m., smoke thickened the mist on the coast line as heavy bombers of the Eighth Air Force rumbled overhead. Not until later did we learn that most of the 13,000 bombs dropped by these heavies had cascaded harmlessly into the hedgerows three miles behind the coast. In bombing through the overcast, Air had deliberately delayed its drop to lessen the danger of spill-over on craft approaching the shore. This margin for safety had undermined the effectiveness of the heavy air mission. To the seasick infantry, bailing their craft as they wallowed through the surf, this failure in air bombing was to mean many more casualties upon Omaha Beach.

Weymouth was the departure point for the force, coffee and doughnuts being dispensed by the American Red Cross on Brunswick Terrace. The plan as envisaged was described in the War Department narrative on the operation published in April 1946: 'The Ranger Group was made up of two battalions: the 2d Rangers, under direct command of Colonel Rudder, and the 5th Rangers, under Lieutenant Colonel Max F. Schneider. Three companies (D, E, and F) of the 2d Battalion were to land from the sea at H-Hour and assault the cliff position. The main Ranger force (5th Battalion and Companies A and B of the 2d) would wait offshore for signal of success, then land at the Point. The Ranger Group would then move inland, cut the coastal highway connecting Grandcamp and Vierville, and await the arrival of the 116th Infantry from Vierville before pushing west towards Grandcamp and Maisy. An alternate plan was ready if the support force of Rangers had not received word, by H+30, of success in the attack on the cliffs at Pointe du Hoc. In this event, the larger Ranger force would land on the western end of Omaha Beach (Vierville sector) behind the 116th Infantry and proceed overland toward the Point, avoiding all unnecessary action en route to its objective. At H-Hour, 0630, the three companies of the 2d Rangers, led by Colonel Rudder, were scheduled to touch down at the foot of the cliffs and deliver their assault. They totalled about 225 men, including a headquarters detachment. During April and May, at Swanage on the Isle of Wight, the personnel had been conditioned by hard practice in rope and ladder work on cliffs like those of the French coast, combined with landing exercises in difficult waters. Personnel of British commando units gave all possible help, based on their experience in coastal raids. As a result of experiment with all types of equipment for escalade, main reliance was places on ropes to be carried over the cliff-tops by rockets; in addition, the assault wave would take along extension ladders. British landing craft (LCAs) with British crews were used both in the training and in the actual operation.'

to knock out the battery of six 155mm rifles that covered our Omaha anchorage from the promontory at Pointe du Hoc.

No soldier in my command has ever been wished a more difficult task than that which befell the 34-year-old commander of this Provisional Ranger Force. Lieutenant Colonel James E. Rudder, a rancher from Brady, Texas, was to take a force of 200 men, land on a shingled shelf under the face of a 100-foot cliff, scale the cliff, and there destroy an enemy battery of coastal guns. 'First time you mentioned it,' Rudder recalls, 'I thought you were trying to scare me.'

To prepare his troops for their mission, Rudder trained them on the stony cliffs of the Isle of Wight. There they experimented with mortar-propelled grapples designed by the British commandos to catapult scaling ropes over the cliffs. In addition to the ropes, they trained with lightweight sectional steel ladders which could be quickly assembled and run up the face of the cliff. To these British devices the Rangers then added a new wrinkle of their own. Four long extension ladders were borrowed from the Fire Department in London and mounted on platforms in DUKWs. The DUKWs were to scramble ashore over the shingle shelf and throw their extension ladders up the face of the cliff. In his plan, Rudder proposed to lead the assault company ashore himself. Huebner objected, reminding Rudder that as commander of the Ranger force he bore responsibility for the operation. 'You can't risk getting knocked out in the very first round', he said.

'I'm sorry, sir,' Rudder replied, 'but I'm going to have to disobey you. If I don't take it — it may not go.'

While Rudder assaulted the cliff, the remainder of his force was to wait offshore for the signal that Pointe du Hoc had been taken. If, after 30 minutes, the signal had not been fired, they were to land with the main Omaha assault force and make for the battery overland.

Meanwhile, of the 32 DD tanks launched off Omaha, 27 had foundered in the heavy surf. Our troops had not yet landed and already two critical supports for the assault had broken down. At 6.45 a.m., 15 minutes after H-Hour, word reached the *Augusta* that the first wave had clambered ashore. It was still too early for news from the beach. I choked down a scalding cup of coffee. By now, it was daylight and because the sun was hidden in a haze overhead, a gray panorama opened about us. So far, we had drawn no return fire from the enemy's coastal guns. 'I don't understand this lack of counterbattery', Kean said. 'He's had time to get us in range.'

Thorson squinted toward a bluff that bulged on the shore line. 'Maybe the Rangers have gotten in', he said. The 2nd and 5th Battalions of Rangers were

No piping hot 'cawfee' or sugary doughnuts on the bleak, wet and windy day we took the comparison.

Above left: **First Lieutenant Edlin beams for the camera. Apart from being publicised as the first American soldier to board a landing craft in an English harbour, he was twice wounded on Omaha and later, during the Brest campaign, led a four-man patrol which captured the Lochrist fortress resulting in the surrender of more than 1,000 men. He was considered for the Medal of Honor, but was awarded the Distinguished Service Cross.** *Above right:* **'Ten LCAs would be sufficient to boat the three small Ranger companies and headquarters party, including signal and medical personnel, with an average of 21-22 men on a craft. Each LCA was fitted with three pairs of rocket mounts, at bow, amidship, and stern, wired so that they could be fired in series of pairs from one control point at the stern. Plain ¾-inch ropes were carried by one pair of rockets, affixed to the rocket's base by a connecting wire. A second pair was rigged for rope of the same size fitted with toggles, small wooden crossbars a few inches long inserted at about one-foot intervals; the third pair of rockets was attached to light rope ladders with rungs every two feet. The rockets were headed by grapnels. The rope or ladder for each rocket was coiled in a box directly behind the rocket mount. Each craft carried, in addition to the six mounted rockets, a pair of small hand-projector-type rockets attached to plain ropes. These could be easily carried ashore if necessary. Extension ladders were of two types. One, carried by each LCA, consisted of 112 feet of tubular-steel, 4-foot sections weighing 4 pounds each; these ladders were partly assembled in advance in 16-foot lengths. For mounting the whole ladder in escalade work, a man would climb to the top of a length, haul up and attach the next 16-foot section, and repeat this process until the necessary height was reached. As a final auxiliary for climbing, four DUKWs would come in close behind the first wave, each carrying a 100-foot extension ladder, fire-department type, with three folding sections. Two Lewis machine guns were mounted at the top of each of these ladders, which would be particularly useful for getting up supplies.'** ***Small Unit Actions,*** **War Department, Washington DC, 1946.**

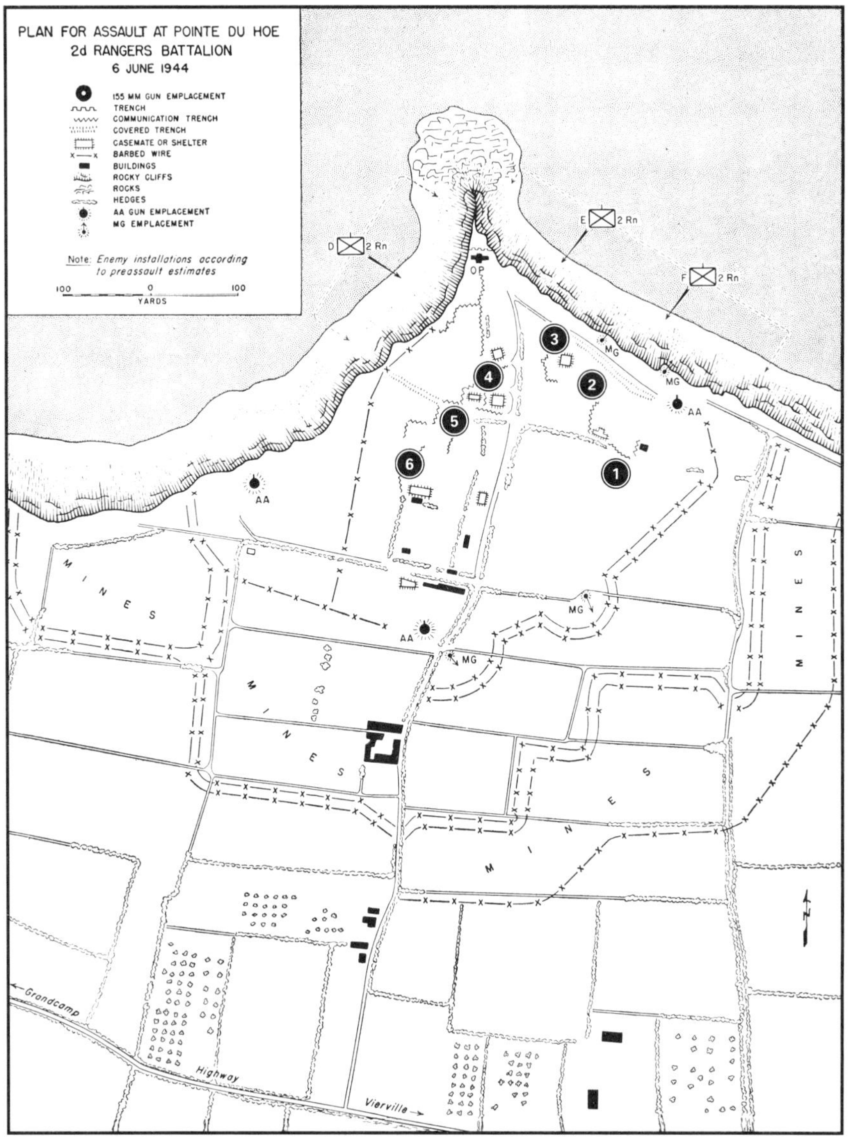

What every official account fails to mention is that it was never intended that Colonel Rudder should personally lead the assault. It was his Executive Officer who had been detailed for that position, but, while aboard the transports in Weymouth harbour, he managed to get himself thoroughly drunk and unruly, and the XO had to be sent ashore. Rudder reported this to Major General Clarence R. Huebner, the CG of the 1st Infantry Division, which was to lead the assault by V Corps, and said that he would now have to take the officer's place. Unfortunately, not to his credit, even General Bradley suppresses the real reason in his explanation on page 329, and the 2nd Ranger Battalion After Action Report of July 22, 1944, fails to mention the last-minute change of command.

Another contretemps occurred during the run in to the beaches, as described to us by Lieutenant Eikner (the Communications Officer) in a letter in April 1994: 'Colonel Rudder's flotilla of ten LCAs was being led in by three small British gunboats. The lead gunboat was doing the navigating. When daylight dawned, it was apparent to Colonel Rudder that we were off course and heading directly towards Pointe et Raz de la Percée some three miles east of Pointe du Hoc (which was to be attacked from the landward side by Company C, 2nd Rangers). Colonel Rudder, in our lead craft, literally forced his boat to break ranks and flank west. The infuriated British officer doing the navigating thought we were trying to abort the mission and tried to run Colonel Rudder's craft down; he soon realised his mistake, however. This error of navigation changed the course of the whole battle and caused us to arrive at Pointe du Hoc 38 minutes late, thereby triggering the option that took the Ranger Main Force to Omaha Beach where they were supposed to pass through the lines of the 116th Infantry and then fight on down to Pointe du Hoc on the double. We expected them to arrive by noon but they did not arrive until noon on the third day, after we had been counter-attacked five times and had suffered casualties of 70 per cent.'

This picture, showing the eight-man tean from the US destroyer *Harding*, under the command of Ensign Bill Carter, scrambling ashore on D+1 to deliver supplies to the Rangers, illustrates the cratered beach which prevented the DUKWs, equipped with the Merryweather extending ladders, from running ashore. One DUKW extended its ladder while still afloat with a brave Staff Sergeant William Stivison at its top, manning the twin Lewis guns. Stivison managed to keep his balance while firing as the ladder swayed horribly some 45 degrees either way some 90 feet up in the air!

'LCA 888. Colonel Rudder's craft, first to hit the beach, had 15 men of Company E and six headquarters personnel, including Lieutenant J. W. Eikner, communications officer. A few enemy troops were seen on the cliff edge as the LCA neared shore, but, when Sergeant Dominick B. Boggetto shot one German off the edge with a BAR, the others disappeared. The Rangers had trouble in getting through the beach craters; neck deep in water, they found it hard to climb out because of the slick clay bottom. A few grenades came over the cliff without causing casualties. The rockets were fired in series, at 35 yards from the cliff base. None of the waterlogged ropes reached the top. When two Rangers, best of the group at free climbing, tried to work up the smashed cliff face without ropes, they were balked by the slippery clay surface, which gave way too easily to permit knife-holds. Bombs or shells had brought down a mass of wet clay from the cliff top, forming a mound 35 to 40 feet high against the cliff. A 16-foot section of the extension ladder, with a toggle rope attached, was carried to the top of the mound and set up. A Ranger climbed the ladder, cut a foothold in the cliff, and stood in this to hold the ladder while a second man climbed it for another 16 feet. The top man repeated the process, and this time Tech. 5 George J. Putzek reached the edge. Lying flat, with the ladder on his arms, he held on while a man below climbed the toggle rope, then the ladder. From there on it was easy. As the first men moved a few yards from the cliff edge to protect the climbers, they found plenty of cover in bomb craters, and no sign of an enemy. In 15 minutes from landing, all the Company E men from LCA 888 were up and ready to move on. Colonel Rudder and headquarters personnel remained for the moment below, finding shelter from enfilade fire in a shallow cave at the bottom of the cliff.' *Small Unit Actions.*

The capture of the camouflaged observation post on the edge of the cliff was assigned to Company E, under 1st Lieutenant Theodore E. Lapres.

As Rudder closed in to Pointe du Hoc, 40 minutes behind schedule, enemy artillery raked his LCAs. The Rangers fired their mortars but many of the grappling hooks fell short as their wet ropes trailed sluggishly behind them. The shelf a the foot of the cliff had been pitted with bomb craters and there the ladder-carrying DUKWs were stalled.

The mortar crews fired again and half a dozen ropes were catapulted over the edge of the cliff. But as the Rangers went up them, hand over hand, the enemy dropped hand-grenades on their heads. A destroyer raced in and swept the top of the cliff with her guns. Within five minutes after they had landed at the base of Pointe du Hoc, the first Ranger had bellied over the top. Seconds later, his companions swarmed up behind him.

The only fighting took place at the tip of the Point. Here, the first men up from LCA 861 found themselves about 20 feet to seaward of a massive and undamaged concrete OP. As Staff Sergeant Charles H. Denbo and Pfc Harry W. Roberts crawled five feet toward a trench, small-arms fire, including machine guns, started up from slits in the OP. The Rangers threw four grenades at the slits, and three went in. The machine gun stopped firing, but Denbo was wounded by a rifle bullet. Lieutenant Theodore E. Lapres, Sergeant Andrew J. Yardley, Pfc William D. Bell, and Tech/Sgt. Harold W. Gunther joined up in the trench. Yardley had a bazooka, and his first round hit the edge of the firing slit; the second went through. Taking advantage of this, the group left Yardley to watch the embrasure and dashed around the OP without drawing enemy fire. On the other side of the structure they found Tech. 5 Victor J. Aguzzi, watching the main entrance from the landward side. Lapres' party pushed on toward gun position No. 4.

Aguzzi had come up from LCA 862, south-east of the OP, with 1st Lieutenant Joseph E. Leagans and Staff Sergeant Joseph J. Cleaves. As they started away from the edge, joined by Tech. 5 LeRoy J. Thompson and Pfc Charles H. Bellows, Jr, they saw a German close to the OP, throwing grenades over the cliff from shelter of a trench. The OP was not their job, but the party decided to go after the grenadier. Bellows crawled over to No. 3 gun position to cover the advance of the party. They threw grenades at the German and moved into the trench when he ducked under the entrance to the OP. Aguzzi found a shell hole from which he could watch the main entrance, while three Rangers tried to skirt the OP on the east and get at it from the rear. Cleaves was wounded by a mine — the only casualty from this cause during the day. Thompson got close enough to hear a radio working inside the OP, looked for the aerial on top, and shot it off. After throwing a grenade through the entrance, Lieutenant Leagans and Thompson decided to let the OP wait for demolitions, and went off on their original mission further inland. Aguzzi, staying to watch the entrance, was surprised a few minutes later by the appearance of Lieutenant Lapres' party, coming from the rear of the OP. Two small groups of Rangers had been attacking the OP from opposite sides, neither aware of the other's presence.

On the afternoon of D+1 the nest was finally cleaned out. Two satchel charges of C–2 were thrown in the entrance, and Aguzzi, still on guard, figured the enemy must be wiped out. But eight unwounded Germans swarmed out with their hands up, and only one body was found inside.

SMALL UNIT ACTIONS, 1946

Pfc Harry W. Roberts was first up the cliff from LCA 861 using the route seen in the picture at the bottom right of page 331, the photo purportedly released through the US Navy on June 12, 1944. Although the *Small Unit Actions*' caption to this photograph claims that it was taken a year later, the US Navy index cards of the original photographs confirm that both pictures were taken on D+1. Five Rangers joined Roberts at the top and all six set out for their objective — the battery observation post. A heavy explosion delayed the ascent of the remainder of the men from LCA 861, but five more Rangers followed Roberts' party. The OP was attacked from two sides but it was not finally secured until late the next day. *Right:* Today the cupola has lost its natural camouflage and unfortunately the cliff is now crumbling away, the edge now fenced with a double row of barbed wire, restricting the area surrounding the position.

This picture, stated as having been taken on the first anniversary of the attack, shows one of the rope ladders still in place just east of the promontory, most probably the same one seen in the picture on page 331.

In 1954, James Rudder took his 14-year-old son 'Bud' back to the same spot for a feature in the now-defunct *Collier's* magazine: 'It was about ten o'clock in the morning when we reached the crossroad just west of Formigny. Ten years had passed since the American had been here, but he remembered the crossroad very well — the Calvary on the one corner and the battle monuments on the three others — and he drove the small gray Peugeot down the narrow, winding blacktop, hemmed in between the thick bulk of the hedgerows, until it widened out, where the new road curves through the center of Vierville-sur-Mer. "The Vierville church", he said now, measuring the words and standing there and looking up at it. The church is gutted still, the roof gone and only a few fragments of stained glass still sticking in the windows, but from the front a new steeple points up into the sky. "Bud, that was one of the old landmarks we studied a lot in England before the invasion. We studied it over and over." The boy said nothing. He was wearing crepe-soled shoes and blue jeans, a blue plaid shirt and a red corduroy jacket. "Now you stay close to us, Bud", Rudder said. "Don't go running off." "I just want to see", the boy said.'

'Rudder had parked the Peugeot on a small patch of level grass at the end of the hedgerowed lane that runs from the blacktop out toward the point of the cliff. We had started along the path between the shoulder-high growth of dark-green thorn bushes. "There wasn't this growth here then", Rudder said. "It was all just ripped-open dirt." The bomb and shell holes, one opening into another and some of them 30 feet across and 10 feet deep, were grown with grass now, and Rudder picked a path between them. "There's still a rope here. Lapres' boat put in there", Rudder said.'

'Then he came upon the concrete blockhouse, standing dome-roofed about eight feet above the ground, open toward the Channel and its floor strewn with concrete rubble. He looked at it for a moment, then called the boy. "Bud", he said, "come back here. I want you to see this." He walked down the two steps among the pieces of broken concrete, and the boy followed him. Then Rudder turned around. "This is where the shell hit", he said, pointing up just above his head to a broken section of the corner where two rusted reinforcing rods protruded. "They say it wasn't from one of our ships, but when you look at the direction, it had to be. The artillery captain, a nice-looking, black-haired boy — I wish I could remember his name — was killed right here. The Navy lieutenant, who was spotting with us, fell right here." He pointed. "It knocked me over right here." He pulled back the right sleeve of his topcoat, unbuttoned his shirt cuff and exposed his forearm and the small red welt on it. "Right under that", Rudder said, "is a piece of the concrete from right here. You carry it around in you for ten years, and you bring it right back where it came from."'

'The boy had found an old red-handled American toothbrush in the dust and broken concrete on the floor. He handed it to his father and his father looked at it and tossed it on the ground. "Come around here with me", he said to the boy. They walked around to the east of the blockhouse. The shelling had ripped half the concrete off the side, exposing horizontal rows of reinforcing rods. Rudder climbed up onto the second one and the boy climbed up beside him, where they could both look toward the lane. "Earlier that morning we were right here", the father said. "The Navy lieutenant was on my right, where you are, the artillery captain was on my left, and we were trying to direct fire over there when I got shot in the leg." "Where was the German?" the boy said, turning. "I don't know", Rudder said. The first time the boy had ever seen the bullet wound had been in the little house on South Bridge Street in Brady, Texas, sitting one night in the parlor. Someone had asked about the wound and his father had rolled up the left pant leg and there, just above the knee, was the pink scar where the bullet had gone in and, on the other side, the pink scar where it had come out. It had been a clean penetration.'

Since that day when Colonel Rudder walked his son around the battlefield, Pointe du Hoc has seen many re-enactments, this particular 'attack' by the US Berlin Brigade on north casemate (the small square just north of the open gun position No. 4 on the plan on page 330) taking place on the 30th anniversary. In January 1979, Pointe du Hoc was officially turned over to the US government and has since been maintained by the American Battle Monuments Commission.

'"This way, Bud", Rudder said now, calling again to the boy. The boy had run ahead, running along the ridges between the bomb craters. " I just want to see the CP", the boy said, coming back out of breath. "You'll see it", Rudder said. "Just be patient." He walked as directly to it as you could, considering the turbulence of the ground. It had been his first command post in France, a hollow scooped out of the edge of the cliff by a bomb, and it was from here that Rudder had sent out his first message: "Praise the Lord", the code meaning: "Rangers up cliff." "Need ammunition and reinforcements", he had sent out later. "Many casualties." Now he stood in the middle of it, and the boy was at the edge, peering down where his father had once climbed, down the sheer drop of about 90 feet, with the narrow stony beach below. "Look, son, I want you to keep away from that edge. You could fall off, and I'd have to go home and face your mother." "Is that where our flag was?" the boy said. "No", Rudder said, pointing. "It was right over here." They had anchored the American flag to the cliff with rocks. When the relief had come on D+2, the tankers had presumed that the Rangers had been annihilated, and so they had started to fire onto the point. He had waved the flag on a stick and the firing had stopped.'

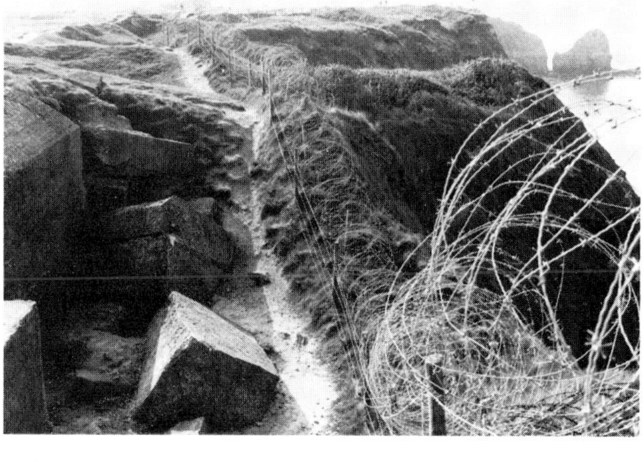

Left: In June 1973, we staged our own simple re-enactment at the Rangers' command post, one of the Second World War's most hallowed spots, virtually unchanged and unspoiled. *Above:* Now, the grassy hollow is collapsing into the sea . . . perhaps in another 30 years' time all will be lost.

'Rudder climbed up now on one side of the scooped earth. He walked around to the side of the buried blockhouse. "We got our first German prisoner right here", he said. "He was a little freckle-faced kid who looked like an American, and we were so proud of him, because when you're trying to get your first prisoner, it's like diving for pearls. Then I had a feeling there were more of them, and I told the Rangers to lead this kid ahead of them. They just started him around this corner when the Germans opened up out of the entrance and he fell dead, right here, face down with his hand still clasped on the top of his head." "How many were in there?" the boy said. "We killed one and got seven or eight out", Rudder said. "We can go down in here", the boy said, calling up from down inside the entrance. "It's open and we might find something in here."' *Above:* This is the rear of the underground shelter which formed the inland side of the CP: being inspected in June 1944 by personnel from the USS *Texas*, and in October 1993 by a nostalgic Jean Paul Pallud.

There they found a desolate table-land bearing the scars of repeated bombings. The big guns, however, were missing; the quarry had skipped. Ranger patrols pushing inland found the guns in an apple orchard 1,200 yards from the cliff. They were mobile, long-barrelled French GPFs with a range of 20,000 yards and they had been sited to fire on both invasion beaches. Quantities of ammunition were stored at the gun sites but the weapons had not been fired. The Rangers killed those remnants of the gun crews that had not yet fled our naval bombardment and disabled the guns by blowing their breeches. By then, however, the enemy had counter-attacked on Pointe du Hoc. There, the Rangers were to be cut off for two days while reinforcements struggled from Omaha to relieve them.

Small Unit Actions: 'By 0725, 1st Lieutenant James W. Eikner had his equipment set up and flashed word by SCR 300 that Colonel Rudder's force had landed. Five minutes later, he sent out the code-word indicating "men up the cliff"; the "Roger" that receipted for this message, again on SCR 300, was Eikner's last communication of D-Day on the Ranger command net. When he sent the message PRAISE THE LORD ("all men up cliff") at 0745, no response was forthcoming. Colonel Rudder had gone on top at 0745, and established his CP in a crater between the cliff and a destroyed anti-aircraft gun emplacement. Most of the assault parties had left the fortified area on their several missions, and Colonel Rudder could only wait for reports. Observation in the churned-up wasteland left by the bombardment was very limited, and for the moment there was little that he could do to exercise control. However, there was some work to do near at hand, as the enemy gave disturbing signs of reviving his resistance close to the Point. Enemy snipers were active, some of them operating inside the fortified area, and steps were taken to eradicate them. Some of the last parties up the cliff, together with headquarters personnel, were sent out to hunt them down. These efforts, repeated many times, were never entirely successful. Through the rest of D-Day, the CP and the whole Point area were harassed by snipers who came out of tunnels and trenches, to find plenty of cover in the cratered debris. Patrols combed over the maze of underground positions, but it seemed impossible to clean them out with the small force available. At no time were the snipers numerous, and there were periods when the Rangers could move in the open with impunity, anywhere on the Point. But these intervals of calm would be broken at any time by scattered small-arms fire from every direction, or by bursts of automatic fire from the German anti-aircraft position, 300 yards west on the edge of the cliff. Colonel Rudder sustained a thigh wound from this fire during the morning.' *Left:* 'It is mid-morning and we have taken a break', wrote ex-Lieutenant Eikner when we sent him this US Navy photo for identification. 'I am seated near the radio aerial drinking from a canteen. In the lower right with the bandaged head is commando Lieutenant Travis Trevor whose helmet had been struck by a bullet as he landed below the cliff right next to Colonel Rudder.' Seated right of Eikner is paratrooper Sergeant Leonard Goodgal of the 101st's 506th Parachute Infantry who had landed near Pointe du Hoc and fought with the Rangers. *Right:* Steve Casely matches the picture exactly 50 years later.

Both the casemates and the open emplacements were devoid of their artillery but, as James Eikner (now secretary of the Ranger Association) explains, 'the publication of Cornelius Ryan's book in 1959, ***The Longest Day***, to be followed by the movie of the same name [seen being filmed at Pointe du Hoc *right*], created a mistaken impression about the mission which haunts us to this day. The book, however excellent, left the idea that the assault, brave and daring though it was, resulted in a needless sacrifice of life since the big guns were not there and had never been mounted. Incorrect! Unfortunately, Ryan had gotten his information from one of our fellows who simply was not that well informed. Six of the guns had been mounted but were pulled back about a mile and carefully camouflaged in an apple orchard. Intermittent bombing had already damaged three of the guns; they were pulled back three days before D-Day to avoid further damage. We found only five of the guns; one of the damaged guns had been removed either for repair or replacement. A two-man patrol consisting of 1st Sergeant Leonard Lomell of Company D, 2nd Battalion, and Sergeant Jack Kuhn, also of the 2nd Battalion, was detailed for their destruction. Kuhn stood guard while Lomell went into the area to destroy the guns — he put thermite grenades into the breech blocks and used the butt of his rifle to damage the sights. About 100 yards away across an open field, the enemy was trying to get organised — this was probably the gun crew. Had we not put the guns out of action, it is certain they would have been used with devastating effect against our troops and ships. A large supply of ammunition was on hand, and the guns were lined up on Utah Beach when we found them.' *Above:* This is the second reinforced concrete casemate which stood just to the south of gun position No. 5, pictured *(left)* by the Signal Corps in September 1944 and *(right)* by Jean Paul in May 1994. *Below:* The emplacement for No. 6 gun, the pictures being taken some 50 years apart.

Although a *Stars and Stripes* photographer landed from LCA 722, there appears to be no trace of any pictures he took, and no 'action' shots are included in the Pointe du Hoc account in *Small Unit Actions* published in April 1946. *Right:* This picture, credited as being taken on June 6 by the Signal Corps, was released on June 12 with the rather vague caption: 'American soldiers who have been training for months, both at home and abroad, apply their training in the "Big Go". Infantrymen level their machine gun to protect their buddies engaged in road building as they take cover behind an earth mound.' All pretty meaningless, but look closely at the helmets: at least three of them sport the 2nd Ranger Battalion diamond insignia. The lump of concrete on the left would also seem to indicate it was taken in a bomb crater beside a damaged bunker or casemate. So it could well be a genuine photo taken during the battle at the Point.

The guns were discovered in an orchard to the south of the Grandcamp–Vierville road. This same orchard later became the location of General Bradley's first command post in France when army headquarters moved ashore from the *Achernar* on June 9. Unfortunately, we have been unable to trace a photograph of the CP, this picture *(above)* being taken in May before the guns were removed from the battery. *Right:* Unlike the terrain around the Merville battery on the eastern flank which was reinstated after the war (see page 235), the cratered landscape makes Pointe du Hoc unique on the Normandy battlefield. By 1991, however, when this picture was taken, the orchard had been greatly thinned out.

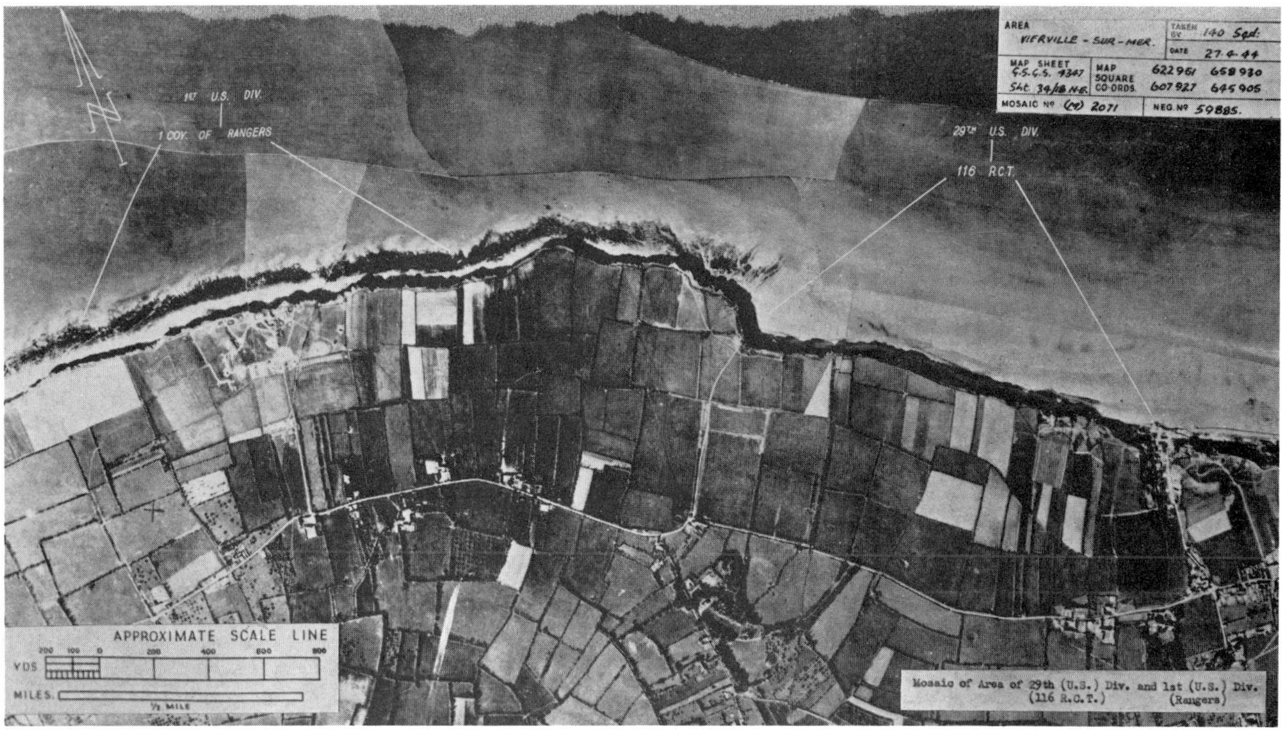

As we have seen, the delay in the landing at Pointe du Hoc caused the 5th Rangers Battalion to be diverted instead to Green Beach of Dog sector. Meanwhile, Company C of the 2nd Rangers had the strong point at Pointe et Raz de la Percée, some three miles east of Pointe du Hoc, as its objective, listed by First Army as Target 137.

More usually described simply as Dog Green, the dividing line between that beach and Charlie sector was the point where the road through the valley to Vierville-sur-Mer met the sea. Company C was probably the first assault unit to reach the high ground and it did so here where the cliffs begin. (Pointe de la Percée can be seen in the far distance.) Rangers under 1st Lieutenant William D. Moody climbed the cliffs using bayonets for hand-holds and toggle ropes to attack the strong point on the summit, the battle for its possession continuing throughout the day.

Along this part of the Normandy coastline, almost every field remains as it could be seen in 1944.

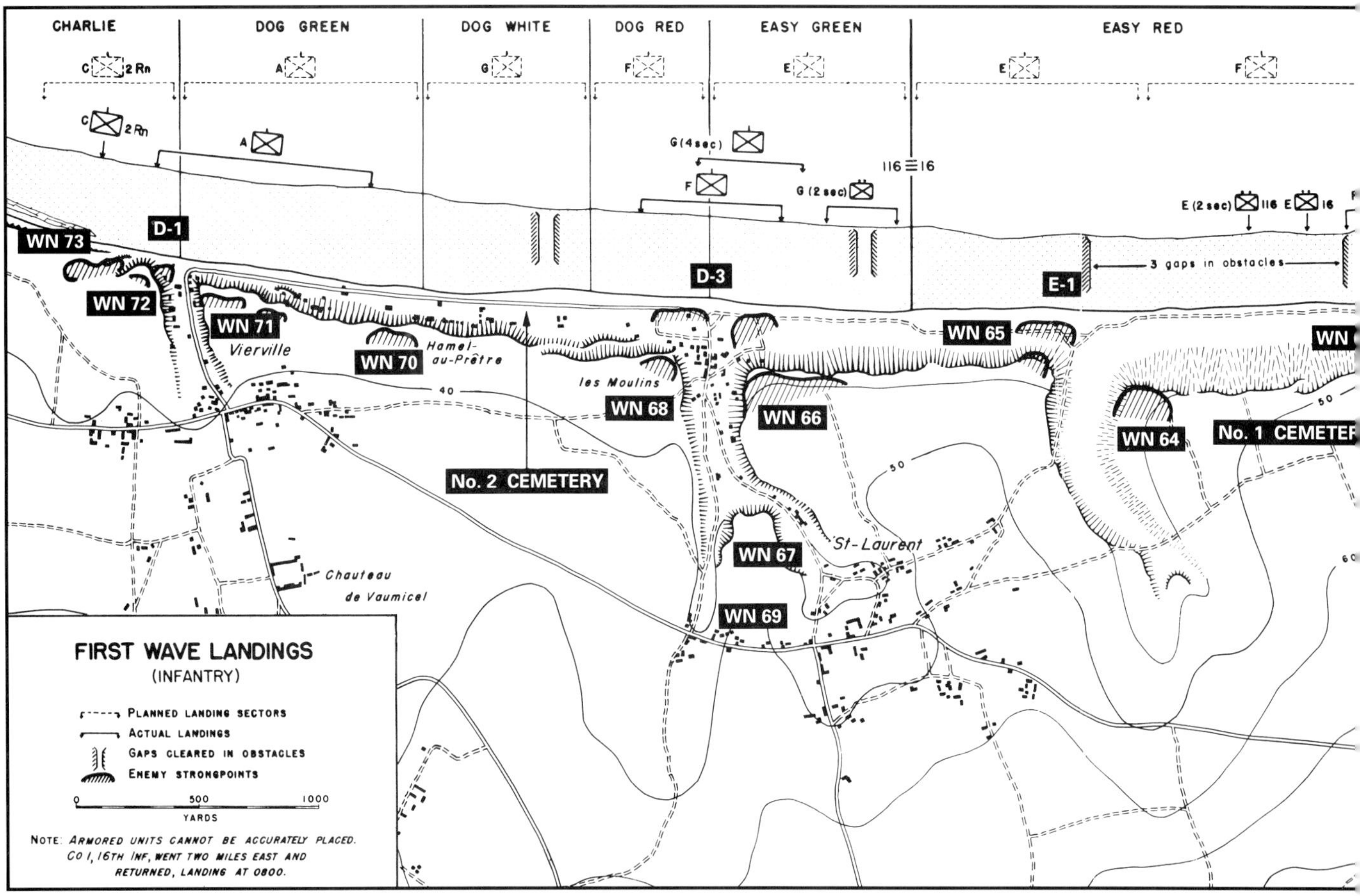

CHARLIE
DOG GREEN
DOG WHITE
DOG RED
EASY GREEN
EASY RED
C 2 Rn
A
G
F
E
E
F
G (4 sec)
F
G (2 sec)
116 ≡ 16
E (2 sec) 116 E 16
3 gaps in obstacles
D-1
D-3
E-1
WN 73
WN 72
WN 71
Vierville
WN 70
Hamel-au-Prêtre
les Moulins
WN 68
WN 66
WN 65
WN 64
No. 1 CEMETER
No. 2 CEMETERY
WN 67
St-Laurent
WN 69
Chauteau de Vaumicel
40
50
60
FIRST WAVE LANDINGS
(INFANTRY)
Planned landing sectors
Actual landings
Gaps cleared in obstacles
Enemy strongpoints
0 500 1000
YARDS
Note: Armored units cannot be accurately placed. Co I, 16th Inf, went two miles east and returned, landing at 0800.

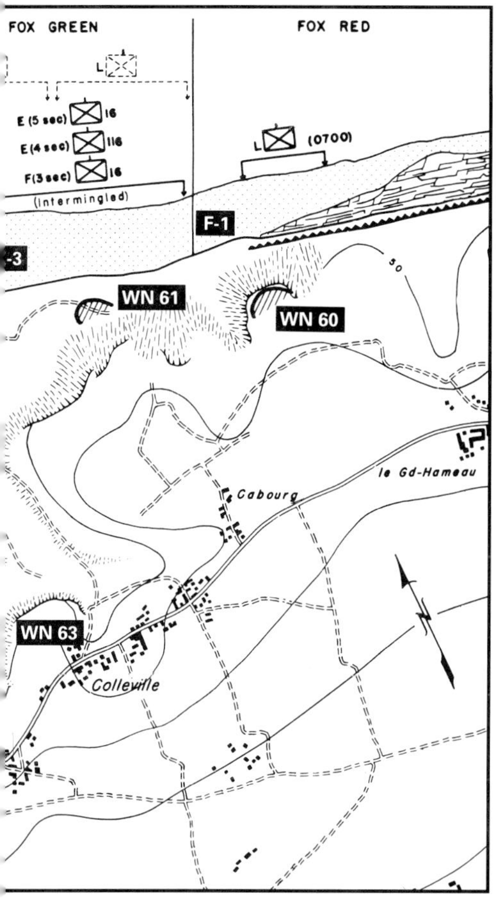

OMAHA AREA

Sector	*Extent*	*Grid Reference*	*Width (yards)*
ABLE	Mouth of River Vire to Pte du Maisy	491878–527935	7,600
BAKER	A to Pte du Hoc (Pte St Pierre)	527935–587940	6,500
CHARLIE	B to road	587940–648917	8,000
DOG	C to mouth of stream	648917–667907	2,400
EASY	D to road	667907–688897	2,900
FOX	E to road	688897–723886	3,900
GEORGE	F to Port-en-Bessin (West breakwater)	723886–750881	3,600

Omaha was the least attractive of the five landing areas and, militarily, had a number of very real drawbacks. Firstly, the available area — some 7,000 yards — was backed by rising ground — the bluffs — some 100 feet high so that the enemy would have the distinct advantage of occupying prepared positions on the high ground. Secondly, movement by vehicles on the eastern two-thirds of the beach was impossible because of a bank of coarse shingle, up to eight feet high, of a similar consistency to that at Dieppe which had spelled disaster for the 14th Canadian Army Tank Regiment in August 1942. Then, at the western end, a sea-wall, four to six feet in height, ran along the edge of the promenade. Small wooded valleys — called 'draws' by the Americans — bisected the bluff and provided natural corridors for the advance inland. The two exits for Dog sector were labelled D-1 (leading to Vierville) and D-3 (Les Moulins), and those for Easy, E-1 to St Laurent-sur-Mer and E-3 to Colleville-sur-Mer. (There was no D-2 or E-2.) A paved road led off the beach at D-1, but the other exits were only rough tracks. At the eastern end, a rough trail leading from Fox was earmarked for development as a fifth exit, F-1. Naturally, the Germans had foreseen the vulnerability of the valleys and each was protected by twin Wiederstandsnest (WN) or 'resistance points', indicated on the map. Behind the dune line or sea-wall lay a flat expanse of marshy ground leading up to the bluff. *Below:* The aerial photo shows the complete expanse of Omaha depicted on the map. However, because of the effects of the bombardment and, more importantly, the work by American engineers after the assault to clear the beach and improve the exit roads, many features were destroyed. The original sea-wall and shingle embankments were completely removed, and the Cemetery No. 1, east of St Laurent, was later developed into the permanent US Normandy Cemetery covering some 172 acres.

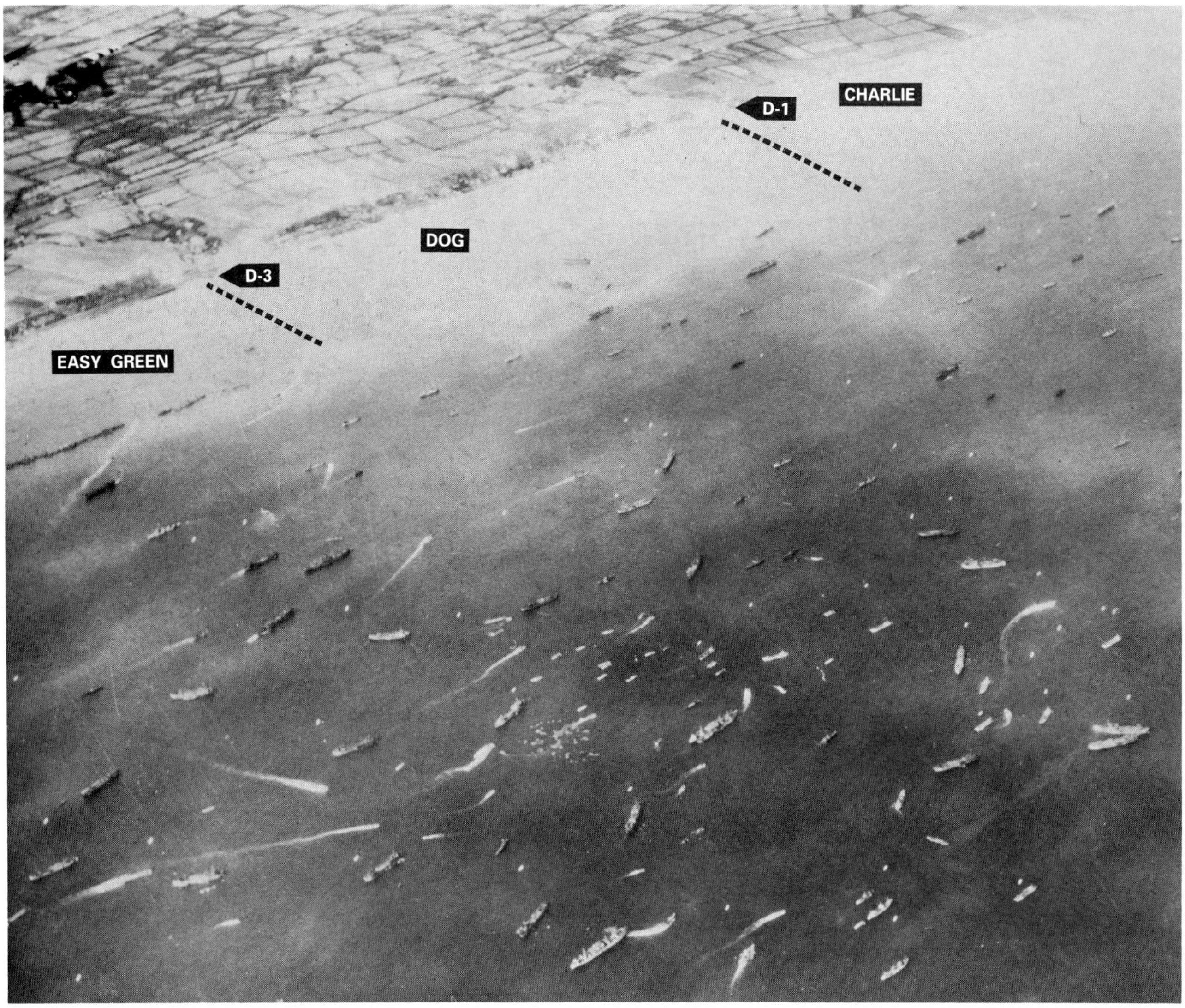

With H-Hour fixed at 0630, the assault on Omaha was to be led by 64 Sherman DDs, 32 each from the 741st and 743rd Tank Battalions, coming ashore at H–5 minutes to deal specifically with the strong points covering the beach exits. In the zone covered by the 116th Regimental Combat Team (RCT), the DDs of the 743rd were not launched because of the rough sea. This picture shows the section of beach allocated to the 116th RCT (Dog Green to Easy Green) including exits D-1 and D-3.

However, the 741st Tank Battalion, scheduled to come ashore further east on Easy Red and Fox Green and clear the vital exits E-1 and E-3, decided to launch its tanks as planned at H–50 minutes when 6,000 yards from the shore. With only one foot of freeboard, the DDs did not stand a chance in the heavy sea and only two made it to the beach. Three more were beached directly from their LCT which could not launch because of a damaged ramp, but the remaining 27 tanks foundered. Two of the DDs had been launched some 15,000 yards offshore — nearly *nine* miles — a fact established 30 years after the war when their hulks were found by a French diver, Jacques Lemonchois. In all, he has pinpointed at least ten of the DDs between four and seven miles out, and in July 1980 prepared to recover two of them lying half a mile apart, 3½ miles off Easy Red in 13 fathoms, a depth of some 80 feet. *Left:* The turret of the first DD and the remains of the second *(right)*, displayed at the Musée Sous-Marin at Commes in 1980 (see also *After the Battle* No. 34).

Following the plan, the third company of each tank battalion was to land its armour (16 Shermans) direct on the beach from eight LCTs at H-Hour. A minute later, the first infantry were to come ashore — the individual companies being shown on the plan on pages 340-341 in their planned and actual positions. The LCVP in this dramatic Coast Guard picture was hit as it approached the shore, according to the original caption 'when machine gun fire exploded a hand-grenade'. The coxswain, Coast Guardsman Dalba L. Nivens, made it to the beach to unload his troops and, assisted by the engineer and bowman, succeeded in returning to his Coast Guard-manned transport under a hail of machine gun and mortar fire.

As the morning lengthened, my worries deepened over the alarming and fragmentary reports we picked up on the Navy net. From these messages, we could piece together only an incoherent account of sinkings, swampings, heavy enemy fire, and chaos on the beaches. By 8.30 a.m., the two assault regiments on Omaha had expected to break through the water's-edge defenses and force their way inland to where a road paralleled the coast line a mile behind the beaches. Yet by 8.30 a.m., V Corps had not yet confirmed news of the landing. We fought off our fears, attributing the delay to a jam-up in communications. It was almost 10 a.m. before the first report came in from Gerow. Like the fragments we had already picked up, his message was laconic, neither conclusive nor reassuring. It did nothing more than confirm our worst fears on the DD tanks. 'Obstacles mined, progress slow . . . DD tanks for Fox Green swamped.'

Aboard the *Ancon*, Gerow and Major General Clarence R. Huebner, commander of the 1st Infantry Division, clung to their radios as helplessly as I. There was little else they could do. For, at the moment, they had no more control than I of the battle on the beaches. Though we could see it dimly through the haze and hear the echo of its guns, the battle belonged that morning to the thin, wet line of khaki that dragged itself ashore on the Channel coast of France. Alarmed over the congestion of craft offshore on Omaha Beach, Kirk ordered his gunnery officer in for a close-up view. I sent Hansen with him aboard a PT boat. They returned an hour later, soaked by the seas, with a discouraging report of conditions on the beach. The 1st Division lay pinned down behind the sea-wall while the enemy swept the beaches with small-arms fire. Artillery chased the landing craft where they milled offshore. Much of the difficulty had been caused by the underwater obstructions. Not only had the demolition teams suffered paralysing casualties, but much of their equipment had been swept away.

Landing two minutes behind the first wave of infantry were to be the men of the special engineer task force, which included 16 joint Army-Navy combat demolition teams, whose job it was to clear 16 gaps through the obstacles, each 50 yards wide. Gap support teams would land not later than H+8 minutes to assist. Such was the plan and, following the overwhelming Allied bombardment of the German positions, the men were told that 'there will be nothing alive on the beach when you land'. The illusion did not last long. Because of the cloud cover, a safety margin had been introduced to prevent aircraft bombing short and, in the event, only two sticks of bombs landed within four miles of the shore defences. The engineers arrived amidst a storm of artillery, mortar and small-arms fire to find troops sheltering behind the very obstacles they were due to destroy. This picture is one of the ten frames which survived out of three rolls of 35mm film taken by Robert Capa who landed with Company E (16th RCT) on Easy Red at 0631. All his other exposures were ruined in the darkroom.

This Coast Guard photo shows LCVPs landing troops of the 1st Battalion, 16th Infantry Regiment, on Easy Red. Captain Edward E. Fritzsche, of the Coast Guard attack transport *Samuel Chase* (APA 26), embarked his landing craft at 0530, and managed to complete the unloading of all his vehicles, including three Piper Cub aircraft, by 1150. (A landing strip was operational by 1800 on D+2.) The *Samuel Chase* then took on board over 300 casualties for return to Weymouth.

FIRST WAVE AT OMAHA BEACH

Able Company of the 116th Infantry of the 29th Division, riding the tide in seven Higgins boats, is still 5,000 yards from the beach when first taken under artillery fire. The shells fall short. At 1,000 yards, Boat No. 5 is hit dead on and founders. Six men drown before help arrives. Second Lieutenant Edward Gearing and 20 others paddle around until picked up by naval craft, thereby missing the fight at the shore line. It's their lucky day. The other six boats ride unscathed to within 100 yards of the shore, where a shell into Boat No. 3 kills two men. Another dozen drown, taking to the water as the boat sinks. That leaves five boats.

Lieutenant Edward Tidrick in Boat No. 2 cries out: 'My God, we're coming in at the right spot, but look at it! No shingle, no wall, no shell holes, no cover. Nothing!'

His men are at the sides of the boat, straining for a view of the target. They stare but say nothing. At exactly 6.36 a.m., ramps are dropped along the boat line and the men jump off in water anywhere from waist deep to higher than a man's head. This is the signal awaited by the Germans atop the bluff. Already pounded by mortars, the floundering line is instantly swept by crossing machine gun fires from both ends of the beach.

Able Company has planned to wade ashore in three files from each boat, centre file going first, then flank files peeling off to right and left. The first men out try to do this but are ripped apart before they can make five yards. Even the lightly wounded die by drowning, doomed by the waterlogging of their overloaded packs. From Boat No. 1, all hands jump off in water over their heads. Most of them are carried down. Ten or so survivors get around the boat and clutch at its sides in an attempt to stay afloat. The same thing happens to the section in Boat No. 4. Half of its people are lost to the fire or tide before anyone gets ashore. All order has vanished from Able Company before it has fired a shot.

Already the sea runs red. Even among some of the lightly wounded who jump into shallow water, the hits prove fatal. Knocked down by a bullet in the arm or weakened by fear and shock, they are unable to rise again and are drowned by the onrushing tide. Other wounded men drag themselves ashore and, on finding the sands, lie quiet from total exhaustion, only to be overtaken and killed by the water. A few move safely through the bullet swarm to the beach, then find that they cannot hold there. They return to the water to use it for body cover. Faces turned upward, so that their nostrils are out of water, they creep toward the land at the same rate as the tide. That is how most of the survivors make it. The less rugged or less clever seek the cover of enemy obstacles moored along the upper half of the beach and are knocked off by machine gun fire.

Within seven minutes after the ramps drop, Able Company is inert and leaderless. At Boat No. 2, Lieutenant Tidrick takes a bullet through the throat as he jumps from the ramp into the water. He staggers onto the sand and flops down ten feet from Private First Class Leo J. Nash. Nash sees the blood spurting and hears the strangled words gasped by Tidrick: 'Advance with the wire cutters!' It's futile; Nash has no cutters. To give the order, Tidrick has raised himself up on his hands and made himself a target for an instant. Nash, burrowing into the sand, sees machine gun bullets rip Tidrick from crown to pelvis. From the cliff above, the German gunners are shooting into the survivors as from a roof top.

Captain Taylor N. Fellers and Lieutenant Benjamin R. Kearfoot never make it. They had loaded with a section of 30 men in Boat No. 6 (Landing Craft, Assault, No. 1015). But exactly what happened to this boat and its human cargo is never to be known. No one saw the craft go down. How each man aboard it met death remains unreported. Half of the drowned bodies were later found along the beach. It is supposed that the others were claimed by the sea.

Along the beach, only one Able Company officer still lives — Lieutenant Elijah Nance, who is hit in the heel as he quits the boat and hit in the belly by a second bullet as he makes the sand. By the end of ten minutes, every sergeant is either dead or wounded. To the eyes of such men as Gilbert G. Murdock, this clean sweep suggests that the Germans on the high ground have spotted all leaders and concentrated fire their way. Among the men who are still moving in with the tide, rifles, packs, and helmets have already been cast away in the interests of survival.

To the right of where Tidrick's boat is drifting with the tide, its coxswain lying dead next to the shell-shattered wheel, the seventh craft, carrying a medical section with one officer and 16 men, noses toward the beach. The ramp drops. In that instant, two machine guns concentrate their fire on the opening. Not a man is given time to jump. All aboard are cut down where they stand.

By the end of 15 minutes, Able Company has still not fired a weapon. No orders are being given by anyone. No words are spoken. The few able-bodied survivors move or not as they see fit. Merely to stay alive is a full-time job. The fight has become a rescue operation in which nothing counts but the force of a strong example.

Above all others stands out the first-aid man, Thomas Breedin. Reaching the sands, he strips off pack, blouse, helmet, and boots. For a moment, he stands there so that others on the strand will see him and get the same idea. Then, he crawls into the water to pull in wounded men about to be overlapped by the tide. The deeper water is still spotted with tide walkers advancing at the same pace as the rising water. But now, owing to Breedin's example, the strongest among them become more conspicuous targets. Coming along, they pick up wounded comrades and float them to the shore raftwise. Machine gun fire still rakes the water. Burst after burst spoils the rescue act, shooting the floating man from the hands of the walker or killing both together. But Breedin for this hour leads a charmed life and stays with his work indomitably.

By the end of one half-hour, approximately two-thirds of the company is forever gone. There is no precise casualty figure for that moment. There is for the Normandy landing as a whole no accurate figure for the first hour or first day. The circumstances precluded it. Whether more Able Company riflemen died from water than from fire is known only to heaven. All earthly evidence so indicates, but cannot prove it.

By the end of one hour, the survivors from the main body have crawled across the sand to the foot of the bluff, where there is a narrow sanctuary of defiladed space. There, they lie all day, clean spent, unarmed, too shocked to feel hunger, incapable even of talking to one another. No one happens by to succour them, ask what has happened, provide water, or offer unwanted pity. D-Day at Omaha afforded no time or space for such missions. Every landing company was overloaded by its own assault problems.

By the end of one hour and 45 minutes, six survivors from the boat section on the extreme right shake loose and work their way to a shelf a few rods up the cliff. Four fall exhausted from the short climb and advance no farther. They stay there through the day, seeing no one else from the company. The other two, Privates Jake Shefer and Thomas Lovejoy, join a group from the 2nd Ranger Battalion, which is assaulting Pointe du Hoc to the right of the company sector, and fight on with the Rangers through the day. Two men. Two rifles. Except for these, Able Company's contribution to the D-Day fire-fight is a cipher.

Baker Company, which is scheduled to land 26 minutes after Able and right on top of it, supporting and reinforcing, has its full load of trouble on the way in. So rough is the sea during the journey that the men have to bail furiously with their helmets to keep the six boats from swamping. Thus preoccupied, they do not see the disaster which is overtaking Able until they are almost atop it. Then, what their eyes behold is either so limited or so staggering to the senses that control withers, the assault wave begins to dissolve, and disunity induced by fear virtually cancels the mission. A great cloud of smoke and dust raised by the mortar and machine gun fire has almost closed a curtain around Able Company's ordeal. Outside the pall, nothing is to be seen but a line of corpses adrift, a few heads bobbing in the water and the crimson-running tide. But this is enough for the British coxswains. They raise the cry: 'We can't go in there. We can't see the landmarks. We must pull off.'

In the command boat, Captain Ettore V. Zappacosta pulls a Colt .45 and says: 'By God, you'll take this boat straight in.' His display of courage wins obedience, but it's still a fool's order. Such of Baker's boats as try to go straight in suffer Able's fate without helping the other company whatever. Thrice during the approach, mortar shells break right next to Zappacosta's boat but by an irony leave it unscathed, thereby sparing the riders a few more moments of life. At 75 yards from the sand, Zappacosta yells: 'Drop the ramp!' The end goes down, and a storm of bullet fire comes in.

Zappacosta jumps first from the boat, reels ten yards through the elbow-high tide, and yells back: 'I'm hit.' He staggers on a few more steps. The aid man, Thomas Kenser, sees him bleeding from hip and shoulder. Kenser yells: 'Try to make it in; I'm coming.' But the captain falls face forward into the wave, and the weight of his equipment and soaked pack pin him to the bottom. Kenser jumps toward him and is shot dead while in the air. Lieutenant Tom Dallas of Charlie Company, who has come along to make a reconnaissance, is the third man. He makes it to the edge of the sand. There, a machine gun burst blows his head apart before he can flatten.

From the level of the tide, with water now covering the lower obstacles, this second shot would time the photographs as having been taken between 0740 and 0800 when the 1st Battalion landed between exits E-1 and E-3. A disabled Sherman, according to the War Department history *Omaha Beachhead* believed to be tank No. 9, from Company A of the 741st Tank Battalion, can be seen on the beach. This was later manned by Captain W. M. King who was ordered to round up as many tanks as possible and get them to exit E-3. King ran along the beach notifying each tank commander as he came to them. When he reached the last one (No. 9), he found the commander wounded and took charge personally. He drove east, weaving in and out of the wreckage before a Teller mine exploded and blew off one of the tracks.

One of the spectacular disasters on Omaha was suffered by LCI 91 which approached Dog White at about 0740 carrying the alternate headquarters of the 116th RCT. The ship was struck by artillery fire as it attempted to get through the obstacles which were barely showing on the rising tide. As the ramps were lowered in six feet of water, a shell hit the forward deck crowded with troops, sending up a sheet of flame from burning fuel. Men, their clothes on fire, jumped into the water to escape the flames. A few minutes later, LCI 92 (which we saw at Weymouth on page 203) came into the same sector and suffered the same fate when an underwater explosion set off her fuel tanks. Both craft burned for the rest of the day, this picture being taken by Bert Brandt of Acme Newspictures around 1600.

Private First Class Robert L. Sales, who is lugging Zappacosta's radio (an SCR 300), is the fourth man to leave the boat, having waited long enough to see the others die. His boot heel catches on the edge of the ramp and he falls sprawling into the tide, losing the radio but saving his life. Every man who tries to follow him is either killed or wounded before reaching dry land. Sales alone gets to the beach unhit. To travel those few yards takes him two hours. First, he crouches in the water, and waddling forward on his haunches just a few paces, collides with a floating log — driftwood. In that moment, a mortar shell explodes just above his head, knocking him groggy. He hugs the log to keep from going down, and somehow the effort seems to clear his head a little. Next thing he knows, one of Able Company's tide walkers hoists him aboard the log and, using his sheath knife, cuts away Sale's pack, boots, and assault jacket.

Feeling stronger, Sales returns to the water, and from behind the log, using it as cover, pushes toward the sand. Private Mack L. Smith of Baker Company, hit three times through the face, joins him there. An Able Company rifleman named Kemper, hit thrice in the right leg, also comes alongside. Together, they follow the log until at last they roll it to the farthest reach of high tide. Then they flatten themselves behind it, staying there for hours after the flow has turned to ebb. The dead of both companies wash up to where they lie, and then wash back out to sea again. As a body drifts in close to them, Sales and companions, disregarding the fire, crawl from behind the log to take a look. If any one of them recognises the face of a comrade, they join in dragging the body up onto the dry sand beyond the water's reach. The unfamiliar dead are left to the sea. So long as the tide is full, they stay at this task. Later, an unidentified first-aid man who comes wiggling along the beach dresses the wounds of Smith. Sales, as he finds strength, bandages Kemper. The three remain behind the log until night falls.

Only one other Baker Company boat tries to come straight in to the beach. Somehow the boat founders. Somehow all of its people are killed — one British coxswain and about 30 American infantrymen. Where they fall, there is no one to take note and report.

Brandt's second shot shows the arrival of LCT 207 carrying the self-propelled guns of the 58th Armored Field Artillery (AFA) Battalion which had made a first attempt to get ashore at 0800. Note that the obstacles are still intact on Dog Red.

Frightened coxswains in the other four craft take one quick look, instinctively draw back, and then veer right and left away from the Able Company shambles. So doing, they dodge their duty while giving a break to their passengers. Such is the shock to the boat team leaders, and such their feeling of relief at the turning movement, that not one utters a protest. Lieutenant Leo A. Pingenot's coxswain swings the boat far rightward toward Pointe du Hoc; then, spying a small and deceptively peaceful-looking cove, heads directly for the land. Fifty yards out, Pingenot yells: 'Drop the ramp!' The coxswain freezes on the rope, refusing to lower. Staff Sergeant Odell L. Padgett jumps him, throttles him, and bears him to the floor. Padgett's men lower the rope and jump for the water. In two minutes, they are all in up to their necks and struggling to avoid drowning. That quickly, Pingenot is already far out ahead of them. Padgett comes even with him, and together they cross onto dry land. The beach of the cove is heavily strewn with giant boulders. Bullets seem to be pinging off every rock.

Pingenot and Padgett dive behind the same rock. Then they glance back, but to their horror see not one person. Quite suddenly, smoke has half blanked out the scene beyond the water's edge. Pingenot moans: 'My God, the whole boat team is dead.' Padgett sings out: 'Hey, are you hit?' Back come many voices from beyond the smoke. 'What's the rush?' 'Take it easy!' 'We'll get there.' 'Where's the fire?' 'Who wants to know?' The men are still moving along, using the water as cover. Padgett's yell is their first information that anyone else has moved up front. They all make it to the shore, and they are 28 strong at first. Pingenot and Padgett manage to stay ahead of them, coaxing and encouraging. Padgett keeps yelling: 'Come on, goddamn it, things are better up there!' But still they lose two men killed and three wounded in crossing the beach.

In the cove, the platoon latches on to a company of Rangers, fights all day as part of that company, and helps destroy the enemy entrenchments atop Pointe du Hoc. By sundown, that mop-up is completed. The platoon bivouacs at the first hedgerow beyond the cliff.

Another Baker Company boat, which turns to the right, has far less luck. Staff Sergeant Robert M. Campbell, who leads the section, is the first man to jump out when the ramp goes down. He drops in drowning water, and his load of two bangalore torpedoes takes him straight to the bottom. So he jettisons the bangalores and then, surfacing, cuts away all equipment for good measure.

Machine gun fire brackets him, and he submerges again briefly. Never a strong swimmer, he heads back out to sea. For two hours, he paddles around, 200 or so yards from the shore. Though he hears and sees nothing of the battle, he somehow gets the impression that the invasion has failed and that all other Americans are dead, wounded, or have been taken prisoner. Strength fast going, in despair he moves ashore rather than drown. Beyond the smoke, he quickly finds the fire. So he grabs a helmet from a dead man's head, crawls on hands and knees to the sea-wall, and there finds five of his men, two of them unwounded.

Like Campbell, Private First Class Jan J. Budziszewski is carried to the bottom by his load of two bangalores. He hugs them half a minute before realising that he will either let loose or drown. Next, he chucks off his helmet and pack and drops his rifle. Then he surfaces. After swimming 200 yards, he sees that he is moving in exactly the wrong direction. So he turns about and heads for the beach, where he crawls ashore 'under a rain of bullets'. In his path lies a dead Ranger. Budziszewski takes the dead man's helmet, rifle and canteen, and crawls on to the sea-wall. The only survivor from Campbell's boat section to get off the beach, he spends his day walking to and fro along the foot of the bluff, looking for a friendly face. But he meets only strangers, and none shows any interest in him.

Dog Green at the end of the day with one of the LCAs carrying B — Baker — Company of the 116th Infantry on the left.

In Lieutenant William B. Williams' boat, the coxswain steers sharp left and away from Zappacosta's sector. Not seeing the captain die, Williams doesn't know that command has now passed to him. Guiding on his own instinct, the coxswain moves along the coast 600 yards, then puts the boat straight in. It's a good guess; he has found a little vacuum in the battle. The ramp drops on dry sand and the boat team jumps ashore. Yet, it's a close thing. Mortar fire has dogged them all the way; and as the last rifleman clears the ramp, one shell lands dead centre of the boat, blows it apart, and kills the coxswain. Momentarily, the beach is free of fire, but the men cannot cross it at a bound. Weak from seasickness and fear, they move at a crawl, dragging their equipment. By the end of 20 minutes, Williams and ten men are over the sand and resting in the lee of the sea-wall. Five others are hit by machine gun fire crossing the beach; six men, last seen while taking cover in a tidal pocket, are never heard from again. More mortar fire lands around the party as Williams leads it across the road beyond the sea-wall. The men scatter. When the shelling lifts, three of them do not return. Williams leads the seven survivors up a trail toward the fortified village of Les Moulins atop the bluff. He recognises the ground and knows that he is taking on a tough target. Les Moulins is perched above a draw, up which winds a dirt road from the beach, designated on the invasion maps as Exit No. 3.

Williams and his crew of seven are the first Americans to approach it D-Day morning. Machine gun fire from a concrete pillbox sweeps over them as they near the brow of the hill, moving now at a crawl through thick grass. Williams says to the others: 'Stay here; we're too big a target!' They hug earth, and he crawls forward alone, moving via a shallow gully. Without being detected, he gets to within 20 yards of the gun, obliquely downslope from it. He heaves a grenade; but he has held it just a bit too long and it explodes in air, just outside the embrasure. His second grenade hits the concrete wall and bounces right back on him. Three of its slugs hit him in the shoulders. Then, from out of the pillbox, a German potato masher sails down on him and explodes just a few feet away; five more fragments cut into him. He starts crawling back to his men; en route, three bullets from the machine gun rip his rump and right leg.

The seven are still there. Williams hands his map and compass to Staff Sergeant Frank M. Price, saying: 'It's your job now. But go the other way — toward Vierville.' Price starts to look at Williams' wounds, but Williams shakes him off, saying: 'No, get moving.' He then settles himself in a hole in the embankment, stays there all day, and at last gets medical attention just before midnight.

On leaving Williams, Price's first act is to hand map and compass (the symbols of leadership) to Technical Sergeant William Pearce, whose seniority the lieutenant has overlooked. They cross the draw, one man at a time, and some distance beyond come to a ravine; on the far side, they bump their first hedgerow, and as they look for an entrance, fire comes against them. Behind a second hedgerow, not more than 30 yards away, are seven Germans, five rifles and two burp guns. On exactly even terms, these two forces engage for the better part of an hour, apparently with no one getting hit. Then Pearce settles the fight by crawling along a drainage ditch to the enemy flank. He kills the seven Germans with a Browning Automatic Rifle.

For Pearce and his friends, it is a first taste of battle; its success is giddying. Heads up, they walk along the road straight into Vierville, disregarding all precautions. They get away with it only because that village is already firmly in the hands of Lieutenant Walter P. Taylor of Baker Company and 20 men from his boat team.

When Baker Company's assault wave breaks up just short of the surf where Able Company is in ordeal, Taylor's coxswain swings his boat sharp left, then heads toward the shore about halfway between Zappacosta's boat and Williams'. Until a few seconds after the ramp drops, this bit of beach next to the village called Hamel-au-Prêtre is blessedly clear of fire. No mortar shells crown the start. Taylor leads his section crawling across the beach and over the sea wall, losing four men killed and two wounded (machine gun fire) in this brief movement. Some yards off to his right, Taylor has seen Lieutenants Harold Donaldson and Emil Winkler shot dead. But there is no halt for reflection; Taylor leads the section by trail straight up the bluff and into Vierville, where his luck continues. In a two-hour fight, he whips a German platoon without losing a man.

The village is quiet when Pearce joins him. Pearce says: 'Williams is shot up back there and can't move.'

Says Taylor: 'I guess that makes me company commander.'

Answers Pearce: 'This is probably all of Baker Company.' Pearce takes a head count; they number 28, including Taylor.

Says Taylor: 'That ought to be enough. Follow me!'

Inland from Vierville about 500 yards lies the Château de Vaumicel, imposing in its rock-walled massiveness, its hedgerow-bordered fields all entrenched and interconnected with artillery-proof tunnels. To every man but Taylor, the target looks prohibitive. Still, they follow him. Fire stops them 100 yards short of the château. The Germans are behind a hedgerow at mid-distance. Still feeling their way, Taylor's men flatten, open fire with rifles, and toss a few grenades, though the distance seems too great. By sheer chance, one grenade glances off the helmet of a German squatting in a foxhole. He jumps up, shouting, 'Kamerad! Kamerad!' Thereupon, 24 of the enemy walk from behind the hedgerow with their hands in the air. Taylor pares off one of his riflemen to march the prisoners back to the beach. The brief fight costs him three wounded. Within the château, he takes two more prisoners, a German doctor and his first-aid man. Taylor puts them on 'a kind of a parole', leaving his three wounded in their keeping while moving his platoon to the first crossroads beyond the château.

Here, he is stopped by the sudden arrival of three truckloads of German infantry, who deploy into the fields on both flanks of his position and start an envelopment. The manpower odds, about three to one against him, are too

heavy. In the first trade of fire, lasting not more than two minutes, a rifleman lying beside Taylor is killed, three others are wounded, and the BAR is shot from Pearce's hands. That leaves but 20 men and no automatic weapons.

Taylor yells: 'Back to the château!' They go out, crawling as far as the first hedgerow; then they rise and trot along, supporting their wounded. Taylor is the last man out, having stayed behind to cover the withdrawal with his carbine until the hedgerows interdict fire against the others. So far, the small group has had no contact with any other part of the expedition, and for all its members know, the invasion may have failed.

They make it to the château. The enemy comes on and moves in close. The attacking fire builds up. But the stone walls are fire-slotted, and, through the midday and early afternoon, these ports well serve the American riflemen. The question is whether the ammunition will outlast the Germans. It is answered at sundown, just as the supply runs out, by the arrival of 15 Rangers who join their fire with Taylor's, and the Germans fade back.

Already Taylor and his force are farther south than any element of the right flank in the Omaha expedition. But Taylor isn't satisfied. The battalion objective, as specified for the close of D-Day, is still more than one-half mile to the westward. He says to the others: 'We've got to make it.'

So he leads them forth, once again serving as first scout, 18 of his own riflemen and 15 Rangers following in column. One man is killed by a bullet getting away from Vaumicel. Dark closes over them. They prepare to bivouac. Having got almost to the village of Louvières, they are by this time almost one-half mile in front of anything else in the United States Army. There, a runner reaches them with the message that the remnants of the battalion are assembling 700 yards closer to the sea; Taylor and party are directed to fall back on them. It is done.

Later, still under the spell, Price paid the perfect tribute to Taylor. He said: 'We saw no sign of fear in him. Watching him made men of us. Marching or fighting, he was leading. We followed him because there was nothing else to do.'

Taylor is a luminous figure in the story of D-Day, one of the 47 immortals of Omaha who, by their dauntless initiative at widely-separated points along the beach, saved the landing from total stagnation and disaster. Courage and luck are his in extraordinary measure.

Thousands of Americans were spilled onto Omaha Beach. The high ground was won by a handful of men like Taylor who on that day burned with a flame bright beyond common understanding.

BRIGADIER GENERAL S. L. A. MARSHALL, 1963

In 1958, Cornelius Ryan was canvassing reminiscences of D-Day for the book he was preparing, and his standard approach was to send out a three-page questionnaire. One was returned by Robert J. Rieske, then the divisional manager with the Shaw-Walker Company in Muskegou, Michigan. in June 1944, he had been a 1st Lieutenant with Headquarters, 1st Infantry Division, serving as Brigadier General Bill Wyman's aide. He responded to Ryan as follows:

What was the trip like during the crossing of the Channel?

'Trip was rough. There were only a few on our LCVP. The General, Major Paul Gale, Don Whitehead and three or four others. I was surprised at the distance to the beach area and the lonesomeness of the trip. We stopped at the navy check-points (picket ships) on the way in to check conditions but received no accurate report. It was considered that the floating tanks had all gone down in the rough water.'

What were the rumors on board?

'The ship I was on with the General was, I believe, totally lacking in rumors. To many, facts were faced with awareness to consider rumor. The facts themselves sounded like something from Buck Rogers. All the beach obstacles — than *(sic)* the beach. The pillboxes. If this and if that.'

Were any of your friends killed or wounded?

'Several.'

Do you remember any conversations you had with them before they became casualties?

'No — as I recall it comes to mind more the silence. The 1st had done this before and you know someone gets hurt. It's the quietness of the experienced man that says all there is.'

Were you wounded?

'Yes.'

Do you remember what it was like?

'I thought it first to be just concussion. There is no pain — this was my second time.'

Do you remember seeing or hearing anything that seems funny now?

'Don Whitehead was inclined to crack funnies. Most of the people going in on the LCVPs got seasick. It did seem peculiar at the time how alone you feel always.'

Do you recall any incident which struck you more than anything else?

'The saddest events were on the beach when troops would not move off. The tragedy of men who wouldn't move. General Wyman moving up and down the beach talking, moving men, redeploying troops. urging them to use their equipment. Trying to locate a radio that operated. Meeting the incoming troops and always exposed. The beach would have gone without him.'

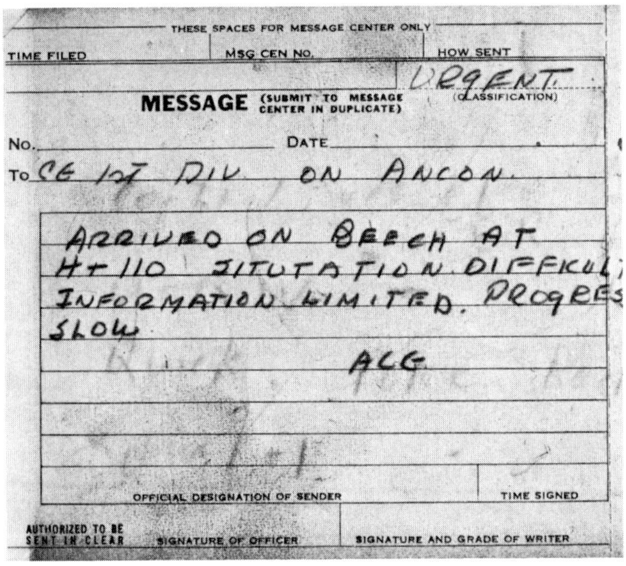
THESE SPACES FOR MESSAGE CENTER ONLY
TIME FILED | MSG CEN NO. | HOW SENT
URGENT.
MESSAGE (SUBMIT TO MESSAGE CENTER IN DUPLICATE) (CLASSIFICATION)
No. DATE
To CG 1st DIV ON ANCON.
ARRIVED ON BEECH AT H+110 SITUTATION DIFFICUL INFORMATION LIMITED. PROGRES SLOW
ALG
OFFICIAL DESIGNATION OF SENDER | TIME SIGNED
AUTHORIZED TO BE SENT IN CLEAR | SIGNATURE OF OFFICER | SIGNATURE AND GRADE OF WRITER

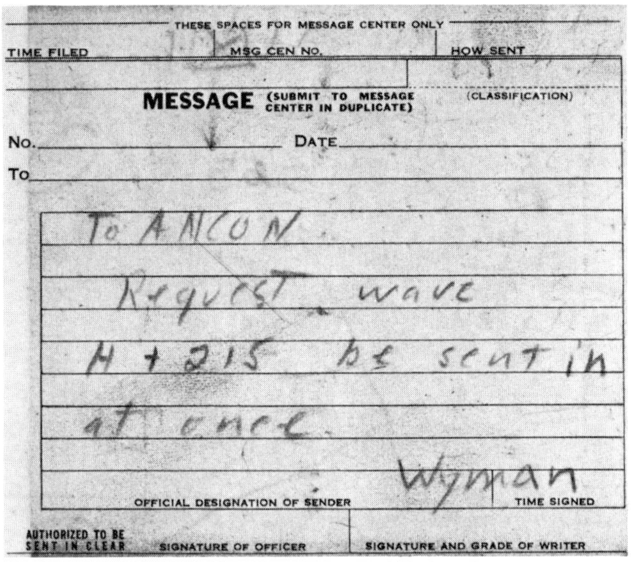
THESE SPACES FOR MESSAGE CENTER ONLY
TIME FILED | MSG CEN NO. | HOW SENT
MESSAGE (SUBMIT TO MESSAGE CENTER IN DUPLICATE) (CLASSIFICATION)
No. DATE
To
To ANCON.
Request wave H + 215 be sent in at once.
Wyman
OFFICIAL DESIGNATION OF SENDER | TIME SIGNED
AUTHORIZED TO BE SENT IN CLEAR | SIGNATURE OF OFFICER | SIGNATURE AND GRADE OF WRITER

Bob Rieske sent Ryan several photographs he had taken personally and also copies of messages that he had written while under fire on Easy Red. Although he wanted them back, Ryan retained them and, when the latter died, they went with the rest of his papers to Ohio University. Doug McCabe discovered them in 1994 and kindly sent them to us. 'As you can see', wrote Doug, 'there are cracks where the negatives were folded and squeezed against file folders for years. Of the two beach photos, the wide shot *(opposite)* is the more interesting to me. You can clearly see ships in the Channel and what appears to be a group of men in the water. There are also several vehicles on the shingle, and one of the very few tanks to make it ashore. At the extreme left of the photo is the antennae of one of the many non-working radios. Note the soldier standing to the right of the tank willing to face fire from beyond the shingle. I suppose the most interesting item in the other photo *(right)* is the tank on the far right. Is that a wedge-shaped plow mounted to the front? Odd. In the deep background at the water line appears to be some kind of amphibious vehicle and beyond that to the right might be a landing craft.'

Other unique pictures taken by Robert Rieske appear in the Editor's Postscript beginning on page 622.

On the morning of June 6, we were up before dawn on the deck of the Chase. I carried my lightweight typewriter strapped to my back, encased in a raincoat for waterproofing. My other impedimenta included a blanket, a canteen of water, a couple of boxes of K-rations, and a notebook and pencil. I was to go ashore in the same landing craft with Brigadier General Willard Wyman, assistant division commander of the 1st, whose job it was to help organise the troops on the beach. His partner in this job was Brigadier General Norman Cota, assistant commander of the 29th Infantry Division.

The first and second waves of troops — scheduled to land at 6.30 and 7.00 a.m. — had been thrown into disorder. Boats swung from their courses and drove through gaps wherever they could find them. This was possible because between 7 and 8 a.m. the tide rose eight feet in the Channel. But units landed far from their assigned sectors. Commanders were separated from their troops. Sections were fragmented. And those who landed were pinned to the beach by heavy machine gun, artillery, and mortar fire.

We rode the rising tide through one of the gaps and waded ashore at 8 a.m. As far as I could see through the smoke of battle, troops were lying along a shelf of shale. Ahead of us stretched mined sand dunes to the bluffs where the Germans were sheltered in their trenches, bunkers, and blockhouses. There was no cover for the men on the beach. The Germans were looking down on them — and it was a shooting gallery.

There were many brave men on Omaha that day — Dutch Cota, Bill Wyman, George Taylor, and scores of men whose names were never imprinted on the honor roll of Omaha Beach. Under the guns of the enemy, they organised small units and established small islands of order in the chaos. In what seemed a formless, confused horde, there did emerge gradually a core of discipline. And even as the Germans believed they were winning this battle on the beach, units of infantrymen were working their way through the minefields and up the bluff.

I remember vividly Private Vinton Dove of Washington, DC [see page 359]. *His name has remained with me to this day. He drove a bulldozer from a landing craft and then he began bulldozing a road from the beach as calmly as though he were grading a driveway at home. He sat there with only a sweatshirt to protect him from bullets and the shell fragments.*

The firepower of the navy was one of our salvations in those first few hours. I recall that we were about 200 yards west of a small draw on Easy Red marked on the maps as E-1 or Exit 1. A blockhouse had been built into the bluff above the dirt road that led inland. The German gunners manning an 88mm weapon had a clear field of fire to the west. They were firing at almost point-blank range at the landing craft and the troops trapped at the edge of the water.

A radio call for help went from an army-navy beach team to a destroyer. We saw the destroyer come racing towards the beach and swing broadside, exposing itself to the fire of the batteries on the bluff. One shell from the destroyer tore a chunk of concrete from the side of the blockhouse. Another nicked the top. A third ripped off a corner. And then the fourth shell smashed into the gunport to silence the weapon. Always, in my mind, the knocking out of this gun was a major turning-point of the battle in our sector.

At 1.30 p.m., General Wyman moved from the beach and set up his first sheltered command post in the knocked-out blockhouse, and this was where I wrote my first story of the landing. As I saw it, that was when the battle of the beach was won — seven hours after the first wave hit the beach.

DON WHITEHEAD,
A CORRESPONDENT'S VIEW OF D-DAY, 1971

Only six paths had been blown in that barricade before the rising tide halted their operations. Unable to break through the obstacles that blocked their assigned beaches, craft turned toward Easy Red where the gaps had been blown. Then, as successive waves ran in toward the cluttered beach-head, they soon found themselves snarled in a jam offshore.

When V Corps reported at noon that the situation was 'still critical' on all four beach exits, I reluctantly contemplated the diversion of Omaha follow-up forces to Utah and the British beaches. Scanty reports from both those sectors indicated the landings there had gone according to plan.

With the Omaha landing falling hours and hours behind schedule, we faced an imminent crisis on the follow-up force. There was due to arrive at noon in the transport area off Omaha Beach a force of 25,000 troops and 4,400 more vehicles to be landed on the second tide. However, only a portion of the assault force of 34,000 troops and 3,300 vehicles had as yet got ashore. Unless we moved both forces ashore on D-Day, the whole intricate schedule of build-up would be thrown off balance. Whatever the improvisation, our build-up would have to be maintained if we were to withstand an enemy counter-offensive. Despite the setbacks we had suffered as the result of bad weather and ineffective bombing, I was shaken to find that we had gone against Omaha with so thin a margin of safety. At the time of sailing, we had thought ourselves cushioned against such reversals as these.

Not until noon did a radio from Gerow offer a clue to the trouble we had run into on Omaha Beach. Instead of the rag-tag static troops we had expected to find there, the assault had run head-on into one of Rommel's tough field divisions.

In planning the assault, originally we had counted upon a thin enemy crust of two static divisions between Caen and Cherbourg. Rommel was known to have concentrated his better reserves behind the beach. Among them was the 352. Infanterie-Division which had been assembled at St Lô.

Just before boarding the *Augusta* in Plymouth harbor, Dickson learned that the 352nd had been moved from St Lô to the assault beaches for a defense exercise. He promptly forwarded this information to V Corps and the 1st Division but was unable to give it to the troops already 'sealed' aboard their craft.

Had a less-experienced division than the 1st Infantry stumbled into this crack resistance, it might easily have been thrown back into the Channel. Unjust though it was, my choice of the 1st to spearhead the invasion probably saved us Omaha Beach and a catastrophe on the landing.

Isolated from the troops ashore, the commanders on their ships could only sweat it out. The intention was to land 34,142 troops with Force 'O', and over 3,300 vehicles, on D-Day, about half of which belonged to the 1st Infantry Division, the other half being attached from the 29th Division. The follow-up troops — Force 'B' — standing by with 25,117 men and 4,429 vehicles were to go ashore on the afternoon of D-Day, but by midday General Bradley was having to contemplate diverting them to Utah. No wonder Major General Charles H. Gerhardt, the 29th divisional commander, looks worried as his staff peer at the coastline from the bridge.

This may well be the indistinct view they had of the beach as the picture appears to have been taken by the same (unnamed) US Navy photographer. Smoke from burning scrub and LCI 91 and 92 obscures Dog Beach where the 115th and 116th RCTs from the 29th Division, temporarily attached to the 1st Division, were ashore with the assistant division commander, Brigadier General Norman D. Cota who had landed shortly after 0730 on Dog White with the main command group of the 116th. (An American regimental combat team, e.g. the 116th Regimental Combat Teams, was basically the 116th Infantry Regiment plus added elements of supporting units, artillery, engineers, armour, etc.)

LCI 553 was disabled by mines and had to be abandoned just in front of strong point WN 62. It was here, on the left of Easy Red, that the Corps of Engineers claims that one of their teams led the entire invasion by at least five minutes. 'The commander of Team 14, 2d Lt. Phill C. Wood, Jr, was under the impression that H-Hour was 0620 instead of 0630. Under his entreaties, the Navy coxswain brought the LCM in at 0625, the boat's gun crew unsuccessfully tying to destroy Teller mines on the upright stakes. Wood and his team dragged their explosive-laden rubber boat into waist-deep water under a hail of machine gun fire. No one was on the beach. The lieutenant charged towards a row of obstacles, glancing backward as he ran. In that moment, he saw an artillery shell land squarely in the center of the craft he had just left, detonating the contents of the second rubber boat and killing most of the Navy contingent of his team. The LCM burned fiercely. Wood's crew dropped bangalore torpedoes and mine detectors and abandoned their load of explosives. Dodging among the rows, they managed to wire a line of obstacles to produce a gap, but here the infantry landing behind them frustrated their attempt to complete the job. Troops, wounded or hale, huddled among the obstacles, using them for cover, and Wood finally gave up trying to chase them out of range of his charges. Leaving the obstacles as they were, he and his team, now only about half of its original strength, rushed forward and took up firing positions with the infantry concentrated at the shingle.'

Easy Red, June 1994. The ruined house which conveniently and characteristically marked Exit E-1, visible just in front of the bow of the LCM on the right in the top photo (which appears to be No. 408), no longer stands.

Of the 16 gapping teams, only four managed to accomplish their missions. On the eastern sector of Omaha, Team 9, landing well ahead of the infantry in the middle of Easy Red, opened a 50-yard gap, and Team 10 created two gaps, one of 50 and one of 100 yards (see plan pages 340-341). This picture, taken late during the morning around 1100 as the tide is approaching the shingle bank, shows LCI 553 from its opposite side looking towards Exit E-3 on the left which is still being hotly defended by German forces.

Although the deadlock had been broken several hours sooner, it was almost 1.30 p.m. when V Corps relieved our fears aboard the *Augusta* with the terse message: 'Troops formerly pinned down on beaches Easy Red, Easy Green, Fox Red advancing up heights behind beaches.'

Fifty years later, a patrolling helicopter overflies enthusiasts driving their preserved military vehicles on Easy Red. Exit E-3 is in the middle distance with the 1st Division memorial obelisk at WN 62.

The battle for the beach-head is over and the detritus of war lies abandoned. In the foreground, a wrecked bulldozer, while LCI 553 lies high and dry. Cemetery No. 1 was established on top of the bluff on the right.

Above: LCI(L) 412 noses up to the shingle below the cemetery. *Below:* The 18th RCT was scheduled to land on Easy Red about 0930 but the congestion delayed their arrival just west of E-1 until shortly after 1000, at which point the LCI(L)s of the 115th Infantry began to touch down on top of them. The 115th, reserve reinforcements for Force 'O', had been due to land on Easy Green and Dog Red but could not find the control vessels for these sectors and they were carried further east by the wind and strong current. This picture, taken at noon just west of E-1, shows swarms of men and vehicles on the narrow strip of shingle. The end of the metalled road on the left marks the dividing line between Easy Green and Easy Red. The anti-tank ditch, seen in the bottom right-hand corner, had only recently been dug to protect WN 65.

As these reinforcements from the 1st Division (probably the 18th Infantry) land later in the morning, the advance from Easy Red up the slope is already under way. Photo sequence taken by Captain Herman Wall (see page 630).

Behind Omaha, the ground rose steeply up brush-covered slopes from 100 to 170 feet high. At four points along the 7,000-yard beach, lightly-wooded draws indented these bluffs to provide exit routes inland. Here, the enemy had concentrated his heaviest fortifications and here he had held out the longest. Only one draw was travelled by an improved road; the others contained nothing but cart tracks. Within days, these cart tracks were to become the most heavily trafficked roads in Europe.

The flag on the skyline marks the present-day US cemetery.

These pictures, taken on Easy Red after the battle, show just how the beach area has changed, much as a result of construction work by engineers who utilised the shingle from the bank for infilling the anti-tank ditch and as road foundations. This wreckage lies just below the shingle bank at the point where the 1st and 2nd Battalion of the 16th Infantry reached the top.

Left: Just behind the bank, engineers quickly constructed a road parallel to the foreshore. On the extreme right is E-1 exit.

Company G, 16th Infantry, led the advance up the bluff from these ruins but no sign of the latter can be seen today *(right)*.

Later, as part of his report examining the part played by US engineers on Omaha on D-Day, Colonel E. G. Paules, the Engineer Member of the War Department Observers Board, inspected the beach-head with Major Allan F. Olson, the Executive Officer of the 121st Engineer Battalion, 29th Division, who had landed at 0838 with the fifth wave. '1st Lieutenant Kays and Private Fitzwater of Company A, 1st Combat Engineers, accompanied me to the beach and traced the path they took with the 16th Infantry on D-Day. This photo *[left]* shows the two men in the garden of the ruined houses. They showed me the route through this yard taken by the 16th Combat Team. After passing through the brush at the rear of the yard, the path swung to the left and up through the little valley shown at the left centre of the photo. Photo *[right]* shows the well-worn path taped out as mines were removed. German fire in this little valley was lighter than in other places and the 16th Infantry reached the top of the bluff at the point shown and then took the beach exit fortifications in the rear. Officers at Engineers HQ of V Corps described Omaha on D-Day as "a scene of indescribable confusion".'

The wooded valley at Easy Red, now forever known as E-1 draw. This picture was taken in June 1943 before very much defensive work had taken place. The western (right) shoulder of the valley became strong point WN 65 centred around a Type 667 50mm casemate which replaced the house [1]. House [2] is the one which characterises exit E-1 and building [3] is another prominent feature seen in many of the D-Day photographs. WN 64 was located on the eastern (left-hand) shoulder.

Reluctant to bank altogether on the laconic reports that trickled in from V Corps, I instructed Kean to go ashore, size up the beach-front congestion, and check on the advance inland that we might calculate our chances on landing a part of the follow-up force that night. With Hansen, he sped off in a PT, closed to 1,000 yards offshore, and transferred to an LCVP for the final trip through the obstacles. High water had reached its mark and the tide was rolling out, leaving the LCTs and hundreds of craft dried out on the beaches. The *Augusta* had now closed in to within 4,000 yards of the beach and the waters about us were strewn with flotsam from the invasion.

Taken on May 19, 1944, WN 65 has been completed and work is proceeding on the installation of beach obstacles using 'horse-power'.

June 1944. Now clearly marked for 'easy' identification, the shingle has been 'dozed away in two places, giving access to the road leading to St Laurent. On the hilltop on the right, the tents and radio masts of V Corps headquarters.

E-1 was cleared fairly early and became the main exit from Omaha on D-Day, largely due to the efforts of the 37th and 149th Engineer Combat Battalions. The 37th suffered 24 men killed including its commander. Two of its bulldozer operators, Privates Vinton W. Dove and William J. Shoemaker of Company C, were both awarded Distinguished Service Crosses for clearing the road through the shingle and filling in the anti-tank ditch while under intense enemy fire, the German gunners having singled out the bulldozers as prime targets. Company C's 1st Lieutenant Robert P. Ross won the third DSC awarded to the 37th on D-Day for helping Company E, 16th Infantry, to silence WN 64 on the hillside overlooking E-1 in a battle in which 40 Germans were killed. After its capture, the engineers took over the 50mm casemate for use as their command post.

Kean's report was more hopeful than I had dared wish for. Despite the congestion of vehicles on Omaha Beach, our troops had penetrated the enemy's defenses between the well-guarded draws, and to the east of Easy Red had pushed one mile inland to cut the first lateral road. Although the strategic draw at Easy Red had not yet been cleared of small-arms fire, bulldozers were already carving a path up its shoulder to the tableland on top of the bluff. And as the tide withdrew from the beach, engineers trailed after it through the debris, blowing new paths through the obstacles as they were uncovered by the Channel.

Having earned three DSCs under fire within yards of the emplacement, it was only fitting that it was chosen soon after the war for the siting of a memorial tablet to the Provisional Engineer Special Brigade Group which encompassed all the engineer units. ***Left:*** **However, the engineers plaque on the western face (the original was later replaced) has since been overshadowed by an obelisk erected by the 2nd Infantry Division (not part of the assault force but a reinforcement for D+1 and 2).** ***Right:*** **Then, just prior to the 50th anniversary, the casemate itself was usurped for the mounting of a plaque directly over the firing aperture to the 467th AA AW Battalion which did not land until 0830 hours.**

Admiral Harold R. Stark, Commander US Naval Forces Europe (COMNAVEU), visited the beach-head on June 14, landing at E-1, and is seen here leaving the engineers CP.

About to face their baptism of fire in World War II, elements of the 2nd Infantry Division climb up past the same bunker on June 7.

How times change! Thirty years after, this section of Easy Red remained virtually unspoiled, with the original breaches through the dunes still visible.

Now seafront development threatens the hallowed ground as two French soldiers carry out a security patrol on the eve of the 50th anniversary.

Strong point WN 64 lay on the opposite side of the valley and, although construction of the casemate had not yet been completed, the Germans were manning trenches nearby overlooking the beach. 2nd Lieutenant John M. Spaulding of Company E, 16th RCT, had reached the top of the bluff (using the small draw depicted on page 357), whereupon he headed west to cut round behind WN 64 and attack it from the rear. In two hours of confused fighting which earned Spaulding the Distinguished Service Cross, Company E managed to overcome the opposition with the help of naval gun-fire directed at the strong point from a destroyer. By mid-morning, just as reinforcements were coming ashore at E-1, the position was neutralised with the capture of 21 of the enemy.

Above: In this shot, looking at the eastern shoulder of E-1 (with building [3] in the middle distance), the uncompleted casemate can be spotted just below the summit. On the left is Exit E-3 on Fox Green. Although the picture is undated, it is obvious that the war has moved inland as French civilians assist First Army quartermaster personnel recover equipment. Prominent are stacks of the M26 life preservers which could be inflated automatically using a small compressed air bottle, or manually through two rubber tubes. However, the lifebelt did not have sufficient buoyancy to support a soldier and his equipment. Consequently, many men drowned when they found that they could not get rid of their packs and ammunition belts without first removing the life preserver.

Looking east towards Fox Green through a tangle of vehicles, landing craft, equipment and stores . . . and the dead.

The fallen, wrapped in blankets, are unceremoniously loaded aboard a funereal DUKW to be taken for burial on the bluff.

Fifty years later, a poignant comparison: anniversary transport on Easy Red with French 'GI' stand ins.

The exit route from E-1 followed the road to St Laurent . . .

Despite the improved situation, however, Omaha had fallen seriously behind schedule. The beach was littered with stoved-in craft, drowned-out vehicles, and burned-out tanks. Scores of bodies sprawled wet and shapeless in the shingle where they had fallen. Only the lightly wounded could be removed to hospital ships through the heavy surf. The more seriously wounded had been bedded down in slit trenches under the sea-wall. And, from one end of the beach to the other, the tidal shelf was littered with the water-soaked debris that washes in with the surf in the wake of any invasion.

The enormous equipment losses on landing had left Omaha badly in need of replacements. 'What do they need most?' I asked Kean.

'Bulldozers,' he answered, 'bulldozers and artillery. They're badly pinched for both.'

Not only were bulldozers needed to clear the debris and obstacles in time for the second tide, but without them our losses mounted as vehicles, ferried ashore on Rhinos from the LSTs, mired in the soft, low-water sands. Of the 16 dozers that had been sent ashore that morning, only six reached Omaha Beach. Three of these were immediately knocked out by enemy artillery fire.

. . . but further up the draw a branch road was cut through to the main road. Today, it has reverted to an overgrown rough track *(below)*.

This incredible panorama was taken on D+1 and it serves as an ideal illustration for an even more amazing event which took place on the afternoon of D-Day as the Corps of Engineers history explains: 'Wading ashore at Dog Green about 1500, troops of the 336th Engineer Combat Battalion assembled at the shingle bank and began a hazardous march towards Fox Red, more than two miles away. The unit moved in a long irregular column, followed by a D-7 tractor that towed an Athey trailer loaded with explosives. As the battalion made its way around bodies and wreckage through smoke and gun-fire, it witnessed the awful panorama of D-Day on Omaha. Artillery fire had decreased at Exit D-1 after destroyers knocked out a strong point on Pointe de la Percée about noon. It grew heavier as engineers approached D-3, several times narrowly missing the explosive-laden trailer. At E-1, the fire let up, but congestion on the beach increased. The worst spot they encountered was at E-3, such heavy machine gun fire and artillery shelling that they had to halt. The commander sent the men forward two at a time; when about half had gone through the area, a shell hit a bulldozer. The 'dozer began to burn, sending up clouds of smoke that covered the gap and enabled the rest of the men to dash across. As the troops proceeded down the beach, they saw a tank nose over the dune line and fire about 25 rounds at a German machine gun emplacement, knocking it out; but artillery barrages continued hitting the beach in front of E-3 every 15 or 20 minutes. At the end of its "memorable and terrible" march across Omaha, during which two men were killed by shell fragments and 27 were injured, the engineer column reached the comparative safety of the F-1 area at 1700.'

Protected also by the two 75mm casemates of WN 62 on the west side of the draw, E-3 yielded only slowly to the persistence of the engineer troops. Now, the 5th Engineer Special Brigade memorial stands proudly on top of one of the Type 669 casemates to record their achievement.

Left: The 88mm Type 677 casemate of WN 61 just east of exit E-3 on Fox Green. It was knocked out at about 0710 by a Sherman DD commanded by Staff Sergeant Sheppard of the 741st Tank Battalion. In this picture, taken on Independence Day, 1944, it is claimed that Staff Sergeant Joseph Harvat is raising one of the first US flags to reach France on D-Day, having been recovered from a landing craft sunk by enemy fire. *Above:* Jean Paul found the casemate now privately owned.

Company L, 16th Infantry, had as its mission the capture of strong point WN 61 on Fox Green, but the easterly current swept them ashore instead at the western end of Fox Red at the point where the bluff becomes a rocky cliff just beyond the high water mark. The company commander was killed and 1st Lieutenant Robert R. Cutler took charge of the assault on strong point WN 60 on the cliff-top (for which he was awarded the DSC). Here, on the narrow strip of shingle, the men reorganised for the assault. The sections were moved out to a position where they were just below WN 60. Two tanks were called upon for fire support as three sections worked their way around the shoulder of the draw, using the thick undergrowth as cover. Despite having to cross a minefield, the men reached the top without serious loss to get in a position to attack the strong point from the rear.

Captain Kimball R. Richmond of Company I, who had just reached Fox Green to find himself the senior officer, began to organise a follow-up to Company L's advance. This comprised a mixed force including the 1st Section of the company (which had actually landed on their designated beach facing WN 61 but was too weak to attempt its capture on their own); some sections of Company E of the 116th RCT which had landed over a mile east of their appointed beach; two sections of Company K; a handful of men from his own Company I, and machine gunners and mortarmen from Company M. Shell-fire from a destroyer which had helped subdue the battery in the early stages of the attack, was lifted to enable both Company L on the high ground and the mixed force from below to attack position WN 60 from two directions. Enemy resistance was soon broken; grenades and satchel charges of explosives cleared out the trenches and emplacements, and by 0900 the position had been secured with the capture of 31 prisoners. *Centre and right:* Risking wet feet and getting cut off by the tide, Jean Paul retraced the steps of Company L to take these comparisons at the foot of the cliff.

Above: From the high ground of the strong point, the entire sweeping curve of Omaha comes into view, with exit F-1 in the foreground. *Below:* This was the remains of WN 60 photographed in February 1945.

The position can be seen — albeit overgrown — just as it was left in 1944.

WN 60 was also the forward observation post of Major Werner Pluskat, the commander of I. Abteilung of Artillerie-Regiment 352. As described by Cornelius Ryan in *The Longest Day*: 'He walked back to the aperture and stood looking out. Wearily, he swung the glasses over to the left again. Slowly he tracked across the horizon. He reached the dead centre of the bay. The glasses stopped moving. Pluskat tensed, stared hard. Through the scattering, thinning mist the horizon was magically filing with ships — ships of every size and description, ships that casually manoeuvred back and forth as though they had been there for hours. There appeared to be thousands of them. It was a ghostly armada that somehow had appeared from nowhere. Pluskat stared in frozen disbelief, speechless, moved as he had never been before in his life. At that moment, the world of the good soldier Pluskat began falling apart. He says that in those first few moments he knew, calmly and surely, that "this was the end for Germany". Then he picked up the 'phone and called Major Block at the 352nd Division's headquarters. "Block," said Pluskat, "it's the invasion. There must be ten thousand ships out here." Even as he said it, he knew his words must sound incredible. "Get hold of yourself, Pluskat!" snapped Block. "The Americans and the British together don't have that many ships. Nobody has that many ships!" Block's disbelief brought Pluskat out of his daze. "If you don't believe me," he suddenly yelled, "come up here and see for yourself. It's fantastic! It's unbelievable!" There was a slight pause and then Block said, "What way are these ships heading?" Pluskat, 'phone in hand, looked out of the aperture of the bunker and replied, "Right for me." Dramatic as all this sounds (the scene in the film was re-created at Longues), it has been challenged by some of Pluskat's former contemporaries. Although he strongly denies it, and has described the scene many times, they say he was never at the front on D-Day but instead was living it up in Bayeux!

In the zone controlled by the 116th RCT, where Brigadier General Cota was the senior officer ashore, both exits — D-1 and D-3 — were not opened until the evening of D-Day. At D-1, at the junction of Charlie and Dog Green, two casemates of WN 72 were sited to enfilade the entire beach. This was the view from the gunport of the 50mm casemate at the base of the headland. The side of the second emplacement, housing a 75mm Pak 40 (although the literature of the period routinely described all German casemated guns as 'deadly 88s'), can be seen just in front on the right with the sea-front road beyond although the wooden sea-wall has already been removed by engineers.

Although Omaha had squeezed through a crisis, she was still on the danger list. With neither depth, artillery, nor tanks, we might easily be dislodged from our precarious footing and thrown back into the Channel by counter-attack. I hurried off to see Gerow aboard the *Ancon*.

However desperate the situation, a senior commander must always exude confidence in the presence of his subordinates. For anxiety, topside, can spread like cancer down through the command.

While splashing toward the *Ancon* aboard a PT boat, I anticipated that Gerow and Huebner might have been unnerved by the prolonged struggle that morning. Both had gone under fire as senior commanders for the first time, and although neither could have averted the crisis, both bore an immediate responsibility for it. Thus, while I was

A side wall, demolished by the time these pictures were taken in September 1944, screened the muzzle blast from observation from the seaward side. The 121st Engineer Combat Battalion was responsible for opening the D-1 exit but during the landing it had been scattered along the beach as far as D-3 and had lost 75 per cent of its equipment. Consquently, the battalion officers had to spend several hours collecting their men and salvaging explosives.

The 75mm casemate, a Type 677, had two flank anti-tank walls; that on the right-hand seaward side joining the sea-wall while the one on the left completely blocked the road. The actual emplacement was silenced just after midday by a Sherman DD of the 743rd Tank Battalion aided by salvoes from the battleship *Texas*.

eager to check on the situation and push the follow-up ashore, I went partly to stiffen their confidence if confidence was what they needed. I found, however, that Gerow's map showed penetrations at five points on the Omaha Beach defenses. The lateral road had been cut at Vierville and again at Colleville on the left. And a force was pushing toward Pointe du Hoc to relieve the Rangers there. With that, we hoisted our tails and went ahead with the original plan to land the follow-up force on Omaha Beach and put five regiments ashore by nightfall.

Huebner was planning to go in and take shore command of his 1st Division that evening.

'How about you, Gee?' I asked. 'When can you move V Corps headquarters ashore?'

'Early in the morning, Brad. We'll have our communications in by then.'

'To hell with your communications', Gerow grinned. 'We'll set up on the beach tonight.'

Engineers set about demolishing the anti-tank wall and the exit was opened to traffic, which had severely clogged Dog Green, by 1700. However, fire from artillery sited inland severely hampered its use until after dark.

With a penchant for siting memorials on bunkers, another American organisation, the US National Guard (the 29th Division was wholly composed of National Guard units) has mounted its own 'blockhouse' on top of the original.

'Along Dog Green and Dog White, a crusty 51-year-old general named Norman Cota strode up and down in the hail of fire, waving a .45 and yelling at men to get off the beach. Along the shingle, behind the sea-wall and in the coarse beach grass at the base of the bluffs, men crouched shoulder to shoulder, peering at the general, unwilling to believe that a man could stand upright and live. A group of Rangers lay huddled near the Vierville exit. "Lead the way, Rangers!" Cota shouted. Men began to rise to their feet. Farther down the beach was an abandoned bulldozer loaded with TNT. It was just what was needed to blow the anti-tank wall at the Vierville exit. "Who drives this thing?" he thundered. No one answered. Men seemed still paralysed by the merciless gunfire that flayed the beach. Cota began to lose his temper. "Hasn't anyone got guts enough to drive the damn thing?" he roared. A red-haired soldier got slowly up from the sand and with great deliberation walked over to Cota. "I'll do it", he said. Cota slapped him on the back. "That's the stuff", the general said. "Now let's get off the beach." He walked away without looking back. Behind him, men began to stir.' Cornelius Ryan, *The Longest Day*.

At 8.30 p.m. that evening, V Corps opened its first CP in a ditch atop the bluffs behind Easy Red. I was anxious that Gerow get his teeth into the beach organisation and speed up unloading of the 2nd Infantry Division on D+1.

Top: **Looking from the gunners' position, one can see how dominating the 75mm position was, covering the whole western end of Omaha. This is another picture from the photographic survey of German defences at Vierville carried out by the Signal Corps on September 3, 1944.** *Right:* **Our photographers, Jean Paul Pallud, Steve Casely and Karel Margry carried out their own photo survey in 1994.** *Below:* **Mine clearing along the D-1 exit road to Vierville — a July 1944 picture showing the remains of Mulberry 'A'.**

Company F, 116th Infantry, came ashore almost exactly on target at D-3 — the strongly-fortified exit at Les Moulins at the junction of Dog Red and Easy Green. However, the fire was so heavy that many men took refuge behind tanks at the water's edge — themselves prime targets for the German artillery emplaced at WN 66 and WN 68. The battalion CO, Major Sidney V. Bingham, came ashore shortly after and he set about trying to rally leaderless sections of Company F. Without a radio to contact his widely-scattered men, he got a party of about 50 across the shingle and occupied this three-storey house right on the foreshore and German trenches which lay just beyond the wire. The house can be seen behind LCT 207 on page 346. Following official US wartime policy in not releasing pictures showing identifiable American dead, the face of the casualty in the foreground has been obliterated on the original negative of this US Navy picture released on June 12.

Not until after the war did we learn that by the evening of June 6, enemy staff officers at the château CP of the German 7. Armee headquartered at Le Mans searched their pencil scorings on the map of France for clues to our intentions. The calm of their long sojourn in occupied France had ended at 1.30 a.m. that morning, when a terse signal from LXXXIV. Korps reported Allied airborne landings from Caen to the Cotentin. News of an Allied attack on the Cotentin instantly alerted the German 7. Armee to the probability of an Allied attempt to isolate the port of Cherbourg by sealing the peninsula behind it. But the German High Command declined to rush into so hasty a conclusion. Both at Rommel's army group and at von Rundstedt's Oberbefehlshaber West, staff officers leafed warily through the first landing reports, hesitant to believe in the all too obvious signs.

Most of them had concluded that an Allied attack would come through the Pas-de-Calais and so confident were they in this assumption that it became difficult for them to accept our Normandy landing as a major effort. From the start, they dismissed it as a 'diversion' designed to throw the 15. Armee off its guard in the Pas-de-Calais. The enemy prided himself on the knowledge by which he had discerned our 'intentions', not knowing that this 'discernment' had been shrewdly encouraged by the 'Overlord' cover plan. Thus, in rejecting as a Yankee trick our landing in the Cotentin, the enemy fell into the trap we had baited for him on the Pas-de-Calais. During the next six weeks, while the German 7. Armee lost the Battle for France as a result of its inability to secure reinforcements, the strategists in Berlin persisted in their fatal miscalculation. Not until after the break-out did they realise how completely they had been misled on the Pas-de-Calais 'landing'. But by then the 7. Armee had been destroyed and France lay open to the German border. Germany's defeat in France derived in part from its own exhaustion and

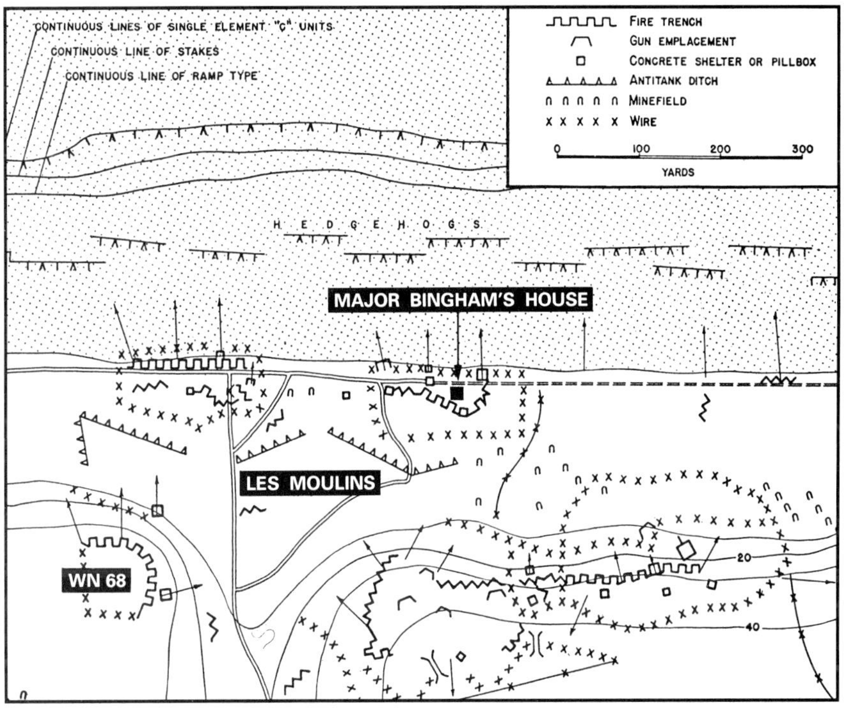

Little of the 1944 shingle bank survives on Omaha, which today is mostly sandy, although a little can still be seen in front of the site of Major Bingham's house.

On the bluff behind the house lay German strong point WN 66 with its elaborate trench system which was assaulted — unsuccessfully — by Major Bingham and a squad of ten men. (The actual house is just out of the picture.)

Hitler's fumbling. But a share of the blame also rests with the German General Staff. For it was German professionals who proved most susceptible to our hoax on the Pas-de-Calais.

As D-Day wore on, 7. Armee's trust in its original estimate on Cherbourg wavered. At 6.45 a.m., just 15 minutes after H-Hour, Army advised Rommel's CP that the naval fire on Omaha Beach might be part of an elaborate diversionary effort to screen a main offensive elsewhere. Shortly before noon, Army made up its mind: the major effort, it reported, had been centered on the British beaches. By then, corps had reported swift British penetrations through the coastal wall toward the rolling tank terrain that led beyond Caen toward the Seine.

The 7. Armee's assumption that the British landing now embodied the main

Trenches are still to be seen in the undergrowth on the bluff above Easy Green.

Left: **One of the WN 66 casemates at Les Moulins photographed on August 4, 1944 by which time D-3 had been transformed into a hardened slipway.** *Right:* **A villa now appears to have been built on top of the shelter, and Karel's comparison, taken on June 8, 1994 just in front of the house, was spoiled by buildings erected for the 50th anniversary.**

Support from naval units , necessarily limited during the first landings, began to count heavily later on. Some of the landing craft had tried to support the debarking troops with the fire from their light guns. When Company G, 116th Infantry, was landing near Les Moulins, the infantry saw a patrol craft stand off directly in front of the enemy strong point to the east of the draw and pump shell after shell into it. German artillery got the craft's range and forced it ashore, still firing; it continued in action until a shell made a direct hit, setting the craft ablaze. Later in the morning, two landing craft made a conspicuous, fighting arrival in front of E-3 draw. LCT 30 drove at full speed through the obstacles, all weapons firing, and continued the fire on an enemy emplacement after touchdown. At the same time, LCI(L) 544 rammed through the obstacles, firing on machine gun nests in a fortified house. These exploits also helped demonstrate that the obstacles could be breached by larger craft, which had been hesitating at the approaches.

Naval gun-fire became a major factor as communications improved between shore and ships. At first, targets were still hard to find; Gunfire Support Craft Group reported at 0915 that danger to friendly troops hampered fire on targets of opportunity; a Naval Shore Fire Control Party in contact with the ships was told by General Cota (about 0800) that it was 'unwise to designate a target'. Between 1000 and 1100, two destroyers closed to within a thousand yards to put the strong points from Les Moulins eastward under heavy, effective fire. All along the beach, infantry pinned at the sea-wall and engineers trying to get at the draws to carry out their mission, were heartened by this intervention.

OMAHA BEACHHEAD, 1945

Left: On the opposite shoulder of the bluff at Les Moulins lay strong point WN 68 with one of its main casemates still under construction. Right: Its remains probably still exist beneath the rampant undergrowth.

threat gained credence that afternoon when corps reported that Allied landings had been smashed from the Vire all the way to Bayeux. This was the sector of Omaha Beach. Indeed, the 352. Division had grown so confident over Gerow's difficulties on that beach that it signalled headquarters at 1.35 p.m. to report that the American assault had been thrown back into the Channel.

Later that afternoon, 7. Armee radioed Heeresgruppe B a cautious estimate of the situation. Its fear of an attack on Cherbourg had not yet materialised, for even by 4.20 p.m. that afternoon 7. Armee had not yet heard of Collins' Utah landing. Our paratrooper drop had severely scrambled and delayed enemy communications. Army, therefore, concluded that perhaps its fears for the safety of Cherbourg were unjustified. The Cotentin air drop could be viewed as a diversion staged to draw off German forces from the British attack near Caen. Within a few minutes, however, Army hastily recanted. Airborne landings had been reported reinforced from the sea.

By 6 p.m. that evening, the badly disorganised 352. Division amended its exaggerated report of Allied difficulties on Omaha Beach. The Americans were not only still ashore but they had infiltrated past strong points on the water's edge and were now shouldering their way inland.

Meanwhile, von Rundstedt demanded the 7. Armee destroy the Allied beach-head by that evening. And from Berlin, Jodl chimed in with an order that all available reserve forces be thrown into the battle. But by 'available' forces he meant only those in north-west France, not the 15. Armee on the Pas-de-Calais where it searched the Channel for signs of still another Allied fleet.

That night the German 7. Armee took stock of its situation. In the Cotentin, German forces looked strong enough to contain the Allied landing there. By some intuitive reasoning, Hitler had ordered the reinforcement in May of that strategic sector.

Nearby, but lower down, a modified Panzer III turret with 7.5cm KwK L/24 gun overlooks the ruins of Major Bingham's house.

The 3rd Platoon of the 607th Graves Registration Company came ashore on D-Day and immediately set up a collecting point on the beach. The 2nd Platoon arrived on D+1 and a cemetery site was selected on top of the bluff between E-1 and E-3 (see aerial shot pages 340-341). Grave digging began but the site was under enemy observation and sniper fire interrupted the work. Strict instructions had been given that no burials were to be made on the beach itself which, apart from carrying the risk of the graves being lost to the sea, would restrict tactical and close-support operations. It was also realised that it would have a demoralising effect on reinforcements coming ashore. However, numerous unburied bodies made their disposal imperative for sanitary reasons, and permission was given for trenches to be dug in the sand by bulldozer at this site just west of D-3, known as St Laurent Cemetery No. 2. This temporary arrangement ceased at midnight on June 10 after 457 interments had been made and, during the next few days, all these bodies were moved to St Laurent No. 1 on top of the bluff.

Along the Normandy coast, from the mouth of the Vire to Bayeux, 7. Armee had not yet discovered the true scale of our Omaha landing. But farther to the east near Caen where British tanks were advancing, the enemy sniffed what he thought to be the main Allied effort. He turned his panzers against that penetration and played neatly into our hands. For while the British baited the enemy to confuse him on our intentions, we were to link our American beaches and secure the port of Cherbourg. However, as Collins pushed inland toward the west coast as though to cut off the Cotentin, the enemy rechecked his findings on Cherbourg as a likely initial objective.

Above: **With the stranded LCI 91 as a backdrop (see page 346), and the 'music' of transport rumbling along the beach road, Father Paul J. McGovern, former pastor at St Mary's Church, Danvers, Massachusetts, conducts Mass at Cemetery No. 2. The date given in the wartime caption is June 25 although that must be suspect for, according to the Quartermaster Corps history, all the graves on the beach had been removed within a week of its closure. Casualties on Omaha on D-Day have never been reliably determined. Without doubt, they were by far the highest of all the five beaches and, as far as can be ascertained, the two assaulting regiments (the 16th and 116th) lost about 1,000 men each.**

On D+2 he confirmed his speedily growing suspicions when he fished from the Channel waters a copy of VII Corps' field order. What he had originally thought an elaborate diversion he now classified as a secondary main effort. To contain that secondary effort, the enemy rushed reinforcements from Brittany into the Cotentin, for at all costs he meant to prevent us from seizing the port of Cherbourg. The German was no less conscious than we of the urgent need for build-up.

We recognised that if the enemy were able to strengthen his defensive ring around Cherbourg, he might seriously delay our capture of that port for weeks. On June 9, therefore, I told Collins to hack through the peninsula to the west coast and seal it off before driving north for Cherbourg. The 82nd's bridgehead west of the Merderet had already cut one-third of the way across. But this Cotentin cut-off was not to be started until first we had established ourselves firmly ashore by linking the Omaha and Utah beaches with the capture of Carentan.

Above: **Equally a casualty of war, LCI 91 was unceremoniously abandoned where she lay.** *Below:* **In February 1945, a Signal Corps photographer returned to Omaha to take a number of 'after the battle' photographs for inclusion in the forthcoming War Department history *Omaha Beachhead*, produced 'especially for the information of wounded men . . . to show these soldiers, who have served their country so well, the part they and their comrades played'. Reaching Dog Red, he paused to take this sad shot as her bones lay rusting in the sea. Perhaps even today her skeleton rests beneath the shifting sands which once were Omaha.**

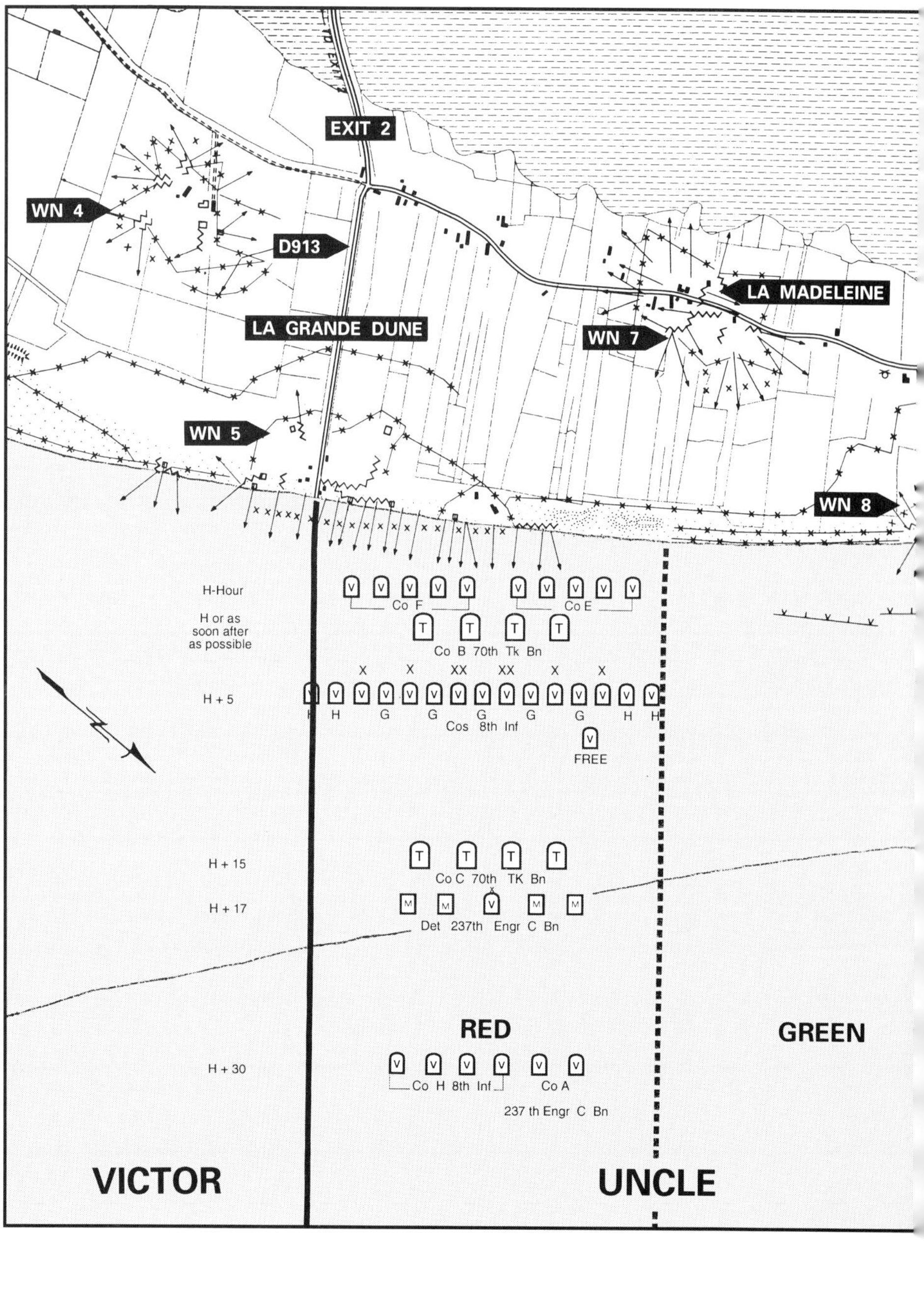

While the 1st and 29th Divisions were fighting for their lives on Omaha, the 4th Infantry Division, commanded by Major General Raymond O. Barton, was coming ashore with ease 15 miles to the westward on Utah. The planned landing beaches fronting St Martin-de-Varreville are shown *above* on this mosaic of April 23, 1944, and *right* in plan view. While Utah was not disadvantaged by the high ground backing Omaha, egress across the inundated marshland behind the beaches was restricted to seven causeways (of which Exits 2 to 4 are shown here). These could be easily defended by relatively-small enemy forces. The beach itself in 1944 was backed by a concrete sea-wall against which sand had piled up to reduce its height from four to eight feet. Behind the wall lay dunes 10 to 20 feet high. There were four main German strong points along Uncle and Tare sectors which had been chosen for the assault, listed by First Army as Target 60 (WN 5) at La Grande Dune; Target 62 (WN 7) at La Madeleine; Target 66 (WN 8) astride Exit 3; Target 70 (Stützpunkt 9) at the junction of Tare Green and Red Beaches; and Target 74 (WN 10) at Les Dunes-de-Varreville. Field Order No. 1 dated May 28 (after the change in the 82nd's drop pattern — see page 262) simply stated that 'VII Corps assaults Utah Beach on D-Day at H-Hour and captures Cherbourg with minimum delay.' The 4th Division, the principal seaborne unit with many other units attached, was to establish the beachhead, then drive on Cherbourg where the port was an essential facet in the chain of supply for the expansion of the campaign into France proper. The 90th Infantry Division would land on D+1 although one of its regimental combat teams, the 359th RCT, would be attached to the 4th Division and land on D-Day for operations on the north-east flank. The 9th Infantry Division would follow up on D+4 and assemble as corps reserve prior to operations to the north-west, while the 79th Infantry Division would land on D+8.

Across the estuary that slashed into the Cotentin neck, our PT rammed through the surf for Utah Beach at full throttle. With two look-outs hugging the deck to warn him of floating mines, the skipper drove his eggshelled craft through blinding spray. Inside the Utah anchorage, we located the *Bayfield* by its topside antennae. As the PT boat pitched to the crest of a six-foot wave, I jumped for the rope net of the *Bayfield* and clambered up its high steel sides. In contrast to Omaha where the shadow of catastrophe had hung over our heads all day, the landing on Utah had gone more smoothly than during rehearsal five weeks before. As G-2 had predicted, the beach was held by second-rate static troops. Except for casemated artillery north of Utah, the resistance quickly collapsed. In tallying up G-1's reports almost a week later, I found that Collins had cracked the wall on Utah Beach at a cost of fewer than 350 casualties in his assault force. This was less than half of what he had lost in the rehearsal on Slapton Sands.

UTAH AREA

Sector	*Extent*	*Grid Reference*	*Width (yards)*
PETER	Village to church	377081–391058	3,200
QUEEN	P to village	391058–407034	3,200
ROGER	Q to chalet	407034–415022	1,900
SUGAR	R to road	415022–430000	3,200
TARE	S to road	430000–443982	2,800
UNCLE	T to road	443982–453966	2,500
VICTOR	U to Carentan Estuary	453966–453906	7,400
WILLIAM	V to mouth of River Vire	453906–491878	7,500

At the outset, however, Utah had got off to an unpromising start. In piloting the assault force ashore, the Navy had missed its guide point and landed the lead regiment 2,000 yards south of its mark. Apparently, Providence had put its hand to the helm. Not only were the underwater obstacles planted less thickly on these beaches but the shore defenses proved less formidable than they were found to be farther north.

Ted Roosevelt, now a spare brigadier with the 4th Division, had volunteered to lead the assault units ashore in the first wave. With the skill and instinct of a veteran campaigner, he quickly improvised an attack to secure an exit across the lagoon that had caused us such anxiety in planning. As the lead regiment pushed across this marshland toward the lateral road three miles inland, it radioed reassuring reports to the 4th Division on the *Bayfield*. Collins promptly passed them on to Army. Thus, while we struggled for a toe-hold on Omaha Beach, we were at least

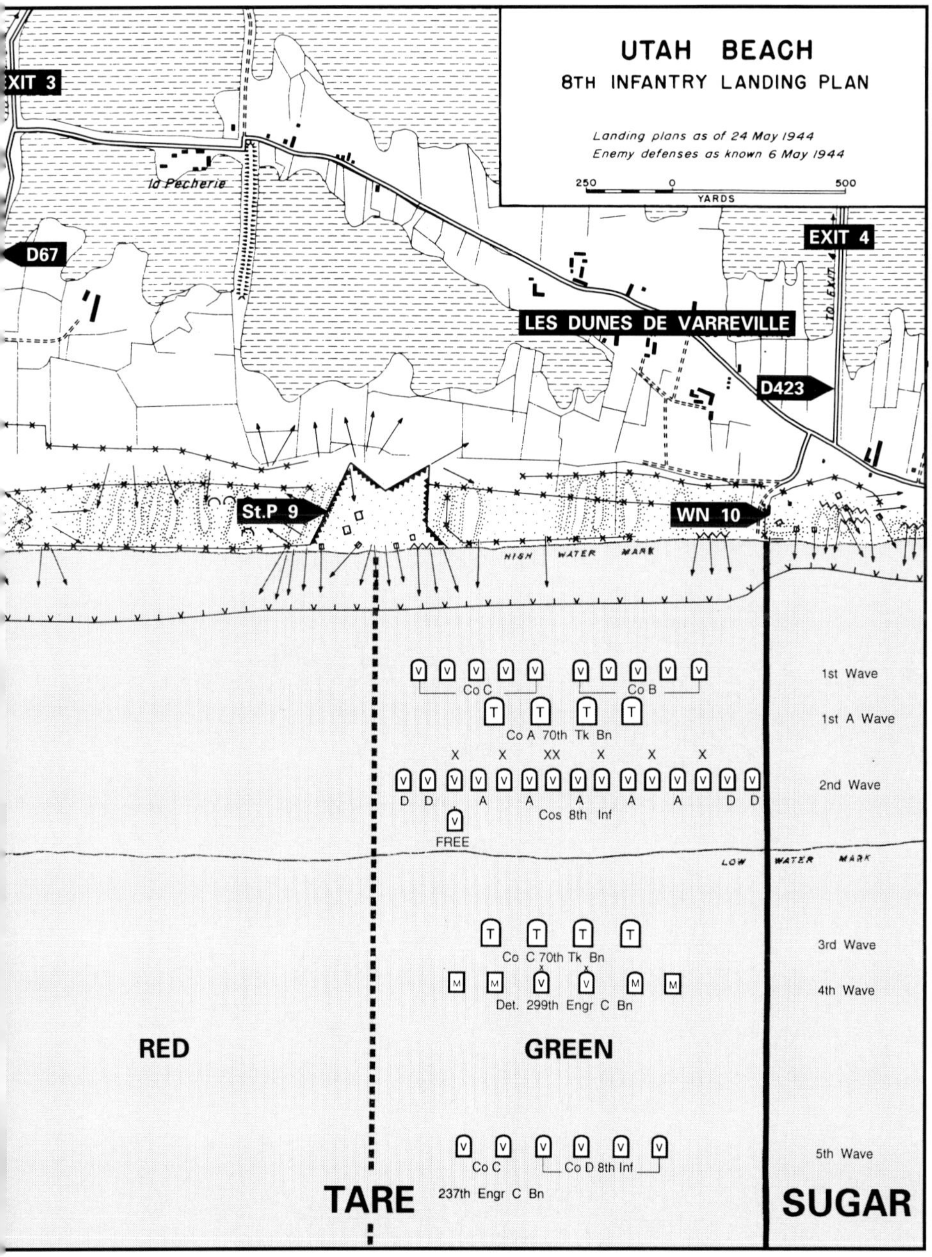

The US attack transport APA 33 *Bayfield* was the headquarters ship for Force 'U' and was also carrying 1,500 troops as part of the Assault Group Red (Uncle Red Beach), together with APA 5 *Barnett*. The Assault Group Green (Tare Green) was headed by APA 13 *Joseph T. Dickman* and the SS *Empire Gauntlet*. The *Dickman* was an apt choice for she was the ex-passenger liner *President Roosevelt*, named after President Theodore Roosevelt, and Brigadier General Theodore Roosevelt, Jr, the President's eldest son, had been chosen as the senior officer to lead the 4th Division ashore. He had fought in the First World War, being wounded twice, and was recalled to the Colours in 1941. He took part in the 1st Division campaigns in Tunisia and Sicily in 1942-43 before General Bradley moved him to the 4th as assistant division commander for 'Neptune'. He died suddenly of a heart attack in July 1944, and in September was posthumously awarded the Medal of Honor.

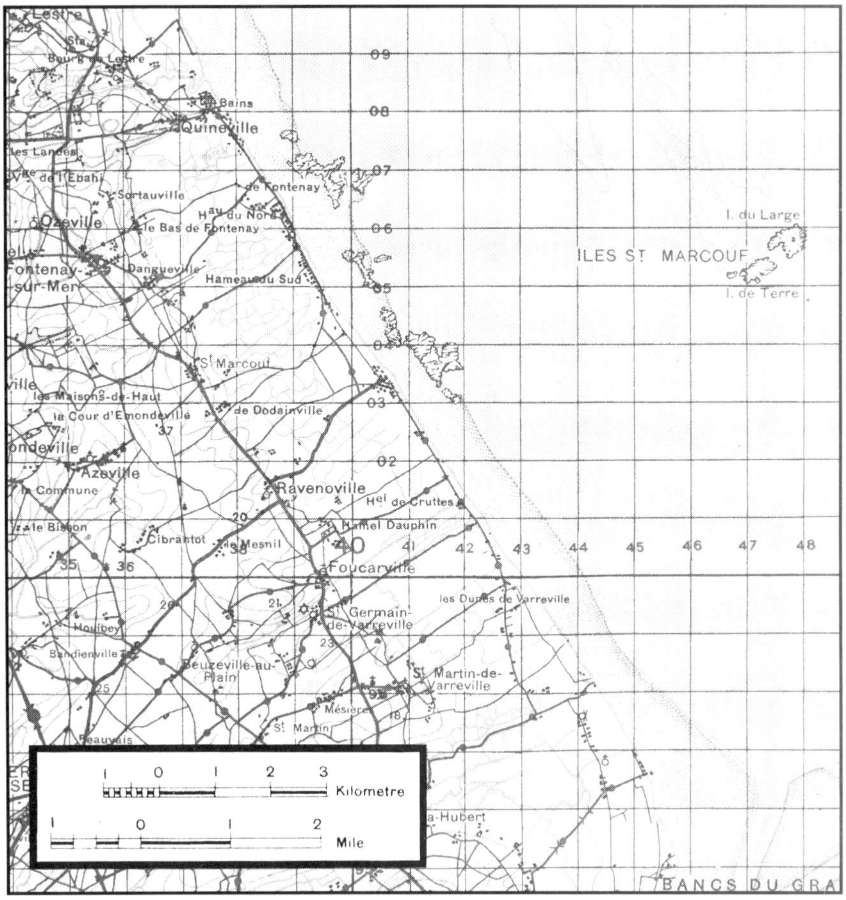

Like Omaha, H-Hour on Utah was to be 0630 but operations would begin with a landing by detachments of the 4th and 24th Cavalry Squadrons under Lieutenant Colonel E. C. Dunn on the Iles St Marcouf at H–2 hours. These two islands lay on a direct line to the invasion beach, and were suspected to house a casemate for remote control of an offshore minefield, or at least an observation post. In the event, no Germans were present although both islands were heavily mined, causing several casualties. The Marcouf islands were secured by 0530 by which time the invasion fleet was approaching. There then occurred a series of mishaps with the beach control vessels whose job it was to make sure the men landed in the correct spot. Potentially, the error was extremely serious, for it resulted in the Tare Green force landing over a mile to the south on Uncle Red, with the troops for that beach pushed over onto Victor (photo *right* taken on the morning of D-Day). *Below:* Utah 50 years on.

DOUVE RIVER
EXIT 2
INUNDATIONS
EXIT 3
TARE
UNCLE

EXIT 4
EXIT 3
TARE

Afterwards, an investigation was made to determine what had gone wrong. The reasons were attributed to the shore being obscured by smoke and dust; the south-easterly coastal current and, more importantly, the absence of three out of the four control craft. Admiral Ramsay's report, published in 1947 after his death, is more specific. This is the relevant extract.

Upon arrival in the Transport Area, PC 1176 took its assigned position as Primary Control Vessel, Green Beach. LCT of Wave 1A carrying DD tanks, scheduled to leave the Rendezvous Area at 0415, due to events not under their control because of storm, did not arrive there until about 0445. At about 0450, PC 1176 sounded 'R' on his whistle, but was unable to hear the signal returned by PC 1261, the Red Beach Primary Control Vessel. After a few minutes delay, it proceeded slowly toward the beach, accompanied by LCC 60, Secondary Control Vessel. The LCH 530 contacted the PC 1261 and learned that it had heard the PC 1176 signal, answered it and got underway for the beach; LCC 80, Secondary Control Vessel for Red Beach, had fouled her screw on a dan buoy and was unable to proceed.

Shortly after getting underway, PC 1261 was observed abreast and both proceeded at six (6) knots, the LCT of Wave 1A following in two columns astern. En route, the engine turns were increased until the maximum speed was obtained at which the LCT could keep up, in order to make up time.

Although the course towards the beach was not a straight line, PC 1176 is believed to have started and stopped in the correct positions, and to have remained within the boat lane, except for about five (5) minutes shortly after departure from the Transport Area, when the course plot lay about one hundred yards to starboard of the right-hand limit.

At about 0555, while about 7,000-8,000 yards from the beach (about 10-15 minutes behind schedule), PC 1261 was hit. She was observed about 30 degrees off course to starboard, mainmast down and dead in the water. Men could be seen going over the side. Witnesses stated she had swung violently to starboard when hit, and that no excessive amount of gun-fire was observed. A few shells were falling in the water before and after the hit and it appeared to have been either a chance shell hit or a mine. Later disclosure of a minefield in that area, and the way in which 1261 acted after she was hit, indicated a contact mine on her port bow.

Shortly thereafter, an LCT directly astern of PC 1176 was hit. It also appeared to have been mined since the entire force of the explosive seemed to go up, with little side effect. The LCT sank almost immediately. PC 1261 settled slowly for a few minutes, rolled over to port and sank, leaving a small portion above water, on which about a dozen survivors were standing.

Due to being late, PC 1176 proceeded to the line of departure before hoisting PETER. On account of the sinkings, the LCT for Red Beach had slowed, and at about 5,000 yards Green LCT also slowed. LCC 60 was sent back to bring them close to the beach and to advise that the LCC 60 would lead all DD tanks in. Wave 1A LCTs proceeded at once to about 3,000 yards from the beach where tanks were discharged. This was 2,000 yards closer than planned, but was done to save time as shell-fire was not heavy.

DD tanks touched down at 0650, slightly south-east of the scheduled beach, and 10 minutes after the first wave of LCVP. The mission of the DD tanks was successfully carried out.

LCC 60, which guided in the DD tanks, reported that the landing point was in error about 500 yards to the south-east. On return from the beach, it was sent to assume Primary Control duties for Red Beach.

Wave Number 1 for both beaches arrived at the point of departure on time and were dispatched abreast. Only a portion of Wave Number 2 arrived and consisted of about 14 to 16 boats for both beaches. Subsequently, the arrival and departure of waves at the line of departure was approximately according to schedule.

Information as to beach conditions was received from Boat Group Commanders, Wave Commanders and Support Craft Commanders (LCS(S)) at an early hour and forwarded promptly. Small arms fire was not encountered on the beaches, but occasional and inaccurate artillery fire from distant batteries was received, which at about 1100 became more accurate and constant and caused casualties on the beach.

No congestion was observed in the water. The beach was crowded, but the excellent traction on the firm sand, and the Army's rapid establishment of good exits, prevented appreciable delay in beach clearance. Beach obstacles were expeditiously cleared by Army and Navy demolition teams. By direction of the Beachmaster, Wave 26 was delayed until the second high tide. During the entire assault, there was never more than one wave at the Line of Departure at any time.

The action of all Wave Commanders and craft as observed was highly commendable. The operation as observed from the Line of Departure progressed well.

NARRATIVE, FORCE 'U' OPERATIONS, 1947
ALLIED NAVAL COMMANDER-IN-CHIEF

As it happened, the error was a blessing in disguise, for the shift southwards increased the range from the big guns inland at St Marcouf (see pages 54 and 154), Azeville and, further along the coast near Quinéville. Apart from sporadic shelling, the landing was completely unopposed, the 1,200 men from the 1st and 2nd Battalions, 8th Infantry Regiment, wading ashore in waist-deep water for the last 100 yards to dry land. The DDs of the 70th Tank Battalion, seen in these pictures waiting on the shoreline for gaps to be made in the sea-wall, played little part in the assault as they arrived some 10 minutes later, four out of the 32 failing to reach the beach when their LCT struck a mine and sank before launching them.

assured success on Utah. But the ease with which Collins had established his seaborne beach-head bore no similarity to the airborne struggle five miles inland where the Battle for France was already five hours old by the time VII Corps landed. By daylight, paratroopers from both the 82nd and 101st Divisions were fighting for their lives deep in the treacherous hedgerows and swamplands of the Cotentin.

Above: The house seen here behind the sea-wall at La Grande Dune lay on the northern edge of strong point WN 5 on Uncle Red (see aerial picture on previous page). *Bottom:* It still stands today, named Le Chalet Rouge, at the end of Baronne Road, Steve Casely specially matching the shot on the morning of June 6, 1994.

Engineer demolitions were to begin at 0635, led by eight 16-man Naval teams, to work on the underwater obstacles. Ten minutes later, eight tankdozers, followed in two minutes by eight 26-man Army demolition teams, would begin to clear eight 50-yard gaps. However, the plan went awry when both Army and Navy demolition men arrived almost simultaneously but without the commander of the Beach Obstacle Task Force, Major Herschel E. Linn, whose craft was sunk. Captain Robert P. Tabb, XO of the 237th Engineers, took charge but he came ashore on Tare Green when his Weasel sank beneath him. By the time he reached Uncle Red, he found Brigadier Roosevelt walking up and down the sea-wall directing operations. Roosevelt had landed with Company E in the very first wave, and is seen here (left) with Major General Barton at the latter's CP 300 yards from the beach. The clearance work went on under artillery fire but casualties were light (six men killed) and the work was unhampered by troops sheltering behind the obstacles as on Omaha. The initial gaps were cleared by 0715 and the entire beach free of all obstacles by 0930.

While the beach obstacles were being dealt with, Companies A and C of the 237th Engineer Combat Battalion were blowing gaps in the sea-wall, removing wire, and clearing paths through minefields in the sand dunes. Later in the morning, bulldozers arrived to open up exit roads through the dunes.

Shortly after noon on D-Day, Collins established contact with Taylor's 101st Division on the southernmost end of his beach-head. But the fate of the 82nd still lay obscured somewhere behind the miles of hedgerow that separated it from the beaches.

'No word from Ridgway?' I asked Collins.

'Nope — but I'm not worried about Matt. The 82nd can take care of itself. How's Gerow getting along? Has his situation over there cleared up?'

'It looks a lot better than it did at noon. But they've been hanging on all day by their fingertips. The 352nd gave us an awful jolt. But the worst seems to be over. Gee is going in tonight. He hopes to get the beach in shape and bring the 2nd in tomorrow.'

Major General Raymond O. Barton, the commander of the 4th Division, had gone ashore earlier that afternoon while Collins remained with his VII Corps staff aboard the *Bayfield* to keep a line on communications — and to hold down Admiral Moon. Alarmed over the

The openings bulldozed in 1944 are still used today by visitors to the beach.

As we have seen, the Tare Green troops came ashore instead on Uncle Red, and the latter force on Victor. However, the history books tend to confuse the issue and still refer to Green Beach troops when, although technically correct, they have become Red Beach men! These nice shots show the latter headquarters set up in the dunes alongside Exit 2. This was the main route off the beach on D-Day as Exit 3 was still under enemy observation.

loss of a few vessels in the assault, Moon had been persuaded by his staff to suspend night-time unloading on Utah Beach. When Collins learned of Moon's decision, he objected strenuously and the admiral was hastily dissuaded. 'Let the Navy expend its ships,' I told Collins, 'if that's what it takes. But we've got to get the build-up ashore even if it means paving the whole damned Channel bottom with ships.'

I went over the rail of the *Bayfield* as dusk was falling. Below me, the PT boat struck savagely at my legs atop each heavy swell. Finally as she reared, I leapt for her wet decks. On the bow, a sailor with a boat-hook grabbed wildly for balance, lost it, and toppled over the side. He fell into the white water that boiled between our boat and the *Bayfield* as the PT slammed its fenders against the merchantman's steel plates. While the skipper backed off to avoid crushing the man, we threw him a rope and hauled him aboard.

Late that evening as we closed in toward the anchorage off Omaha, a destroyer challenged us with a blinker through the darkness. Slipping into the Omaha anchorage from the estuary near Carentan, we might easily have been mistaken for a German E-Boat.

'Now hear this!' One can almost hear the Tannoy announcement from the Navy CP a few yards along the beach.

'What in hell's the recognition signal?' the skipper bellowed below as he scrambled for a lantern. 'Give it to me quick, or well have the whole damn navy sweeping us with a broadside.'

'I hope he finds it', I said to Hansen. 'This would be a helluva way for a doughboy to end the war — skewered on the end of a 5-inch shell in 15 fathoms of water.'

Picking our way through the transport area, we located the *Augusta* just as a star shell broke in the sky. A line of tracers arced skyward. The enemy had come in for its nightly raid.

Sadly, the sea-wall on Uncle Red, which typifies so many of the Utah photographs, is crumbling but fortunately the chimney of the house on the right enabled Steve Casely to pin-point the exact spot on D-Day+50.

The skipper grabbed for his megaphone and hailed the *Augusta*.

'Ahoy — can we come aboard?'

'Lie off!' the deck called back. 'Lie off until we get an all clear.'

I had confessed before to uneasiness in an air raid afloat. But if afloat we were to be, I preferred the 9,000-ton *Augusta* to this sea-going hot-rod. For 20 minutes, we idled in a tight circle. When the raid appeared to slacken, we hove to the *Augusta* once more.

'Lie off!' the answer came back. 'Lie off!'

'But we've got passengers aboard', our skipper shouted through the darkness.

'Prisoners?' the deck called, with a note of curiosity. 'Stand by to bring the prisoners aboard.'

I climbed a rope ladder up the *Augusta*'s side and crawled over the rail, cold, wet, hungry, and tired.

The crew pressed forward to see its 'prisoners'.

'Oh, hell,' a sailor grunted, 'it's only General Bradley.'

Despite the confusion that still existed in many of the smaller isolated units, our situation had materially improved by the morning of June 7.

Members of the 2nd Beach Battalion of the US Navy. One of the advantages of the American system of beach control was that many of the specialised personnel required for the assault soon became redundant during the subsequent build-up phase, allowing the whole battalion to be relieved in one go. However, the drawback was that when the organisation of the Naval Officer in Charge (NOIC) took over from the beach battalions, problems were created during the transition and there could even be a confusing period of dual control. The British, on the other hand, introduced the NOIC headquarters as soon as possible after the landing had taken place, giving continuity from the assault phase to the build-up. The American NOIC organisations were established ashore about D+6.

'US Navy, Utah Beach, June 11, 1944. Taking captured radio-controlled German "Beetle" tanks apart, to see what makes them "tick".' A rather loose caption to describe the Goliath tracked demolition charge, technically the Leichte Ladungsträger (SdKfz 303). This was not radio-controlled but *remote*-controlled, the guidance wire — seen on the drum at the rear of the model on the right — allowing the tank to travel 650 metres. They were powered by a Zündapp 703cc motor cycle engine and had a top speed of 12 kilometres per hour with a range of 12 km. The Goliath had two forward gears and one reverse, controlled from the hand-set being inspected by the sailor on the left. Two models were built, the 303a carrying a demolition charge of 75kg, and the 303b with 100kg of explosive. The body was constructed of 10mm plate which would be proof against small-arms fire. All told, 4,604 were produced by Zündapp from April 1943 to September 1944, with a further 325 of the modified version.

This photograph, while giving all the indications that it is a combat picture, is dated June 9. More likely, it shows troops taking shelter from the shelling which harassed the unloading of men and supplies right up until the big batteries at St Marcouf and Azeville to the north were captured.

On the other hand, we were not yet out of danger. On the thin five-mile sliver of Omaha Beach, we had fallen far short of D-Day objectives. German artillery still pounded the beaches where traffic had congealed in the wreckage. And we had not yet reached the Caen-Carentan road that was to have strung our Allied landings together. Nevertheless, we took some comfort in the fact that five regiments had been put ashore on Omaha by dawn, a miraculous achievement in view of the disordered condition of the beach. But to get them ashore we had sacrificed bulk tonnage. Had it not been for the 90 preloaded DUKWs that waded ashore on D-Day, we might have been hard put for ammunition.

This picture is dated as being taken on June 11, at which stage shells were still hitting the beach.

However, the enemy had paid dearly for our delay on Omaha Beach. His 352. Infanterie-Division had been mauled at the water's edge, depriving Rommel of one more field division. Meanwhile, during our first 12 perilous hours

Another picture which could easily be mis-captioned as something along the lines of 'enemy troops captured during the assault'. If so, they have been sitting on the beach for ten days, for this picture was taken by the US Navy on June 16 as they await evacuation to Britain.

ashore, the enemy had failed to mount a single co-ordinated counter-attack against our beach-head. The omens were better than our progress.

On Utah, Collins had fared better than Gerow. Although unable to extend his beach to the north and overrun his D-Day objective, Collins had expanded to the south. There, he anchored his landing tightly on the neck of the Cotentin where we were to force a junction between both beach-heads. During the night, he had linked up with Ridgway's 82nd Airborne Division.

By the end of D-Day, over 20,000 troops and 1,700 vehicles had reached Utah, and on D+1 this total was boosted by another 10,000 men with nearly 1,500 vehicles. However, the unloading was about 36 hours behind schedule for by now nearly 40,000 men, 5,000 vehicles and 7,000 tons of supplies should have come ashore.

The main problem at Utah was the shallow beach gradient, which shelved from 1:100 to 1:200, which made unloading exceedingly slow because of the difficulty in beaching landing craft far enough up the beach. There were also troubles with the functioning of the ferry control organisation. The sand was firm but there were still difficulties reaching dry land. Although not a casualty of the anti-tank gun seen *above*, *Cannon Ball* *(right)* has not lived up to its name and has come a cropper in a pocket before it could come into play.

The same 50mm KwK 39/40 gun — one of the five at WN 5 — still stands in its open 'Tobruk' emplacement.

A Navy pontoon landing stage was constructed on D+1 but German artillery prevented its use. By D+3, the practice had been adopted of drying out LSTs by beaching them on a falling tide, and two days later additional DUKWs were made available.

It was still too early to evaluate the success of the airborne drop. The dispersal had so shaken our confidence in night-time airborne operations that we never again attempted a night-time drop. In the initial count, casualties looked excessively high and some feared Leigh-Mallory might be vindicated in his prediction. But as 'lost' units trickled in through our lines, we discovered that airborne losses for the drop and the first day aground did not exceed 20 per cent.

On the morning of D+1, the enemy's high command in Berlin awaited word from Rommel that the Allied landing had been roped off and would soon be flung into the Channel. But with the passing of D-Day, the enemy had lost his best chance to destroy us. By the morning of D+1, we had not only got a tight grip on the beach-head, but Allied build-up was already beginning to swell.

I had long ago anticipated that the enemy would dash his Luftwaffe against our landing with every plane Göring could put into the sky. For it was while we were hanging precariously to a slender beach-head that we could have been most critically hurt by enemy air.

Two landing craft approach the beach opposite Le Chalet Rouge — Red Beach HQ can just be picked out on the extreme left.

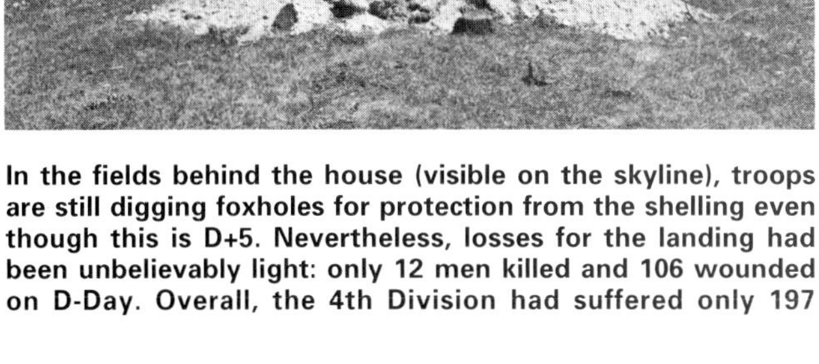

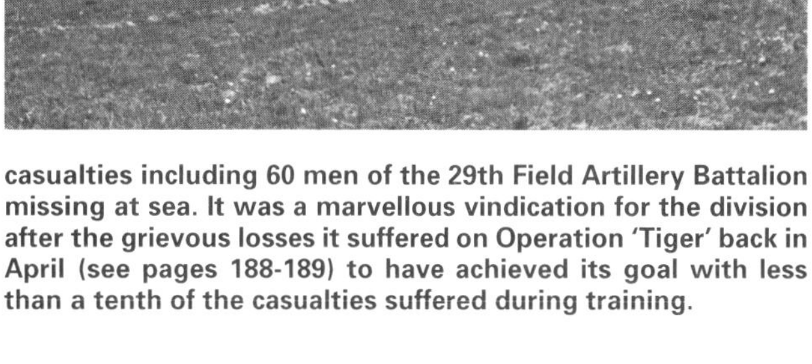

In the fields behind the house (visible on the skyline), troops are still digging foxholes for protection from the shelling even though this is D+5. Nevertheless, losses for the landing had been unbelievably light: only 12 men killed and 106 wounded on D-Day. Overall, the 4th Division had suffered only 197 casualties including 60 men of the 29th Field Artillery Battalion missing at sea. It was a marvellous vindication for the division after the grievous losses it suffered on Operation 'Tiger' back in April (see pages 188-189) to have achieved its goal with less than a tenth of the casualties suffered during training.

After the capture of the coastal positions, the 8th Infantry moved inland: the 1st Battalion north then west along Exit 3; the 2nd Battalion south to Exit 1 and Pouppeville, where they made the first contact with elements of the 101st Airborne; and the 3rd Battalion west via Exit 2 towards Ste Marie-du-Mont. *Above:* This picture, taken on D+2, shows Exit 2 (now the D913) on the far side of the house, leading inland. The troops are from the 286th Joint Assault Signal Company who had also landed at H+60.

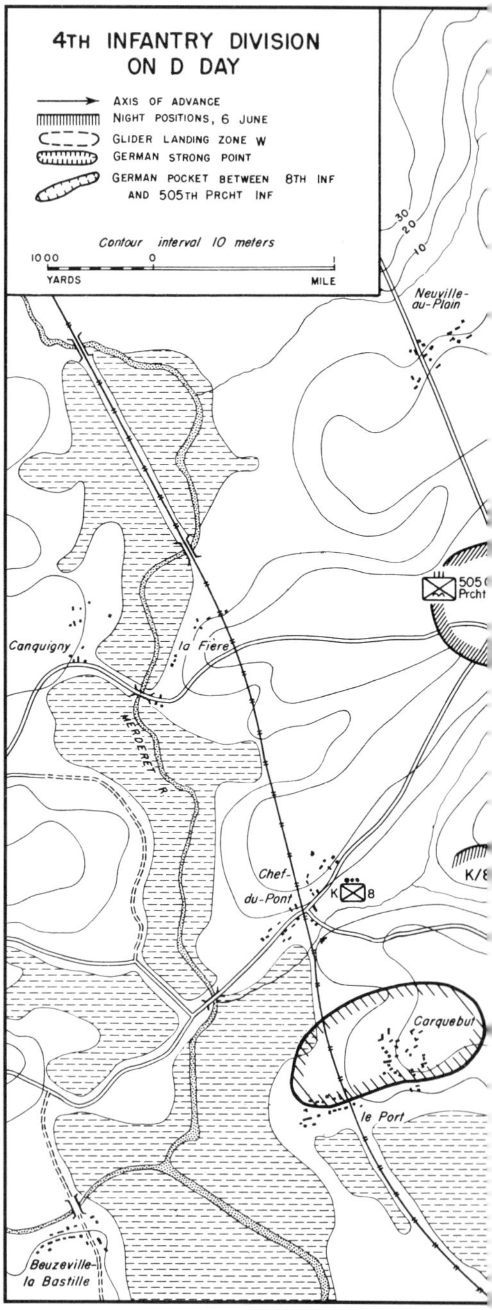

The house still survives, albeit now in the guise of a beach café.

The caption to this US Navy photograph is less than helpful, simply: 'US Army soldiers beside a road somewhere in France'.

Good job therefore that we have Jean Paul Pallud on our side: he recognised it immediately as the rear of the beach café!

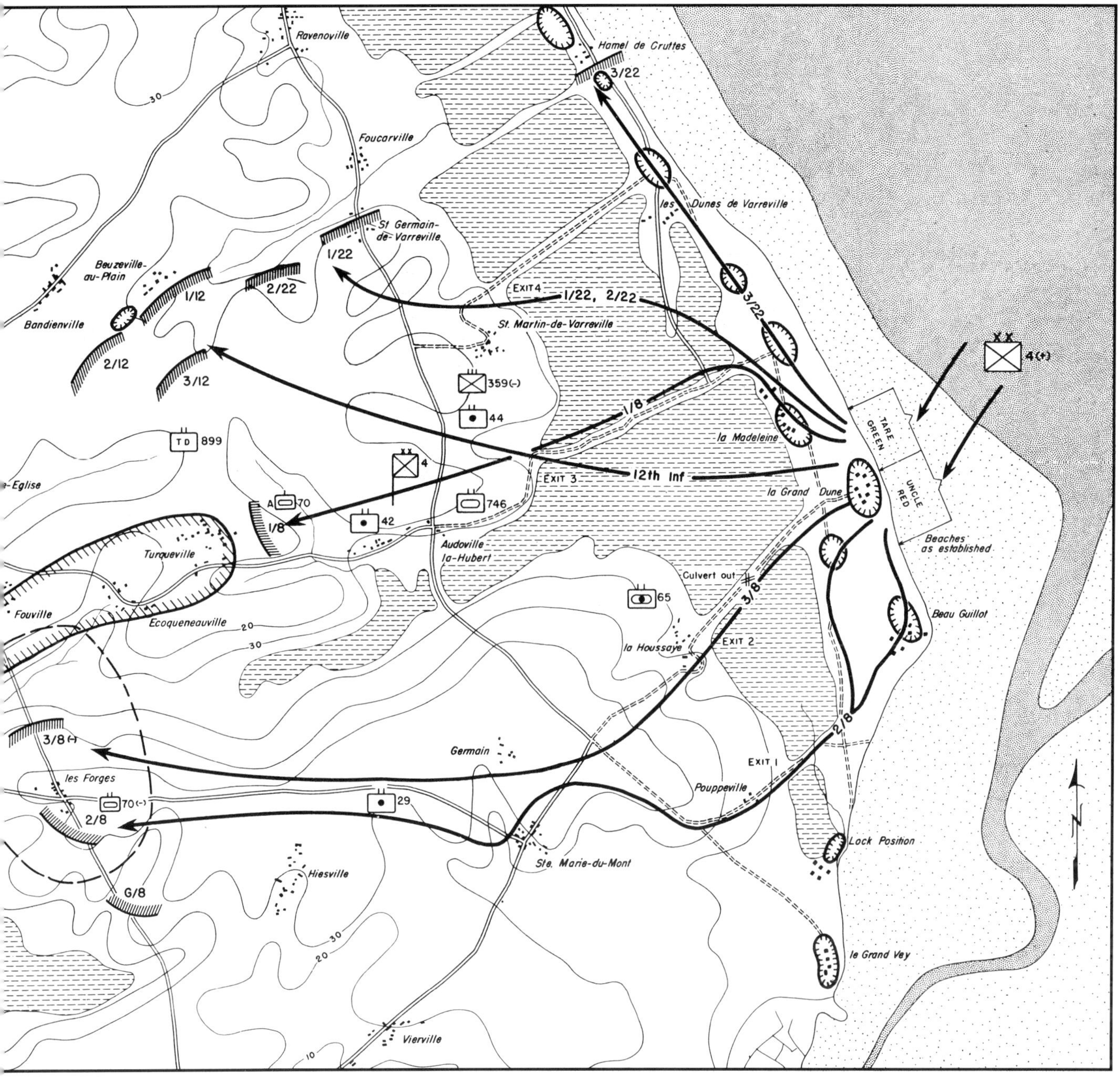

Riflemen attached to an advance party of a heavy weapons unit of the 90th Infantry Division, which came ashore in force on D+1, take a break during their advance from Red Beach.

It is a difficult shot to match with certainty but, after inspecting all the possibilities, Steve Casely believes it could have been taken here on the D67 (Exit 3) to Audouville-la-Hubert.

Throughout the daylight hours of June 6, only a few enemy Jabos broke through our fighter cover for ineffectual passes at the beach. And during the night-time raid that had stranded us aboard the PT, a meagre force was all that the Luftwaffe could muster against us. Not only had the Allied air forces whittled the German down to 400 first-line aircraft in the west on D-Day, but the concentrated attack on his French fighter bases had driven him back to the German border. To conserve his fast-waning strength, Göring had flinched at the very moment a bold blow might have saved him.

Shortly after 6 p.m. on June 7, Montgomery came alongside the *Augusta* aboard a British destroyer. He was anxious that the Allied beaches be joined before Rommel could concentrate his forces against any single beach and there break through. While we perspired through the D-Day crisis, the British dashed ashore and quickly pushed inland for a penetration of seven miles near Bayeux. Their primary objective at Caen, however, had eluded them. Sensitive to the British attack against that vital communications centre, the enemy had attacked out of Caen in a panzer counter-offensive.

Eisenhower signalled that he would arrive in the transport area at 11 a.m.. Meanwhile, I slipped ashore on Omaha to prod Gerow on Montgomery's order for an early link-up of the beaches. Gerow was to push Major General Charles H. Gerhardt's 29th Infantry Division to the right toward a juncture with Collins on the Cotentin neck while Huebner's 1st made contact with the British on their left.

V Corps had hidden its headquarters in a ditch behind the hedgerow on the exit road from Easy Red. I hitched a ride on a truck up a road still under construction. A column of infantrymen trudged up the hill, enveloped in dust from a line of trucks. On the flat top of the bluff, engineers were already levelling an airstrip for the evacuation of wounded to England.

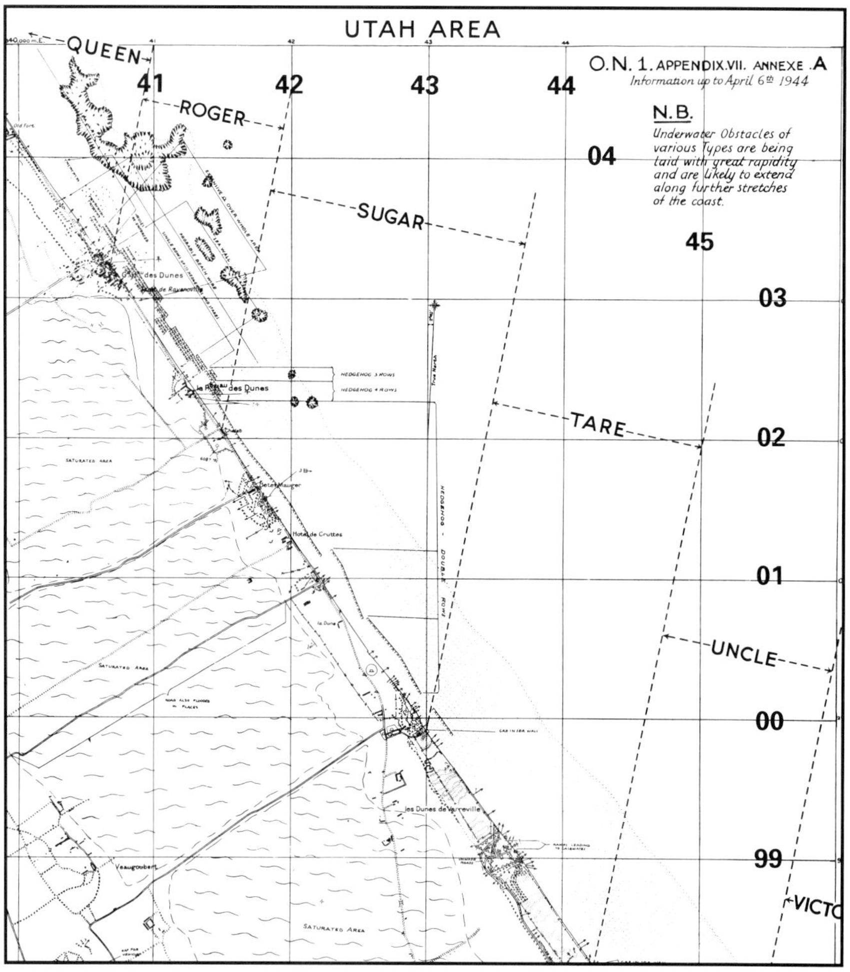

While the infantry moved off inland, the supply position had still not been resolved, and the more men that came ashore only made the problem worse as they in turn had to be kept supplied. It was a vicious circle and on D+6 a joint Army-Navy meeting examined various means of expediting the unloading. A third beach, Sugar Red, had already been established above Tare Green by the 531st Engineer Shore Regiment, and the arrival of the 38th Engineer General Service Regiment on June 10 heralded the beginning of the beach maintenance phase of engineer operations. Within two days they had blasted holes in the sea-wall in Roger sector and cleared obstacles from the tidal flat so that a fourth beach — called Roger White — was available on June 12. By the 14th, an average of 4,000 tons of stores was coming ashore daily compared with 1,500 tons during the first three days. By now, some 87,000 personnel, 9,800 vehicles and 25,000 tons of supplies had come across the Utah beaches.

Each sector — be it on Utah or Omaha — was marked with large, colour-coded panels — we have seen a good example at Omaha on page 362. American engineers had adopted the so-called British World Wide System of the military alphabet so that there was a unified marking system in both landing areas. For night identification, the Omaha beaches first had lights blinking the Morse code for Dog, Easy or Fox, but this caused confusion so they were replaced with boards with nine-foot-high lettering, outlined in coloured lights, matching the beach names. On Utah, barrage balloons, painted to correspond to Uncle Red and Tare Green, were flown directly over the beaches. A second red balloon was added above Sugar Red.

The 3rd Battalion of the 22nd Infantry Regiment had been assigned the task of advancing northwards along the coast to reduce the beach strong points. The first, situated at the junction of Tare Red with Tare Green, was Stützpunkt 9 — Strongpoint No. 9 — at Les Dunes-de-Varreville. Two casemates (Type 677) for 88mm guns faced north and south.

Gerow had gone forward to Huebner's CP and I went on to see him. The 1st Division had bypassed small enemy pockets in its advance on D-Day and was now rooting them out to prevent snipers from harassing the rear.

'These goddam Boche just won't stop fighting', Huebner complained. He was impatient to clean up the beach-head that he might drive inland and secure his immediate objectives. 'It'll take time and ammunition,' I told him, 'perhaps more than we reckon on both.'

This is the northward-facing casemate, the inscription '28th' — no longer visible today — if referring to the 28th Infantry Regiment of the 8th Infantry Division, is rather a cheek as this unit did not reach Normandy until July.

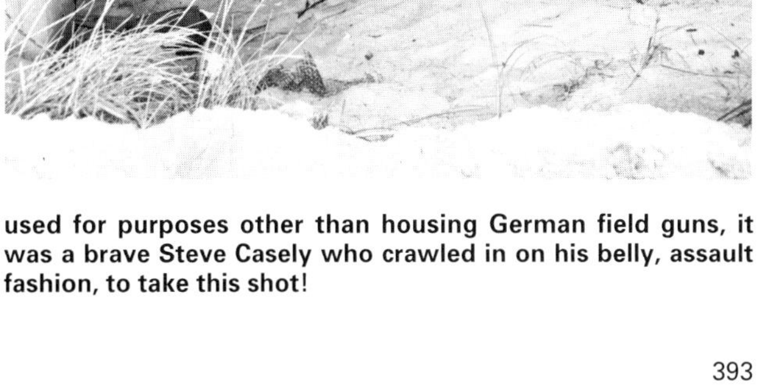

A comparison to match this interior shot is not so easy for the dunes are progressively swallowing the bunkers. As bunkers and casemates on French beaches these days are very often used for purposes other than housing German field guns, it was a brave Steve Casely who crawled in on his belly, assault fashion, to take this shot!

A Type 633 mortar bunker at Stützpunkt 9 where, amazingly, unknown hands have repaired the top of the wall on the right; ready for the next invasion perhaps?

A few hundred metres inland lies the Bertot farm which Jean Paul visited in May 1994. 'The farm was, and is still, owned by the Bertot family', he reported back. 'M. Raymond Bertot and his wife kindly welcomed me, and from him I learned the background to what happened in 1944. The farm was then held by his father, Jean-Baptiste Bertot. Early on June 6, a shell from one of the naval vessels crashed on one of the buildings and killed six to eight horses. Hoping to shelter them from further shells, he rushed to gather in his cows that were in the fields. This done, he took shelter behind the silo (the tower in the background) to smoke a cigarette, whereupon another shell then exploded in the yard, killing or wounding a dozen of the cows.' Unfortunately, the original caption gives little further detail, merely stating that 'American troops plan their attack on the next objective on the road to victory.'

'A tree planted in the middle of the yard has grown in front of the window from which the picture was taken, now preventing an exact comparison', said Jean Paul. 'However, I managed to obtain a ladder to climb onto the roof of the barn just beside the house and I took this near match.'

WN 10 lay at the seaward end of Exit 4. The 3rd Battalion, under Lieutenant Colonel Arthur S. Teague, had been specially constituted as a task force to attack the beach fortifications using the methods developed at the Assault Training Center in England (see pages 182-184). Nevertheless, the strong points proved very difficult to crack, even with the assistance of naval gun-fire, tanks, 57mm anti-tank guns and chemical mortars. By nightfall on the evening of D-Day, the battalion had knocked out one fort and reached the southern edge of Les Cruttes, some 1,500 metres further north.

Even if 'beautiful' is hardly a word which can be applied to a weapon of war, it can certainly be said in this case of Jean Paul's comparison. The 50mm Tobruk emplacement still overlooks the so-called Emerald Coast of the Bay of the Seine. In the hazy distance, the Iles de Marcouf.

As Admiral Ramsay's flagship manoeuvred into position abreast of the *Augusta*, the coxswain swung our LCVP under the ship's Jacob's ladder. I jumped for it and climbed aboard. Ike greeted me at the rail.

'Golly, Brad,' he exclaimed, grasping me by the hand, 'you had us all scared stiff yesterday morning. Why in the devil didn't you let us know what was going on?'

'But we did.' I was puzzled. 'We radioed you every scrap of information we had. Everything that came in both from Gee and Collins.'

Ike shook his head. 'Nothing came through until late afternoon — not a damned word. I didn't know what had happened to you.'

'But your headquarters acknowledged every message as we asked them to. You check it when you get back and you'll find they all got through.'

Aboard the *Augusta* 20 minutes later, I double-checked our journals. Not only

It was hardly the Côte d'Emeraude in 1944. Even when this shot was taken by the Signal Corps in August, the beach just south of Hameau du Sud, cleared by the 39th Infantry (9th Division) on June 12-13, was littered with the refuse of war.

The picture was taken from this casemate of WN 14. It had two embrasures: a 50mm port to the south ***(above)*** **and a 47mm aperture looking north.** ***Below:*** **This is the view today looking northwards towards Le Hameau du Sud.**

A kilometre further up the coast, Jean Paul struck gold. During his early research into the liberation of his country, he had come across this picture *(left)* in the French Army collection of captured German photographs in Paris. There was no caption and no location — it could have been taken anywhere — but then he spotted the shot *(above)* taken by the US Signal Corps. Recognising it as depicting the same building, the American caption gave the clue: Utah. However, it was still a case of checking every blockhouse and bunker along the coast . . . until he reached the Café La Brèche *(below)* at Quinéville, nearly five miles north of the landing beaches. This was part of the former Stützpunkt 19 and, although the false roof to camouflage the bunker as a house had disappeared, Jean Paul realised it was the same place.

had the messages been sent but each had been properly acknowledged. Later, I heard that the decoding apparatus had broken down at Montgomery's CP. So heavy was the D-Day radio traffic that code clerks fell 12 hours behind in deciphering the incoming reports.

However, Ike's vigil could not have been any more agonizing than the one we suffered aboard the *Augusta*. For the reports, if anything, were no less worrisome than the fears that are spun out of silence. A week later, I confessed to Monty that I would never admit to Ike just how worried I was that morning we waited in the mist off Omaha Beach.

The café lies at the end of the Avenue de la Plage and customers can now enjoy their drink outside, sheltered from the wind by the original German anti-tank wall. Nearby, is the Musée de la Liberté and a kilometre stone indicating one of the several beginnings of the Voie de la Liberté which mark the routes taken by the Allied armies across France. The capture of Quinéville and the ridge named after it did not come until June 14 but proved to be the turning point in the northward push up the Cotentin. Meanwhile, the inland batteries still harassing the beaches had to be destroyed.

After landing, the main priority of the 4th Division was to make contact with the 82nd Airborne. On the morning of D+1, the 8th Infantry attacked towards Ste Mère-Eglise on a three-battalion front against a pocket of Infanterie-Regiment 795 between them and the airborne force. The 2nd Battalion, under Lieutenant Colonel Carlton O. MacNeely (who had already made contact with the 101st at Pouppeville — see page 301) advancing in the centre broke through at Ecoqueneauville (see map pages 390-391) but had no sooner made contact with the 505th Parachute Infantry in Ste Mère-Eglise than a German threat developed from the north. Colonel MacNeely, together with Colonel Vandervoort (2nd Battalion of the 505th), quickly planned a co-ordinated attack north up the N13. Earlier in the afternoon, a German armoured thrust was beaten back on the very edge of the town by a task force of the 746th Tank Battalion which the corps commander, General Lawton Collins, had ordered north as soon as he came ashore that morning.

Steve Casely matched the shot of this knocked-out Sturmgeschutz 40 of SS-Panzer-Jäger-Abteilung 709 of the 709. Infanterie-Division just 100 metres from the St Mère-Eglise town sign. It was disabled by Company H of the 505th Parachute Infantry. The new bypass now cuts in on the left.

The link-up between the seaborne and airborne forces having been made, 'US soldiers relax for a few minutes outside a French café. Street scene in Ste Mère-Eglise'. So reads the US Navy caption to this picture, but unfortunately it is wrong! Jean Paul pinpointed it as having been taken in Baudienville, two kilometres to the north-east. The café owner, Jacques Philippe, stands in the doorway with the young Jacqueline Hochet. Although the censor would rather us not know the unit, having blacked out the shoulder patches on the negative, he has missed one: it is the 90th Infantry Division, so these are most probably troops of the 359th Infantry which was concentrated in reserve near the village at the end of D+1.

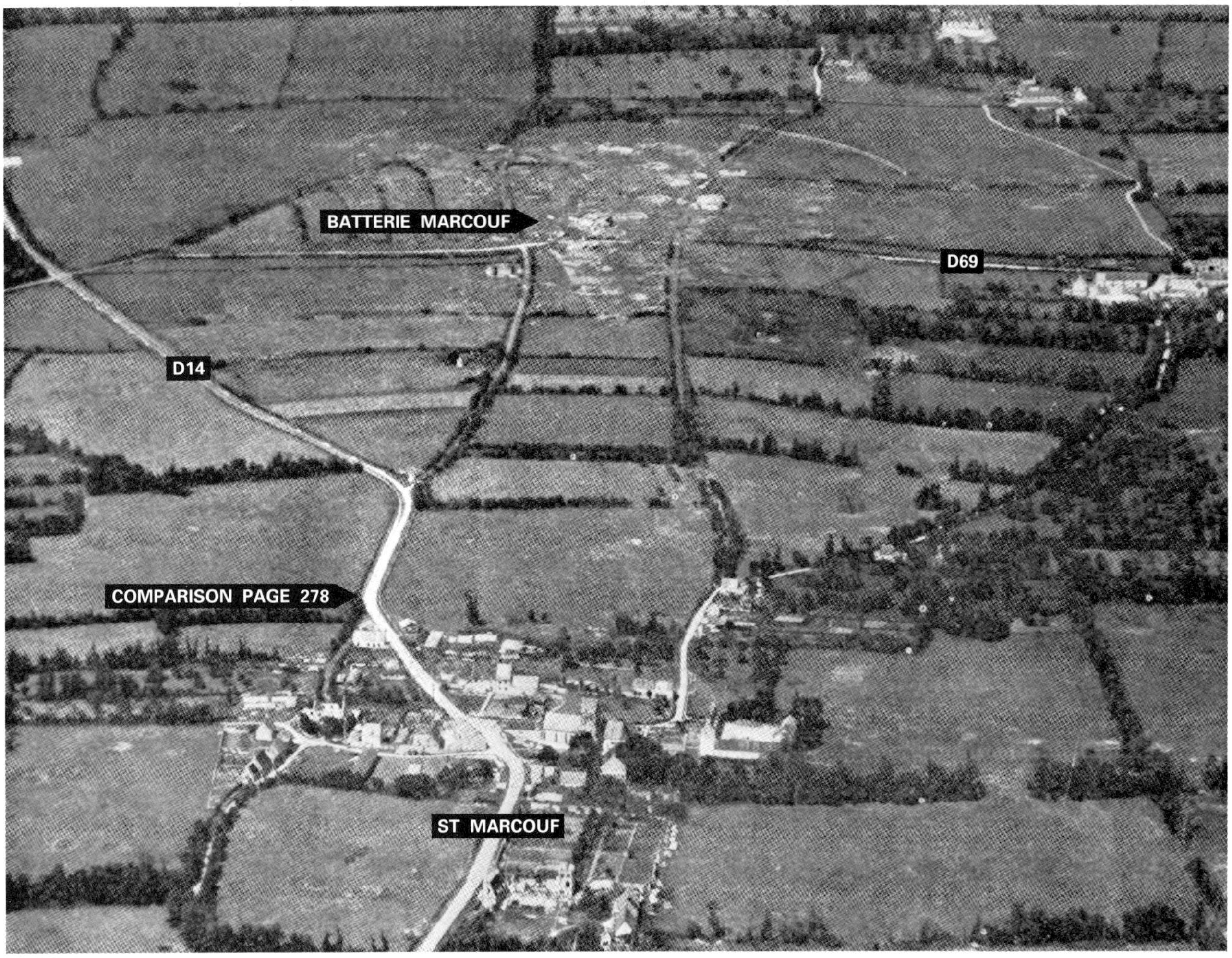

Meanwhile, north-east of Ste Mère-Eglise and inland from the coast, still lay the troublesome fixed batteries of Crisbecq and Azeville and a strong point at Ozeville. The task of eliminating the Crisbecq battery, sited north of the village of St Marcouf (see pages 54 and 154), belonged to the 22nd Infantry Regiment. The 1st Battalion launched its first attack against the German position on June 7 via the two tree-lined trails leading directly to the forts from the village of St Marcouf.

Later on the afternoon of June 7, Kirk ferried me to Utah aboard the *Augusta*. I hailed a lift ashore aboard a passing LCM draped with the coxswain's washing. Near shore, we spotted a DUKW and I called the driver for a lift dry-shod to the beach.

'Can you run me on to General Collins' headquarters?' I asked.

The driver shook his head. 'Like nothing better, General,' he answered, 'but my captain would give me hell. He told me to hustle right back from this run.'

I did not dispute his captain's orders; on D+1 rank could not compete with the priority importance of tonnage. Pleased at having avoided a soaking in the surf, I jumped off onto the beach and then hitched a ride on a passing Weasel.

Known as Marinebatterie Marcouf, with four 210mm guns (in German parlance 21cm K39/41), the position was manned by the 3. Batterie of Heeres-Küsten-Artillerie-Abteilung 1261. Two guns were protected by casemates, and two were in the open. *Left:* **This German picture shows the effects of Allied air attacks, although casemated guns were virtually impossible to destroy by bombing.** *Right:* **The peculiar camouflage impressions in the concrete help to identify the correct casemate.**

The same Type 683 casemate after its capture. As the 1st Battalion moved out against the position, it received heavy artillery fire from the Azeville battery a mile or so to the south-west. When the advance reached the outer wire defences, a German infantry counter-attack hit their left flank and the Americans retreated in a disorganised withdrawal. Nineteen men were left behind and were probably captured. At 10 a.m. on June 8, the battalion renewed the attack, drove the Germans out of the village which they had re-occupied in the night, and prepared to assault the battery again. At 1330, a 20-minute preparation of naval, field artillery and mortar fire gave way to a rolling barrage which the infantry followed 200 yards behind. However, when the companies reached the wire, the battle developed much as it had done the day before.

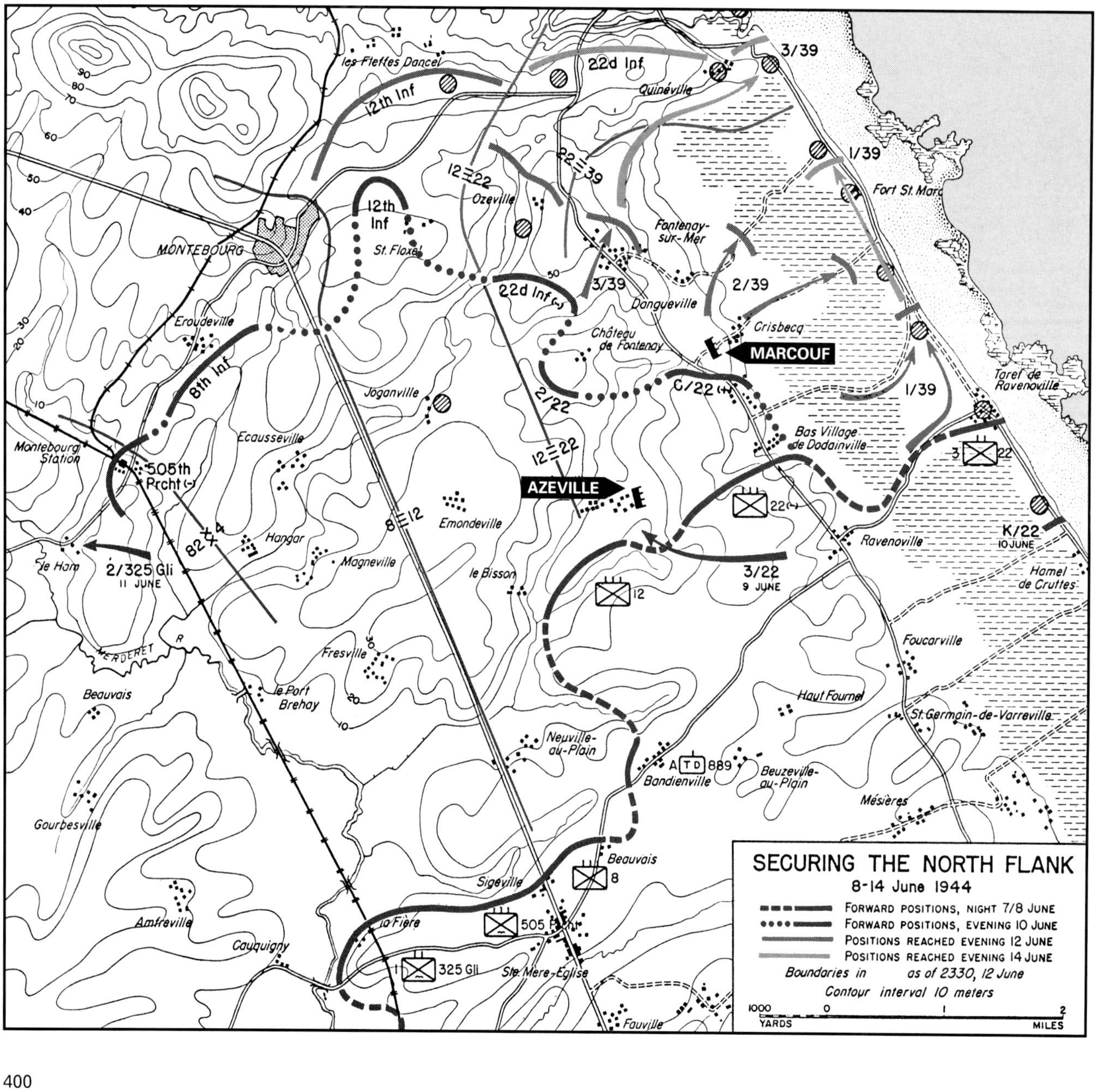

The assault sections exhausted their pole charges without having made any impression on the main fortifications which included bunkers, pillboxes and shelters. Hand-to-hand fighting developed in the trenches and a German counter-attack from the left flank again forced the Americans to pull back under the cover of smoke. With the failure of the second attack, Marcouf was surrounded but temporarily bypassed. Twice the besieging force pulled back for scheduled bombing missions which failed to materialise because of unfavourable weather. The epic defence by the garrison continued until June 11 when the battery commander, Oberleutnant zur See Walter Ohmsen, ordered his men to withdraw. The following day, General Collins charged a fresh division, the 9th, with its reduction but when the 2nd Battalion of the 39th Infantry pushed patrols to St Marcouf, they found the battery site abandoned.

Left: Although, seeing this casemate today, one would jump to the conclusion that it was demolished by the Germans themselves before they left, the picture at the top of the page, taken by the US Coast Guard after its capture, proves otherwise. The War Department history ***Utah Beach to Cherbourg*** simply states in its caption to the aerial picture *below* that the casemate was 'destroyed by demolitions', so possibly it was as a result of an American engineers' test project after the battle. While the attacks against Batterie Marcouf were taking place, similar attempts were being made by the 2nd Battalion of the 22nd Infantry to capture the battery at Azeville. It, too, was driven back by counter-attacks on the 7th and 8th.

As can be seen from the Allied intelligence overlay of Azeville (Interservice Target 9/J/180), the position encompassed the east edge of the village of the same name. This was manned by

2. Batterie of Heeres-Küsten-Artillerie-Abteilung 1261 with four 105mm guns, all in concreted casemates. (The 1. Batterie of the HKAA was at St Martin-de-Varreville.)

On June 9, the 3d Battalion, 22nd Infantry, assembled about 1,000 yards south-east of Azeville, and at 1100 it crossed to the draw south-west of the village. Company L moved farther west in a wide arc in order to enter the village from the west and capture any reserves the enemy might have to the rear of the fort. Company I, organized into five assault sections, moved north inside the arc of Company L, and advanced up the draw and through the fields to approach the fort from its right rear. The 44th Field Artillery fired 1,500 rounds in preparation for the attack. The company started out with the support of tanks, but mines held up all except one of them. At noon, Company I came in sight of the first outlying pillbox. The men did not attempt to lift the mines, but, after cutting the wire, they picked their way through the fields and orchards. They buttoned up pillboxes with rifle fire and then blew them. Enemy return fire was not heavy. The Germans had neglected to clear good fields of fire and to cover the approach from the south-west.

Company I concentrated on the nearest blockhouse. First bazookas and the lone tank opened fire from behind a hedgerow, but accomplished little more than to chip the concrete. An assault team was then sent in to blow the rear entrance, which was recessed in the blockhouse and out of reach of direct fire. The team worked its way to its objective, emptied its flame-thrower, and set off a pack charge. But this had no effect, nor did a second attempt, nor a third with a still heavier satchel charge. In a last effort, Captain Joseph T. Samuels, commanding Company I, sent Private Ralph G. Riley to the blockhouse to 'give it a few more squirts'. With the flame-thrower on his back, Private Riley ran 75 yards under fire and dropped into a shell-hole for cover. The flame-thrower would not work, and he tried to think of the proper 'immediate action'. He opened the valve, held a lighted match to the nozzle, and trained the stream of fire on the base of the door. At just this time, enemy artillery fire from Crisbecq [Marcouf] *began to come in and Captain Samuels thought the attack had failed. Suddenly, Private Riley heard a popping sound, different from the sound of the rifle fire around him. It was soon followed by explosions within the blockhouse. The enemy's ammunition had been fired by those 'few more squirts' of the flame-thrower. Soon a white flag was raised and, after the firing had ceased, the rear door of the blockhouse swung open to let out an American parachute officer followed by two Germans. The German commander surrendered all four forts with their garrison of 169 men.*

UTAH BEACH TO CHERBOURG, 1947

Left: **The battery was photographed for French Navy records in 1946. This shows one of the 10,5cm K 331(f) guns still in situ.**

Right: **Jean Paul identified the correct emplacement, now almost lost to sight in a Normandy hedgerow.**

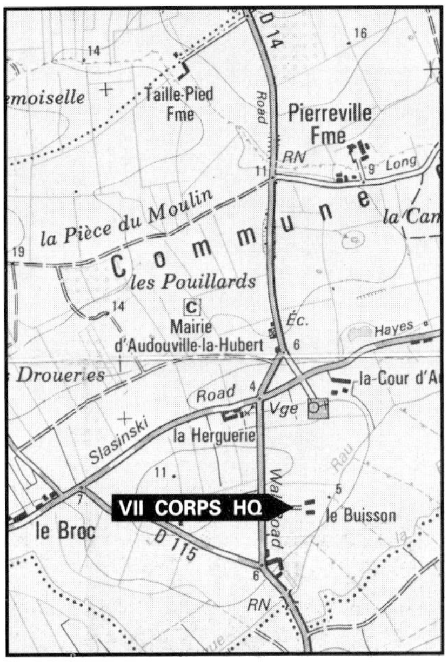

On D-Day itself, the corps and army commanders afloat could participate very little in the initial beach-head operations. Consequently, all activity centred around the divisions and their subordinate units. Although an advance detachment of VII Corps Headquarters under Major General Eugene M. Landrum had come ashore late in the afternoon, the corps commander, Major General J. Lawton Collins, was still afloat on the *Bayfield*. At this stage, it was preferable that he did so as the ship was fitted out with communications equipment to enable contact to be maintained with General Bradley; V Corps under Major General Leonard T. Gerow; First Army headquarters on the *Achernar*; directly with the two airborne divisions and with the 4th Division. Furthermore, General Collins wanted to be close to Admiral Moon, the Force 'U' commander. General Landrum set up a command post for VII Corps in a farmhouse near Audouville-la-Hubert, near the CP of the 4th Division, and General Collins went ashore on the morning of D+1. The plaque mounted on the gateposts to the Buisson farm to record its use by VII Corps rather wildly claims it as the 'first command post of the American Army in France'.

Collins had established his VII Corps CP inside a walled Norman farmyard. He had gone forward leaving behind his deputy corps commander, Major General Eugene M. Landrum. We checked the situation map in a stall in the barn. The 4th Division was pushing north to clear the beach of fire while the 101st shoved south for its link-up with V Corps. Although Ridgway had collected his 82nd east of the Merderet, units west of that river were still reported cut off.

'Heard anything from Matt today?'

Landrum showed me a typewritten situation report from the 82nd Division.

'Matt must be in pretty good shape. At any rate he's got a typewriter in action.'

Ridgway had organised a strong position north of Ste Mère-Eglise. There, firmly astride the Carentan–Cherbourg road, he covered the left flank of the 4th Division.

'Well, Gene,' I called to Landrum before starting back to the *Augusta*, 'you people are going to have to win this war in a hurry if I'm going to make my daughter's wedding.'

'When is it?' he laughed.

'Tomorrow — D+2.'

Landrum threw up his hands.

On Friday, June 9, army headquarters moved ashore from the *Achernar* to establish its first CP in an orchard behind Pointe du Hoc where the Rangers had tracked down the battery of French heavy guns that the Germans had earmarked for the cliff-top battery. With communications ashore, there was no longer need for me to remain aboard the *Augusta*, and Saturday morning when I disembarked, we closed down our floating CP.

General Bradley confers with Major General Collins and General Eisenhower.

The Supreme Commander sailed with Admiral Ramsay from Portsmouth at 0800 on June 7 in HMS *Apollo*, first visiting the USS *Augusta* off Omaha. Returning to the *Apollo*, they cruised to the British beaches where General Montgomery came aboard from HMS *Faulknor*. However, the tour along the invasion beaches was brought to an abrupt halt when Captain John Grindle embarrassingly rammed a sandbar. In his anxiety to free his ship, instead of stopping engines to let the bow float free, he gunned the ship forward to try to force her across, causing even more damage. During the voyage, the *Apollo* had flown a special four-star general's flag which had hastily been run up on Admiral Ramsay's instructions. The flag was now transferred to the destroyer HMS *Undaunted* for the return journey to Portsmouth and, before he left, Eisenhower autographed the flag and presented it to the ship. On the 20th anniversary of the Normandy landings, *Undaunted*, still in service, returned once more to the D-Day beaches, proudly flying the General's flag.

In 1970, it was handed over to the National Trust for Scotland for safe keeping and put on display in the Eisenhower Room of Culzean Castle, in Ayrshire, in which the Trust had given the General a suite for his personal use for life in 1946. The *Apollo* was scrapped in 1962 and as for the poor old *Undaunted*, she became a practice target for an Exocet missile in 1974.

The first meeting on French soil between American and British commanders took place at Port-en-Bessin — on the dividing line between Omaha and Gold — on Saturday, June 10. The pictures were billed as being taken in 'a quiet pastoral setting, a field on the roadside'. Montgomery met with General Bradley and General Miles C. Dempsey of the British Second Army.

Monty had called a meeting that morning at the fishing village of Port-en-Bessin to co-ordinate First Army movements with those of the British Second Army. Dempsey had plotted an attack south of the unspoiled town of Bayeux, partly to extend his beach-head and partly to envelop Caen from the west. I found Monty waiting with Dempsey in a field where British MPs had been posted as out-guards. He wore a faded gaberdine bush jacket, a gray turtleneck sweater, corduroy trousers, and a tanker's black beret. A map case had been spread on the flat hood of his Humber staff car. Two panzer divisions were dug in before Caen, and Dempsey sought to outflank them in his attack from Bayeux. We were to parallel this British attack and drive south in the direction of Caumont. There, Gerow was to establish a strong defensive outpost for V Corps. An attack on this end of the lodgement, we estimated, might also help divert enemy reinforcements from Collins' attack toward Cherbourg.

Monty was flying back to his headquarters in Portsmouth that afternoon.

'Anything I can bring you?' he asked.

'Why yes, sir, a newspaper — any one at all.' I felt strangely cut off from the news of the world without a paper at breakfast.

Jean Paul found the photograph had been taken beside the Gendarmerie on the eastern side of the D2 just as it leaves the town. Unfortunately, a new house has since been built on the field where the conference took place and a new hedge planted.

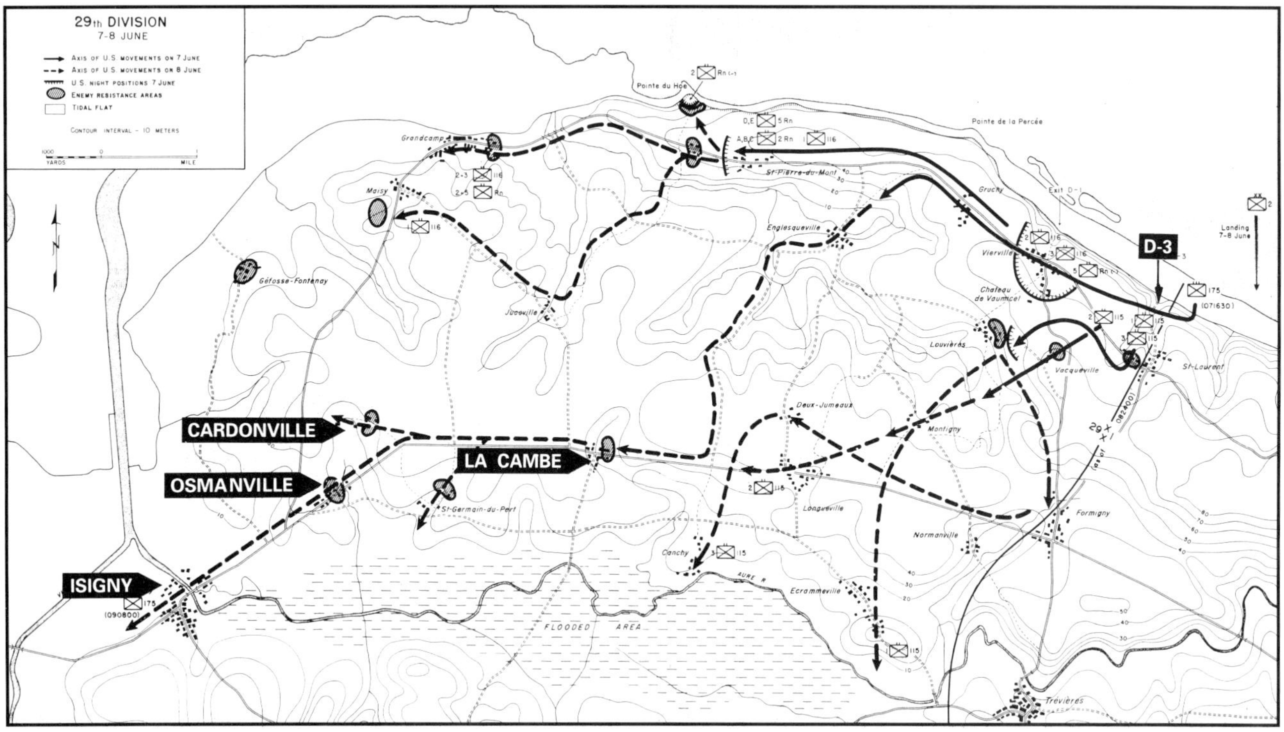

The 175th Infantry of the 29th Division had landed east of D-3 on Omaha on the afternoon of June 7. Anticipating the arrival of these reinforcements, V Corps issued their Field Order No. 1 at 2100 to cover the next phase of operations, giving Isigny as the division's chief objective. The capture of the town was vital to achieve the link-up between the two American beaches, and the 175th Infantry, together with two companies of the 747th Tank Battalion, was to advance westwards via the N13 highway to La Cambe and Osmanville. The advance echelon of armour reached La Cambe early the next morning only to be promptly strafed by Allied aircraft which inflicted 20 casualties. Aided by naval gun-fire from HMS *Glasgow*, the 2nd Battalion had reached Cardonville by late evening. The march was continued throughout the night by the 3rd Battalion, Isigny being entered around 3 a.m. on the morning of June 9.

The town was in flames as the result of the heavy naval bombardment. This is the Rue Emile Demagny looking west towards the Place Gambetta.

By Saturday morning, June 10, Gerow had parlayed his original thin holdings on Omaha into a substantial beach-head. Not only had he linked forces with Dempsey but he had thrust beyond the lateral road that tied their landings together. On his right, the 29th Division had pushed through the burning streets of Isigny to reach the flatlands of the Carentan estuary. A few miles across the estuary, glider infantry manoeuvred in a move to outflank Carentan from the north-east. Meanwhile, paratroopers of the 101st advanced toward that pivotal city down the highway that led south from Cherbourg to Carentan. The road ran through a vast marshland, flooded by the enemy in an effort to restrict us to the narrow roads.

'We've got to join up with Gerow just as quickly as possible', I had told Collins, anticipating difficulty in those marshlands. 'If it becomes necessary to

Using a 'buckeye gas shovel' and a bulldozer, men of the 1055th Engineer Port Construction and Repair Group clear the streets.

save time, put 500 or even 1,000 tons of air on Carentan and take the city apart. Then rush it and you'll get in.'

Later that afternoon, word reached Army that Omaha and Utah had been joined together over a back country route across the estuary. The company of glider infantry from Utah had forced its way to the village of Auville-sur-le-Vey where reconnaissance troops of the 29th Division waited a few miles beyond Isigny. With Hansen, I drove down through Isigny to see if we could get through on this overland route to Collins.

A small dairying town of 2,800 known for its Camembert cheese, Isigny lay charred from its shelling the day before when the 29th called for naval gun-fire to drive the enemy out of the town. A few villagers searched sorrowfully through the ruins of their homes. From one, an aged man and his wife carried the twisted skeleton of a brass bed. And down the street, a woman carefully removed the curtain from a paneless window in the remaining wall of what had been the village café. For more than four years, the people of Isigny had awaited this moment of liberation. Now, they stared accusingly on us from the ruins that covered their dead.

Beyond the Vire, we pulled up short of Auville-sur-le-Vey. In the intersection ahead, an armored car had engaged a sniper with its 37mm gun. The ping of his rifle was lost in the crash of the car's cannon.

A Jeep pulled up with Brigadier General Edward I. Timberlake, Jr, commander of an AA brigade.

'You're crazy as hell to go through, sir', he said. 'The road may be mined. Let me go on in front.'

'Nope — but thanks anyhow', I said. 'I'm not going to go through.'

As my driver wheeled the Jeep around, I turned back to Hansen.

'Be kinda silly to get killed by a sniper while out sight-seeing', I said. 'We'd better stick to the PT boat until Carentan is opened.'

By dawn on June 12, Taylor's paratroopers had encircled Carentan in a brilliant pincer movement. At 6 a.m. that day, they drove into the city's streets to open the main road between Omaha and Utah. On our seventh day ashore, we had linked the Allied forces together in a beach-head 42 miles wide.

Post-war redevelopment has transformed the centre of Isigny. This picture was taken by Steve Casely in June 1994 looking from the Place Gambetta — now renamed the Place du Général de Gaulle — across Square André Mignot towards the town hall.

Bradley greets General Marshall at E-1 on the morning of Monday, June 12. General 'Hap' Arnold (right), the commanding general of the US Army Air Force, had sailed to Normandy aboard the destroyer USS *Thompson*, but he was able to return to England by air from the landing strip constructed at St Laurent (see page 608) which had just opened to traffic.

On the evening of June 11, Kirk's aide ferried ashore bringing with him a gallon of ice cream and the news that Admiral King and General Arnold would visit us the following day. Later that evening, a signal reported that General Marshall would join them. Eisenhower was to escort the Chief-of-Staff from England. I begged off a 10 a.m. conference with Monty for the following day and unpacked my first clean change of clothes.

'Gee, we're running behind schedule', Eisenhower must have been thinking. On the right, Admiral Ernest King, the US Navy chief, and in the background the 'E-1 house'. On the left is the anti-tank ditch into which, General Bradley says, was swept all manner of 'rubbish' from the beach — an unbelievable treasure trove now just waiting to be uncovered.

The party came in at Easy Red early the next morning. This meeting with General Marshall was to be the third of my four brief conversations with him throughout the war. He jumped down from the DUKW that carried the group ashore, looked up and down the beach, then seaward toward the Channel where a vast armada swung at anchor. Within a week, Omaha Beach had been

Thirty years after the battle, mouldering Nissen hutting could still be seen at the rear of the filled-in anti-tank ditch.

tions and herded their vehicles bumper to bumper.

'They're practical soldiers', I explained. 'If they're strafed or bombed just once, they'll never again bunch up this way. But if I were to give them the devil now for closing up the way they do, they'd probably look at me and say to themselves: "Doesn't that damn fool know the Luftwaffe is *kaput*?" '

In a caravan of recon cars we serpentined through traffic that churned the Normandy roads into a trail of choking white dust. It parched our throats, watered our eyes, and chalked King's neat blues. From Omaha, we turned toward Isigny, past the dry, malodorous tidal basin at Grandcamp-les-Bains where the enemy had destroyed a dozen fishing craft and damaged the tidal gates. From offshore, a salvo echoed across the beach as the battleship *Texas* lobbed its broadsides into the Carentan flats where the enemy had withdrawn behind that city.

After having so persistently badgered the navy for capital ships in the bombardment, I was anxious that King see the effects of his big guns in the streets of Isigny. Hansen had parked two armored cars in the village square to cover our party with their guns. With General Marshall, King, Arnold, and Eisenhower all bunched together in three open cars, an enemy sniper could have won immortality as a hero of the Reich.

We lunched on C-rations and biscuits in a mess tent at the First Army CP. After I had outlined our plans for the capture of Cherbourg, General Marshall briefed us tersely on the global war. Later that day, he mentioned the Navy had asked for me by name to command a Pacific landing. I must have looked startled for he quickly added that he had informed the Navy I was already booked for another job. He referred, of course, to the Group command that would become operational after the breakout. After ferrying to Utah for a brief visit with Collins that afternoon, the chiefs boarded their minesweeper for the return trip to England.

combed of its D-Day debris and had become the major port of Europe. Bulldozers had swept beach obstacles, barbed wire, charred trucks, and the flotsam of the assault into a wide anti-tank ditch behind the high-water mark. Unloading points had been flagged and traffic was being routed by MPs in neat columns toward the beach exits. And yet, with each successive tide, a dismal ring of D-Day refuse was left stranded on the shore. As General Marshall's DUKW waded in, it splashed past a broken tennis racket half hidden in the wet sand. Near it, a water-soaked boxing glove lay torn in the deep impression made by the tread of a tank.

Offshore, a line of Liberty ships and obsolete naval vessels had been scuttled to form a breakwater for unloading by lighter inshore on Omaha Beach. Gooseberry, as the breakwater was called, was the forerunner of a massive artificial harbor that had been contrived by the British and prefabricated in England. Inside the protected anchorage, Rhino ferries, loaded to the water's edge with vehicles and guns, chugged peacefully from the gaping prows of the LCTs to the beach where engineers had laid steel matting to form unloading hards.

The bluffs from which the enemy had pinned down Huebner's troops on D-Day were now honeycombed with foxholes. Here, the naval shore parties and beach engineers had burrowed into the sand for protection against the falling flak of the enemy's nightly raids. The more resourceful GIs had roofed their shelters with wreckage and leftovers from the beach. Atop the bluff, the litter-carrying C-47s turned in through a jungle of barrage balloons to pick up the wounded that were to be flown to England. Within two weeks, more than 15,000 wounded were evacuated from Omaha Beach. And on the hill across the draw that identified Easy Red, the dead lay in white mattress covers awaiting burial in a cemetery overlooking the beach.

Although Carentan had fallen that morning to the 101st, the city had not yet been cleared and the arterial road between Omaha and Utah still lay under fire. After touring Omaha by car, we had planned to cross the estuary by PT boat to Utah Beach. Hansen had reconnoitred the route very early that morning, but the traffic that tangled those overloaded roads made it impossible for us to station enough MPs on the route to speed us through. In the cramped Omaha beach-head, a tie-up anywhere on a critical road would back up traffic to the water's edge and slow up unloading. I knew that General Marshall would rather have hiked than displace a truckload of ammunition.

Anticipating that General Marshall might look critically on these tightly-packed truck columns, I thought it better to explain the offence soon after we started. Originally, we had sought to enforce road discipline on the beach-head by insisting upon the conventional 70-foot interval between trucks. The drivers simply ignored these instruc-

Lieutenant General J. C. H. Lee (right) congratulates Private (now Corporal) W. Barrett on the award of his Medal of Honor in November 1944. Brigadier General R. B. Lord has just finished reading the citation.

PRIVATE CARLTON W. BARRETT
18th Infantry, 1st Infantry Division

For gallantry and intrepidity at the risk of his life above and beyond the call of duty on 6 June 1944, in the vicinity of St Laurent-sur-Mer, France. On the morning of D-Day Private Barrett, landing in the face of extremely heavy enemy fire, was forced to wade ashore through neck-deep water. Disregarding the personal danger, he returned to the surf again and again to assist his floundering comrades and save them from drowning. Refusing to remain pinned down by the intense barrage of small-arms and mortar fire poured at the landing points, Private Barrett, working with fierce determination, saved many lives by carrying casualties to an evacuation boat lying offshore. In addition to his assigned mission as guide, he carried dispatches the length of the fire-swept beach; he assisted the wounded; he calmed the shocked; he arose as a leader in the stress of the occasion. His coolness and his dauntless, daring courage while constantly risking his life during a period of many hours had an inestimable effect on his comrades and is in keeping with the highest traditions of the Army of the United States.

1st LIEUTENANT JIMMIE W. MONTEITH, Jr
16th Infantry, 1st Infantry Division

For conspicuous gallantry and intrepidity above and beyond the call of duty on 6 June 1944, near Colleville-sur-Mer, France. 1st Lieutenant Monteith landed with the initial assault waves on the coast of France under heavy enemy fire. Without regard to his own personal safety, he continually moved up and down the beach reorganizing men for further assault. He then led the assault over a narrow protective ledge and across the flat, exposed terrain to the comparative safety of a cliff. Retracing his steps across the field to the beach, he moved over to where two tanks were buttoned up and blind under violent

1st Lieutenant Jimmie Monteith. Brigadier General Frank Dorn, Headquarters Army Ground Forces USA, presented the award to the Lieutenant's widowed mother at her home. He now lies buried in St Laurent Cemetery.

enemy artillery and machine gun fire. Completely exposed to the intense fire, 1st Lieutenant Monteith led the tanks on foot through a minefield and into firing positions. Under his direction, several enemy positions were destroyed. He then rejoined his company and, under his leadership, his men captured an advantageous position on the hill. Supervising the defense of his newly-won position against repeated vicious counter-attacks, he continued to ignore his own personal safety, repeatedly crossing the two or three hundred yards of open terrain under heavy fire to strengthen links in his defensive chain. When the enemy succeeded in completely surrounding 1st Lieutenant Monteith and his unit, and while leading the fight out of the situation, 1st Lieutenant Monteith was killed by enemy fire. The courage, gallantry, and intrepid leadership displayed by 1st Lieutenant Monteith is worthy of emulation.

TECHNICIAN 5th Grade JOHN J. PINDER, Jr
16th Infantry, 1st Infantry Division

For conspicuous gallantry and intrepidity above and beyond the call of duty on 6 June 1944, near Colleville-sur-Mer, France. On D-Day, Technician 5th Grade Pinder landed on the coast 100 yards off-shore under devastating enemy machine gun and artillery fire which caused severe casualties among the boatload. Carrying a vitally important radio, he struggled towards shore in waist-deep water. Only a few yards from his craft, he was hit by enemy fire and was gravely wounded. Technician 5th Grade Pinder never stopped. He made shore and delivered the radio. Refusing to take cover afforded, or to accept medical attention for his wounds, Technician 5th Grade Pinder, though terribly weakened by loss of blood and in fierce pain, on three occasions went into the fire-swept surf to salvage communication equipment. He recovered many vital parts and equipment, including another workable radio. On the third trip he was again hit, suffering machine gun bullet wounds in the legs. Still this valiant soldier would not stop for rest or medical attention. Remaining exposed to heavy enemy fire, growing steadily weaker, he aided in establishing the vital radio communication on the beach. While so engaged, this dauntless soldier was hit for the third time and killed. This indomitable courage and personal bravery of Technician 5th Grade Pinder was a magnificent inspiration to the men with whom he served.

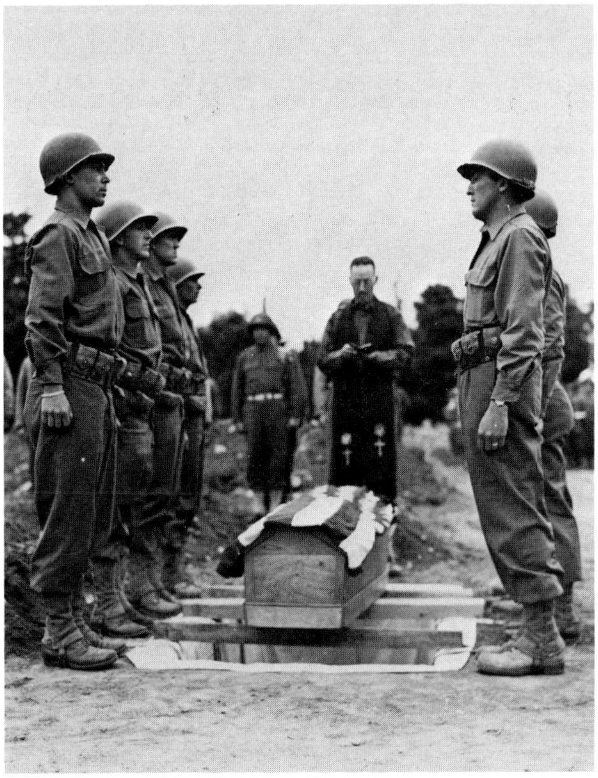

'The body of T-5 John J. Pinder, Jr, son of John Pinder, Sr, of Burgettstown, P.A., will arrive in Burgettstown (this) Thursday morning at 10 o'clock on the Pennsy train from Columbus, O. The casket will be met by a guard of honor of World War II Veterans at the station and escorted in the Jeep caisson to the Lee and Wilson Funeral Home, where it will remain until Sunday at 2.30 p.m., when services will be held in the First Presbyterian church, Burgettstown. The sermon will be preached by Legion Chaplain Stone. Burial will be in Grandview cemetery. The award of the nation's highest honor was made posthumously in January 1945 by Major General Phillip Hayes, commanding Third Service Command.' — *Burgettstown Enterprise*, April 29, 1948.

BRIGADIER GENERAL THEODORE ROOSEVELT, Jr
4th Division

For gallantry and intrepidity at the risk of his life above and beyond the call of duty on 6 June 1944, in France. After two verbal requests to accompany the leading assault elements in the Normandy invasion had been denied, Brigadier General Roosevelt's written request for this mission was approved and he landed with the first wave of the forces assaulting the enemy-held beaches. He repeatedly led groups from the beach, over the sea-wall and established them inland. His valor, courage and his presence in the very front of the attack and his complete unconcern at being under heavy fire inspired the troops to heights of enthusiasm and self-sacrifice. Although the enemy had the beach under constant direct fire, Brigadier General Roosevelt moved from one locality to another, rallying men around him, directed and personally led them against the enemy. Under his seasoned, precise, calm and unfaltering leadership, assault troops reduced beach strong points and rapidly moved inland with minimum casualties. He thus contributed substantially to the successful establishment of the beach-head in France.

Brigadier Roosevelt died in his sleep on July 12 after suffering a heart attack in a captured German truck he had made into his CP. General Bradley was on the point of giving him the ill-trained 90th Infantry Division whose commander had been removed as a result of its poor performance since landing. Roosevelt was buried in Ste Mère-Eglise Cemetery No. 2 on July 15 at a ceremony attended by Bradley and Patton, anti-tank guns being fired in salute. His remains were transferred to St Laurent in 1948.

Gold Area

By Brigadier Harold Pyman

CHIEF-OF-STAFF, XXX CORPS

I came back to England early in 1943 to find myself Brigadier General Staff (BGS) Training at HQ Home Forces, soon to be called 21st Army Group. In April when I took up my job, we were stationed at St. Paul's School, London, but soon after moved to Wentworth.

I had enjoyed my time at the Staff College as training instructor very much and I loved training my own unit but training as meant by General Staff Duties seemed to me to imply something quite different. Maybe it was because I could not get my own way all the time! My duties as BGS Training in normal times would have been mainly concerned with the allocation of training materials to the formations in the commands, perhaps interspersed with criticising training manuals and exercises. I maintained that training should be the prerogative of the commander at whatever level and, as I have already said, I enjoyed and made much of the training of my own units. Now, as may be imagined, I was not very happy in my new job, but times were not normal — with the invasion of Europe so close, training took on a new importance and I was out of my office visiting units at work all over the country.

In spite of this, I found myself in trouble on more than one occasion, once with no less a person than the Naval Chief Staff Officer. It was over the size of a corps/naval force training area. We, at Headquarters, suddenly decided that we could do with a smaller area but I failed to inform the Navy of this until I aired it at a senior staff meeting. I was promptly accused by the Navy of courting favour in high places. A sad setback to inter-service co-operation. Luckily, I had discussed the whole question earlier with I Corps Commander, Sir John Crocker, who was an old friend of mine. He assured the Navy that it was a correct decision and peace was restored, for no one ever doubted 'Honest John's' word.

Sir John Crocker, who was in my own regiment, was a man with a remarkable record. He finished World War I as a lieutenant colonel with a DSO, MC and Croix de Guerre. 'Honest John' was not really a good nickname for him because it caught only one facet of a very rich and varied character. As well

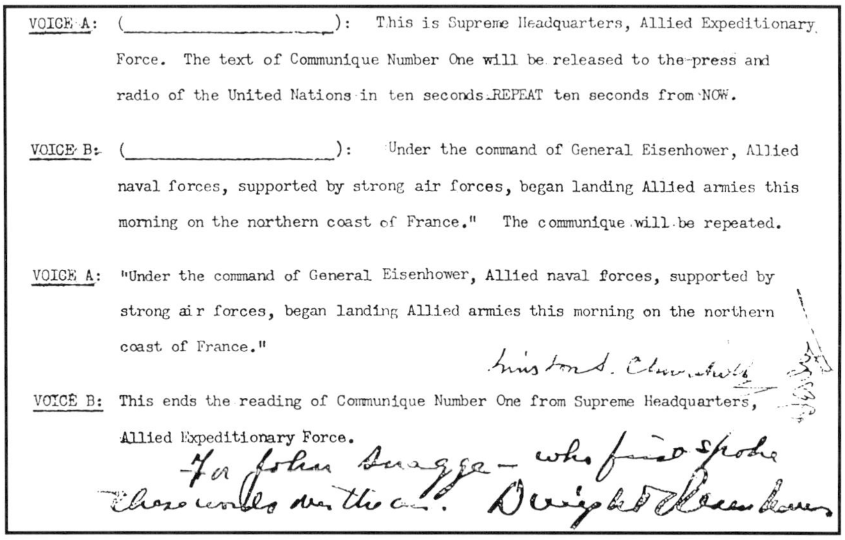

VOICE A: (____________________): This is Supreme Headquarters, Allied Expeditionary Force. The text of Communique Number One will be released to the press and radio of the United Nations in ten seconds. REPEAT ten seconds from NOW.

VOICE B: (____________________): Under the command of General Eisenhower, Allied naval forces, supported by strong air forces, began landing Allied armies this morning on the northern coast of France." The communique will be repeated.

VOICE A: "Under the command of General Eisenhower, Allied naval forces, supported by strong air forces, began landing Allied armies this morning on the northern coast of France."

Winston S. Churchill

VOICE B: This ends the reading of Communique Number One from Supreme Headquarters, Allied Expeditionary Force.

For John Snagge – who first spoke these words on the air. Dwight D. Eisenhower

Top: **Having addressed the House of Commons at noon, after lunch Churchill, accompanied by HM The King, motored to Leigh-Mallory's headquarters at Bentley Priory, where they were able to see the unfolding of events in Normandy in the underground ops room. Leigh-Mallory had telephoned Eisenhower at 'Sharpener' around 6.45 a.m. with news of the airborne landings, and Ike, in turn, contacted Major General Bull (the SHAEF G-3) to get out a communiqué. However, Joseph Goebbels, the German propaganda chief, broadcast the news to the world at 7 a.m., pre-empting the Allies by some two hours. SHAEF's Communiqué No. 1 was not put out by the BBC until 9.32 a.m., John Snagge reading the bulletin. This is his original copy which he gave to the Imperial War Museum in 1994.**

297

TOP SECRET

SH 202

REF. NO. S.52420
SCAF 33
DATED: MAY 221850

OUTGOING MESSAGE SHAEF

IMPORTANT

From: SHAEF

To: AGWAR

SCAF 33 22nd May 1944

"EDITED LITERAL TEXT"

INTERIOR ADDRESSES:

TO: AGWAR FOR COMBINED CHIEFS OF STAFF

FROM: SHAEF, SIGNED EISENHOWER

SAC proposes broadcasting the following statement as soon as the D Day communique is released:

1. 'People of Western EUROPE.

2. "A landing was made this morning on the coast of FRANCE by troops of the Allied Expeditionary Force. This landing is part of the concerted United Nations plan for the liberation of EUROPE, made in conjunction with our great Russian Allies.

3. "I have this message for all of you. Although the initial assault may not have been made in your own country, the hour of your liberation is approaching.

4. "All patriots, men and women, young and old, have a part to play in the achievement of final victory. To members of resistance movements, I say, 'follow the instructions you have received'. To patriots who are not members of organised resistance groups, I say, 'continue your passive resistance, but do not needlessly endanger your lives until I give you the signal to rise and strike the enemy. The day will come when I shall need your united strength.'

Until that /

298

- 2 -

Until that day, I call on you for the hard task of discipline and restraint.

5. "Citizens of FRANCE.

6. "I am proud to have again under my command the gallant forces of FRANCE. Fighting beside their American and British comrades, they will play a worthy part in the liberation of their homeland.

7. "Because the initial landing has been made on the soil of your Country, I repeat to you with even greater emphasis my message to the peoples of other occupied countries in Western EUROPE. Follow the instructions of your leaders. A premature uprising of all Frenchmen may prevent you from being of maximum help to your country in the critical hour. Be patient. Prepare.

8. "As Supreme Commander of the Allied Expeditionary Force, there is imposed on me the duty and responsibility of taking all measures necessary to the prosecution of the War. Prompt and willing obedience to the orders that I shall issue is essential.

9. "Effective civil administration of FRANCE must be provided by Frenchmen. All persons must continue in their present duties unless otherwise instructed. Those who have made common cause with the enemy and so betrayed their country will be removed. As FRANCE is liberated from her oppressors, you yourselves will choose your representatives, and the government under which you wish to live.

10 "In the course of this campaign for the final defeat of the enemy you may sustain further loss and damage. Tragic though they may be, they are part of the price of victory. I assure you that I shall do all in my power to mitigate your hardships. I know that I can count on your steadfastness now, no less than in the past. The heroic deeds of Frenchmen who have continued the struggle against the Nazis and their Vichy satellites, in FRANCE and throughout the French Empire, have been an example and an inspiration to all of us."

THE PARAGRAPHS OF THIS MESSAGE WERE SCRAMBLED FOR TRANSMISSION.

Circulation

Foreign Secretary
First Sea Lord
C.I.G.S.
C.A.S.
C.C.O.
Defence Office

The Allies should have won the race to be first with the news as statements had been prepared and approved weeks in advance. This message *(above)*, from General Eisenhower personally, was pre-recorded, and was broadcast after Communiqué No. 1 had been issued, being also relayed to the peoples of Norway, Denmark, the Netherlands, Belgium and France in their own languages.

as being utterly honest, John Crocker was a man with a most penetrating insight into character and behaviour. Anyone who tried to hoodwink him was on a forlorn and dangerous path. He was, too, a very strict disciplinarian. I once saw him take a guard commander aside and give him the shock of his life for the state he and his men were in. I personally spent the rest of the day glancing in mirrors and keeping out of John Crocker's way — and this although I was his Chief-of-Staff at the time. I did notice, too, that a different, and cleaner, guard commander saw him off.

At the time of my 'naval engagement', John Crocker was I Corps Commander, Second Army, and so under my military boss at 21st Army Group, Sir Bernard Paget. He was another remarkable man. In his time as Commander, Home Forces, he had prevented us losing the land battle for

Supreme Headquarters
ALLIED EXPEDITIONARY FORCE
Public Relations Division

6 June 1944

PRESS CONFERENCES MINISTRY OF INFORMATION

The following procedure will be followed in the Press Conferences:

1. The opening conference on D Day will be held in Macmillan Hall. Subsequent conferences will be held in the Information Room, Chancellor's Hall.

2. Program for D Day is on reverse.

3. Communique No. 1, and order of the day will not be released for publication until authorized. The time of this release is not known, and may not be until 1100 hours.

4. Correspondents will be kept locked up in Macmillan Hall until after the release of the communique, and will leave the Hall only in emergency and under escort.

5. It is proposed that correspondents should write their first stories between 0825 and 0900. Later articles can be written from 1025 until the release of the communique. Stories should be handed in in duplicate to the SHAEF Press Copy Control. This control will log all stories in the order they are received, and pass them to Censorship.

6. SUBSEQUENT CONFERENCES

These will be held daily in the Information Room Chancellor's Hall, at 1030, 1700, and 2330 hours. At the 1030 conference, a communique will be issued and released at 1100 hours. A senior officer will elaborate the communique, give background, and answer questions, assisted by Naval and Air Officers. The same procedure will take place at the 2330 conference with the exception that the communique will be released at that hour. At the 1700 conference, high ranking officers of the various forces and arms taking part in the operation will give addresses on over-all guidance, the progress of the operation, and on military subjects of interest.

7. The Information Room is available for use by correspondents for obtaining information, but not for typing their articles. This room will probably have to be closed daily one hour before each conference, and notices will be exhibited to that effect.

Elaborate rules had been drawn up by Bull's deputy, Major-General John Whiteley, to govern the release of details about the landings to the press.

General Whiteley gives the first news to journalists at the press conference held at Senate House — the Ministry of Information's headquarters in the University of London building in Malet Street — on the morning of D-Day.

The production of training pamphlets was part of my job and I wrote a great number, incorporating the points I had learnt with the Eighth Army in battle. Paget approved of these and later let them go forward for general acceptance, which they got. But I was less successful with him when I initiated a pamphlet on the Army Group's view of infantry and tank co-operation. It was never published and the more is the pity, for of the many pamphlets I wrote it was undoubtedly the best.

When I first returned from the desert, I was amazed to find that everyone on this little island was not afraid nightly of having his throat slit by a seaborne or airborne German invader.

I was, of course, quite wrong. Indeed, the time for the Germans to launch such an attack had long passed but until I really understood the problems which had to be overcome before we could attack the beaches on the Continent, and understood too how few divisions we were ultimately to employ, I could not understand why neither side could do anything.

this island by his watchfulness and his organisation of our very limited resources. Paget had though (in my eyes) one major fault, and that was that he was too much of a stickler for staff duties, which is hardly possible in the speed of modern fighting. I have spent, and enjoyed, half an hour's discussion with him over where a comma should be placed in a sentence but, while this is an academic point, it is not one on which to hold up the issue of a signal. Orders must be got out on time, even at the sacrifice of grammar and staff duties. Paget so appointed his mess that remarkable people came to drink, to dine and to talk. He was himself a magnificent debater and I shall always be grateful for the opportunity of sharing in the entertaining and educative discussions at his table.

Looking back on this period, I see it as one of immense and varied activity, of which certain aspects — some unrelated and not all by any means of equal importance — present themselves most clearly to my memory. There was, for instance, the 'Field of the Cloth of Gold', the re-appearance of Montgomery, the pamphlets on infantry and armoured fighting and the training of the beach groups.

OPENING PRESS CONFERENCE   MACMILLAN HALL MOI

Approx Time	Speaker	Subject
0800 - 0805	Colonel R. Ernest Dupuy Acting Chief of Division	Opens Conference and Explains Procedure
0810 - 0825	Colonel E. H. Carkeet-James Chief Briefing Officer, Prd, SHAEF	General Guidance
0827 - 0900	Write Articles	
0902 - 0909 0909 - 0916	Captain J. Creswell and) Captain L. P. Lovette, USN)	Naval Background
0916 - 0925	Air Commodore L. F. Heald	Air Background
0925 - 0945	Senior Officer, SHAEF	Elaboration of Communique 1.
0945 - 1015	Write Articles	
1015 - 1025	Colonel R.D.Q. Henriques	General Background
1025	Write Further Articles until release of Communique 1.	

As the timetable shows, the press conference was held in the Macmillan Hall *(below)*, now once again a lecture hall of the university.

La bataille suprême est engagée . . . Bien entendu, c'est la bataille de France, et c'est la bataille de la France! . . . Pour les fils de France, où qu'ils soient, quels qu'ils soient, le devoir simple et sacré est de combattre l'ennemi par tous les moyens dont ils disposent . . . Les consignes données par le gouvernement français et par les chefs français qu'il a qualifiés pour le faire doivent être exactement suivies. . . . Derrière le nuage si lourd de notre sang et de nos larmes, voici que reparait le soleil de notre grandeur!

GÉNÉRAL DE GAULLE,
BROADCAST JUNE 6, 1944

The decisive battle has begun . . . Of course, it is the battle of France, and it is France's battle! . . . For the sons of France, whoever they may be, wherever they may be, the simple and sacred duty is to fight the enemy with all available means. . . . The directives issued by the French Government and by the French leaders who have been delegated to issue them must be followed to the letter. . . . Behind the heavy clouds of our blood and our tears, the sunshine of our greatness is presently reappearing!

As has been recounted earlier (see pages 159-160), Général de Gaulle had been told about the Supreme Commander's broadcast to be made to France when he visited 'Sharpener' on Sunday, June 4. Eisenhower had given de Gaulle a copy of the text (on page 413) whereupon the Général pointed out that it failed to mention either himself as leader of the Free French or his movement. Eisenhower fobbed the Frenchman off by saying that it was only a draft (although copies had already been mass-produced eight days earlier for air dropping over France). When the Général came up with revisions to the text the following morning, he was then told it was now too late! De Gaulle flatly refused to follow Eisenhower on the air or to submit his script in advance for approval. Early on June 6, he finally agreed to record his speech at noon at the BBC's Bush House studios, the disc being subsequently checked before it was broadcast. But even for their special midday bulletin that Tuesday — also read by John Snagge — the BBC were still scratching around for something worthwhile to say (see page 569). ***Below:*** **The Allies may have got in first in Normandy, but Goebbels reached America first at 12.37 a.m. (local time, Washington) via his Transocean News Agency. Allied reports followed at 3.32 a.m. Soon after 4 p.m. on the afternoon of D-Day, President Roosevelt, having previously been briefed by Generals Marshall and Arnold and Admiral King, gave over 180 pressmen the latest news from Europe.**

Los Angeles, three hours and 2,600 miles away to the west, greets D-Day in typical Californian style — or at least as interpreted by a *Life* magazine photographer!

Last night, there were air attacks on the remaining forces in the Calais-Boulogne-Caen area. Constant air raids since midnight in Le Havre, Caen, Cherbourg and air landings at six o'clock.

The invasion of the above areas began at 1.30 a.m. last night. Paratroopers on Guernsey and Jersey; landing craft at the Cap de la Hague; paratroopers at Cherbourg; landing craft at Barfleur; airborne troops in the area of Carentan. Landings all along the coast from Isigny to Caen, and at Arromanches-les-Bains. Arrival of tanks; more paratroopers north-west and north-east of Lisieux, airborne troops from the north at Le Havre. Six battleships and 20 destroyers identified in the Seine Bay.

The situation at Dieppe is unclear. It is not yet known whether there are troops at sea outside Dunkirk. There are still landing troops outside Calais and Dunkirk.

Already during the night, the first reports regarding the beginning of the invasion in the West have arrived. Since we were the first to get hold of the relevant information, we were able to send out a message all around the globe. The English and Americans held back in the beginning. Then a Reuters message on the subject, namely that they have undertaken to land on the fortified west coast of France, and (more specifically), that this landing has taken place between Le Havre and Cherbourg.

The Führer is more than happy about this. I notice in him a process which I have often seen before in difficult crises, namely that he is in low spirits as long as the crisis had not been resolved, but when the crisis is resolved it is as if a heavy burden is lifted from him.

The enemy is sending airborne troops behind the lines. Sometimes they land in our minefields, but sometimes they are deployed in such a way that operational reserves must be used against them.

Eisenhower addresses his troops in one broadcast and the people of Europe in another. Both are without the slightest propaganda value. They contain the same old accusations. In the USA, our message is a great sensation.

De Gaulle also speaks to the people of France. All these broadcasts have the common aim of asking the people not to act rashly under any circumstances since success is not yet guaranteed. 'Great battles are before us' — the entire English propaganda and broadcasting strategy is based on this slogan — 'the German war machine has not yet been defeated. There will be a large number of casualties.'

Churchill spoke up fairly early. It's obvious he's scared as hell. As usual with great operations he rushes into the House of Commons and offers his words of wisdom. He explains that the English would have to reckon with 20,000 losses at the bridgehead at Anzio. He waffles on about the capture of Rome and then gets on to the invasion. Four thousand naval units have supposedly set off for Western Europe. He is already talking about a tactical success, which of course in reality cannot be in the slightest bit true. As well as him, prominent opposition figures are appealing to the public. King Haakon, the exiled Dutch government, and I don't know who. But the loud notes of jubilation take on a more modest tone during the afternoon.

JOSEPH GOEBBELS, JUNE 7, 1944

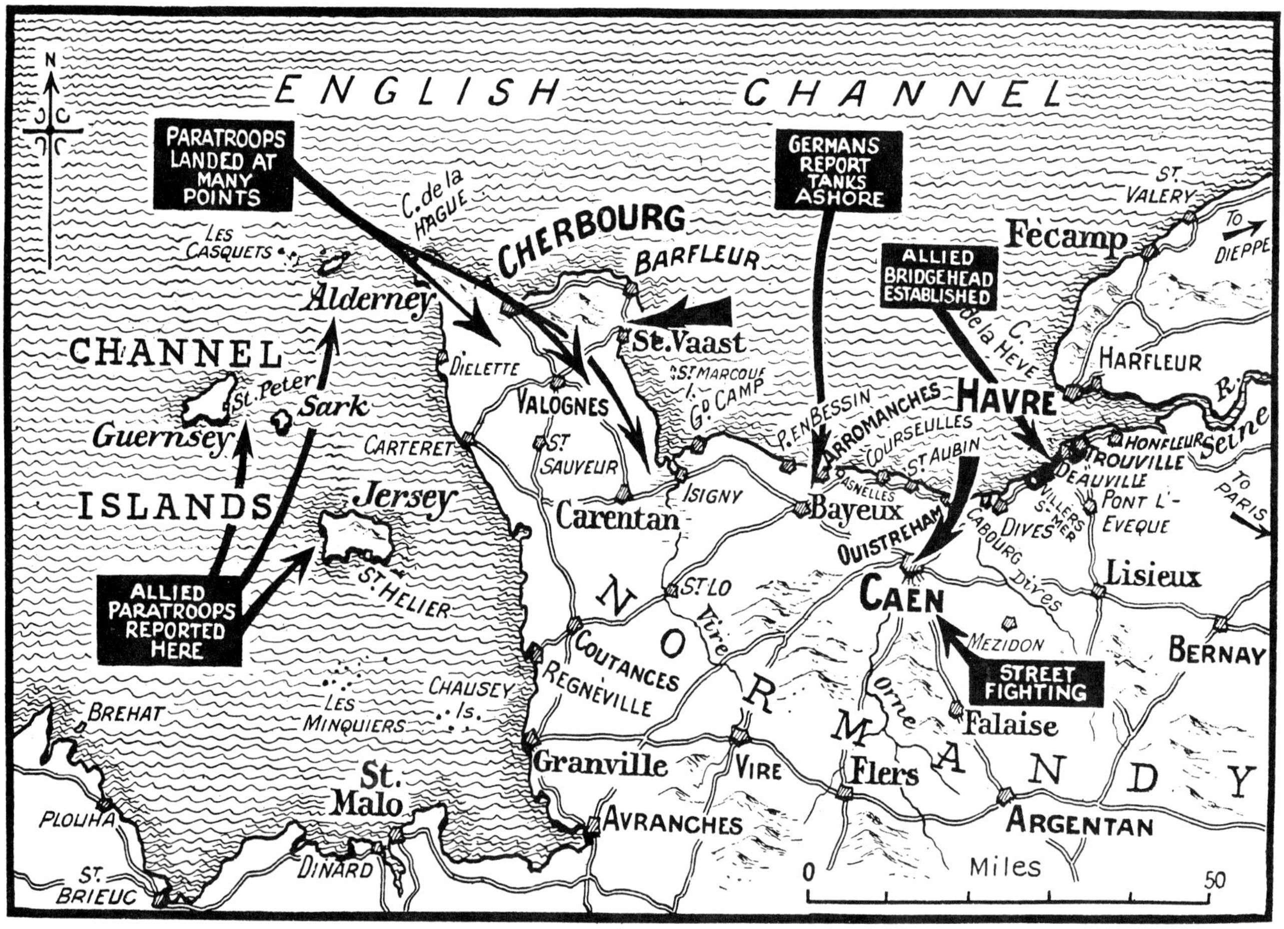

SHAEF issued its second communiqué shortly before midnight on Tuesday as Frank Phillips was reading the late-night news. (Last-minute pencilled alterations are shown in square brackets.) 'Now here is tonight's communiqué — Communiqué No. 2 — issued a few minutes ago from SHAEF: "Shortly before midnight on the 6th of June 1944, Allied night bombers opened the assault. Their attack in very great strength continued until dawn. Between 06.30 and 07.30 hours this morning, two naval task forces commanded by Rear-Admiral Sir Philip Vian, flying his flag from HMS *Scylla*, and Rear Admiral Alan Goodrich Kirk, US Navy, [launched the assault forces]. The naval forces who had previously assembled under the overall command of Admiral Sir Bertram Ramsay made their departure in fresh weather, and were joined during the night by a bombarding force which had previously left northern waters. Channels had to be swept through the large enemy minefields. This operation was completed shortly before dawn and while minesweeping flotillas continued to sweep towards the enemy coast, [the entire naval force swept channels behind them towards their objectives]. Shortly before the assault, three enemy torpedo boats with armed trawlers in company attempted to interfere with the operation and were promptly driven off. One enemy trawler was sunk and another severely damaged. The assault forces moved towards the beaches under cover of heavy bombardment by destroyers and support craft while heavier ships gave enemy batteries which had already been subjected to air bombardment. Some of these were silenced. Allied forces continued to engage other batteries. Landings were effected under cover of the air and naval bombardment [and] gliders carrying large forces of troops also made [successful landings] at a number of points. Reports of operations so far show that our forces succeeded in their initial landings. Fighting continues. Allied heavy, medium, light and fighter-bombers continued the air bombardment in very great strength throughout the day with attacks on gun emplacements, defensive works and communications. Continuous fighter cover was maintained over the beaches and for some distance inland and over naval operations in the Channel. Our night fighters played an equally important rôle in protecting shipping and troop carrier forces and in intruder operations. Allied reconnaissance aircraft maintained continuous watch by night over shipping and ground forces. Our aircraft met little fighter opposition or anti-aircraft gun-fire. Naval casualties were regarded as being very light, especially when the magnitude of the operation is taken into account."' With such brief details to go on, it is not surprising that this map in Wednesday's *Daily Telegraph*, based on German reports, was somewhat wide of the truth.

I realised very early on after my return to England that the Services in the United Kingdom regarded themselves as the real students of war and we who had been in the desert as 'cowboy-and-indian' soldiers. There was something to be said on both sides and it was made clear to me that one must never allow one theatre of war to become exclusive — your characters must be mixed up from the start of the operations, so I agreed wholeheartedly with Montgomery's policy when, on arriving in 21st Army Group, he switched a number of his senior personalities around. That was right, but he should have done more. Units should all have a baptism of fire early in any war without regard to other factors such as movement, however difficult this may be to achieve. Otherwise, in the main attack, you cannot make the best use of the offensive moment. This may sound as though I am criticising the readiness of the Army. Let me just say this. Going around England as I had to, and spending a lot of my time talking to Britain's servicemen, I found a firm and unanimous determination to win the war, at any price. I have never known anyone so hated as Hitler and his gang with him.

But let us turn to the subject of 'Overlord' and Lords and go on to the conference held at Callander Hydro in 1943 and known popularly as 'The Field of the Cloth of Gold'. It was there that I saw Lord Mountbatten in action for the first time. He was much the most junior of the *élite* but he chaired that conference, and banged some heads together, in a way I had never seen anybody do before. I am convinced that without that conference we and the Canadians would either have had to delay our attack for further months waiting for equipment and training or would have lost many more men on the beaches. Mountbatten, with his knowledge and drive, made everyone 'see' that invasion and how we would have to do it.

The Eastern Task Force assaulted three areas: Gold, Juno and Sword under the overall command of Lieutenant-General Sir Miles C. Dempsey (see page 105), commander of the British Second Army. His assault force was split into two corps: XXX Corps for Gold and I Corps for Juno and Sword. The commander of XXX Corps was Lieutenant-General Gerry Bucknall, seen here in the pullover with his Chief-of-Staff (and our author for this chapter), Brigadier Harold Pyman, better known as 'Pete' Pyman. General Bucknall was commissioned with the 1st Battalion, The Middlesex Regiment, in 1914 and served throughout the First World War, being wounded and awarded the Military Cross. Between the wars, he was in the Middle East and Canada, but was back with his old regiment in 1939 and later commanded the 5th Division in Sicily and Italy in 1943.

Some time after my appointment to 21st Army Group, I visited a beach group training exercise outside Edinburgh.

A beach group's functions were in the main administrative, and beach groups themselves were normally based on a specific unit of one arm with detachments of various others to make the amalgam a workable instrument. Virtually they were responsible for administration of every kind over the beaches. The day on which I visited this particular group was very cold and wet but the unit was training with all its heart. A unit so mixed must have presented the commanding officer and the orderly room with many problems, but military difficulties are there to be overcome, not overlooked, and it was in that spirit that this beach group was at work. That it later distinguished itself in battle came as no surprise to me. It had based its plan on bringing up stores at the rate at which the fighting units it was serving would need them and it was well within its timings.

It would have broken my heart if I had not been used in the campaign in north-west Europe, but my fears were soon allayed. Monty came back from Eighth Army in Italy and took over his rightful position as leader of our liberation army. He soon told me that he did not want a BGS Training and made me Chief-of-Staff of XXX Corps, which had been made an assault corps on its return from the Mediterranean. This suited me admirably, although I had to turn down a midnight offer to be Director Royal Armoured Corps (DRAC) to Oliver Leese who, in the reshuffle, was by then in command of Eighth Army.

GOLD AREA

Sector	*Extent*	*Grid Reference*	*Width (yards)*
HOW	G to road (Cap Manvieux)	750881–836873	8,900
ITEM	H to Asnelles	836873–878868	4,800
JIG	I to road	878868–907871	3,200
KING	J to mouth of stream	907871–929868	2,500

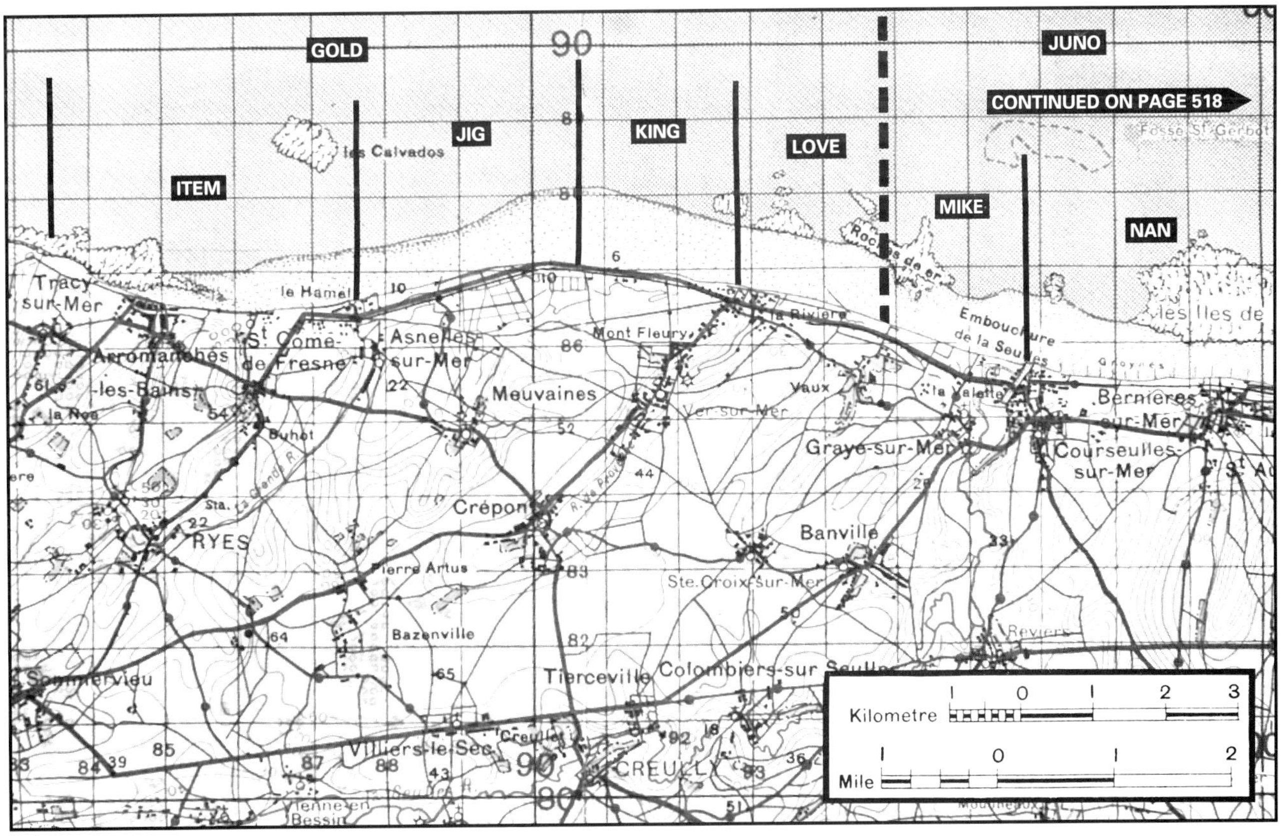

So off I went to XXX Corps at Six Mile Bottom, close to Cambridge, with George Webb [Brigadier i/c Administration] and many old friends around me. The chief characteristic of XXX Corps headquarters was that it was thoroughly battle-worthy and, whether you were talking to a brigadier or a captain, he knew his job from A to Z. They also knew me well from the desert days, so introductions and interviews were hardly necessary. They wanted to get on with knowing their soldiers and so did I and left it at that.

The corps had until lately been commanded by Oliver Leese, a man of great and well-earned reputation. He had just gone to Eighth Army and Jerry Bucknall reigned in his stead, a man equally well-known and liked. Both men have their critics but of one thing I am certain, and that is that Oliver Leese will always be known as a soldier who saw the need for mobility in war. I am only sorry I never had the opportunity of serving on his staff.

One of my first jobs in the Headquarters was when we needed a replacement. They (the Military Secretary's Branch) proposed Lord Lewes of the Life Guards. I was stupid enough to say I would 'have no flipping peer from the Life Guards here'. Mercifully, I was overruled. John Lewes, later the Marquess of Abergavenny, was a first-class and very hard-working G-2 and his later promotions had no objections and every possible recommendation from myself.

The administration of XXX Corps was outstanding and throughout all campaigns allowed us a great degree of manoeuvre. It is difficult to place a finger on what was the key and it is difficult to mention names. Webb was a wizard — that we know — but who were the other men? It does not matter. Their teamwork was unbeatable and selfless, and, as a result, we had a corps which could do nearly as much with its administrative troops as it could with its fighting units. This scheme of things was a peculiarity of Second Army whose team was led by Brigadier Cecil Roberts, their Brigadier i/c Administration and a man of great modesty and charm as well as ability.

Our main run-through of the plan for the assault of XXX Corps on the beaches was held in the Union at Cambridge, and many of those attending that rehearsal stayed in Trinity College. They will have happy memories of these days, and I myself was particularly glad to be able to introduce my own university to the corps. The run-through itself was of the greatest value and I was extremely grateful for the facilities and help we were given.

As General Smith outlined on pages 21-22, the primary duty of a chief-of-staff is to relieve the commander of the day-to-day running of the command — almost the office manager — of a division, corps or army, and this was Brigadier Pyman's rôle with XXX Corps. He had joined the army in 1930 as a subaltern with the Royal Tank Corps (then commanded by Major-General Percy Hobart who led the 79th Armoured Division in Operation 'Neptune') and ended his career as NATO Commander-in-Chief Allied Forces Northern Europe. Here, on the Normandy battlefield on June 15, 1944, Brigadier Pyman briefs unit commanders at XXX Corps HQ on the latest situation.

Unfortunately, only one AFPU photographer was officially assigned to cover the XXX Corps landings on Gold — Sergeant Norman Midgley. His first frame *(left)* shows the men of the 6th and 7th Battalions of The Green Howards boarding the SS *Empire Lance*, an LSI(L) sailing from Southampton with Assault Group G2. Commodore Cyril Douglas-Pennant was the Force 'G' commander in HMS *Bulolo* (see pages 174 and 177), with Major-General D. A. H. Graham commanding the 50th (Northumbrian) Division. *Right:* The last frame Sergeant Midgley took aboard ship: prayers before battle.

Touchdown on Gold was to be at 0725 — 55 minutes after the planned H-Hour for Omaha, the adjacent US beach some 15 miles to the westward. Force 'G' arrived at the lowering position and the *Bulolo* and the leading LSIs anchored at about 0535. Twenty minutes later, the battery on the cliffs backing How Sector at Longues (see page 54) opened fire on the *Bulolo*. No hits were scored and the guns were silenced by return fire from HMS *Ajax*. (In 1961, the observation post on the cliff edge doubled up for Major Pluskat's OP at WN 60 when depicting this scene in *The Longest Day* — see page 367.)

So after all it was to be a four-corps effort (two American, two British), each of the corps containing follow-up reserves. The Navy was to be our taxi of the day, so to speak. It had to clear minefields and keep secure its own forces. In true naval fashion, they said they would put us on the beaches and they did. The Royal Air Force was used in its rôle of bombing and protecting.

'ENDIX VI SECRET

MASSIVE CONCRETE POSITIONS

Page 3

Strong concrete gun emplacement with bomb craters. (Longues battery)

15cm. gun at Longues

Control tower at Longues battery from the front

Left: **After the war, Longues (WN 48) was subjected to a detailed examination, Admiral Ramsay stating in that 'this battery came to life again later and was engaged by the *Argonaut*. It was subsequently found that two guns had been put out of action by direct hits with 6-inch shell through the embrasures. These hits must be attributed to chance, since the density of craters around the guns was not high. The remaining two guns were undamaged, though in one case the casemate had been hit. In all, 150 rounds of 6-inch (*Ajax*) and 29 rounds of 5·25-inch (*Argonaut*) were fired at Longues battery.'** *Right:* **Captured by C Company of the 1st Battalion, The Hampshire Regiment (231st Brigade), on D+1, the battery has been progressively restored in recent years. Although the cliff is slowly eroding, the OP is still about 30 feet from the cliff edge.**

The 50th (Northumbrian) Division assault area — then and now. Gold actually extended from Port-en-Bessin to the mouth of the River Provence at La Rivière (on the left of the picture) but it was the easternmost sectors — Jig and King — that were chosen for the initial assaults. This section was enfiladed by strong German positions at both La Rivière to the east and Le Hamel to the west. The 5th Battalion, The East Yorkshire Regiment would land on King Red; the 6th Green Howards on King Green; 1st Battalion, The Dorsetshire Regiment, on Jig Red; and the 1st Battalion, The Hampshire Regiment, on Jig Green.

The success of the landing on Jig Green all depended on the neutralisation of strong point WN 37 at Le Hamel *(above right)*, coded in Allied documents as 'Dart'. It escaped damage in the bombardment because 75 tons of bombs planned to be dropped on it by the Eighth Air Force fell in fields 3,000 yards south. In addition, the navigational and control vessels for the 147th Field Regiment of self-propelled artillery, which was to engage the target on the run in, fell astern due to weather conditions. The emplacements were also fully protected from the seaward side against low-trajectory fire by destroyers.

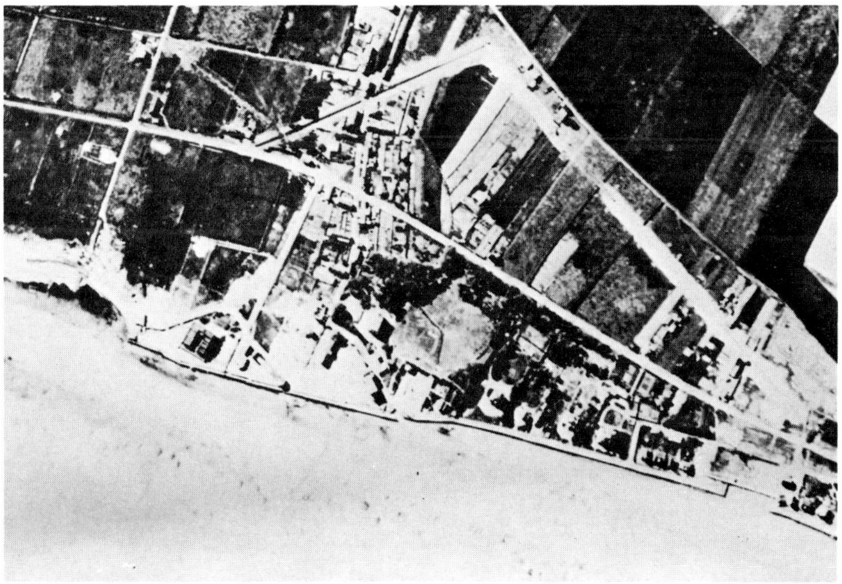

The crumpled print, reproduced at the top of the page, was part of the planning brief for the attack on 'Dart'. Apart from the main emplacement, which was fitted with a French 75mm gun on a swivel mounting (although invariably referred to elsewhere as an 88mm), 'Dart' comprised eight concrete pillboxes for infantry weapons (seven facing seaward and one inland), two concrete shelters, and a trench system linked in with the large adjacent building known as the sanatorium. The picture *above* shows the late addition of an anti-tank ditch to the rear. Six lanes were to be made through the defences by assault teams from B Squadron, Westminster Dragoons, and No. 82 Assault Squadron, Royal Engineers (all part of the 79th Armoured Division). Lane 1 was to be made from the small beach on the left of the picture, right in front of the 75mm gun which enfiladed the entire length of Jig Green.

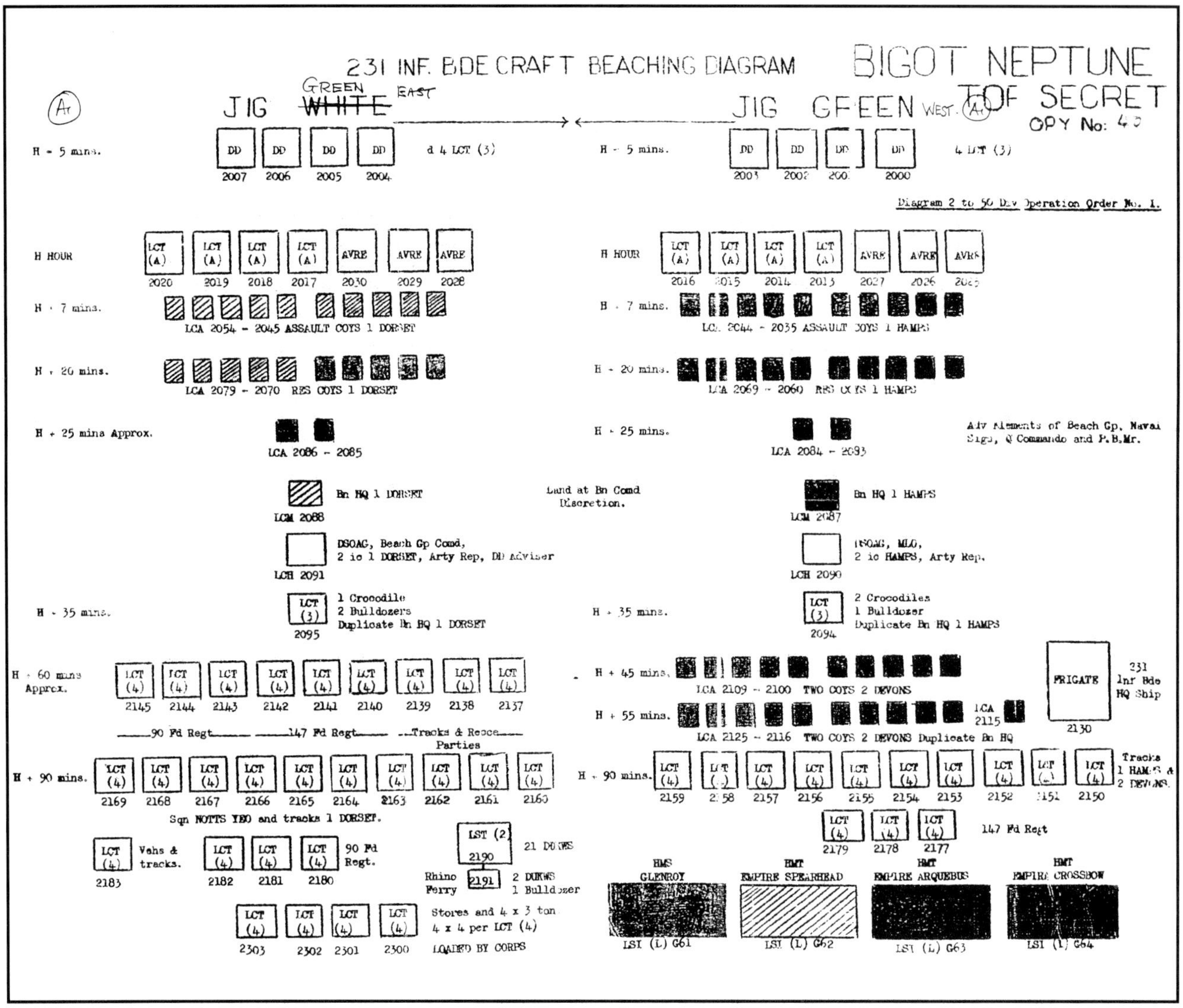

A schematic extract from the 50th Division Operational Order No. 1 — note the amendment made on May 1 to the beach designation for the Dorsets. It is important to remember that the vessel numbers given are not the ship's pennant number but its Landing Table Index Number (see page 208). David List looked into LTINs for us at the Public Record Office: 'They were fixed on a master document which was compiled by using standard pro-formae with each landing unit figuring out its own loads according to agreed criteria and after much discussion (argument actually, and the ships still sailed overloaded). Each naval unit, such as an LCT flotilla, embarking troops was given a pro-forma scheduling their vessels by fleet or pennant number in naval seniority order and it was up to the flotilla commander to allocate vessel to load and to assign the loading vessel the relevant LTIN to be displayed for the movement concerned. The LTIN would change after each movement was completed and could be altered if a vessel became u/s prior to loading. This assignment was done in pencil at the last possible moment but, unfortunately, no comprehensive record appears to have been retained of the allocations.'

I have kept brief the period when I was Chief-of-Staff to XXX Corps before the invasion because it *was* brief. In actual fact, my G-1, Victor Balfour, and my G-2, Lord Lewes, had to work extremely hard. They knew exactly what was wanted in all the forces for the early assault boats and they ensured that sufficient room was left for the Army members. I am glad to say they did not overcall their hand. There just was not room for reserves and only the essential elements could be called forward.

Then came the day when we presented our plan. Our corps commander, Gerry Bucknall, was away immediately before the conference, and so Webb and myself wrote down what we thought our corps commander should say in the seven minutes allotted to him; but he thought differently and after 17 minutes he was told to sit down.

It was about this time that I met our new army commander. With his usual courtesy, he rose from his seat as I entered the room. His name was Miles Dempsey, and he subsequently became one of my best friends as I was one of his greatest admirers. I will not attempt to give a full description of his personality. Let me just say that I grade him as the perfect British officer, without peer. Self-assured yet modest, he had all the essential qualities of a great commander and a great soldier without any of the unnecessary distracting qualities.

Our boss was, of course, Bernard Montgomery. At times, he could be quarrelsome, and at times he got very angry indeed with the turn of events, but he was always magnificent, a land commander that we trusted and we knew, and my goodness, he knew us. He led the British, Canadian and at times American divisions with unerring skill. The British Army may think slow and act slow at times, but woe betide the man who tries to belittle the achievements on the battlefield of our Monty.

D-Day was an exciting day. Second Army was to assault across the beaches around the townships of Caen and Bayeux, with its two corps, I Corps on the left with a Canadian and British division, and the all-British XXX Corps with one division, the 50th Northumbrian, on the right, each corps having follow-up reserves.

To go into the assault in any detail would be to travel along an already very well worn garden path. We did what we had to do and we did it very well. It was a day when everyone was at their best. It hardly needs saying, however, that to try to do it again now in the same way would be disastrous. A beach landing on the D-Day scale would offer the perfect nuclear target.

As the Editor-in-Chief of Second Army's official history, written while it was still fresh in our minds, I feel that it is my pleasure and my duty to the officers and men to quote from that work of how the landing went.

The first of only four frames exposed by Sergeant Norman Midgley on D-Day. The LTIN (on large boards affixed to the front of the bridge) are visible on the original print for two of these vessels: LCT 710 bears '2163', and LCM 164 to her port side '2164', which would place this picture as being taken around H+60 minutes when the SP guns of the 147th (Essex Yeomanry) Field Regiment landed.

'As the leading ships of the great invasion armada swept across the Channel, they experienced no enemy interference. Yet the voyage was by no means uneventful, and a number of craft, particularly LCM, were forced to turn back owing to the rough weather. In the grey dawn of June 6, the LSI of assault groups hove to in their lowering positions. Quickly, efficiently, the troops — their faces grim with determination — took their places in the LCA. 'Lower away', and these smaller craft were launched into heavy seas which broke over them as they churned their way towards the beaches.

'As they neared the shore, the landing ramps in the bows were held half open in readiness. Then, as the keels grounded, down went the ramps and the troops leapt out to charge through 18 inches of water and storm the beaches. The Second Front had begun.

'Tribute to the qualities of the men of all three services who took part in the invasion has been paid by Rear-Admiral Sir Philip Vian [the commander of the Eastern Naval Task Force] in his official report, in which he writes: "Conditions of wind and sea on the day of sailing were, in my appreciation, unexpectedly severe for the launching of an operation of this type and imposed a high test on the landing craft crews. It may probably be that the weather conditions had some part in what must ever be a matter for wonder — that the embarkation, sailing and passage of the force by day, should have been carried through without so great a movement being detected. That this should have been achieved is a lasting tribute to the admirable work of the Allied Air Force and the excellence of the cover plan." '

Rear-Admiral Vian also explained that the weather conditions were on the border line for the swimming DD tanks. In all the assaults, these arrived after the first landing craft had touched down.

Left: **This 'after the battle' shot reproduced in the 79th Divisional history shows the Fascine AVRE destined for Lane 3. It was hit in the vision port, the driver being killed or wounded, and the fascine dropped. As the tank was still in gear, it slowly climbed on top of the bundle of chespaling and overturned.** *Right:* **The seafront has totally changed at Le Hamel since the war and the sanatorium, visible in the extreme left background of the wartime shot, has been demolished.**

It was too rough to launch the DDs of the Nottinghamshire Yeomanry and they were landed directly onto the beach after the AVREs had come ashore from the LCTs. The plan shows the intended landing positions of the six lane-clearance teams, but the LCTs beached some 400 yards further to the east than intended and Teams 2 and 3 were reversed. The first AVRE for Lane 1 was launched into deep water and promptly drowned with its stern still on the ramp. It was impossible to move either the AVRE or the LCT which swung broadside and became a sitting target. Consequently, no vehicles could be disembarked from it until 1300. Major Harold Elphinstone, commanding the 82nd Assault Squadron, was killed in the turret of his AVRE and, within minutes of the arrival of the Hampshires at H+5, their CO, Lieutenant-Colonel David Nelson-Smith, had also become a casualty, together with the forward observation officer and the battery commander from the field artillery.

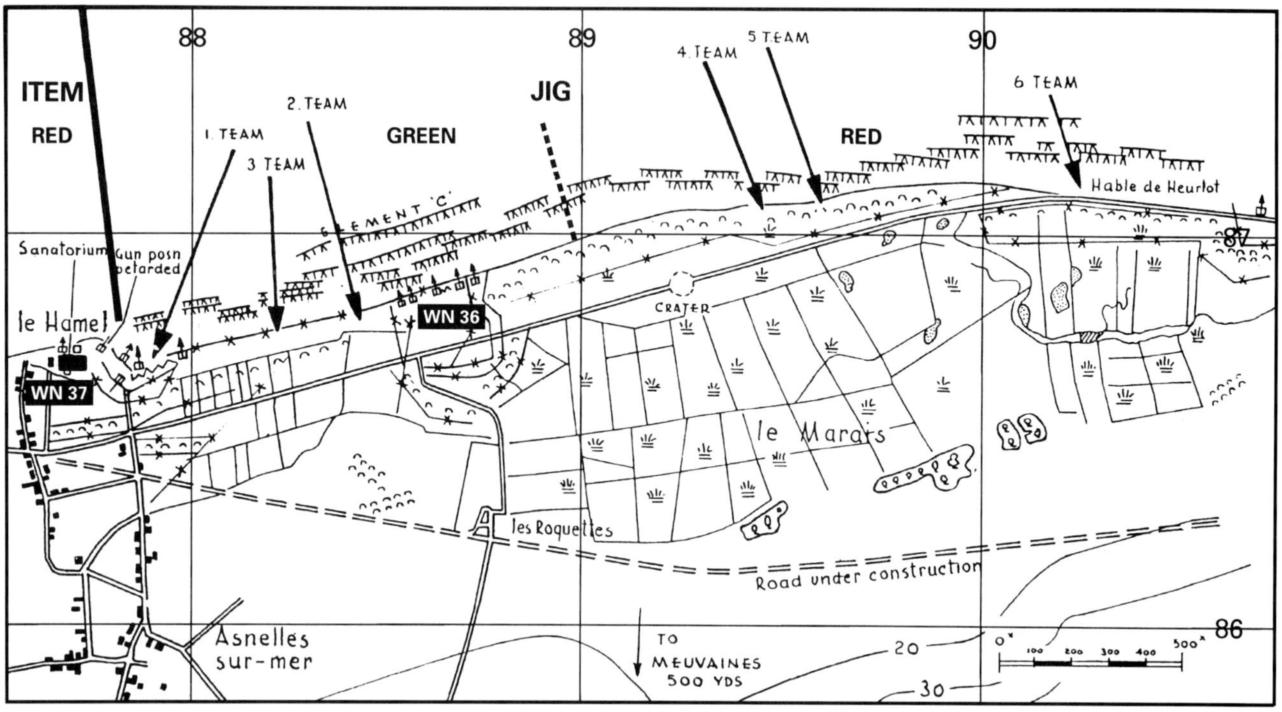

The comparison *(right)* with the sanatorium *(top)*, was taken by Karel Margry on June 5, 1994 from a little further back to show the notorious 75mm casemate (Allied code-name 'Asnelles 7') which accounted for at least six tanks. Today, the emplacement is a memorial to the Essex Yeomanry with particular mention of the destruction of the 88mm *(sic)* 'at a range of 300 yards by a 25-pdr SP gun commanded by Sergeant R. E. Palmer'. However, contemporary reports state that it was an AVRE from the 82nd Assault Squadron which finally put the casemate out of action 'by placing a Petard round through the rear entrance, shattering the interior and causing ammunition to detonate'. An after-action report stated that 'there was slight damage to the top south side of the embrasure caused by shell-fire from the beach'. The 'Dart' position was finally cleared by B Company of the 6th Battalion, The Border Regiment, at 1530.

Major-General Percy Hobart, for some time now commander of 79th Armoured Division, had been preparing for this day for a long time and it was splendid to see his efforts succeed. As Winston Churchill told the House of Commons: 'Certain ingenious modifications had been used.' 'Hobo's division went in as the first wave and, rightly, he used all his armour, not the Tank Regiment alone this time. In his division, he had famous cavalry and yeomanry regiments in which every man, from the commanding officer down, had done the most extensive and arduous training for these particular conditions. 'Hobo' never envisaged failure and no more did his troops, although a Force 5 wind gave them an untidy run-in when a Force 4 wind was supposed to be the maximum they could work in. Here were the Yeomanry, the Westminster Dragoons, considered by Dempsey and 'Hobo' alike as worthy of being in the first wave. Their tanks, fitted with flails, were planned to operate as mine removers and in squadrons, but as well they got most of the surprises which war can inflict and had to operate as normal tanks against other tanks and go forward in support of the infantry. But they retained throughout the standard we had come to expect from our Yeomanry. I have particular pleasure in recording this as I was later the Honorary Colonel of the Westminster Dragoons.

In general, lane clearance teams comprised two Flails, a Roly Poly AVRE, Bobbin AVRE *(above)*, a Fascine AVRE, SBG AVRE and a D7 armoured bulldozer. *Below left:* This discarded Type C Bobbin core lies just east of the junction of the old lateral road with the road to Asnelles, but it is difficult to say with any certainty to which team it belonged. Team 2 did not lay their Bobbin because the frame was twisted and the explosive release charges would not blow out the release pins, and Team 3 did not need it laid because the ground where they landed was firm enough. *Below right:* Karel took this comparison from the D514 looking towards the sea at a part of Le Hamel now called Roseau Plage. Only the end house on the left remains.

In comes the 1st Battalion of the Dorsets. Sergeant Midgley's next D-Day shot shows the vessels which brought in the SPs of the 147th Field Regiment, Crocodiles of 141st RAC, 'dozers and the non-swimming Shermans of the Nottinghamshire Yeomanry.

Instead of landing on Jig Green West, with their first objective the strong point 'Dart', A and B Companies of the Hampshires landed without the supporting DD tanks on Jig Green East where they found that 'the aerial bombardment did not seem to have been so effective as they expected. Enemy machine gun nests survived the aerial, naval and artillery bombardment and made the fullest use of their underground, well-concealed and well-built positions. The narrowness of the beach and the presence of mines added to the difficulties of the battalion's task. In spite of heavy casualties, however, the battalion drove the enemy from the beach . . . inflicting heavy casualties'. The strong point they captured was really the objective of the 1st Dorsets on the left. B Company of the Hants was street fighting in Le Hamel all morning and the area was not secured until 2000. Meanwhile, the other companies were advancing westwards.

Jig Green as seen from the German gun position (WN 39) on the cliffs between Le Hamel and Arromanches. This sector of the coastline — in effect Item Red — could not be assaulted frontally, yet it was of vital importance because of it having been earmarked for the siting of Mulberry 'B', the Eastern Shore Arm of which would line up with the conspicuous lookout tower beside the Le Hamel casemate. The view shows how this position, overlooking the beach from the dress circle so to speak, brought further devastating fire down onto the Hampshires below.

The corps commander and myself crossed on the afternoon of D-Day on board a destroyer, HMS *Beagle*. On board, my appointed place was on the bridge but I soon began to go green. A kind soul came up to me and said 'You are going to be sick'. I replied 'I know, you fool — get me a bucket.' 'I'll get you a bucket if you will take this pill', he answered. He gave me a minute white pill which I hastily swallowed. True to his word, he returned with the bucket but I never needed it. I blessed him on many subsequent occasions for letting me into the secret of this pill.

My naval hosts were amazed that I knew the coastline so well. I had to. I had learned it off by heart. Monty altered the plan when he enlarged it, but the objectives were never changed.

Today, two caissons of the Eastern Shore Arm of the Mulberry point towards Le Hamel. In the foreground, vehicles of the period provide a fitting link with the past.

By mid-June 1944, the beach was alive with activity as more and more supplies poured in to support the advance on its way inland.

Right: In the 1st Hampshires' operational plan, the capture of the Giant Würzburg on the eastern headland overlooking Arromanches was detailed to B and C Companies. It was believed the radar would only be lightly held by the station personnel plus a few infantry. Troops were particularly ordered to preserve the equipment from damage, as its examination would be followed up by No. 30 Assault Unit which was a joint services commando unit specially set up and trained in the seizure of intelligence objectives and placed under the direct operational control of ANCXF. *Below:* The modern vertical takes in a wider area to show the relationship of the radar station to the town. (We shall see the Mulberry in detail later on.) The position was captured with some 40 prisoners. Arromanches itself had been bombarded by HMS *Scylla* which fired 40 rounds between 0924 and 0931, and later by the guns of the 147th Field Regiment. The town was finally clear by 2100 when C Company went on to capture Longues.

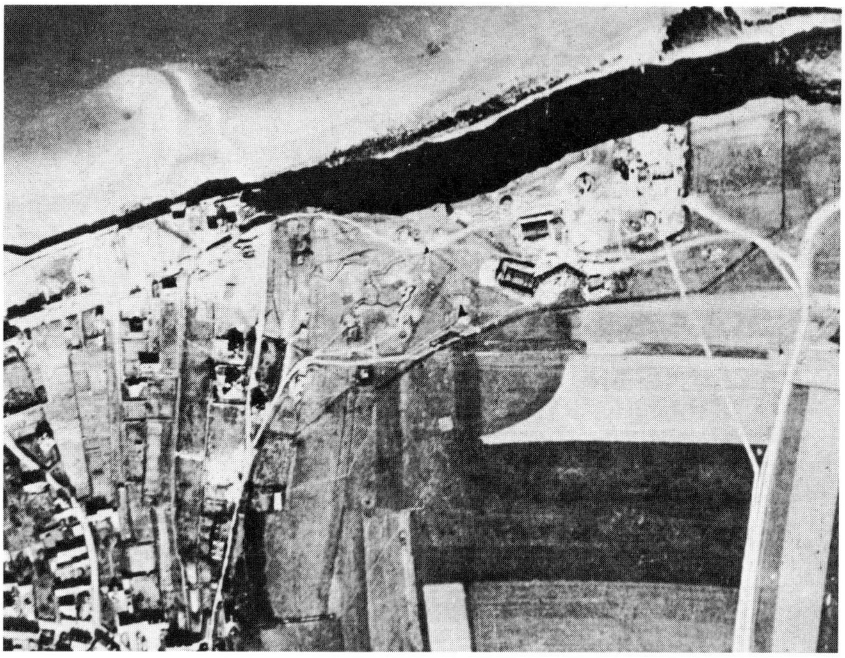

As such, No. 30 Assault Unit had carte blanche to take anything of interest, and some of its finds included charts showing swept channels, cipher and code-books, infra-red signalling apparatus, miniature tanks, a night gunsight, a W/T van, vital parts of radar installations and samples of a new German mine. Having been given official blessing to plunder to order, the work of the unit was hampered by the ruthless way in which captured equipment was looted for souvenirs or mishandled from sheer destructiveness. Initially, two main objectives were assigned to it, viz., (a) the radar station at Douvres and (b) the naval headquarters and arsenal at Cherbourg. Subsidiary tasks were the prevention of demolitions at Port-en-Bessin, Ouistreham and Courseulles, and examination of the radar stations at Arromanches and Englesqueville (west-south-west of Bayeux). For these purposes, the unit was divided into two: one landing early on D-Day on Juno, the other on D+4 on Utah. The main body concentrated on flying bomb sites in the Cotentin peninsula, subsequently assisting in the capture of the German naval headquarters at Cherbourg on June 26.

Mission accomplished. These Hampshire lads occupy a former German position at Arromanches. Comparison by Brana Radovic.

Above: **At 0950, No. 47 (Royal Marine) Commando, commanded by Lieutenant-Colonel C. F. Phillips, landed on Jig Green East with an estimated strength of 300 after three of their LCAs had been sunk by mines on the run in, causing over 40 casualties. Their task was a special one and well suited to the Special Service troops: to cross the beach and then to straightaway advance through enemy lines in a wide arc, bypassing Arromanches, and capture Port-en-Bessin, ten miles to the west, from the rear. Their move would also more than likely link up with the US V Corps. Sergeant Midgley took these two pictures of the commandos coming ashore before they concentrated at the back of the beach. No casualty figures on the beach are available, but 12 were suffered en route to Port-en-Bessin.**

The battle for the small fishing port on the inter-Allied boundary began early on D+1 and continued throughout the day, supported by fire from HMS *Emerald* and three squadrons of rocket-firing Typhoons. One or the other most probably sank the flak boat. The port was secured at 0400 on June 8 but, according to American sources, the first contact between British and US forces had occurred the previous evening between the commandos and the 3rd Battalion of the 16th RCT.

However, General Dempsey did not record the link-up in his Army Commander's diary until 1630 on June 8: 'Saw commander 231 Brigade. There is now complete touch Longues—Port-en-Bessin—5 American Corps which is most satisfactory'. *Above left:* This classic shot, taken by Sergeant Morris on the same day when Montgomery met General Bradley just outside the town for their first meeting on French soil (see page 405), shows the General touring the harbour and speaking with navy personnel. *Above right:* A timeless comparison save for the fading advertisement. *Left:* Commander Cowley Thomas, RN, had opened his headquarters as Naval Officer in Charge at first light on June 8. The capacity of Port-en-Bessin for handling stores greatly exceeded all expectations, and within six days the port was averaging 1,000 tons per day. *Below:* No. 47 Commando lost 50 per cent of their strength in the battle for the town, and a new memorial was erected to their memory in June 1994.

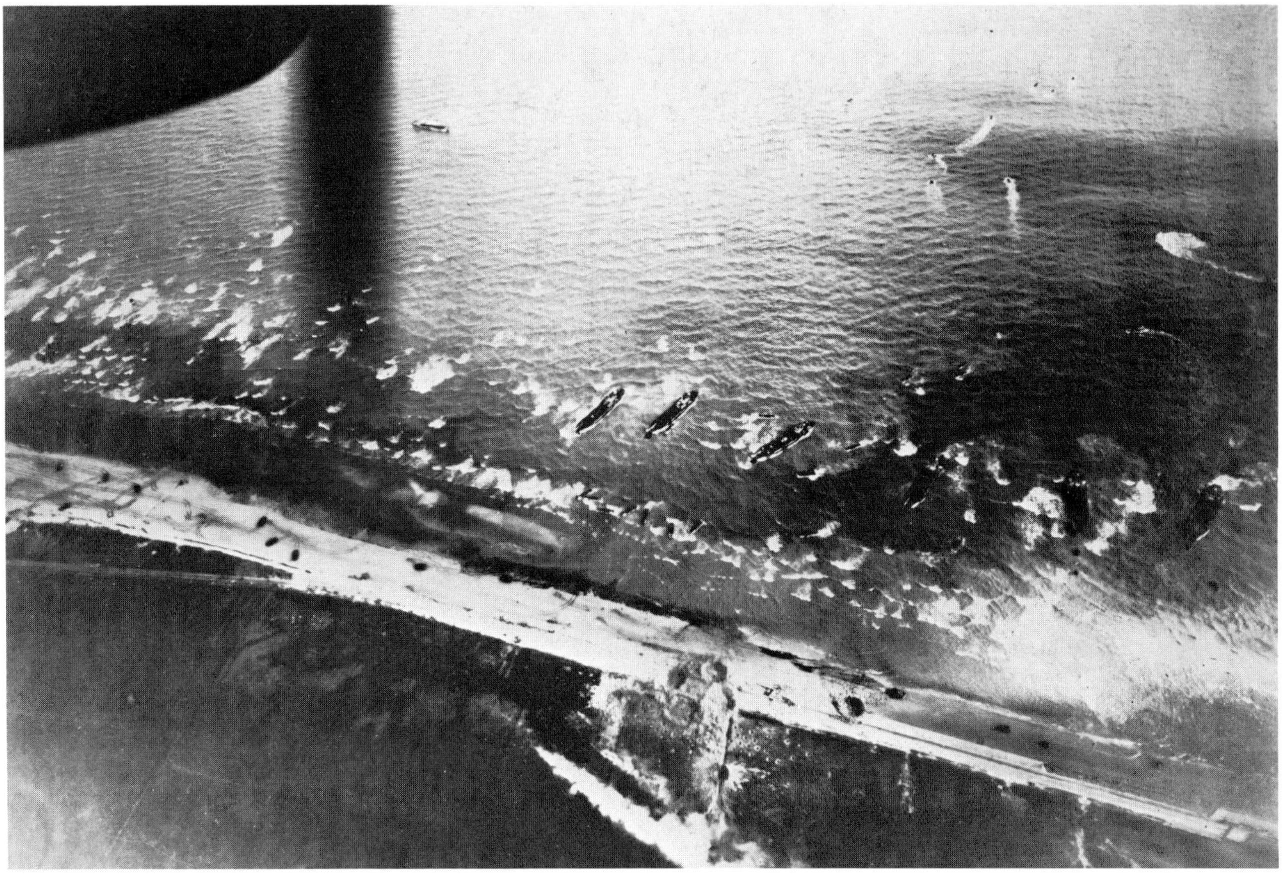

On Jig Green East, a series of defensive positions (WN 36) at what was called in the operational order, Cabane des Douanes, was the first objective of the 1st Battalion of the Dorset Regiment. However, all the landings were hundreds of yards east of the designated spots, with the result that the Hampshires landed in front of the Dorsets' strong point, while the Dorsets came ashore 'somewhat east of the correct position'. A and B Companies touched down at 0725 and 0737 respectively, and A Company on the right 'pushed forward to the line of the lateral road without opposition . . . the company commander, Major A. A. E. Jones, Lieutenant Ellis and CSM Howell all wounded soon after landing by shell and mortar fire'. Touching down behind B Company at 0750, D Company suffered several casualties from mines and mortar fire when getting clear of the beach, after an LCA had hit an underwater obstacle. It is thus clear that, on this beach, which was apparently Jig Red West, the only opposition encountered was from shelling and mortaring. This is borne out by the remark that the day had passed 'not without considerable fighting, not so much on the beaches themselves as further inland'. In the US picture *above*, the LSTs have beached just to the east of where the coast road bends inland. Team 6 landed here and two Flails of B Squadron, Westminster Dragoons, had cleared the lane (seen on the left) by H+22 minutes.

Since craft were beached on a rising tide, congestion was inevitable until more lanes could be cleared through the minefield. The latter were marked with both yellow and white 'Achtung Minen' signs; only much later was it discovered that the white signs were dummies. This picture, [1] on the oblique opposite, was taken at the extreme eastern end of Jig, almost into King Green. In spite of 'kedging', both LSTs have drifted broadside on from the effect of wind and current.

Right: Picture [2] clearly shows a track across the dunes but it must be impassable or mined. This could be Lane 4 where the two Flails bogged down in the marshy ground — there are two objects visible on either side. This team contained two Fascine AVREs which then took hull-down positions at the head of the beach. A Roly Poly AVRE proceeded west to Lane 5 (just out of the picture to the left) and joined the lateral road (see picture *below*) and turned west. Some 200 yards along the road it was halted by a large crater, 50 feet in diameter and 9 to 10 feet deep until three Fascines were called up to drop their bundles of chespaling into the opening. (B Squadron of the Westminster Dragoons reported that the crater had been caused by a shell.) The Flails then continued to the crossroads to clear a gap to the south side of the road which was later extended through a minefield.

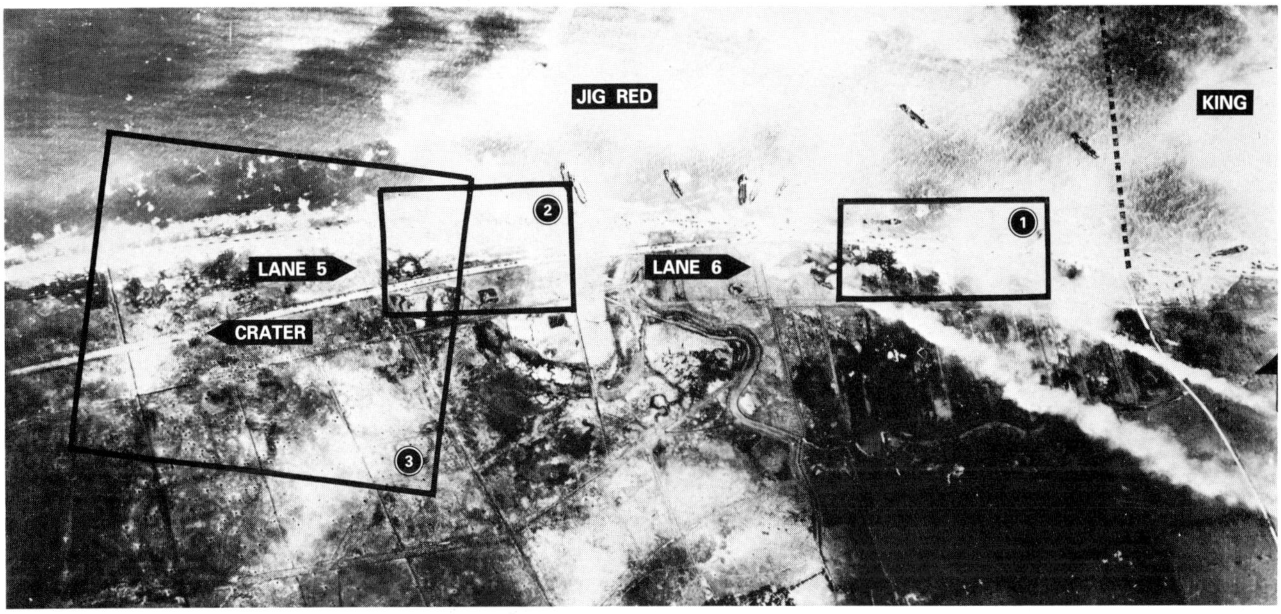

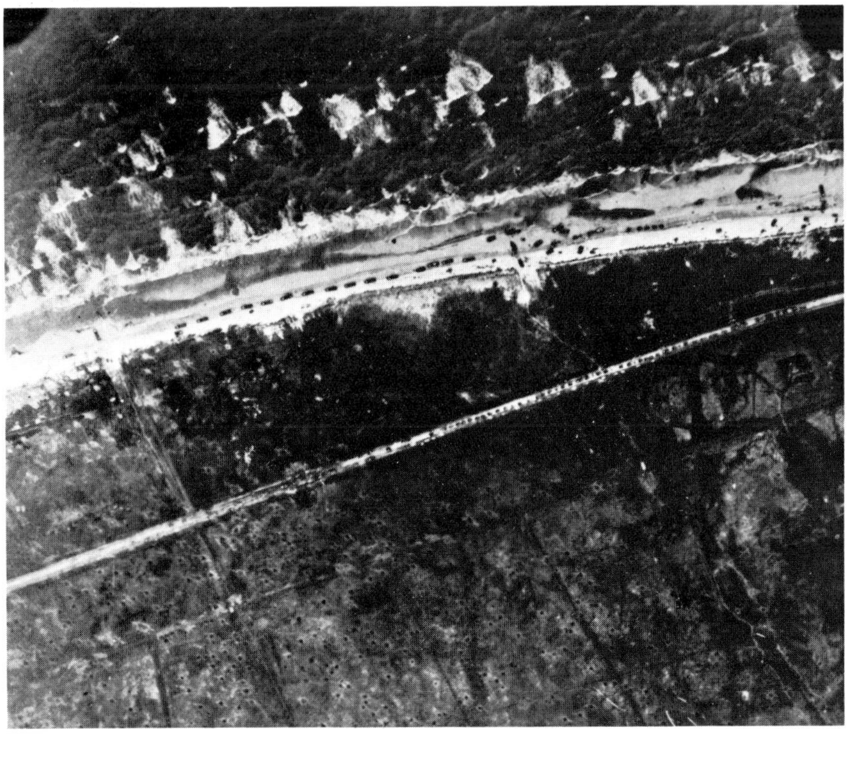

Left: Picture [3] shows the crater in the process of being bridged. The Army Operational Research Group report states that although Jig Red was 'not so unsatisfactory as on Jig Green, the situation here was rather difficult, particularly in the early stages of the assault. There were some exits from the beach at about H+15 minutes, though they are described as being bad, and such a concentration of traffic is reported at H+15 minutes that it was impossible to move guns for some considerable time. Perhaps the most eloquent statement on the comparison between Jig Red and Jig Green is that of 6th Border [part of the beach group organisation for Jig] who report that their "first tide personnel landed on Jig Red" and that there were "no landings on Jig Green as planned as it had not been possible to clear all the underwater obstacles". Clearance evidently later proceeded much more rapidly on Green than on Red, for at H+10 hours the latter was officially closed down. Despite the presence of obstacles, from some of which the mines had fallen to be buried in the sand, naval units insisted on landing at Jig Red even after it had been closed.'

We were called well before dawn, and, driving across the darkened airfield to the Ford mess for an early breakfast, we heard the roar of powerful engines as the first formations of day fighters made their way to Normandy to relieve the night patrols. After a hurried meal, we strapped ourselves into the cockpits of our Spitfires. I took the three squadrons across the Channel, over a choppy grey sea, to patrol the line of beaches being assaulted by British and Canadian troops.

From the pilot's viewpoint, flying conditions were quite reasonable — better than we expected after the gloomy forecasts of the previous two or three days. The cloud base was at about 2,000 feet and the visibility between five and six miles. Calling the wing leader of the formation we were about to relieve, I told him that we were already on our appointed patrol line. Had he seen anything of enemy fighters? 'Not a bloody thing,' he replied, 'although the flak is pretty hot if you fly a few hundred yards inland.'

Amongst the mass of shipping below us was a fighter direction ship. I called the RAF controller on my radio and asked if he had any plots of enemy formations on his table. The controller came back with the guarded reply that for the moment he had no positive information for me.

We swept parallel to the coast beneath a leaden grey sky, and I positioned the wing two or three hundred yards offshore so that we should not present easy targets to the enemy gunners. Our patrol line ended over the fishing village of Port-en-Bessin, while farther to the west, beyond our area of responsibility, lay the two American beaches.

Offshore, the sea was littered with ships of all sizes and descriptions, and small landing craft ploughed their way through the breakers to discharge their contents at the water's edge. We could see a fair number of capsized vessels, and afterwards learnt that the various obstacles erected by the Germans below the high-water mark were considerably more formidable than had been expected. Not content with the erection of these steel obstacles, the Germans had attached underwater mines to them and so added to the hazards of our landing craft. Further out in the bay, cruisers and destroyers manoeuvred to lie broadside on to the assault beaches: we could see the flashes from their guns as they engaged the enemy defences well inland. As I watched the naval bombardment, I realised that we flew constantly in an air space between the naval gunners and their targets. No doubt the shells were well above our height of 2,000 feet, but I made quite certain that we did not exceed this altitude.

WING COMMANDER 'JOHNNIE' JOHNSON
No. 144 WING

The casualty rate in Jig Sector had been surprisingly light. Although accurate figures were not kept for D-Day by most of the regiments involved, out of the 4,000-odd men who landed in the assault phase, casualties (i.e. dead, wounded and missing) were estimated at 171. The Hampshires were given as '60?'; the Dorsets '20?'; the Devons '20?', and No. 73 Field Squadron, RE, at 26. The time of 0820 was the cut-off point for the end of the assault phase, by which time the majority of the beach defences had been neutralised. Typical of the observations set down after the battle was this one by the commanding officer of the 120th Light Anti-Aircraft Regiment: 'My main reaction to D-day and night was surprise at the lack of opposition from enemy ground troops and almost entire absence of the Luftwaffe. The mass of shipping offshore and the jam of traffic on the beaches must have been a perfect target, and yet the enemy made no real attempt to attack. I was also surprised at the small amount of casualties by drowning and enemy action. I saw less than 50 dead between both sectors [King and Jig].' The Luftwaffe certainly had not been in evidence, and it is believed that the total effort by the German air force amounted to less than 100 sorties during daylight, of which 70 were flown by single-engined fighters. However, after dark, a major effort was directed at the beach-head, mainly by long-range bomber and torpedo-bomber forces. Those Allied fighters and fighter-bombers detailed to give close support to the assaulting troops were controlled from the headquarters ship HMS *Bulolo*. On board were a number of air force officers whose duty it was to despatch aircraft patrolling above onto particular targets. It was rather ironic, therefore, that the *Bulolo* herself was singled out for attack early on June 7. Shortly after dawn, a 250lb phosphorus bomb scored a direct hit on the ship, killing three officers (two RAF and one RN), and blowing a 5-foot hole in the foremost bulkhead of the operations room *(right).*

Above: **The Ninth Air Force's 10th Photo Group F-5 Lightning continues its sortie along the beach-head. At this point, it has reached King sector which began at the road on the right. Burning tanks spread plumes of smoke low over the battlefield; one of these must be the Flail from the LCT (LTIN 2029) which belonged to the Breach Commander for Lane 5 on Jig sector. As the two Flails cleared the gap beyond the crater, his was hit in the petrol tank by a heavy mortar or gun shell and immediately went up in flames. King sector was assaulted by the 69th Infantry Brigade on a two-battalion front with the 6th Green Howards on the right on Green Beach, and the 5th East Yorkshire Regiment on Red Beach, close to La Rivière. The 7th Battalion, The Green Howards, was in reserve due to land at H+20 minutes and advance through the 6th to capture a gun position inland at Ver-sur-Mer. At touch-down at 0725, there was a wade of 100-150 yards, but at high tide (approximately three hours after H-Hour) the beach was only 20-30 yards wide which made manoeuvring very difficult.**

This US vertical looks down at the Jig-King sector boundary road beside which a group of pillboxes formed strong point WN 35.

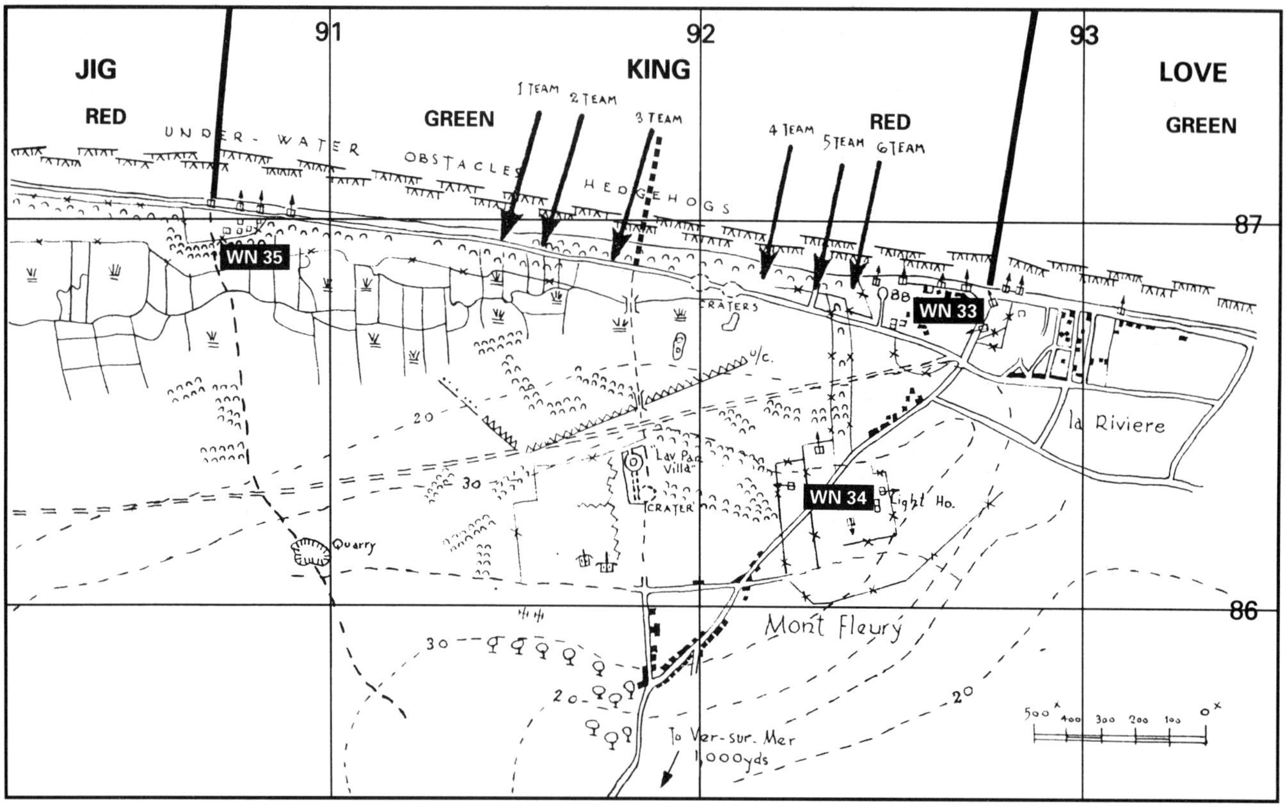

As in Jig sector, there were to be six breaching teams comprising C Squadron of the Westminster Dragoons and the 81st Assault Squadron, RE, divided into two: X Squadron on King Green and Z Squadron on King Red. All the LCTs touched down at their correct positions, but one AVRE was run over by an LCT while wading. When launched, each Roly Poly was carried east by the rough sea and had to be abandoned. All the other AVREs and Flails reached the water's edge satisfactorily.

To keep in communication with the forward divisions, we next boarded HMS *Bulolo*, of which I remember Cecil Kershaw of English Rugby fame, who played for England in 1920-23, as the central figure. They looked after us very well and I remember, as we climbed into the LCT to go ashore, Kershaw leaning down to say jocularly 'You'll never do it.' I must admit that the landing craft looked very small from the deck of HMS *Bulolo* and the thing

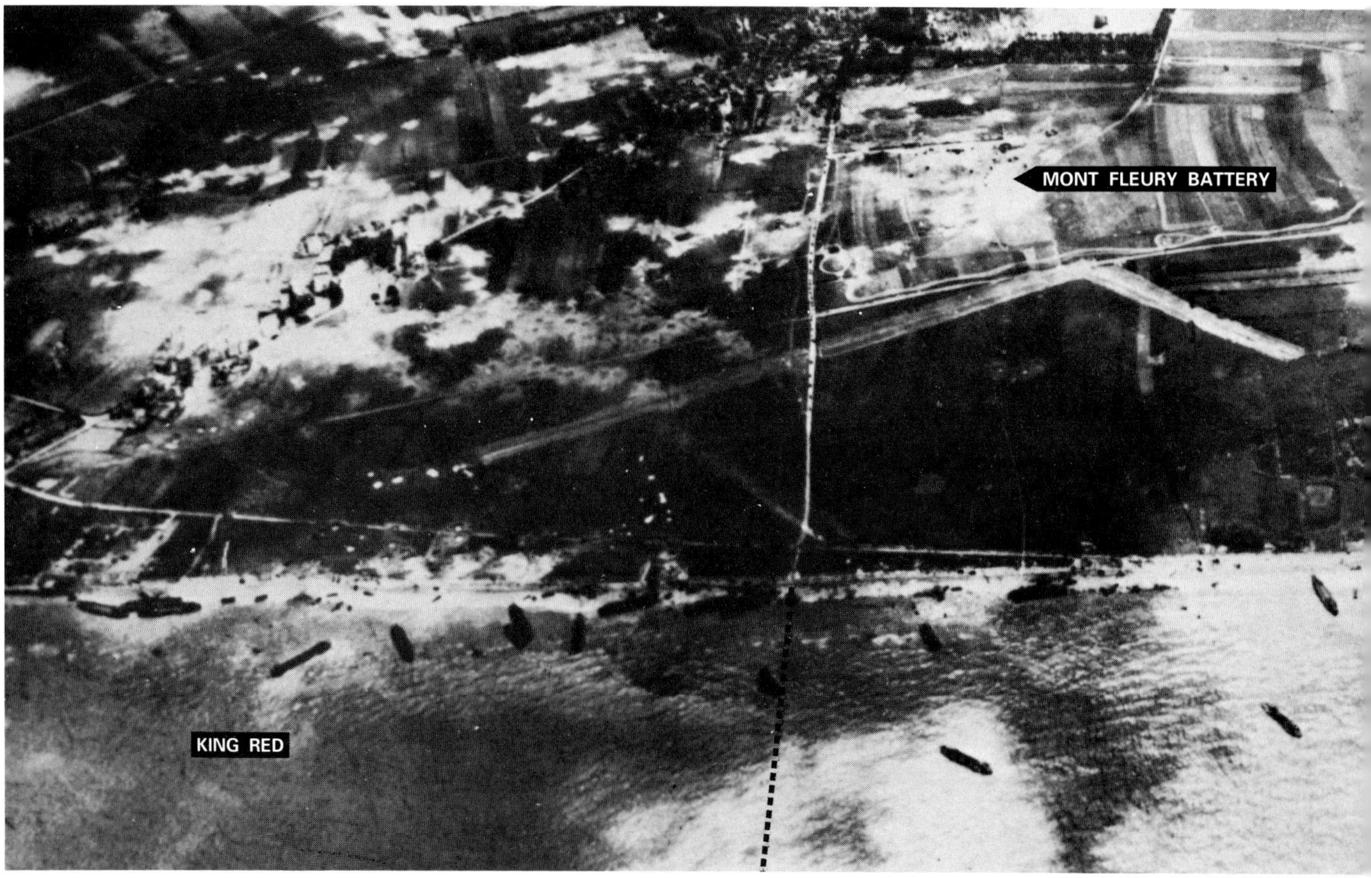

was bouncing about like a pea on a drum. But we did it and were soon at the coast and the beach, over which thousands of troops had passed that day. And there was I, Chief-of-Staff to an assault corps, in France on D-Day. My cup was full when eventually I drove into corps headquarters, where as a Chief-of-Staff I do not think I had any right to be at that moment.

During the morning, the Deputy Senior Air Staff Officer of the Second Tactical Air Force, Air Commodore Andrew Geddes, took off (probably from Northolt) in his Mustang fitted with a camera with an 8-inch lens to photograph the beaches. This is what he reported: 'TOA 1020–1100. OUISTREHAM ALL GOING WELL. Own tps ½ way to CAEN and passed rd DOUVRE–COLLEVILLE. Beaches clear of vehicles, smoke screen SEINE estuary. J K & L beaches W of COURSEULLES FIGHTING IN CLOSE PROXIMITY TO BEACHES. OMAHA beach very little progress beaches congested with vehicles. Smoke & dust within 1000 yds of sea. UTAH little progress bad flooding. *Warspite* off LE HAVRE ??? CABOURG. Beaches photoed 1200 ft. Destroyer blew up houses east of PORT EN BESSIN. Destroyers in very close VIREVILLE many vehicles.'

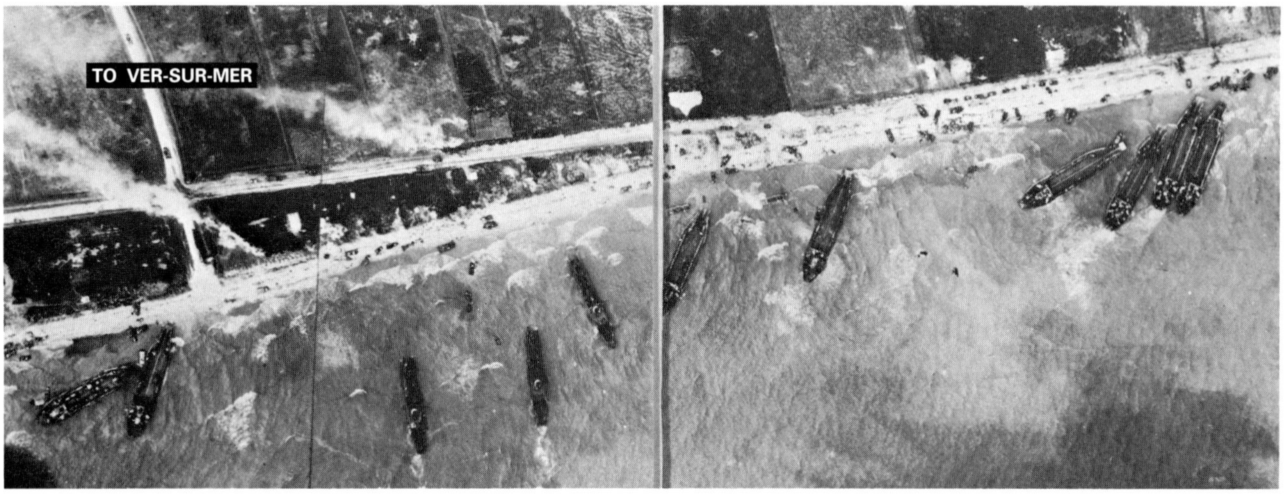

With the aerial photography of the D-Day beaches, it is surprising how the same picture can emanate from different sources. The montage *(above)* was found in file AIR 34/836 at the Public Record Office but with no caption. However, we were able to pinpoint it as showing, on the right, King Green with the beach exit on the left (denoting the boundary with King Red), the clearing of which was the mission of Team 3. Their two Flails were both knocked out by the 88mm gun enfilading the beach from La Rivière, as they began to cross the minefield behind the beach. (Unfortunately, their hulks cannot be readily distinguished in the dark shadow.) Team 2 managed to clear their lane to the beach road (possibly the track just to the right of the crude join) but both Flails bogged down on turning right. Team 1 lost one Flail in the clay on the beach, but the second, commanded by Lieutenant B. Pear, was ordered to turn east (left) to clear Team 3's road to Ver-sur-Mer.

The second print *(above)*, virtually the same but with the join not so prominent, is accredited to the collection of Squadron Leader P. Lamboit. His caption, although stating incorrectly that it was taken 'along Gold Beach at Asnelles' (which is to the west on Jig Green), added the detail that it was taken at '1030 hours on D-Day'.

I remember seeing, as we crossed the beaches, the price that our forces had had to pay; no unopposed landing this. I remember, too, seeing the beach groups whose training I had watched, already settled down and functioning smoothly. I thought briefly on a number of people who should have been there with me but whose fight was over. But such thoughts were swiftly driven from my mind by a flash from a hostile 88. Here I was again, with my Jeep, making too much dust under enemy observations, as I had done only too often in the desert in my tank.

The third photograph, a 10x8 glossy from USAF sources, states that it was taken by the 3rd Bomb *(sic)* Division of the Eighth Air Force, but the Eighth's photo unit was the 7th Photo Group. It is obviously exactly the same print as most of the left-hand part of the one at the top of the page, but does not have the join and shows an extended view inland. We can pick out artillery towing guns on the road and, more importantly, the bridge over the stream which, much to his surprise, Lieutenant Pear found had not been destroyed. Amazingly, the road across the anti-tank ditch (visible on the panorama on pages 434-435) had also not been blown.

Teams, 4, 5 and 6, landing closer to La Rivière, were subjected to direct fire from an 88mm casemate built into the sea-wall. This was part of German strong point WN 33 at the eastern end of King Red and included a 50mm (referred to in some accounts as a 37mm) anti-tank gun, two machine gun posts, a light machine gun or mortar position and an open mortar pit. As a result of the preliminary bombardment, one of the machine gun posts was 'completely destroyed either by a hit from a destroyer or by a bomb', and the anti-tank gun was 'knocked out probably by fire from an LCG(L)'. This position put up stout opposition to the landing and the 88mm damaged two Flails and two AVREs of the breaching squadrons and, with the aid of the MGs, pinned down D Company of the 5th East Yorks causing heavy casualties. The gun was silenced fairly early on by Captain R. F. Bell of C Squadron, Westminster Dragoons. Nevertheless, stiff fighting continued until 1000 when the position was finally secured.

It was well after dark by the time we reached corps headquarters where, by a miracle of good management on the part of the staff, we were in communication with all the elements of the corps and our maps were beautifully up-to-date.

The troops had done magnificently that day. They had been superbly led and they had answered every call with gallantry. Surely, there was a glory in being in France on D-Day. Eisenhower made the right decision when he chose June 6 but what a decision for one man to have to make.

Although the last few weeks' preparation had been performed in perfect summer weather, on June 4 it became apparent that the weather would not be favourable on June 5, the day chosen for the assault. Therefore, on June 4, Supreme Headquarters signalled a 24-hour postponement. An uncomfortable day was spent during which certain historians recalled that the last major invasion armada to sail the English Channel had 365 years previously come to grief through just the same south-west wind that was delaying Operation 'Overlord'.

Christopher Buckley of *The Daily Telegraph* once told a story of a press interview I gave at the time. As the English are inclined to do, I was describing a battle in cricketing terms — how the earlier batsmen had the job of wearing down the bowling and how, when they had done so, we would send in Chapman to hit the Germans for six (or some similar expression). A Russian observer jumped up at this point and asked: 'And who is this General Chapman, please, and what does he command?'

Whether dealing out death and destruction or equipment for the sailing fraternity, the 88m casemate at La Rivière soldiers on.

The British Army did not do nearly so well after D-Day. I have often wondered what the reasons were and I still stick to my first opinion. We lost many of our commanding officers in those first days, and to units so carefully trained by one man this meant a great deal. It made the tree shake, so to speak, and it was a few weeks before a real recovery was made.

The 5th East Yorks had as their objectives to eliminate the La Rivière defences and then capture the strong point at the lighthouse at Mont Fleury (not to be confused with the heavy gun battery a little to the west) which was equipped with a 50m and 75mm gun. WN 34 lay some 600 yards up the road from the seafront to Ver-sur-Mer and was distinguished by a nearby lattice-work radio mast. The position was attacked from H–10 minutes to H–5 minutes with 500 and 1,000lb bombs, and taken by A Company with eight casualties and the capture of 30 prisoners. The battery commander was found to have committed suicide. Major F. W. Anderson of the Special Observer Party from Combined Operations Headquarters landed on D+6 to investigate the effect of fire preparation for 'Neptune' and he noted that 'the bombing was on the target and concentrated, but the only certain damage to weapons was to one MG, possibly to a second, and there was some damage to auxiliary buildings east of the road. The 50mm anti-tank gun was in an open concrete emplacement 40 feet from the edge of a 1,000lb bomb crater. Except for a small amount of debris in the emplacement, this gun was not harmed. The 75mm gun, also in an open emplacement, was 30ft from the edge of a 1,000lb bomb crater. The gun platform had been buried in debris which had subsequently been cleared away. No damage was caused. One underground concrete dugout east of the road had a direct hit on the entrance which was partly blocked. Between this and a second, undamaged, dugout, the ground was completely ploughed up by bomb craters. A concrete pill box along the western side of the road had a machine gun housing and was undamaged.'

Above: One of 4th/7th Royal Dragoon Guards' Sherman DDs on the road in front of the strong point, now named the Avenue du 6 Juin. *Below:* Nice comparison by Karel Margry on 6 Juin in 1994 with restored military transport descending the hill to La Rivière. The lighthouse still stands midst the trees.

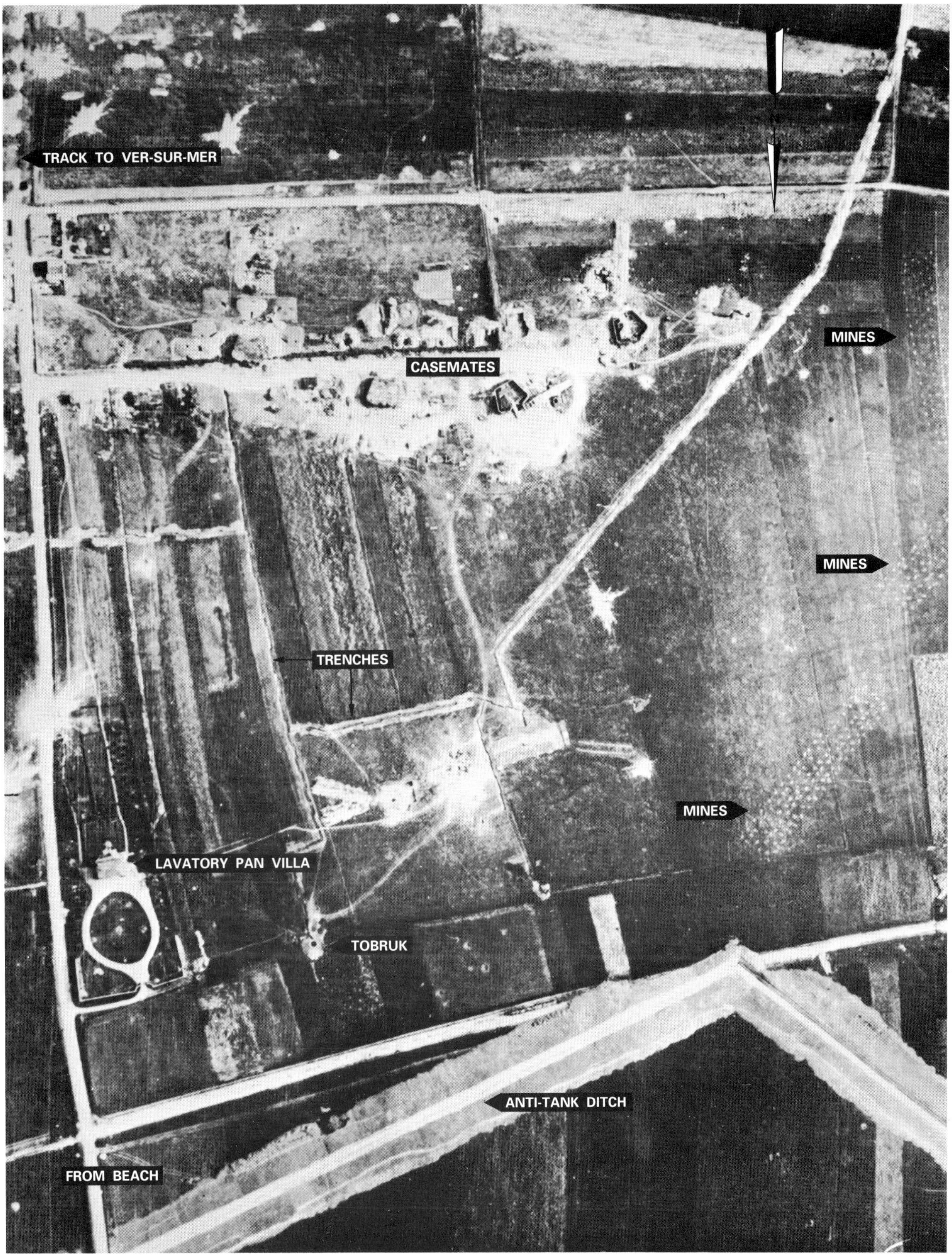

Major Anderson went on to inspect the Mont Fleury gun battery position just over a quarter of a mile to the west. It lay 800 yards inland from the coast road, protected to its seaward side by an anti-tank ditch — the same one which Lieutenant Pear crossed advancing up Lane 3 over the stream bridge. This picture, taken pre-D-Day, extends northwards from where the picture at the bottom of page 436 leaves off. The house with the circular drive was dubbed, in the idiom of the British soldier, 'Lavatory Pan Villa'. Lieutenant Pear passed this house, believed to have been used as the battery OP, and proceeded up the road until he came to a large crater. He informed his squadron commander, Major S. P. M. Sutton, and he ordered up an AVRE which successfully laid its SBG bridge across the gap. Major Anderson reported that the Germans had begun the construction of four casemates but only two had been completed and only one was fitted with a 122mm gun. This had been hit by a 500lb bomb but not put out of action, although he said it appeared that it had fired off all its ammunition.

Above left: This RAF photograph, taken shortly before D-Day, was used for briefing all the members of the 6th Battalion of The Green Howards whose task it was to capture the battery. This lane was to be the axis of advance by D Company of whom the Company Sergeant-Major was Stan Hollis. *Above right:* The casemates themselves lay just over the hill — Lavatory Pan Villa still stands on the left of the new houses which have since been built on and around the battery site. (See also the present-day aerial on pages 420-421.) The white tent on the hill has been temporarily erected for the events in June 1994. When he was about a mile from the shore, CSM Hollis was able to recognise the details from the briefing photographs, but the small building on the left appeared to him to be a pillbox — right beside their exit from the beach. Balancing a Bren gun on top of the ramp of the landing craft, he fired several bursts at the building, only to discover on landing that it was a bus shelter! (Until recently, the spang marks from Hollis' shooting could still be discerned in the brickwork.) Having crossed through the minefield, D Company moved up the road towards Lav Pan Villa but, as they emerged through a gap in the hedge, they came under fire from a pillbox at the right-hand end of the wall in front of the circular drive. Two platoons pushed on quickly past the house while CSM Hollis tackled the pillbox. Without having received any orders, he jumped up and ran towards the Germans — a distance of some 30 yards — firing his Sten as he ran. He reached the pillbox unscathed and pushed his submachine gun through the firing aperture and sprayed the inside. He then lay down on top of the pillbox and posted a grenade. As soon as it exploded, he rushed the doorway at the rear to find the occupants either dead or wounded. By now, the rest of the platoon had moved on, but there was yet another pillbox about a hundred yards away at the far end of the communicating trench but as he approached it, Germans emerged with their hands up. All told, CSM Hollis's bag here was 25 to 30. *Centre:* Fortunately, the 7th Photo Group despatched an aircraft from the 27th Photoreconnaissance Squadron to survey the situation on the beaches on the evening of D-Day and they photographed Mont Fleury battery around 2100. Fifty years later, Robert Voskuil surveyed the position only to find that a new house now occupies the site of the first pillbox, but Robert followed the line of the trench to the second *(right)*.

When the Green Howards reached the battery site itself, they found the casemates all abandoned. Major Anderson reported after his own inspection that the 'target was well hit. The main weight of the attack fell on the emplacement and on the auxiliary buildings; and though the only active gun was not put out of action by this means, the efficiency of the battery should have been considerably impaired. There is no evidence that the bombing caused many casualties but the moral effect may have been considerable.' *Above left:* The two westernmost (unfinished) casemates and *above right* the eastern one, now incorporated into the garden of one of the new residences. *Right:* This Tobruk stand lay on the lower slope of the hillside and may still remain hidden in the flourishing crop which covered the field when Robert took his photograph. Following the capture of the Mont Fleury position, the Green Howards pushed on as there was still the Meuvaines Ridge behind the battery to be taken en route to their final objective: St Léger, lying astride the Caen–Bayeux road. So far, casualties had been 'surprisingly low', around ten men all told out of a total strength of 850, but they comprised several key men including two company commanders. Also, Sergeant William Hill of No. 16 Platoon had been run over by a landing craft on the beach, and the platoon commander, Lieutenant John Kirkpatrick, was killed during the advance to Crépon. At this point, Major Ronnie Lofthouse, the company commander, detailed Sergeant Major Hollis to take charge of the leaderless platoon.

We last saw our AFPU photographer, Sergeant Midgley, on Jig Green, but on D+1 he popped up on King Green to picture these armour reinforcements moving past Lavatory Pan Villa.

Jean Paul Pallud's comparison looking back to the hedge — now a tree-line — where D Company came under fire. The crossing track has now been upgraded to a metalled road.

Sergeant Midgley pictured 'the first German prisoners being marched along the beach', so these could well be some of those who surrendered to CSM Hollis.

Two major points came out of this assault which I would like to stress, for I think they hold good for opposed landings at any time. First, you must operate in an air situation which is favourable, and you must control the waters in which you operate. Secondly, you must make your D-Day objectives distant and ambitious. What you fail to get on D-Day may take weeks and many lives to capture later, whereas if you attempt the deeper objective on D-Day, you may well achieve and hold it. Caen provides the perfect example: it was so near and yet so unobtainable for a time. No one was really to blame. XXX Corps virtually obtained every one of its objectives but I Corps in an ambitious endeavour just failed with Caen. We had to look at Caen for a number of weeks and various attempts were made

Once the leading assault troops had left the beach via the lanes cleared for them through the obstacles and minefields, there still remained the huge task of making the rest of the beach safe. In King sector, this job was accomplished in a surprisingly short space of time by No. 280 Field Company, RE. This is an extract from their diary.

'0730 hrs. All LCT touch down and AVRE tanks proceed ashore. LCOCU [Landing Craft Obstacle Clearance Unit — see page 184] beach and commence demolishing obstacles on KING RED and KING GREEN beaches. The folding boats in which sappers were being towed ashore by AVsRE prove too flimsy for the heavy seas, and most of them capsize. Heavy enemy opposition encountered from MGs, mortars and 88mm gun. No flank protection from DD tanks owing to heavy seas. In spite of this, all ranks carried on with the job and two 200-yard gaps were cleared for craft in the underwater obstacles before the advancing tide made further work impossible. The enemy were still very active and several men fell about this time as a result of hand-grenades lobbed over the sea-wall. After about half an hour, however, an assault party succeeded in disposing of all the enemy with the exception of a few snipers operating from inland.

'0830 hrs. Further work being impossible for the time being owing to the tide, etc., roll was called and it was found that 8 men were killed and 26 wounded, 1 officer was seriously wounded, 1 naval rating was killed and 4 wounded from LCOCUs under command.

'1300 hrs. The tide having receded, work was again commenced on the demolition and removal of obstacles, and by 2030 hrs when the tide again made further work impossible, 1,200 yards of beach had been completely cleared of enemy obstacles.'

'Types of obstacle dealt with were: (1) HEDGEHOGS each with either a Tellermine or a shell attached (both fitted with a DZ 35 igniter); (2) WOODEN RAMPS approx 10ft high (fitted with AA Shells); (3) WOODEN STAKES approx 10ft high (fitted with shells and Tellermines); (4) CONCRETE TETRAHEDRA. June 7th 0300 hrs. Work again commenced on clearance of obstacles. By the end of D+1, nearly two miles of beach had been cleared, involving the destruction of approximately 2,000 obstacles.'

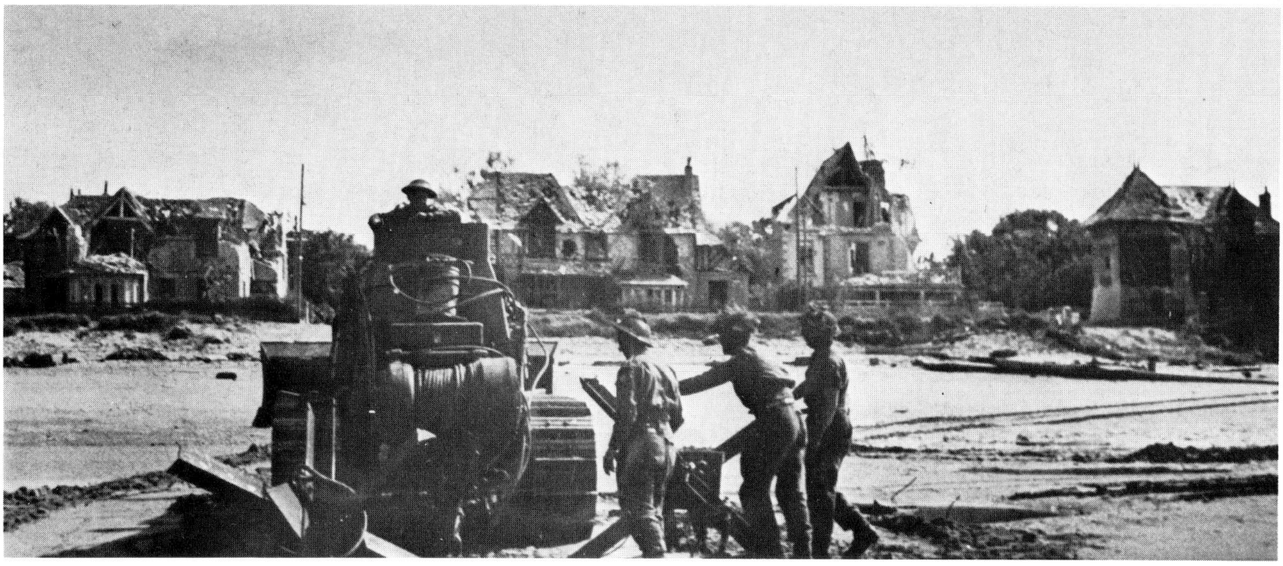

104 Beach Sub-Area (responsible for Gold): 'The development of the beaches during 6 June, from 1000 hours in the morning, continued throughout the day according to plan. The opposition encountered by the Assault Division and the leading elements of the Beach Coys, and recce parties of depots, somewhat disorganised the swift deployment of beach organisation. In addition, the surface of the beach was considerably worse than had been expected. As a result, stranded and disabled vehicles and craft, and the complexity of the beach mining and obstacles, added to the difficulties of quick development. Clearing of the beaches by RE and LCOCU personnel continued steadily under the direction of CRE [Commander, Royal Engineers] but, owing to the mass of stranded craft, the volume of traffic continually landing and the general confusion brought about by parties not knowing exactly where they were when they landed, it cannot be said that the beaches were under control, but each individual party knew what it had to do and got on with the job without further direction from higher HQ.'

to capture it. But D-Day was our real chance and many lives and much material had been lost before we eventually did capture Caen.

Never forget that D-Day is the attacker's day. He is strung up to a high pitch and ready to make big sacrifices, whereas the defender has been waiting, waiting, waiting. The job of our assaulting troops looked so very difficult and yet our waiting enemy was deeply uneasy — and how correctly that uneasiness was founded.

The German Army divisions on D-Day were very short of men, sometimes only having 25 per cent of their proper order of battle; so much of his manpower was deployed against the Russians. Even so, as Dempsey said in his forecast of the opposition which Second Army could expect to meet, the enemy had a good assembly with which to challenge us; although we outnumbered him in tanks, we came about level with him in under-strength divisions.

The bulldozer of No. 9 Beach Group is working on the eastern half of La Rivière beach — Love Green to be exact. None of the original buildings remain, and a new sea-wall runs along this part of the promenade, but the position was established by Karel Margry by the elimination of all the other options. The exit roads between the houses are, left, Rue Gabriel Pellain, and, right, Rue Suzanne Hélène.

A report by No. 24 Beach Recovery Section for June 7 stated: 'Plenty of recovery of all types. Most of the work due to vehicles bogging in clay and being overtaken by the tide. Over 100 tanks recovered yesterday.'

D+1 and Commodore Douglas-Pennant, the Force 'G' commander, comes ashore from the *Bulolo* to inspect 'his' beach. The build-up began on June 7 with the arrival of the first eight convoys although unloading was severely restricted due to a Force 5 wind. A special system had been formulated to designate 'Neptune' convoys now that there was two-way traffic across the Channel. Each was allocated a three-letter prefix:

1st Letter — Country of departure:

E — England	F — France

2nd Letter — Area of arrival or departure in United Kingdom:

T — Thames	C — Cornwall and Devon
X — Newhaven (Sussex)	B — Bristol Channel
W — Isle of Wight area	M — Miscellaneous
P — Portland	

3rd Letter — Nature of convoy:

P — Personnel	L — LST
M — MT ships	C — Coasters

The three-letter prefix was followed by a serial number, for example:

ETP1 — 1st Personnel ship convoy from the Thames;

FWM2 — 2nd MT ship convoy from France to the Isle of Wight area.

Ships joining outward-bound convoys from ports on the south coast, or leaving homeward-bound convoys for those ports, were indicated by the appropriate self-evident letter as a suffix showing area of departure or arrival, e.g. ETM4W — Ships from the Isle of Wight area joining 4th MT ship convoy from the Thames; FBC2W — Ships for Isle of Wight area leaving 2nd Coaster convoy from France to Bristol Channel. Suffixes 'Y' and 'Z' were used to denote different sections of a convoy which, owing to its large size, was sailed in two sections, and convoys sailing direct from the Isle of Wight area to France were given suffixes 'A' or 'B', according to whether their destination was the American or British area.

Above: **Transport moving freely at last — this is D+2 on King Red west of La Rivière. The 50mm PaK 38 anti-tank gun emplacement is in the centre, but unfortunately rather burned out on the negative of this print.** *Below:* **King Red 50 years on. The pillbox has now been converted into a small beach house.**

The weeks immediately after D-Day went as anticipated. Indeed, Dempsey had already forecast for us the enemy's reactions and movements with the same accuracy as he employed for his own troops. We manoeuvred around far too neatly to be taken off balance, but unfortunately with insufficient speed to upset the enemy seriously, though we achieved our object of holding the weight of the enemy armour against Second Army.

It is interesting to recall that our troops landed with only just over 50 per cent of their established vehicles, which was quite enough for the job in hand. This matter of supply is always difficult. To wait too long for supplies to build up gives the enemy a chance to build up his. In this event, we were just about right, and the enemy fell back as we broke out of the bridgehead at full fighting strength. This was not until some weeks after D-Day but he just could not stop us.

One aspect we have not discussed is the balloon cover provided as an additional air defence. The Mk VI (VLA) was chosen because of its lightness; the fact that it could be transported while flying; and its economy of operation as only two airmen were required for each balloon. They were flown at 2,000 feet by night and just below the cloud base by day. There were practically no reports of low-level bombing during the periods that the balloon barrage was flying and only one German aircraft was destroyed by balloons over the beach-head (in the US sector). Nevertheless, in spite of the lack of results, Air Chief Marshal Leigh-Mallory considered that the presence of the balloons gave a definite morale value for both naval and army personnel.

'Lance Corporal Wallis D-Day H-Hour'; 'Sergeant Hughes, RM 47 Commando'; 'Unidentified'; 'Lance Corporal Barber B Coy 2nd Bn Hertfordshire Regt KIA 6.6.44'; 'PO/X Scott, RN', 'Capt Lynn Green Howards'. Thus the honoured dead are laid to rest on the battlefield on which they fell. A memorial service held by Padre C. R. Scott — the burial ground once a florist's nursery. Casualties on King Sector during the assault phase — 0725 to 0810 — were estimated at 184 out of the 4,200 men landed, the 5th East Yorks being given as 'circa 91' and the 6th Green Howards as '10?' (Accurate totals for casualties on Gold as a whole were not maintained, the best estimate being around 300 on the beaches themselves, and 1,000 overall during D-Day.) This temporary cemetery was established in La Rivière at the inland end of the two streets seen at the top of page 443.

It is always an unhappy event when a corps commander has to go. So it was with Gerry Bucknall at the end of July. He had done a great deal for the corps and he was a fine D-Day commander. But the open warfare was not nearly so much up his street. He kept getting out of position. He and those who were with him went with great dignity. In fact, it was altogether a very dignified affair. Army Commander for his actions and Corps Commander for his reactions alike lost nothing in my young eyes. We got in Gerry's place 'Jorrocks', Lieutenant-General Brian Horrocks, so the corps lost nothing.

On August 7, Mont Pinçon fell at last and with it the bridgehead was opened.

Bayeux had been the D-Day goal of XXX Corps and it was to Bayeux War Cemetery that the fallen were taken in December 1944 . . . and where they now rest in perpetuity. *Left:* Lance Corporal George Postgate's grave can be seen in the foreground of the La Rivière cemetery. *Above:* The old houses have all been replaced, but the plot beside the D514 is still empty.

The dead are buried and the advance continues. AFPU photographer Sergeant Parkinson believed he had taken this photograph near St Gabriel (mis-spelled as St Gabrielle) which lies over half-way to the Caen–Bayeux road, but in actual fact he was on the road between Ver-sur-Mer and Crépon. This was the line of advance of CSM Hollis and the 6th Green Howards, with B and C Companies in the lead, D Company behind, and A Company in reserve. Just outside Crépon, the force came under intense fire, possibly from the same position which the 86th Field Regiment, RA, had to reduce the next day with the aid of two Shermans and a Crocodile. (The 141st Royal Armoured Corps reported that the Germans surrendered immediately on the sight of flame, and over 50 prisoners were captured together with four 75mm and one 88mm guns.)

From this point, Bayeux is still 12 kilometres away; it was not reached by the 56th Brigade until later on D+1.

When his men came under fire here at the entrance to Crépon *(above left)*, Lieutenant-Colonel Robin Hastings, the battalion commander, was anxious to press on to his assigned objective — St Léger on the Caen–Bayeux road — lest his advance get bogged down in lengthy — and costly — house-to-house fighting. He therefore ordered B and C Companies to bypass the village while D Company was to stay behind to clear the road ahead. 'Don't get caught up in trying to clear every German out of the village', Hastings told the D Company commander, Major Lofthouse. 'It may well be held in some strength. Just do the minimum necessary to open the road for us to use.' Major Lofthouse briefed his platoon commanders as to their duties, and Sergeant-Major Hollis *(above right)* was given this farm *(below)* on the far side of the village to search. He found the farmhouse itself empty, save for a small boy aged about ten sheltering in the corner of one room. *Below right:* That same boy, now M. Lahaye, still lives at the farm, and, 50 years later, he kindly allowed Robert Voskuil to follow in Hollis's footsteps. *Right:* The aerial photo was taken on June 22, 1944.

After the war, Sergeant Major Hollis, together with Lieutenant-Colonel Hastings and Major Lofthouse, was a participant speaker at the 50 Div Battlefield Tours organised by the Army Staff College at Camberley, Surrey. Stan Hollis was then the landlord of The Green Howard inn in North Ormesby, Yorkshire, which had been renamed in his honour. (When that pub was demolished in 1970, he moved to the Holywell View in Liverton Mines.) Stan Hollis's on-the-spot description of events in Crépon which led to his award of the Victoria Cross was filmed and these stills are illustrated with his own words. *Left:* Finding the farmhouse itself empty, the Sergeant-Major decided to search outside. M. Lahaye indicates the route Hollis took. *Right:* Hollis: 'I was leading the platoon along this alleyway, when I took a careful look round, here, just as I am now . . . '

' . . . and straightaway a shot and a bullet hit here *(left)*, knocking this bit of corner off. Now I got back pretty smartly, stood few seconds had another look round and I saw two dogs in the hedge . . . in the far hedge *(right)* . . . and they were jumping up and down and wagging their tails, obviously very friendly with someone that was there.'

'So, I went out and told the company commander what I had seen. I had seen, in fact, a field gun in that gap that you can see there. What size it was I don't know. So I told the chaps — seven or eight of them — to dash out of here, across there, and start firing at that hedge, while I went down a patch of rhubarb that used to stretch — there is a little bit of it left there *(left)* — from here right down to the end of this wire.' *Right:* Alas, no rhubarb left for tea today.

'I got a PIAT gun from the company and I brought two Bren gunners up with me. These seven or eight chaps dashed across here, to give me covering fire while I crawled through the rhubarb, and they were immediately killed . . . down here . . . all of them *(left)*. And I crawled through the rhubarb to the forward edge and put the bomb in the PIAT, and fired it, but it was no good and it fell short. The field gun then fired a round — I thought directly at me — and it hit the house behind me *(right)* as a matter of fact. So I thought, no, hell with this, I'm getting out of this. So I crawled out of the rhubarb with my PIAT and rejoined the company on the road. When I got back to the company we heard a hell of a noise going on back here, and I realised then that the two Bren gunners who came with me hadn't come back. So I said to the company commander, "Well, I took them in, I had better go and get them out". So I got a Bren gun this time . . . came along the passage . . . and I ran out here with the Bren firing it from my hip and I shot up the far hedge. At the same time, I shouted to those two lads to come back out of it. They did, and by the time I had emptied the magazine of the Bren gun, they were able to get back here and we all made a smart move back to rejoin the company.' Company Sergeant-Major Hollis's Victoria Cross was the only VC to be awarded for gallantry on D-Day. The 'rules' for the award dictate that the battalion commander is the initiating officer who puts a name forward for consideration. The actual exploit has to have been witnessed by at least three people and, if the application is successful, the regiment then writes up the citation. Unfortunately, all the Victoria Cross files for the Second World War at the Ministry of Defence were destroyed some years ago, so it is no longer possible to add any further background information in Stan Hollis's case. Stan Hollis died in February 1972 and his VC was sold at auction in 1983 for £32,000. By comparison, it is difficult to put a price on a Medal of Honor — the equivalent American award instituted for the US Army in 1862 for bravery in action — because, until very recently, US Federal law prohibited the purchase of military decorations and none of the four D-Day Medals of Honor have ever come on the market.

WARRANT OFFICER STANLEY ELTON HOLLIS

The King has been graciously pleased to approve the award of the Victoria Cross to No. 4390973 Warrant Officer Class II (Company Sergeant-Major) Stanley Elton Hollis, The Green Howards (Alexandra, Princess of Wales's Own Yorkshire Regiment) (Middlesborough).

In Normandy on 6 June 1944, during the assault on the beaches of the Mont Fleury battery, CSM Hollis's company commander noticed that two of the pill-boxes had been bypassed, and went with CSM Hollis to see that they were clear. When they were 20 yards from the pillbox, a machine gun opened fire from the slit and CSM Hollis instantly rushed straight at the pillbox, firing his Sten gun. He jumped on top of the pillbox, re-charged his magazine, threw a grenade in through the door and fired his Sten gun into it, killing two Germans and making the remainder prisoner. He then cleared several Germans from a neighbouring trench. By his action, he undoubtedly saved his company from being fired on heavily from the rear and enabled them to open the main beach exit.

Later the same day, in the village of Crépon, the company encountered a field gun and crew armed with Spandaus at 100 yards range. CSM Hollis was put in command of a party to cover an attack on the gun, but the movement was held up. Seeing this, CSM Hollis pushed right forward to engage the gun with a PIAT from a house at 50 yards range. He was observed by a sniper who fired, and grazed his right cheek, and at the same moment the gun swung round and fired at point-blank range into the house. To avoid the fallen masonry, CSM Hollis moved his party to an alternative position. Two of the enemy gun crew had by this time been killed, and the gun was destroyed shortly afterwards. He later found that two of his men had stayed behind in the house and immediately volunteered to get them out. In full view of the enemy who were continually firing at him, he went forward alone using a Bren gun to distract their attention from the other men. Under cover of his diversion, the two men were able to get back.

Wherever fighting was heaviest, CSM Hollis appeared and in the course of a magnificent day's work, he displayed the utmost gallantry and on two separate occasions his courage and initiative prevented the enemy from holding up the advance at critical stages. It was largely through his heroism and resource that the company's objectives were gained and casualties were not heavier, and by his own bravery he saved the lives of many of his men.

Company Sergeant-Major Hollis's award of the Victoria Cross was announced in the *London Gazette* on August 15, 1944.

And so to Bayeux. Anthony Eden, Foreign Secretary, D+1: 'I told Général de Gaulle that we wished to discuss with the French committee the problem of civil affairs in France. We would keep the United States government informed and would do what we could to encourage them to participate. The Général then made a long lament. He said he had never been so unhappy about our relations as now. He had been grateful for the Prime Minister's action in receiving him on his arrival and telling him of the battle [see page 159] but still nothing had been arranged about civil administration in France. I told the Général that our intention was to discuss just this problem. It would be days, perhaps weeks, before we commanded any territory except the beaches. In the meantime, let us work together to agree a plan. The Général asked what would be the value of such a plan unless the Americans would also agree and made further complaints . . . I continued that what we were asking him to do was to work with us so that the civil administration of France could be set up.'

Bayeux, June 14, 1944. Four years to the very day when German troops marched into Paris, Général de Gaulle set foot in France. The way back had been tortuous and full of argument with Churchill, and still there was a lack of any formal agreement on the future civil government for the people of France. Because of this, Churchill stipulated that 'it would not be possible for de Gaulle to hold a public meeting there, or gather crowds in the streets. He would no doubt like to have a demonstration to show that he is the future President of the French Republic. I suggest that he should drive slowly through the town, shake hands with a few people, and then return, leaving any subsequent statement to be made here.' *Above:* The Général leaves the Mairie on — yes, you've guessed it — the Place du Général de Gaulle!

De Gaulle: 'We proceeded on foot, from street to street. The inhabitants stood in amazement, then burst into cheers, or into tears. Coming out of their houses, they escorted me amidst an extraordinary display of emotion. The children surrounding me, the women smiling and sobbing. The men with hands outstretched. We thus walked on together, fraternally, overwhelmed, and we felt the joy, pride, and faith in the nation surging again from the abyss.'

The original H-Hour on the Canadian front was 0735 for the 7th Brigade and 0745 for the 8th. However, the lateness of certain craft groups resulting from the weather caused the two assault group commanders to defer H-Hour ten minutes more in each case. Thus, the final H-Hour was 0745 and 0755 respectively. This was unfortunate, in that the higher tide made it more difficult to deal with the beach obstacles; to quote Commodore G. N. Oliver, the Force 'J' commander aboard HMS *Hilary*, 'craft beached amongst the obstacles instead of short of them, and clearance of the outer obstacles was not practicable until the tide had fallen'. The obstructions, and the mines attached to them were, in fact, to take a heavy toll of our craft.

The combination of the rough sea, the obstacles and the enemy's fire made an unpleasant prospect for the crews of the landing craft; but they were not daunted. In the words of Admiral Vian: 'Their spirit and seamanship alike rose to meet the greatness of the hour and they pressed forward and ashore, over or through mined obstacles in high heart and resolution; there was no faltering, and many of the smaller landing craft were driven on until they foundered.'

The fire that came down upon the leading craft as they ran in was actually much less than had been feared. There was not much firing by the heavy inland batteries and, of what there was, little if any was directed at the ships of Force 'J'. Nor were any enemy aircraft to be seen. As for the artillery weapons mounted in the beach defences, they were so emplaced as to enfilade the beaches, and in almost all cases could not bear upon craft any distance offshore. In consequence, it was in the

Juno Area

Lieutenant-Colonel Charles P. Stacey
HISTORICAL SECTION, GENERAL STAFF

main only small arms and mortars that fired upon the approaching craft. Admiral Vian reported that opposition began to manifest itself only when the leading craft were about 3,000 yards from the beach; and even then the fire was 'only desultory and inaccurate'. Heavy fire directed at the craft while still afloat was, in fact, the exception rather than the rule; Commodore Oliver wrote that 'in general, apart from some inaccurate mortar fire, very little shooting was directed on craft before touch-down'. It was after the actual landings that really fierce opposition began to manifest itself.

Top: **Lieutenant-General John Crocker (holding the map board), commanding I Corps, was responsible for the landings on both Sword and Juno areas, and both, rather confusingly, carried out by divisions bearing the same number: the British 3rd Division on the former and the Canadian 3rd Division, commanded by Major-General Roderick Keller *(left)* on the latter.**

The Canadian assault was to be spearheaded by the 7th Brigade under Brigadier Harry Foster and the 8th Brigade, commanded by Brigadier Kenneth Blackader. Bringing up the reserve 9th Brigade was Brigadier D. G. 'Ben' Cunningham, seen with General Crocker and *right* with his brigade headquarters staff.

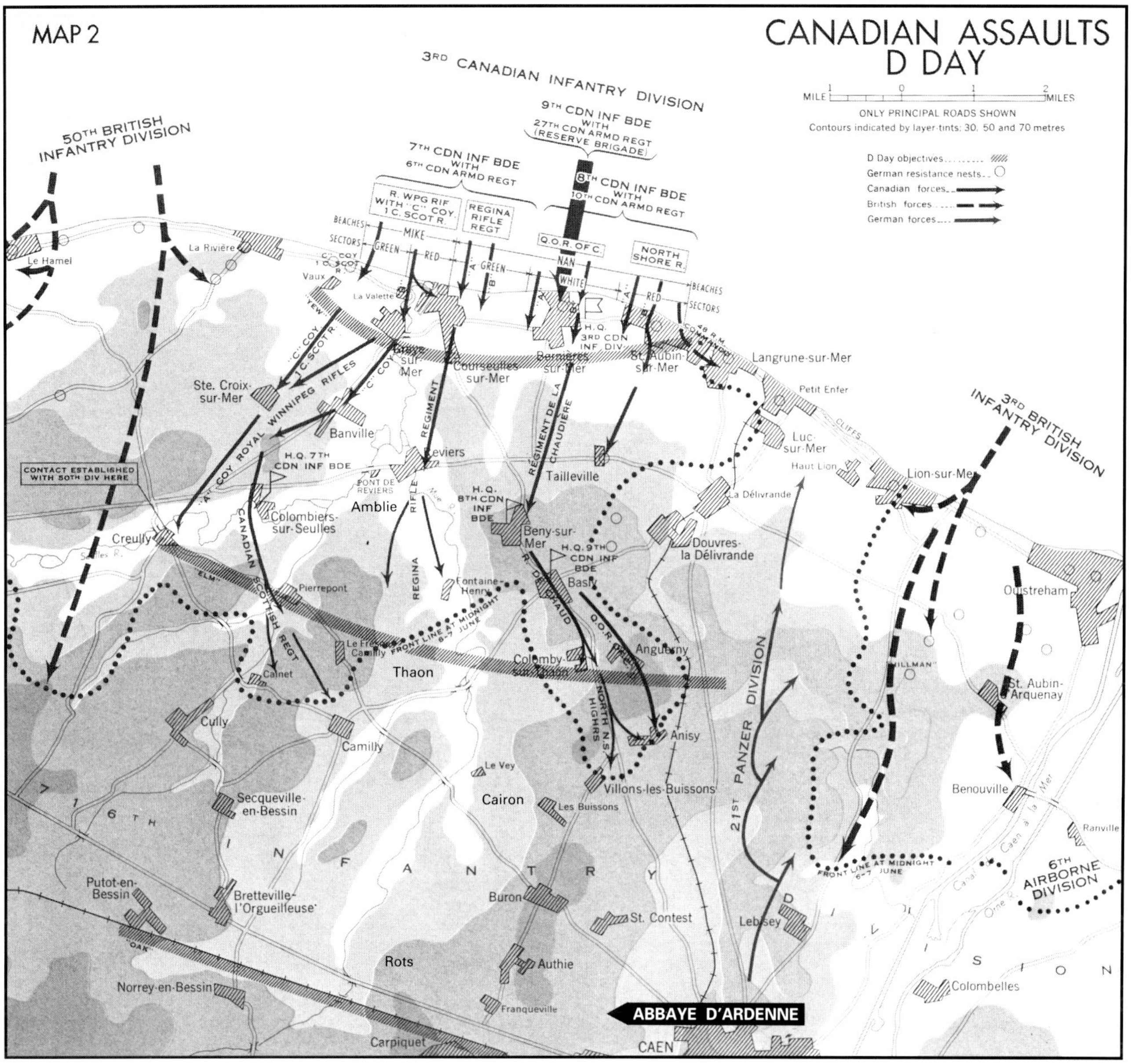

Landing on Mike and Nan sectors, the 7th Brigade was to capture the port of Courseulles and secure the high ground in the area of Pierrepont, south of the River Seulles, while the 8th Brigade would capture Bernières and take up a firm position in the vicinity of Anisy to cover the landing of the 9th Brigade. The 9th would then pass through the 8th Brigade and secure the left half of the divisional objective while the 7th Brigade continued its advance on the right. Meanwhile, the 2nd Armoured Brigade was to push forward to Bretteville-l'Orgueilleuse on the Caen–Bayeux road. There were two subsidiary operations. The 4th Special Service Brigade would land at St Aubin-sur-Mer and make contact on the inter-divisional boundary with one of its commandos landing with the British 3rd Division on Sword, and also capture La Délivrande and Douvres. Then, RE demolition parties, speeding inland on armoured cars of the Inns of Court Regiment, were to blow bridges on the River Orne south of Caen.

In these circumstances, it was during the landing craft's sojourn on the beach, and still more their withdrawal from it, that they suffered most of their casualties. The commander of Assault Group J2 (8th Brigade) reported: 'The LCAs had had to beach amongst the hedgehogs. Although no difficulty was experienced in steering the craft in through them, going astern out of them proved more difficult. A high percentage of LCAs of all the three flights set off mines in this way, causing them to founder.' In Force 'J' as a whole, 36 LCAs (25 per cent of the whole number engaged) were lost or damaged in the assault. Force 'J's casualties in total craft lost or disabled were by a small margin the heaviest in the Eastern Task Force, numbering 90 craft as against 89 for Force 'G' and 79 for Force 'S'. Force 'G' however had heavier losses in LCAs — 52 — while Force 'S' lost only 29.

The orders for the operation conjure up a picture of groups of vehicles and craft going ashore in orderly planned succession. They called for the first landing to be made, five minutes before H-Hour, by the two squadrons of DD tanks assigned to each brigade sector; these were to be launched from their tank landing craft well offshore and to swim in. At H-Hour itself, the plan called for two LCT groups to land on each brigade front: one carried the AVREs of the 5th Assault Regiment, Royal Engineers, the other the tanks of the 2nd Royal Marine Armoured Support Regiment (RMASR) and a proportion of armoured bulldozers manned by Royal Engineers. The RMASR was equipped with Centaur tanks armed with 95mm howitzers, plus one Sherman tank for each troop. These tanks were not intended to fire during the run-in unless self-defence required it; their rôle was to land and engage targets that had escaped the main bombardment with observed fire from hull-down positions in the water.

The assault companies of the forward infantry battalions were to hit the beach in assault landing craft five minutes after H-Hour, by which time, it was hoped, the tanks and the engineers would have made some progress in clearing the obstacles and in overcoming such opposition as had not been beaten down by the bombardment. The reserve companies of the assault battalions were to land 15 minutes later.

The intention of blowing bridges across a 15-kilometre stretch of the Orne between St André-sur-Orne and Thury-Harcourt was to further extend the protection of the bridgehead on the left flank where the introduction of the 12. SS-Panzer-Division was most feared. General Dempsey, the Second Army commander, had spoken to General de Guingand (Montgomery's Chief-of-Staff) at 1115 on D-Day morning 'to put the air on movement into Caen from south and east' following intelligence reports which showed that while 21. Panzer-Division was operating south-east of Caen, the 12. SS-Panzer-Division might also be on the move. Earlier that morning, preparation for attacks by fighter-bombers had already been made should any movement in the German armoured forces be detected. At 1000 hours, a 21st Army Group 'Tac flash' reported 30 tanks near Poussy (south-east of Caen) which linked up with intercepted wireless traffic which indicated that a '21 Pz Recce Unit' was in the Bretteville-sur-Laize area at 0640 hours. The German messages stated that patrols were to be sent to St Sylvain (at 0945 hours); two to Estrées-la-Campagne (at 0940); and one to Ouilly (0958). *Above:* Reinforcements move 'zur Front'. *Below:* Brana Radovic placed their location here at St Martin-de-Fresnay, 35 kilometres south-east of Caen.

My recce patrol consists of the eight-wheeler armoured car under command of Hans Krapf and another under Heinz Dahmann. Both are experienced armoured recce commanders who have served in Russia. I give my men a quick briefing on our intention and orders and on intercommunication en route. It has already got a bit lighter and the visibility is over 100 metres now. Since our target area — Bayeux and Courseulles — is some 80 km away, I am choosing the quickest route through Broglie and Lisieux to Caen. We are now helped by our knowledge of roads gained from our recce and training exercises over the last few months. After an hour, we are moving through Lisieux.

Air recce as a result of General Dempsey's request was largely negative: '1130 hours area Villers-Bocage—Thury-Harcourt—Flers—Domfront NMS' [no movement seen]; '1210 hours, road Falaise—Argentan—Alençon—Mortain NMS', but fighters from Lee-on-Solent reported a column of '100 plus MT moving in neighbourhood of Livarot' and the US Eighth Air Force reported a truck convoy, two to three miles long, travelling south-west from Bernay. *Above and below:* This PzKpfw IV Ausf. C has halted for a moment in the centre of the village — as Brana did five decades later to take these perfect comparisons.

Off we go now on the Route Nationale to Caen. Visibility has improved and the sun should soon be penetrating the fog and clouds. My eyes are watering from the cold damp morning mist. We are distinctly meeting more Wehrmacht transport, so the road is clear. We soon reach Caen. At the entrance to the town, there is a busy to-ing and fro-ing of transport of every description. Wehrmacht units at platoon strength have taken up their positions. A Leutnant asks us where we have come from and whether we have had any contact with the enemy. He is willing to take me to his commander a few streets to the north. At the same time, he draws my attention to the sounds of battle and reports that enemy parachutists have attacked the Orne bridges some 10 kilometres to the north and that fighting is taking place. I can now understand both the great activity on the roads and the massing of infantry on the edges of the town. They are panzergrenadiers of the 21. Panzer-Division. A Hauptmann in this defence company asks where I am from and informs me that strong British airborne units have landed on both sides of the Orne estuary and that the bridges are in all probability in enemy hands, since there is no longer any telephone connection with Ranville. The sounds of battle, which can be clearly heard, will be coming from there. Even as we talk, fighter-bombers are attacking, shooting up the town at random. Panic-stricken French civilians are deserting their houses and thronging out of the town.

We drive through the centre of Caen to the western exit. It's the same picture here: the streets are almost jammed, particularly with anti-aircraft troops with or without vehicles. They come from the direction of the airfield to the left of the road. A thick pall of smoke drifts off to the south-east, presumably from a successful hit by the fighter-bombers. If I could have done with a bit more light, even some sun earlier on, I would now welcome even more of this mist which is blowing over from the coast on the right of the road. It's a good thing, however, that the Bayeux road, which is almost as straight as a die, is lined with trees and that there are leafy plots surrounding the villages lying on the road.

Another 20 kilometres and we will have reached our destination — Bayeux. Because of the heavy traffic coming towards us, no Tommies can have landed here, so we step on it at 80 kph. Civilians are running from the first houses lining the road. Elderly soldiers, who could have been our fathers, stand by the garden fences and chat with the locals. The nearer we get to the centre of the town, the market square, the denser grows this mass of humanity: baggage trucks, Kübelwagen cars, motorbikes, uniforms of every branch of the service — only the Kriegsmarine is missing. A detachment of military police is trying to create some order. I want to get to the Stadtkommandant, but it's no use. Then I hear that artillery has already been pounding Bayeux. If the fighter-bombers get here too, all hell will be let loose.

A Feldwebel tells me that there is heavy fighting in the bay of Arromanches and that the Englanders have been offloaded on the coast by hundreds of ships. Judging by the sounds of battle, things must really be hotting up there, for you can distinctly hear the crump of the artillery. We must see this! So these are not just airborne landings, but seaborne landings as well!

I brief SS-Unterscharführer Dahmann that we are avoiding roads from now on and only driving along terrain which is under cover. North of the town, the country rises gently with pastureland and farmsteads.

In the early afternoon, reports began to reach 21st Army Group of something more definite. More wireless intercepts about 21. Panzer showed that their reconnaissance unit had elements in the area Caen—Tilly-sur-Seulles—Balleroy—Bayeux—St Lô (1137 hours); Falaise and Démouville (1200); and between 1500 and 1600 hours, air reports showed tanks near to Caen on the south side. Then, at 1610, came an interception report of wireless activity from 1515 onwards in the area of 12. SS-Panzer. The division was at last on the move, although at 1628 another intercept picked up was: 'Where is Div HQ?' The German account reproduced on these pages is by SS-Obersturmführer Peter Hansmann, the commander of 1. Kompanie of SS-Aufklärungs-Abteilung 12 of 12. SS-Panzer-Division. Little did he know it but through their 'Y' Service wireless intercepts, Monty's men were on to him and his reconnaissance mission to the 'Invasionsfront'.

As we proceed, keeping our eyes open and watching both sides, to the little village of St Sulpice, we can see spouts of earth and burning houses in the direction of the coast at Tracy. As yet I can't see anything of the sea. We have to go about another 1000 metres before we reach the ridge. We drive dead slowly, keeping to the stone walls and the hedges, until we reach the high ground (about 50 metres) of Magny-en-Bessin, just a farmhouse with trees and a barn. A view opens up here over the bay of Arromanches. Our armoured cars keep to the reverse slope and, thanks to the good camouflage which Hans Krapf and Heinz Dahmann draped round our vehicles like leafy bushes back at the exit from Bayeux, we can stand up and look down on to the great unknown, the improbable, the incomprehensible. What sort of grey expanse is this, stretching out in front of us? I have once more to orientate myself: there, on the left, to the west, is the steep cliff of the bay of Arromanches, and there is the heaviest artillery fire. Spouts of earth as high as houses spring up and then die down. To the east, a seemingly endless dark grey expanse — the sea — and, equally endless, the horizon, only rather lighter in colour than the sea.

I look through my binoculars and now I can pick out the outlines of individual ships. Next to one another, behind one another, reaching to the horizon: ships — ships, masts, command bridges. From behind them, lightning spots lit up at irregular ranges and from different places — naval artillery! Between the beach and the dark armada in front of us lies the dark grey sea, and in these dark expanses of water all the way from the steep coast of Arromanches to the horizon east of the Orne mouth, white lines are advancing from the endless bank of ships — coming toward us! They are fast boats with high white foaming bow waves, landing craft which then spew out brown globules of soldiers on to the beach. I can also see white fountains of water spraying up among the landing ships too, presumably from our own coastal batteries. Then, I hear the distinct splutter of German MG42 machine guns. So our coastal defences have not yet been entirely overrun!

SS-Unterscharführer Dahmann points out to me some brown shapes slowly crawling through the sand-dunes. They are wearing flat steel helmets, so they must be British! Groups of men in platoon strength, even whole companies, are advancing towards us through the dunes, apparently meeting no resistance. They are still a good 3000 metres away from us, only recognisable through binoculars. Some houses are alight in Arromanches; the smoke drifts over us and from time to time screens the whole bay.

Then I spot tanks — one, two, three of them, a whole bunch, oddly shaped. They come from the bay, follow the coast road up to us, and then branch off to the east, zigzagging through the dunes, firing without stopping to aim. Presumably they are neutralising individual resistance nests. I can, however, clearly make out long blades on the tanks which they bulldoze in front of them. Are they intended for the construction of an immediate coast road or for digging out mines? Imperturbably, other tanks emerge straight from the sea. Is this really happening? At first, all you see are the turrets and then the whole tanks emerge like dinosaurs from the primordial deeps. And no one seems to hinder them. Aren't there any 8.8cm flak guns there? Well, no, for fighter-bombers attack the reverse slope of the coastal cliff with impunity. They unload their rockets on the concrete walls of the defence installations.

I take another look at our lightly armoured scout cars, are they camouflaged enough? For, if we are spotted, they will cut us to pieces. Even our Tiger tanks are powerless against these 'bluebottles'.

But now my report has to be got through quickly! Division must know as soon as possible what's going on here! This must be the invasion! What else can it be? Soon there will be more ships than water! But who will believe this, if he hasn't seen it himself?

So let's make a cool count . . . and where exactly are we? '0745 hours, bay of Arromanches, my own position 3 kilometres south of Magny. (Then I count, between two degrees of my binoculars, the ships, about 50×8=400.) Over 400 ships, with a wall of barrage balloons, stretching over a 30-kilometre length of coast east as far as the mouth of River Orne. British are putting ashore troops and heavy equipment continuously and unimpeded. Have observed 11 heavy tanks. Coastal defences neutralised and overrun. Infantry to battalion strength advancing south towards Bayeux. Enemy naval artillery firing on Bayeux and its approach roads. Fighter-bombers attacking resistance nests in the coast cliff. Am making further recce in direction of Creully. Ende.'

Suddenly, the ground rocks all around us, almost without warning — a slurping sort of noise as if bombs were falling, but then we haven't seen a plane. Then I realise it is the naval artillery. Tremendous explosions: whole mounds of earth fly through the air and rain down over a radius of several hundred metres. We lie down on the ground and would like to get back into our steel tubs, which at least keep the splinters off. But the side hatches are closed; I half get up, knock on the plating, and shout — but the gunner, driver and radio operator just don't understand that we want to climb in from underneath and not through the turret through which we got out, since the pressure waves from the explosions alone would blow us off. And then, finally, they get the message. The eight-wheeler weaves to the right and left, lumps of earth splatter against the armour and, as long as we still hear that, all is well, since, if it were a direct hit, we would no longer hear anything!

I am just wondering how they could have seen us. This good camouflage, this distance away — even the advancing Tommies, two kilometres away, can hardly have seen us. If so, the tanks would certainly have immediately opened up on us. Or has somebody ratted on us from a nearby farmhouse? But then they wouldn't have ordered this hellish fire down on themselves, would they? I press my forehead against the narrow observation slit: nothing stirring in the farmhouse. The roof looks pretty odd: pockmarked, yet still with a few tiles on the roof supports. Then it's all quiet again apart from distant sounds of battle on the coast. The cows, which were grazing separately near us, now huddle together in a corner some way off.

We leave our positions one by one and drive along the edges of the fields and the hedgerows eastwards past Ryes and Bazenville in the direction of Creully. In Creully, houses are burning and enemy artillery is shooting it up. I halt once or twice to make observations and establish that despite the murky weather conditions and the smoky atmosphere along the coast road, the broad sandy beach to the west of Courseulles is clearly visible from time to time. Along the full extent of the coastline, for some 20 kilometres, the bright bow-waves from the fast landing craft are hitting the beach ceaselessly. Hundreds of craft lie beached in the shallow waters and are offloading; trucks just take off into the sea and wade ashore.

In Creully, our own artillery must be in position 'plastering' that section of the coast. Their hits in the water and on land are clearly very effective: the beach is bursting with much equipment and the Tommies try to reach the first houses on the beach as quickly as possible. Whole bundles of men at company strength are massed round some of the houses: the front line must still be holding here. But tanks are already driving on the coast road and the stubby shape of a Sherman makes it quickly identifiable as an enemy tank.

Intelligence were by now of the opinion that while 21. Panzer would be fully committed north and north-west of Caen by evening, 12. SS would not be arriving that night. By early evening, larger columns began to be seen west of the Dives. At 1820, 'a very large column of AFVs' with its head almost at the outskirts of Caen was seen moving on the Lisieux road and, at 1945, a flash reported a convoy on the Falaise road, well dispersed in groups of 10 to 15 vehicles. Its head was also just south of Caen. ***Above and opposite:*** **These shots show the 12. SS-Panzer-Division passing through St Pierre-sur-Dives, six kilometres or so up the road to Caen from St Martin, as Brana follows their move towards the coast.**

At 1715, several trains were spotted in 12. SS-Panzer-Division's area: one at Gacé; four at Verneuil; another at Tillières-sur-Avre; seven at Evreux, and a similar number at Pont-Authon. All this activity was supplemented by wireless interception which indicated a 12. SS radio net working at 2010 hours with two outstations for panzergrenadier regiments and one for a panzer regiment. *Above:* **Circumventing Caen, the 12. SS 'Hitlerjugend' pass through Verson south of the city towards their assembly area around Authie, enabling Brana to secure another timeless comparison** *below.*

Heavy enemy artillery is systematically churning up the inshore area, the roads leading up this height to Caen. And then there are the Jabos, the fighter-bombers; despite the low clouds, they dart in at lightning speed and blaze away into the village of Creully from the south. We nudge our way from cover to cover, ready for any enemy patrol which might be a target for our guns.

In these few hours, I have already seen how a wave of 10,000 soldiers has rolled ashore; and every second fresh ships are landing, bearing soldiers like ants.

Back to division. I must make a personal report to the commander. Otherwise no one will believe this. And whoever still has doubts then, will have to go and see for himself. But in a few hours' time, they shan't be able to stand on this spot any more, since British tanks will be rumbling around here!

SS-OBERSTURMFÜHRER PETER HANSMANN,
Chef de Panzerspähkompanie
SS-Aufklärungs-Abteilung 12, 12. SS-Panzer-Division

The Abbaye d'Ardenne at Authie, just west of Caen, was taken over by SS-Panzergrenadier-Regiment 25 of SS-Standartenführer Kurt Meyer. *Top left:* **Here, SS grenadiers with a Pak 40 75mm anti-tank gun enter the grounds via the northern gates.** *Top right:* **Brana took this remarkable series of comparisons during a trip to Normandy in 1989.** *Above:* **Three battalion commanders prepare for the counter-attack on June 7, 1944. L–R: SS-Sturmbannführer Eric Urbanitz (I. Abteilung, SS-Panzer-Artillerie-Regiment 12); SS-Sturmbannführer Karl-Heinz Prinz (II. Abteilung, SS-Panzer-Regiment 12); and SS-Sturmbannführer Karl Bartling (III. Abteilung, SS-Panzer-Artillerie-Regiment 12).** *Right:* **Members of Brana's battalion: Jeremy Bergbaum, Malcolm Fisher and Chris John. The Abbaye was (and still is) a collection of medieval buildings including a church and huge stone barn set inside enclosed gardens.**

Since the 1920s, it had been occupied by M. Roland Vico and his family, but their activities in the Resistance led to his arrest and that of his wife Francine in December 1943. M. Vico's son, Jacques, who was also in the Maquis, quickly moved a cache of arms stored at the Abbaye with the help of his younger brother Jean-Marie, and then went into hiding. *Above:* To the officers of the SS regiment it was known as Kloster Ardenne. Pictured in the courtyard is the heavyweight SS-Sturmbannführer Franz Steineck, appropriately, in view of his bulk, the CO of the schwere (heavy) Artillerie-Abteilung 101; SS-Sturmbannführer Hubert Meyer, the 12. SS Ia. Next to him, SS-Standartenführer Kurt Meyer (no relation), the commander of SS-Panzergrenadier-Regiment 25. The two men in the right background are SS-Obersturmführer Bernhard Meitzel, the O1 (1. Ordonnanzofficier), and SS-Hauptsturmführer Günther Reichenbach from the staff of SS-Wirtschafts-Bataillon 12. *Right:* The regimental commander (left), better known to his men as 'Panzermeyer', with his divisional commander, SS-Brigadeführer Fritz Witt (centre) and the commander of SS-Panzer-Regiment 12, SS-Obersturmbannführer Max Wünsche. (He had served as Hitler's ordnance officer in 1938-40 until he was dismissed and returned to an active service unit.) At dawn on D-Day, 12. SS-Panzer-Division 'Hitlerjugend' passed into the control of Rommel's Heeresgruppe B, having been until then in the OKW reserve. Its orders were to assemble east of Lisieux. SS-Panzer-Regiment 12 was to be split in two: I. Abteilung going to SS-Panzergrenadier-Regiment 26, with its II. Abteilung joining up with SS-Panzergrenadier-Regiment 25. At 3 p.m., the division was ordered to regroup west of Caen to carry out a counter-attack, passing under the command of LXXXIV. Armeekorps (whose HQ was at St Lô). The various units took up positions during the night.

Above: War correspondent Herbert Reinecker stands behind Hubert Meyer who converses with SS-Obersturmbannführer Karl-Heinz Milius, the commander of the III. Bataillon of SS-Panzergrenadier-Regiment 25. On the right SS-Obersturmführer Meitzel. Witt was killed on June 14 when naval gun-fire targeted the 12. SS-Panzer-Division's headquarters at Venoix on the western outskirts of Caen, and Prinz lost his life just north of Falaise on August 14, the same month when the Vico family were able to move back into their home. Lying directly behind Juno, the Abbaye battlements also provided an excellent vantage point to watch the Canadians approaching. Their armoured spearhead was aiming almost straight for Authie, advancing towards the airfield of Carpiquet beyond, seemingly totally unaware of the presence of the 'Hitlerjugend' panzergrenadiers or their armour, then preparing their own counter-attack. The clash would come soon, tank versus tank, in a pitched armoured battle around Buron on D+1.

The 7th Brigade beaches, the dividing line between Nan sector (on the left) and Mike the breakwater of Courseulles harbour.

JUNO AREA

Sector	*Extent*	*Grid Reference*	*Width (yards)*
LOVE	K to road	929868–949862	2,100
MIKE	L to Courseulles (West breakwater)	949862–968858	2,200
NAN	M to St Aubin	968858–016851	5,500

THE 7th BRIGADE'S BEACH BATTLE

The 7th Canadian Infantry Brigade was to be landed by Captain A. F. Pugsley's Assault Group J1 on the right or western sector of Juno area. The Royal Winnipeg Rifles, with one company of the reserve battalion (the 1st Battalion Canadian Scottish Regiment) attached, landed on Mike Red and Mike Green Beaches, west of the river-mouth at Courseulles, while The Regina Rifle Regiment landed on Nan Green immediately east of the river. The DD tanks of A Squadron of the 6th Armoured Regiment (1st Hussars) were to support the Winnipegs, while B Squadron performed the same service for the Reginas. The 6th Armoured Regiment was commanded by Lieutenant-Colonel R. J. Colwell.

There was some disagreement as to precisely when the DD tanks landed. Admiral Vian asserted that in all cases they arrived after the first landing craft touched down; but the weight of evidence supports the statement of Commodore Oliver that on the 7th Brigade front the tanks touched down first, '20 minutes before the infantry', although it seems evident that this was the case on only one battalion sector.

What happened was this. After the decision not to launch the DDs at 7,000 yards, the craft proceeded towards the beach, 'wasting' time so as not to arrive before the moment planned. When at a distance from the beach (which Major J. S. Duncan, commanding B Squadron of the 6th Armoured Regiment, estimated at 4,000 yards), the flotilla officer of the LCT flotilla, after consulting the squadron commander, decided to launch the tanks. All the 19 tanks of B Squadron left the craft and, when about 2,000 yards from the beach, the squadron commander gave the order to deploy into line. Fourteen of the tanks duly landed on the proper beach, in Duncan's words, 'somewhat later than was intended but still well in advance of either AVsRE or infantry'. Another

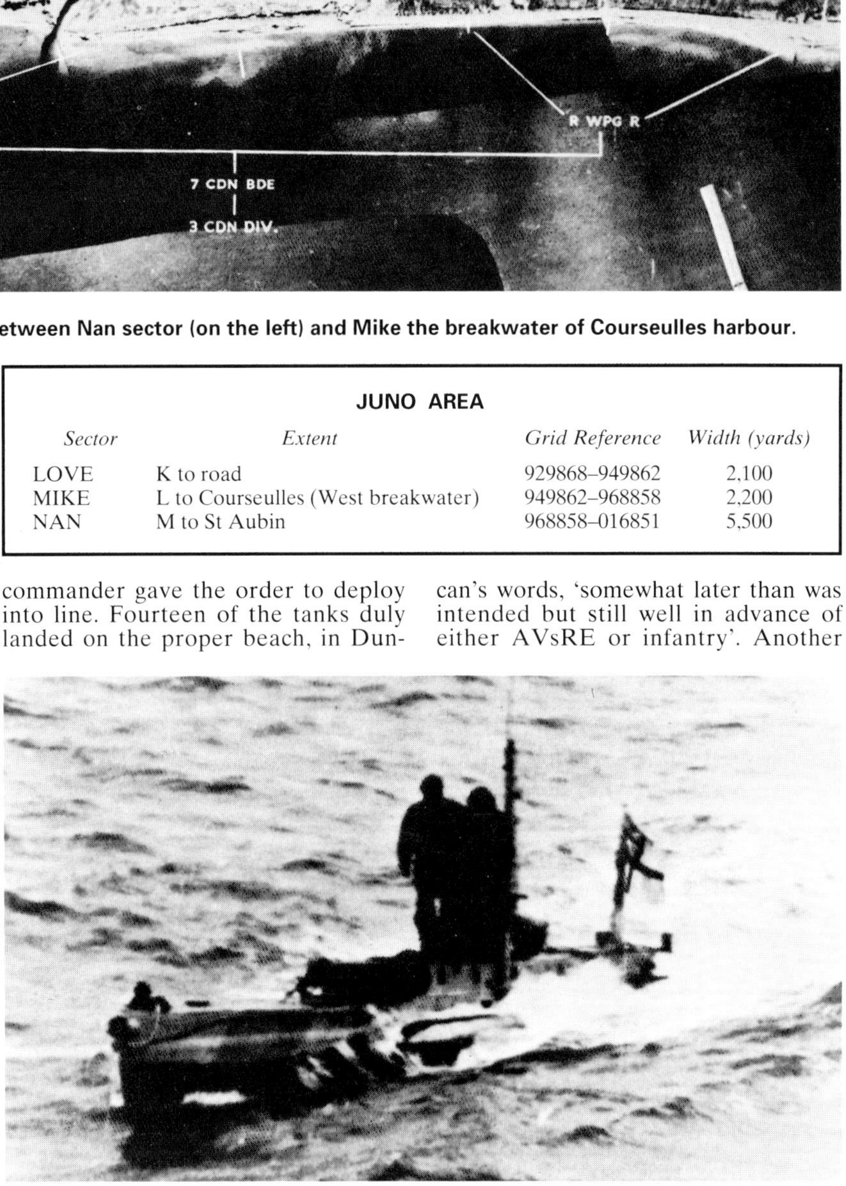

At a fairly late stage in the planning, it was reported that outlying rocks off Nan sector of Juno dried at around five feet instead of three feet as had previously been believed (see page 200). As a result, H-Hour, compared with the adjacent Gold and Sword areas, had been fixed at 10 minutes later for Assault Group J1 landing the 7th Brigade on Mike Green and Red, and Nan Green. Offshore, lay the midget submarine *X.20*, commanded by Lieutenant K. R. Hudspeth, whose task it was to mark the launching position for the DD tanks and provide a useful check on the position of the leading flotillas. Together with her sister midget (the *X.23 above* commanded by Lieutenant G. B. Honour, seen returning to Britain) off Sword, their crews had spent 64 hours dived out of 76 hours spent at sea — the first Allied vessels to arrive in the assault area.

The matching section of invasion coastline from a French survey carried out in 1991. The river is the Seulles.

landed later some distance to the east. There seems no doubt of the tanks being the first element ashore, for at 0758 The Regina Rifle Regiment's headquarters received and logged from its B Company the code-word 'Popcorn' meaning 'DD tanks have touched down'. B Company's message reporting its own touchdown came in at 0815.

A Squadron's experience was less fortunate. The order to launch was longer delayed than in the case of B Squadron; it was given, according to the senior officer of Group 311, when the craft were about 1,500 yards from the beach. 'The launching', he reported, 'took too long, and the LCTs drifted down on the tide.' Major W. D. Brooks, the squadron commander, wrote: 'All craft at this point were not in the proper formation for launching and all were being subjected to mortar and other enemy fire.' The chains holding the door of one LCT were shot away after one tank had been launched. Another craft with five tanks aboard landed them directly on to the beach. Only 10 tanks of A Squadron swam off the LCTs and of these, seven reached the beach. The commander of Group 311 states that they were six minutes after the assaulting companies. The war diary of The Royal Winnipeg Rifles confirms that the tanks were late; but an extremely warm letter from the Winnipegs' commanding officer (Lieutenant-Colonel J. M. Meldram) attests the value of the support they gave him in his beach battle, 'and for the gallantry, determination, dash and skilful use of fire-power on the part of Major Brooks and his squadron'.

Owing to the heavy weather, and to several groups using the wrong channels, at the last minute the assault group commanders found it necessary to retard the H-Hour times by 10 minutes. However, both Deputy Senior Officers for the Assault Groups (Captain A. F. Pugsley for J1, and Captain R. J. O. Otway-Ruthven for J2 landing the 8th Brigade on Nan White and Red) decided it was too rough to launch the DD tanks at the planned 7,000 yards from the shore. However, on the 7th Brigade front, the senior officer of the group carrying the DDs revised his decision and launched them when about 1,000 yards out. In the case of one squadron, those tanks which reached the beach arrived after the assaulting infantry. The LSTs carrying the AVREs landed a few minutes behind the assault companies.

The two squadrons between them lost seven tanks during the run-in, the majority evidently as a result of the roughness of the sea. One was run down by a rocket craft, all but a single member of the crew being saved, and one tank was sunk due to its canvas screen having been damaged by mortar fire. Most of the men in the sunken tanks were rescued, thanks to the tanks' rubber dinghies.

It seems evident from the accounts written by members of the 1st Hussars that the procedure followed by the tanks in most cases after touching down was to stop in the water on the seaward side of the beach obstacles, deflate the flotation gear, and open fire on the nearest pillbox. While thus engaged, a number were flooded and immobilised by the rising tide.

This is the western end of Red Beach in Mike sector — two pictures taken by an American aircraft a few seconds apart. *Above:* **Tanks have backed up on Exit M2 on the right which led across flooded land to the lateral road. Just over the dunes, it had been deliberately obstructed by a tank trap, 16 feet wide and about 9 feet deep, and, a little further along, at the point where it crossed a stream, the culvert had been destroyed by a stick of bombs. This water-filled crater was over 60 feet across but was covered with wind-blown sand. The 26th Assault Squadron, RE, under Major A. E. Younger, had two gapping teams to clear the exits, M1 (600 yards to the west) and M2, but No. 1 Troop touched down in the wrong position; in fact opposite No. 2's proposed M2 exit. The 22nd Dragoons flailed as far as the tank trap, which was filled by a fascine, and then proceeded to the culvert crater. However, not realising its size, the OC No. 1 Troop, Captain E. J. Hewitt, ordered up another Fascine AVRE but it over-ran the edge and slid into the crater where it was submerged. The crew of six managed to get out, but three were killed and the others seriously wounded before they could reach the shelter of the dunes.**

The clearance of exits from the beach was the business primarily of the AVREs and bulldozers of the assault engineers (the 5th Assault Regiment, RE) and 'Crabs' of the 22nd Dragoons (79th Armoured Division). There was great difficulty in opening exits on the 7th Brigade front. A line of low sand dunes, and beyond it a flooded area, were the causes of the trouble. On Mike Red, one exit was opened across the dunes just west of Courseulles and the flooded area behind them, a bridge being laid and a rough causeway built across an AVRE which had become submerged at a cratered culvert on the track which it was planned to use. Some tanks got across about 0915, then the causeway failed and traffic had to be stopped. This exit was not working satisfactorily until noon or later.

A second one, on Mike Green further west, gave less trouble and was working fairly well by about 0930. In the meantime, the assault infantry had made good progress inland, but very few tanks or other vehicles were available to support them, and the beach was extremely congested.

The second shot clearly shows two SBG AVREs, one on the shoreline, the other about to advance up the track to bridge the crater.

The REs worked frantically to open the route from the beach as Major Younger explains: 'The sequence of operations that followed were, firstly, the fascine was released from the sunken AVRE by placing explosive charges on the retaining steel wire. Great credit is due to Captain Hewitt and his men, who, at this stage, had to work in the open to fix these charges, Lance Sergeant Snelling and Lance Corporal Gall being particularly worthy of mention. Secondly, the 1 Troop bridge was dropped from the seaward side on to the sunken tank which acted as a pier. Beyond this was the now-released fascine. The gap was still incomplete on the far side, so the OC organised the available troops on the beach to bring up logs which had been dumped nearby by the Germans presumably for use as craft obstacles. Gradually, and with the help of chespale fascines from various sources, a causeway was built out and, at about 0915 hours, the first DD tank got across close behind the assaulting companies. Six tanks were got across before the bridge started to slide off the turret of the sunken AVRE. Traffic therefore had to be stopped while the bridge was chocked up and improved. Another four tanks then got across until a 17-pdr Sherman slightly misjudged the track across the logs on the far side and became bogged. He was towed out by Lance-Sergeant Snelling's tank which had been the first across, and the opportunity was taken to bring up further logs. The next incident was that of the first SP gun which totally misjudged the bridge, and bellied itself firmly on it in such a way that when its tracks turned they could grip nothing. Three bulldozers were linked together but failed to pull it off, two AVREs were therefore brought up and, after a lot of trouble, succeeded in getting it off. During this time, a horse and cart had been "acquired" from a disinterested farmer and was impressed into bringing rubble from damaged houses to the gap. The work proceeded steadily under OC 2 Troop, Captain Hendry; traffic was leaving the beach with occasional breaks of two or three minutes when fresh cart-loads of rubble were brought up. The work here was finally handed over to the Beach Group in the afternoon, when the AVRE crews were withdrawn.' Later, the road was concreted over by No. 85 Field Company and in 1955 Captain P. C. Gray, second in command, returned to inspect the work his men had carried out back in 1944. He found that the turret was still visible beneath the concrete slab *(above left)*. The road subsided in 1969, but even after its repair, the tarmac cracked in a tell-tale square which we photographed in 1973 (*above right*).

In November 1976, Royal Engineers from the British Army of the Rhine (the post-war successor to 21st Army Group), carried out a major operation to dig out the AVRE.

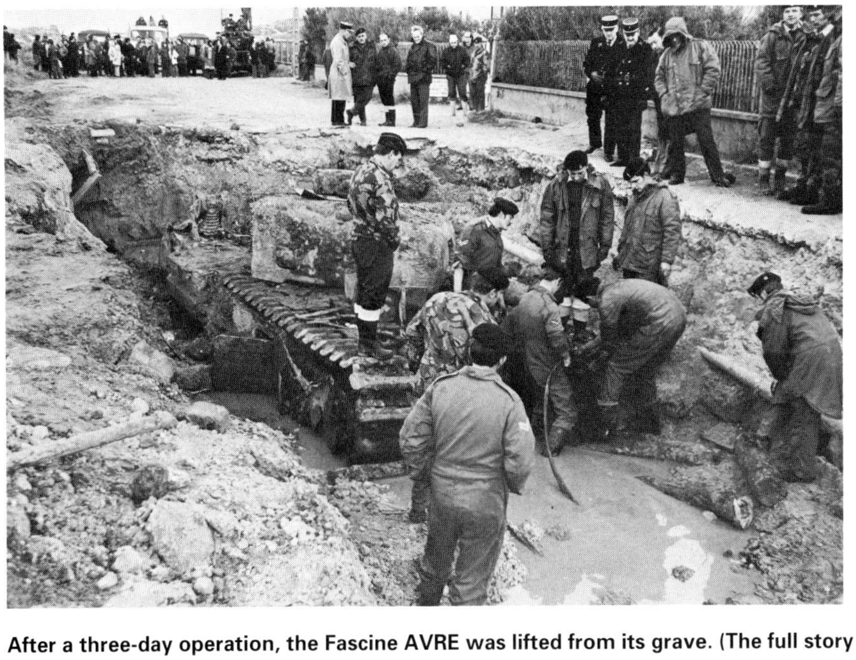

After a three-day operation, the Fascine AVRE was lifted from its grave. (The full story was told in *After the Battle* No. 15.)

The interior was a unique D-Day time capsule, as it still contained the complete contents it had carried into battle: including a Sten; a Bren with an unusual 100-round drum magazine; 600lbs of various explosives including *(top left)* General Wade charges (see page 241); 26 disassembled Petard bombs *(centre and right)*; demolition charges and '808' plastic explosive, all of which was taken away by the French authorities and blown up on Omaha. There were also complete sets of tools, and the personal kit of the crew — right down to a tin of Uruguayan corned beef! *Right:* The three men killed by a mortar shell: Lance-Sergeant Cecil Ashton, and Sappers Alf Battson and Roy Manley were first buried beside the road, but now rest at Bayeux, Two of the wounded survivors, the driver Bill Dunn, left, and demolitions NCO Bill Hawkins, were able to return for the unveiling of the refurbished AVRE the following year. *Below:* Now displayed close to the spot where it came to grief, one of the most remarkable relics of the battle to be seen today.

Above: **The delay in completing the two exits — M1 on the right and M2 on the left — caused congestion on the beach as vehicles landed but were unable to get off — the DDs being held up from being able to support the infantry for up to 90 minutes. The engineers frantically working on the exits were hindered by snipers on the crest of the hill behind the beach and P Troop of the 2nd Royal Marine Armoured Support Regiment, landing at around H+2 hours, found 'things were chaotic; as yet there were no exits for vehicles, tracked or otherwise. The tide was in and an enormous amount of equipment was jammed in a narrow strip of sandy beach. The troop commander made a recce of several exits during the course of the day but was unable to get the troop off the beach'.**

The infantry's experience on the right battalion front of the Canadian division was a mixture of good and bad. The Royal Winnipeg Rifles state that they touched down at 0749, all three assault companies landing 'within seven minutes of one another'. On the far right, C Company of the Canadian Scottish, which was prolonging the Rifles' front here, reported that it landed with slight opposition, and the platoon which had the job of knocking out the 75mm casemate north of Vaux approached it 'only to find — thanks to the Royal Navy — the pillbox was no more'.

While the picture at the top of the page was taken at the height of the problem — also by Air Commodore Geddes — that *(above)* is another of those US photos from around 2100 hours on the evening of D-Day. By that time, the crater on M2 has been filled in and some vehicles can be seen inland on the lateral road.

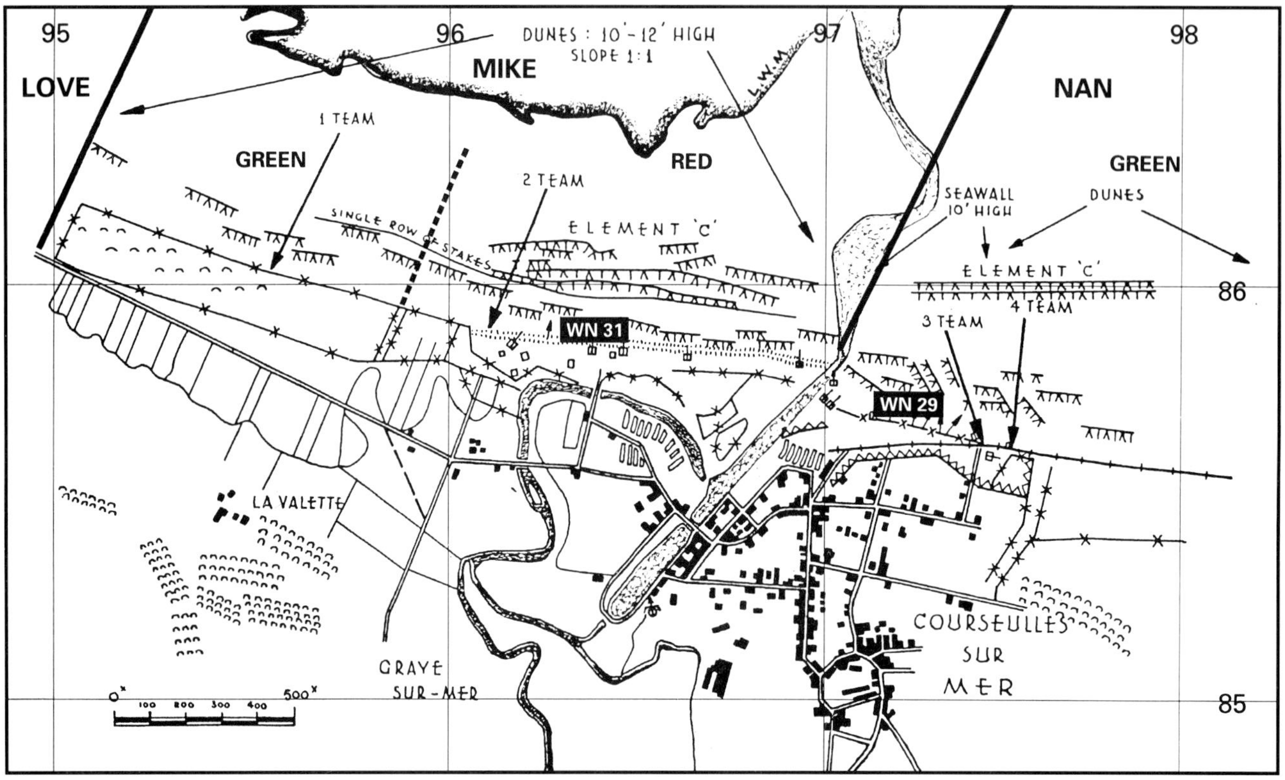

Quite different was the experience of B and D Companies of The Royal Winnipeg Rifles, a short distance to the left, whose task it was to deal with the western portion of the Courseulles strong point. The battalion diary remarked grimly: 'The bombardment having failed to kill a single German or silence one weapon, these companies had to storm their positions "cold" — and did so without hesitation.'

Very little shooting, apart from some inaccurate mortar fire, was directed at the landing craft before touchdown. Reports about the reception encountered on the beaches are conflicting. No. 5 Field Company, RCE, stated that 'there was no opposition to the landing in this sector [Mike Red]', whereas No. 7 Beach Group (8th Kings) reported that A Company on Mike Green 'carried out their initial reconnaissance under great difficulties owing to the enemy fire and numerous mines' and that 'much the same experience fell to B Company on Mike Red'. When A and C , the reserve companies of the Royal Winnipeg Rifles, landed with portions of the battalion headquarters, the beach and dunes were still under heavy mortar and machine gun fire to the extent that the companies were pinned down for two hours. The total casualties for the regiment for the day was almost 130, most of them being suffered by B Company.

B Company touched down on Mike Red beach where they were greeted by enemy mortar fire: 'One of their craft received a direct hit [which] caused several casualties before they were able to land. B Company and attached troops were pinned down with a shower of directed mortar fire which was being directed by an enemy pillbox ([1] on picture *below*) at the extreme left of Mike Red beach. The troops were getting hell as the mortar fire peppered the beach causing several casualties'. *Right:* Karel found this Mike Red casemate [2] slowly turning turtle some distance to the west of the entrance to Courseulles harbour, sited in such a position to enable it to enfilade the beach to the north-west. The wartime picture was taken in July 1944 when it had been taken over as living quarters for beach commanders from the Royal Canadian Navy.

B Company met heavy machine gun, shell and mortar fire beginning when the LCAs were 700 yards from the beach. This continued until touch-down, and as the men leapt from the craft many were hit 'while still chest high in water'. But the Little Black Devils were not to be denied. B Company, with the aid of the tanks, captured the pillboxes commanding the beach; it then forced its way across the Seulles bridge and cleared the enemy positions on the 'island' between the river and the little harbour. The fierceness of the fight on the beach is attested by the report of the Special Observer Party which later examined the German positions: 'Big guns in this area were probably all put out of action by close-range tank fire, and the machine gun and mortar positions gave up when surrounded by infantry.' When the strong point was clear, B Company had been reduced to the company commander (Captain P. E. Gower) and 26 men. Gower, who had set a powerful example of leadership and courage as he directed the clearing of the successive positions, received the Military Cross. An assault party of No. 6 Field Company, Royal Canadian Engineers (RCE), which landed with the infantry, had similar losses; the company had suffered 26 casualties during the day.

The Americans certainly won the air photo war over Normandy on D-Day. The picture *below* — another from the 7th Photo Group evening series flown by Captain Lawrence McBee of the 27th Photo Recon Squadron — is a remarkable comparison to that *opposite* taken at the height of the assault. Unfortunately, the latter is captionless, but it will either have been taken by the 7th, which belonged to the Eighth Air Force, or the 10th Photo Group which was part of the Ninth Air Force.

Once the beach had been secured, a lateral track was swept along the entire front of Mike sector although no mines were found. In this picture, the track has been upgraded with Pierced Steel Planking (PSP), an American product made out of No. 10 US gauge mild steel plate.

D Company met less fierce opposition when landing, since it was clear of the actual strong point area. It had relatively little difficulty in 'gapping' a minefield at La Valette and clearing the village of Graye-sur-Mer beyond it. When the reserve companies landed, the beach and dunes were still under heavy mortar and machine gun fire. A Company pushed inland towards Ste Croix-sur-Mer, starting at about 0805, while C Company advanced on Banville. The latter village fell comparatively easily, but machine gun fire held up the advance in front of Ste Croix. Assistance was asked from the 6th Armoured Regiment, which with 'cool disregard' of mines and anti-tank guns, beat down the opposition and permitted the advance to continue. By 1700, the battalion was consolidated in and around the village of Creully.

Although it had been the most difficult exit to clear, Mike M2 became the focal point for VIPs visiting the British and Canadian sectors. It was fairly central to the Eastern Task Force beach-head, and was only about six kilometres from 21st Army Group TAC HQ, established at Creully on June 8. ***Centre:*** **General Montgomery had stepped onto French soil — or rather sand — at 8.45 a.m. that morning, D+2, to be greeted by the CO of No. 7 Beach Group, Lieutenant-Colonel W. J. Humphrey (whom we heard quoted on page 468).** ***Right:*** **Naturally, we had to be historically correct with this comparison which Karel took on June 8, 1994 at 8.45 a.m. precisely!**

Above: Exit M2 had even been flagged 'Personnel Exit' although by the time HM King George VI arrived *(above right)* on June 16, No. 7 Beach Group had straightened up the sign. Note also how Sommerfeld tracking, which was basically a large-gauge chicken wire braced with 3/8-inch mild steel rods, has been overlaid on the sand to give vehicles a grip. The King was accompanied by Admiral Ramsay; Admiral of the Fleet Sir Andrew Cunningham (Chief of the Naval Staff and First Sea Lord); Marshal of the Royal Air Force Sir Charles Portal (Chief of Air Staff); Lieutenant-General Sir Hastings Ismay (Churchill's Military Chief-of-Staff), and His Majesty's private secretary and equerry, Sir Alan Lascelles and Captain Sir Harold Campbell. The party had left Portsmouth at 8 a.m. and arrived in the Juno area at 12.50 p.m. to be greeted by the Force 'J' commander, Commodore Oliver, and the NOIC Juno, Captain Colin Maud, who had set up his advanced headquarters east of Courseulles at 1330 on D-Day. Churchill had wanted to cross to France with the invasion armada on June 6, and, back in May, after the big conference at St Paul's School (see page 110), he had asked Admiral Ramsay to make plans for him to witness the first day's bombardment from a warship and to set foot in France at the earliest possible moment. The Admiral replied that the best ship to ensure the Prime Minister's safety would be the cruiser HMS *Belfast*, the flagship for Bombarding Force 'E', and that it might be possible for him to go ashore on D+1. However, when Eisenhower heard of Churchill's scheme, he was firmly against it, arguing that 'the chance of him becoming an accidental casualty was too important from the standpoint of the whole war effort'. Churchill replied that the Supreme Commander had no jurisdiction over the British Prime Minister, but it was The King who settled the issue by stating that he would accompany Churchill on the venture as titular head of his troops. Now it was the Prime Minister who objected strongly on safety grounds. The King only agreed not to go if Churchill did likewise. In the end, the Prime Minister set foot in France on D+6 *(right)*, beating The King by four days!

Now one of the characteristic D-Day monuments, which have been erected by the Comité du Débarquement all along the Normandy coast, stands at Exit M2. In the background, the Churchill (tank this time!) rescued from beneath 'Pont d'Avre'.

Although the Canadian division and its brigades set up their command posts ashore early on D-Day, it was not until June 18 that General 'Harry' Crerar (see page 104) was able to move Canadian First Army headquarters to Normandy. This was established at Amblie, three kilometres east of Creully, in the same village where Lieutenant-General Guy Simonds located the corps HQ. Meanwhile, the main Canadian military HQ remained in London in the offices of the Sun Life Assurance Company of Canada *(left)* in Cockspur Street. This comprised four main sections: Military Intelligence, Staff, Historical, and Public Relations, and it was as head of the historical section that our author for this chapter, Lieutenant-Colonel Charles Stacey *(right)*, had served since 1940. He supervised the historical programme of the Canadian Army Overseas and produced the first of several histories in 1948. Publicity-wise, Canada received a raw deal over the D-Day publicity and Colonel Stacey (who died in 1989) would have been closely involved in a contretemps which blew up ten days after the landings.

The rumpus concerned the rocket ships, an item of specialised D-Day equipment which we have not so far illustrated. Rocket Projectiles (RP) had been used in an anti-aircraft or air-to-ground rôle for several years, but it was not until 1943 that a proposal was made to install banks of the army's 5-inch rockets on board a naval vessel. The LCT(R) carried 792 rockets on launcher rails angled at 45 degrees. They were set up in stands of six and could be fired in 24 salvoes in quick succession by electrical igniters. With a range of 3,500 yards, the RPs could blanket an area 750 yards by 160 yards with a 36lb explosive charge bursting on every 150 square yards. Aiming was arbitrary and depended on the accurate positioning of the LCT(R) in relation to the shore target, so the vessels were fitted with extra navigational equipment including a radar tower aft of the bridge which was protected from blast by a screen. Even if the weapon was not very accurate, it was considered a marvellous morale-booster for the troops about to land, and eight LCT(R)s — four per brigade front — were employed on Juno.

Unfortunately, at Juno, a passing Typhoon met a pattern in mid-air and was destroyed. While we are not claming this to be that low-flying aircraft — for it looks more like a Spitfire — the still comes from the same sequence of film which caused the rocket ship rumpus and the Canadian contretemps.

On January 29, Major George C. Stevens, the US chief of the Motion Picture Department Special Coverage Production Unit, had received the following cable: 'For civilian showing in the United States require 4-reel rough cut of picture showing forces preparing for assault to come. This film to be sent to United States for final 2-reel version to be released in the United States on the day of the announcement of initiation of assault operations.' This was the offending sequence in the first post-D-Day newsreel film: *The Eve of Invasion*, which was the subject of a telephone conversation between Colonel J. B. L. Lawrence, head of public relations for ETOUSA, and Major General A. D. Surles, his opposite number in Washington, on June 14, 1944 at 1740 hours British time. The rumpus also threatened to sour relations with the Canadians.

COLONEL LAWRENCE: Hello! This is Colonel Lawrence talking.

GENERAL SURLES: Hello, this is General Surles.

LAWRENCE: There was a meeting of this committee today, Anglo-American Committee, at which certain matters came up which we thought you should know. The Royal Navy representative at the Anglo-American Film Committee registered an official protest by the Admiralty against the release in the United States of the 'Eve of Invasion' without the censorship cuts guaranteed by Colonel Mitchell, as the War Department representative.

SURLES: All right.

LAWRENCE: They stated that they had had sharp repercussions from the Press because of the use of rocket gun shots.

SURLES: Right.

LAWRENCE: Regarding which there have been Naval censorship cuts here. The Royal Navy first officially requested the War Department to insure that no stills are released regarding the rocket gun shots on 'The Eve of Invasion'.

SURLES: All right.

LAWRENCE: The Royal Navy then protested the release of the picture on D+3 when they say it was decided that the release should have been on D+4. Now the next — the representatives of the Air Ministry, the British War Office protested against the failure to include in the picture the requirements for a proper Canadian representation. They stated that the impact on Canada was very dangerous politically. The Royal Navy then requested officially that this point be made to the War Department, that there is a danger of the matter being brought up in Parliament here, and by the Canadian High Commissioner as to why proper Canadian representation was not included. They went further and stated that it was evident that the release of the picture through the newsreel channels in the United States meant that this would include release in Canada by the newsreels so that Canada saw the picture in the US version rather than in the version desired by the Canadian Government.

SURLES: Well, now let me tell you the story of that particular picture. You can relay this to them and they will have exactly the circumstances that attended its showing here.

LAWRENCE: Yes, sir.

SURLES: In the first place, we had requested a long time before, a considerable time before, that the picture be made up.

LAWRENCE: Yes, sir.

SURLES: Nothing developed on it and I think the Chief-of-Staff inquired as to where the material was, a couple of weeks before. Whereupon, it is my understanding that a picture was hurriedly thrown together, by a British director, I believe, and sent over here. Now, it arrived here about one or two days before D-Day. I showed it to the Chief-of-Staff. It was both his opinion and mine that unless that picture was shown immediately after D-Day we might just as well throw it in the waste basket because people would not be interested in the pre-operation after the pictures of the actual invasion came out. The picture was made, as my understanding was, principally by the British so we assumed that it was going to be satisfactory to them.

We did know about the request for concealment of the rocket gun sequence but our Navy here had prepared material for release on D-Day of rocket material. So far as censorship in the United States was concerned, the stuff on rockets was off on D-Day.

It did a remarkably good job here in the United States in showing the people the great preparations that were made for this effort, the great care and the training, and it was a very valuable document to put in before the public just at the time it was put in. Furthermore, it did a very good job in the way of Anglo-American relationship because it was a very strong representation of what the British were doing in this thing. You see what I mean?

LAWRENCE: Yes, sir.

SURLES: Now, with that in mind, we sent our picture representative to New York to talk to the War Activities Committee. The War Activities Committee says frankly that unless the film was shown at once it wouldn't get 500 dailies to show it later on after the time interval had passed. Then they talked the matter over up there and a decision was made by the film people themselves that they would put it in the newsreels on the spot for the following Thursday. Now, that is the story.

LAWRENCE: Excuse me. There is only one more question, Sir. They were very perturbed about the Canadian situation. They were very worried for fear there would be political questions because of the lack of Canadian material. Is there anything we could tell them on that, sir?

SURLES: Nothing except that the Canadians could have done what they pleased with the picture. I mean as far as their distribution and value is concerned, I think it was up to the Canadians themselves as to when they wanted to show it.

LAWRENCE: In other words they had — .

SURLES: They were in on it here. They knew what was going on here.

LAWRENCE: They did. They were aware of what was going on?

SURLES: That is right.

LAWRENCE: One more moment, sir. Could we ask you this for our own information. In the film were they British or American rocket ships? Do you happen to know, sir?

SURLES: Oh, I don't know. I haven't the faintest idea. The rocket sequence was very much in the picture. They couldn't possibly tell what ships it came from or what points. All you see is in the distance four or five sheets of flame and you can't see even the ships that they are fired from.

In dealing with the other half of the Courseulles strong point, east of the river, The Regina Rifle Regiment, as we have seen, had the advantage of the fact that their DD tanks reached the beach ahead of the infantry and in larger numbers than on the Winnipegs' front. Here, as at most points, however, the results of the preliminary bombardment had been disappointing. During the planning, the village of Courseulles had been partitioned into blocks numbered 1 to 12, each to be cleared by a designated company; at the same time, careful study of aerial photographs and maps had familiarised the troops with the ground to such an extent that, as the commanding officer, Lieutenant-Colonel F. M. Matheson, said: 'Nearly every foot of the town was known long before it was ever entered'.

Here, on Nan Green, there was rather less difficulty with beach exits than on Mike Red: the Crabs dealt with the mines, an anti-tank ditch was filled with fascines dropped by the AVREs, armoured bulldozers improved the lanes, and both planned exits (leading into the East Courseulles strong point) were working by about 0900. All across the brigade front, the engineers and the 22nd Dragoons had done yeoman service, and the former in particular had had a considerable number of casualties.

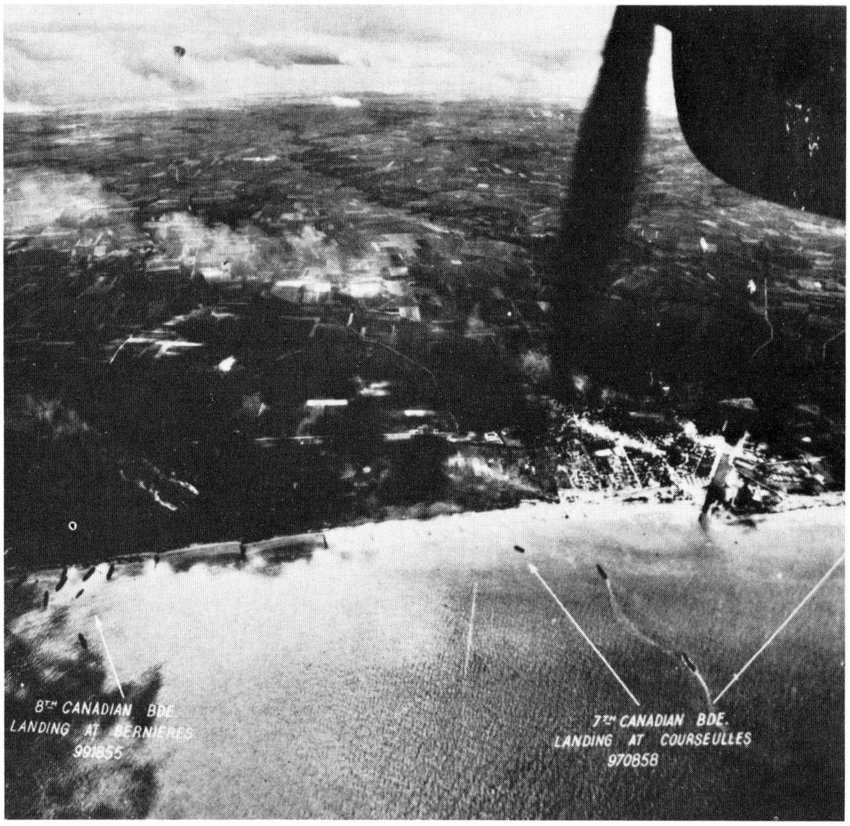

Above: **A rather poor quality shot, but it is important as it shows the relationship between the 7th Brigade beaches at Courseulles and the 8th Brigade a mile to the east at Bernières. Nan Green Beach lies just to the left of Courseulles harbour — three vessels can be seen approaching the shore.** *Left:* **Nan Green in close-up. This pre-invasion photographic cover illustrates the strong point WN 29 directly facing the planned landing spots for Teams 3 and 4 (see map page 468) backed by an anti-tank ditch.**

The two assault companies (A and B) reported touching down at 0809 and 0815 respectively. A Company, which was directly opposite the strong point, immediately met heavy resistance. The strong point gave it a hard struggle, and Colonel Matheson testified that the help of the tanks of B Squadron of the 6th Armoured Regiment was invaluable. This observation is supported by the later examination of the German positions by the Special Observer Party, which reported, with respect to the 75mm position at the east end of the strong point: 'The gun had fired many rounds (estimated 200 empties) and was put out of action by a direct hit which penetrated the gun shield making a hole 3"×6" . . . It is probable that the gun was put out by a direct shot from a DD tank.' Similarly, the 88mm position by the riverside was reported as 'probably silenced by direct hits with guns from DD tanks', although the concrete and

Left: **The same area today shows the realignment of the esplanade (now the Promenade de Dartmouth); the disappearance of any trace of the anti-tank ditch, and the associated casemates of the East Courseulles strong point.**

The WN 29 defences at the east end of Courseulles centred around an 88mm (for the purist it is an 8·8cm Pak 43/41) in a Type 677 concrete emplacement at the harbour entrance.

gun shield were marked by shells probably fired by destroyers and LCGs. The nearby 50mm gun's shield had been pierced by holes 'probably caused by aimed fire from tank at short range'. Of the strong point generally, the observers reported that 'the guns had fired a considerable quantity of ammunition and were put out of action by accurately placed fire from close range by tanks'.

Touch down! Claim to be first on Nan Green Beach was made by B Squadron of the Canadian 6th Armoured Regiment. The DD tanks were launched at 4,000 yards, and 14 out of 19 touched down. Four were lost by shell or mortar fire or by being run down by other craft; the other one came ashore further to the east later. Two out of the 14 which got ashore were drowned on the beach owing to the rapid rise of the tide after they deflated their flotation gear. The other tanks immediately went into action against the beach defences under continual mortar and shell-fire although they suffered very few crew casualties. On the other hand, the assaulting companies of The Regina Rifles, one of them carried in five LCAs of the 505th LCA Flotilla, met a considerable volume of machine gun fire as their ramps went down. The matter-of-fact reports by each craft make them all the more poignant: 'No. 1 Craft: "All troops got clear of the water and then three were seen to fall when running up the beach." No. 2 Craft: "Two were hit as soon as they attempted to leave the craft. The remainder of the troops sustained a few casualties when running up the beach." No. 3 Craft: "Six seen to fall whilst running up the beach." No. 4 Craft: "A number seen to be hit when crossing the sand." No. 5 Craft: "A few casualties among the troops once they were clear of the water."' A Company bore the brunt of the assault, the battalion diary confirming that 'it was evident to all that, due to adverse flying conditions, the air support had not been as great as had been expected', and that 'pillboxes and other emplacements were still open for business when our troops touched down'. The company was held up by the strong point, clearly visible in the centre of the photo *above*, for several hours. However, after its capture, the company failed to leave a small force behind to prevent its re-occupation, and the Germans soon returned to the south-west corner, whereupon the Canadians had to begin the whole disheartening business of recapturing the position over again.

When the obstacle clearance units — No. 5 Field Company, Royal Canadian Engineers, and No. 262 Field Company, Royal Engineers — reached the beach, the water was already too high, so that work could not begin until the tide fell. No. 3 Platoon of 262 Field Company arrived at H+20 minutes, by which time the obstacles were covered, and their LCM hit a fuzed shell on the last row of hedgehogs, blowing off the front of the craft and injuring four men. Despite tremendous difficulties, all were rescued, including the wounded, by dragging each man ashore using a line. The Armoured Breaching Teams of the 26th Assault Squadron, RE, were late, No. 3 Team not beaching until 0815 and No. 4 Team even later at 0831. By this time, the infantry had arrived, but could not get off the beach. Both troops completed their gaps (east of the planned locations) by 0900 — the next obstacle to be overcome being the anti-tank ditch *(above left)*. *Above right:* Karel Margry traced the line of the excavation, the bend to the right coming at the end of this road. In the field beyond, his countrymen from the Dutch 'Keep 'em Rolling' military vehicle preservation society are appropriately camped to commemorate D-Day+50 years. *Right:* The ditch was breached by an AVRE's SBG bridge — this picture being taken looking westwards and at a right-angle to that above. Fortunately, a single house remained in the background as a common reference point. *Below:* After a good deal of searching, Karel found the spot where this Flail had come to grief which lay off the present-day D514 to Bernières, the wood being masked by new houses. This is more or less on the boundary between Nan Green and Nan White.

Left: Guarding the east bank of the harbour entrance was this 50mm. In the main, the guns were silenced by the DDs of B Squadron (6th Armoured Regiment) which certainly knocked out the 88mm and this 50mm which still bears its wartime scars. *Right:* Technically, it is a converted 5cm Kampfwagen-kanone (KwK) — a converted tank gun on a pivot mounting.

For the assault, Courseulles itself had been partitioned into blocks numbered 1 to 12, each to be cleared by designated companies, and training in street fighting had been carried out in anticipation of resistance in the town. The strong point engaged by A Company of The Regina Rifles was contained in Block 1, and while the company was held up here, B Company cleared Blocks 2, 3 and 4. The reserve companies now commenced to come ashore. C Company touched down without mishap and moved through the town to clear Block 8. D Company's craft were blown up in the water by mines and only 49 survivors reached land. C Company reported Block 8 clear and, within a short time, Blocks 9, 10 and 11. A Company now reported Block 1 in their hands and were ordered to take on 5, 6 and 7 on the lock bank *(above left)*. Shortly afterwards, B Company had cleared 4 and was sent on to 12. Then, as we have seen, A Company had to go back to recapture the strong point, after which they returned to complete clearing Block 5. The battalion commander, Lieutenant-Colonel F. M. Matheson, was of the opinion that Courseulles contained more troops than had been expected from intelligence reports and, in any event, about 80 Germans were taken in the town. Many more had been killed or had managed to escape.

Left: 'Loyalty is the essence of Honour' — '(The) Victory is our belief'. The writing was on the wall in the pock-marked German officers' mess in the harbour. *Right:* Canadian war photographer Lieutenant Ken Bell pictured this German sand table of the beach and its defences — amazingly covering the exact area assaulted by the 7th Brigade — in the Mairie.

Sergeant Leo Gariepy, who claimed that his was the first of B Squadron's DDs to come ashore, was pictured by Lieutenant Bell in 1944 *(left)* driving through the town in his tank and *(right)* on the same spot 25 years later.

More by accident than by design, I found myself the leading tank. On my way in, I was surprised to see a friend — a midget submarine who had been waiting for us for 48 ours. He waved me right on to my target and then made a half-turn to go back. I remember him very distinctly standing up through his conning hatch, joining his hands together in a sign of good luck. I answered the old, familiar Army sign — To you too, bud!

I was the first tank coming ashore and the Germans started opening up with machine gun bullets. But when we came to a halt on the beach, it was only then that they realised we were a tank when we pulled down our canvas skirt, the flotation gear. Then they saw that we were Shermans. It was quite amazing. I still remember very vividly some of the machine-gunners standing up in their posts looking at us with their mouths wide open. To see tanks coming out of the water shook them rigid.

My target was on the seafront. A 75mm which was in a position of enfilade fire along the beach like all the guns. The houses along the beach were all full of machine-gunners and so were the sand dunes. But the angle of the blockhouse stopped them firing on me. So I took the tank up to the emplacement, very close and destroyed the gun by firing at almost point-blank range.

We ended up in a narrow street and there was one of those funny looking trucks with a charcoal burner on the running board. I couldn't get my tank by, and I saw two Frenchmen and a French woman standing in a doorway, looking at us. So I took my earphones off and told them in good Quebec French: 'Now will you please move that truck out of the way so I can get by?' They must have been frightened because they wouldn't budge. So then I called them everything I could think of in the military vocabulary. They were amazed to hear a Tommy — they thought we were Tommies — speak French with the old Norman dialect!

SERGEANT LEO GARIEPY, 1974
B Squadron, Canadian 6th Armoured Regiment

Gariepy had stayed on in Courseulles after the war, and in 1970 was instrumental in promoting the recovery of one of the five DDs which had failed to make it to the shore. Salvage rights were then held by M. Jean Demota, and his company carried out the actual recovery *(left)*. The following year, *Bold* was dedicated on the seafront *(right)*.

The choked streets of Courseulles pictured on D+1. Unfortunately, no caption details are given, but Jean Paul Pallud discovered that the column of vehicles *(above)* are approaching from the beach along the Rue de la Mer . . .

When at last A Company had cleared the strong point after breaking through by 'a left flanking attack', its troubles were not over. It moved on to its next task without leaving any force in occupation, and the Germans promptly filtered back into the positions 'by tunnels and trenches'. The work of clearance began again, with the assistance after a time of an additional troop of tanks. In the meantime, B Company, landing on the left of the battalion front east of the strong point, had met only slight resistance and had cleared a succession of the assigned blocks in the village.

The fortunes of the reserve companies were similarly mixed. C Company reported that it touched down at 0835 and moved inland without difficulty. D Company, on the other hand, met catastrophe. Coming in late (it reported landing at 0855), several of its craft were blown up on mined obstacles concealed by the rising tide and only 49 survivors reached the beach.

As the companies overcame resistance in their areas, they pushed inland towards the village of Reviers, where the battalion gradually concentrated in the course of the afternoon; the last to arrive was A Company, which had finally overcome the stubborn resistance in Courseulles. About 1700, the Reginas began to advance southward from Reviers. Before 2000 hours, both Fontaine-Henry and Le Fresne-Camilly were in their hands.

The 7th Brigade's reserve battalion, the 1st Battalion of The Canadian Scottish Regiment, commanded by Lieutenant-Colonel F. N. Cabeldu, found opposition still alive as its three companies approached Mike sector about 0830. The leading companies came under mortar fire on the beach, and one of them was held up there for some time while waiting for an exit to be cleared of mines. Soon after 0930 the

. . . before turning left down the Rue Emile Heroult. At this point, we are looking eastwards towards Bernières.

Once D Company of the Reginas had re-organised following their mishap on landing, the survivors set out inland as planned for Reviers. The leading troops reached the village around 1100, being joined in short order by C Company having finished with Block 11 in Courseulles. By 1500, battalion headquarters had also established itself in Reviers, followed by the arrival of B Company and then A Company although Colonel Matheson could not be sure of the exact time of each arrival.

battalion was able to start its advance across the fields towards Ste Croix-sur-Mer. En route, it picked up its C Company, which had landed in the assault wave. There were a considerable number of casualties from machine gun fire during the advance, which was pushed with all possible speed. After dealing with snipers in Ste Croix, the battalion continued through Colombiers-sur-Seulles, passing through The Royal Winnipeg Rifles. Little or no opposition was now being encountered, and the Scottish could have gone further, but under orders from brigade headquarters they dug in for the night around Pierrepont, with patrols out well in front of Cainet and Le Fresne-Camilly, the latter village having been taken over from The Regina Rifle Regiment.

A troop of tanks of C Squadron of the 1st Hussars, commanded by Lieutenant W. F. McCormick, which was supporting The Royal Winnipeg Rifles, helped them through Creully and then 'just kept on going', pushing on through Camilly to the north edge of Secqueville-en-Bessin. En route, they shot up a German scout car and inflicted casualties on parties of infantry; and Lieutenant McCormick was punctiliously saluted by a German soldier who evidently did not expect to meet the enemy so far inland. The fact that these few tanks — which probably got closer to the final inland objective than any other element of the Allies' seaborne assault forces that day — were able to push so far and return is evidence of how slight the resistance on the 7th Brigade's front was during the afternoon.

Delay in opening exits from the beaches on the 7th Brigade front prevented the field artillery from moving inland as soon as had been planned. In these circumstances, Lieutenant-Colonel R. H. Webb brought the guns of the 12th Field Regiment ashore about 0900 and put them into action actually on the beach. Deployed side by side amid the confusion of men and vehicles, they opened fire in support of the advancing infantry. In the late afternoon, the regiment was able to move to

With B Squadron tanks in the lead, the Regina Rifles set out south from Reviers at around 1700, but five out of their remaining ten tanks were lost to two 88mm guns before the latter were silenced. Nevertheless, one troop of the reserve C Squadron pushed ahead and got close to their D-Day objective, namely Bretteville-l'Orgueilleuse, without suffering any losses. However, being out on a limb without infantry support, the tanks pulled back, yet the 6th Armoured Regiment believed that these were the only troops of the Allied forces to achieve their objective on D-Day along the whole Normandy battlefront. It would have been nice to illustrate that drive with genuine pictures taken en route, but, as none were taken, we will have to settle for second best. ***Above:*** **A Sherman moves through Reviers some time later in June; Brana Radovic matched the shot** ***(below).***

Next stop Thaon, half-way to Bretteville, though these Canadian Shermans were pictured by Lieutenant Frank

Dubervill on June 20. Comparisons taken by Jean Paul Pallud on the Place de la Criée at the eastern end of the Grand Rue.

its planned gun area between Ste Croix and Banville. The 13th Field Regiment had landed somewhat later. The first battery to land established itself south of Courseulles. By evening, the whole unit was in its designated position adjacent to the 12th Field Regiment's.

The Centaurs of the Royal Marine Armoured Support Regiment had comparatively little to do on the 7th Brigade's beaches. Some of the Centaurs were lost at sea, and others landed late. They received few calls for fire, though one troop, answering a request received through a 13th Field Regiment observation party, silenced a beach position which was harassing the Reginas.

Because of the late landings, and the state of the tide which was higher than had been predicted, the arrangements made for clearing the beach obstacles were badly disrupted. This task was to be shared by army engineers and special naval parties. As it turned out, little could be done until the receding tide uncovered the obstacles.

On D-Day, Lieutenant McCormick pressed on through Camilly to the northern edge of Secqueville-en-Bessin *(above)*.

Although this is a shot of a 23rd Hussars British Sherman on June 26, it was taken by none other than Sergeant Midgley.

Just over a mile to the east of Courseulles lay the 8th Brigade beaches at Bernières-sur-Mer. The Queen's Own Rifles of Canada came ashore on Nan White (on the right) with The North Shore Regiment on Nan Red.

THE 8th BRIGADE BEACHES

The 8th Canadian Infantry Brigade Group was to lead the assault on the eastern sector of the Canadian Division's front, with The Queen's Own Rifles of Canada, commanded by Lieutenant-Colonel J. G. Spragge, landing on Nan White Beach, on the right, and capturing the resistance nest at Bernières, while The North Shore (New Brunswick) Regiment, under Lieutenant-Colonel D. B. Buell, landed on Nan Red on the left and cleared the similar strong point at St Aubin. The brigade's reserve battalion was Le Régiment de la Chaudière under Lieutenant-Colonel J. E. G. P. Mathieu. Armoured support in the assault phase would be provided by the DD Shermans of the 10th Armoured Regiment (The Fort Garry Horse), which was commanded by Lieutenant-Colonel R. E. A. Morton, with B Squadron supporting the Queen's Own and C Squadron the North Shore.

The DDs on the 8th Brigade front had a quite different experience from those with the 7th; no real attempt was made to swim them in; instead, they left their craft close inshore and landed behind the infantry assault companies. The DD equipment was inflated, and the tanks used their propellers, but the operation was 'really a wet wade'. Captain R. J. O. Otway-Ruthven, whose naval Assault Group J2 landed the brigade, reported: 'The LCTs with the DD tanks touched down at 0810 and, except for one craft which beached on Love sector and was missed, all the tanks got ashore and the LCTs got clear of the beach without much damage'. The war diary of the 10th Armoured Regiment implies, rather than states, that the tanks landed before the first infantry, but gives no time. All other

Red and White Beaches of Nan sector as they appear today. (This coverage links in with that on page 474.)

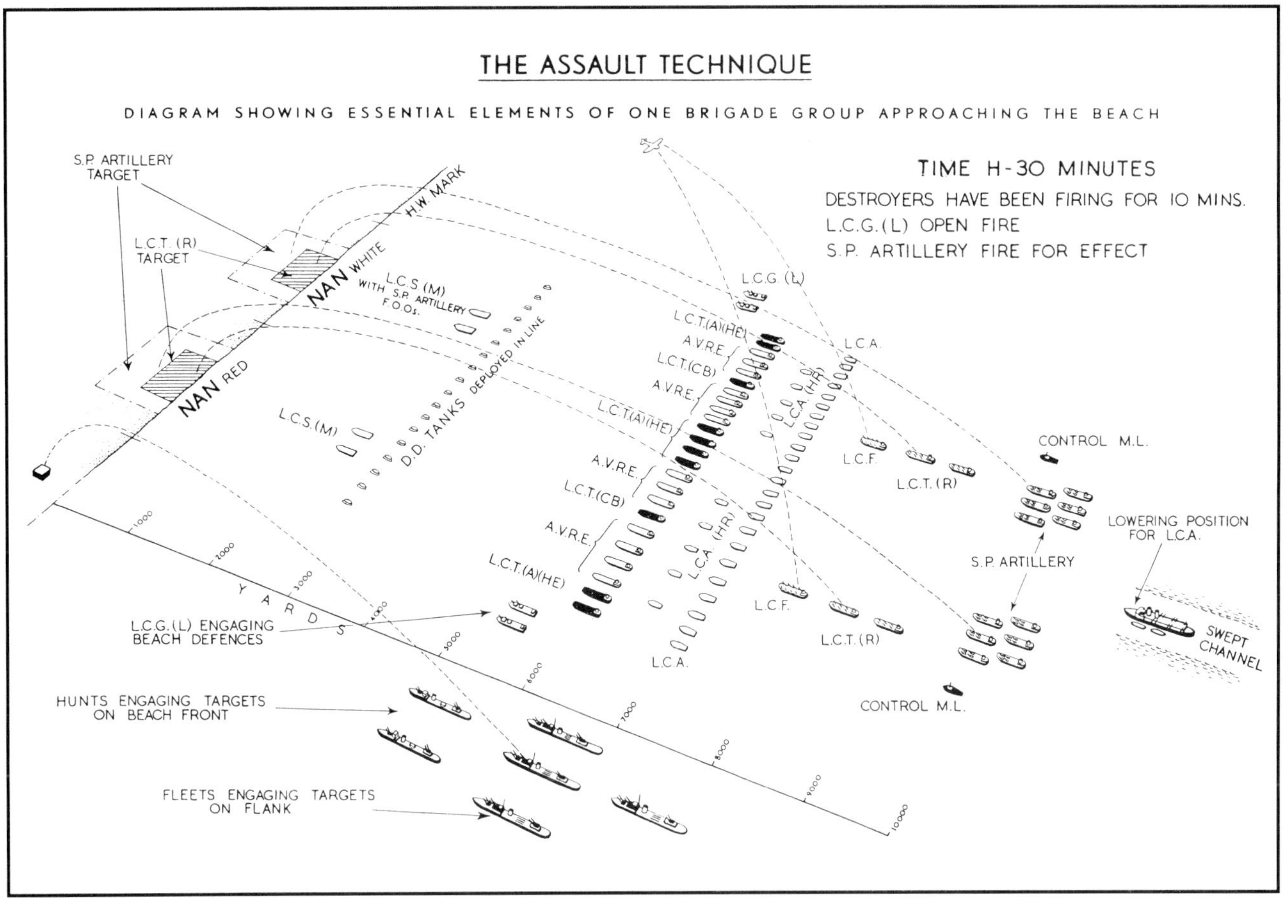

General Montgomery's illustration from *Normandy to the Baltic* of the text-book assault . . . only it never happened like this in real life! The opinion of the Queen's Own Rifles on the fire preparation was that 'the support all round has been very disappointing so far as we are concerned, for none of the beach defences have been touched, and this has caused very high casualties among the assaulting coys'. Naval sources reported that the DDs came in ten minutes behind the infantry. The breaching teams of AVREs, due to touch down at H-Hour (set at 0755 in this sector), were also late and, as a result, the infantry assault had to be postponed for 30 minutes, with the LCAs circling offshore, and even at 0830 the Queen's remarked: 'By now, the DDs and AVREs are on the beach but do not seem to be getting any place'.

The main defensive position at Bernières was a strong point (WN 28) just east of the railway station. It comprised two anti-tank emplacements, one of wood, the other of concrete; seven machine gun emplacements and two mortar pits. Although the bombardment of the coast had destroyed or damaged 90 per cent of the buildings between the railway and the sea, in the vicinity of the strong point there was no trace of bomb, shell or rocket fire. This picture is another of the briefing photographs. At this point, the beach is backed by a sea-wall some six to ten feet high into which pillboxes had been constructed. Reference with the present-day situation *(opposite)* shows that the strong point area has since been built over, while the railway line has been dismantled and the line of the track turned into a road.

evidence is that the infantry were earlier. The Queen's Own Rifles indicate that the tanks were behind the assault companies. Evidence from the North Shore Regiment is that neither tanks nor Centaurs were present at the moment of the first infantry landing, which the officer commanding one of the assault companies puts at 0805, but the battalion diary at 0810. The 5th Assault Regiment records are similar. The 80th Assault Squadron indicates that on the right the infantry were first, followed by the AVREs and later by the tanks; on the left, it reports the DD tanks did not arrive until H+60 minutes. It seems evident that on both battalion fronts, the DD tanks were behind the leading infantry, but likely that most of them landed only a few minutes later.

According to our author, Colonel Stacey, the Queen's' assault of Nan White was the most difficult and costly of all the Canadian landings, coming ashore as it did right in front of the strong point. However, one post-battle account says that it was believed that the 50mm guns probably had not fired; nor had the mortars, yet the Queen's war diary says that as soon as A Company (which came ashore just to the right of the strong point) hit the railway 'they came under very heavy mortar fire and are pinned down'. Whatever the truth, it was the machine gun positions which took the heaviest toll, decimating B Company. The infantry scaled the sea-wall and the remnants of the company outflanked the position. Finally the garrison surrendered. The battalion lost 36 men in storming the strong point, the majority from B Company.

If you are familiar with the area, the sharp bend in the wall, with the pill-box, was on our right front. My section was first from the LCA, and we were slaughtered.

For some peculiar reason, as we approached the beach, our craft did an about turn, making a large loop, then came in for the landing. How long? Who can say, but the defences were manned as our craft grounded. Our support craft were knocked out so we had no heavy weapons. The DD tanks had not come ashore. My platoon, approximately 36 strong, went through what we believe was enfilade fire from five machine guns.

We landed in our proper area, but no specialised gear reached the wall. All our assault engineers were killed in action. We were still in the water when the section was cut down. Most of us had deflated the Mae Wests we were wearing, and possibly those that died had drowned. I was a Lance-Jack, Bren crew, loaded with around a total of 300 rounds, plus 36 Mills grenades. The sea was red. One lad was hit in the smoke bomb he was carrying. Another, a human torch, had the presence of mind to head back into the water. Our flame-thrower man was hit and exploded, and we couldn't even find his body.

ROLPH JACKSON, 10 PLATOON, D COMPANY, THE QUEEN'S OWN RIFLES OF CANADA, 1993

This pillbox was one of the forward positions protecting the strong point assaulted by the Queen's Own Rifles who lost so many men in its capture. However, today it stands instead as a memorial to Le Régiment de la Chaudière — the reserve unit which came ashore some 30 minutes later —'A Tous Nos Morts'.

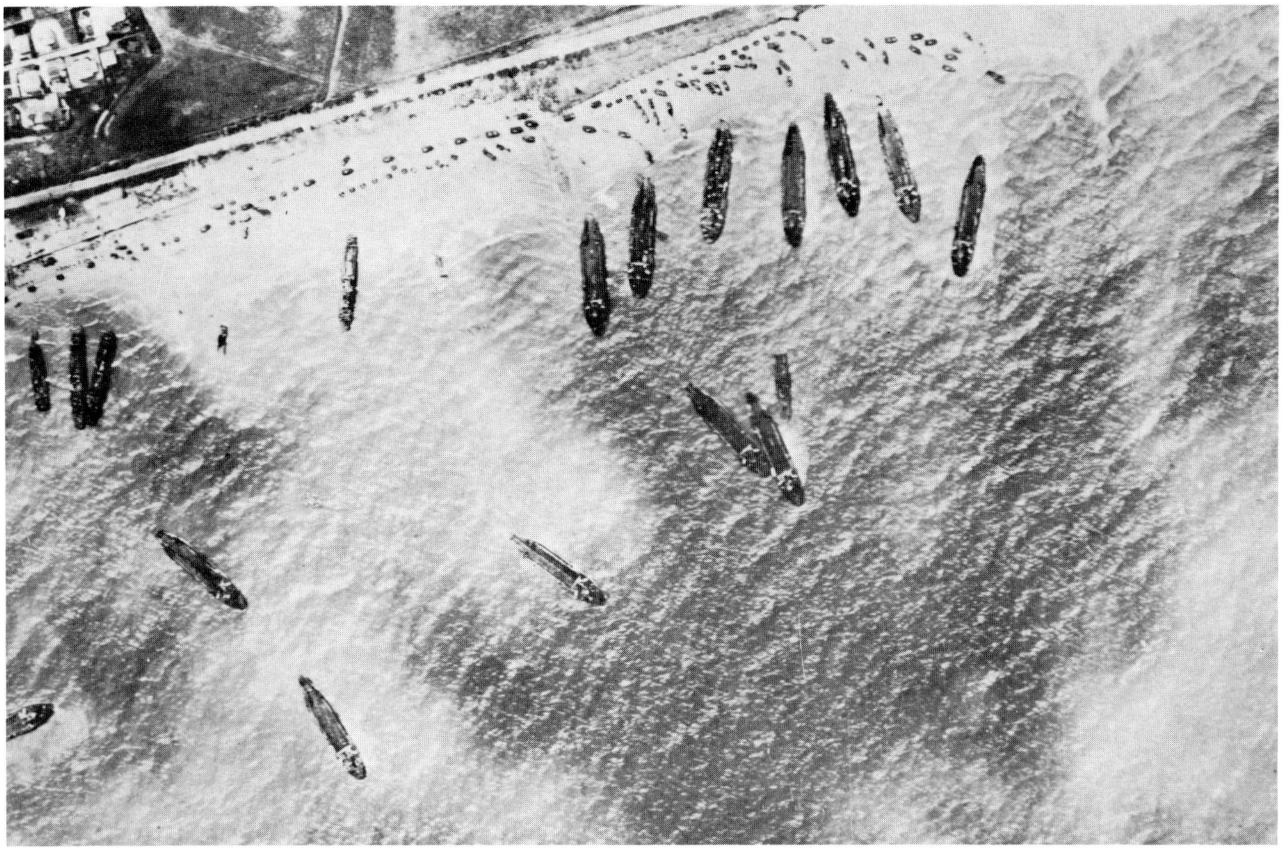

On the right sector of the 8th Brigade front, B Company of the Queen's Own ran into difficulty. Captain Otway-Ruthven reports that the assault companies 'touched down about 200 yards east of their correct position'. B Company landed directly in front of the 'resistance nest' at Bernières: 'Within the first few minutes there were 65 casualties'. Then, Lieutenant W. G. Herbert, Lance-Corporal René Tessier and Rifleman William Chicoski dashed at the pillbox [assumed to be one of the sea-front positions east of Bernières railway station in front of the strong point] which was causing the losses, and put it out of action with grenades and Sten gun fire. This opened the way for clearing the rest of the strong point. In other respects, the battalion's experience paralleled that further west.

Centre: **However, the Queen's do get proper credit, having claimed the 50mm anti-tank gun emplacement a few yards away as 'their' memorial.** *Left:* **Jean Paul took this picture in September 1993 but, when Karel rephotographed it on June 6, 1994** *(right)*, **the Fort Garry Horse, not to be left out, had introduced their own memorial between the two!**

The other assault unit, A Company, landing west of the strong point, had much less difficulty in getting off the beach, but shortly came under mortar fire and also suffered casualties. The reserve companies, like those on other sectors, suffered heavy casualties to their craft by mines as they came in but, fortunately, losses among personnel were not numerous. By the time these companies arrived, the Bernières strong point was being mopped up, and they were able to get through to the southern edge of the village. During the afternoon, they led the battalion's advance southward towards Anguerny, which was captured after some resistance had been overcome.

The 50mm casemate was a focal point for several other pictures taken on D-Day. At this early stage in the battle, both adversaries appear — on film at least — to be good natured with each other. It would soon change.

This was the only Canadian assault battalion front where tank support was reported as ineffective. The 10th Armoured Regiment itself recorded that the QOR suffered severely 'before B Squadron could support it'. The Special Observer Party, which did not report any visible damage by tank fire, got the impression that it was possible that 'very good tactical surprise was achieved here'. But this was not in fact the case, and the troop of assault engineers working on the beach 500 yards east reported being heavily fired on by the two 50mm anti-tank guns in the Bernières strong point, which, they said, were silenced only after some 15 minutes, when they were captured by the infantry. Men of No. 5 Field Company, RCE, also had heavy casualties on both Nan Red and Nan White.

Fifty years on, the beach has risen to all but cover the sea-wall.

Although 21st Army Group had budgeted for handling 500 prisoners per day in the early stages, rising to 1,000 per day after D+10, this estimate far exceeded the total number of captured, which, even by July 26, had amounted to only 12,153, of whom around 10 per cent were not German. Impressed Russians and Poles predominated, who took 'an early opportunity of giving up the fight'.

Le Régiment de la Chaudière, the brigade's reserve unit, began to land at Bernières about 0830. Its craft had a difficult time with the beach obstacles. Captain Otway-Ruthven described A Company's experience: 'The LCAs of the 529th Flotilla (HMCS *Prince David*) struck a very bad patch of obstacles and mortar fire on Nan White and all foundered before touching down. The troops, however, discarded their equipment and swam for the shore. They still had their knives and were quite willing to fight with this weapon.' This was only a slight exaggeration; Canadian naval records indicate that just one of *Prince David*'s five assault craft made the beach undamaged. Luckily, most of the men reached it safely. The battalion, however, was held up along the sea-wall for some time while the Queen's Own Rifles finished dealing with the strong point. It then advanced through the village, meeting opposition, and assembled in the wooded area on its south edge. The people of Bernières were surprised and delighted to find themselves liberated by men who spoke their own tongue. The regiment's diarist wrote: 'Les français sont assez accueillants et beaucoup nous acclament au milieu des ruines de leurs maisons'. Two years later, the present writer, visiting Bernières, found the recollection of Le Régiment de la Chaudière still strong among the people of the village.

Two gaps through the obstacles should have been cleared by H+75 minutes, but by the time the two units concerned (No. 5 Field Company, RCE, and No. 262 Field Company, RE) had arrived, the tide was too high. Of the AVRE breaching teams, No. 1 Troop landed late and, because the infantry were already on the beach, Petard operations were limited. The first Flail reached the sea-wall to the west of the strong point followed by an assault bridge, but the first AVRE over hit a mine and blocked the exit *(above)*. Two Flails then cleared a second path where the sea-wall had broken down.

On clearance of obstacles, the story on the 8th Brigade beach was much the same as on the 7th's. By the time the engineers arrived, the tide was too high to permit much work on them. 'It was obvious from the outset', recorded No. 80 Assault Squadron, RE, 'that beach obstacles could not be cleared'. Neither the sappers nor the naval Landing Craft Obstacle Clearance Units were able to make headway with the task until the tide fell.

Four beach exits were planned for the brigade front: two at the village of Bernières and two between Bernières and St Aubin. The set of the tide caused most of the engineers' craft to touch down some distance east of their planned positions. In the Bernières area, the high sea-wall caused some trouble, which was made worse by the effects of enemy fire. However, four exits were opened here by the 5th Assault Regiment, RE, one with the aid of a 'small box girder' assault bridge placed over the wall by an AVRE; one at a point where the wall had been broken down; one by clearing an obstructed ramp, and one in a manner not described.

This well-known sequence, taken by the Canadian photographer, Lieutenant Gilbert Milne, has often been used to illustrate the first touch down but, as we can see, the No. 1 Troop assault bridge is now in place and the mined AVRE has been cleared. Also, the troops coming ashore are the Stormont, Dundas and Glengarry Highlanders which formed part of the reserve 9th Brigade which did not arrive until 1140. The battalion commented that 'the damage to the village [Bernières] is not as great as we imagined it might have been'. Points of interest are the prominent timbered house on the foreshore which still stands, and the railway station (with the white name board on its end wall) which also survives but is hidden in the comparison *(below)* behind the new building. The planned exit for No. 2 Team was some 400 yards to the east (left) near the strong point, but instead they landed several hundred yards beyond that, almost on Nan Red. (See map page 503.)

All alone on Nan White early on D-Day 1994, Karel matched the comparison, lacking only an LSI for extra height.

Lieutenant Milne had sailed to Normandy aboard LCI 306 (part of the 1st Canadian Flotilla) embarking the North Nova Scotia Highlanders and the Highland Light Infantry of Canada, all of the 9th Brigade, but when they arrived the exits had still not been properly cleared.

Have bicycle . . . will travel: then and now on Nan White.

THE RESERVE BRIGADE LANDS

While the 7th and 8th Brigades were fighting their way forward, the craft carrying the reserve brigade, the 9th, were circling offshore waiting their turn to go in. At 1050, divisional headquarters ordered the brigade to land. As was natural in the state of the beaches, it was sent in through the 8th Brigade sector in accordance with the primary plan. However, it was considered necessary to land the entire brigade on Nan White beach. (Craft had been diverted from Nan Red since about 1030, since 'the craft casualties were getting serious'; the opposition still being offered by the St Aubin strong point may also have had some influence.) This meant that the whole brigade had to land through Bernières and make its way southward over one road only, that leading to Bény-sur-Mer.

The battalions actually began to land about 1140. At 1205, brigade headquarters reported, 'beaches crowded, standing off waiting to land'; but 15 minutes later it signalled that the brigade commander had landed and the units were moving to their assembly area near Bény. However, the 8th Brigade's slow progress and the severe congestion around Bernières retarded the movement. The battalions halted on the outskirts of the village, and The North Nova Scotia Highlanders (Lieutenant-Colonel C. Petch) who were in the lead, did not move on towards Bény until 1605. They were accompanied by the 27th Armoured Regiment (The Sherbrooke Fusiliers Regiment), commanded by Lieutenant-Colonel M. B. K. Gordon, and were followed by the other battalions of the brigade, The Stormont, Dundas and Glengarry Highlanders (Lieutenant-Colonel G. H. Christiansen) and The Highland Light Infantry of Canada (Lieutenant-Colonel F. M. Griffiths).

Meanwhile, the Régiment de la Chaudière (8th Brigade) records that it spent two hours in the assembly area (it reported itself still there at 1356) and then pushed southward towards Bény-sur-Mer, supported by A Squadron of the 10th Armoured Regiment. Traffic congestion slowed the advance. A Company captured a battery described, apparently inaccurately, as consisting of 88mm guns and, evidently somewhat later, B Company took what may have been the position known as the Bény-

The Highland Light Infantry of Canada: 'A number of LCAs from the assault wave were lying under water where they had hit mines. The beach itself was in a terrible confusion. There was only about 25 yards of beach in front of the promenade which was heavily wired, so there were only the exits put up by the Beach Group. The beaches were jammed, troops with bicycles, vehicles and tanks all trying to move towards the exits. It was an awful shambles. One gun ranged on the beach would have done untold damage, but the brigade landed without a shot fired on them.' Note the SBG bridge mid-way along on the left. The Shermans probably belong to the Sherbrooke Fusiliers (27th Armoured Regiment), attached to 9th Brigade. When the tide receded, the engineers managed to clear 1,800 yards of beach by 2200.

Above: **The station at Bernières is one of the significant landmarks of the Juno battlefield; fortunately, although the track has been lifted, the building remains, now taken over by the local Office de Tourisme.** *Bottom:* **This shot shows the opposite side and the end of the anti-tank ditch.**

sur-Mer battery. Bény-sur-Mer itself was captured by C Company, apparently about mid-afternoon, though the actual time seems nowhere to have been recorded.

The two self-propelled artillery regiments employed on the 8th Brigade front, the 14th Field Regiment and the 19th Army Field Regiment, Royal Canadian Artillery, began to land at 0925 and 0910 respectively. They had no great difficulty in getting off the beach. The 14th had 18 guns in action near Bernières by 1130; the 19th had its first gun in action at 0920. Both regiments had casualties in men and guns from enemy artillery fire. It appears that both spent most of the day in action in improvised gun areas close to Bernières. In the evening, the 14th, at least, moved forward to a planned area a mile or so north of Bény.

Above right: **The Régiment de la Chaudière cross the railway line on their way to Bény-sur-Mer, a rather ambiguous name for a village which is situated five kilometres from the coast. The railway station lies just out of the picture to the left.** *Right:* **The road along which they are advancing has now been renamed Rue du Régiment de la Chaudière in their honour.**

Major-General R. F. L. Keller, the commander of the Canadian 3rd Division, had left HMS *Hilary* with part of his staff at 1145, and divisional headquarters was set up in a small orchard at Bernières. Here, at 1435, General Keller held a conference which was attended by the commanders of the 8th and 9th Infantry Brigades and the 2nd Armoured Brigade. No changes of plan resulted. It was confirmed that the North Shore Regiment was having trouble in Tailleville and that the 8th Brigade would push on to take Bény-sur-Mer, while the 9th would pass through it on the GOC giving the codeword 'Kingston'.

At 2115, General Keller sent out his orders for the night by liaison officer. The 7th Brigade on the right was to occupy the area Le Fresne-Camilly—Cainet. The 8th was to hold the area Colomby-sur-Thaon—Anguerny and to contain La Délivrande and Douvres-la-Délivrande with a view to clearing them both at first light in the morning. The 9th Brigade was to occupy the area Villons-les-Buissons—Le Vey. This was generally equivalent to ordering the brigades to hold the ground on which they found themselves.

Above: **The other symbolic building, which appears in so many Juno pictures, is the large timbered house on the esplanade; it also still survives although the adjacent one just to its rear has been demolished** *(bottom).*

Major-General Rod Keller, the GOC, Canadian 3rd Infantry Division, came ashore on Nan White at 1310 on D-Day to set up his HQ in a grove of trees at Bernières.

That night, General Keller's forces prepared for the inevitable counter-attack. To have had maximum effect, it should have been mounted on D-Day itself but, as we have seen, the opportunity for a swift counter-blow was lost. At 0645 on June 7, OB West made Panzergruppe West operational, being responsible for the area between the Orne and Vire rivers (i.e. covering Omaha to Sword). However, Panzergruppe West did not assume command until 2100 on June 9 and, as we have seen (page 72-75), its HQ was dealt a fatal blow the following day.

Meanwhile, it was the 12. SS-Panzer-Division which was preparing to give the Canadians a surprise. Brana Radovic did the impossible and pinpointed this cover shot (taken by SS-Kriegsberichter Zschäckel) of SS-Schütze Otto Funk of SS-Panzergrenadier-Regiment 25 to a small alleyway in the village of Rots in the direct path of the Canadian advance to the airfield at Carpiquet and the high ground south of Caen. This is one of a series of pictures taken by accredited war photographers Zschäckel and Wilfried Woscidlo.

WAR DIARY, 7. ARMEE, JUNE 6, 1944

The enemy launched a large-scale attack in the early hours between the Seine estuary and the Cherbourg peninsula. Following an attack from midnight by large forces of enemy bombers against coastal defences, especially against coastal batteries, paratroop and glider forces came down in strength from 0030 hours on either side of the Orne estuary, at Caen and Bayeux and on either side of the Vire, as well as around Carentan and Ste Mère-Eglise.

At 0115 hours, the Army ordered the immediate implementation of Alarm State II for the sector of LXXXIV. A.K. [Armeekorps] *and of Alarm State I for the sectors of the other corps and II. Fallschirmjäger Korps. The Army staff was also alerted.*

Following a report to the Army commander, the Chief-of-Staff gave the following provisional situation report to H.Gr. B [Heeresgruppe B] *at 0215 hours: all indications are that the focal point of the enemy's airborne assault is on 716. I.D.* [Infanterie-Division] *in the southern sector of the east coast of Cotentin and in the Carentan narrows. In contrast to the view of H.Gr. B and OB West, the Chief-of-Staff considers the airborne landings a prelude to greater enemy action and requests that 91. I.D. be subordinated to the Army. This subordination is approved and the Army attached 91. I.D. to LXXXIV. A.K.*

By means of subsequent heavy on-going landings from the air, the enemy has been reinforced, especially in the area of the Orne estuary (Caen) and Ste Mère-Eglise. Following a report from the commander of LXXXIV. A.K., G.R. [Grenadier-Regiment] *915 (of 352. I.D.) in corps reserve has been committed to engage enemy airborne forces in the Carentan area, with orders to establish and maintain contact across Carentan. Contact with Ste Mère-Eglise has been lost.*

In the opinion of the Chief-of-Staff, the enemy seems to intend cutting off the Cotentin peninsula at its narrowest point.

21. Pz.Div. [Panzer-Division] *was alerted by H.Gr. B and committed at 05.00 hours, being placed at the same time under the command of the Army and directed at the airborne landing area by the Orne estuary, with its main effort to the east of the Orne.*

At 0515 hours, the Chief-of-Staff gave a further evaluation of the situation to H.Gr. B:

The depth of penetration (up to 20 km) of enemy glider landings on the Orne and in the south-eastern part of the Cherbourg peninsula and the taking of the crossings over the Carentan—Pont-l'Abbé channels, coupled with defined maritime targets off the Orne estuary between Port-en-Bessin and the Vire estuary as well as to the north of Cherbourg and to the north of the Jobourg peninsula point to an imminent landing and large-scale attack against Normandy.

The following counter-measures were taken to dislodge enemy airborne bridgeheads established in the early hours of the morning:

a) counter-attack by 21. Pz.Div. to clear the area to the east of the Orne,
b) Kampfgruppe Meyer (G.R. 915, 352. I.D.) is to fight and clear the area Isigny—Carentan,
c) by means of a counter-attack by 709. I.D. with subordinated G.R. 1058 (of 91. I.D.), the clearing of the area to the east of the dyke line Carentan—Le Ham,
d) counter-attack by 91. I.D. with G.R. 1057 and parts of Panzer-Ersatz und Ausbildungs Abteilung 100 to effect the clearing of the area to the west of the dyke line Carentan—Le Ham. (Enemy strength from Carentan to the north as far as Montebourg is estimated at approximately one division),
e) Schnelle Brigade 30 to be moved towards Périers,
f) disposition of 243. I.D. in accordance with the report of the commander of LXXXIV. A.K. in such a way that it can be committed to the east while leaving protection on the coast.

The focal point of the airborne assault turned out by 06.00 hours to be the area of the Orne estuary and the south-eastern part of Cotentin. Given the depth of the enemy dropping zone, it must be taken into account that a heavier attack is to follow in conjunction with the expected sea landing. At the present time, it cannot be ascertained whether this is a major attack or feint and secondary attack.

From 0530 hours, the enemy suddenly opened fire on the coastal defences along the whole Calvados front with several hundred naval guns. From 0600 hours, the seaborne landing began, with its main thrust between the Orne and Vire estuaries. The enemy landing occurred shortly after low tide with the result that the operation on the level beach was not hindered by the foreshore obstructions, which remained uncovered by the sea. Our minefields were detonated ahead of the main combat zone by the enemy's use of new forms of mortars, carpet bombing and heavy fire from naval guns. Due to massive superiority in the air and at sea, the enemy managed to get through strong points and resistance nests in a surprisingly short space of time and thrust relatively fast deep into the main battle zone. Under cover of smoke screen, large numbers of tanks were suddenly brought forward which enabled the enemy to pass between our all-round defensive positions and achieve surprise penetration into our artillery positions.

By midday, the enemy had thus managed to establish a beach-head, 25 km wide and 5 km deep from the estuary of the Orne north to Ryes. At this time, 21. Pz.Div. was attached to 716. I.D. and the bringing up in the Caen sector of 12. SS-Pz.Div. and of staff of XXXXVII. Pz.Korps was requested to Heeresgruppe B. The Army further requested the clearing of the position to the east of the Orne by units of 711. I.D. and also heavy air strikes against the beach-head to the west of the Orne estuary.

In the sector of 352. I.D., small beach-heads were cleared, only Colleville-sur-Mer was contested. For the main part, this coastal defence sector is firmly held by our coastal defence forces.

While counter-attacks by 91. I.D. with support by Fallsch.Jg.Rgt. 6 against major concentrations of enemy airborne forces to the north of Carentan and around Ste Mère-Eglise were developing, the enemy managed to effect a seaborne break-through by tanks in the Madeleine coastal defence sub-sector with the object of linking up with the airborne bridgehead at Ste Mère-Eglise.

During the afternoon of D-Day, German armour had probed the gap between Juno and Sword but it was not until the Canadians reached Buron early on D+1 that they ran into serious opposition. Some of the Sherbrooke Fusiliers' tanks bypassed the village and actually came within sight of the airfield — their objective — before the 12. SS hit them with a battalion of PzKpfw IVs and SS-Standartenführer Kurt Meyer's three battalions of panzergrenadiers. He had watched the Canadians approach from the Abbaye, and by mid-afternoon the opposing forces were locked in their first major battle of the invasion.

Looking back up the alley, we see SS-Unterscharführer Wick (with the field glasses), who was a member of the 15. (Aufklärungs) Kompanie — the reconnaissance arm of SS-Panzer-grenadier-Regiment 25.

As a further measure, the Army ordered the Kampfgruppe of 275. I.D. to readiness at Alarm State I and the one of 265. I.D. at State II for move to the sector of LXXXIV. A.K. The deployment of 266. I.D. and 77. I.D. still seems premature as the arrival of transport gliders in Brittany renders the development of the situation in this area unclear. The Chief-of-Staff has further ordered Alarm State II in the zone of LXXIV. A.K.

Since, at 1500 hours on day one of the attack, the situation in the Calvados sector is proving critical and cannot be maintained with local reserves, the assignment of I. SS-Pz.Korps with corps troops as well as 12. SS-Pz.Div. and Pz.Lehr-Div. into action against the bridgehead in the sector of 716. I.D. ensues on the proposal of the Army through H.Gr. B.

The Army has accordingly issued the following operational order:

a) I. SS-Pz.Korps will be deployed to the right next to LXXXIV. A.K.; the boundary line to be the right flank of 352. I.D.,

b) the corps will take command of 716. I.D., 21. Pz.Div. and 12. SS-Pz.Div.,

c) the corps has the order, while cordoning off the eastern bank, to attack and throw back into the sea those enemy units which have broken through to the west of the Orne.

12. SS-Pz.Div. to transfer immediately north of the line Alençon—Flers in the area either side of Evrecy. Pz.Lehr-Div. to move simultaneously south of the said line to reach initially the area Flers—Vire.

Meanwhile, 21. Pz.Div. has with its forward sections arrived to the north of Caen and awaits imminent contact with the enemy.

By late evening, the Germans had entered Buron and captured a number of troops from the North Nova Scotia Highlanders. Officially, the Canadian total of losses was 84 killed and 158 wounded or taken prisoner but, of the latter, over 20 were shot out of hand after surrendering, bringing the first excesses to the battlefield. The Fusiliers had lost 21 Shermans but claimed to have accounted for 30 to 35 enemy tanks. Meanwhile, the Royal Winnipeg Rifles had reached Putot, just west of Bretteville, on the far side of the Caen–Bayeux road. On the morning of June 8, they were attacked by SS panzergrenadiers, who encircled and captured most of the battalion, and again it was later discovered that over 40 Winnipeggers taken prisoner had been shot in cold blood, creating a no-holds-barred situation between the Canadians and the 12. SS-Panzer-Division.

A mile to the east, and in the early evening, the panzergrenadiers then attempted to overrun the Regina Rifles who were by now established in the key town astride the Caen–Bayeux highway with the tongue-twisting name: Bretteville-l'Orgueilleuse. Lieutenant-Colonel J. M. Meldram, the Winnipeg Rifles' commanding officer, takes up the story: 'Some tanks continued forward to Bretteville to within about 300 yards of battalion headquarters. There they remained for one and a half hours, shelling and machine gunning the town. About midnight, two Panthers entered the town. One came opposite battalion headquarters and was struck by a PIAT bomb fired from behind a low stone wall at 15 yards range, safe from the tank's huge gun. It halted for a moment, started again and after 30 yards was hit again by a second PIAT bomb. It stopped, turned around and headed out of town. A third PIAT hit finished it off so that it slewed around, out of control, running over a necklace of No. 75 grenades which blew off a track. The crew dismounted and attempted to make off, but were killed by small-arms fire. During this incident, the second Panther had remained further up the road. Seeing the fate of its companion, it commenced to fire both 75mm and MG wildly down the street "like a child in a tantrum", doing no damage whatsoever except to set fire to the first Panther.' This picture, taken by Lieutenant Don I. Grant, shows the PIAT gunners of the Regina Rifles who knocked out the tank. L–R: Riflemen J. E. Lapointe and G. A. Carmie and Lance-Corporal C. V. Hewitt. (Note that there were two Canadian photographers named Grant operating in Normandy at this time — the other being Sergeant W. G. Grant who landed at 0900 on D-Day with the Canadian 12th Field Regiment.)

The Chief-of-Staff reports to H.Gr. B. at 1620 hours with an up-dated overall impression of the current situation:

At the point of break-through, strong enemy forces are present. Operationally there is at present still no particular cause for concern since, to cut off Normandy, the east coast of Cotentin has still to be taken. Cotentin can probably be cleared with our forces. It is noticeable that here airborne troops have been committed without direct support from the sea. There is the suggestion of a possible feint attack, which is supposed to divert our forces.

Since 1630 hours, the enemy has carried out heavy follow-up landings from the sea in the Madeleine sector and in the Vire estuary and reinforced himself to such an extent that contact could be possible with enemy airborne forces in the area of Ste Mère-Eglise. Our own counter-attacks by Fallsch.Jg.Rgt. 6, by reinforced Gren.Rgt. 1057 and by reinforced Gren.Rgt. 1058 (of 91. I.D.) are advancing only slowly through difficult hedge-covered terrain. For this reason, the Army's Sturmbataillon [assault battalion] was additionally committed from the north.

At the same time, the situation has also worsened in the sector of 352. I.D. Here, the enemy has also pushed through the resistance nests with tanks and infantry and its advanced units have reached the Colleville-sur-Mer—Louvières—Asnières line. The direction of the thrust appears to be aimed at Bayeux, which the enemy is also trying to reach from the Calvados bridgehead. Upon this, the Army ordered the Kampfgruppe of 275. I.D. to be released immediately, with initial transportation by rail from 1900 hours to the Lison—Bayeux area: the unit is to be placed under the command of LXXXIV. A.K. upon arrival. Further rail transport was ordered if possible since insufficient MT was available in the area and disruption from enemy aircraft is not expected initially since they are committed to the coastal sector.

The proposal of the Army commander to 15. Armee that parts of 711. I.D. be committed to attack airborne forces between Dives and the Orne has, following initial rejection through the 15. Armee commander, been approved by H.Gr. B and an attack ordered.

The Army has ordered the transfer by route march of the Kampfgruppe of 265. I.D. to the area of LXXXIV. A.K. The battle group is to be reinforced by the panzerjäger battalion of 353 I.D. and a heavy anti-tank platoon from 265. I.D. and to be conveyed to St Lô by LXXXIV. A.K.

They came this way . . . General Crerar, the Canadian First Army GOC, passes the same Panther from 4. Kompanie of I. Abteilung of SS-Panzer-Regiment 12, still lying where it had been hit, during a visit to front-line troops on June 23.

These pictures were taken in Rots on the afternoon of June 9 after the 3. Kompanie of SS-Panzer-Regiment 12 had been bloodily repulsed from an attack on Norrey, two kilometres from Bretteville. *Left:* SS-Obersturmführer Rudolph von Ribbentrop, son of the German Foreign Minister and commander of the 3. Kompanie, being driven by a bandaged Max Wünsche.

With the arrival of dusk, the enemy is trying by means of massive airborne landings to crush our battle groups which are engaged in a counter-thrust in the Calvados bridgehead. 21. Pz.Div., which in its counter-thrusts had already opened up a narrow corridor to the coast, was prevented from developing the situation further by numerically superior airborne units, which have been freshly dropped, and has been forced over to the defensive.

Because of this situation in the Calvados bridgehead, which is becoming increasingly difficult, Pz.Lehr-Div. is additionally placed under the command of I. SS-Pz.Korps and the following order issued to the corps:

a) having fought itself into a position where it has freedom of movement, 21. Pz.Div. is to continue an attack in the direction of Riva-Bella—Lion-sur-Mer,

b) the combination of 12. SS-Pz.Div. and Pz.Lehr-Div is to attack and destroy as soon as possible the enemy forces which have broken through the Bayeux-Caen road,

c) Flak-Rgt. 32 is assigned to a co-operation rôle.

On the opposite side of the street, the gunner of Panther 326, SS-Rottenführer Gerd Krieger, cleans off the blood after the commander, SS-Unterscharführer Friedrich Eismann, had been decapitated in the turret.

Wünsche, right, with his bandaged head, has just emerged from the alleyway while a Flakpanzer 38(t), most probably from SS-Panzer-Regiment 12, moves through Rots along the N13, eastwards in the direction of Authie and the Abbaye d'Ardenne.

OB West informs the Chief-of-Staff of the demand of OKW that enemy forces in the Calvados bridgehead must be eliminated by the evening of 6.6 and that the chief of Wehrmachtführungsstab, Gen.Ob. Jodl, has ordered a concentration of all available forces at the break-through point. The Chief-of-Staff has explained that, given the vast superiority of enemy forces there, a removal of the bridgehead is no longer possible during the course of this evening. However, all steps have been taken to proceed with a counter-attack as soon as possible.

At 2340 hours, the Army commander informed the commander of H.Gr. B, Feldm. Rommel, of the situation in the army's theatre of operations and requested permission to release the Kampfgruppe of 266. I.D. and of 77. I.D. Feldm. Rommel decided that the Kampfgruppe of 266. I.D. and of 77. I.D. should initially only be placed on stand-by.

With the agreement of OB West, the commander of II. Fliegerkorps, Bülowius, is instructed through Luftflottenkdo. 3 to co-operate immediately with 7. Armee.

We have already briefly touched on the emotive issue of the killing of prisoners (see also page 315). Max Hastings, whose father Macdonald was a war reporter in 1939-45, is himself no stranger to war, having covered several, including the Falklands in 1982. Two years later, he put the whole subject into perspective in his book *Overlord*: 'Much has been made of the shooting of prisoners — most notoriously, Canadian prisoners — by 12th SS Panzer and other German units in Normandy. Yet it must be said that propaganda has distorted the balance of guilt. Among scores of Allied witnesses interviewed for this narrative [*Overlord*], almost every one had direct knowledge or even experience of the shooting of German prisoners during the campaign. In the heat of battle, in the wake of seeing comrades die, many men found it intolerable to send prisoners to the rear knowing that they would thus survive the war, while they themselves seemed to have little prospect of doing so. Many British and American units shot SS prisoners routinely, which explained, as much as the fanatical resistance that the SS so often offered, why so few appeared in PoW cages.'

The Authie–Buron area. Panzergrenadiers bring in captured Canadians who are helping to carry wounded SS men.

Max Hastings: 'Once a definable atrocity had been discovered, as with the bodies of the Canadians killed by 12th SS Panzer, and the conscious decision taken to respond in kind, it is difficult with hindsight to draw a meaningful moral distinction between the behaviour of one side and the other on the battlefield.'

Seven Canadian prisoners of war were murdered in the grounds of Meyer's own regimental headquarters at the Abbaye d'Ardenne during the course of June 8, and another eleven over the following two days. This is the main entrance — revisited by Brana Radovic in 1989 to investigate where the killings took place. (The Jeep is Malcolm Fisher's.)

The battlegroup commanded by SS-Obersturmbannführer Karl-Heinz Milius *(left)* had been the first SS element to make contact with Canadian forces during the battle on June 7. *Above:* Wilhelm Mohnke (whose reputation for meting out callous treatment to prisoners in France went back to 1940); Wünsche, 'Sepp' Dietrich and Kurt Meyer.

Brana retraced the explanation given by a 17-year-old SS despatch rider of Polish origin by the name of Jan Jesionek who had witnessed the killings of the seven prisoners on June 8 and who testified later at the trial of Kurt Meyer. Brana: 'Jesionek, waiting for his motorbike to be repaired, saw the prisoners being marched into the Abbaye grounds and bustled into a stable *(right)* under the watchful eye of an escort of two soldiers from SS-Panzergrenadier-Regiment 25, and it was he who led one of the guards into the old chapel of the Abbaye to report the arrival of the prisoners to Meyer. He was perceptibly angered by the arrival of the prisoners. "Why do you bring prisoners to the rear?" he asked the guard. "They only eat up our rations." Meyer turned to another officer standing nearby and spoke to him briefly in tones too low for Jesionek to catch. Then he announced in a voice loud enough for all to hear: "In future no more prisoners are to be taken!" The officer and the guard then left the chapel and made their way towards the stable where the prisoners were being kept. Jesionek followed them as far as the stable courtyard.'

'He had intended to take a wash at the water pump there, but he was directed instead to the concrete pool near an archway leading to a garden, and from there he had a perfect view of the prisoners, who were being interrogated one at a time in English by the officer at the stable entrance.'

Jesionek's testimony related that 'one of the prisoners had tears in his eyes, and the officer laughed at him in a sneering manner. The officer seemed to be enjoying himself and frequently burst out laughing as he spoke to the prisoners. He took their papers from them and returned to the chapel. The guard who had spoken to Meyer took up position at the archway leading to the garden. Each of the seven prisoners was then called by name and in turn had to walk from the stable entrance to where the guard was at the archway. They were then directed up some steps and into the garden. Here, each made a left turn, and as he did so an Unterscharführer, who had previously gone into the garden and was awaiting the prisoners, shot him in the back of the head. As each of the prisoners came out of the stable, he shook hands with the others before walking into the garden. They all seemed to know what was about to happen, and the sound of the shots and occasionally a scream could be clearly heard.' The Vico family (see page 460) had returned to the Abbaye in August, but it was not until December that Michel, while playing in the garden, found what appeared to be a human jaw bone. A piece of disturbed ground was investigated by the civil authorities in February 1945 and it was found to contain the remains of six Canadian soldiers. All had been posted missing on June 7. Over the following months, four more unmarked graves were discovered, bringing the total of bodies found to 18. In the meantime, Jan Jesionek had reported what he had witnessed to the Canadian authorities. The call went out to find the man whose headquarters had been there in June 1944, and Kurt Meyer was indicted and brought to trial at Aurich, Germany, in December 1945. His death sentence was commuted and he was released in September 1954. Before he died in 1961, Meyer returned to his former HQ, where Jean-Marie accompanied him to the garden. There, Meyer concurred with what had happened, but said it was difficult for an officer to admit such things to an enemy court.

Back to D-Day and the 8th Brigade landings. The assault craft of The North Shore Regiment (New Brunswick) under Lieutenant-Colonel D. B. Buell, were to land on the left flank of Nan sector on Red Beach. The latter stretched from La Rive in the west to include St Aubin-sur-Mer further to the east. The village of St Aubin backed right onto the sea-shore and comprised mainly masonry buildings with slate or tile roofs. Several houses at the western end had all their windows bricked up on the seaward side, and some had walls strengthened by internal sandbags at floor level, beneath the windows, to provide facilities and protection for snipers. The central defence position was WN 27 — located on Allied intelligence maps at grid reference 014851 — its 50mm anti-tank gun *(above)* having exceptional command of the beach.

On the left sector of the 8th Brigade front (Nan Red), the North Shore Regiment found that the St Aubin strong point 'appeared not to have been touched' by the preparatory bombardment. B Company had the task of dealing with it, and this was done with the assistance of the tanks and later the AVREs, which used their Petards with effect. 'The co-operation of infantry and tanks was excellent and the strong point was gradually reduced.' The battalion diary records that the area was cleared by 1115, four hours and five minutes after landing. It appears, however, that there was still sniping going on after this time, and the OC B Company stated that the enemy in the strong point did not finally give in until 1800.

The 50mm anti-tank gun in the resistance nest here caused serious trouble in the early stages of the assault. B Company's commander recorded that it knocked out the first DD tanks to arrive (as already indicated, no real attempt was made to swim the DD Shermans in; they came off their LCTs close inshore behind the leading infantry) and subsequently two other tanks and an AVRE dealt with it. The Special Observer Party reported that the concrete of the emplacement bore the mark of a 95mm shell, evidently fired by a Centaur. The gun had been put out of action by tank fire, but 'about 70 empty shell cases' around the emplacement attested the resolution with which its crew had fought it.

The North Shore's A Company, landing to the west of B Company, suffered some casualties in booby-trapped houses, but in general made good the beach-head objective without great difficulty. The reserve C and D Companies likewise had comparatively little trouble in the beginning. D Company carried out its task of securing the south end of St Aubin, and C Company, which was to seize the inland village of Tailleville, met no opposition until it reached the actual outskirts. Here the enemy, well dug in, fought long and hard; in spite of early optimistic reports, it was 'nearing evening' before the company, with tank support, finally cleared the place, taking over 60 prisoners. Divisional headquarters logged the report of its capture at 2010 hours.

Jean Paul Pallud's comparison shows a scene virtually unchanged save for the omission of the DD tank and the Thunderbolt which force-landed on the beach.

The 5cm gun position was the subject of a water-colour by Captain O. N. Fisher — Jean Paul matching it in September 1993.

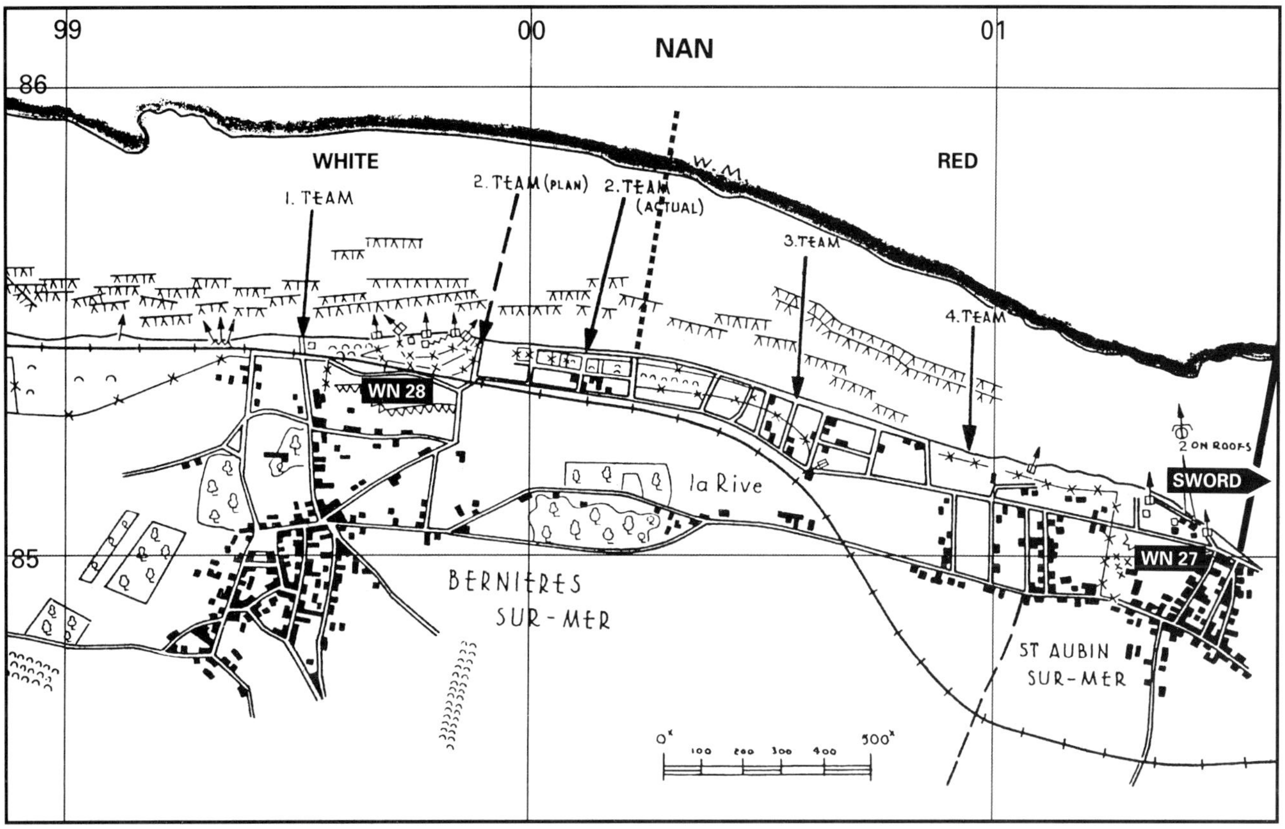

The strong point held out for several hours against B Company, all the time bringing heavy fire on the beach and, in the end, the company had to call for armoured support. The commander of the 5th Assault Regiment, RE, late wrote that 'the pillbox and the compartment beneath it in the cliff were destroyed by Petard and some houses were silenced by both Petard and 75mm gun-fire'. At 1115, the area was finally cleared with 48 prisoners having been taken and an equivalent number believed killed. Apart from the anti-tank gun enfilading the beach, the St Aubin strong point included several positions for machine guns and 8·1cm mortars. We have heard mention of mortar pits several times in our narrative; this is what they looked like. *Right:* Inspecting a mortar position at St Aubin (we could not find any trace of it today), and, *below*, two kinds of pit at Courseulles (WN 31 and WN 29).

The grid references given (refer to the map on page 468) for anyone keen enough to put a spade in the ground, are 965858 for the mortar pit *(left)*, described as 'West Courseulles No. 9 with mount and aiming points', and 973857 for the '5ft diameter Tobruk-type machine gun post, East Courseulles No. 11' *(right)*.

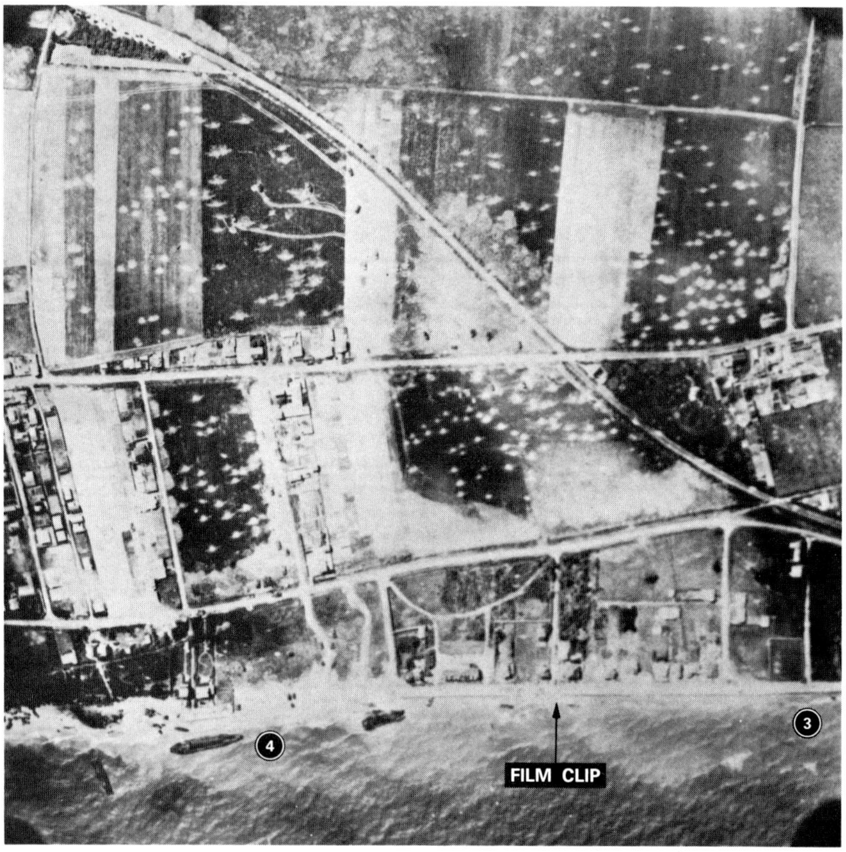

We sent Robert Voskuil, armed with a set of stills and his own camera, to walk along Nan and Mike sectors until he found the same houses. He struck 'gold' on Nan Red at La Rive, proving that the film shows men of either A or B Companies of the North Shore Regiment which touched down at 0805. The breaching teams from Nos. 3 and 4 Troops of the 80th Assault Squadron, RE, preceded their landing by 25 minutes. The planned breaching positions are shown, but it is not clear from the records whether No. 3 Troop [3] actually completed their gap at the projected place. No. 4 Troop touched down 150 yards east of their target [4]. (Note the swathe of rocket strikes behind the first lateral road.)

The moment of reality . . . the armoured doors to the landing craft open . . . the ramp drops . . . It is a film sequence that all of us remotely interested in D-Day have seen replayed over and over again . . . but the question for us: where exactly was it taken? The earliest use of the clip, which in its edited form runs for only a few seconds, is in *The True Glory*, SHAEF's own documentary premièred in August 1945. Back on page 473, we described the beginnings of Major Stevens' involvement in its production in January 1944. On March 3, he submitted a draft script to Colonel Lawrence with the tentative title *A Single Instrument* based on a phrase taken from a speech in the script written 'in anticipation of a statement of the character of General Eisenhower'. Five days later, the Joint Anglo-American Film Planning Committee was formed to facilitate collaboration between Major Stevens' special coverage unit and the British Army Film and Photographic Unit. It was jointly agreed that a full-length film *Assault on the Continent* should be made with a new script although 'it was impossible at this point to decide where the film should end, or what date it should be released'. After many months of trans-Atlantic discussion and argument as to what was to be included to give an even balance and avoid a repetition of the earlier slight against the Canadians, the film was finally released under the 'sponsorship' of SHAEF as *The True Glory*. This film clip is included and one has the impression that it is the *British* 3rd Division landing on Sword that is depicted . . . but we would be wrong. The original footage, taken with a camera in a fixed position on the LCA, emanates from Canada: ergo it must show one of the landings on Juno.

It is possible that the gaps through the minefields were not completely cleared, for at H+45 minutes (0840), C Squadron of the 10th Armoured Regiment reported: 'By now the support companies of infantry are coming in and the assault RE had still made no gaps, so the squadron leader made the decision to push through the minefield himself. This he did, losing three more tanks but he led the remainder through.' The 558th LCA Flotilla, RM, which brought in A and B Companies of the North Shore Regiment, said that 'troops were put down into 1 foot 6 inches to 2 feet of water. All troops were put ashore and, although looking very green, went off in good order, the majority calmly walking up the beach and getting under the shelter of the sea-wall.' The infantry themselves said they crossed the beach itself with only a few casualties, though an officer and several other ranks became casualties in houses along the beach which had been booby-trapped. A Company reached the line of the beach-head at 0948, having incurred 24 casualties.

'To you who now, living in love and hope, who sense the future in the surrounding air, this testament is offered. Here you may look on the violent fragments of our age, and the once-thinness of the little thread that made us then the citizens of freedom. For dark was Europe, and the face of man, when this begins . . . ' The opening lines of SHAEF's film, first heard by your Editor at school in the 1950s, struck a deep chord: who were those men and where precisely was it that they dashed forward to assault Hitler's 'Fortress Europe'?

Fifty years later, thanks to Robert's diligence, all is revealed. 'Now the time has come to put our victory to the tests of peace . . . in company with men of many lands to sift from ashes what the struggle taught. In the rebuilding of a broken earth, may we keep in our hearts this ancient prayer: "O Lord God. We now givest to thy servants to endeavour any great matter. Grant to us also to know that it is not the beginning, but the continuing of the same until it be thoroughly finished . . . which yieldeth . . . The True Glory".'

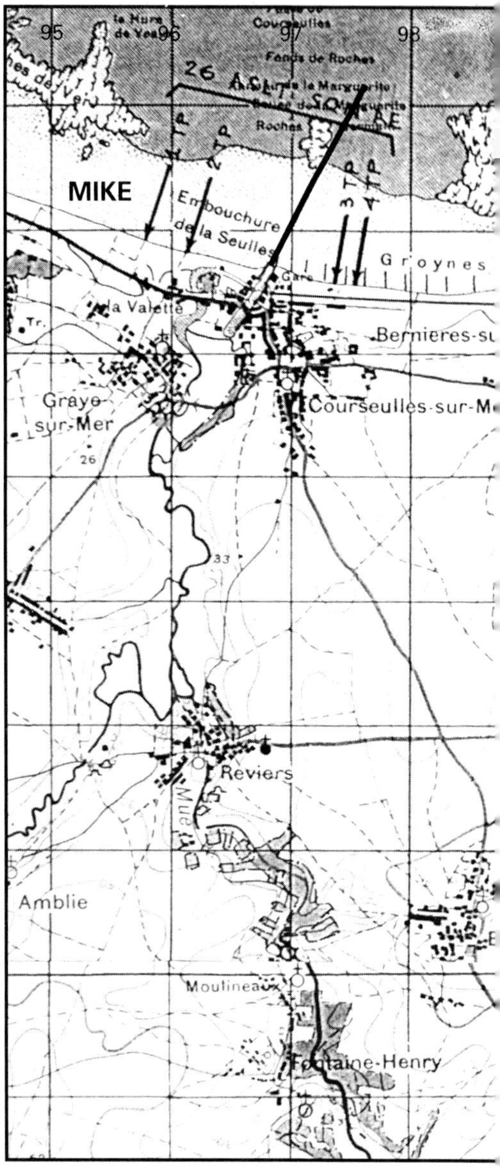

A quarter of a mile to the west of *The True Glory* 'set', there was anything but glory for the 500 Royal Marines of No. 48 Commando. Their disastrous landing at St Aubin, under the guns of WN 27, reduced their strength by 50 per cent, some three-quarters of the losses occurring on the beach. They landed close to the boundary between Nan sector with Oboe, but let us allow the commanding officer, Lieutenant-Colonel James Moulton, to explain what happened: 'Between the Canadian 3rd Division on Juno beach and the British 3rd Division on Sword beach, there was a gap of five miles, caused by a reef off the coast which prevented landings; No. 48 Commando was to land immediately behind the North Shore Regiment, the left battalion of the Canadians, wheel left, and clear the beach defences opposite the reef — until it met No. 41 Commando, who would be doing the same thing, coming the other way, after landing behind the right battalion of the British 3rd Division. We were to meet at a group of houses on the stream which runs through a village, engagingly called Petit Enfer. Our landing, at the village of St Aubin, would be covered by the North Shore Regiment and, of course, by the enormous number of bombs and shells which were to precede the whole landing. When we started off on our task, a squadron of light support craft would work along the shore ready to support us.' The Marines' flotilla moved towards the shore at 0730 with the easternmost landing craft almost opposite the strong point (014851) and perhaps 200 yards from the northernmost craft. The Commandos landed at 0843, HQ of the 4th SS Brigade *(above)* following at 0900.

When the Brigadier, Bernard 'Jumbo' Leicester [the OC of 4th Special Service Brigade], *had finished, I* [Lieutenant-Colonel James Moulton] *took over and described my plan. As we should not be under fire when we landed, and as our transport would not be available for the first day, we would land carrying a fairly heavy load of ammunition and explosives. We would dump this at St Aubin and then, lightly equipped, would move down a road parallel to the shore to Langrune. This would be our firm base, and from it we would tackle the coast defences from the rear.*

As we closed the beach, Lieutenant-Commander G. C. L. Timmermans [commanding the LCIs carrying the commandos] *and I tried to pick up the beach signs and beach parties. The beach seemed confused and they were difficult to spot, but it was clear that there were a lot of people there, and we could see some signs of work on the beach exit, to the right of the houses. Now we were very close. No one seemed to be shooting at us. It was probably all right. Our motion checked sharply, and Timmermans swore as we hung rolling on the beach obstacle we had fouled; then a wave caught our stern, swung us, and carried us forward to beach at a bad angle and rolling. As we struck the obstacle, the enemy opened fire with mortars and machine guns from the esplanade, a little more than a hundred yards away. The sailors replied with crashing bursts of Oerlikon fire.*

I looked around and saw the other landing craft of the squadron in confusion. Our craft and the three next to us on our left had got through to beach reasonably close in; further left, the other two were hung up on beach obstacles, helpless and well out from the beach. In the noise and confusion, I realised that the enemy were firing at us and that men were being hit. No question now of our smoke upsetting the Canadians' battle or interfering with the work on the beach — that had all too clearly gone very wrong — and I looked for the mortar men to fire the smoke. Thinking that they would not be wanted when we were not fired at on the way in, they had dismounted their mortars and gone forward ready to land. I shouted to them, realised that my voice was powerless against the noise, jumped down from the bridge on the port side and ran forward a few paces to grab one of them by the arm. He looked around, saw me, said something I could not hear, then ran back to the sandbags and started to mount his mortar. Someone had done the same on the starboard side. Back on the bridge, I realised with a sinking heart that the Commando was meeting something like disaster. Then the mortars popped, and seconds later, hissing out of the sky on to the esplanade to windward, came the blessed smoke bombs. The other craft, seeing our smoke, joined in with theirs, and in a minute or two we were in dense white smoke, and the Germans were firing blind.

My adjutant, Captain Dan Flunder, had gone forward to see that there was no delay in landing. When the craft checked on the obstacle and seemed to beach, he and some of Headquarters and Signals helped the sailors to get the first brow out, then started down it. As he led the way, the wave hit the stern, the craft rolled, and the brow, jolted from its rollers, threw him and others on it into the sea.

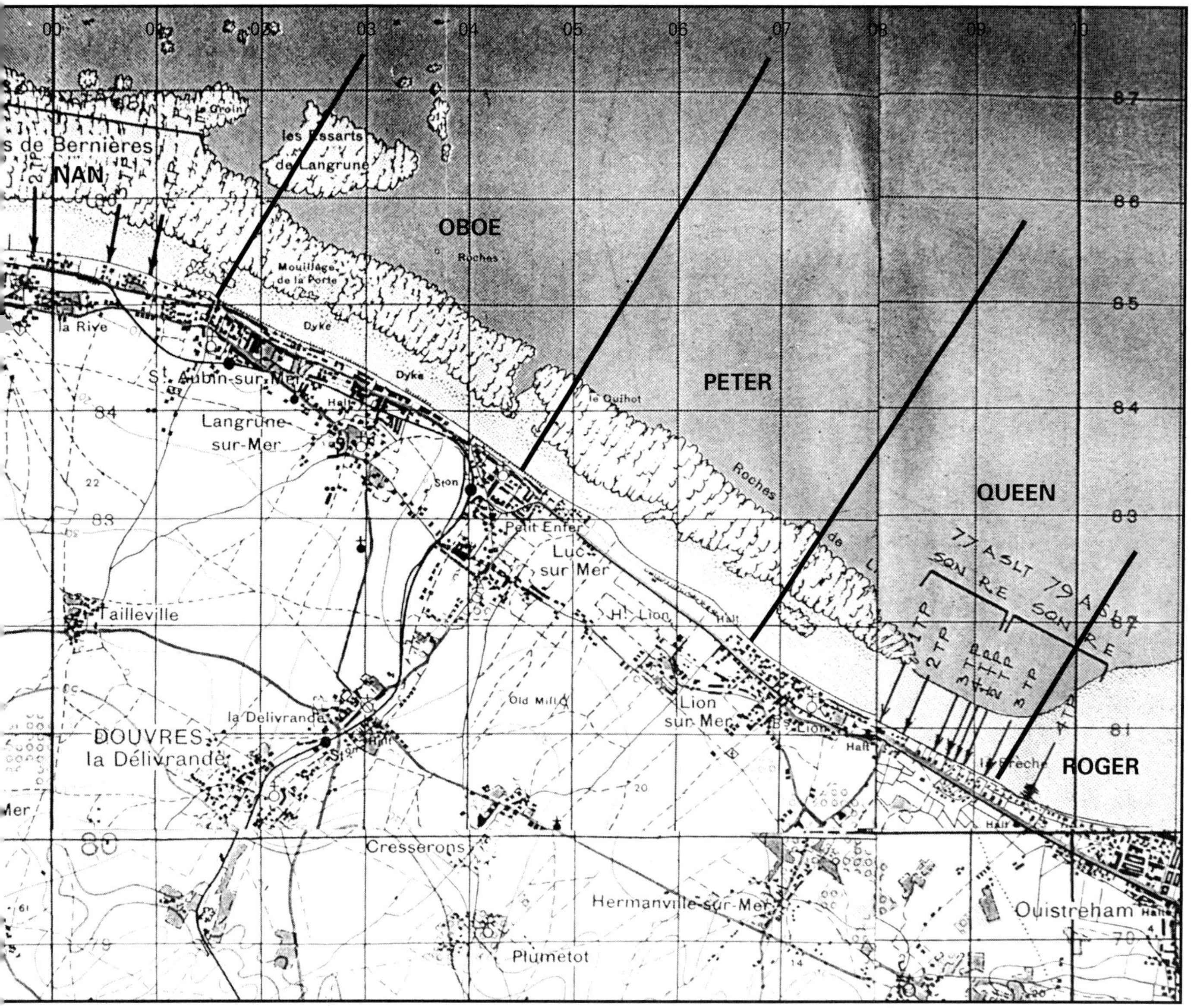
NAN
OBOE
PETER
QUEEN
ROGER
s de Bernières
les Essarts de Langrune
Mouillage de la Porte
la Rive
St. Aubin-sur-Mer
Langrune sur-Mer
Petit Enfer
Luc sur Mer
Tailleville
la Delivrande
DOUVRES la Délivrande
Old Mill
Lion sur Mer
Cresserons
Hermanville-sur-Mer
Plumetot
Ouistreham
77 ASLT SQN R.E
79 ASLT SQN R.E

A squadron of tank landing craft wallowed in to an untidy beaching, hampered by the beach obstacles and our stranded craft. Their steel hulls were less vulnerable to the obstacles than those of our wooden craft, but the beach was getting very congested now, and they seemed to have trouble in beaching. The tanks came out blindly and bogged down in the shingle. Flunder saw one run over some wounded men lying in its path, shouted to it to stop, then, as it paid no attention, deliberately broke one of its tracks with an anti-tank grenade. Other tanks began to burn, with their smoky yellow flames. For the moment we could see no more of our men, so we went back through the taped exit and on to the assembly area: again the contrast from the din and confusion of the beach.

What had gone wrong? First and foremost, the much vaunted pre-H-Hour bombardment was, on our beach, almost completely ineffective. A few days later, I walked around St Aubin and the strong point which had done the damage; I counted two, and only two, houses which had been hit by anything larger than light projectiles. This meant not only that the defenders, in their well-protected defences, were unharmed and unshaken; but that the Canadians, once ashore, found it an exceedingly slow and costly business to get into the esplanade strong point; and did not do so until that evening. We were soon to have similar difficulties. The time allowed for the Canadians to silence the beach defences, before we landed in unarmoured craft, was very short, and in these circumstances quite impossible. We realised this from the first and never had any inclination to blame the Canadians for our bitter medicine.

Secondly, the Landing Craft Infantry (Small) were quite unsuitable and unnecessarily dangerous for landing against beach obstacles or under fire. The gallant leading-seaman, who ferried ashore Z Troop in his assault landing craft, convincingly demonstrated that smaller, lightly armoured craft could negotiate the beach, in spite of its obstacles and fire, with success and without unreasonable risk. There were, it is true, not enough of these craft for everyone to have them; reserve brigades landed in the heavy, steel Landing Craft Infantry (Large). Neither type of landing craft should have been sent forward without first ensuring that the beach was reasonably clear of obstacles and aimed machine gun fire — as far as I know this was done for the larger craft. Any delay which might have been caused by holding back the small infantry landing craft, and if necessary deflecting them or ferrying from them, would in our case have been more than compensated for by our added effectiveness once ashore.

The 4th SS Brigade: 'About 0730 hrs the flotilla moved in towards the shore. At first it appeared that the landing would be unopposed and most craft dismounted the 2in mortars which were prepared to cover the landing with smoke. Then MGs opened up from the strong point at St Aubin, which was almost opposite the easternmost landing craft and perhaps 200 yards from the westernmost and the craft were subjected to mortar and shell-fire. The Z Troop craft received a direct hit amidship. The Oerlikons replied and HQ craft put down smoke on the beach with 2in mortars. 0843 hrs. Beach obstacles had not been cleared and were well below the water when the Commando landed. Two craft (Y and Z Troops) struck obstacles and were unable to beach. HQ craft struck an obstacle but was fairly close inshore. A, B, X and HQ troops were able to wade ashore in about 3 feet of water but Y and Z troops could only get ashore by swimming. Many officers and men attempted to swim ashore from these craft and a high proportion of these were lost from drowning in a strong undertow.'

'On reaching shore, troops made for the cover of the earth cliff and sea-wall. Here they found a confused situation. The cliff and sea-wall gave some protection from SA fire but any movement away from them was under MG fire. The whole area was under heavy mortar and shell-fire. Under the sea-wall was a jumble of men from other units including many wounded and dead. The beach was congested with tanks, SP guns and other vehicles, some out of action, others attempting to move from the beaches in the very confined space between the water's edge and the sea-wall. LCTs were arriving all the time and attempted to land their loads, adding to the general confusion. A quick recce showed that the beach exit to the right of the isolated houses was free from aimed SA fire, except for occasional shots, and that a gap had been cleared through the mines.'

'As this was the quickest way to the assembly area, orders were immediately passed for troops to move out to the assembly area by this route. B Troop led, followed by A Troop, HQ and X Troop. The assembly area was much quieter. The CO returned to the beach to contact X and Z troops. A considerable number of men of mixed troops were found still under the cliff and these were moved off to the right. He found Y Troop attempting to get ashore from an LCT in which they had transferred from their LCI. However, the landing of Y Troop was very slow and few man managed to get ashore before the LCT shoved off, taking with her about 50 men of the Commando to England, despite their energetic protests. Z Troop was more fortunate and about 40 men were eventually collected in the assembly area. In the assembly area it was found on calling for reports that A, B and X troops each had about 50 to 55 men available. HQ had had about 20 casualties but was working satisfactorily. The five men of Y Troop present were joined with Z Troop (about 40).'

Although the house has been replaced, part of the garden wall still survives.

Above: **Although we cannot claim that these pictures of 'troops of the 4th SS Brigade taking cover from sniping at St Aubin-sur-Mer' depict the precise action described by Colonel Moulton, they are *his* men and they *do* illustrate the battle against the strong point so well. Fortunately, Brana Radovic arrived just in the nick of time and took the photograph *below* on the very day in October 1993 that the tell-tale piece of sloping buttress was to be demolished.**

Lieutenant Peter Handford, of No. 5 Army Film and Photographic Unit, took the photographs in 1944, coming ashore with the commando brigade in the first wave at H+25 minutes. This is the Rue Canet leading directly to the sea and the 50mm anti-tank gun we saw on page 502. The DD is from C Squadron of the 10th Armoured Regiment (The Fort Garry Horse) and the range from here about 200 metres. The records state that 'crew commanders directing fire were subjected to sniping' and that, out of the 20 tanks of C Squadron, four had already been lost. Sporadic fighting in St Aubin itself went on for some time, but, 'dominated by the tanks, the infantry soon cleared the town satisfactorily up to a strong point where the enemy held out stubbornly. A troop of tanks was allotted to the infantry here but the strong point held out all day and finally gave in at 2000 hrs that night. The remainder of the squadron helped the infantry on many occasions during that day'.

As we moved through the landward part of St Aubin, we found the Canadians, with a few tanks, vainly trying to fight their way into the esplanade strong point. I saw Lieutenant-Colonel D. B. Buell [CO of the North Shore Regiment], *stopped and exchanged a few words, then we were out of the village and on our own. A Troop was leading as vanguard and I sent B Troop off, to start clearing the sea-front houses.*

On the far and inland side of Langrune, we found the strong old walled farmhouse and garden, which I had selected from the air photographs to hold as a firm base for our house-clearing operations. I ordered Z Troop to organise its defence and X Troop to start on their sector of house clearing. At some time about then, I sent an officer's patrol to our junction point with No. 41 (RM) Commando.

Apart from this, B and X Troops had met nothing but snipers and patrols, which withdrew before their advance; a little later, B Troop rejoined us at the farm, Captain Jim Perry confident and in command of the situation. X Troop reported that it was held up, and then the new troop commander came in to report. Moving along the sea-front, he had reached the St Aubin or west side of Langrune, but could make no further progress. I pressed him for more definite information about what was holding him up, but all he could say was that he was losing a lot of men to snipers. Feeling rather futile, I told him to keep on trying to hunt the snipers out of the houses; and then told Perry, whose confidence I found as reassuring as X Troop Commander's lack of it was depressing, to take B Troop and work down the road leading to the sea-front on the east side of the village, so getting behind whatever it was holding up X Troop. I gave him our one mortar, under Lieutenant Mike Aldworth of S Troop, who had now reached us from the beach, in case he met opposition.

Soon, he reported that he was in contact with the enemy, and Dan Flunder and I went down to have a look. We walked through the back gardens, scrambling over walls and pushing our way through side doors, passed Aldworth starting to range his mortar, and came up with the men of B Troop. They were having a good many casualties from light mortar fire, we could see the tails of the bombs lying about, and I told them to keep inside the houses until they were wanted. At last, we reached a house where we were told Perry was, and were directed upstairs to find him in the loft. I started to haul myself up through the hatch, but my arm and shoulder felt very sore from mortar bomb splinters, so I stood with my head and shoulders in the hatch, talking to Jim. He said he could see right into a German post, and was quite confident he could capture it as soon as he had a fire plan arranged. I was glad to leave things in his confident hands, and went back to Commando Headquarters to see what other reports were coming in.

In actual fact, the tanks in Colonel Moulton's battle were Centaurs as by now he had reached Langrune-sur-Mer (see map pages 506-507): 'I did my best to see what I could of the enemy position, then went back perhaps a hundred yards to give my orders. B Troop, assisted by the Centaurs, must push on a little way further, to secure the next crossroads, the last before the sea-front, with the two houses on the far side of it. A Troop, now under its senior subaltern, Lieutenant R. G. Mackenzie, would follow down the houses and, on my order, pass through B, swing left, and start clearing down the houses parallel to the sea-front. X Troop commander had been wounded by now, and it was led by Lieutenant D. G. Goodlet, its junior subaltern. It must continue its pressure on what now seemed to be the other end of the German position. There had been a warning of a possible counter-attack from inland, so Z Troop should secure our rear.'

Reducing the range, the Sherman closes on the strong point . . . but this is at St Aubin . . .

B Troop started well, supported by the Centaurs, which I watched from a little way back down the street. Then, having run out of ammunition, the first Centaur came back; and the other, going forward to take its place, struck a mine, lost a track and blocked the road. The handful of B Troop men dashed across the lateral road, and tried to get into the houses on the far side of the crossroads. They seemed unable to get in. I watched them crouch under the ten-foot wall which blocked the street, and saw half a dozen stick grenades come over it to fall among them. Miraculously, it seemed, there were no casualties. Shortly afterwards, they came back into the houses on our side of the road. Much later, I was to hear that some of them had forced an entry and then fallen foul of anti-personnel mines. I should have had more men close up, ready to back up their momentary success.

We were nearly back where we had started, one Centaur less, and the road blocked to tanks. Worse, we now knew that the enemy had built and wired themselves into the block of houses they were holding. It seemed that, until we could knock something down, it was physically impossible to enter; while, by demolishing the last house on our side of the crossroads, they had given themselves a clear field of fire to prevent our close approach. While I was digesting these unpleasant facts, 'Jumbo' Leicester came up and told me to call off further attempts on what we now began to call the Langrune strong point, and to organise the rest of the village for defence; German armour was moving up towards the coast, and Langrune was on its axis.

It was now getting dark. The patrol had come back from our junction point with No. 41 Commando, reporting that they had seen nothing of 41, but had met no enemy either; so we seemed to be on our own. We ate some rations and went to our defence stations for the night. I was in the farmer's pleasant ground-floor study; I put my automatic pistol and torch handy and tried to find a comfortable position on the floor to sleep without hurting my sore places.

The problem of the strong point had now resolved itself into that of somehow forcing an entrance. As the Germans had so arranged things that they could shoot at us while we were doing so, it was not going to be simple for us, and could be very costly.

The Brigadier came up and confirmed that we were free from the threat of counter-attack and that our job was to finish off the strong point. I realised our duty, both to the military world at large and to our own self-respect, to capture it ourselves and not to leave it to someone else; it would make a great deal of difference to the Commando's future morale to finish the job — and we all, by now, had a personal score to settle. But then weakness: the strong point was beginning to seem impregnable; and it would be nice to stop and lick our wounds, without the prospect of more casualties, more danger and perhaps another failure. Jumbo Leicester's matter-of-fact order was just what I needed, and I recognised not only its correctness, but the moral stiffening, which I needed, and which it gave me. I tried not to show all this, as I acknowledged his order in what I hoped was an imperturbable way.

. . . while Colonel Moulton has moved on to Langrune where the strong point there demanded their attention. One of the Centaurs of the Royal Marine Armoured Support Regiment provides cover for the commandos.

With the Centaur immobilised up ahead, the Canadian M10s approach the crossroads. Colonel Moulton on the left takes a quick peek before one of the tank destroyers makes the detour through the field on the right to the strong point beyond. 'I was close enough to talk to the commander', wrote Colonel Moulton in his book *Haste to the Battle*, 'and after some time he reported that his ammunition was running out; I could see a lot of small holes in the wall, but it still looked inaccessible and strong. The M10 withdrew the way it had come, and the Sherman came forward to have a go with high explosive again, now that the wall was weakened by the holes in it. In a little while, the wall and the house on one side of it began to crumble.'

The Brigadier also gave me some tanks to replace the Centaurs: two Canadian M10s and a troop commander's Sherman from the Royal Marine Armoured Support Regiment. It would be more correct to call both the newcomers and the Centaurs self-propelled guns. The M10s were anti-tank guns on a tank chassis. The Centaurs were obsolescent tanks, which had been brought into the invasion operation to fire from tank landing craft, thus making them into improvised support craft to increase the volume of fire for the landings. This was the reason for the Marines manning them. It had been intended to de-engine them and leave them in the craft; but Monty heard about it, and very reasonably said that a tank was a tank and he might be short of them, so they must keep their engines and come ashore in case they were wanted. So Royal Armoured Corps drivers were added to their Royal Marine crews, and come ashore they did. They were a great help to us, but they could hardly be as good as a fully trained armoured unit, especially in this most difficult job for armour, street fighting.

The tanks, for that is how we used them and how I shall continue to call them, could blow us a hole in the masonry and thus get us into the strong point, but we must first get them past the disabled Centaur. Luckily, there was an open field on the far side of the road; it was mined, but we would use a bangalore torpedo to cut a lane through the mines. A bangalore torpedo is a metal pipe, filled with high explosive, primarily intended to cut barbed wire, but also effective in detonating mines over which it is exploded. We used some smoke; Lieutenant R. G. Mackenzie, with some of A Troop, rushed across the road behind the Centaur and into the field, placed the bangalore torpedo, checked its placing and lit its fuze, then rushed back into the cover of the houses, and the bangalore exploded with an almighty bang.

Covered against possible anti-tank weapons by our men in the houses, one of the M10s went forward, swung clear of the Centaur, followed the line of the bangalore past it, then swung back into the road. I watched, heart in mouth, fearing to see another mine go up under it; but nothing happened, and now it could blow us a hole in the masonry. It started to fire at the wall across the street. Yesterday, the Centaurs' high-explosive shells had burst on the thick, concreted wall and hardly dented it; now, the M10's solid, high-velocity anti-tank projectiles went right through it.

These photographs are amazing, depicting as they do the precise events described in the text. Jean Paul rounded off the story nicely with his comparison taken on the Rue du Colonel Harival, but why is it not 'Rue du Colonel Moulton'?

'After a bit, I judged we could make it and gave the word', continues Colonel Moulton. 'Lieutenant Mackenzie led the way with A Troop, and I followed with B, then 'Skinner' [Major D. H. W. Sanders] with X and a working party from Headquarters with shovels and explosives. While A and B Troops worked through the houses along the sea-front, 'Skinner's working party blew down what was left of the wall, and shovelled the debris into the trenches and fire positions around it, so that a tank could pass. Germans were firing down the open promenade, but Mac seemed to be getting along well through the houses. The Sherman ground its noisy way across the debris of the wall onto the promenade, slewed to fire along it, and as it did so put a track into a trench on the promenade and wrenched it off. Hell! Were we going to fail now? The tilted Sherman fired as well as it could down the promenade, and I tried to follow Mac down the houses to see if I could do anything to help him. Then, suddenly, grey figures began to emerge with their hands up. RSM C. H. Travers fell them in and checked to see that they were unarmed, and the officer in charge was brought to me, but we had no language in common. As we looked at each other, I saw one of 48 kick a German bottom, and shouted to him to shut up being a fool. Mac came along and reported no further opposition; the prisoners were marched off; and that was that.'

On the 8th Brigade beaches, as on the 7th's, the Royal Marine Centaurs had not a very great deal to do. One troop came into action on the beach against targets in St Aubin and subsequently gave assistance to No. 48 Commando in its struggle to clear Langrune-sur-Mer just to the eastward. A number of Centaurs intended for these beaches did not arrive until D+1 or D+2.

The armoured cars of the Inns of Court Regiment had not been able to carry out their task of destroying bridges over the Orne. Some of the squadron's vehicles were lost before landing or on the beaches. It landed at Courseulles, and was one of the victims of the slowness in opening beach exits there. An isolated message from it appears in the division's log at 1140: 'Left exit clear, priority to be given to anti-tank guns'. It seems to have got off the beach about noon, and the greater part of it crossed the Seulles at 1500, apparently at Creully, but the armoured cars did not get through to the Orne, or the nearer Odon, which the I Corps operation instruction had prescribed as an alternative objective. (See also page 625.)

Top: **Jean Paul found that the prisoners had been lined up with their backs to a wall which still exists off a small overgrown garden on Rue du Capitaine Pool in Langrune.** *Centre:* **He then followed Lieutenant Handford back to St Aubin to discover that these prisoners, captioned as having been captured by Royal Marines, i.e Commandos, were marching down the Rue du Maréchal Foch. The planned link-up on the coast with No. 41 (RM) Commando advancing westwards from Lion-sur-Mer never took place, No. 41 being delayed capturing a strong point on their patch until D+1 just as No. 48 were held up by theirs at Langrune.**

A post-action report on the casualties suffered by each unit landing on Nan White and Red estimated No. 48 Commando's at 100 plus with a note than most were by 'drowning when landing craft mined' — a high price indeed when set against the 340 dead suffered by the Canadians as a whole on D-Day. *Above:* **The temporary Commando cemetery was in this garden — not as stated in St Aubin but a few hundred metres further east in the Rue Anatole Duval in Bernières.**

The casualties suffered by the Canadian 3rd Division on D-Day, though heavy, were fewer than had been feared. For the whole day, Canadian losses in the seaborne force amounted to 340 all ranks killed or died of wounds, 574 wounded and 'battle injuries', and 47 taken prisoner. It is not possible to distinguish between casualties suffered on the beaches and those in the later stages. There was not much difference between the casualties of the two assault brigades. The infantry unit that suffered most heavily was the Queen's Own Rifles of the 8th Brigade, which lost 143 men; this loss was presumably mainly caused by the strong point at Bernières, captured without tank assistance. Next came The Royal Winnipeg Rifles, which had 128 casualties. This reflects the bitter fight at Courseulles. The North Shore Regiment lost 125 men, chiefly undoubtedly in the prolonged fighting at St Aubin and Tailleville.

One thing we had to do was to clear up the St Aubin beach. It was a shocking sight. Many corpses, some of them badly dismembered, were lying among the rest of the debris of the assault: wrecked and burnt-out tanks; equipment and stores of every sort, scattered on the beach or drifted up along the water's edge; wrecked landing craft broached-to on the beach or in the sea among the beach obstacles. Three of our landing craft were still there, wrecked and abandoned; I never heard what the squadron's casualties were in men. Among all this, several French women were walking about, picking up what tinned food they could find — incredibly they had small children with them, who gazed with indifferent curiosity on the shattered corpses, the broken equipment and the scattered tins of food.

Skinner took charge of a burial party, set up a cemetery in a little garden near our assembly area, and buried, of ours, the Canadians and the sailors, about eighty. He hung the green berets won at Achnacarry on the rough wooden crosses of our men, and the French people brought flowers for the graves, which later we were to find renewed whenever we revisited the cemetery. It was our first burial party, and they must have been glad when it was over; but the seemly burial of the dead had a noticeably good effect on morale.

LIEUTENANT-COLONEL JAMES MOULTON,
HASTE TO THE BATTLE, 1963

Perhaps, as a final tailpiece to the No. 48 Commando operation, we ought to comment on the unfortunate abbreviation 'SS' when applied to the Special Service Brigade. When Churchill had first proposed the formation of 'Striking Companies' in 1940, he had chosen an even more contentious name for them: 'Storm Troops'. The title eventually settled upon was 'commando', although even this had bitter connotations as it had been the name of an earlier enemy of the British Army — that of the swift-moving Boer groups in the South African war. After six months campaigning in Europe in 1944, much of it against the Waffen-SS, the title 'Special Service' was quietly dropped and the official name became 'Commando Brigade'.

Sword Area

By Brigadier David Belchem
CHIEF OF STAFF, 21st ARMY GROUP

After General Montgomery departed from Italy, I remained to assist the new team under General Sir Oliver Leese, but I knew I was destined to join the inter-service planning team which was being organised at home.

On January 8, 1944, a signal arrived from the War Office to say that I was urgently required in London, and I left Vasto the following day. We landed in England on January 14 at an RAF station near Bristol and in no time were waiting on the platform at Temple Meads for a train to London. At Paddington, a movement control officer told me I was to report forthwith to St Paul's School, Hammersmith.

I first went to see the Military Secretary, Jack Gannon. He welcomed me home and said that Monty wished to see me. I was ushered into the General's office. Freddy de Guingand, his Chief-of-Staff, was not around but the Master was at work.

'Have a good trip back?' he enquired.

'Yes, Sir, thank you.'

'Time is short and there is such a lot to do, David. I shall put you in charge of the Operations Staff, but initially you will be BGS Special Planning Section.'

Right: **Brigadier David Belchem was one of General Montgomery's principal staff officers for the invasion of Sicily and, at the conclusion of Operation 'Husky', was appointed BGS (Brigadier General Staff) Operations and Plans for the Eighth Army. When Montgomery returned to England to become commander of the 21st Army Group, Brigadier Belchem was summoned to London to serve as BGS (Operations) for 'Overlord'.** *Top:* **The official group photo for GSOs (General Staff Officers) Grade 1(Ops) was taken at the advanced HQ at Southwick (see page 102) on D-Day. Standing L–R: Lieutenant-Colonel R. G. S. Lewthwaite (GSO1 Ops.B); Colonel E. L. Bols (Ops.B); Brigadier Belchem; Colonel R. G. S. Hobbs (Ops.A); Lieutenant-Colonel D. G. Jebb (GSO1 Ops.A); Colonel G. C. Mudgett (US) (Ops.A). Kneeling L–R: Lieutenant-Colonel H. N. Llewellyn (GSO1 Liaison); Lieutenant-Colonel M. D. Losey (US) (Ops.B), and Lieutenant-Colonel F. N. W. Gore (GSO1 Ops.B). (Basically, the Ops 'A' Branch dealt with tactical operations, whereas the 'B' Branch looked after strategy and deception matters.)**

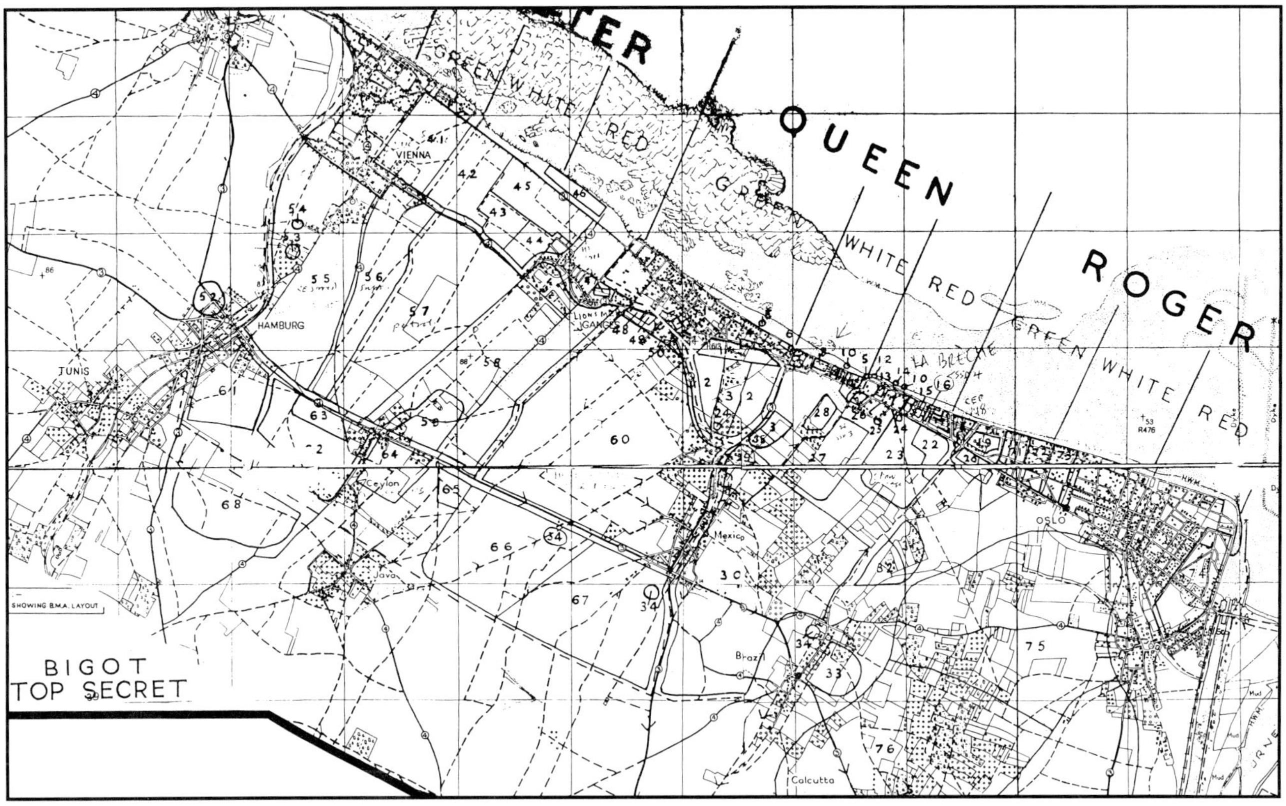

According to Brigadier Belchem's writings, he personally chose the code-names for the British and Canadian invasion areas from a standard army code-book, but said that the American names were picked by the two corps commanders after their home states in the United States. However, General Collins came from Louisiana, not Utah, and General Gerow from Virginia, not Omaha. Unfortunately, the truth of the matter is now unlikely to be resolved as Brigadier (by then Major-General) Belchem died in 1981. For security reasons, the early planning maps replaced real locations with fictitious code-names; thus, in the Sword area, Luc-sur-Mer became 'Vienna'; La Délivrande 'Tunis'; Hermanville-sur-Mer 'Mexico'; Colleville-sur-Orne 'Brazil', and Ouistreham 'Oslo'. Stephen Sykes, ex-Captain in No. 5 Beach Group HQ, who kindly supplied this plan, added the written notes at the time. The more interesting locations are: 1. Transit areas D-Day personnel. 5. DUKW control point. 10. Beach Coy HQ. 12. No. 5 Beach Group CP. 14. No. 101 Beach Sub-Area CP. 20, 33, 46 and 65. Burial areas. 23. PoW cage. 26. Sector Stores Dump 3. 31. RE HQ. 35. 73rd LAA Regt. HQ. 48. REME HQ. 61. Casualty Clearing Station.

'Sir.'

'Now tell me', said Monty. 'What are you planning to do — you have not been home for some six years?'

'First I would like to see my mother and father.'

'Where are they living?'

'Folkestone, Sir.'

'Ah, that is some way out of London. You may have tomorrow off. Let us start work on Tuesday.'

Obviously not my day: I had expected at least a week's leave!

I found that my deputy in the Planning Section was Colonel Leo Russell, who explained to me the studies which had been made to date of the problem of re-entry into western Europe. Our work at St Paul's began at 8 a.m., and we finished any time between 7 and 10 p.m., seven days a week.

There was some delay before the command set-up for Overlord was decided but, once the top command appointments had been made, the C-in-Cs made up their own staffs and, in general terms, the planning personnel who had worked together in the Mediterranean (for the invasion of Sicily and Italy) were brought back to the UK. This greatly facilitated getting down to work, since we knew one another well and because we had already some experience of seaborne assault operations (and, in the case of those who were in Greece and Crete, of the opposite — evacuation techniques, in which we had worked closely with the Royal Navy).

When Eisenhower decentralised to Montgomery the responsibility for planning and executing the first stage of the invasion, a new element was introduced into our staff at St Paul's School; we became an Anglo-American staff and staff-trained American officers joined us, for Montgomery was responsible not only for 21st Army Group but also for US First Army of 13 divisions, plus three airborne divisions, and contingents of French, Czechs, Belgians, Dutch and Poles. In the case of my own (planning) section, I was given an American deputy, Colonel Gilman C. Mudgett from General Bradley's G-3 section, who now became G(Ops)(US) 21st Army Group, and two other US officers.

With the assault sectors settled, and the boundaries of the lodgement area determined (on the Seine and Loire), Montgomery applied himself to the master plan for handling the Battle of Normandy. This was evolved from an appreciation of the vital strategic importance of Caen. It was the rail and road communication centre where the routes from the east and south-east converged, and continued westwards to Cherbourg and to the Brittany peninsula. The bulk of the potential German reserves which the enemy could send to the Normandy sector were located north of the Seine, and to reach the combat zone would have to pass through Caen. Any reserves transferred from Italy or the East would be routed through Paris and Caen.

Montgomery argued that if the Allies developed and sustained a major threat to Caen, the enemy would react strongly, and reserves arriving in Normandy would tend to be committed in the Caen sector. Moreover, indications that it was the Allies' intention to break out of the bridgehead in the Caen sector would

SWORD AREA

Sector	*Extent*	*Grid Reference*	*Width (yards)*
OBOE	N to Luc	016851–046835	3,900
PETER	O to Lion (West outskirts)	046835–068818	3,000
QUEEN	P to settlement	068818–093805	3,000
ROGER	Q to Ouistreham (West breakwater)	093805–119798	2,900

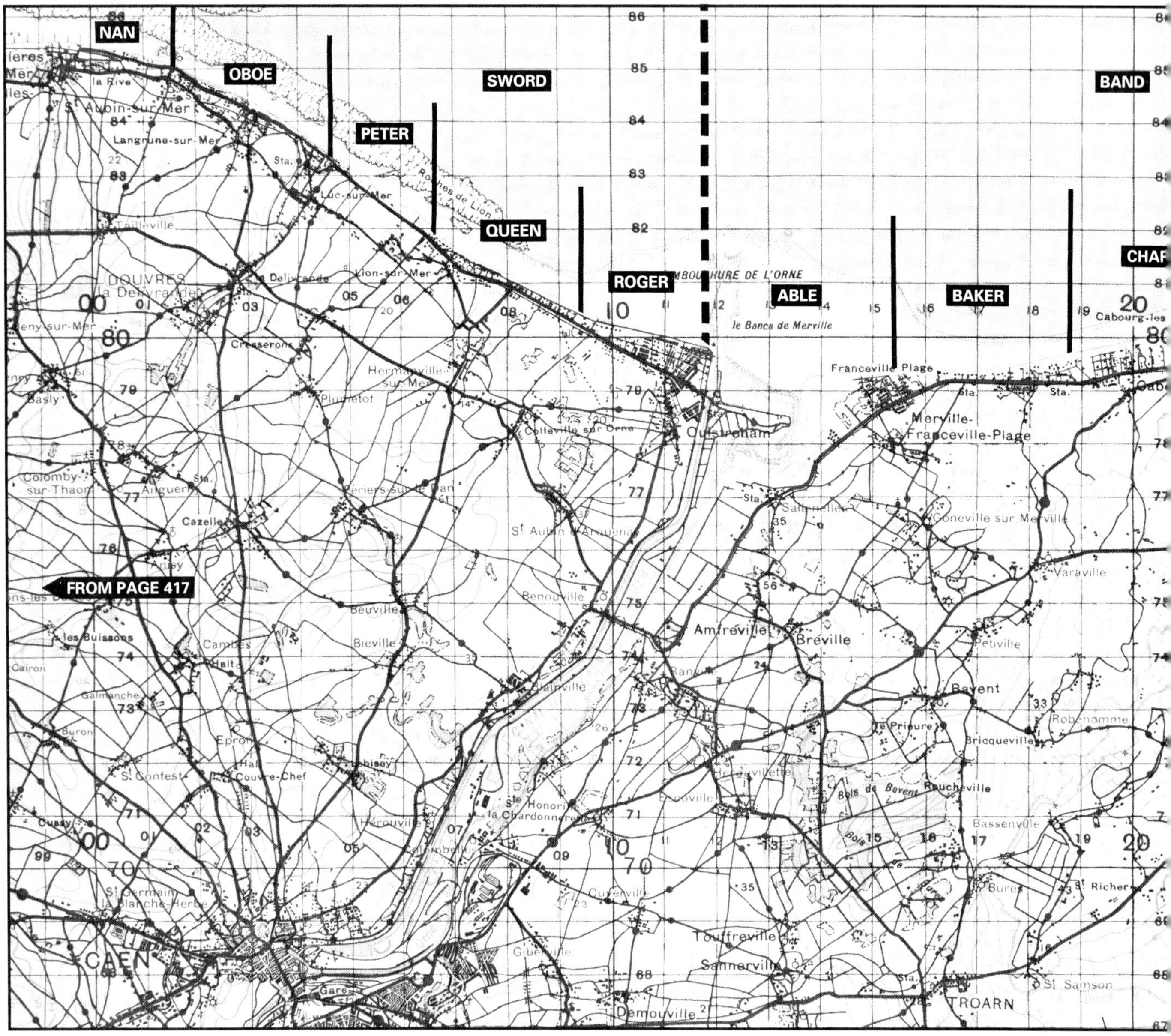

increase the enemy's determination to resist our offensive there, in order to prevent us from deploying our armoured forces in the open country to the south-east, and striking towards the Seine and Paris. Apart from any political significance, Paris has traditionally been the objective for invaders of France, if only because it is the point towards which virtually all main routes in the country converge.

From these considerations, Montgomery decided that the master plan for Normandy would be based on drawing the bulk of the enemy's mobile reserves to the Caen sector. This could only be done by very strong and very persistent offensive action by British and Canadian forces on our eastern flank. If successful, this concept would not only gain time for the US forces to clear the Cotentin, and capture Cherbourg, and then to regroup south of the peninsula on the general line St Lô–Coutances, but it would also facilitate a break-out from the American sector, as long as the British/Canadian forces could hold the main enemy mobile armoured forces on the eastern front. The American break-out could then be developed into a wide sweep down to and along the line of the River Loire, and thence up to the River Seine, the whole movement hinging on Caen. From the start of our post-assault planning, this was the concept that Montgomery adopted, and through the normal staff channels, this was the briefing which was given to all the senior subordinate commanders, and to the planning staff.

The fire plan for the assault was an intricate combination of the resources of the three services. The object was to destroy or neutralise the coast defence artillery, the strong points in the Atlantic Wall, and the batteries located in rear. We had made a scale model of the coast area, with the position of all targets modelled upon it; each of the forces involved were given a different colour of skeins of wool, and strands were attached to the targets at one end, and the source of fire at the other. The programme began with Bomber Command which was to deliver 6,000 tons of bombs, commencing a few hours before daylight.

There was a complicated system of Army-Air Force co-operation communications; in brief, calls for support from the troops going ashore were channelled to a detachment of our staff at Uxbridge. Pre-arranged air support was handled through my links, and passed to Uxbridge by Air Vice-Marshal Kingston McCloughry, who shared a caravan office with me until the Army-Air Staffs were established normally again on the Continent.

Since my activities were frequently concerned with problems demanding Air Force co-operation, I will give just one example of how we operated together. I recall the occasion when I discovered that the Germans in Normandy were confining their movements (e.g. of replenishment convoys and reinforcements) to the secondary roads. From our photographs, it was possible to discern the main traffic routes, though sometimes it was not easy to follow them on our British maps of Normandy. It occurred to me to get a French Michelin map of the area: first class main roads are in red on a Michelin map, and second class roads are in yellow. The pattern of German move-

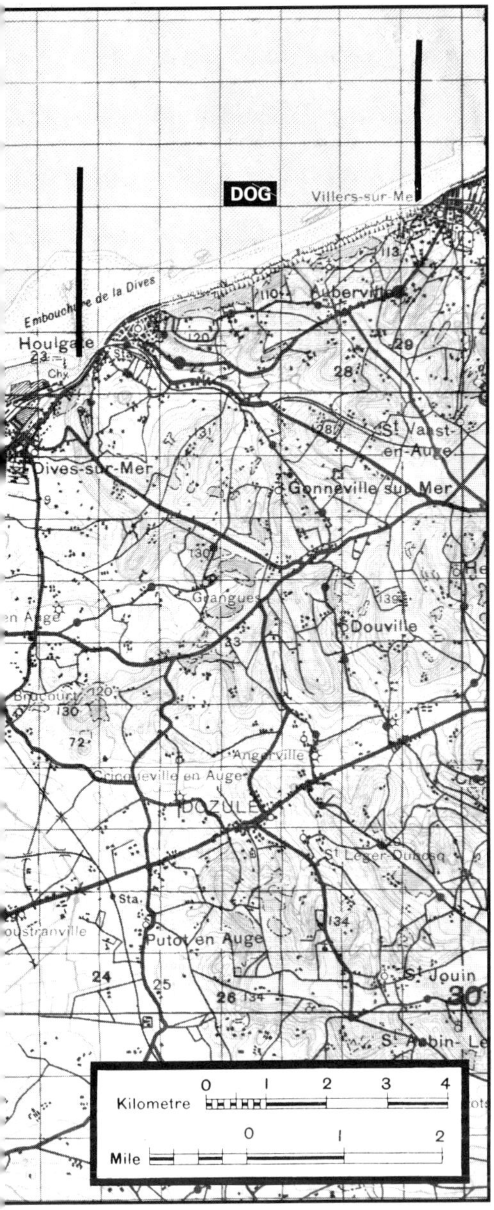

BAND AREA

Sector	*Extent*	*Grid Reference*	*Width (yards)*
ABLE	Ouistreham (West breakwater) to road	119798–154794	4,000
BAKER	A to road	154794–189797	3,100
CHARLIE	B to Houlgate (mouth of river)	189797–237805	5,400
DOG	C to Villers-sur-Mer (west outskirts)	237805–293831	7,100

While Band Area was designated east of the Orne river, it was not used for the seaborne assault and we have included its boundaries here merely for the sake of completeness.

ments observed by us were, in virtually all cases, on yellow roads. From this point, we pin-pointed the main bottlenecks on yellow routes leading to the rear areas of the enemy's known positions, where delivery by night of ammunition, stores and rations was probably made.

Kingston then requested the RAF to arrange bombing raids at these bottlenecks, as late in the day as possible. He also arranged fighter-bomber sorties to the same bottlenecks at first light the following morning. The plan proved successful because the fighter-bombers found heavy traffic congestion at the target areas, which were chosen where reversing the convoys would be most difficult, and the finding of alternative routes in order to by-pass the cratered area would involve long detours.

To those who study the progress of the Battle of Normandy, I must emphasise one imponderable which went against us to an extent not always appreciated by those who took no part in it. In the planning period, we assumed average weather conditions in the operational theatre for the summer and autumn. But the adverse weather we had to contend with in 1944 was unprecedented (at least compared with the previous 20 years). This accounts on a number of occasions for serious delays in the developments of the Allied operations. However, to quote Montgomery, 'the plan proved capable of implementation and workable in practice'.

Before leaving the planning period, I must refer to one of the worst experiences in my life. As the head planner, I held (and was responsible for) the one and only map upon which was marked the landing areas in Normandy, together with the forces destined to go ashore. This precious map was always locked in my safe. If a senior officer wished to borrow it, I had a register board which he personally had to sign.

The day came when the map 'disappeared', and I had no signature for it. The whole of St Paul's School was searched under Leo Russell's guidance. I went to Norfolk House and took the whole building to pieces in my search. After 24 hours, Freddie de Guingand told me that if the map was not found by the following morning it would be necessary to call in Scotland Yard and I would probably finish up in the Tower of London! The deadline for this fate was noon next day. During that morning, I was at Norfolk House when Leo Russell rang me up at eleven. 'I've found it', he said. Thus I was saved from the Bloody Tower. While I was in no doubt about to whom I had lent the map, the fault was mine for not having insisted on a signature; in trusting a colleague I might have got myself shot! The map was in fact found where he put it — in the draughtsman's cupboard!

Destination Sword. The 1st East Riding Yeomanry (of 27th Armoured Brigade) underway for their landing scheduled for 1255 hours but delayed in the event for over an hour. Captain Derrick Knight of the AFPU went with them and took this shot aboard their LST. Because the assigned beaches — Queen Red and White — were very narrow, restricted by the steeply shelving beach before Roger on the east, and low cliffs to the west, the British 3rd Division had to land on a single brigade front. To ensure that there would be no navigational error, the second of the two midget submarines, *X.23*, was to be stationed 7,000 yards offshore. There was a particular danger on Sword from the heavy batteries to the east on either side of the Seine estuary. Those further to the west at Villerville, Mont Canisy and Houlgate — all of which covered Sword area, but were outside the sphere of military operations — were to be neutralised by HMS *Warspite*, *Ramillies* and *Roberts* respectively. Those at Le Havre were not included as primary targets, as it was intended that they should have been put out of action by bombing prior to D-Day.

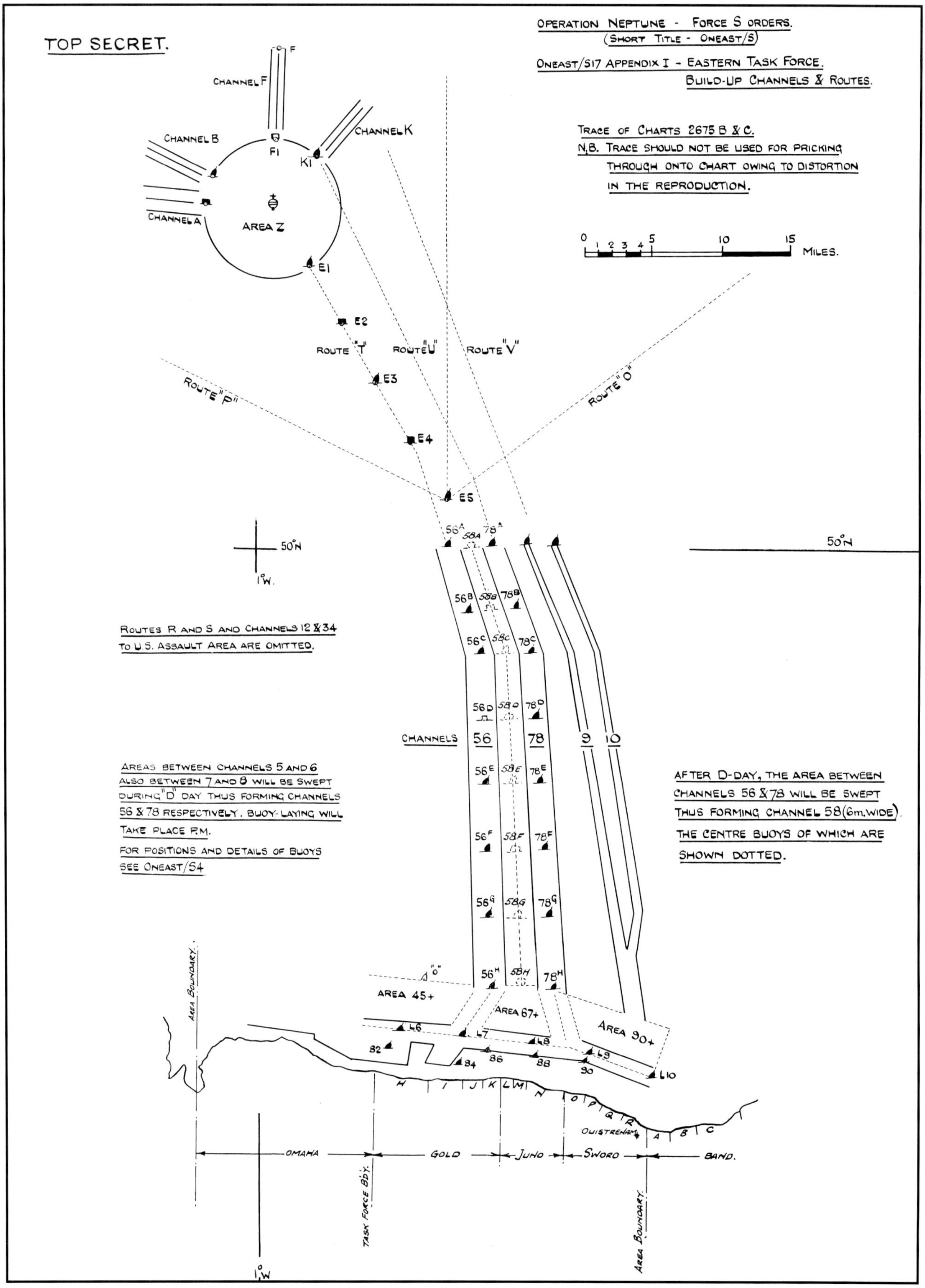

It was known that a moored mine barrier existed from about Lat. 50° N to within some seven to ten miles of the French coast. To the southward of this area ran the enemy coastal channel, which was expected to provide a clear area unless mined at the last moment. The lowering positions for the assault forces were accordingly sited in this channel. Inshore of the coastal channel there was no evidence of mines, but it was necessary to make provision in this area and on the flanks for the safety of the bombarding ships. The minesweeping was the largest such operation ever undertaken in war.

The plan adopted fell into four phases, viz: clearing and marking two channels for each assault force through the mine barrier, using one fleet minesweeping flotilla for each channel; finding or making clear areas for the bombarding forces and anchorages close inshore; widening the approach channels through the mine barrier and clearance of mines from neighbouring areas in order to give sea room; and the clearance of mines laid after the assault. A vital aspect of these operations was the marking of the areas cleared. This was done in the first instance by lining each channel on both sides with lighted Dan buoys, spaced at intervals of about one mile. These buoys were replaced by ocean light buoys on D-Day and D+1. The clearance of areas for the bombarding forces and shore anchorages followed, using a proportion of the flotillas released after the sweeping of the approach channels. On arrival in the assault area, bombarding ships formed part of the assault forces to which they were allocated. Flag and senior officers commanding British bombarding forces were therefore requested to exercise only such control over ships of their force as necessary to implement the intentions of task or assault force commanders. Rear-Admiral W. R. Patterson was the Senior Officer of Force 'D', the Bombardment Force covering Force 'S'. His most powerful battleship was HMS *Ramillies* *(above)*, fitted with eight 15-inch guns which could lob a shell of 1,938lbs some 32,000 yards — over 18 miles. She carried 110 rounds per gun. In addition, she had twelve 6-inch guns, each with 130 112lb shells. (HMS *Warspite* also mounted eight 15-inch guns, but only her 'A' and 'B' turrets were in action.)

Arguably, the most powerful ship off Normandy was HMS *Rodney* with her nine massive 16-inch guns which could fire a shell weighing over a ton for a distance of over 20 miles. She was in the Eastern Task Force reserve and, according to the Admiralty caption to this photograph, was pictured 'supporting the Caen beach-head', i.e. Sword, on D+1.

Queen sector was to be assaulted by two battalions: the 2nd of the East Yorkshire Regiment on the left coming ashore on Red Beach, and the 1st Battalion, South Lancashire Regiment on White Beach to their right — rather a poor choice in the light of the 15th-century Wars of the Roses when the House of Lancaster fought under the banner of a red rose and York under one of white! The dividing line between the two beaches was at the road marked 18; Red Beach covering roads 18-26 and White 11-18. The capture of the strong point WN 20, right in the centre (Allied code-name 'Cod', but also known to the troops as '0880' after its map square grid reference) was assigned to both the East Yorks and South Lancs.

The British 3rd Division, in the Sword area, assaulted on a one-brigade front. The landing beach selected was to the east of Lion-sur-Mer in Queen sector on White and Red Beaches. The orders were that the division should make straight for Caen and seize a bridgehead there over the River Orne; the first objective was the feature near Périers-sur-le-Dan, which the leading brigade was to hold, while the follow-up formations passed through, on the line of the road to Caen.

H-Hour was at 0725 and the first-wave craft arrived on time, preceded by the strongest and most effective air and warship bombardment on any of the D-Day beaches. In spite of heavy seas and bad visibility, 31 out of 34 launched DDs of the 13th/18th Hussars together with Flails of the 22nd Dragoons (and Westminster Dragoons) landed, together with the AVREs of the 5th Assault Regiment, RE, ahead of the infantry.

There was a second German strong point (WN 20A) at map square 0681 on the extreme right flank at Clos Colas on the junction between Queen and Peter sectors (see also aerial photo on page 135). Code-named 'Trout', it was 1,400 yards from the nearest beach to be assaulted and was made the objective of No. 41 (RM) Commando who were to advance along the coast to meet with No. 48 (RM) Commando landing at St Aubin (see pages 506 and 514). The force allotted to clearing it proved to be too weak, and the position was not captured until D+2. As a result, the planned commando link-up at Petit Enfer failed to materialise, British and Canadian infantry joining forces further inland near Cambes. ***Below:*** **Queen sector today.**

The clearance of the foreshore presented no great problems, but along the sand dunes behind lay a maze of fortifications, obstacles and mines. Thanks to the timely arrival of the tanks and engineers, by 0930 the assaulting 8th Brigade had captured Hermanville-sur-Mer, about a mile and a half inland. Here, however, they found the Périers feature held by infantry and 88mm guns of the 21. Panzer-Division. The gun line obliged the British tanks to fall back, and the infantry battalions went to ground (as stipulated in the orders).

Back at the beach, the onshore wind drove the tide in so fast that the engineers had insufficient time to clear all the underwater obstacles before the follow-up wave (185th Brigade) arrived, and great skill was needed to bring the craft in safely. And on Queen, there followed traffic congestion as experienced elsewhere; indeed the 9th reserve Brigade did not get to the shore until midday.

On page 208 we saw Sergeant Mapham departing from Gosport in LCT 610; now we see his craft about to ground on Red Beach. White Beach lies 200 yards away to the right. The time is H+35 minutes (0800) and he is approaching the shore in the company of the 27th Armoured Brigade. This was his third roll of film but of the 11 exposures only five survive. A knocked out AFV appears to be brewing up in front of the houses. Although the sea was considered too rough, Captain E. W. Bush, commanding Assault Group S3, ordered the launch of the 13th/18th Hussars' DDs at 5,000 yards. Two sank immediately and the following LCTs carrying the AVREs had to slow to avoid running the others down. However, Bush ordered the LCTs to proceed through them, resulting in one DD being rammed by an overtaking landing craft. On Red Beach, four lanes were to be cleared by the 79th Assault Squadron, RE, with the assistance of Flails from A Squadron, 22nd Dragoons.

Fortunately the twin sea-front villas still stand on the corner of Rue de Rouen to make a perfect comparison.

If Jimmy Mapham, an ex-*Leicester Mercury* press photographer who died in September 1968, had taken no other pictures than this one, it would remain his enduring epitaph. Many attempts have been made over the years to put names to the individuals depicted, yet it was not until the 50th anniversary was upon us that they were at last correctly identified. David List, our photographic interpretation specialist, always believed that the Battle Jerkins indicated Royal Engineers, and he thought the most likely time the picture had been taken was around 0845 as No. 84 Field Company, RE, which wore Beach Group formation signs (the red anchor in a light blue circle) landed in small parties throughout the morning — a total of 160 men coming ashore between 0745 and 0825, and another 52 from 1030 to 1230. Fifty years later, Fred Sadler (walking on the right) contacted the *Sunday Mirror*: 'My job was to search for land mines. I remember the photographer walking past me on the beach, then turning round and taking a picture. I know I look calm, but I was quaking in my boots.' Fred first saw the picture in the *Sunday Despatch* two weeks later, showing in the foreground two of his mates: Cyril Hawkins and Jimmy Leask. David List confirmed from the nominal roll of No. 84 Field Company that all three men had come ashore from the same landing craft at 0815 hours, tying in nicely with his earlier research.

It appears that Sergeant Mapham walked a few hundred yards to the west to take the picture while standing on White Beach looking back towards Red, the heavily-laden troops with the rucksacks in the centre being from the 8th Field Ambulance, RAMC, attached to the 8th Brigade, who were most probably helping wounded from the wrecked carrier on the right of the 2nd Battalion, The Middlesex Regiment. We may also be seeing men of No. 41 (RM) Commando in the background. The casualties of the 2nd Battalion, East Yorks on Red Beach are unknown, but the 1st Battalion of the South Lancs which landed on White Beach sustained 126 casualties during the assault phase of the landing. *Below:* Karel Margry stands in for Fred Sadler at 8.45 a.m. on June 6, 1994.

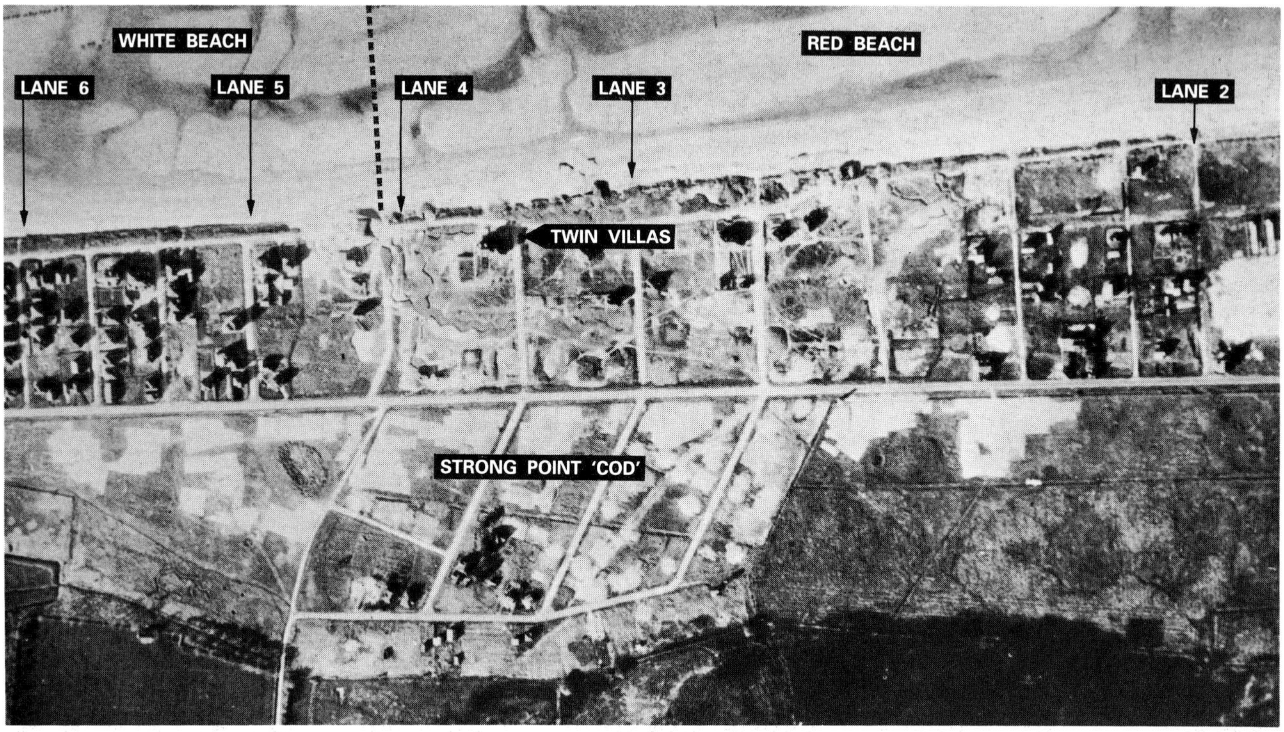

Each of the two assault squadrons was split into two teams, one to deal with the beach and underwater obstacles, the other to do the gapping. Both the Flails and the AVREs disembarked and waded onto the beach — the time would appear to have been 0720 as the 79th Squadron remarked that 'DDs have not touched down and no infantry are in sight. For a minute or two there is no fire from the enemy.' The four lanes were tackled as follows: LANE 1 'Beached at H-Hour. Flails cleared up to low dunes. Log carpet and chespale were laid and road clearance began. One Flail knocked out and the other completed clearance to lateral. Bangalore hit side of craft on disembarkation and had to be jettisoned.' LANE 2 'Landed at H-Hour. Both Flails knocked out. Mines were cleared by hand by dismounted crews. Bridge was dropped and later blocked by DD falling off the side of it. A second gap was made by D7 [bulldozer].' LANE 3 'Landed at H-Hour and Flails began to clear lane to top of beach. They were both knocked out. Bomb release on bridge was hit prematurely and bridge fell. Gap was made with hand-placed charges and improved by D7. Bobbin was damaged and had to be jettisoned.' LANE 4 'Landed at H-Hour and Flails flailed up beach until one Flail was knocked out. Second Flail continued lane. Bridge was dropped but badly placed. Second lane was started and carpet laid, lane completed. Eventually both lanes made good. Bridge was jettisoned.'

The film used by the AFPU photographers during the war did not have modern edge numbering and the negatives were cut into individual frames after development. Poor shots were then discarded so that of Sergeant Mapham's ten rolls of film, each of 11 exposures, only 60 frames remain (at the Imperial War Museum, London). David List comments that 'the images have been sequenced by the old Ministry of Information picture editors into a story which is actually in the film roll order 5, 8, 7, 10, 6, 4, 2, 3 and 1'! In addition, odd negatives appear to have been transposed so it makes it somewhat difficult to re-create the original exposure order. All one can say of this picture is that it is from Roll 4 and, because Karel established where the following shots were taken, it most probably shows East Yorks troops amidst the chaos at the top of Red Beach.

These two frames are obviously taken from the same spot — in front of Lane 2 looking in a westerly direction — but one appears in Roll 4 *(above)* and the other in Roll 6 *(right)*. The AVRE on the left is an SBG carrier having laid its bridge, and that on the right, a Petard, both of 79th Assault Squadron. A subsequent technical analysis showed that the most effective weapon against the assaulting infantry was the 8.1cm mortar (which had an effective range of over 2,500 yards) which caused $6\frac{1}{2}$ per cent casualties from every $5\frac{2}{3}$ bombs fired. This compared with a 2 per cent casualty rate from machine gun fire for which 65 rounds would be necessary. From the attitude of the troops, it would appear that strong point 'Cod', which lay just behind the houses in the distance, had not yet been captured. It made life extremely hazardous on Red Beach and it was not finally subdued by the East Yorks, with help from other units, until 1000 hours.

The two end houses on the right still stand amidst the new villas which have sprung up along the sea-front since 1944.

Above: 'Cod', at the junction of the two beaches (extending 400 yards along Red Beach and 100 yards into White) was described as a 'hedgehog' comprising 20 individual positions: a 7.5cm gun; two 5cm anti-tank guns; three 8·1cm mortars; a 3.7cm machine gun; five other MG posts, one with two or three machine guns, and various observation posts and shelters. One position received a direct hit from a 105mm self-propelled gun, and the 7.5cm crew were killed by a tank shell. One anti-tank gun appeared to have been hit from the seaward side and the other was knocked out by tanks. The infantry — the East Yorks, South Lancs, with help from No. 4 Commando and the 5th Battalion, The King's Regiment (of No. 5 Beach Group) — took nearly three hours to capture the position and, although precise casualty figures are not given, they were reported to be 'heavy'.

Captain Knight took the wartime pictures; Karel Margry the comparisons.

Three of the dead lie close to the wire barricade protecting the position from the beach.

Captain Stephen Sykes of No. 5 Beach Group (whom we met on page 517) took these snaps about three hours after touch-down as his men were working on the north-western edge of what he still describes today as 'strong point 0880' *(right)* to improve Lane 4 *(below)*. (It ought to be explained that, in army terminology, a 'lane' is a path clear of obstacles and mines to the first lateral road which may only be sufficient for infantry to assault over, while an 'exit' has a surface suitable for either tracked or wheeled vehicles with traffic control so that transport may proceed inland in an orderly fashion.) 'The exit track was being frantically worked on, to surface it with wire mesh to stop vehicles sinking into the soft sand', says Stephen, 'although some tanks must have made their way off the beach some time before.'

'We had come ashore from our LCT a long way to the right of the twin villas beside 0880 and we started to run from the cover of one stationary vehicle to another, feeling very exposed to the tall villas overlooking the beach. As we went along, we kept seeing the familiar faces of other members of our group, but when I sheltered beside other figures lying beside tanks or trucks, I realised that some were dead. The large German blockhouse was sited to face westwards but when we reached it, it had already been captured and turned into a casualty clearing station, and the turf covering its concrete top pushed off. There was a dead German lying on his back in front of the seaward side.' *Right:* In 1962, Stephen went back to Queen, and there he matched his 1944 picture exactly, although the gun emplacement had already disappeared.

The move inland. Two more Mapham shots which make for beautiful comparisons. *Above:* The two tall villas — the landmark beside strong point 0880 which lies over to the right. These men appear to be predominantly No. 5 Beach Group troops. *Bottom:* Jean Paul found the twin villas, now named Tancrède and Le Petit Quinquin, standing beside Lane — or rather Exit — 4, now upgraded to a metalled road congruously called the Boulevard de la 3ème D.I.B. (British 3rd Division).

Left: This carrier driver (unfortunately one cannot be positive as to which unit he belongs) has halted on the lateral road behind the houses — then the N814, a Route Nationale, but now downgraded to a Chemin Départemental, the D514.

With all the confusion on Red Beach, it is difficult to accurately identify all the various troops shown in Sergeant Mapham's pictures. This photo was taken at the Colleville end of the beach and even Mapham is taking cover while taking the shot. Captain (later Major) Eric Lummis landed with the 1st Battalion The Suffolk Regiment at around 1100 hours, and he explains that there are always important distinguishing features to look for like the 'Normandy' pattern steel helmet which had been issued to most, but not all, of the assault formations in 21st Army Group. Technically, this was the Mk III helmet, developed in 1941 but not recommended for adoption because of its similarity to some foreign helmets. Thus, troops wearing the old pattern are most probably Beach Group personnel. 'My First Reinforcement Company travelled down from Scotland a week after the main body and missed being issued with the new helmet which the others received in their camps near Portsmouth and Newhaven. Assault troops also had their big packs in company transport but we carried ours with us.'

Having moved just beyond the beach, Sergeant Mapham is equally of no help in identifying these men, merely captioning the picture: 'troops with bicycles'! However, Karel established that the picture was taken on cross-route 23 on the aerial picture on pages 522-523 (a similar post on the right still surviving) now called the Rue Jolivet *(right)*. Eric Lummis believes that they are possibly the bicycle company of the 1st Battalion The Royal Norfolk Regiment of the intermediate 185th Brigade, or possibly the 2nd Battalion of The Royal Ulster Rifles, one of the units of the reserve 9th Brigade, who came ashore at this end of the beach at 1000 and were also carrying bicycles. The Royal Ulsters were to move west behind White Beach along the N814 to their assembly area at Lion-sur-Mer before advancing south to Caen which it had been hoped would be captured by nightfall.

Now we are on White Beach — the oddly-shaped white patch, bottom right, showing the overlap with the Red Beach aerial on page 526. On this end of Queen, the lanes were the responsibility of the 77th Assault Squadron. LANE 5: 'Beached on previously chosen exit. Leading Flail disembarked, second Flail was hit by anti-tank fire and the remainder could not disembark. An explosion occurred on board killing Lieutenant-Colonel A. D. B. Cocks and wounding Lieutenant F. G. Charlton. LCT was ordered back to UK.' LANE 6: 'Grounded on top of a DD and, after clearing, beached to the left instead of the right of 4 Troop (Lane 5). Flails cleared tracks, carpet was laid and bridge [marked as [1] in picture] was dropped on attacked exit which was cleared to lateral. Bobbin hit by mine and anti-tank fire and was drowned. D7 hit mine.' LANE 7: 'Beached to the right of 1 Troop (Lane 8) instead of to left due to drift whilst LCT lay off to allow DD to go in. Bangalore was placed in dunes but was blown prematurely by enemy fire. Gap was made and Flails surmounted dunes. One Flail blew tracks on mines but a route was cleared around it. The bridge [2] was dropped right on top of gun position. The bobbin was damaged and jettisoned. D7 (the armoured bulldozer) was not used.' LANE 8: 'Landed at place previously chosen at H-Hour. Obstacles were six to eight feet high sand dunes. The Flails flailed up the beaches and crossed the dunes unaided. The bangalore was jettisoned. Mines were cleared from the inland roads by Flails and hand clearing teams. One AVRE hit by anti-tank gun broke track and drowned. Crew dismounted and forced their way into Hermanville killing many enemy.'

SBG bridges [1] *above* and [2] *bottom* at La Brèche. Karel took both the comparisons exactly 50 years after they were laid.

This AVRE Petard standing in Lane 8 is a fitting memorial to the 5th Assault Regiment who started out to clear the lanes with 34 AVREs and 8 bulldozers. All told, four AVREs and one bulldozer (plus two Flails) failed to get off one of the LCTs, and a further five AVREs were knocked out after landing, two on White Beach and three on Red, with one bulldozer on each. Eight Flails were lost, six on Red Beach and two on White. The Petard now displayed on Queen sector came from Germany.

The two leading companies of the 1st Battalion of the South Lancashire Regiment touched down on White Beach at 0720 and, although met by machine gun and mortar fire, they had overcome all the opposition by 0810 except for the occasional sniper *(right)*. Losses were given as 18 killed, 89 wounded and 19 missing. While A Company turned right to Lion-sur-Mer, towards strong-point 'Trout' at the west end of Queen Green, the remainder of the battalion moved inland to Hermanville-sur-Mer. The lateral road to the cross-roads at Hermanville-la-Brèche was jam-packed with men with bicycles and vehicles from 185th and 9th Brigades and from No. 5 Beach Group as they moved inland to their assembly areas around Hermanville. Sergeant Mapham was following in their footsteps *(below)*.

Left: With the traffic at a standstill, Sergeant Mapham has dismounted at La Brèche d'Hermanville (sometimes just abbreviated to La Brèche — 'the gap'). *Above*: Much of the light railway, (classed as an 'intéret local'), which then ran right along the inland side of the N814 from the Orne at Ouistreham, was ripped up on D+1 to widen the carriageway.

Ahead lies the junction with Lane 8 (which could also be termed Exit road 11 according to the aerial on pages 522-523) from the beach on the right. We can tell from the number M4923763 on the Willys MB ahead that it was built under contract SM 2275 in 1944, and from the identification plate that it belonged to the 9th Infantry Brigade HQ.

Left: Approaching the crossroads, the '94' sign on the right denotes the direction of the 185th Infantry Brigade headquarters. *Right:* This is now the Place du Cuirassé Courbet and Karel specially took the comparison on June 6, 1994.

The Petard AVRE from the 77th Assault Squadron is parked on the corner of what had now become a main exit from the beach. The AVRE's name *Bulldog* has appropriately been adopted for the similar model now displayed a few yards away (shown on page 533). The number '64' on the carrier turning inland towards Hermanville-sur-Mer (another 'by-the-sea' village yet a mile inland) signifies that it is from the 2nd Battalion The Middlesex Regiment (Machine Gun).

Above: Sergeant Mapham has stood with his back to the beach to show us the view down the road to Hermanville. The traffic appears to be now under the control of the sergeant from No. 5 Beach Group armed with a Sten. The number '69' on the carrier denotes the 2nd King's Shropshire Light Infantry (185th Brigade). *Below:* In this case, the '50' reveals that the vehicle belonged to No. 246 Field Company, RE. The British unit serial numbering system was deliberately designed to confuse the enemy — and later historians! Tables of numbers — the same for each division — were produced but one has to know, first, the division concerned and also the precise order of battle at the particular date in question, before being able to then determine to what unit the number refers. The men in the foreground, wearing 3rd Division formation patches, have been described elsewhere as belonging to the 2nd Royal Ulster Rifles (9th Brigade).

Ironically, on the 50th anniversary, French gendarmes established a road-block on the very same spot — this time to *prevent* vehicles approaching the beaches!

A Ninth Air Force Marauder overflies Queen sector — a picture which now sets the scene for the next phase in the operation.

'Twenty miles from the coast and 12 to lowering point,' shouted Lieutenant-Commander Rupert Curtis, the flotilla commander, against the wind. I nodded respectfully, trying a shivering smile with eyes on the duffle coat. The navigator had done his job well — on course and ahead of the clock. Nautical twilight was past and the sea changing colour to oystershell in the grey dawn when an Aldis lamp blinked on our port bow. 'Good morning, commandos, and the best of British luck.' Curtis and his yeoman spelt out the signal. We made a suitable reply: 'Thanks; think we are going to bloody well need it.' Rupert ran up his battle ensign. War was becoming personal again.

At 0530 hours, Warspite and Ramillies opened fire. The men came up from below to stretch legs, and sea-sick soldiers gulped in fresh air. Muzzle blast from the turrets of the ironclads lit the dawn with a yellow glare as 15-inch guns hurled their one-ton shells into the batteries round Le Havre. The fearsome salvoes screamed over like trains coming out of a tunnel. 'That is just an overture', I said. 'Listen to the racket starting on the starboard side; old Ajax with destroyers are way on ahead, shooting up defences. At six o'clock, some real noise will startle the Herrenvolk.'

BRIGADIER THE LORD LOVAT, 1978

Lord Lovat, commanding the 1st Special Service Brigade: 'The 6th Airborne Division and 1st SS Brigade would be responsible for holding the left flank of the Allied bridgehead. The brigade, consisting of four commandos, was to land on the extreme left on Queen Beach and cut inland to join forces with two brigades dropped inland overnight by glider and parachute. No. 4 Commando was to destroy a battery and garrison in Ouistreham, then later rejoin. The rest of the brigade, landing 30 minutes after No. 4, was to fight through enemy defences to reach and reinforce brigades of the 6th Airborne Division, meeting astride bridges spanning the River Orne and Caen Canal at Bénouville. We had been assigned a formidable task.' *Right:* En route for Normandy. Captain Leslie Evans is our photographer aboard Brigadier Lord Lovat's LCI(S) 519.

The commandos came in directly opposite the distinctive three-storey Maison de la Mer (since demolished) which lay between today's Rue de Pont l'Evêque and Rue de l'Amiral Courbet. The DDs are from B Squadron of the 13th/18th Hussars.

The run-in took 40 minutes. At the lowering position, we changed formation. The flotilla divided into equal flights, landing ten minutes apart. I did not want the whole brigade boiling on the beach at the same time.

The first wave — 12 motor launches [actually Fairmile LCI(S)] *in line abreast — closed to arrowhead formation as we picked up landmarks in the last mile.*

No. 6 Commando, the point element in the encounter phase, rode on the port quarter of No. 519 (the command craft), keeping station, a cricket pitch apart. No. 41 Royal Marine Commando (attached passengers in transit) rode to starboard on the right flank.

Ahead, No. 4 Commando and the Free French were landing, passing through the toe-hold hopefully seized by the 8th Infantry Brigade. They had the benefit of steel landing-craft — slow movers, but proof against the small-arms fire expected on arrival. Hutchie Burt's troop went in singing 'Jerusalem', like the fierce Covenanters of old. With them rode the brigade major and his wireless operators. In the event, communication from ship to shore was a wash-out. No. 4 landed at the double, with no help from the first arrivals. The heavy casualties sustained by the infantry on Sword came from mortars and artillery, ranged (as predicted) on the tide-mark and controlled by observation points on high ground behind.

Our own approach, which had the legs of the field, relied on speed rather than protection. The thin skins of three-ply wooden hulls did not stop machine gun bullets, and we knew it. As a precaution against trouble, I had divided headquarters, with Max in charge of the other party. Derek rode within hail, wrapped in a wet oilskin and taking a lot of spray as he searched for landmarks.

The big ships had made an impression on my subconscious mind but noise spoiled the conversation, and commandos were busy with immediate personal affairs. They looked green after the rough crossing. As we came under heavier shelling, Salsbury (who happened to be a mimic) suggested, in an Oxford accent, that the piper should get on with that blank-blank fanfare and find himself a trumpet. From a breastwork of protective rucksacks, a voice restored order. 'Watch it, mate — the old man's farting fire this morning.'

Half-seen through palls of smoke, boats were burning to our left front.

Then, with much shouting, Derek picked up his landfall: a conspicuous building, still standing, with a pitched roof. No. 6, who had trained over a stiff course, here took a tot of rum; Curtis made a slight alteration to starboard.

A tank landing-craft with damaged steering came limping back through the flotilla. The helmsman had a bandage round his head and there were dead men on board, but he gave us the V-sign and shouted something as the unwieldy craft went by. Spouts of water splashed a pattern of falling shells.

Out among the offshore obstacles — heavy poles and hedgehog pyramids with Teller mines attached — we started to take direct hits. Curtis picked his spot to land, increased speed and headed for the widest gap, our arrowhead formation closing station on either side. The quiet orders — a tonic from the bridge — raised everybody's game: 'Amidships. Steady as she goes.' The German batteries mistakenly used armour-piercing ammunition in preference to high explosive and bursting shrapnel. Derek's landing brows were shot away and beyond him Ryan Price's boat went up with a roar. Max had an unpleasant experience when a shell went through his petrol tanks without exploding. Rear headquarters got away with minor casualties. Our command ship took two shells in the stern. It happened in the last hundred yards. There was no time to look back. The impact must have swung round the two boats, Max's and mine, touched down side by side. Each carried 4,000 gallons of high-octane fuel in non-sealing tanks aft of the bridge. Had Max blown up we would have gone with him. Five launches out of 22 were knocked out, but the water was not deep and commandos got ashore wading; a few took a swim in the shell craters.

The smoky foreground was not inviting. The rising tide slopped round bodies with tin hats that bobbed grotesquely in the waves. Wounded men, kept afloat by life-jackets, clung to stranded impedimenta. Barely clear of the creeping tide, soldiers lay with heads down, pinned to the sand. Halfway up the beach, others dug themselves into what amounted to a certain death-trap. Half left, middle distance, Doc Patterson's No. 4 Commando stretcher-bearers were still struggling, under heavy loads, up to the shelter of the dunes.

'I am going in', said Curtis. He gunned his engines and bumped over the shallows. 'Stand by with the ramps!' Four able seamen sprang to the gangways. 'Lower away there', and the brows ran sweetly down at a steep angle. The command craft had a comfortable landing. On these occasions, the senior officer, stepping cautiously (rather than attempting a headlong dive), is first off the boat. Surprisingly, it is as safe a place as any. The water was knee-deep when Piper Millin struck up 'Blue Bonnets', keeping the pipes going as he played the commandos up the beach. It was not a place to hang about in, and we stood not on the order of our going. That eruption of 1,200 men covered the sand in record time.

BRIGADIER THE LORD LOVAT, 1978

Another priceless moment captured for ever on film by Captain Evans. Piper Bill Millin (we saw him earlier on page 245), in the right foreground, strikes up *Blue Bonnets* and the commandos splash ashore to the skirl of the pipes. Brigadier Lord Lovat is said to be the figure in the water just to the left of Millin's left arm. The time is shortly after H+1 hour.

As we ran up the slope, tearing the waterproof bandages off weapons, the odd man fell, but swift reactions saved casualties. My O group did well through the soft sand and flung themselves down behind the nearest pillbox taken single-handed by Knyvet Carr. The job had been the responsibility of the East Yorks; Carr (a skinny but determined subaltern known as 'Muscles' in No. 4) would have won a VC in less demanding circumstances as he bombed his way into the enemy wire.

Others were less fortunate: Max's brother-in-law, Eric Kiaer, was killed before we reached the dunes. Wounded and half drowned in landing, pulled over by the heavy rucksack, then picked out and dragged over the sand — Brian Mullen the artist, like a broken doll, lay with both legs shattered, at the end of a bloody trail. He was beyond speech but out of pain; a glance showed a hopeless case and death was busy with him. A gifted man, Mullen should have landed later with the reserves, but he would not hear of it. No volunteer in the whole brigade was prouder of his beret.

David Wellesley Colley, a Downside boy with a cheerful smile, lay against the pack of a sergeant who had pulled him into shelter. He was shot through the heart. Tears were running down the NCO's face. 'Mr Colley's dead, sir. He's dead. Don't you understand? A bloody fine officer,' he repeated in shock as a field dressing was wrapped round a broken arm. Little Ginger Cunningham, RAMC, with the flaming red hair, had his legs shot from under him as he ran up the beach, but he was picked up by big Murdoch McDougall and got clear. His swearing between lamentations is recorded: 'To think they could miss a big bugger like you, those f—ing Germans, and then blank something well chose to pick on me!' After patching up more wounded, and with the help of my wading stick, he set off after the commando and stayed with them through D-Day.

There was no time to catch the breath. A hot reception — in terms of noise. Destructively, it could have been worse. Except for direct hits, the long-range heavy stuff wasted each shell burst, bunkering deep into the dunes. During the saturation bombing, Monsieur Lefèvre, a Resistance leader, risked death to walk from Ouistreham and cut cables connected with flame-throwers in the beach defences. He did more than the 8th Brigade, who landed to our immediate front. A poor showing in the last rehearsal was faithfully repeated on the battlefield.

As well as Captain Evans with his stills camera, Sergeant George Laws was shooting ciné: 'I took several shots of the other assault craft on the way in, and as we neared the beach everybody was ordered to crouch below the top edge of the craft for the final run in. The din of covering gun-fire and the screech of the rocket-launching ships, and the oncoming return fire, was terrific. About 30 yards from touch-down, with mortar bombs dropping around us, there was an almighty explosion which caused the LCA to lurch sideways, throwing everybody into a heap.'

We passed through them, leaving platoons scrabbling in sand where the shelling hit hardest, digging holes which would be drowned when the tide returned. No. 6 Commando led the way. Alan Pyman, commanding the point element with Donald Colquhoun, bombed a path through the built-up area, widening the gap where No. 4 had previously forced a passage. Throwing down rucksacks, the troop moved fast, mopping up pillboxes and the immediate strong points with hand grenades and portable flame-throwers; supporting Bren guns sprayed lead at every loophole and casement aperture. Houses not destroyed by bombardment were occupied by a few Germans; firing small arms, they sniped from roofs and windows. These pockets of resistance were wiped out by selected marksmen.

The landing was a soldier's battle — total confusion which favours spirited assault — and it was soon over. Above the crash of shells and mortars, Derek shouted among the buildings like Marshal Ney leading the Old Guard at Waterloo. Soon a trickle of grey uniforms appeared: bewildered men in shock, their hands clasped behind bare heads. (The captured Germans seemed pleased to throw their hats away.) Some scuttled in a bee-line back into concrete positions already captured. Others hurried towards the beach, where Peter Young and No. 3 Commando were landing in the second flight with No. 45 Royal Marines under Reis. I heard later that, humping some wounded as they ran, the demoralised Germans splashed to the boats, crying: 'Engeland, Engeland!'

We were almost through the Atlantic Wall. The immediate defences were laid out with German thoroughness: they warrant a description. They were not, as it were, a continuous row of grouse butts, but rather a system of ingeniously interlocked defence works equipped with every weapon, from underwater obstacles and devices to set the sea on fire to wire and minefields at the water's edge, ranging back through strong points laced with machine guns and anti-tank guns to distant artillery and self-propelled half-track cannon — all bearing on the beach. Beyond lay German infantry dug into weapon pits — again with interlocking fields of fire. The tanks and armour were held some distance to the rear. It was a question of how long they would stay there!

A Commando, of which there were four in the 1st Special Service Brigade (Nos. 3, 4 and 6, and No. 45 Royal Marine) comprised a nominal strength of 24 officers and 440 other ranks divided, not into companies like an infantry battalion, but into 'troops' each of three officers and 60 men. No. 4 Commando was to pass through the 8th Infantry Brigade leading the assault on Queen sector and move east to capture the gun batteries at Ouistreham before rejoining the rest of the 1st SS Brigade. No. 6 Commando was to advance inland by way of the GC35 through Colleville-sur-Orne and St Aubin d'Arquenay direct to Bénouville to relieve the forces holding the bridges, while Nos. 3 and 6 Commandos were to follow up at H+90. As we have seen from Major-General Gale's account in the chapter on the 6th Airborne, the 1st SS Brigade was under his overall command, bearing in mind its duties fell within the objectives of that division to secure the eastern flank of the beach-head.

Each pillbox was a citadel of reinforced concrete, sunk hull-down and half-buried in the ridges of the dunes. Walls two feet thick stood six feet above ground level, their height made up by a very solid roof giving further feet of concrete head cover. They were certainly bomb- if not blast-proof and made equivalent precautions at home appear inadequate. Positions sited in depth, 100 to 150 yards apart, were surrounded with barbed wire, with minefields in between. No pillbox faced directly to the front, but each was at an angle to either side, sited to enfilade the wire and deal effectively with approach from the flanks. Each was manned by a crew of half-a-dozen men firing 75mm cannon and light automatics.

All this was seen before smoke blinded the last nests of resistance. The furious pace quickened and determination turned the scales. Our teamwork went well. Men remembered that 'he who hesitates is lost'. No. 6 Commando moved like a knife through enemy butter.

Bobby Holmes (my demolition expert) hated marching, but he must have been uncommonly strong in the arm. To a slung Tommy gun, a pack of explosives and regulation rucksack (50lb in weight) he added a motorbike borne across his shoulders. Bobby took cover at my side behind another pillbox. He was wet from head to foot, after disappearing in a shell crater below the churned-up surface. But he held on to his wheels. They provided our only transport for some time to come.

The proximity of the Chief Royal Engineer was an embarrassment as more sappers, laden with gelignite, struggled into the O group. 'Are those bags liable to get touched off?' The brigade major moved hastily round the corner, muttering, 'HQ's going to blow up so fast that nobody will know what hit them.'

Bobby assured us plastic charges were harmless, though detonators (he tapped a hand grenade) were unpredictable. 'And who the hell controls the fuses? Let's get out of here and shake out, you're crowding headquarters.' Even as I gave the order and moved on, a shell pitched among the last REs to get to their feet. Sand partly contained the burst of shrapnel. The 'gelly' behaved correctly, but three of Bobby's men were killed and we left another sitting head down with hands pressed to his middle as blood started to seep through weakening fingers. The poor fellow was beyond speech: nothing could be done for him except the shot of morphine.

Prisoners were forced to hoist packed explosives; here also we collected a windy gentleman in officer's uniform, smoking a pipe at the bottom of a shell-hole and taking no part in the battle. The pipe annoyed me and he was kicked up, told to join the party and consider himself under arrest: Salsbury, who enjoyed any untoward occurrence, put a rifle to his back and we pushed blindly on.

BRIGADIER THE LORD LOVAT, 1978

There was one other unit we must mention within the brigade: two French troops (Nos. 1 and 8) of No. 10 (Inter-Allied) Commando led by Commandant Philippe Kieffer, but under the command of No. 4 Commando, who were to lead the attack on the Ouistreham strong point: Stützpunktgruppe Riva-Bella, which comprised six 155mm guns. The East Yorks were also to turn left along the lateral road to clear two positions near the south-west corner of Ouistreham. No. 4 Commando came ashore on Red Beach in two waves at H+30, to be followed by the HQ (Lord Lovat) of the 1st SS at 0840. Then came No. 3 Commando and No. 45 (RM). Captain Evans' picture shows commando troops — they scorned the wearing of steel helmets — moving towards the assembly area which was located in a pre-war holiday camp at the west end of the beach (between Roads 24 and 26 on the aerial photograph on pages 522-523).

Above: **The holiday camp was hard by Lane 2 (photo page 526) — the SBG bridge can be seen in this shot just in front of the beach villa. Possibly the bulldozer is the D7 described as clearing the adjacent gap.** *Right:* **The commandos regroup beyond the villa before moving off** *(below)* **to their assigned missions.** *Below right:* **Today, this whole area has been redeveloped, with no trace left of the old prefabricated buildings.**

Meanwhile, the left-hand sector battalion, the 2nd East Yorks, had first to attack and neutralise a series of strong points, and freedom from machine-gun fire was only achieved when No. 4 Commando broke into the west side of the small town of Ouistreham. While No. 4 Commando cleared Ouistreham, the rest of the 1st Special Service Brigade marched straight to the Orne river and canal bridges to link up at 1330 hours with the 6th Airborne Division.

George Laws continues his account: 'Seconds later we grounded, the ramp at the front of the craft crashed down and out we went up to our waists in water. I had already put my ciné and still cameras in waterproof bags as a precaution against a wet landing. When clear of the water's edge, I stopped to film the scene, only to find my camera had been accidentally switched on by the thump of the explosion in the LCA from a mine or underwater shell and the clockwork motor had run down. Worse still, it meant about a third of my 100ft roll of film had been wasted while running inside the rubber bag, but at least the camera was dry. Quickly winding the motor up, I proceeded to take shots on the beach, but by this time the commandos were well up the beach, so I chased after them to their assembly point' *(right).*

Above: Back to Captain Evans and this interesting shot that he took just as the commandos move out. The time is most probably around 1000 hours because this is a scene very closely described by Major Peter Young who was commanding No. 3 Commando: 'We were in touch with No. 45 Commando in the brigade's first forming-up place, but progress was delayed by minefields, confining the brigade to one track which had to be followed in single file [as seen in the background]. No. 6 Commando was ahead, but the advance was still maddeningly slow.' *Left:* Karel Margry discovered that the picture had been taken at the junction of the beach exit road — now appropriately named the Avenue du No. 4 Commando — with the N814/D514. Here at the crossroads also stands a memorial to Commandant Kieffer and the French forces of No. 4 Commando.

The men in the picture with folding parachute bicycles could well be from No. 3 Troop of No. 3 Commando who, as a follow-up unit, could trade off the burden of bikes against the advantage it offered in mobility. Those in the background were moving along what is today the D60a to Colleville-sur-Orne.

These two shots from the series proved somewhat difficult to find, not least because the original captions are none too helpful! *Top left:* Captain Evans thought he was in Ouistreham when he took this picture but Brana Radovic proved otherwise when he found the comparison *(top right)* three kilometres away in Colleville-sur-Orne! This was the village that so loved the 21st Army Group commander that after the liberation it added his name to theirs to become Colleville-Montgomery. These commandos are moving south towards Bénouville — we saw their arrival on page 244 where Captain Evans also took the pictures. *Above:* Although Evans' film rolls are out of order, and he merely captions this as 'a badly damaged village', Jean Paul believes the commandos were advancing with the Sherman DDs of the 13th/18th Hussars through the next village on the route to the river: St Aubin d'Arquenay *(right)*.

Left: We must now return to the N814 to follow in the footsteps of Commandant Kieffer and the men of the East Yorks (who were to capture strong point 'Daimler') to Ouistreham. Sergeant Laws was the cinematographer. *Right:* Robert Voskuil retraced the same route and found that a small piece of the same stone wall still stands on the left-hand side of the road.

George explains that 'while they sorted themselves out, I changed to a fresh roll (a 100ft roll only lasted one minute), laboriously threading the film round the sprockets through the film gate and finally to the take-up spool. In that rush up the beach, the commandos had suffered some 40 casualties including their Colonel [R. W. P. Dawson] who had been wounded twice. Having regrouped, the commandos set off along the coast road *(above)* to their objective — the gun battery at Ouistreham. Heavy machine gun and sniper fire was encountered, positioned in various houses along the road. At one point, in open ground, harassing fire came from inland, and this is the spot where the picture *(below)* of the Sherman giving covering fire was taken, reproduced in 1994 as one of the D-Day stamps *(right)*. Fighting continued until the battery was reached. The final assault went in with severe casualties on both sides and eventually the position was taken. It was now time to move inland and support the 6th Airborne. As we started to retrace our steps back along the road, a German plane, flying at low level, strafed us. It happened so quickly there was no time to take cover as the bullets splattered along the road — a few more casualties. Reaching the road leading to St Aubin d'Arquenay we proceeded inland. Several times we dived into the roadside ditch as mortar and shell-fire caught us and it was on one of these occasions I heard a horrible clonk within my camera and, to my horror and chagrin, I found that the spring on the motor had broken. What a climax to all my training!'

Above: The casino at Ouistreham — a venue much frequented in more peaceful days before the war as a rival to those in the fashionable resorts like Deauville-Trouville further up the coast. *Right:* In October 1942, the Germans razed the building as it stood in the field of fire to the west of the Riva-Bella strong point which commanded entry to the Caen Canal. Here, six casemates were sited just behind the beach to house the guns, with two smaller positions to the rear. Commandant Kieffer: 'Two 20mm guns fired at us non stop from the concreted roof of the casino, while snipers harassed us from the belvedere [flak tower]. Two attempts to put our Piats in position against the guns of the casino failed, leaving the crews wounded. It would have been suicide to assault the casino with the company reduced to half and without artillery support. While the commandos, sheltering as much as possible, continued to keep the casino under fire, I worked my way back along the street.'

'It was 0925 when the Centaur arrived. Climbing and breaking through an adjacent wall, the tank positioned itself facing the casino and opened fire over open sights. The first two shells hit the cupola of the casino square on and the enemy guns fell immediately silent, but their automatic weapons continued to fire. It was at that moment that, standing on the tank to direct its fire, I was wounded for the second time in the lower arm. Halted at 150 metres from the casino, the Centaur sent off another dozen shells. Without giving the adversary time to react, we launched the attack, [Maître-Principal Hubert] Faure's section on the left and [Second-Maître Louis] Lanternier's on the right. The belvedere stopped the right-hand section so the tank moved in that direction and silenced it with four shots. The assault moved across anti-tank ditches and barbed wire obstacles, and clearing the resistance nests of the casino's defensive system with bayonets and grenades slowly broke the enemy opposition.'

'On June 14, I visited the casino strong point which had been taken by the French', wrote Captain Sykes of No. 5 Beach Group (see pages 517 and 529). 'There was a heavy coastal battery under construction beside the area where the demolished casino had stood. Very crude dummy guns made of telegraph poles and junk had been put in the completed emplacements *(below)*. Flame-throwers *(above)* and tanglefoot wire protected the seaward side.'

'Just behind them stood a curious tall concrete tower *(below left)*, the walls blank of any apertures or loopholes except at the top. There, facing out across the Channel, was a wide open slot designed to house a large rangefinder. It had received a direct hit dead centre above the opening in the naval shelling. To enter the Keep, as it was called, one had to follow a narrow passage below ground level and round a couple of corners, then through a heavy metal door which was covered from the angle in the passage by a loophole. This was closed by a heavy spherical metal plate through which a machine gun was mounted. It would have been costly to try to capture the tower by assault and unnecessary, as it could no longer play an active rôle or threaten the Beach Group troops. It was believed that a small handful of Germans had sealed themselves inside.' Lieutenant Bob Orrell of No. 91 Field Company, RE, investigated at 2200 on June 9 with three men. They blew open the armoured door and were surprised to hear a voice in English inviting them upstairs. Orrell insisted they came down and over 50 Germans surrendered. *Below right:* Today, the OP serves as a museum specialising in the Atlantic Wall.

'The casino battle was featured in the film *The Longest Day* and,' Stephen comments, 'quite understandably, has been made much of by the French. When I visited the beaches 18 years later I noticed that this action had been publicised out of all proportion but, when one thinks what the British attitude would have been to being liberated by the French from the Germans, I do not suppose we would have failed to overemphasise the part played by a sole British commando.'

The re-creation of Kieffer's attack by Darryl Zanuck for the film, even if overplayed (astonishingly, the assault on the casino does not even appear in Cornelius Ryan's book) still merits inclusion here, if only for its spectacular action played out in another Normandy location. *Above left:* We saw Port-en-Bessin captured on page 428; now engineers — both British and American — demolish fortifications alongside the harbour on June 10. Note the building in the background, originally an hotel, but from 1931 the town's anti-tuberculosis preventorium. *Right:* It no longer exists today but . . .

. . . in 1961 it was still standing with its wartime damage intact. Zanuck had acquired the film rights in December 1960 for $175,000 from French producer Raoul Levy, who had purchased them soon after the book appeared in 1959. Determined not to use any stock footage, the re-creation of D-Day was to cost close to $10 million with sequences such as the landing on Omaha (filmed on Corsica with the help of the US Sixth Fleet and 3rd Battalion of the 6th Marine Division and cross-cut with additional footage shot on the Ile de Rhe) alone costing $1,500,000. However, many sequences — Pegasus Bridge, Ste Mère-Eglise and Pointe du Hoc — were shot on the actual locations, which, we feel, justifies their inclusion in this book.

Although the Ouistreham assault was not filmed in that port, it was, nevertheless, 're-fought' over ground in another port captured by another commando unit 17 years previously. The main inaccuracy was the inclusion of the casino, which the set designers had already started to erect on a car park *(bottom left)* beyond the ruined building *(bottom right)*, when Zanuck was told that it was not standing in 1944. The wartime damage to the corner was repaired, only to be blown out again in spectacular fashion! *Right:* The action begins on the Quai Félix Faure as Christian Marquand, playing Philippe Kieffer, and Georges Rivière as the fictitious Sergent Guy de Montlaur, begin the advance. A dramatic 90-second pan from a helicopter then follows the attack along the harbour, past the building with its painted sign (see page 429), changed by the art department to 'Port de Ouistreham', and across a footbridge to the Quai Baron Gérard and towards the 'Casino'. The ground action then centres around a line of dragon's teeth *(below)* in front of the 'strong point'.

Right: **Back to reality, this is one of George's last clips — taken, he believes, of two French commandos with a sleepy resident after Ouistreham had been liberated.** *Bottom:* **Jean Paul Pallud found the Auberge du Cheval Blanc still in business at the main crossroads in the town; the Avenue de la Mer leading to Riva-Bella is on the left.**

The record of the 3rd Division is the most disappointing of all the assault sectors. Having started off with commendable élan, with the rapid capture of Hermanville, the progress of the division afterwards gave the impression of over-cautiousness. All three British assault divisions had had previous battle experience, but the 3rd Division had not previously taken part in a seaborne invasion assault. A more dynamic formation would not have dug in at Hermanville, but would have devised a plan, with the tanks, supporting artillery and tactical air force, designed to outflank the enemy at Périers. This should not be taken as criticism of the troops, but rather a comment on the lack of training and battle experience of some of their officers.

On the airfield near Lille, Wing Commander Josef 'Pips' Priller and Sergeant Heinz Wodarczyk ran for their two solitary FW 190 fighter planes.

The Luftwaffe's 2nd Fighter Corps headquarters had telephoned. 'Priller', the operations officer had said, 'the invasion has started. You'd better get up there.'

Priller had exploded: 'Now you've dropped it! You damned fools! What the hell do you expect me to do with just two planes? Where are my squadrons? Can you call them back?'

The operations officer had remained perfectly cool. 'Priller', he had said soothingly, 'we don't know yet exactly where your squadrons have landed, but we're going to divert them back to the field at Poix. Move all your ground personnel there immediately. Meanwhile, you had better get up to the invasion area. Good luck, Priller.'

It was 9 a.m. when they took off. They flew due west, hugging the ground. Just over Abbeville, high above them, they began to see Allied fighters. Priller noticed that they were not flying in tight formation as they should have been. He remembers thinking that 'if I only had some planes, they'd be sitting ducks.' As they approached Le Havre, Priller climbed for cover in the clouds. They flew for a few more minutes and then broke through. Below them was a fantastic fleet — hundreds of ships of every size and type, stretching endlessly, it seemed, all the way back across the Channel. There was a steady procession of landing-craft carrying men towards shore, and Priller could see the white puffs of explosions on and behind the beaches. The sands were black with troops, and tanks and equipment of all sorts littered the shoreline. Priller swept back into the clouds to consider what to do. There were so many planes, so many battleships offshore, so many men on the beaches, that he figured he'd have time for just one pass over the beaches before being shot down.

There was no need for radio silence now. Almost light-heartedly, Priller spoke into his microphone. 'What a show! What a show!' he said. 'There's everything out here — everywhere you look. believe me, this is the invasion!' Then, 'Wodarczyk, we're going in! Good luck!'

They hurtled down toward the British beaches at over 400 mph, coming in at less than 150 feet. Priller had no time to aim. He simply pressed the button on his control stick and felt his guns pounding. Skimming along just over the men's heads, he saw upturned, startled faces.

On Sword, Commander Philippe Kieffer of the French commandos saw Priller and Wodarczyk coming. He dived for cover. Six German prisoners took advantage of the confusion and tried to bolt. Kieffer's men promptly mowed them down.

CORNELIUS RYAN, *THE LONGEST DAY*

The attack on Colleville by the 1st Suffolks (8th Brigade) took longer perhaps than would have been expected, for the German force in the village were from the 716. Infanterie-Division — coastal defence troops who were spread over a wide area from north of Bretteville right across to the area east of the 6th Airborne Division. The whole sector in which the 3rd Division was operating had been saturated with sustained fire by aircraft and warships, and, apart from II. Bataillon of Panzergrenadier-Regiment 192 on the west side of the Caen canal (belonging to the 21. Panzer-Division, which was attacking the 6th Airborne holding the Bénouville bridge), there was no concentrated enemy force to impede the British advance.

We have now travelled the entire length of the invasion coast — a distance of about a hundred kilometres — although, as we have seen, only a small fraction of that was actually assaulted at H-Hour. Now we must return — as George Laws did — along the N814 to Hermanville to follow the main thrust to Caen . . . and it was while he was walking back along the road that George was strafed by a German aircraft — he believes by Adolf Galland, but more probably by Oberst Josef 'Pips' Priller of JG 26.

But first the capture of the strong points 'Morris' and 'Hillman'. These lay just inland from Sword and were garrisoned by the 716. Infanterie-Division — in fact 'Hillman' turned out to be the regimental headquarters of Grenadier-Regiment 736 — this plan coming from German archives. 'Information about the two main positions to be taken was fairly detailed', writes Eric Lummis who took part in the operation. '"Morris" was a four-gun 105mm battery, three guns of which were housed in two-metre thick concrete casemates; the fourth was under construction. It was surrounded by two belts of wire, the outer 9ft wide, the inner 3ft, and in between were anti-tank and anti-personnel mines. There were six machine guns and an anti-aircraft gun. "Hillman", less than a mile away, was described to us as the battle headquarters of the right-hand coastal defence battalion with a strength of 80 to 100 men. There were a number of concrete emplacements with seven machine guns and possibly two light infantry guns and an anti-tank gun manned by a platoon. Pillboxes for four heavy anti-tank guns were believed not to be occupied. Trenches connected all positions. The whole area some 600 by 400 yards was surrounded by two belts of wire, the inner 12ft wide, the outer 8 to 12ft with 40ft between them containing a minefield in four rows.'

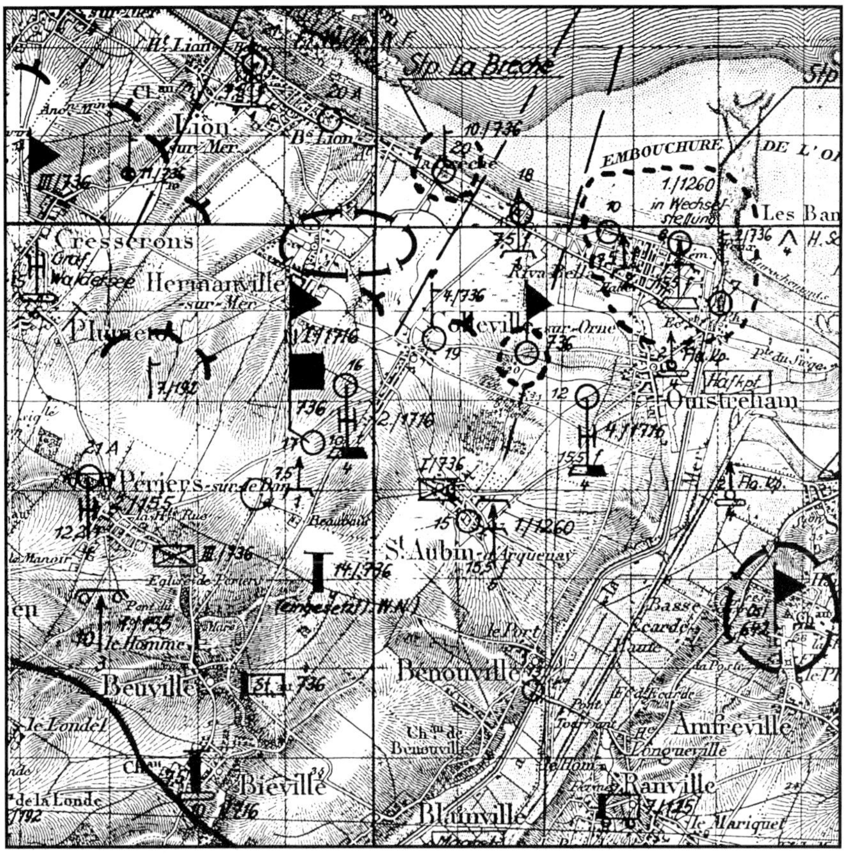

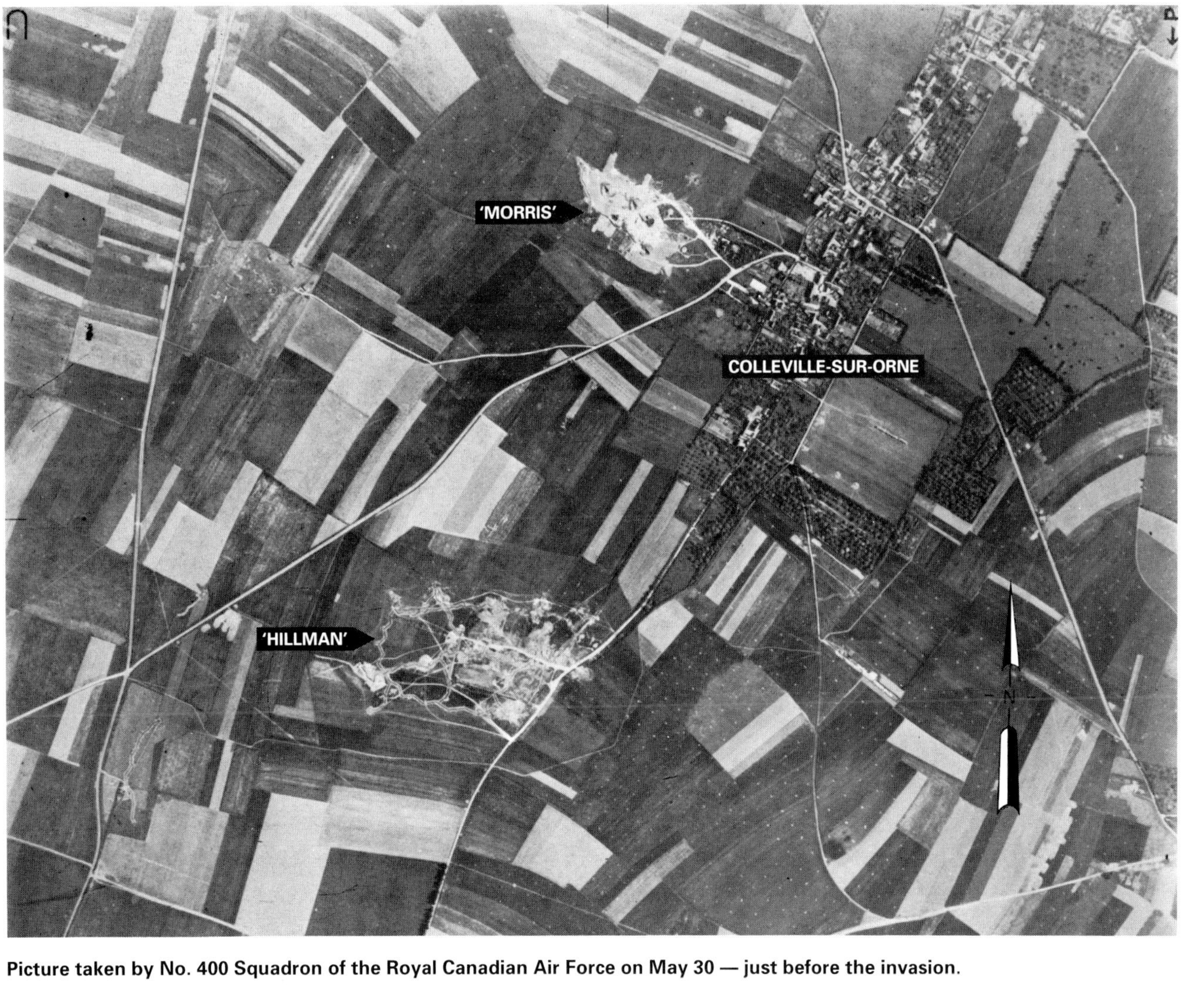

Picture taken by No. 400 Squadron of the Royal Canadian Air Force on May 30 — just before the invasion.

The Royal Mail would have us believe that this 50th anniversary commemorative issue — based on Sergeant Mapham's picture *(right)* — shows the 1st Battalion of the Suffolk Regiment. Ex-Suffolk veterans were flattered at being singled out — so much so that they didn't have the heart to tell Royal Mail that they were wrong!

As the LCAs got near the beach, they moved into line abreast and drove on at full speed. Through the thick pall of smoke along the beach, features of houses which had been picked out as landmarks began to be recognised. Then, the beach obstacles could be seen with Teller mines lashed to the top of them. The cox'ns of the LCAs who were Royal Marines skilfully weaved their way through them and other obstacles such as derelict tanks. The LCAs grounded in about 18 inches of water and those in them waded ashore some 40 yards. As they landed, though there was much noise of guns and small-arms fire, there was nothing falling on that part of the beach. Shortly afterwards, enemy guns opened up from the right front, shells whistled overhead and bursting among the beached craft. The CO, Lieutenant-Colonel Dick Goodwin, believed one had landed on the LCA he had just quit, while Major C. A. Boycott, commanding C Company, was told that his LCA had received a direct hit just as the last man left it. The crew would have gone up with it. The general impression was one of burning vehicles and craft and houses on fire beyond the beach creating a general smell of explosive and burnt metal.

Companies moved off to the right to find a way off the beach. Having found prepared exits off the by now-crowded beaches, companies moved to the assembly area about 800 yards inland. Bullets and shells were flying about in all directions but casualties were few. C Company had one man slightly wounded. Sergeant Ling from Lieutenant Mike Russell's platoon of D Company was badly wounded in the thigh just off the beach by a bullet which came from behind and another man was killed. More seriously, Captain Llewellyn, RA, the Forward Observer, Bombardment, and his party were hit by a mortar bomb as they left their LCA and had all been killed or wounded. As a consequence, without the FOB, it was not possible to call on the fire for the attack on 'Hillman'.

On arrival, the assembly area was found to be devoid of cover. The trees which had been there had all been cut down, perhaps to make 'Rommel's asparagus'. This was not unexpected as the battalion had been told at the last moment that photo reconnaissance had shown the clearing of the wood. A sniper was among the piles of brushwood left but he was either killed or made off. The CO decided to move further inland 200 or 300 yards to an orchard where companies soon assembled.

It was from here that Captain Harry Elliott, commanding the anti-tank platoon, was sent on a special mission to make contact with the 6th Airborne Division which had captured the bridges over the River Orne and the Caen Canal. He covered some eight to nine miles which he described as 'rather like walking across the front of the butts at Bisley during a rapid fire practice' and successfully completed his lone mission.

Eric Lummis, who took over A Company on D+1, explained to us that while it was nice that the picture had been credited to them, their signals unit — for the group certainly have wireless sets — made straight across the beach without stopping. Also, the Suffolk signallers did not carry toggle ropes although they wore the 'Normandy' helmets. He feels the picture probably shows part of the Beach Group. *Right:* Fortunately, Karel Margry located the spot for us among the new dwellings backing on Red Beach by the short stretch of railings which still remain. This is just a few yards east of Lane 6, the road in the foreground being the promenade — the Boulevard de la Mer. The Suffolks' assembly area was at the bend in the road where the Hermanville War Cemetery is now located.

Left: **On June 22, Sergeant Christie visited 'Morris', this picture showing the centre casemate, now completely incorporated into the house of the Maresq family** *(above).*

In the assembly area, the CO confirmed orders and companies moved off accordingly. D Company, less the two breaching platoons, moved south to a position where they could observe and bring fire upon 'Morris'. They met minefields marked with 'Achtung Minen' signs but they did not hinder progress unduly. C Company moved off immediately after with a troop of tanks south-eastwards towards Colleville, followed by the remainder of the battalion.

C Company had already started on the clearing of the village, assisted by a troop of C Squadron, 13th/18th Hussars. Under Major Charles Boycott, a clear-thinking, brave leader, later wounded, the company did its work of ensuring that the village was cleared quickly and efficiently. It was plain that they knew what had to be done and were well trained for it. They found no Germans and, therefore, had no problems as they worked through the buildings.

In the meantime, Major Philip Papillon, an imperturbable commander who inspired confidence, had reported from his position with C Company on the right that C Squadron of the 13th/18th Hussars were in position to his right and were exchanging some shots with 'Hillman'. He also reported that there appeared to be no movement from 'Morris'. As C Company was meeting no opposition in clearing the village, the CO sent for Major D. W. 'Mac' McCaffrey commanding B Company and told him that it was possible that the enemy had already deserted the battery position. He was instructed to be prepared to put in his attack as arranged in case it was a trick. Major McCaffrey ordered his company quickly up into the village behind C Company and, directly he had elbow room, he moved towards the battery.

B Company started preparing for its assault on 'Morris' and the guns of the supporting battery began to register on their target. In view of the lack of fight shown so far, Major McCaffrey decided to quicken the procedure by blowing the outer wire before calling for his artillery concentration. However, just as the bangalore torpedoes were being placed for this task, a white flag was put up and the garrison emerged from their concrete emplacements with their hands up. There were 67 in all. They were brought back into the village by four highly delighted soldiers who moved them along the street at a smart pace. They were not in good shape. They had suffered some heavy air raids on June 1 and 2, one of which we now know caused a lot of casualties.

That morning, they had again been attacked by the USAAF though there had not been any direct hits. The navy had then started their bombardment with the 6-inch guns of HMS Dragon and those of the destroyer Kelvin. Their fire was to be controlled by a naval air spotter but they reported that there was difficulty in communications with the spotting aircraft. Dragon therefore was unable to engage 'Morris' except by blind fire. It was found later that the guns were still serviceable. A photograph taken a fortnight later showed one of the guns apparently intact except for a small jagged hole in the shield presumably from a shell or a bomb splinter. Despite the strength of their two-metre-thick concrete, the positions can be seen today in very much the state they were in in 1944 with no apparent damage from all the explosive hurled at them. The effect, however, was enough to make them give up without a fight.

CAPTAIN ERIC LUMMIS, 1989

Left: **Driver R. P. Turnham hangs out his washing — this time on the Atlantic Wall. This is the rear entrance of the western-most casemate. 'Morris' may have given up without a fight, but this was not to be the case at 'Hillman'.**

Although Sergeant Christie had taken four pictures all told of 'Morris', unfortunately he did not visit the more important position, only half a mile away, of 'Hillman'. Its capture took over six hours, the Suffolks suffering in the process over 20 killed and a similar number of men wounded. It was certainly the strongest position in the 3rd Division sector — its strength greatly under-estimated by the planners — and it was possibly the most formidable in the whole Second Army area. Having 'purchased' the battery with their blood, it was very appropriate that The Suffolk Regiment Association should acquire part of the title in actuality. In February 1989, through the generosity of the land-owner, Madame Suzanne Lenauld (whose father-in-law had been the wartime Mayor of Colleville), the association purchased one of the concrete bunkers *(above)* on which they affixed a memorial plaque: 'In 1944 this bunker formed part of the strong point known as "Hillman", covering an area of 600×400 metres. "Hillman" consisted of 12 emplacements, with concrete up to 3½ metres thick. It was armed with anti-tank and machine guns, some in armoured cupolas immune to all tank guns. It was the Regimental HQ of the coast defences of the area, defended by over 150 men. Despite the absence of the planned heavy air bombing and naval gun support the position was taken by 1st Bn The Suffolk Regiment on 6th June 1944 with the support of C Sqn 13/18th Royal Hussars (QMO), A Sqn Staffordshire Yeomanry [recalled before they could take part], 2 batteries of 33 and 76 Field Regiments Royal Artillery, a detachment of 246 Field Coy Royal Engineers, and a machine gun platoon of 2nd Bn The Middlesex Regiment.'

Captain Geoff Ryley, commanding A Company, went off to make a closer reconnaissance; C Company pushing one platoon forward to protect the reconnaissance and deployment of A Company and another platoon through the orchards on the left where they could see the open country so as to form a defensive flank for the operation on that side. Thus, with B Company on the right, A Company was reasonably secure.

At the same time, the platoon of D Company with company HQ collected the breaching platoon which had been with B Company, and waited in reserve at the top of the village.

The battery commander was now registering his guns on this enemy strong point and the battalion 3-inch mortars were doing the same.

Just before 1300 hours, Captain Ryley told me that he was ready and I laid on 'Grab' for 1310 hours, giving this out over the air. At 1310 hours, the HE came down, laid on by artillery, mortars and tanks; the breaching platoon with A Company under Lieutenant Mike Russell, ready to move forward to the outer wire. Then, with the lifting of the HE and under cover of smoke, the platoon crawled forward through the corn; the bangalore torpedoes were placed under the wire and blown. Next, the mine clearance sheep tracking party made their three-foot-wide lane through the minefield and laid the white tape for the troops to follow. When these reached the inner wire, the second bangalore section came up and placed their torpedoes. Here Lieutenant Russell had bad luck as the first initiating device to fire the torpedo failed to go off, and he had to go back and fire another one. This was successful and the breach was made. This platoon of D Company carried out their task extremely well, working just as they had done on training many times before; but in this case they were within 50 yards or so of the enemy. They were then pulled back into company reserve.

The first assault platoon of A Company then moved forward through the breach, crawling under cover along a narrow sunken lane which enabled the troops to get within about 30 yards of the outer wire. The platoon got through the gap, the enemy opening up with machine guns; but the platoon went on into the trenches. These proved of little value for, when they moved again, the Germans from their shelters and emplacements brought heavy machine gun fire to bear at short range.

The enemy now had the gap in the wire taped and any movement brought bursts of automatic fire; casualties began to mount up. However, by use of 2-inch mortar smoke, the second platoon got into the enemy's trench position but were brought to a standstill like the first platoon. Captain Ryley was killed and Lieutenant Trevor Tooley mortally wounded, also Corporal F. Stares, his leading section commander. It was not possible to bring these two latter in as no movement across the open was possible. Other wounded from the vicinity of the gap were dragged back through the corn to the sunken lane, where the stretcher bearers carried them back to the Regimental Aid Post.

By this time, my carrier and the battery commander's tank had arrived; this gave us a No. 19 set, a link on the tank squadron net, and on the battery commander's tank, his proper communications to his guns, both of which were great assets. The smaller sets had not been working well due to the great number in use over the area.

As there appeared to be no enemy anti-tank guns left in action in the position, I ordered the tanks up to the outer wire in order to give the troops close support.

At this time, the 2nd Norfolks, who were to pass through us, started to move out to the left and bypass the position; as it was obvious that it would be some time before it was finally subdued.

The divisional commander, Major-General Tom Rennie, came up to my OP and asked how we were getting on. On being told the situation, he said: 'Well, you must get it before dark; and in time to allow you to dig in on your consolidated positions. Enemy armour is about and they will probably counter-attack at first light.' I assured him we should succeed. He left with a cheery 'Good luck'.

The arrival of the tanks at the outer wire did not materially improve the situation; they prevented any enemy movement across the open, but they could not penetrate the emplacements or cover our men from the enemy machine gun fire. The steel cupola which was causing most of the trouble was not even penetrated by several rounds of 17-pdr armour-piercing shot, though no doubt the occupants suffered from a severe headache. It was obvious that it would not be possible to capture the position unless the tanks went inside the wire to enable the infantry to get up close to the emplacements and winkle the Boche out. In the absence of enemy anti-tank guns, this seemed a justifiable task for the Shermans, and accordingly I decided to make a vehicle gap and lay on a fresh attack with a short preliminary bombardment.

I ordered Lieutenant K. G. Perry, who had taken over command of A Company, to withdraw his men from the position to the sunken lane so as to get them clear of the bombardment. Then I ordered the Royal Engineers' officer, Lieutenant Arthur Heal, to widen the gap to nine feet. This he proposed do with a British Mark III mine buried deep; a job that would have taken at least an hour. It was only possible to work lying full length on the ground as any exposure drew machine gun fire.

Meanwhile the Squadron Liaison Officer and the battery commander went off in the battery commander's tank to look at the left of the position. They returned about 20 minutes later and the Liaison Officer sat down saying that he had a slight headache, as the tank had just gone up on a mine. The tank was in fact a complete wreck, one track being blown off and the tank completely burnt out.

The Brigadier [E. E. E. 'Copper' Cass] arrived and I asked him for two Flails which would speed up the process of mine clearance and make a wider track. This he arranged to do. But we did not stop work on the gap, and this was just as well as the gap was open before there was any sign of the Flails. The Squadron Leader agreed to take a chance with the gap, even though the sapper had only been able to give it a 50-50 chance of complete clearance.

Time was getting on and I called for a preliminary bombardment of five minutes HE from the tanks and two batteries at Rate Four. When this lifted, the tanks went through, negotiating the gap safely. The troops followed them up and set about cleaning up the complicated position — one platoon from each of C and D Companies assisted A Company with this task. It was a slow business and, at the start, the tanks drew away too far from the infantry; but were called back and then were of great assistance.

Whatever had been the state of the morale of the enemy we first encountered, there was no doubt that the men in this strong point had been told and were determined to fight it out to the end. They continued to fire from their emplacements while the mopping up was going on and in some cases they had to be blown out with heavy explosive charges which the battalion pioneers were carrying.

When it appeared that resistance was decreasing and the situation under control, I ordered B and D Companies forward to their previously arranged consolidation areas, as it was essential that they should have as much time as possible for digging in before dark.

The last resistance on the strong point ended about 2015 hours and our men moved on as quickly as possible to get on with consolidation.

LIEUTENANT-COLONEL R. E. GOODWIN,
CO, 1st BTN, THE SUFFOLK REGIMENT, 1944

The battleground has mellowed; the habitations expanded. This picture covers the same area as that on page 551.

***Left:* Over 250 prisoners were captured including the regimental commanding officer, Oberst Krug. These men are being marched through the centre of Hermanville on June 7 back towards the coast. *Right:* Jean Paul apologises for the van, but on every occasion that he visited the Grande Rue it was parked right outside the critical spot.**

Meanwhile, the leading troops of the division, a mobile column consisting of the 2nd King's Shropshire Light Infantry (185th Brigade), riding the tanks of the Staffordshire Yeomanry, were still on the line Biéville–Blainville, three miles from the outskirts of Caen. The division had made few calls on the air forces for direct support, which was of course a mistake, but the air cover had rendered a valuable contribution to the 3rd Division's operations since there had been no intervention by the main tank force of the 21. Panzer-Division during the morning of D-Day.

By mid-morning, the 3rd Division assault was falling behind schedule. The 185th Brigade — the 2nd Battalion, The Royal Warwicks; the 1st Battalion, The Royal Norfolks; and the 2nd Battalion, The King's Shropshire Light Infantry — was to head for Caen, but their tank support was still trying to clear the beach.

The number '50' borne by the carrier which once stood on this corner of the road to Colleville refers, as we have seen, to No. 246 Field Company. The REs have completed (or are about to begin) mine clearing. Meanwhile, the half-track (no unit identifier visible, but most probably part of the 27th Armoured Brigade) pushes on southwards towards Caen.

Left: **A hundred yards from the crossroads, the commander of the brigade, Brigadier G. E. Prior Palmer on his scout car gives instructions to Captain E. H. Palmer, his staff captain. In this case the '50' denotes the headquarters of the 27th Brigade. The armour of the Staffordshire Yeomanry had been detailed to support the advance but, at 1100 hours, the tanks had still not cleared the beach. Frustrated at the delay, by 1200 the Shropshire commander, Lieutenant-Colonel F. J. Maurice, was given permission by Brigadier K. P. Smith to set out on foot via the GC60 (now the D60) through Beuville and Lébisey. From Hermanville, Caen was 12 kilometres away, but the troops had barely covered a third of the distance when they came upon a German battery near Périers. However, the Yeomanry had now caught up so, leaving a company and a squadron of tanks to deal with the position (which held out until evening), the remainder of the force bypassed it and had reached Biéville by 1600. However, the reconnaissance troop of the Yeomanry now spotted the approach of German armour — the expected counter-attack by 21. Panzer-Division. The Yeomanry and Shropshire anti-tank gunners deployed for the attack.**

The battle groups of panzergrenadiers had, since the early hours of D-Day, made repeated counter-attacks against the 6th Airborne Division, on both sides of the Orne. These had all been repulsed. We now know that tank groups of Panzer-Regiment 22 had been destined to reinforce the efforts against 6th Airborne but, when the seaborne landings became known, the commander of 21. Panzer-Division, Generalmajor Edgar Feuchtinger, recalled them and ordered that they should cross the Orne at Caen and at Colombelles to concentrate on the north side of the city. Any movement of these tanks observed from the air at once received the attention of the tactical air force. At General Dempsey's request on the morning of D-Day, all German troop movements in the vicinity of Caen were subjected to almost continuous air attack.

Supporting the Shropshire's own 6-pounders at Biéville were a few 17-pounder self-propelled guns of the 20th Anti-Tank Regiment. Pictures taken during the actual battle at Biéville and on the Périers ridge, so decisive for the outcome of D-Day, do not appear to exist — but at this point, before we leave Hermanville, perhaps this is the next best thing — anti-tank gunners deployed facing south for the expected German armoured counter-attack. Jean Paul discovered that they were lining the Rue de la Croix Rose. When the approach of the German armour was spotted, the Yeomanry colonel immediately asked for the release of his A Squadron, which had been ordered to 'Hillman' but had not yet arrived there. This squadron had just taken up position to the west of Biéville when about 40 enemy tanks, moving very fast, attacked.

Generalmajor Feuchtinger claimed that from the south-west side of Caen his Panzergrenadier-Regiment 125 — reduced by a combination of air attacks and breakdowns to 90 serviceable panzers — together with two infantry battalions, advanced northwards to oppose the Allies. It was not until 1600 hours that British tanks of the Staffordshire Yeomanry, scouting south of Biéville, reported German tanks advancing northwards.

About 40 panzers put in a 'cavalry charge' attack, apparently not expecting

The 21. Panzer-Division had split its force into three. Belatedly opposing the 6th Airborne Division was Kampfgruppe von Luck, under Major von Luck, the CO of Panzergrenadier-Regiment 125, comprising von Luck's own regiment (less one battailon), the 4. Kompanie of Panzer-Regiment 22, Panzer-Aufklärungs-Abteilung 21 and Panzerjäger-Abteilung 200. The force attacking on the western side of the Orne towards Lion-sur-Mer was Kampfgruppe Rauch, under Oberst Rauch of Panzergrenadier-Regiment 192, comprising his own regiment (less II. Bataillon), the 2. Kompanie of Panzer-Pionier-Bataillon 222, and II. Abteilung of Panzer-Artillerie-Regiment 155. *Above:* This PzKpfw IV belonged to Panzer-Regiment 22, whose I. and II. Abteilung (less the 4. Kompanie) formed part of the eastern force, Kampfgruppe Oppeln, under Oberst Hermann von Oppeln-Bronikowski of Panzer-Regiment 22. The other units in his task force were I. Bataillon of Panzergrenadier-Regiment 125 (minus one company), 1. Kompanie of Panzer-Pionier-Bataillon 222 and III. Abteilung of Panzer-Artillerie-Regiment 155. This force mustered over 70 PzKpfw IVs.

The picture at the top of the page defied all efforts to trace its location until Brana Radovic decided to check every level crossing over the now-dismantled railway line between Caen and Cabourg (we saw a section of it in the aerial shot on pages 242-243). Altogether, he counted 26 places where the picture could have been taken; he struck lucky just east of Démouville.

the quickly-established gun line comprising a squadron of the Staffordshire Yeomanry tanks, some 17-pounder self-propelled anti-tank guns of the 20th Anti-Tank Regiment, RA, together with the 6-pdr anti-tank guns of the Shropshire Light Infantry. Four leading German tanks were brewed up and the enemy swung away into the cover of some neighbouring woods. They were pursued by the Yeomanry and artillery fire, and suffered further casualties, whereupon they made a wide detour to the east and came in again towards the Périers ridge. A squadron of the Staffordshire tanks was awaiting them 'hull down' by Point 61, and at least 13 were knocked out: the German tanks again withdrew. Feuchtinger stated after the war that he had started the day with 124 tanks, and that by nightfall he had only 70 runners left. This seems an

The force spotted by the British at Biéville was Gepanzerte Gruppe Oppeln. As the first German tanks left the Lébisey woods, the British troops opened fire. Two PzKpfw IVs were knocked out by the Staffordshire Yeomanry and two by the Shropshire anti-tank guns. The German tanks turned away back into the woods, pursued by the Yeomanry tanks and by field-gun fire. However, von Oppeln's I. Abteilung under Major Wilhelm von Gottberg made a wide detour through Epron and Cambes and came in again, this time near Mathieu. Here, although they managed to knock out one of the 17-pounder SP guns of the 20th Anti-Tank Regiment, the Germans lost another six panzers. A Squadron of the Yeomanry knocked out four and one SP gun of the 20th Anti-Tank knocked two more. Again, the Germans broke off the attack, but they did not give up. Making another short left swing, von Gottberg came in yet again, now trying to take the Périers ridge. This time, he ran into B Squadron of the Staffordshire Yeomanry which had been left posted on the ridge at Point 61 (where the Hermanville–Caen road reaches the crest) for just such an occasion. Three more PzKpfw IVs were knocked out and again the Germans drew off. Von Gottberg later said: 'My tanks were knocked out by the British even before their tanks were within our firing range. We had to give up.' The Germans broke off their attack. Von Oppeln and his commanders were very surprised to find the Périers ridge in enemy hands, since 88mm guns of Panzerjäger-Abteilung 200 of their own 21. Panzer-Division had been in position on the ridge, and from there had stopped the Allied infantry moving inland from Hermanville earlier in the day. They were unaware that these guns had been ordered to move westwards in the course of the morning. His tanks now turned back three times, von Gottberg received orders to dig in on a line from Epron to the Orne. Still, several tanks were later knocked out, the one *(top)* by a shell through the 30mm side armour, and the one *(centre and right)*, belonging to 3. Zug of 1. Kompanie of von Gottberg's battalion, by a direct hit through the 50mm front armour.

Meanwhile, Gepanzerte Gruppe Rauch, advancing northwards on von Oppeln's left, had had more luck. Moving precisely into the gap between the British and Canadian forces, and joining up with III. Bataillon of Grenadier-Regiment 736, this force actually reached the sea at Lion-sur-Mer at 1900 hours. However, when at 2100 hours they saw massive glider forces (the reinforcement lift for 6th Airborne) passing overhead, and apparently landing behind their backs, they thought it was designed to cut them off, so Rauch decided to pull back from the coast, first to Anguerny, later that evening to von Oppeln at Epron. The evening glider landings brought cheer to the British troops but despair to the Germans: 'From the hills east of Caen, we saw the gigantic Allied armada', wrote von Luck, 'the fields littered with transport gliders. In view of this superiority, I thought, on seeing the landing fleet, there was no longer much chance of throwing the Allies back into the sea.'

The location could be Beauvais Farm which lies on the Périers ridge just east of Point 61 and just one kilometre south of 'Hillman' (which had been captured just before the glider landings began). However, the extant buildings are not conclusive evidence, hence no comparison.

When Sergeant Laws lost the use of his cine camera, he shot a few still pictures with an old Voigtländer he was carrying. This picture when released was merely captioned: 'Commando troops resting in a narrow lane near Caen'.

The 6th Airborne Division, without much of its heavy equipment, had had little enough assistance during the day, but had fought off numerous counter-attacks — the most determined and dangerous of which were made by the panzergrenadier battalions. The 1st Special Service Brigade had arrived in the afternoon and its three commando units had reinforced the airborne troops. But now, at last, the remainder of the airborne division had arrived, virtually doubling the fighting strength of the formation. In addition to two strong battalions, the glider convoy included the armoured reconnaissance unit, some light artillery, anti-tank guns and a medical unit. Stores and ammunition were also dropped by parachute.

exaggeration: our troops counted 20 abandoned tanks and the RAF knocked out six in a Typhoon aircraft rocket attack on the outskirts of Caen. There is no record of the successes achieved by the RAF in the other rocket attacks they had made.

The Shropshires made a further sortie southwards from Biéville along the Caen road, but found that there was a strong enemy force astride the highway at Lébisey: it was growing dark, and because of the danger of a renewed attack on their exposed right flank they returned to Biéville for the night.

Almost at last light, the leading company of 2nd Royal Warwickshires from 185th Brigade reached the outskirts of Blainville, having previously cleared the enemy in Le Port and Bénouville who had been attacking the Parachute Regiment's 7th Battalion all day. This coincided with the passage at 2100 hours of Allied transport aircraft towing gliders, strongly escorted by fighters.

With George's help, almost by intuition, Brana found the 'narrow lane' five miles north of the city in the little hamlet of La Basse Ecarde on the east bank of the river not far from Amfréville.

Walking wounded in the Rue du Pré de l'Isle in Hermanville. For some, the war — at least for the time being — was over.

. . . but for others it was ended for good. Last respects for a fallen comrade killed in action against 21. Panzer-Division. The Reverend Victor Leach, padre of the 13th/18th Hussars, reads the burial service. Jean Paul tracked down the location of the grave to a corner of this well-kept garden on the crossroads of the Grand Rue and Rue du Bac du Port.

The arrival was fortuitous. The 7. Armee telephone records include a report that states: 'Attack by 21. Panzer-Division rendered useless by heavy concentration of airborne troops', and the report which was sent to Rommel was in similar terms. In due course, the Allies determined from radio intercepts that the 21. Panzer-Division, less the battalions east of the Orne, had been ordered to withdraw to a line running eastwards from Cambes-en-Plaine to the Caen canal.

Regrettably, it was not until towards evening that the 3rd Division finally relieved the 6th Airborne Division at the Bénouville bridge. It was 1830 hours when the 2nd Warwicks, having cleared Le Port, took over the bridge from the airborne troops which had held out there since the early hours.

Left: **The early beginnings of the radar station. Although undated, this American sortie must have been taken circa 1942 as the northern complex (see plan *opposite*) has not yet been started. The US annotations are: 'Traces of buried mines [A], and barbed wire fence [B] to prevent accidental detonation of mines on each side of mine belt'.**

It was too early to appreciate the manner in which the enemy would react to the Allied landings. For Montgomery and Dempsey, it was a surprise that the 21. Panzer-Division had taken so long to intervene in strength in the battle, and that the tank thrust made at last around 1600 hours had lacked tactical skill and been so readily repulsed. It was not known to the Allies that the division had experienced not only an exhausting day, having been alerted around 0130 hours, but also endless frustration at being 'pushed around'. To begin with, its commander, Feuchtinger, was not sure whether he was under command of LXXXIV. Armeekorps, or under the newly formed XLVII. Panzerkorps, the commander of which had not yet been nominated; or under the HQ of Panzergruppe West. However, Feuchtinger had standing orders that, in the event of an Allied landing, he was to send two battalion groups of Panzergrenadier-Regiment 125 with his anti-tank battalion to engage the enemy east of the River Orne. This he did, and their

Below: **The same area just south-west of Douvres-la-Délivrande in 1991.**

Report by the Supreme Commander to the Combined Chiefs-of-Staff, 1946: 'In the British-Canadian sector, chief interest centred in the thrust by the British 3rd and Canadian 3rd Divisions toward Caen. Exploiting the success achieved on D-Day, they pushed southward and succeeded on June 7 in reaching points some two or three miles north and north-west of the city. However, the enemy fully appreciated the danger in this sector and, employing the tanks of 21st Panzer and 12th SS Panzer Divisions, counter-attacked successfully in ideal tank country. This counter-attack penetrated nearly to the coast, and drove a wedge between the two Allied divisions, preventing a combined attack on Caen for the time being. Subsequent events showed that the retention of the city was the key to the main enemy strategy and, during the struggles of the following weeks, the Germans fought furiously to deny us possession. Meanwhile, the Allies had their first experience of the enemy's skill and determination in holding out in fortified strong points behind our lines. Although German claims of the effects of these strong points in delaying the development of our operations were greatly exaggerated, it was undeniably difficult to eliminate the suicide squads by whom they were held. The biggest of these points was at Douvres in the Canadian sector, where the underground installations extended to 300 *(sic)* feet below the surface. It was not until June 17 that the garrison here was compelled to surrender.'

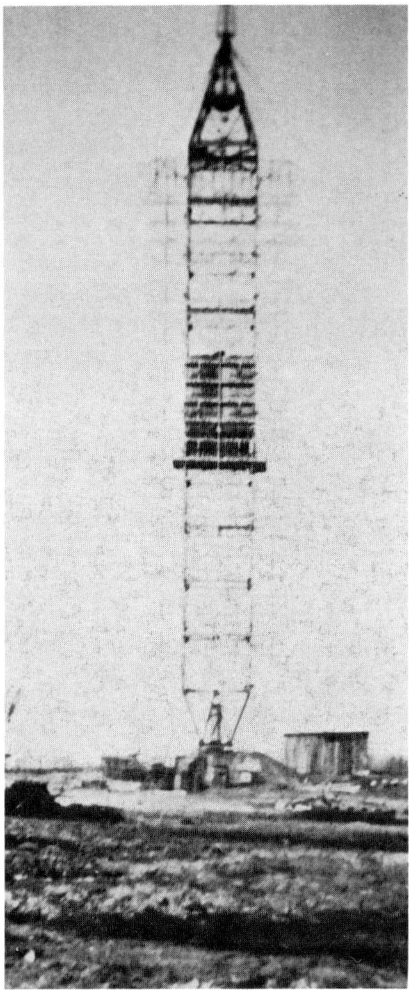

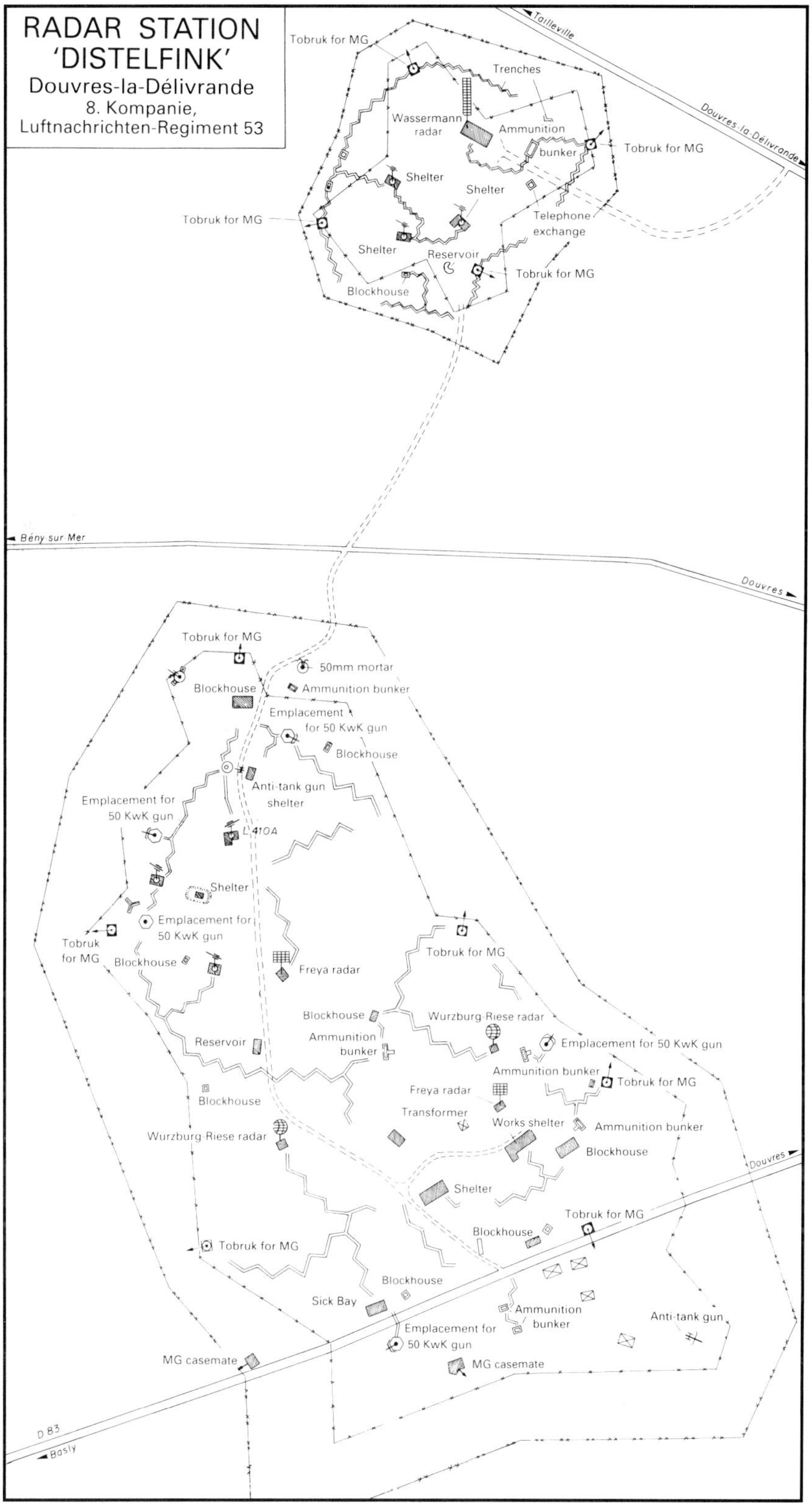

The southern installation consisted of both a Freya, the original German defence radar working on a wavelength of about 2.5 metres, and a Würzburg Riese (Giant Würzburg) with a 7.5-metre diameter paraboloid on a 53-centimetre wavelength. A Wassermann long-range early warning installation stood on the northern site. ***Above:*** **The tall antenna of the latter, which also provided a height-finding facility, gave it its Allied code-name of 'Chimney'. After the capture of the station (its German code-name was 'Distelfink'), which had been the objective of the Canadian 8th Brigade on D-Day, No. 30 Assault Unit (see page 427) was to take it over in their rôle of the intelligence seizure unit. Although the capture of Douvres was much delayed, nevertheless a section of the unit was present at its fall on D+11. However, by that time the installations were in a sorry state.**

counter-attacks on the 6th Airborne Division have been mentioned earlier. His orders also specified that he should send his Flak-Abteilung 305 to Caen, where it would join the local Flak-Kommando.

Time passed, and finally on his own personal initiative, presumably because his units on the Orne called for assistance, Feuchtinger sent a battle group including tanks to join the panzer-grenadiers on the east side of the river. It was not until 0845 hours that a message was received placing the 21. Panzer-Division under LXXXIV. Armeekorps. The commander, General der Artillerie Erich Marcks, told Feuchtinger that he wanted to send his division north and north-west of Caen, but that he was still awaiting permission to do so through the normal channels from OKW. At 1030 hours, Feuchtinger received his first clear order: he was to proceed north and north-west of Caen and restore the situation developing on the German front between Caen and Bayeux.

The battle group, which was on its way north, on the east side of the River Orne, had therefore to be diverted to the west side of Caen in order to link up with the main body, which was starting off from its location some 15 miles south of the city, near Falaise. These tank movements were quickly spotted by the Allied air forces, and were attacked repeatedly by the tactical air force and harassed by naval gun-fire. A number of tanks were destroyed before the two columns of the 21. Panzer-Division were clear of Caen, by which time it was nearly 1500 hours.

Although Douvres was basically a radar station — and an elaborate one at that which the Allies had bombed repeatedly during the previous weeks — in view of its strong defences the Germans also looked upon it as a strong point: Stützpunkt Douvres. It was occupied by a garrison of the 8. Kompanie of Luftnachrichten-Regiment 53, with a total strength of 160 split between admin; the technical personnel working on six-hour shifts; and the troops manning the Flak positions. From the beginning of May until D-Day, the site had been subjected to bomb, machine gun and rocket projectile attacks from Thunderbolts, Typhoons and Spitfires. A rather nice pair of contrasting comparisons taken by Sergeant Mapham when he visited the site on July 1. *Left:* A German 50mm anti-tank gun and a British Bofors *(right)* which is captioned as 'now occupying one of the gun pits in "Hindenburg Bastion". A German 88mm gun formerly stood on the site.'

The radar station at Douvres-la-Délivrande had been a D-Day objective, but proved more strongly defended than had been expected, and the initial attacks failed. Accordingly, the station was bypassed. It proved to be a thorn in our side, occupying a commanding position and being able to pass information regarding activities going on in the area. The job of wiping out the station was given to my own unit, a squadron of 22nd Dragoons and a Royal Marine commando. I was at that time a Lance Corporal, and my job was that of tank driver. I should mention here that the vision of the driver of a Churchill tank in action is very limited and I cannot do more than give my own account of the attack.

On the afternoon of June 17, the squadron moved up to the forward start line which was about half a mile from the radar station and concealed from it by trees and a farm. We arrived here at about 1600 hours, and it was a gloriously warm sunny afternoon. Having moved up into position, we dismounted, and had a meal and some tea. While we indulged ourselves in this manner, the station was being subjected to a bombardment by heavy artillery.

At about 1700 hours, we moved in to the attack. We were to make a direct attack across the minefield, and, to clear lanes through this belt, which was about 40 yards deep, Flail tanks or 'Crabs' of B Squadron 22nd Dragoons were employed. Each Crab was followed by three AVREs, my own being second in line.

We had penetrated about one-third of the minefield before anything happened. But then we came under heavy anti-tank fire. The fact that I was wearing headphones, together with the noise of the engines, prevented me hearing the noise of the gun-fire. But every now and then I could see a column of dust and smoke go up as a shell landed, and the flashes from the 75mm guns of the Crabs as they replied. As we moved through the minefield, I removed my gloves to light a cigarette. Smoking inside tanks is strictly against orders, and I was to suffer for this later.

When we got through the belt of mines, the Crabs pulled to one side and we opened up at short range with both Besas and the Petard at any target we could find. I remember seeing two direct hits on concrete shelters by my gunner, which completely demolished them.

When the initial attempts to capture the station on D+1 proved abortive, the position was bypassed. On D+11, the 26th Assault Squadron, Royal Engineers, was given the job of capturing 'Hindenburg' with the assistance of B Squadron of the 22nd Dragoons, with troops of C Squadron under command, and the support of No. 41 Royal Marine Commando. Seeing that this was still basically the Canadian sector, Sergeant Ken Bell was on hand to picture the preliminary bombardment.

It would be nice to be able to claim that these commandos passing through nearby Douvres-la-Délivrande are from No. 41 (RM) Commando on their way to attack 'Hindenburg' but, as the picture was taken ten days before the attack, they are most probably from No. 46 Commando. Nevertheless, it is an appropriate picture to include at this point because the tower of the church on the left was used by the various commanders to give them a fine grandstand view of the coming assault.

The AVRE in front of me succeeded in getting its offside track in a deep trench and was stuck there immovable. My commander gave me the order to overtake on the left. As I did so, there was a terrific concussion and my vehicle gave a lurch. My instrument panel lights went out as well as all the interior lights. My first impression was that we had hit a mine, and I tried the steering to see if the tracks were intact. As I did so, I saw my co-driver lying with a terrible wound in his head. He was unmistakably dead, and I then realised we had been hit by a shell. The next moment, the whole of the driving compartment caught fire. I was almost suffocated by flame, but managed to open the hatch over my head enough to scramble through. As I was climbing out, the ammunition in the hull Besa was exploding and a piece of shrapnel hit me in the right leg. I jumped clear and ran for a bomb crater about 15 yards away. I was joined by my wireless operator and my gunner. Hardly had we dropped into it than my tank blew up. The force of the explosion blew the turret, which weighs about ten tons, 50 yards away.

When we had recovered from the first effects of shock, we found we were all severely burned about the hands and face, the burns on my hands being due to the fact that I had removed my gloves to light that cigarette! I decided to try and get to the ditched tank to get the first-aid kit which is carried outside an AVRE in the rear. Imagine my feelings when, after having crawled about 20 yards, I found the container for the first-aid kit full of nuts and bolts. On my way back, I saw the other tank crews place their 70lb charges on top of the underground emplacement and lie doggo until they were blown.

I joined the crew of the ditched AVRE and we set out to see if we could winkle out any enemy that might be above ground. We were joined by men of the Royal Marine commando, who had come in to mop up. The white flag appeared and the job was done.

LANCE CORPORAL H. B. SORENSEN,
26th ASSAULT SQUADRON, RE, 1946

This shot was even taken from that tower, although not of the scene described by one eye-witness on June 17 when 'interested commanders leaned out to see the battle looking, to an observer on a hillside a few hundred yards away, curiously reminiscent of a part of a battle scene from an illuminated manuscript of the Middle Ages'.

'There is still one German strong point which is holding out within six miles of the Normandy coast and many miles behind our front line. The Navy have had a try at smashing it. The Air Force had a try. But still the German garrison held out. We've called off all big-scale attempts to clear it up because the commander in the area has ruled that no heavy casualties must be risked in smashing it. But the point is that this strong point of the West Wall which the Canadians swept past in the first day is still intact. All you can see of it is ordinary fields, with a few grass mounds here and there indicating defence points. You can see a concrete tower hidden amongst trees, and through binoculars you can see the signs: "Achtung. Minen". Beware of mines. This is a sample of what the Germans hoped to prepare for us along the coast. We've surrounded it, we've shelled it, we've bombed it, and it's still unopened.' Robert Barr, BBC, June 17, 1944.

'You have heard of that colossal strong point just along the coast at Douvres where getting on for 200 Germans held out till last night. That's a place to see. Somebody this morning called it an inverted skyscraper. That's not an unreasonable description. Fifty feet and more into the ground it goes — four stories deep. On the surface you barely notice it. The top's almost flush with the ground. But going down those narrow concrete stairways you think of going into the vaults of the Bank of England. And the Germans did themselves well down below there — central heating, electric light, hot water, air conditioning, radios, telephones, comfortable well-furnished rooms and offices, well-equipped workshops, and ample supplies of food and of ammunition. The Germans who were standing here on this ground 14 days ago certainly must have thought that they had little to fear, and yet what a change now!' Frank Gillard, BBC, June 18, 1944.

Surprisingly little damage had resulted from the pre-D-Day attacks, and up to June 6 only one barrack building had been burned out. The radar installations themselves, protected by concrete, were practically undamaged. The RP attacks were particularly ineffective, but the machine gun fire into the radar cabins was feared and effective, and eight men had been killed prior to D-Day. Apart from short intervals spent repairing cables and aerial severed by MG fire, the installations were kept continually in operation. On the night of June 6/7, the radar personnel had been busily employed monitoring Allied shipping and at 0100 hours, the Würzburg plotted around 100 ships, the information being passed to Jafü 5. The Würzburg and Freya were kept operating even through the later artillery and tank attacks, and it was only when capture became imminent that all the technical apparatus was destroyed by explosive charges. The garrison put up a spirited defence and not until Allied tanks broke through the minefields did the station finally surrender.

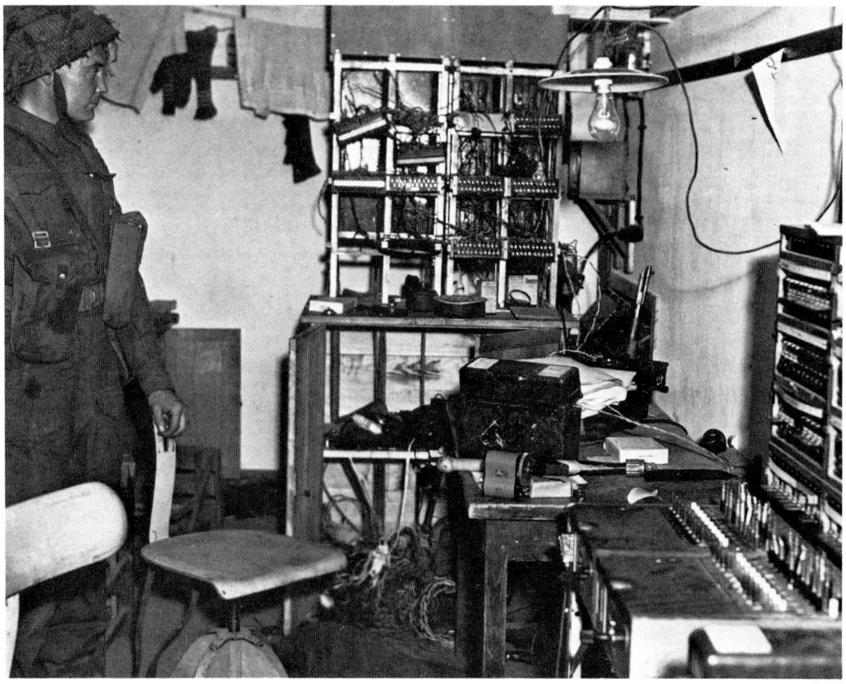

XXII Dragoons, 1760-1945: 'In clouds of dust, and with a shattering clanking of chains, the flails moved into the minefield. German machine guns stuttered away here and there, swishing around them apparently at random. From a patch of dead ground, a group of supporting flails, hull down, loosed off machine guns and 75mm shell to keep the German heads down. For half an hour and more, the flails moved smoothly on, biting through the minefield and touching off mines that sent up tall pillars of heavy black smoke. Then they were through, and in the most leisurely manner the AVREs rolled up the lanes to the mouths of the fortresses, where their crews jumped out and placed their stinging "beehives". Suddenly, one of their tanks went up with a roar and was swallowed up in flame and smoke. But there was little opposition; there could not be, for the whole area was swept by fire from the flails.'

'Again a sudden quiet as the commandos closed in; and then an astonishing sight. From all the trenches and underground shelters, Germans began to pour out, hands up, finished with their war. Turret lids popped open. Crews scrambled out on their tanks and waved, or leapt down to take prisoners. Down below in the fortress-like yard of a farm, where the prisoners were being assembled, some of the Frenchmen were more demonstrative. There was one small boy dancing hysterically in the road screaming: "Cut their throats; cut their throats!" The prisoners, however, were for the most part badly shaken and dispirited men, glad to be out of it all. Meanwhile, flail crews were scrambling down among the shambles of the radar station's fortresses for souvenirs and the legitimate spoils of war. A lucky few found bottles of indubitable champagne and tins of paté-de-foie-gras. All found a trophy of some sort in the rubbish that was thickly piled along the fortress floors. They had certainly earned them.'

'In this model operation we suffered no damage whatever to our men, and lost only tracks on five tanks. The engineers lost three men killed and seven wounded, and had to write off four Churchills. That was the total cost of an operation that wiped out a stronghold of considerable local nuisance value in under two hours and yielded over 200 more prisoners for the cages down by the beaches. Of deeper importance to us was the fact that in their first land assault on a strong point in battle, our machines, our methods, and our training had had a brilliant success. That night, the BBC war reporter, whose record was played in the nine o'clock news bulletin, was the victim of poor staff work at Portland Place. He informed his large public that the Germans were holding out in Douvres. He described the strength of the defences and the tenacity of their defenders. "We've surrounded it," he concluded, "we've shelled it, we've bombed it, and it's still unopened." In the orchard at Cresserons we took leave to disagree.'

What would the men who assaulted the position in June 1944 say if they returned 50 years later to find that a Giant Würzburg once again stood at Douvres? This one came from the Observatoire de Paris and was set up at what is now called Le Musée Radar.

At the end of the day, General Montgomery could claim with some justification that 'we had achieved surprise, the troops had fought magnificently, and our losses had been much lower than had ever seemed possible. We had breached the Atlantic Wall along the whole "Neptune" frontage, and all assaulting divisions were ashore. In spite of the bad weather, the sea passage across the Channel had been successfully accomplished and, following this, the Allied naval forces had given valuable support by fire from warships and craft; the Allied air forces had laid the foundation of success by winning the air battle before the invasion was launched, and by applying their whole collective striking power, with magnificent results, to assist the landings.

'In spite of the enemy's intentions to defeat us on the beaches, we found no surprises awaiting us in Normandy. Our measures designed to overcome the defences proved successful. Although not all the D-Day objectives had been achieved — in particular, the situation on Omaha beach was far from secure — and in all the beach-head areas there were pockets of enemy resistance, and a very considerable amount of mopping-up remained to be done, we had gained a foothold on the Continent of Europe.'

After lying forgotten by everyone except the most faithful, its bunkers and casemates buried as more peaceful pursuits overtook the battery site, Douvres was resurrected from the ashes by the Caen Mémorial and inaugurated on June 5, 1994. Further work will be undertaken to reinstate much of the site as it was in 1944. ***Top:*** **Casemate 'Anton', in the centre of the southern site, was uncovered and converted into a museum, although unfortunately with the addition of an additional set of metal stairs to mar the comparison.** ***Above:*** **Sergeant Savage commanded the Bofors crew (see page 564) from the 102nd Light Anti-Aircraft Regiment.** ***Right:*** **'His' bunker still remains, but time and the elements have served to extinguish 'Hindenburg'. However, does the good sergeant's own graffiti still remain below ground? Perhaps, some day, we will know.**

REFLECTIONS AT THE END OF D-DAY

Winston Churchill described the assault on Normandy as 'the most difficult and complicated operation that has ever taken place'. Because of the changing technology and weaponry of warfare, no action of its kind may ever take place again. Yet there are lessons to be learnt from it which, for all time, will influence the study of war.

There is no doubt that the most important single factor in the success of the invasion was the mastery in the air established by the Allied air forces before D-Day, and subsequently maintained throughout the operation. This dominant air supremacy had an adverse effect on every aspect of the Germans' defence philosophy, planning, conduct of operations and logistical capability. Strategic bombing of oil installations and industrial plants affected the enemy's sources of essential equipment and vehicle fuel. Allied air power had played the major part in the campaign against U-Boats; it had protected the UK invasion bases from bombing attacks; and it had obstructed Luftwaffe air reconnaissance to the extent that the assembly and Channel crossing of the massive armada of ships and craft had not only been unmolested but took place unnoticed until its arrival in daylight off the French coast. It had been an important element in the pre-D-Day deception plan, and had provided the vitally effective radar deception plan during the night of D–1. Its interdiction programme had immobilised the railways in the essential areas, and

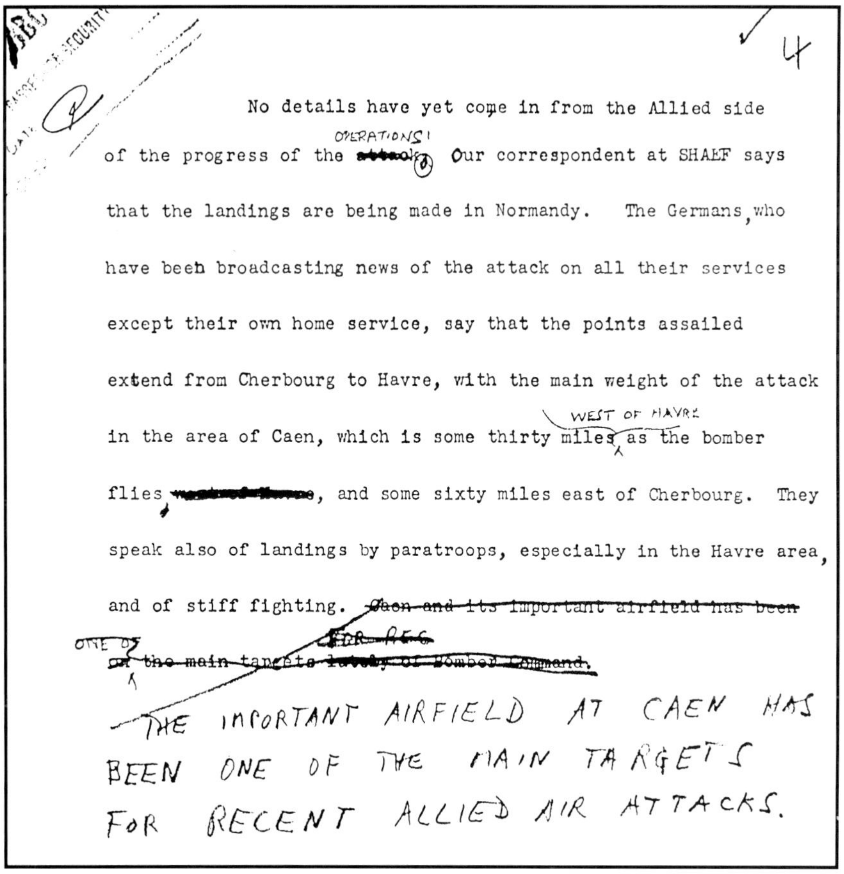

4

No details have yet come in from the Allied side of the progress of the [redacted] OPERATIONS. Our correspondent at SHAEF says that the landings are being made in Normandy. The Germans, who have been broadcasting news of the attack on all their services except their own home service, say that the points assailed extend from Cherbourg to Havre, with the main weight of the attack in the area of Caen, which is some thirty miles WEST OF HAVRE as the bomber flies [redacted], and some sixty miles east of Cherbourg. They speak also of landings by paratroops, especially in the Havre area, and of stiff fighting. ~~Caen and its important airfield has been~~ ~~FOR REC~~ ONE OF ~~of the main targets lately of Bomber Command.~~

THE IMPORTANT AIRFIELD AT CAEN HAS BEEN ONE OF THE MAIN TARGETS FOR RECENT ALLIED AIR ATTACKS.

Even at midday on June 6, apart from repeating Communiqué No. 1 and General Eisenhower's message to the people of Western Europe, the BBC had little news to impart on the progress of the invasion. This is the original transcript read by John Snagge. (See also page 415.)

Apart from vessels lost to passive defences like mines, the only direct attack on the 'Neptune' fleet was launched from Le Havre against Force 'S' by 5. Torpedobootsflottille *(left)* commanded by Korvettenkapitän zur See Heinrich Hoffmann. Rear-Admiral A. G. Talbot, the Force 'S' commander, describes what happened: 'As *Largs*, bringing up the rear of the LSI convoy, approached the coast of France, the sense that we had achieved a large measure of tactical surprise became apparent. No air attacks, no E-Boat attacks, no radar or W/T jamming worth mentioning. The air plot showed enemy aircraft on patrol away to the eastward in the Pas-de-Calais area. A glance to starboard showed the assault convoys on time as far as could be judged. The operation was proceeding with unreal precision. . . . As we approached the lowering position, *Warspite*, *Ramillies*, *Roberts* and *Arethusa* were already anchored in their bombarding positions to port of us, down the extension of Channel 10 [see plan page 520] swept by the 40th Minesweeping Flotilla, *Scylla*, *Mauritius*, *Danae*, *Dragon* and *Frobisher* disposed at anchor along the swept "Loop" channel joining the lowering position to the southern extremity of Channel 10 extension. The bombarding squadron had opened fire, but were only being engaged by the enemy in a desultory fashion, few shots falling anywhere near them. The bombarding destroyers, under the command of Captain (D) 23rd Flotilla (Captain P. G. L. Cazalet, DSC, Royal Navy), in *Saumarez* were waiting, as ordered, clear of the swept channels where they merged, to be swept into their inshore positions by the 165th BYMS. The "DD" LCT convoy was just coming up to the lowering position — on time, but the LCT(A) convoy was obviously late. Such was the picture at 0510 as we ran down from the knuckle to join Channel 9. Then events started to move swiftly. In accordance with plan, our own aircraft streaked low across the eastern flank at about this time and laid a most effective smoke screen to shield the force from the heavy batteries at Havre. Unfortunately, three German torpedo boats took advantage of this to carry out a torpedo attack, and though engaged by the bombarding squadron, were able to make good their escape in the smoke. Two torpedoes passed between *Warspite* and *Ramillies* and at 0530 one hit *Svenner* close on the port beam of *Largs*. Another torpedo was seen approaching *Largs*; her engines were put emergency full astern and the torpedo passed a few feet ahead of her. It then came to rest and sank just short of *Virago*. She had, however, seen *Svenner*'s signal "Torpedo Port" and with the remainder of the starboard division of bombarding destroyers, waiting stopped in a group, went emergency full ahead. The *Svenner* had apparently been hit immediately under her boiler room. There was a burst of steam amidships and her funnel fell aft as the whole ship lifted out of the water. She broke her back and sank rapidly; the greater part of her ship's company were picked up. The *Warspite* followed the enemy in by radar and opened fire at 14,000 yards; she reported one torpedo boat sunk. The *Mauritius*, *Ramillies* and *Arethusa* also opened fire, the former claiming one trawler sunk and one damaged.' *Right:* Korvettenkapitän Hoffmann was awarded the Knight's Cross for his exploit.

destroyed the bridges on the lower Seine and the Loire. It was only in the bombing of beach defences during the pre-assault stage that results were largely disappointing, due to the incidence of cloud and bad visibility.

Throughout D-Day, in addition to the maintenance of air cover over the Channel and the combat area, tactical air forces were engaged in supporting the ground troops during the daylight hours. The Second Tactical Air Force logged over 100 attacks and long-range fighters of the Eighth Air Force, normally used to escort the heavy bombers, were active in attacking ground targets over a wide area of the battle in the south and east. The Eighth also provided 600 heavy bombers for attacks on towns through which enemy reinforcements and supply columns were likely to pass, and the Ninth Air Force employed over 2,700 aircraft for similar attacks in the Cherbourg peninsula and south and south-west of Omaha.

Then, although out of the direct assault area, the Liberty ship *Sambut* was hit by the German gun batteries on the French coast in the Straits of Dover on D-Day.

The Luftwaffe was a spent force, and throughout the day our men on the ground, or afloat at sea, saw little sign of enemy aircraft. In fact, the Luftwaffe did make 36 sorties over the British sectors; only 12 of the aircraft showed fight, of which seven were shot down and the remainder turned back. The Ninth Air Force claimed five enemy aircraft shot down and, just before last light, four Heinkel bombers were all shot down by RAF Spitfires after scattering some bombs near Juno. It is thus difficult to account for the German claim to have made 319 sorties on D-Day with the loss of 31 aircraft destroyed and 16 damaged.

Statistics on Luftwaffe air operations over Normandy on D-Day are much at variance. The strafing attack described by Cornelius Ryan on page 550, and experienced by Sergeant Laws on his way back from Ouistreham, has been documented, but how many sorties were there over the beach-head all told? Less than a hundred is the generally accepted figure. Without being able to see any identifying markings, it is difficult to say when this Bf 109G was shot down. Both a Canadian and a British photographer pictured the wreckage (Sergeant Ken Bell *above* on June 16 and Sergeant 'Jock' Laing *below* three days earlier) although this is no indication of the date it crashed. The location given is 'west of Tilly-sur-Seulles'. Armed with these two photographs, Jean Paul Pallud drew a complete blank in the area stated, and it was only when he was en route to General Montgomery's TAC HQ, over ten kilometres away, that his photographic memory suddenly pulled him to an abrupt stop. There, on the D22 opposite a petrol station, was the perfect comparison.

In air operations on the night of D–1 and on D-Day, Allied aircraft of all types had flown no less than 14,000 sorties, and suffered relatively light casualties: 127 aircraft lost, and 63 damaged.

The most successful attack on the Normandy beach-head by the Luftwaffe was also against Sword when a lone FW 190 scored a direct hit on the main sector stores dump in No. 101 Beach Sub-Area (No. 26 on the plan on page 517). At the time, the dump contained 100,000 gallons of petrol and 400 tons of ammunition, and the resulting firework display carried on burning and exploding for a day. The lateral road had to be closed for 12 hours and a considerable number of vehicles in the dump were also lost. Captain D. G. Tugwell of No. 91 Field Company, writing of June 7, says that 'some time that afternoon I was in the platoon area when a terrific sheet of flame shot up from the petrol dump about a quarter of a mile up the road, while I saw a plane making off inland. The whole dump of petrol and ammunition seemed to have gone off at once, and is was not possible to approach this place for many hours owing to exploding ammunition'. It is possible that Captain Tugwell got the date wrong, as other accounts state June 8, although Captain T. L. Clark of No. 18 GHQ Troops also recalled it happening on the same day that the Beach Sub-Area HQ was bombed in a separate incident which was June 7. One of a flight of Ju 88s dropped its bombs across the command post during a conference, the personnel narrowly escaping annihilation when one of the Ju 88s was shot down almost on top of the CP.

The preparations made by the Allied navies for the assault reached a climax on D-Day, when 130,000 men, with their vehicles and stores, were landed on the French coast. At this time, the total number of naval personnel involved in the warships, landing ships, craft and barges was 112,800 British and 53,000 American, with some 5,000 personnel of other Allied navies. In addition there were some 25,000 Merchant Navy seamen manning the transport vessels, making an overall total of approximately 196,000.

The accomplishment of putting the armies ashore in such adverse sea and wind conditions, without interference by German naval forces, was a remarkable achievement. The distribution of the personnel landed was approximately: Gold 25,000; Juno 21,500; Sword 29,000; Utah 23,250; Omaha 34,250; Total of British and Canadians: 75,000; American: 57,500

The numbers of personnel were of the order of magnitude planned beforehand, but there was a short-fall in vehicles and stores. Taking only the British sector as an example, since comparable figures are not available for the US sector, the number of vehicles landed was 6,000, including 950 tanks and armoured vehicles (out of 1,050 planned), 240 field guns, and 280 anti-tank guns; altogether about 60 per cent of planned deliveries. The total of 4,000 tons of stores unloaded was about 75 per cent of the target. The main shortfall was in medium artillery (which was greatly missed by the assault forces) and AA artillery, which fortunately was not in demand, given the absence of the Luftwaffe.

Bringing the craft ashore, and returning from the landing beach after unloading, in the heavy swell and gusty wind, demanded not only skill but also an element of good fortune, because of the underwater obstacles which, in varying degrees, were a problem on all beaches. The magnitude of the clearance task can be understood from a typical example: on a run of three and a quarter miles of coastline, 2,500 obstacles were counted, set in three lines. It was calculated that they weighed 900 tons and nearly all had fuzed mines or large shells attached. It is therefore remarkable that in the British sector around 250 craft were lost, with a slightly higher number in the US sector.

The naval anchorage defence was based on a cordon of minesweepers stationed at half-mile intervals, ready in particular to deal with mines dropped from aircraft. There were also roving patrols of destroyers and motor torpedo boats in the Channel, watching for surface craft encroachment. The system included, of course, fighter aircraft cover by day, and up to six squadrons of RAF Mosquitos by night.

The incalculable importance of the fire support afforded to the ground troops by the Allied navies throughout the operation has seldom been adequately emphasised. After the pre-arranged naval bombardment before H-hour, the warships engaged the innumerable strongholds and defensive positions which had survived the preparatory air bombing raids. During the assault phase, a 7. Armee report recorded that 'counter-attacks, successful at first, later suffered unusually high casualties in the neighbourhood of the coast through enemy naval gunfire'. More significant in this context is a report which von Rundstedt sent to Hitler personally.

Stephen Sykes took both these pictures, the one *(top)* after the bent and buckled jerrycans had cooled sufficiently to approach the dump. He returned to Normandy in 1962 — D-Day+18 years — and took the comparison more or less from the centre of the 0880 strong point which he found was 'à vendre'. The water tower in the background serves as a common reference point.

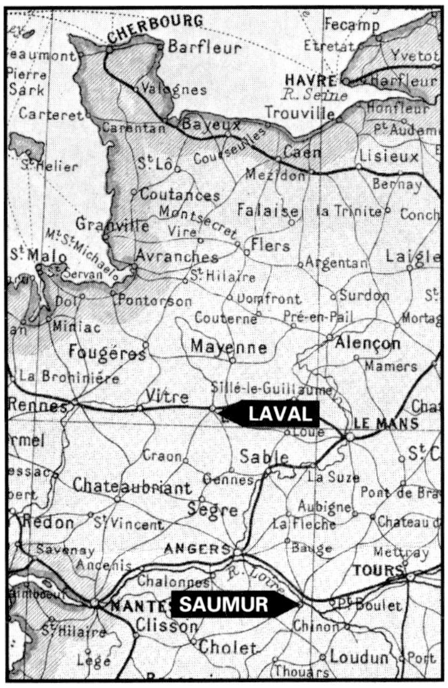

As the stores dump burned and exploded itself to destruction, the RAF mounted its own spectacular raid 125 miles from the battlefield. When Ultra revealed on June 7 (see page 71) that the 17. SS-Panzergrenadier-Division was to be moved to Normandy from Thouars, it was perceived that an attack on the railway tunnel at Saumur, 40 kilometres to the north, just before the line crossed the Loire, might stop the division in its tracks.

A raid was quickly planned for the following night (June 8/9) using the RAF's latest weapon: the 'Tallboy'. This was a large bomb weighing 14,000lbs which had the explosive force of a high-capacity blast bomb coupled with the penetrative power of an armour-piercing missile. When it hit the ground, travelling at around 3,500 feet per second, the Tallboy penetrated deep before exploding and displacing 5,000 tons of soil, each bomb producing a crater comprising over 30,000 cubic yards. Nineteen Tallboys were carried to the target by Lancasters of Bomber Command's specialist squadron, No. 617, led by Wing Commander Leonard Cheshire. Four Lancs from No. 83 Squadron were to mark the target and also attempt to hit the bridge over the river with ordinary 1,000lb bombs, but both these and the flares were dropped wide of the mark so Cheshire himself marked the south-western end of the tunnel. In the picture *above*, 17 craters can be counted with one direct hit on the tunnel itself. The Germans made no attempt to repair the damage, and the line was still out of action when Saumer was captured by American forces at the end of August. (It was officially reopened in 1948). However, the advance guard of the 17. SS-Panzergrenadiers — the men of 'Götz von Berlichingen' — had already crossed the river before the attack and its SS-Panzer-Abteilung 17 under SS-Sturmbannführer Ludwig Kepplinger was in action south of Carentan less than a week later, fighting in this sector until the American break-out on July 18.

German photographs of the beach-head are understandably thin on the ground. Leutnant Hans Ertl, the 'Jimmy Mapham' of the Deutsche Kriegsberichter, is seen *left* with Rommel on one of the inspection tours and *right* camouflaged with a long-lensed camera at the Orne estuary. One of the pictures he took on that occasion is reproduced *below*.

At one o'clock in the morning on June 6, the telephone on my bedside table rang. It was Oberleutnant Maisch from Rommel's HQ informing me that we were at Alarm State II. I asked what was up and his reply was brief. 'Enemy airborne landing in the Caen area.' I dutifully woke my pals in the cottage and passed on the message with the order to wake the drivers and get ready for action. It seemed the moment we'd been waiting months for had finally come. In a way, we'd been looking forward to it: we all knew it would bring the final outcome of this war. So I sat there on my camp bed ready to go, sweating with apprehension. I tried to get a tumbler of herbal calming remedy up to my mouth but trembling hands made the liquid spill over. Nothing like this had ever happened to me before. From the mouth of the Seine, just 60 to 90 miles away as the crow flies, salvoes thundered from naval guns and from the coastal batteries at Cherbourg and Le Havre. The thudding and blast waves from the explosions reached this far, the ground trembling again and again as if in an earthquake.

Leutnant von Esebeck, reporter; Feldwebel Fred Rieder from the photographic section and Feldwebel Dahlmeier responsible for cine film, were the first from our group to set off that night towards the invasion area. Our good wishes went with them. All three were recognised in their fields as tried and tested, sensible enough to know their capabilities and limits; this, in contrast to some young colleagues who charged off medal-hunting, only to end up under a wooden cross. The Air Force correspondent, Dettmann, had started it all. As a fully-trained air gunner, he'd earned himself an Iron Cross, not just by snapping enemy aircraft with his camera but also by shooting several down with a machine gun; since then, various correspondents had wishfully set their sights on that same decoration.

On the afternoon of June 8, von Esebeck, Rieder and Rob Dahlmeier got back from their first operation at the invasion front. Although they had received a dose of the heavy stuff at Branville during a successful battle against enemy airborne forces, which involved our tanks and assault artillery, they were well and truly pepped up. The reason was the booty which they'd brought back in the form of — as they put it — 'unique' stills and film footage. As a result, they hardly took time out for a proper tea break but were dead set on finishing their reports and sending off their film. On the way out, Rob stuffed a piece of fruit cake into his mouth before racing off in our fastest car, spurred on by journalistic ambition, to be first to the communications flight to Paris and, incidentally, also hurrying to his girl friend, Ruth, who was employed there as a 'Blitzmädchen', as the female signals auxiliaries were known. She would certainly reward her hero following his active service on the invasion front.

Later, on the evening of June 11, I planned to set out for the sector of the front to the east of the Orne estuary in order, if the opportunity presented itself, to take shots of the invasion fleet: that was the order from the propaganda section of the Armed Forces High Command (OKW/WPrV). 'Why don't the Air Force or Navy film correspondents do it?', wondered Heini Gleiman. 'They

Ertl's pictures were not that interesting, but he obviously went down to the beach for this shot of one of the Landing Craft, Personnel (L) — the 38-footer which could carry 25 — usually used as a commando-type assault craft.

only need to fly overhead or whizz by in a speedboat and leave their cameras running', he added sarcastically. 'But those smart-arses are conspicuous by their absence, just like the whole Navy and Air Force!'

Basically, he was right but, despite all this, the order was there for me. I could put it off for a bit but not for too long, otherwise I'd end up on the war correspondents' list of slackers and run the risk of being transferred to an active service unit. So far, on D-Day plus 5, I'd only been able to come up with my flak story. However, at least with that those characters in Berlin would have something of mine to cut up and paste in. Robert at once volunteered to take my rolls of film to the communications flight although he'd only that morning got back from Paris.

In the course of our attack on the Orne, we were able to straighten out the existing salients and throw the enemy back over the river. However, another effective pile-driving thrust into the enemy's flank failed due to concentrated defensive fire from his large-calibre naval guns and the hail of bombs from his aircraft. The hard fighting in the Forest of Bavent was even mentioned in the official Wehrmacht communiqué of June 15. There was, however, no mention of the heavy losses.

The following day, we managed to record something of it with our cameras when we crept forward to Hill 130 to get a look at the assembly of part of the invasion fleet. Too bad I hadn't brought my 1000mm telephoto lens; but even with the 650mm lens, the picture was impressive. Battleships, heavy cruisers and destroyers of all sizes were lying at anchor or cutting casually backwards and forwards under a curtain of steel cables held up by massive barrage balloons which shielded the fleet from low-level air attack. But, in any case, those manoeuvrable fighters, circling continuously overhead, would have immediately foiled any attack from the air. Again and again, there were flashes from the battleships and cruisers each time they sent a broadside over to the front line; and all this without a single shot being returned by our artillery. As a war correspondent, I had never before felt our impotence as I did then.

During a sortie in the sector to the east of the Orne estuary, we arrived at Dozulé on the morning of June 15, just as they were bringing the first captured British paratroopers into the divisional command post. Naturally enough I took the opportunity of filming the interrogations, complete with sound track, but the sessions were continually interrupted by low-flying enemy fighters, which fortunately held back from bombing us, presumably because they'd recognised their own prisoners.

Whereas the ordinary British soldiers willingly replied to the questions put by our interrogators, the officers behaved in a downright arrogant, even insolent, manner. There was no more of that 'the fight is over' attitude; no longer any trace of the fairness and comradeship which I remembered from the battles in Africa in 1941. There, the first thing you did was offer the captured enemy a cigarette in order to smoke a 'pipe of peace'. Here, you had to reckon with one of these hate-filled British officers possibly knocking the proffered cigarette out of your hand, deliberately to provoke a serious argument.

The Anglo-Americans seemed to have learned from their Bolshevik allies that targeted hate-propaganda can in certain circumstances be decisive in a war since troops in such a psychotic state fight like maniacs and thus take the place of divisions.

LEUTNANT HANS ERTL,
KRIEGSBERICHTERSTATTER, 1985

This frame appears towards the end of the same roll of film and fits in with Ertl's description although this soldier from the 51st Highland Division is hardly 'one of the first captured paratroopers'! The 51st, a follow-up division, sailed as part of Force 'L' from the Thames Estuary on D–1, its leading elements coming ashore on the afternoon of D-Day, later units not arriving until D+7.

Before the Highland Division returned to England to take part in 'Overlord', it had been in action in Sicily where one of its brigade commanders had been Brigadier Tom Rennie who had served in various capacities with the division since 1940. Once back in Britain, Rennie (left), promoted to Major-General, was appointed to command the British 3rd Division which, as we have seen, failed to make an auspicious start following their landing on Sword. On June 12, General Montgomery visited the divisional HQ which had been established in the château at Hermanville, and the following day General Rennie was out visiting his troops with the commander of the 9th Field Ambulance, Lieutenant-Colonel Wood. As they entered Cambes, where the Regimental Aid Post of the Royal Ulster Rifles was situated, their Jeep struck a British mine, recently laid due to a change in forward positions.

Von Rundstedt wrote that 'the guns of enemy warships have so powerful an effect on areas within their range that any advance into the zone dominated by fire from the sea is impossible . . . '

In the first days of the invasion, fire support was provided by all types of naval vessels, from battleships to gun-carrying craft. As the fighting moved inland, the bombardment forces were reduced, but there remained at all times an average of two battleships or monitors, several cruisers and some destroyers in readiness for calls from the armies ashore.

In spite of all the preparations that the Germans had made during the previous two years, including the elaborate systems designed to give timely warning of any seaborne attack, the Allies had achieved complete surprise. The Atlantic Wall had been breached, and the coastal defences on much of the total assault frontage cleared by the end of D-Day. The losses sustained by the Allies on D-Day were far less than had been feared. Among seaborne troops the British and Canadian casualties were around 2,700 (killed, wounded and missing); the total American casualties about 4,700 of which some 2,000 were incurred on Omaha. A later estimate of the total number of Allied troops killed on D-Day itself was 2,500 [but see page 620]. Fortunately, many of the 'missing' eventually rejoined their units; this applies particularly to the airborne troops.

The medical arrangements to provide rapid attention to the wounded were extremely well-organised. Serious cases, able to travel, were evacuated to hospitals in Britain by air, in the care of nursing sisters in the aircraft, and it has been recorded that no army ever went overseas with such a comprehensive and skilled medical service as that provided for the Normandy invasion. Between June 6 and August 31, 57,500 casualties were evacuated from France by sea and a further 22,500 by air.

Colonel Wood suffered a badly injured foot, and General Rennie a broken arm. The next day (June 14), the General was evacuated to the Force 'S' command ship, HMS *Largs*, but the wound proved more serious than at first thought and he had to be flown to Britain four days later. Brigadier E. E. E. Cass of the 8th Brigade temporarily took command of the division until June 23 when Major-General L. G. Whistler, standing by in Britain ready to take over the first vacant divisional commander's appointment, arrived in France. Even before General Rennie was fully recovered, he was sent back to Normandy to take command of his old division, the 51st Highland, which had made a poor showing in Operation 'Goodwood' (designed to try to break the stalemate in front of Caen). Its commander, Major-General C. Bullen-Smith, was relieved of his command and General Rennie, still with his arm in a sling, took over on July 26. Under his command, and now fighting alongside the Canadians, the 51st Highland Division became once again the formidable force it had been in North Africa and Sicily, but General Rennie was not to see the final victory. On March 24, 1945, during the operation to cross the Rhine near Rees, he was again travelling in his Jeep driven by his ADC, Lieutenant Douglas Tweedie, when it received a direct hit from a mortar bomb. Tweedie was unhurt, but Rennie died almost immediately. In the presence of the corps commander, Lieutenant-General Brian Horrocks, and the commanders of the British 3rd and Canadian 3rd Divisions, he was buried at Appeldorn, but transferred in October 1946 to Reichswald Forest War Cemetery (Grave 1, Row D, Plot 61) near Cleves.

This is the Gin Gordon's Stands Supreme Maximum Prices Per bott 25/3 Half bott 13/3 Gt. Britain and N. Ireland only

Daily Mail

4 A.M. EDITION

UTILITY FOOTWEAR A98 with CC41 George Webb FOOTWEAR FOR MEN MADE BY CRAFTSMEN IN NORTHAMPTON

NO. 15.008 ONE PENNY FOR KING AND EMPIRE FRIDAY, JUNE 9, 1944

ALLIES FIVE MILES BEYOND BAYEUX

Beachhead 36 Miles Wide: Tank Clash Coming

THERE—TO STAY

MORE eloquently than any words, this magnificent picture, taken on the British beachhead in the Caen sector, illustrates the solidity of our hold there. Great masses of shipping of all descriptions are drawn up on the waterline; piles of equipment lie on the beaches guarded by ack-ack guns. The troops stand around or rest on the ground, unconcerned — clearly free of enemy interference either from the air or from guns.

We Capture Thousand Prisoners

Enemy Use 'Beetle and Hornets'

From ALEXANDER CLIFFORD

21st Army Group H.Q., Thursday

THE crisis in the battle of Normandy is not far off now. The race is on. It is all a

CAEN DESTROYED BY BIG GUNS OF FLEET

TWENTY divisions — ten on each side — were reported early this morning to be locked in battle in Normandy, but the Germans are still using only local reserves. They have been in action all along the beachhead front, and have been repelled everywhere.

Supreme Headquarters communique issued at midnight said British and Canadian troops are continuing to make progress. Repeated attacks against the Sixth Airborne Division have been held. The American

Auderville

Lord Louis Planned it

PLANS for the invasion of Normandy owe their origin to Lord Louis Mountbatten, when he was Chief of Combined Operations.

Lord Louis' Commando raids revealed the weaknesses of the enemy defences. His plans

GERMAN VERSION OF THE FIGHTING

British Try To Cut Off Peninsula

Below is the story of the fighting from the German side. It is interesting in that it places the scene of much of the fighting.

BERLIN last night reported that large forces of British tanks and infantry, fed from a beachhead now 36 miles wide, were thrusting westwards from Bayeux to link up with the Amer-

LEAP ON GERMAN BATTERY

'Pin-point Attack Saved Beach

A PICKED force of paratroops were revealed last night as the men who laid open the invasion road across the beaches of Normandy.

They were dropped well ahead of "H" hour to smash, in a pin-point, split-second attack, a powerful German battery which commanded the entire strip of coastline.

Extent of the landing depended on their lone battle, for which they had trained for weeks with a life-size model of the battery built on a lonely English hillside.

Nothing has been heard of the paratroops, but when the

'BEGINNING OF THE END'

Washington, Thursday — Mr Ralph A. Bard, Assistant Secretary of the Navy, said today that the invasion of Europe marks the beginning of the end for the Nazis and the Japs. — Exchange.

BIG JAP CRUISER

Canadian photographer Frank Dubervill was first to get a photo published when his picture of German prisoners on page 486 was wired to the *New York Times* in time for their June 7 issue. The London *Evening News* repeated the picture the following day when Bert Brandt's photo on page 346 was published in the *News Chronicle* and *Glasgow Herald*. On Friday, Eddie Greenwood's unique panorama *(above)* appeared in *The Times* — the first picture to have been taken by a British civilian photographer. He had been at sea with the Navy and went ashore courtesy of his Admiral on D+1.

However, the intended objectives for the divisions for D-Day had not been achieved, except for the evacuated town of Bayeux, which was not occupied until after dawn next morning. The main preoccupation of the Allied commanders was the situation at Omaha, which remained highly vulnerable to a concentrated enemy counter-attack. The beach-heads had not yet been linked up into a continuous bridgehead; there remained gaps between Utah and Omaha, and from the east of Omaha to the 50th Division at Port-en-Bessin; and there was still a narrow enemy salient between Juno and Sword, embracing the very strongly organised enemy defensive system at Douvres.

Other immediate preoccupations were the uncertainty of the weather, and the fact that the overall build-up tables were already eight to 12 hours behind schedule.

On the other hand, the very favourable situation in the air gave cause for confidence and, in spite of the dispersion of the airborne divisions in the Cherbourg peninsula and the presence there of two first-line German infantry divisions, together with other reinforcements sent in May by Hitler's orders, there was every indication that operations were progressing well. This was important for the capture of Cherbourg port was a high priority requirement, and also because the Allied front would not be 'tidy', and ready for the development of Montgomery's master plan, until the whole of US First Army was concentrated facing south, in a cordon across the base of the peninsula.

Horrocks had been brought in to take over XXX Corps following General Montgomery's weeding out of inefficient commanders at the end of July. The Gold corps CO, Lieutenant-General Bucknall, right (with General Dempsey, centre, and the I Corps commander, Lieutenant-General Crocker) was sacked along with the 7th Armoured Division CO, Major-General W. R. 'Bobby' Erskine, and Brigadier Hinde of the 22nd Armoured Brigade. This picture was taken at Second Army HQ at Banville (a mile inland from Graye-sur-Mer) on June 10. General Dempsey: '1700 — Conference with Commanders 1 Corps, 30 Corps and Airborne Forces at my HQ to tie up the operations of both Corps for the next four days, and to plan the landing of 1st Airborne Division in conjunction with either 1 Corps or 30 Corps on 13 June. The decision as to which Corps 1 Airborne Division will co-operate with depends upon the progress made tomorrow morning by 7th Armd Div in the Tilly area, and the recces sent out by 3rd Cdn Div on their front.'

As we saw on page 470, General Montgomery arrived in France on June 8. These pictures were taken by Sergeant Morris after he left the beach at Graye and drove to Creully but, although Jean Paul and Karel retraced every possible route they might have taken from the beach inland, they could not positively identify the roof of the house seen behind the trees.

At 1.30 p.m. I moved off with the reconnaissance party, a skeleton staff of about six men representing transport, defence, signals and operations personnel, to the new site, the park of the Château de Creullet at Creully. I interviewed the owners, a retired colonel and his wife, descendants of the old French nobility, who were allowed to remain in residence. A list of names of permanent residents and employees on the estate was obtained from them, and actually only comprised the proprietors, an aged gardener and five other regular employees who came from the village. I made out passes for these eight people and gave a list of their names together with a specimen pass to the Colonel G(Ops), to the Camp Commandant, to the Officer Commanding Military Police at TAC HQ, and to the OC Defence Company.

Before issuing the passes I went to the Mairie, the office of the mayor, to check up on the character and reliability of the civilians concerned. The mayor was a prisoner in Germany, so I went to the gendarmerie. The gendarmes of this village had enjoyed a reputation for trustworthiness during the years of occupation and, as I was the only Intelligence Corps representative, I had to rely on local informants. They had co-operated with the local inhabitants in deceiving the Germans, helped the local youth to dodge slave labour in Germany, and gave assistance to French patriots in hiding. This information was given to me, not by the gendarmes themselves but by numerous inhabitants of at least three villages. As a result of my visit to the gendarmerie, it appeared that all the civilians to whom passes had been made out were inhabitants of long standing, good citizens, and of no danger from a security point of view.

On my return, I warned the lady of the château that she must keep all shutters overlooking the caravans closed. This was done forthwith. It was now 9.15 p.m. and at the invitation of the Major G(Ops) I attended a conference at our newly established Creully camp on the defence of TAC HQ. The problem was that, situated as we were in a large park with several entrances and an extensive perimeter, it was difficult not only to control but even, at times, to be aware of unlawful entry. The number of guards and sentries in our small headquarters was naturally limited and we did not use barbed wire or other physical obstacles; so, as I had learnt at Dundee, the best kind of security was provided, not by material defences, but by the quality and vigilance of human beings. The problem therefore centred upon the most effective use of personnel. As a result of this discussion I later, during a stand-to, accompanied officers on a tour of inspection of the defence layout, to decide upon the positioning of the tank and the armoured cars, the placing of sentries, the patrolling by guards, and the most efficient methods of ensuring the security of the perimeter — always, of course, with the safety and survival of our vital Chief in mind.

SERGEANT NORMAN KIRBY, JUNE 8, 1944

On June 11, General Montgomery held his first press conference for Allied correspondents at his TAC HQ: 'When the Americans landed east of the Carentan estuary they found the sector being defended by a German division which was not a coastal division. There was very heavy fighting on that beach for the rest of D-Day, and in the evening the leading American troops were no more than 100 yards inland. They were hanging on by their eyelids. There is no doubt that the American troops in that sector fought absolutely magnificently. They recovered from that very unpleasant situation, and today those same troops are over ten miles inland. The situation was retrieved by three things: first, the gallantry of the American soldier, who is a very brave man; secondly, the very fine supporting fire of the Allied navies; and thirdly, very good support by the fighter-bombers. The retrieving of that situation and the advance to the present very good situation are one of the finest things done in this operation.'

On June 12, Churchill set foot in France (page 471). Field-Marshal Sir Alan Brooke, Chief of the Imperial General Staff and Chairman of the Chiefs-of-Staff Committee, wrote in his diary that 'the PM had called me up, stating he proposed to visit Monty on Monday and wanted me to come with him. Smuts also coming. We are to leave by train on Sunday night and make an early start by destroyer on Monday. At 10.15 p.m. [on June 11], I left the flat and drove to Ascot station where I picked up the PM's train. We got off to bed at a fairly reasonable time as we had to leave the train at 7.30 a.m. to catch the destroyer *Kelvin* and leave Portsmouth at 8 a.m. Monty met us on the beach with a team of Jeeps which we got into and drove off on the Courseulles–Bayeux road to about half-way to the latter place. There we found Monty's HQ and he gave us an explanation on the map of his dispositions and plans.' Churchill later recalled that 'we lunched in a tent looking towards the enemy. The General was in the highest spirits. I asked him how far away was the actual front. He said about three miles. I asked him if he had a continuous line. He said "No". "What is there then to prevent an incursion of German armour breaking up our luncheon?" He said he did not think they would come. The staff told me the château had been heavily bombed the night before, and certainly there were a good many craters around it. I told him he was taking too much of a risk if he made a habit of such proceedings. Anything can be done once or for a short time, but custom, repetition, prolongation, is always to be avoided when possible in war. He did in fact move two weeks later, though not till he and his staff had had another dose. It continued fine, and apart from occasional air alarms and anti-aircraft fire there seemed to be no fighting. We made a considerable inspection of our limited bridgehead.' *Right:* Before he left, the Prime Minister added another entry in Montgomery's autograph book (see page 120) which the General later titled 'Chapter VI'.

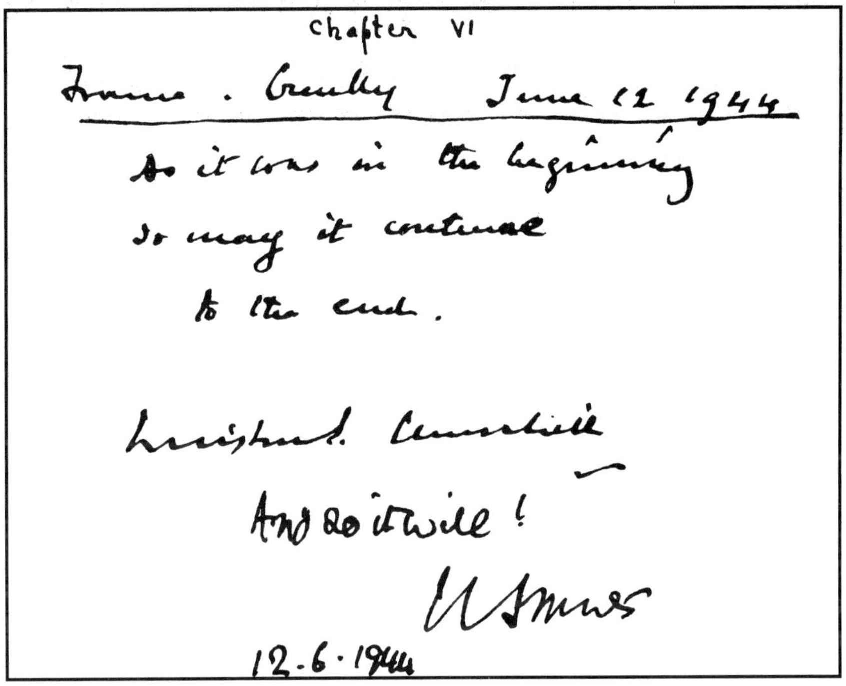

Chapter VI

France. Creully June 12 1944

As it was in the beginning so may it continue to the end.

Winston S. Churchill

And so it will!

J C Smuts

12.6.1944

'After lunch we drove round to "Bimbo" Dempsey's HQ', continued Brooke. 'I was astonished to see how little affected the country had been by the German occupation and five years of war. All the crops were good, the country fairly clear of weeds, and plenty of fat cattle, horses, chickens, etc. As usual, Winston described the situation in his inimitable way when driving with me. He said: "We are surrounded by fat cattle lying in luscious pastures with their paws crossed!" This is just the impression they gave one. And the French population did not seem in any way pleased to see us arrive as a victorious army to liberate France. They had been quite content as they were, and we were bringing war and desolation to the country.' *Left:* Creullet château just north of the River Seulles (not Creully château just south of it as is sometimes stated) was the location of General Montgomery's TAC HQ from June 8 to June 23 when he moved to Blay to be closer to the American sphere of operations.

Gooseberry and Mulberry

By Captain Harold Hickling
CHIEF-OF-STAFF, MULBERRY/PLUTO

When it came to invading the Continent we had two enemies to reckon with: one was the Germans, the other was the weather. Of these two enemies by far the most unpredictable, the most uncertain, was the weather. As the Sailing Directions — the sailors' Bible, say, 'The weather in the English Channel is seldom calm.'

The landing of a huge army, with a build-up of millions of tons of equipment and stores, called for all the features and appliances of a major port. We might, of course, land over open beaches but that would put the build-up at the mercy of the weather. Neither of these courses of action was acceptable to Lieutenant-General Morgan planning the invasion in those far-off days of August 1943. Hitler had said, 'If we hold the ports, we hold Europe', and the Germans meant to hold the ports: we had had a taste of assaulting a major port at Dieppe. To have attacked Cherbourg, for instance, would have been a costly, a lengthy and bloody business forfeiting any element of surprise. Nor was the alternative of landing over open beaches acceptable because no prudent commander was going to leave his build-up to the mercy of the weather in the English Channel.

I saw the shining, blue sea, Not an empty sea, but a sea crowded, infested with craft of every kind: little ships, fast and impatient, scurrying like water-beetles to and fro, and leaving a glistening wake behind them; bigger ships, in stately, slow procession with the sweepers in front and escort vessels on the flank — it was a brave, oh, an inspiring sight. We are supplying the beaches all right — no doubt of that. We flew on south-west, and I could see France and Britain, and I realised how very near to you all at home in England is this great battle in Normandy. It's a stone's throw across the gleaming water.

I saw it all as a mighty panorama, clear and etched in its detail. There were the supply ships, the destroyers, the torpedo boats, the assault craft, leaving England. Half way over was another flotilla, and near it a huge, rounded, ugly capital ship, broadside on to France. There in the distance was the Cherbourg peninsula, Cherbourg itself revealed in the sun. And there, right ahead now, as we reset course, were the beaches. Dozens, scores, hundreds of craft lying close inshore, pontoons and jetties being lined up to make a new harbour where, six days ago, there was a empty stretch of shore.

RICHARD DIMBLEBY, BBC BROADCAST, JUNE 11, 1944

The two prefabricated harbours, Mulberry 'A' off Omaha, and Mulberry 'B' on Gold, were each to cover an area equivalent to that of Dover harbour and were to provide sheltered water by D+4 and to be fully established by D+14. The daily disembarkation target for the two Mulberries was 3,000 tons of stores by D+4; 7,000 tons and 2,500 vehicles by D+8, building to 12,000 tons and 2,500 unwaterproofed vehicles. Initially, it was intended that they would have a life of 90 days, at which point captured ports would take over. Rear-Admiral William Tennant was placed in overall charge of the naval aspect, both in the British and US areas, with our author, Captain Harold Hickling, as his deputy and Chief-of-Staff. Admiral Ramsay explained the basic Mulberry plan on pages 196-199; *above* we see the early beginnings of Mulberry 'A' with the sinking of blockships, code-named 'Corncobs', to form Gooseberry No. 2.

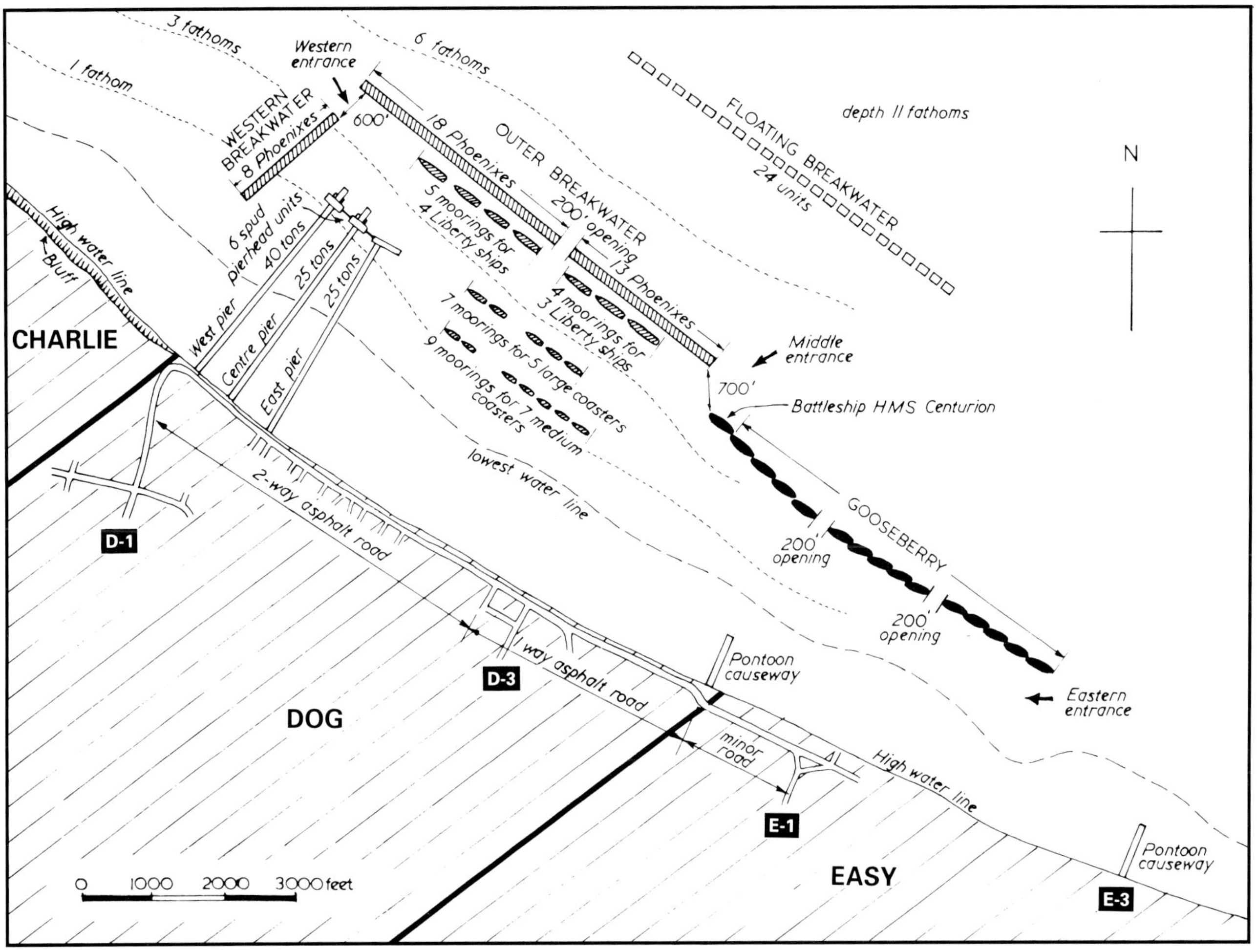

Although Gooseberry No. 2 was off Easy sector (Exit D-3 can be seen in the photo *opposite*), the Mulberry which followed lay to its west off Dog sector. Although Royal Navy experts warned that the strength of the ship breakwaters would be severely impaired, the Americans insisted on leaving two 200-foot gaps in the line of blockships to give easy access for small craft. The warning proved correct when bad weather blew up on June 19, as the gaps allowed the sea to pound through and wreck the harbour. Later, Captain Hickling commented that if blockships ever had to be laid again, 'the ships should be locked well, i.e. they should overlap; there should be no gaps otherwise scour will take place, the ends of the ships will become unsupported and, as happened in the American harbour, they will break their backs.'

THE PLAN

So General Morgan conceived a plan whereby he would assault over the open beaches, where the defences were relatively weak, and take a couple of harbours along with him. His plan was calculated to spring a major surprise on the enemy which, as we know in the light of later events, it most certainly did.

The crux of the plan which Morgan submitted to the Chiefs-of-Staff was 'Sheltered Water'. Without that, he was not prepared to invade the Continent. A secondary requirement was to provide within that sheltered water means of rapid discharge of stores to the shore.

That plan was submitted to the Combined Chiefs-of-Staff at the Quadrant Conference in Quebec in July 1943, and was approved. On September 4 that year, we who were waiting in London received the 'Bigot, Most Secret' signal telling us to get busy with two artificial harbours, one in the American sector at a place called St Laurent to be known as Mulberry 'A', and one in the British sector at Arromanches, ten miles to the eastward, to be known as Mulberry 'B'. The harbours were to be prefabricated in the United Kingdom, towed across the Channel and put down in 14 days, and were to supply between them at least 12,000 tons of stores a day irrespective of the weather. That was only one-third of the total the armies required each day, which was of the order of 40,000 tons.

Owing to the flatness of the foreshore off the Normandy coast, ships could not anchor closer in than four to five miles from the beaches, which meant that there had to be thousands of landing craft, barges, etc., ferrying the Army's stuff ashore. If it came on to blow from the north, and there was no protection for these craft, they would be driven ashore and wrecked, so that when the weather abated there would be nothing left to ferry the stores ashore. Then the Army's life-line would fail and they would be at the mercy of the Germans. So, not only were two artificial harbours — the Mulberries — required, but also five small-craft shelters, which were known as Gooseberries, one for each beach. These five shelters were needed from the word 'Go', not only to provide protection from the weather but also to give facilities for landing craft to be serviced and repaired and for their crews to get meals and rest. They were provided by blockships, some nine to twelve per beach, sunk in about 12ft of water, which made a breakwater about a mile long.

RESPONSIBILITIES

In so novel a project, it was inevitable that there should be considerable doubt at the outset as to who was to do what. In the very early days, I do not think the Navy fully realised the immensity of the task, nor the very large part which they would have to play. 'Transportation' at the War Office, with Brigadier Bruce White and Colonel Steer Webster in the van, were much more alive to the various problems. After a lot of back-chat, it was decided broadly that the Navy should be responsible for the Bombardons (floating steel breakwaters) and blockships; assembly of *all* parts of the harbour on the southern side of the United Kingdom, and for towing them across the Channel and constructing the breakwaters. The Army, on the other hand, should be responsible for the construction of the Phoenix caissons and Whale floating pierheads and roadways and for the erection of these units on the 'Far Shore', and also for the technical side of operating the Phoenix, such as opening the sinking valves.

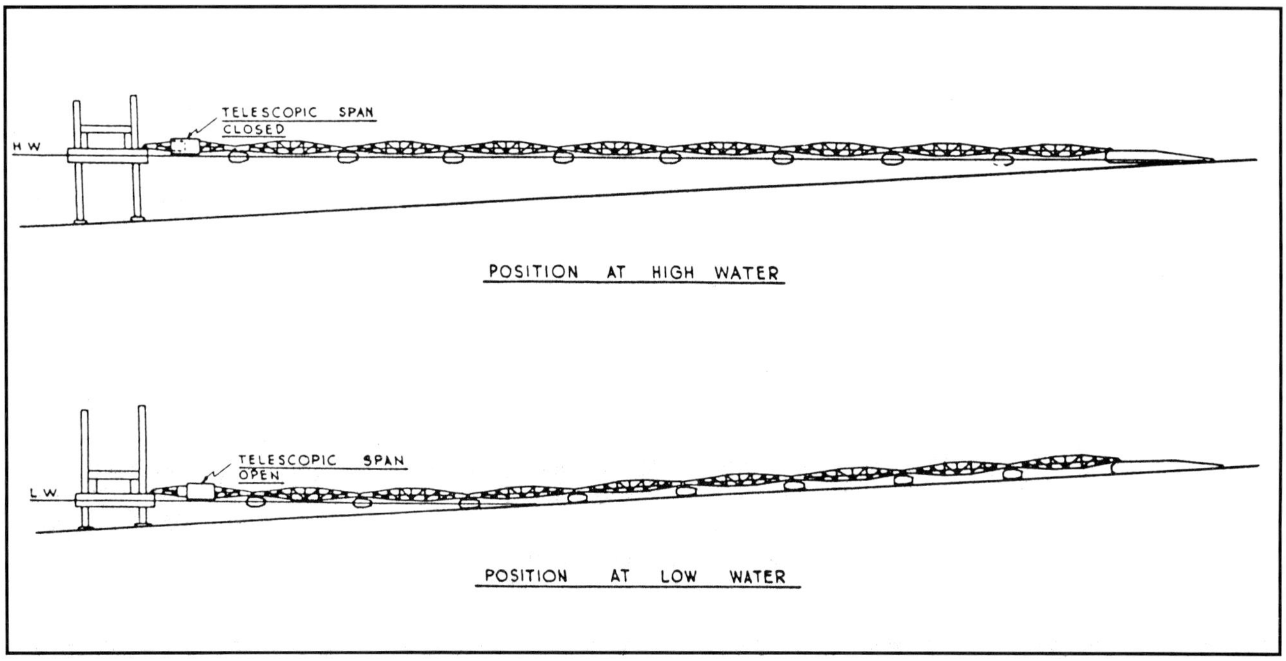

Early in 1941, the Director of Transportation at the War Office, Major-General Donald McMullen, created a special branch to deal with port engineering, called Transportation 5 (Tn5), with Major (later Brigadier) Bruce White, an ex-WWI Royal Engineer, in charge. To the new department fell the construction of military ports; from Winston Churchill came the directive in May 1942 (page 588 — also 196 in facsimile) to produce a structure which would float up and down with the tide.

Although there was some bickering in Whitehall, once we got down to Admiral Ramsay's headquarters at Southwick everyone worked in very well together. Soldiers, sailors (Royal Navy and Merchant Navy); British and Americans; Ministry of War Transport; Ministry of Supply; sappers; Seabees; tugmen; local authorities — they all had but one object: to get ready in time for D-Day. That object was achieved with about ten minutes to spare!

CO-ORDINATION

The co-ordination of all the various authorities and Ministries concerned in this vast building programme was a formidable task. The Phoenixes employed 25 contractors and 25,000 men in prefabricating the best part of a million tons of reinforced concrete. There were 240 different firms in the United Kingdom concerned with the 50,000 tons of highly-specialised steelwork of the Whale; the parts for the 115 Bombardons had to be taken from all over the kingdom to be assembled — 20 every three weeks — in the King George V dock at Southampton.

This task of co-ordinating the Admiralty, the War Office, Ministries of War Transport, of Supply, of Production, and of Labour, to mention but a few of the parties concerned, fell to Major-General Sir Harold Wernher as Co-ordinator of Ministries and Services Facilities. He was also responsible for all the Hards over which the assault loaded up. With a single assistant, Colonel T. B. Bunting, and a military and a naval liaison officer — Colonel E. V. Daldy and myself — he carried out a very difficult job in a most able fashion. Above all, he kept the peace between the more irascible members and reconciled the often conflicting interests and priorities.

I think it is fair to say that in those early days we found no difficulty in getting a straight answer out of the Admiralty — often a very straight one — from the Controller when we cast covetous eyes on his docks or the steel for his frigates.

Sir Jack Gibson, the master contractor on Phoenix, acting for the Ministry of Supply, was a tower of strength and was always as good as his word, but with our friends on the other side of Whitehall it was not so easy to get down to brass tacks. We never seemed to be able to find one individual, except Colonel Webster, who could speak with full authority and give quick decisions. As the construction stage gave way to the operational stage, i.e., the assembly and the operation itself, so the burden of co-ordination passed from Major-General Wernher to Rear-Admiral William Tennant (Rear-Admiral Mulberry and Pluto, abbreviated to RAMP). It was on January 3, 1944, that Admiral Ramsay made Tennant directly responsible for both Mulberries and Pluto, with me as his Chief-of-Staff.

Pluto was a separate undertaking which laid submarine fuel pipe-lines across the Channel and is another story.

Tn5 formed a special unit — No. 1 Transportation Fixed and Floating Equipment, Development and Training Depot, RE, which was given the responsibility for the development and installation, and a remote base was established on the Solway Firth in Wigtown Bay where the Scottish coastline resembled Normandy. Major White made contact with Henry Lobnitz, the managing director of Lobnitz & Co., based at Renfrew, who had built a dredger with attached legs or 'spuds' to stabilise the craft while working at all states of tide and weather. His design was adopted for the Mulberry pierheads, giving them their alternate name of Lobnitz pierheads. By April 1943, a prototype had been constructed and erected in Wigtown Bay at Cairn Head, together with a section of roadway supported on pontoons.

SURVEYS

While we were building the million tons of prefabricated ports, the Navy was making surveys of the coast of Normandy where the harbours were to be constructed. All we had to go on was an Admiralty chart based on a survey dated 1836 — a year before Queen Victoria came to the throne. The coast between Le Havre and Cherbourg — that is to say the Bay of the Seine — was not one much frequented by mariners; it was more a place to which rich financiers took their girl friends for the week-end; but that was not the information we wanted. We sent out reconnaissance parties in bitterly cold weather right under the noses of the German sentries to obtain the information we required. They carried out surveys, obtaining soundings, tidal information and, most important of all, information about the composition of the sea-bed, so that we should know whether we were building our harbour on rock or on sand.

This information was all collected and analysed, and a large model of each harbour was constructed under the greatest secrecy. That for Mulberry 'B' was first mounted in the War Office and later in a cellar of the Automobile Association at Fanum House in London's Leicester Square, and was accessible only to a very few senior officers directly concerned. On these models with movable pieces, many 'games of chess' had to be played before the best layout was arrived at. It was indeed remarkable how closely the finished harbour followed the final arrangement of this model.

The initial idea was merely to erect the piers and discharge directly onto the beaches from the open sea, and in July 1943 the Combined Chiefs-of-Staff ordered six pierheads and four miles of pier for delivery by February 1, 1944. However, the need to protect the piers with a breakwater of some kind to provide sheltered water for unloading was seen as a pre-requisite, and the Chiefs approved the plan for the two Mulberry harbours in September 1943. Captain Hickling explains that 'the harbours had to be able to accommodate deep-draught Liberty ships and were to provide, at the earliest possible moment, shelter for the minor landing craft working the ferry service from ship to shore on the adjacent beaches. This last requirement was extremely important because the capacity of the harbours was only about one-third of the maximum daily tonnage estimated as necessary for full-scale offensive operations; consequently, the balance would have to be landed over the open beaches by ferry craft. Finally, the harbours had to last for a minimum of 90 days.'

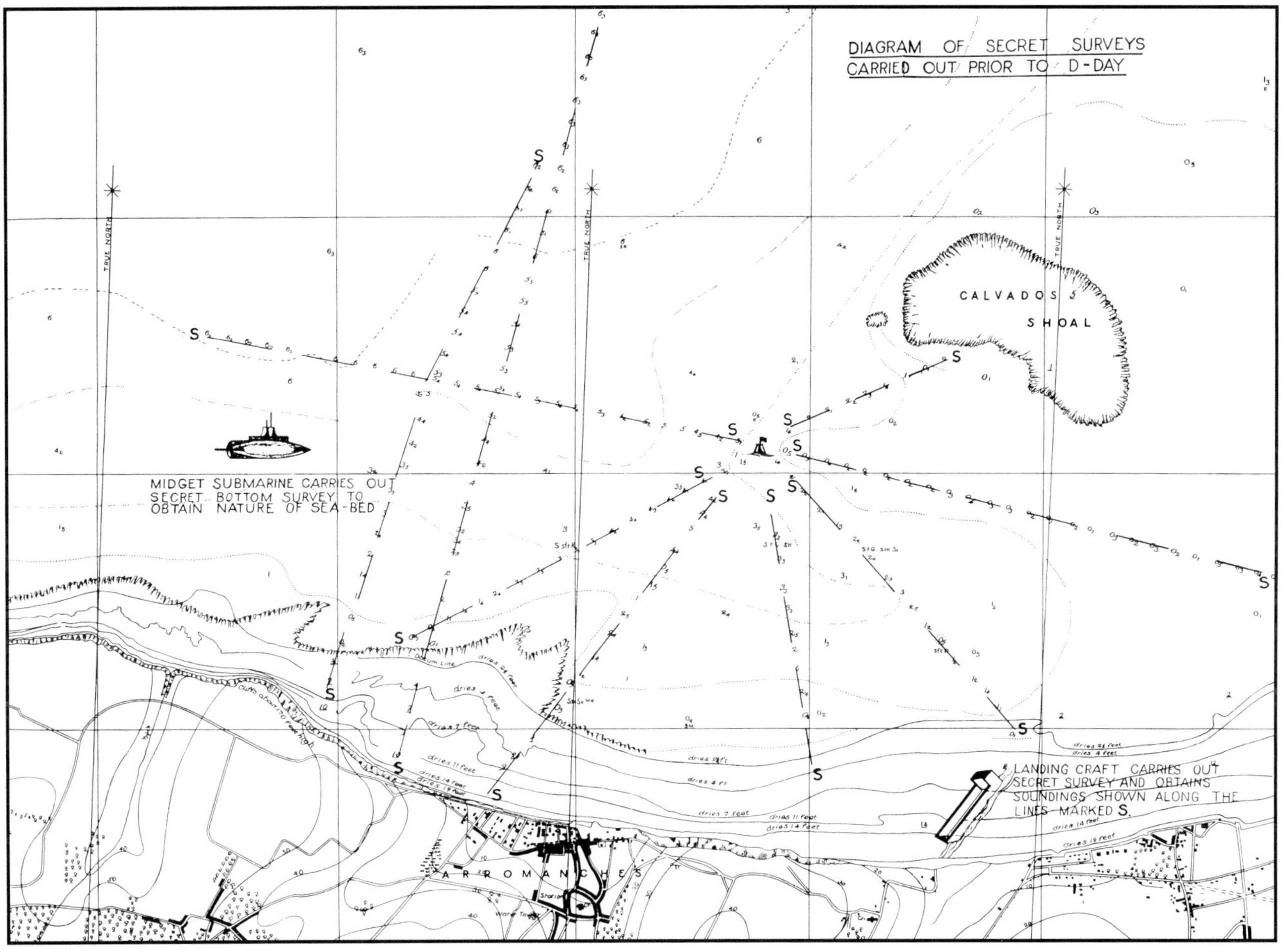

'The capacities and sites for the harbours were specified in the outline plan (12,000 tons of cargo and 2,500 vehicles by D+14); the next step was to plan in detail the layout, the programme of erection, and the method of operation of each harbour. For this purpose, two planning teams were set up, one composed of US officers for Mulberry 'A' and the other of British officers for Mulberry 'B'. The principal need was for accurate topographical and hydrographical information; the available maps and charts — particularly the latter — were not very up-to-date, the existing charts being based on the last French survey dated 1836 — over a hundred years previously. This was done by secret surveys; the diagram *above* indicates the method. On dark nights with suitable weather and tide, small landing craft would come in under the noses of the Germans and run a "base" from the shore from which they could fix accurately, using the taut wire method, the location of a buoy which had been dropped at about the centre of the area to be surveyed. Once the buoy had been fixed the party would take a series of soundings on lines radiating from it — rather like the points of a star. In addition to the underwater shape, it was also essential to know the nature of the sea-bed and under-bed; were we to build our "house" on sand, or rock, or mud, or a combination of them? To ascertain this, a midget submarine, or sometimes a small landing craft, was sent in by night and a major and a sergeant of the Combined Operations Pilotage Party swam ashore on each occasion and took sample borings of the bottom. On two occasions, the submarine found itself in what was apparently the target firing area of the defences, some of which opened fire in its direction, but it was able to withdraw unscathed, its mission seemingly unsuspected.'

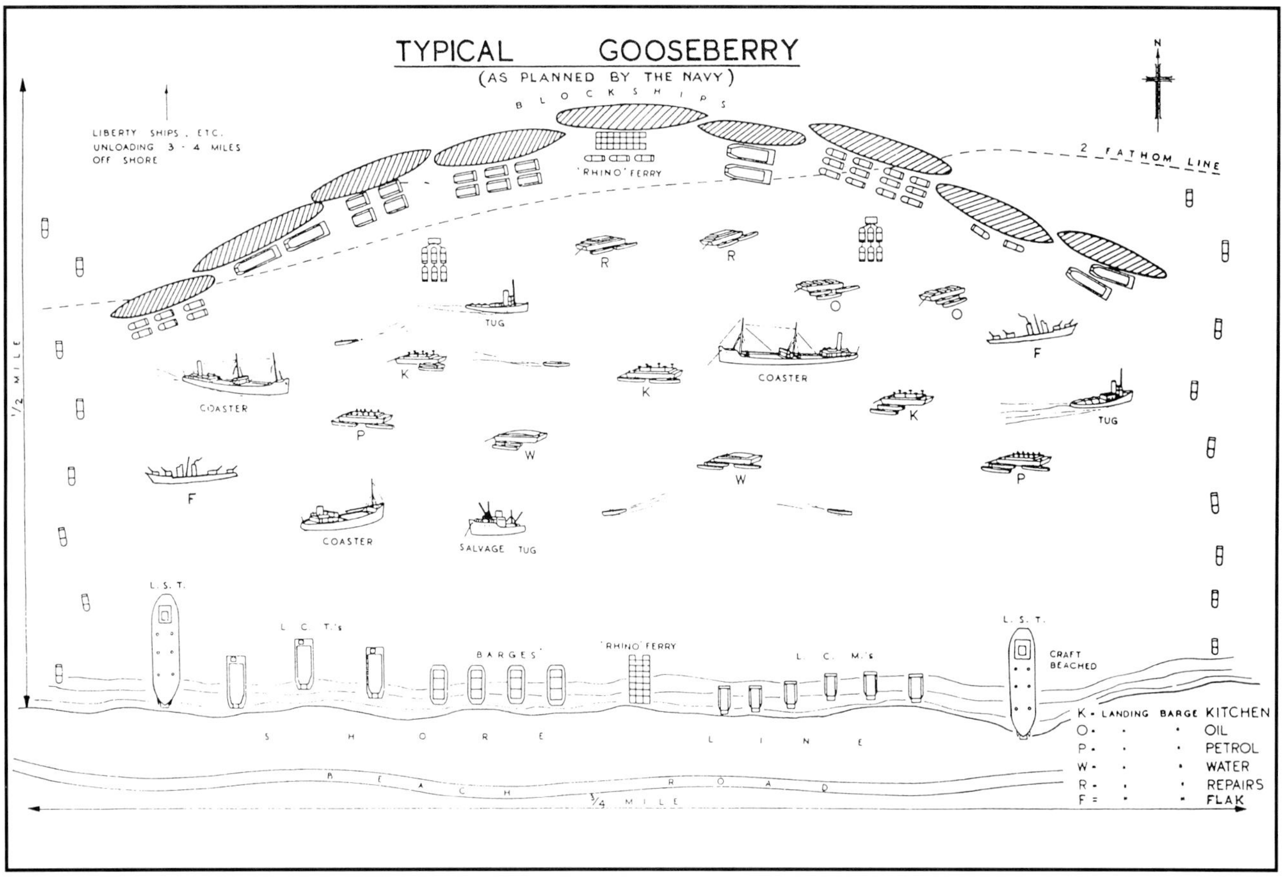

'When the scope of the assault was increased by two divisions (one US and one British)', explains Captain Hickling, 'and the assault area was extended on either flank, the speed of the follow-up and build-up was also stepped up. It was then too late to take any action to increase the size and capacity of the two Mulberries, but it became apparent that additional shelters for the minor landing craft were essential, particularly on the flank beaches which were too far away from the Mulberries for the latter to be reached by small craft in the short time likely to be available between the warning of bad weather and its commencement. In any case, the enlarged scope of the assault and build-up involved a material increase in the number of minor craft to be employed and the Mulberries by themselves would not be able to shelter them all. It was therefore decided to provide a craft shelter, called a Gooseberry, for each assault beach. Reading from west (right) to east (left), these were: Utah area, No. 1 Gooseberry at Varreville; Omaha area, No. 2 Gooseberry at St Laurent; Gold area, No. 3 Gooseberry at Arromanches-les-Bains; Juno area, No. 4 Gooseberry at Courseulles; and No. 5 Gooseberry at Ouistreham for Sword area. No. 2 and No. 3 Gooseberries were on the same beaches as Mulberries 'A' and 'B' respectively, and the proposal was that these two Gooseberries, when established, should grow into Mulberries — no mean horticultural feat!'

BREAKWATERS

During the pre-planning stage we had been considering various types of breakwater, but I will not go into details of all the different types, such as the Bubble breakwater and the Liberty ship floating breakwater, as they did not play any part.

BLOCKSHIPS

The first form of breakwater and probably the simplest was the blockship (code-name 'Corncob') which was used for the Gooseberries. They consisted of such old merchant ships as we could get hold of and they had the great advantage that, being mobile, they did not require any tugs, for in this venture tugs were worth their weight in gold. They could move under their own steam and manoeuvre themselves roughly into position and so provide essential protection from D-Day onwards. They were ballasted to draw about 19ft of water, and filled with explosive charges of ten pounds of amatol on each side of each hold, which were connected up electrically to a central firing key. When they were in the right place to be 'planted' as we called it, the charges

At the extreme eastern end of the beach-head facing Ouistreham, Gooseberry No. 5 comprised nine blockships: six merchantmen and three warships: the 33-year-old French battleship *Courbet* (from which this picture was taken); the old British cruiser *Durban*, dating from 1919, and the hulk of the Dutch cruiser *Sumatra*, built in 1920. The *Courbet* had to be towed to her watery grave but the Germans, not appreciating her true purpose, reported her grounded, believed damaged.

GOOSEBERRY SHELTERS

No. 1 (Utah)	No. 2 (Omaha)	No. 3 (Gold)	No. 4 (Juno)	No. 5 (Sword)
Benjamin Contee	*Artemas Ward*	*Alynbank*	*Belgique*	*Becheville*
David O. Saylor	*Audacious*	*Aghios Spyridon*	*Bendoran*	FFS *Courbet*
George S. Wasson	*Baialoide*	*Elswick Park*	*Empire Bunting*	*Dover Hill*
Matt W. Ransom	HMS *Centurion*	*Flowergate*	*Empire Flamingo*	HMS *Durban*
West Cheswald	*Courageous*	*Giorgios P.*	*Empire Moorhen*	*Empire Defiance*
West Honaker	*Flight-Command*	*Ingman*	*Empire Waterhen*	*Empire Tamar*
West Nohno	*Galveston*	*Innerton*	*Formigny*	*Empire Tana*
Willis A. Slater	*George W. Childs*	*Lynghaug*	*Manchester Spinner*	*Forbin*
Victory Sword	*James W. Marshall*	*Modlin*	*Mariposa*	HNMS *Sumatra*
Vitruvius	*James Iredell*	*Njegos*	*Panos*	
	Olambala	*Parkhaven*	*Vera Radcliffe*	
	Potter	*Parklaan*		
	West Grama	*Saltersgate*		
	Wilscox	*Sirehei*		
		Vinlake (ex-*Csikos*)		
		Winha		

Note: Later additions not listed

were fired and blew a hole 3ft below the water-line, and down the ships went. We also had alternative methods of firing by time fuse. HMS *Vernon* [the Torpedo and Mining School] took every sort of precaution to avoid any hitch, but one thing was overlooked: rats that ate the insulation of the electric wires. Fortunately, we spotted this in time.

The depth of the average tramp, such as we got, was of the order of 40ft from keel to upper deck. This meant that, with a rise of tide of 23ft, the depth in which the blockships could be sunk to make effective breakwaters was about 15ft at low water. A breakwater which is submerged at high water is not much use.

It was a comparatively simple business to fit out these blockships, but to obtain the 60 old ships we needed was not so easy. At this time — December 1943 — the heavy sinkings of Allied shipping by the U-Boat packs in the Atlantic were still fresh in people's minds, and when Admiral Tennant and I went to the Admiralty and said we wanted all those ships just to sink off the coast of Normandy to make the five Gooseberries, we were very nearly thrown out. As we came away somewhat chastened, I said to Tennant: 'Bill, we came here to get a Gooseberry and all we seem to have got is a raspberry!'

However, the request was considered by the Chiefs-of-Staff the following day and, although I was not present myself, I have a pretty shrewd idea that the argument must have gone something like this: 'Supposing for a moment we do get one of those infrequent summer gales and supposing the landing craft ferrying the stuff ashore to the beaches are driven ashore and cast up high and dry and the Army's life-line fails, are we, the Chiefs-of-Staff, prepared to face the country and say the invasion has been defeated because we were unable to provide Admiral Ramsay with 60 old merchant ships?' So we got them. We also got a few old warships, including the French battleship *Courbet*, the Dutch cruiser *Sumatra*, and the old target ship HMS *Centurion*.

The intention was to sink the blockships in shallow water, say 15ft, and then to extend that breakwater east and west into deeper water by means of concrete caissons — the Phoenixes, which I will describe shortly.

At the western extremity lay Gooseberry No. 1. The sinking operation off Utah was interrupted by German shelling so that the *George S. Wasson* swung round just as she was settling. The German guns hit the second and third ships, but they sank more or less in the correct positions, though slightly too far apart. As a result, it was decided to scuttle the remaining ships to form two crescent-shaped breakwaters. Two unloading jetties, constructed of Naval Lighter Pontoons, were added, and eventually Gooseberry No. 1 was berthing up to 25 Liberty ships. (See also pages 388-389.)

BOMBARDONS

Outside each harbour, however, it was decided to put down a mile of floating breakwater called the Bombardon. This was an entirely novel form of breakwater. The idea came to a fellow called Lochner, Lieutenant, RNVR, who was sitting one summer's afternoon in his garden alongside the swimming pool where a Lilo, one of those rubber mattress affairs, was floating. Through his half-closed eyes, he noticed the wavelets breaking up against the windward side of the Lilo while on the lee side it was quite calm. That is how the Bombardon started. We actually got three mammoth rubber Lilos, each 200ft long and about 15ft in diameter — the biggest rubber job Dunlops ever made. The concrete keel alone weighed 750 tons. They worked quite well while they lasted, but no practical seafaring man wants to go into an operation of this sort with a lot of rubber hot water bottles hung round his neck!

The theory of these Bombardons was that when the sea hit the freeboard they would start to oscillate, but they were so designed that the period of these oscillations would never come into phase with the period of the waves which it was intended to suppress. The wave for which they were designed, and which we expected off the Normandy coast with a wind of Force 6 to 7, was 200ft crest to crest. The Bombardon had the advantage that it could be moored in comparatively deep water, say 60ft, which would enable deeply-laden Liberty ships to anchor in its lee and discharge their cargoes under those difficult half and half conditions. A mile of Bombardons was laid by D+8 at each Mulberry, and so long as the conditions for which they were designed, i.e., half a gale, were not exceeded they worked fairly well, and gave a wave suppression of about 40 per cent. But on June 19 came the great storm, when they broke adrift from their moorings, and were wrecked on the beaches of Normandy. By some miracle, they did not damage any ships as they drove ashore, nor did they damage any of the breakwaters, as some people have stated.

The Bombardon was a massive floating outer breakwater, anchored a mile to seaward of the Mulberries, to give a first line of protection to the main harbour. Secondly, it was to provide a sheltered area where ships could lie up before unloading. The idea was first mooted by Lieutenant Robert Lochner, in charge of the Heavy Engineering Section of the Department of Miscellaneous Weapons and Devices — aptly nicknamed 'Wheezers and Dodgers'. Experimenting on his garden pond *(above)* at Hammer in Sussex, he discovered that if weights were added to a rubber Lilo, it was capable of reflecting waves to give calm water on the leeward side.

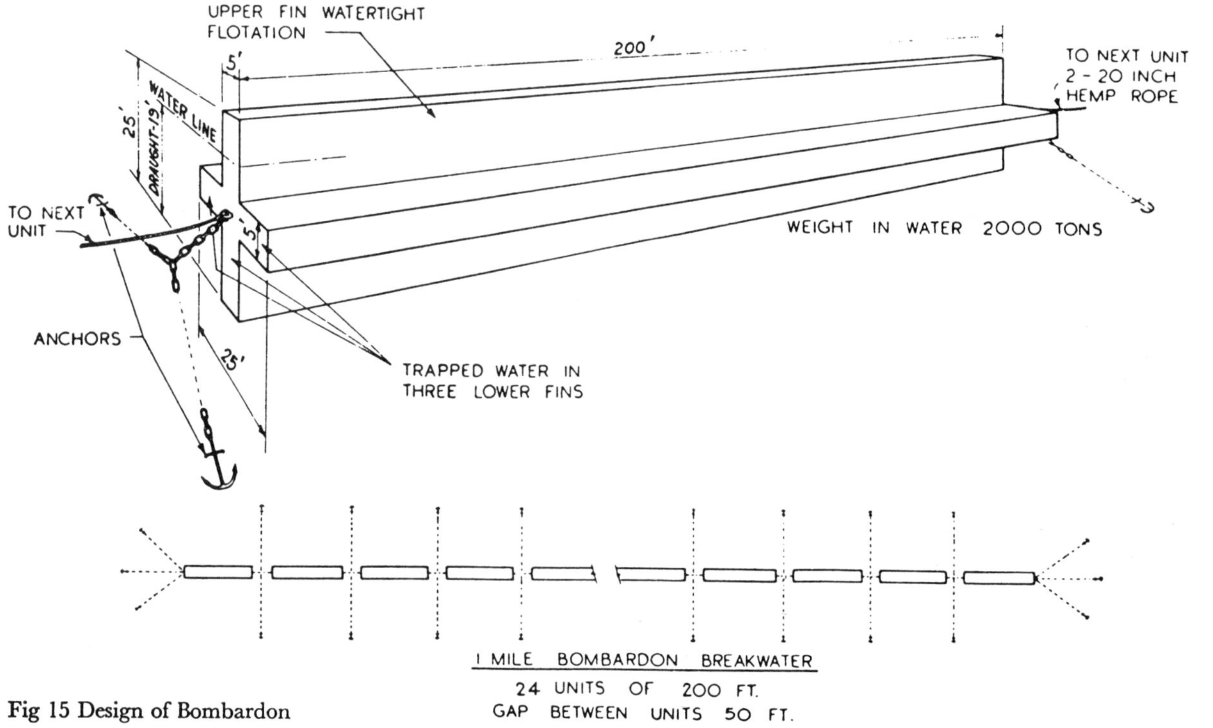

Fig 15 Design of Bombardon

While rubber was impractical, Captain Hickling explains that 'it was evident that if a design in steel or concrete could be produced to perform the same duty, then a floating breakwater formed from such units would be less vulnerable and easier to maintain. So a variety of designs in steel were developed and the one ultimately adopted is shown in the diagram *above*. It is 200 feet long and of cruciform cross-section, having a width and breadth of 25 feet. The top fin is enclosed and provides the floatation while the remaining fins are open and contain trapped water which gives the whole structure, when afloat, a mass of some 2,000 tons. The Bombardons were quite satisfactory in practice in the conditions for which they were designed (half a gale), but they were not designed to stand up to the conditions which occurred during the storm which blew up on D+13, and they all finished up on the Normandy coast, never to be used again.'

PHOENIXES

As I have said, the blockships and the Bombardons were a naval commitment. Now we come to the Army's part — the concrete caissons known as Phoenixes and the Whales.

The depth of the blockships confined them to comparatively shallow water and, in order to provide breakwaters behind which Liberty ships drawing 26 or 27ft of water could berth, we had to go into the concrete business. The War Office designed the Phoenixes, which were nothing more nor less than concrete ships or hulks. They were not the best design but they were the best that could be made in the time. Always we were working against time: remember we had only seven months in which to do the job — a job which had never been done before, for our target date was May 1, 1944. We had to go into production before the blueprints were off the drawing board, and we certainly had some teething troubles.

There were half-a-dozen different sizes of Phoenixes (see page 198), depending on the depth of water in which they were to be planted, for they formed not only the outer breakwater but also the side arms. The A1 — the biggest, was 200ft long, by 60ft high and 40ft beam. These 'blocks of flats' had to satisfy various conditions, the first of which was that they had to be towable, which is why they were given swim (upswept) ends. They also had to be stable, that is, they had to remain on an even keel while they were being planted for we did not want them capsizing. But, most important of all, so far as the Navy was concerned — and it was the Navy who had to 'plant' them — was that they should sink quickly. You can imagine that 'planting' a 6,000-ton hulk with 40ft freeboard to catch the wind in any sort of breeze and with a cross tide is no mean feat of seamanship, for they had to be placed with an accuracy not of feet but of inches. The first designs were going to take the best part of an hour to sink, but eventually the War Office brought it down to about 15 minutes: that is all except two which were being towed across the Channel after D-Day, one of which was torpedoed, and one mined; they sank in 30 seconds!

The question was where to build these things, especially as we only had six months in which to do the job. We tried to get dry docks but the majority of these were already in use on shipping repair and also on a lot of jobs in connection with the assault itself. Remember, the assault was not a separate business from all this Mulberry operation, the Mulberry was a sort of poor relation and about as popular in assault circles. However, big holes were scratched out on the banks of the Thames, and the first were built there. When this was done, the bank was broken down to let the water in, and the sections were floated out and taken to adjacent wharves where they were completed. This process introduced all sorts of difficulties: for instance, the Phoenix was designed as a complete structure, like a ship; building a bit of it and then floating it meant setting up all sorts of unfair stresses. It was only by a great deal of clever calculation, a certain amount of good fortune and prayer, that it proved possible to fit the sections together without the whole structure breaking up. The first unit took about four months to build, but as things went on this was reduced to two months.

To be wise after the event, I think it would have been better if the Navy instead of the Army had undertaken the Phoenixes, as I have said, they were concrete ships or hulks and, whereas it is part of naval routine to 'accept' ships when they leave the builder's hands to carry out equipment trials, handling trials and so forth, such things naturally are not provided for in the War Office. Amateurs, however enthusiastic and with the best advice in the world, cannot have the same knowledge and experience as those who have made seafaring their profession. As it was, when D-Day approached, the Navy took over the equipment of the Phoenixes and prepared them for the passage across the Channel.

'The target date, by which the whole of the equipment for the two Mulberries and five Gooseberries had to be ready, was set at May 1, 1944. This gave little more than seven months in which to complete the planning, designing and provision of a vast quantity of specialised material in a country then in its fifth year of war, with its total productive capacity already fully committed. With so little previous experience, it would not have been unreasonable, even under wartime conditions, to take some three months in the research and design stage before the blueprints came off the drawing board; thereafter, normally some six weeks or two months might well be fully taken up in developing practical construction details and getting out contracts. But in this case we could not afford three, let alone five months before construction started, and the whole was telescoped into a period of 14 days. Perhaps', says Captain Hickling, 'the greatest construction project of all was the production of over a hundred of the huge reinforced-concrete caissons which were to form the semi-permanent breakwater to Mulberry 'A' and 'B'.' (See also pages 197-198.)

However, Captain Hickling goes on to explain that 'the Whale equipment was far more complex than the Phoenix and it is quite certain that, if a prototype had not already been built and undergone successful trials by the summer of 1943, it would not have been possible to complete the design and provide the required quantity in the time available. The problem set by the Prime Minister to the technicians in May 1942 was to produce a pier which could be quickly erected and which would provide continuous alongside discharge on flat beaches with a tide range of up to 30 feet; moreover, the equipment must be able to withstand rough weather. Continuous alongside discharge, even for coastal vessels, would require some 20 feet of water at the pierhead at low tide; with a tidal range of 30 feet this involved a depth of 50 feet at high water. The average slope of the Normandy beaches was about 1 in 100 (some were as flat as 1 in 150); but, even at 1 in 100, the pierhead would have to be 50 x 100 feet out to sea from the high tide mark at the top of the beach. This means a mile of pier and quite clearly any rigid structure of the necessary strength would be extremely difficult to erect in a week or ten days which was the period contemplated. A further objection to a rigid structure was the difficulty of designing a pierhead so that the discharge is convenient at all stages of the tide. The solution consisted of two principal parts: (a) the spud pontoon pierhead, and (b) the flexible floating roadway. The pontoon pierhead was 200 feet long, 60 feet wide and 10 feet deep and, when complete with fittings, it weighed approximately 1,000 tons. It was constructed with compartments much like a ship and was fitted with a diesel-driven electric power plant. Four stiff steel legs or 'spuds' fitted in guides, one at each corner of the pontoon, and four electric motors were provided to raise and lower the legs as required.'

WHALE PIERHEAD

Sheltered water having been provided for, the next most important thing was the means for rapid discharge of stores, vehicles, etc. Early in the war, the Prime Minister had realised that wherever we landed in Europe we should have to land over flat beaches, and if ships were to discharge at all states of the tide, piers would have to run out a very long way to seaward. You will recall the chit the Prime Minister sent to Lord Louis Mountbatten, then Chief of Combined Operations (see page 196): 'They must float up and down with the tide. The anchor problem must be mastered. . . . Let me have the best solution worked out. Don't argue the matter. The difficulties will argue for themselves.'

The result was the 'Whale' — probably one of the finest pieces of bridge engineering the world has ever known, and one of the most ingenious pieces of engineering of modern times. It consisted in the main of two principal elements: the pierheads, of which 23 were made, and the floating pier roadway, which connected the pierheads to the shore. Ten miles of this equipment was ordered.

The pierheads — known as spud pierheads on account of their four long legs or 'spuds' — consisted of a rectangular steel ship, 200ft long, 60ft beam and about 11ft deep. At each corner, a leg or spud, 90ft high and 4ft by 4ft cross-section, was fitted and, by means of winding machinery, it was possible to move these legs up and down. When we wanted to tow the thing over to France, all we had to do was to press a button and wind the legs up into and above the body of the hull. When we got it to where we wanted it, the man would press another button and the legs would be lowered down until their spud feet buried themselves in the sea-bed. As the four legs were independent, no matter what the inequalities of the sea bottom, they would take up their own level and moor a pier weighing in all about 1,000 tons which could go up and down with the tide.

A Stores Pier, which could take a load of 5 tons, consisted of seven pierheads placed in a continuous line in a depth of 18ft at low water. There coasters could berth and discharge at all states of the tide.

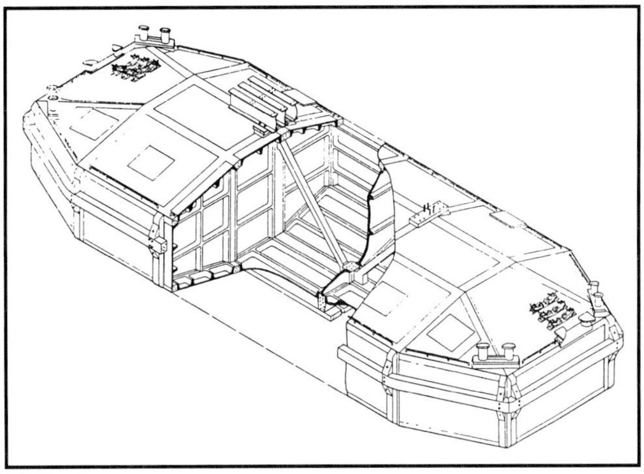

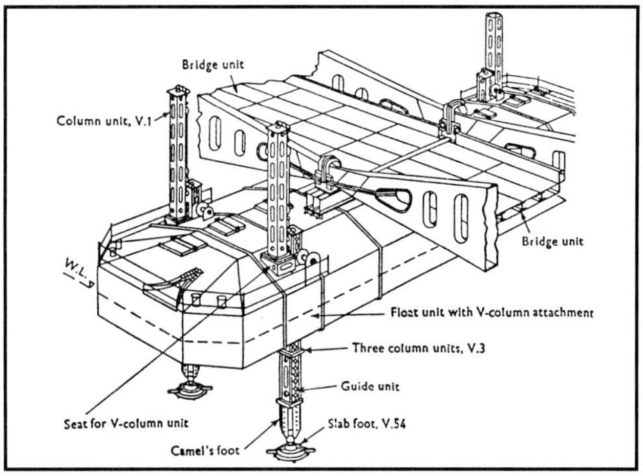

'The floating roadway was perhaps the most difficult problem of all to solve', recalled Captain Hickling. ' It is well known that when waves come up against any rigid structure tremendous forces are developed, but if that structure can be arranged to give slightly to the waves and then come back into position again, the forces are greatly reduced. That is very broadly the principle on which the floating roadway was designed and it may be called one of controlled flexibility.'

Left: **The pier pontoons to support the floating roadway were nicknamed 'Beetles' because of their turtle-back shape designed to reduce resistance when towing. To avoid a further demand on steel, they were constructed of reinforced concrete divided into six watertight chambers with wooden fenders to protect the skin — only 1¼in thick — from damage.** *Right:* **For rocky foreshores, a float similar to a Beetle but with adjustable legs had to be manufactured out of steel.**

BEETLES

These pierheads were connected to the shore half a mile away by means of the floating pier roadway. The latter consisted of 80ft steel spans supported on specially designed floats known as Beetles.

If you try and resist water you set up very big stresses; it is much easier to give to the sea than to resist it. The principle of the floating pier roadway is one of flexibility — controlled flexibility, and there was nothing rigid in these spans. But of course if you go and flex a structure too much you are apt to fatigue the metal and fracture it. It was necessary to damp down the motion of the waves and this was achieved by designing the Beetles on the principle of the carapace of a turtle. If you have ever been bathing with a turtle you will notice that the seas break over it and under it, with the result that instead of a rapid jerky motion it has a slow leisurely movement.

Owing to the rise and fall of tide and various other things, the pier roadway was always varying its length and, to compensate for this while the pier was under traffic, telescopic spans were introduced at intervals. These spans also enabled the shore end, known as the shore ramp float, to be winched up the beach as necessary, tide after tide.

LST PIER

At Arromanches, we also had an LST pier which could take a 40-ton load such as a tank. This consisted of two pierheads, one at right-angles to the other alongside which two LSTs at a time could come and discharge their cargoes. This pier ran out to provide a depth of about 14ft at low water. The tank landing craft lowered its ramp on to what was called a buffer pontoon and unloaded its lower deck; simultaneously the upper deck was cleared of motor transport by means of an overhead ramp. Our best time for unloading an LST with about 70 tanks and trucks at Arromanches was 18 minutes.

The main Beetle assembly area was No. 1 Port and Inland Water Transportation Repair Depot at Marchwood, Southampton.

Sections of floating roadway attached to the Beetles moored off the Isle of Wight ready for towing. Other assembly areas were strung out along the south coast with Phoenixes and pierheads at Dungeness and Selsey; Bombardons at Portland, and Corncobs at Poole.

THE ASSEMBLY

By March 1944, the various units of Bombardon, Phoenix, Whale and Corncob were nearing completion. It was the intention to assemble them on the south coast of England so as to reduce as far as possible the tow to the 'Far Shore'. The Navy had viewed with growing concern the problems which the towing of these monstrosities was likely to involve. The soldiers had said that they would probably tow 'like drunken sailors', to which the sailors wittily replied, 'You mean drunken soldiers', so all were satisfied.

In practice, the units, with certain exceptions, towed remarkably well. It required the service of 200 tugs, mustered from all over the United Kingdom and the United States for nearly four months, to collect the 600 units from all round the British Isles and bring them down to the south coast. This was undoubtedly the biggest towing operation ever undertaken and, but for the unremitting efforts of the tugs and the Admiralty Towing Section, combined with a fine Spring, I doubt if we should have been ready for D-Day. As it was, when the tugs had accomplished their task, they only had a few days in which to clean their boilers, refit their towing gear, and be ready for the passage across the Channel.

The south coast of England was already filled to overflowing with the assault forces and it was no easy matter to find suitable places to park the Mulberry units. All had to be protected from the south-westerly blows and from attacks by the enemy both surface and air. Moreover, the Phoenix units had to be sunk on a flat and sandy bottom as no quays or moorings were available. This, of course, meant a big pumping job when it came to refloating them.

In the event, the Bombardons, 115 of them, were parked at Portland, the blockships at Poole, and the Whale roadway — some 84 tows, each 480ft long (six 80ft sections) — were moored on the Peel Bank near Ryde. The 150 special Mulberry tugs were based at Lee-on-Solent and were administered by Captain Edmund J. Moran, US Navy, and a fine job he made of it.

Of the Phoenixes and the Whale pierheads, two-thirds were parked at Selsey and one-third at Dungeness.

The month of May was very hectic, for all the units had to be got ready for the crossing. The pier roadways were put together at Marchwood and Richborough and were then towed to the Peel Bank, and it was during this assembly stage that we realised they were going to give trouble. Erection tanks were a weak spot and some of the tows came to grief while crossing the Solent. No proper provision had been made for mooring the 84 Whale tows at Peel Bank but fortunately the Commander-in-Chief, Portsmouth, came to the rescue. The preparation of the units for sea involved a very large amount of boat work taking parties and stores to and from the shore. The British were lamentably short of water transport and appealed to the Americans, who helped us out considerably with the loan of DUKWs and small tugs.

There was very nearly a major disaster over the pumping equipment for raising the Phoenixes, eight to ten of which it was intended to raise and send across the Channel daily. Four little Dutch schuyts had been fitted out with a Heath Robinson arrangement of pumps in which none of us had very much confidence. A lucky accident had put one of the Phoenixes aground on the Bramble Bank in Southampton Water, and it had taken a salvage tug a week to get it afloat again. As time went on, and the Dutch schuyts did not materialise, Tennant took drastic action. He took over responsibility for the whole of the pumping-out equipment and appealed to the Admiralty, but only just in time. For a month, work under Captain J. B. Polland, the Deputy Director of the Admiralty Salvage Department, went on night and day and, by mobilising the whole of the salvage organisation, the situation was saved; but it was a near thing.

When, on the eve of D-Day, only 108 tugs were available for towing the various sections of the harbours to France, reluctantly it was necessary to postpone the target date for completion by seven days — from D+14 to D+21.

THE CROSSING

By superhuman efforts, the assembly was completed and the units made ready for sea just about the time the assault forces were leaving harbour on D–1. The first Mulberry left harbour in the evening of D-Day. For purposes of planning, we had worked out an integrated towing programme because each unit had to be moved into the harbour in its proper place and proper order at the proper time. Of course we realised that with so many unknown factors, including enemy action, our programme would never be strictly adhered to, but it provided a very good guide. In our planning, we had allowed a towing speed of three knots — actually an average speed of four knots was achieved. We allowed one day in four when bad weather would prevent towing, but unfavourable weather prevailed most of the time. We allowed for the loss of 15 tugs, but only two went to the bottom. We allowed for a 20 per cent loss of the units to be towed: our losses of Bombardons, Phoenix and pierheads were negligible; but our loss of pier roadways, due to bad weather, was of the order of 50 per cent.

Each night, depending on the weather forecast, the following units were despatched to each Mulberry: 4 to 5 Phoenixes; 6 Bombardons; 2 or 3 pierheads; 4 or 5 sections of pier roadways.

It was so arranged that they should not enter the combat area during dark hours owing to the presence of enemy E-Boats. When the units arrived on the far side, they were taken over by harbour tugs so that the sea-going tugs could return for another tow. The Whale units would then be turned over to the Sappers, while the Planter — Lieutenant-Commander A. M. D. Lampen, RN, and his team would board the Phoenix and, if conditions were right, plant it. It was quite remarkable with what accuracy the Phoenix breakwater was placed, often under difficult conditions of wind, tide and light.

Captain Hickling: 'The towing factor dominated both the assembly on the south coast and the subsequent movement of all the components across the Channel to Normandy. Some tugs were also required permanently on the 'Far Shore' for the erection and operation of the harbours. For the assembly, some 200 tugs of all shapes and sizes were obtained by combing all the ports, harbours and naval dockyards in the UK; some 150 were selected as suitable for the Channel crossing and were marked with an "M" for Mulberry on their funnels; all took great pride in their "M". There were about 90 large tugs — in the 1,000–1,500 horse-power range — mostly British; the remainder were smaller, around 750 horse-power, and were mostly US. There were also a small number of ocean-going Dutch tugs. The British tugs were a mixture of White and Red Ensign with some dockyard tugs thrown in, while the US tugs were both Navy and Army (Transportation Corps).'

The Mulberry control ships and mooring forces left the UK on the morning of D-Day; the Bombardon tows from Weymouth and Corncobs from Poole during the afternoon, with the first Phoenix tows leaving during the evening. On D+1, the laying of the anchorages for the Bombardons was begun by boom defence mooring vessels, an operation which proceeded so well that the first Bombardons were able to be placed in position the next day. That afternoon too, a start was made on the first blockship sinkings. The following day (D+2), the Whale tows began.

At Omaha, work could not begin on the necessary survey to confirm the earlier soundings until D+1. Thereafter, construction of Mulberry 'A' by Force 127.1, more usually referred to as Force Mulberry, comprising Seabees of the 108th Construction Battalion (CB) from the 25th Naval Construction Regiment, continued apace. Three blockships were sunk the same day, although they immediately came under enemy fire which caused some casualties among the merchant marine crews. On D+2, three more ships were sunk and three Phoenixes put in position to begin the harbour proper. The first Bombardons were also moored. By D+4, the Gooseberry was completed, 10 Phoenixes were emplaced; 12 Bombardons were moored and all the survey work completed. By June 17, all 24 Bombardons were in position; 32 out of the planned 51 Phoenixes had been sited, with berths prepared for two Liberty ships. Meanwhile, work was proceeding on the 3,000-foot floating roadways and, by June 16 when these pictures were taken, the centre LST pier was complete and in operation.

Both the eastern and western piers were well under way and two of the Lobnitz pierheads had been installed. On the first day that the centre pier was used, a tank landing ship spent an average of 64 minutes unloading, the LSTs discharging their vehicles at a rate of one every 1 minute 16 seconds. D-1 draw can be seen on the right.

The first Whale roadway was completed on D+4, the second, begun the next day, being completed three days later. Although Mulberry 'A' was not scheduled to be fully operational until D+18 (June 24), by D+12 a total of 314,504 out of the planned 358,139 men had crossed the American beaches and 11 of the planned build-up of 12 divisions were ashore. In this, the harbour played a vital part even if not fully completed. The Gooseberry breakwaters can be seen on the extreme right of this picture, which is dated June 23, although that must be wrong as by then it had been largely destroyed by the gale.

The empty beach seen from the western shoulder of the Vierville draw with the Hotel du Casino now standing on the site of the ruined house. Karel Margry took the comparison on June 8, 1994 — see also page 370.

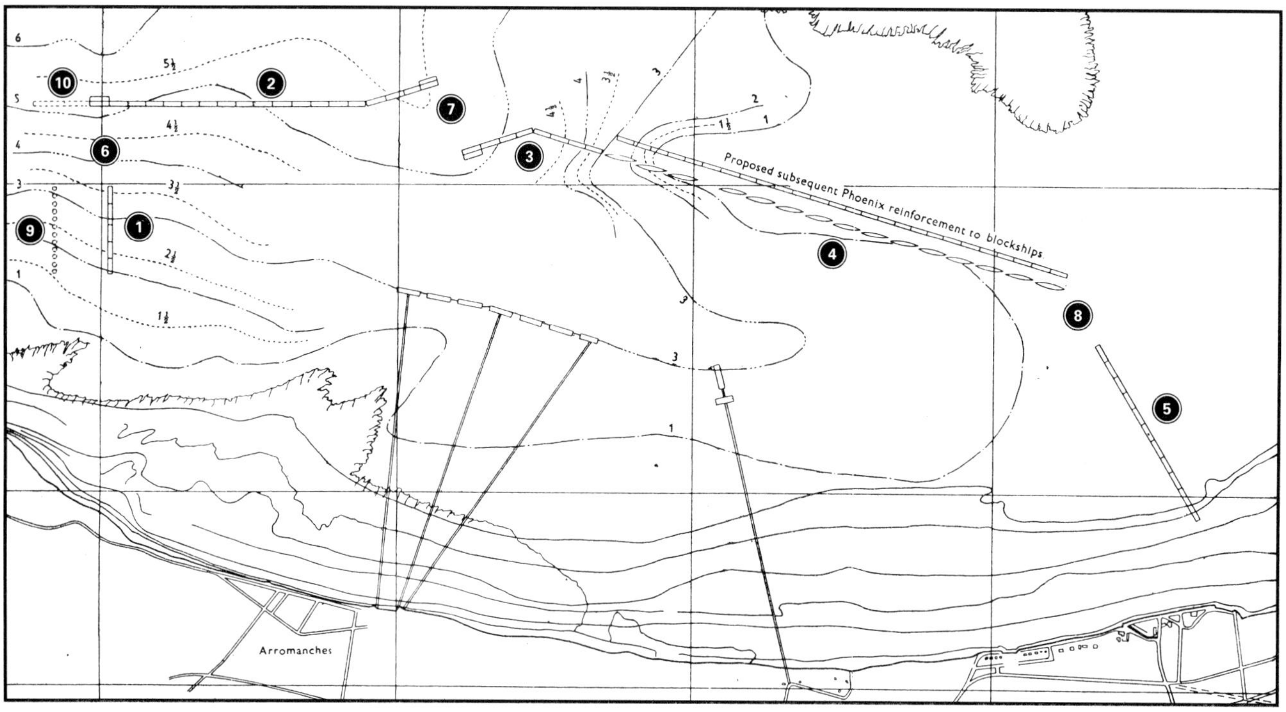

The planned layout of Mulberry 'B' based on the pre-D-Day surveys. [1] Western Shore Arm. [2] Detached Mole. [3] Blockship Extension West. [4] Blockship Breakwater (subsequently reinforced with concrete caissons). [5] Eastern Shore Arm. The entrances were the Western Entrance [6]; the Northern Entrance [7], and the Eastern Entrance [8]. The Detached Mole was sited so as to skirt a suspected deep patch immediately north-west of the northern entrance. The Blockship Breakwater was sited so as to keep all the component ships above the one-fathom contour, but as near to it as possible, with the exception of the first two ships at the western end of the line for which slightly deeper hulls were available. The Blockship Extension West continued the line of blockships as far as possible until it became necessary to deflect it southwards so as to maintain a 700-foot entrance with the eastern end of the Detached Mole. An alternative position for the Western Shore Arm is shown dotted [9], and was to be used if the three concrete caissons, indicated as double headers for the eastern and western ends of the Detached Mole and the western end of the Blockship Extension West, respectively, were diverted from those positions to provide a westward extension of the Detached Mole, which is also shown dotted [10].

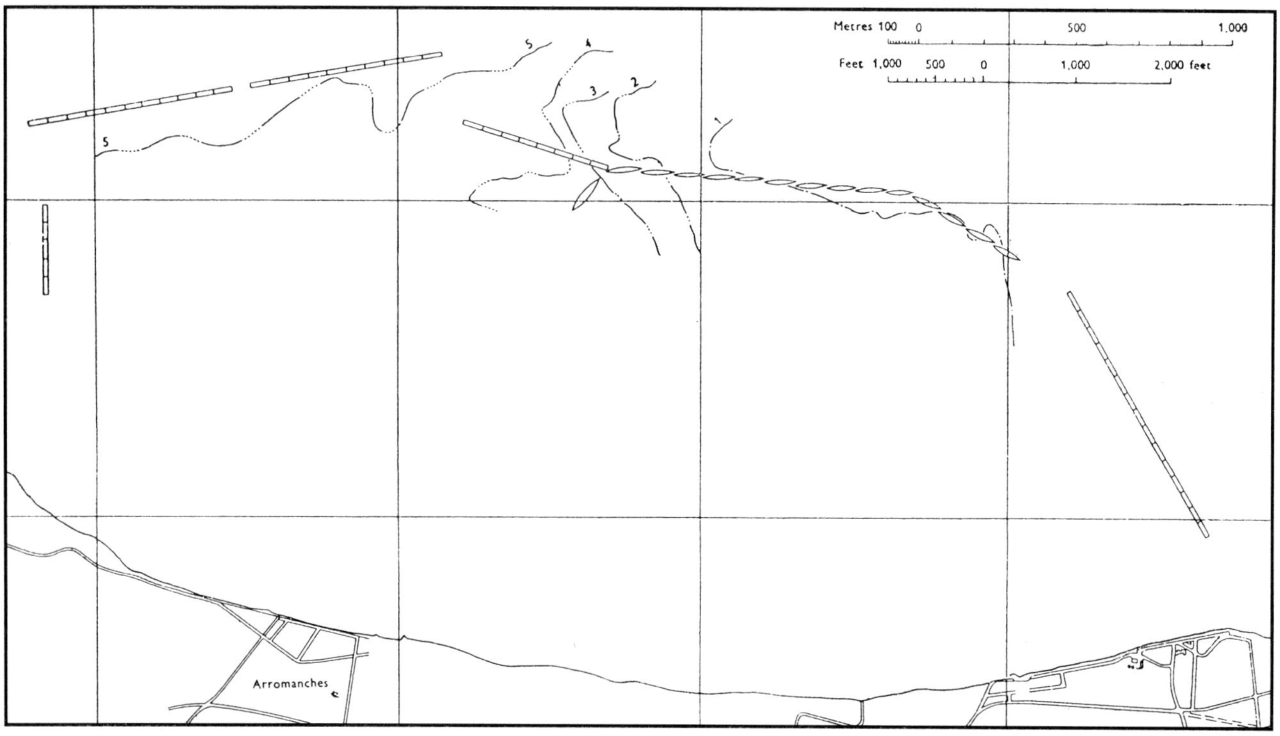

Revised layout prepared after the sites of the breakwaters had been surveyed and the sinking of the first units had commenced. The deep patch of water north-west of the Northern Entrance was found not to exist, which allowed the Detached Mole to be swung seawards and straightened and the Blockship Extension West to be straightened, so as to continue the original blockship alignment for its whole length. The three double-heading units are shown in their final positions at the western end of the Detached Mole, and the Western Shore Arm is shown in its alternative position. The discovery of somewhat deeper water than anticipated in the centre of the blockship line necessitated the swinging of that line northward and then south again from a point four ships from the end, as shown.

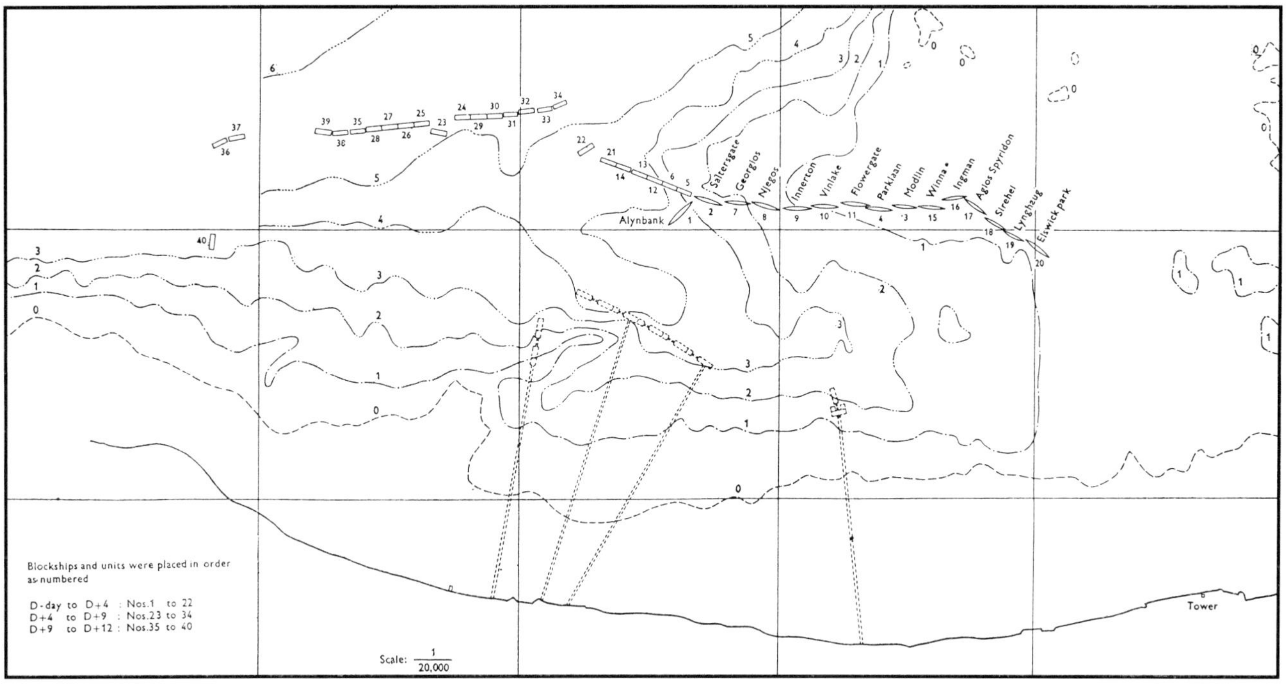

The line of blockships was sunk approximately as intended. Block-ship No. 1 (*Alynbank*) went down completely out of line in the position shown, owing to the unexpected length of time taken to sink. The delay enabled the current to take hold of the ship and swing it out of position. However, the sinking of subsequent ships was facilitated by the presence of the previously sunk ship as a fixed point to secure one end, while tugs were provided to control the other. Phoenix No. 22 sank out of place through being damaged by a tug in the course of the sinking operation, which had to be conducted at night in somewhat unfavourable weather. On D+9, work commenced on the Detached Mole, leaving completion of Blockship Extension West (one unit only) to a later date. Unit 23 settled out of position on account of the difficulties in the placing of an initial unit as none of the tugs could hold the massive structure against the current, but the placing of subsequent units was simplified by using the previously sunk unit as an anchor. Units 24 and 25 were therefore successfully sited and it was decided to leave 23 in its position and use the opening thus created for small boat access. The diagram *above* represents the stage reached on D+9 with the Detached Mole completed at the east end, leaving only the extension westward to continue. Since that would have restricted sinking operations to the west-going tide only, Unit 36 was laid with the intention of working from both ends of the gap between it and Unit 35. However, Unit 36 was sunk considerably out of the intended line to the northwards. Units 37, 38 and 39 represent the start of operations to close the gap. Unit 40 was the first unit laid of the Western Shore Arm. It would have been preferred to begin that length of breakwater starting from the shore end but, unfortunately, the initial caisson which arrived was one of the very few of the particular size required for the northern end and therefore had to be placed first.

While construction of the harbour was proceeding, a trans-shipment service using DUKWs was established using one of the existing exits from the beach at its western end. The painted crosses mark the Beachmaster's headquarters. Sergeant Harrison took the picture in July 1944 — Brana Radovic 50 years later.

D+4 and the first section of Whale is drawn ashore to begin the easternmost roadway for the Stores Pier.

By June 14, a spud pierhead had been attached to the end of the roadway which then reached out around three-quarters of a mile from the shore. Discharge of cargo began immediately and within three days was up to 2,000 tons per day.

Today, these mouldering Beetles remain to mark the line of the Whale roadway.

No. 1 Port Construction and Repair Group was responsible for building Mulberry 'B', the actual work-force for the piers and pierheads coming from the specially-formed Nos. 969 and 970 Port Floating Equipment Companies. *Above left:* Sappers were responsible for the beach exits and roads leading inland, this picture being taken on D+3 as an opening is made in the anti-tank wall backing the Place du 6 Juin in Arromanches ready for the centre roadway. *Bottom left:* The first section is beached on June 11. *Bottom right:* Brana took the comparisons, a section of the German wall still surviving.

The work of building the harbour went reasonably well for the first few days, the Gooseberries being finished on D+5, to what Admiral Vian described as 'the great satisfaction of all'. By D+8, the Bombardon had been finished and was giving very good results with a wave suppression of about 40 per cent. By D+10, the Mulberry breakwaters were about half completed and the Whale piers about one-third finished. The Americans at Mulberry 'A' were building somewhat faster than we were at Mulberry 'B', but my impression when I was over there on D+5 was that they were not taking so much care. I did not think the blockships were locked close enough in together and I reported to Admiral Tennant that some of the Phoenixes had been planted in too deep water. Some of them had barely a foot freeboard at high water. The trouble with the Phoenix was that the units were weak to internal pressure, not as might be expected to external attack by the sea. They would fill up with water and then, due to the difference of hydraulic head inside and out, would burst. This structural defect was overcome by fitting roofs.

Work continued day and night — this picture being taken on June 12 — but the storm interrupted the assembly and the centre roadway was not completed until July 7. By then, it had been decided to restrict the length of the Western Stores Pier (see plan page 595) into a jetty for discharging barges.

Captain Hickling explains that 'up to D+10, the progress of erection had been satisfactory with the exception of the piers and roadway, the despatch of which had been held up by the weather. However, the arrival of this equipment, particularly the Class 40 roadway, had now become urgent as it was most desirable to commence the discharge of vehicles from LSTs in each harbour. Consequently, the officer responsible for despatch from the UK was delighted to be told on the morning of D+12 (Sunday, June 18) that there was an almost perfect weather forecast. The crystal-gazers were enthusiastic; everything pointed to a 48-hour spell of fine weather. There were no ominous areas of low pressure and the high pressure wedges were all as they should be. So arrangements were put actively in hand; all possible tugs were mobilised and set out with a record number of units including 22 tows of roadway, each 480 feet long, making a total of nearly two miles.'

Sunday, June 18. *Left in Faulknor* [the destroyer HMS *Faulknor*, repaired since running aground when putting General Montgomery ashore on June 8] *for Western Task Force Area at 0745, accompanied by Bieri and Courage.* [Almost certainly Captain Richard Courage, RN, Fleet Wireless Officer, Home Fleet, on secondment to 'Neptune'.] *A fine sunny day. Arrived off Augusta at 1145. Kirk met me and took us to see Mulberry and beaches. The anchorage and beaches looked very orderly after the confusion of a week ago. The piers were progressing well and unloading going apace, 8,500 tons being said to have been landed in the previous 24 hours. Lunched (well) in Augusta and then by PT boat to Utah area where we were met by Admiral Moon and General Hoge* [*sic* although Brigadier General William M. Hoge was commander of the Provisional Engineer Special Brigade Group on Omaha.] *who took us round his anchorage and beaches. But before this we had gone ashore in Omaha area and inspected the set-up and some of the German defence system. I was much impressed by all that I saw and the Americans have made great progress, more in fact than the British, though starting slower. The Utah was a grand beach of firm sand and things were obviously going well. We drove from end to end and then inland and back the other side of the inundations and across the causeway. The country looked prosperous. Meadows with fine cattle and mares with foals. People friendly. Embarked in Faulknor and arrived Portsmouth 2150. A very satisfactory and enjoyable day.*

DIARY OF ADMIRAL SIR BERTRAM RAMSAY

That same Sunday, Admiral Ramsay in Normandy was inspecting the Western Task Force areas. The weather was fine and everything was proceeding satisfactorily but it was — literally — the lull before the storm.

THE GREAT STORM

It was about D+11 that, as usual, I went along to the Meteorological Office to get the weather forecast which determined what should be sent over that night, and for once the weathermen were all smiles. There was a really good weather forecast: for 48 hours it was going to be fine, not a breath of wind, not a ripple on the water. This was just what we had been waiting for. Not only would we get across the daily ration of units but all the backlog, all the accumulation of pier roadway which had been held up by indifferent weather. Altogether we sent over 22 tows of roadway — about two miles in all. It arrived on the other side, but was sunk in sight of the harbour by the storm.

About 3.30 a.m. on Monday, June 19 (D+13), it started to blow and it blew for three days and three nights such a summer gale from the north as had not been known for 80 years. It was a gale

However, not one yard of the roadway was to reach France, for at 0330 on Monday, June 19, the north-easterly increased to Force 7 (29-36 miles per hour — a 'High Wind' — on the Beaufort scale) by the afternoon. Although never reaching even a half-gale, the waves of up to 12 feet were twice the design strength of the Mulberry components and great destruction was wrought, both directly against the assembled structure and indirectly by hundreds of vessels of all sizes which were torn free of their moorings and tossed against the piers. Mulberry 'A' caught the full force of the weather and, towards evening, an American salvage barge and five British LCTs (seen on the right in the picture *below*) struck the centre pier. All the Bombardons broke free, some crashing into piers, others ending up on the beach. The Whale bridging was damaged and the centre roadway ended up twisted in a great arc, its Beetles smashed and filled with water.

After 0900 on Wednesday (June 21), the wind moderated to Force 5-6, enabling Signal Corps photographer Bacon to venture out along the centre pier almost as far as the spud pontoon. The half-submerged, broken-off section of Whale *(below)* can be seen between the two piers in the *bottom* photo, which also makes a good comparison with that on page 592.

Above: **This massive section of pierhead and Whale roadway has been swept over half a mile from its mooring and thrown on top of a trawler. The picture was also taken on Wednesday, the same day that Admiral Ramsay drafted in Captain Hickling to take charge at Arromanches: 'The Allied beaches were a sorry and disheartening sight. Hundreds, almost thousands, of craft and small ships — some up to 1,000 tons dead-weight — were lying ashore at and above high-water mark, in a shambles which had to be seen to be believed. Craft were actually piled on top of each other two and three deep.'**

Monday, June 19. *A day of fresh or strong northerly winds which played havoc with work off and on the beaches in the Assault Area. The Gooseberries much in request. Some Phoenix units starting to break up.*

Tuesday, June 20. *Strong north-easterly wind prevented all sailings to Assault Area and caused stoppage of work there except behind the Mulberries and Gooseberries. Large numbers of craft beached and many anchors lost. This is second day of stoppage and the results are serious on the build-up. No hope of improvement comes from the Met Office . . .*

Wednesday, June 21. *Still blowing hard but Met people hold out a faint hope that things may be better tonight. US Army making good progress towards Cherbourg, now only 4–5 miles off. . . . Creasy* [Rear-Admiral George Creasy, Ramsay's Chief-of-Staff] *went over to see Vian and discuss arrangements for the turn-over to Rivett-Carnac* [Rear-Admiral James Rivett-Carnac, due to relieve Vian as naval commander in the British Assault Area at the close of the assault phase of 'Neptune']. *Arranged for Hickling to go across as NOIC Arromanches as an emergency measure, as Vian says Petrie cannot make the pace.* [Captain Christopher Petrie, RN (Retd), the officer responsible for Mulberry 'B', who appears to have been broken by the experience of the storm.] *The evening weather report indicated no change! The three days gale is extending now to a four days gale; phenomenal for this time of year. Creasy returned after dinner having had a rough time but having done useful work. This is a damnable spell we are going through.*

DIARY OF ADMIRAL SIR BERTRAM RAMSAY

Captain Hickling says that 'Mulberry 'A' was in a very bad way indeed (compare the photo *above*, taken on June 24, with that on page 592). More than half the Phoenix in the main harbour wall had disintegrated and could only be seen at low water. Nearly all the blockships had settled two or three feet, thus reducing their effectiveness at high tide, while a few had shifted positions and one or two had broken their backs. Inside the harbour, some of the piers and much of the floating roadway had been smashed beyond repair and all had been damaged. The number of craft and ships which had been damaged or destroyed also far exceeded that of any other sector. Some ten days later, when the full extent of the damage had been assessed and the repair requirements of both harbours estimated, it was decided to write off Mulberry 'A' and to concentrate all the remaining equipment, including that which could be salvaged, on Mulberry 'B'. However, it was decided to restore the Gooseberry at Mulberry 'A' and to make it into an enlarged craft shelter by double banking the blockships with suitable Phoenix units.'

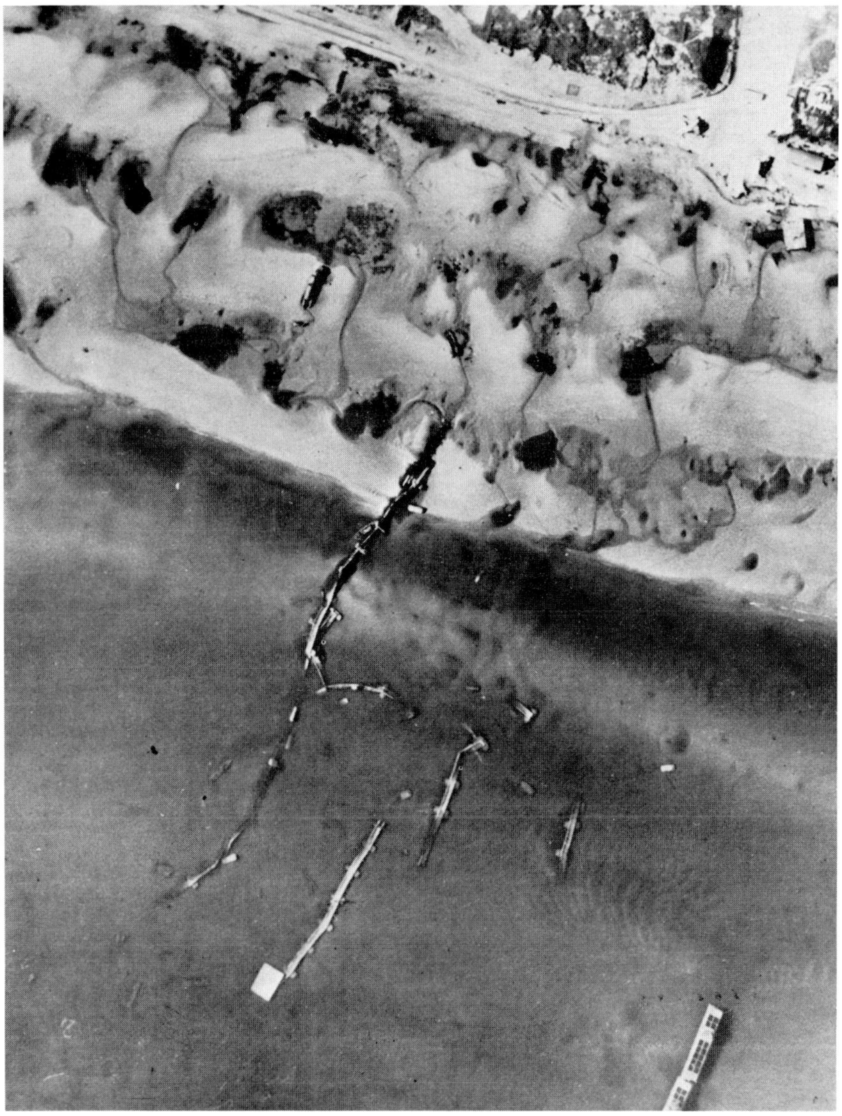

which was comparable only to that which in 1588 dispersed the Spanish Armada, and had we not had the Gooseberries and the half-completed Mulberries, I think the Allied armada would have shared the same fate as the Spanish; it is a solemn thought that so much hung on that slender thread.

The gale destroyed the American harbour Mulberry 'A' almost completely. However, as Cherbourg was soon likely to fall, it was decided not to repair it, although the Gooseberry part of it continued to do good work right up to the time we packed up in Normandy at the end of 1944.

Friday, June 23. *Left for France at 0745 in HMS Serapis and had a fine-weather trip there and back and a satisfactory day. The mine menace necessitated slowing down nearing the Assault Area and I didn't arrive until about 1225. Went on board Scylla off Arromanches and had early lunch with P. Vian. H. Hickling, Cyril D.P.* [Commodore Cyril Douglas-Pennant] *and Jim R.C. there. After lunch inspected Mulberry and Gooseberry, where damage is not too bad but there were very many craft inactive for one reason or another and a general air of floppiness prevalent. However, Harold* [Captain Hickling] *will soon put that right. Landed at pier and drove along Gold beaches. Numbers of craft washed up ashore, including Fury* [which was mined and driven ashore] *and too little apparent repair work going on. Fixed up all my business with Vian and left in Serapis for Omaha beach at 1630. Counted over 50 MT ships and as many or more coasters lying off. Kirk came to fetch me in a PC Boat and we visited the Mulberry beaches. The sight of the latter was frightful with so many craft ashore. Much worse than Gold Beach. As for the Mulberry Gooseberry, it was in a shocking state. Impressed my views on Kirk as to stopping priority unloading and left for Portsmouth. Arrived 2200. Roney* [Ramsay's personal assistant, Lieutenant Ernest Roney] *met me at Landing Place and told me Creasy had collapsed and had been taken to Haslar Hospital. Arrived to find lots of questions to be answered and calls on 'phone to Ike. However, squared off and got to bed at 1230. A long day.*

DIARY OF ADMIRAL SIR BERTRAM RAMSAY

Top: **HMS *Fury*, pictured the day after Admiral Ramsay inspected the damage.** *Above:* **'All hands set to work to clear up the mess', recalled Captain Hickling, 'and to recommence the discharge of stores and vehicles. Four days after the storm, the daily overall discharge had risen to 40,000 tons of cargo and the backlog of MT ships — there were 55 on the British sector alone — had been cleared in addition to subsequent current sailings. These rates of discharge, however, could only be achieved by using all remaining craft continuously and by diverting some of the LCTs from the cross-Channel service to beach work; further spare craft were essential if discharge rates were to be maintained because the remaining craft must get relief for repair and maintenance. Such spare barges and craft as had been left in the UK were sent over; stranded craft were re-floated, some being pushed down to the water by bulldozers, and those which only required light repairs were speedily made fit to work. The protective value of the Gooseberries and the partly-finished harbours was really demonstrated by the way in which sufficient craft survived to restore discharge rates so quickly and by the comparatively low number which were destroyed or damaged beyond repair — perhaps 20 per cent of the total craft available before the storm.'** *Right:* **Karel's comparison taken just in front of Captain Hickling's old HQ on the sea-front at Arromanches.**

Captain Hickling explained that two principal factors led to the decision to abandon Mulberry 'A'. 'Firstly, the total amount of spare or salvageable equipment would not really be sufficient to cover the requirements of both harbours; one or both would have to be reduced in some respects and, even if that course had been adopted, some spare equipment would have to be held in reserve against future bad weather of which everyone, at that time, was apprehensive. Secondly, Cherbourg was about to fall and, once opened, it should provide far better, and it was hoped far more quickly, sheltered discharge for the US sector than could ever be expected from a repaired Mulberry 'A'.' *Above:* The LST pier, which lay over half a mile east of Arromanches, was also badly damaged. It came ashore right beside strong point WN 39 where a section of double double Bailey bridge led up the bluff *(below)*.

At Mulberry 'B', a certain amount of damage was done. Of course we had the protection of the Calvados Shoal, but that was by no means the only reason why the British harbour survived.

Nevertheless the harbour began to take shape, and by about D+30 it was very much as you see it in the diagram (on page 604). We were working up to an average discharge of about 9,000 tons a day: 2,000 tons more than the harbour was designed for.

We, at Arromanches, where Colonel Pat Leaper was Port Commandant and I was NOIC, had one object and one object only, that was to maintain the discharge of stores at the maximum rate.

The whole time, shipping, lying in a dense mass off the Normandy coast, was being attacked in one way or another. Every night, about 30 to 40 aircraft dropped either mines or torpedoes. I was somewhat concerned when it was reported one night by the mine watchers stationed round the harbour that a parachute mine had come down between the Stores Pierhead and the breakwater. It was the very worst place it could have fallen; in a narrow bottleneck between the East Coaster Anchorage and the West Coaster Anchorage through which nearly all the traffic had to pass. In order that the rate of discharge should not be affected, I let it be known that it was not a mine but a dud Ack-Ack shell. I may say we buoyed the position of the supposed mine (incidentally a boat made fast to the buoy and proceeded to have their lunch until they were asked to move on)

'The fine weather which followed was particularly favourable to discharge over the beaches and, in order to allow the port construction to proceed as quickly as possible, imports through the port were restricted to that which could not be handled over the beaches. The work went so well that by the end of the third week, the port could have been used to its planned capacity but it was decided to continue to work it lightly for a further week in order to increase its capacity to the maximum to offset, as far as possible, the loss of Mulberry 'A'. This decision was wise because, from D+28, the discharge figures jumped to treble those of the preceding week.' *Below:* Après la deluge. Canadian reinforcements land on the repaired pier on July 23.

Below: **This plan shows the damage sustained during the gale. As a result of the destruction of Units 36 and 37, the original line of the Detached Mole was resumed, working westward from Unit 39. After the arrival of Unit 40, the remaining units for the Western Shore Arm proceeded to arrive, starting from the shore end, which was at that time anticipated to be approximately in the position shown by Unit 41. It was therefore necessary to start working from the shore end which, on account of the inaccuracies inevitable in sinking, produced the gap between Unit 53 and Unit 40. That gap had to be covered by Unit 67. Units 68 and 76 on the Western Shore Arm represent additions made possible by the surplus arising from the cessation of operations on Mulberry 'A'. Unit 77 represents a similar addition seawards, which was laid at the angle shown partly to give additional lee down the inside of the Western Shore Arm.**

Above: **Captain Hickling, as Naval Officer in Charge at Mulberry 'B', was based in Navy House — a tall building on the seafront to the east of the Western DUKW exit.** *Bottom:* **Lovely comparison by Karel Margry in June 1994 with a preserved DUKW descending the same exit.**

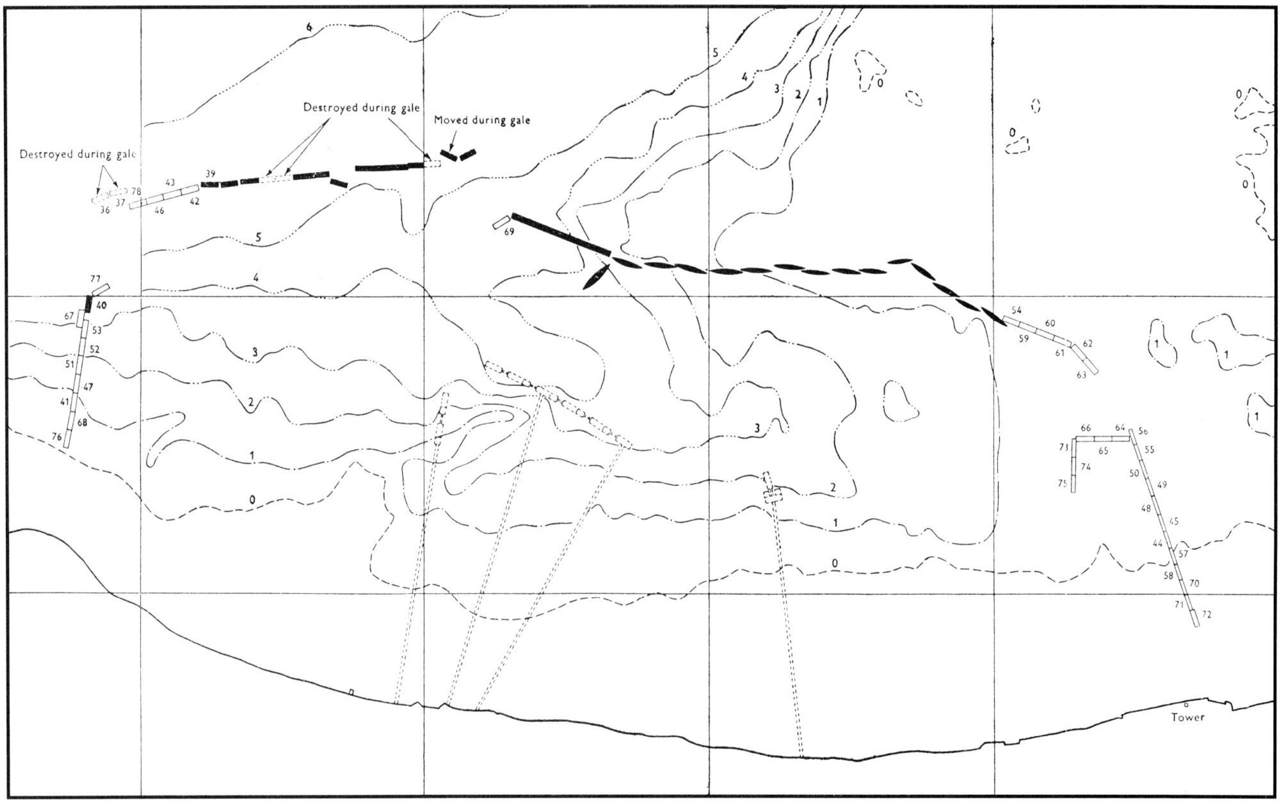

It was also intended that this angle would partly reduce the narrowing of the Western Entrance to something less than the full length of the unit. At the eastern end of the harbour, the additional units from Mulberry 'A' made possible the alteration shown, whereby the Blockship Breakwater was extended by six units comprising the Blockship Extension East and a small boat camber was constructed just inside the eastern entrance. Unit 69 was placed at the western end of the Blockship Extension West, but it had to be deflected out of the existing line on account of uncertainty as to the exact position where the wreck of Unit 22 lay (see plan page 595). In the event, the actual degree of deflection achieved was excessive, being indicative of the exaggerated caution exercised by the sinking party.

with a view to putting the mine disposal boys on to it. Nothing, however, happened that day but the following day as I went into my office in Navy House about 8 a.m., there was a terrific explosion. We were fairly well accustomed to explosions at Arromanches — we had the sappers there and they never seem to be happy unless they are blowing up something — but when I looked out of my window there in the very spot off the Stores Pierhead was the plume of a mine — a mound of water some 200ft high. To my horror, on the side of the plume was a DUKW (we had three or four hundred of them) and I thought that was the end of that particular DUKW but not a bit of it. It slid off the side of the plume, wagged its tail and proceeded to come ashore under its own steam right under my window. Overcome with relief and astonishment, I sent a hand to get the number of the

Wednesday, July 12. *Left for Eastern Task Force Area by air with Bob Mansergh and Bill Tennant. Arrived 1045 and met by Paynter F.L. to FOBAA.* [Lieutenant Horace Paynter, RNVR, Flag Lieutenant to Flag Officer, British Assault Area.] *Drove to Port-en-Bessin. Met Cowley Thomas* [Commander Cowley Thomas, RN] *NOIC, and was shown round by him. Found five coasters and six small tankers unloading. All going very well. Went back to Arromanches where we had an excellent lunch with Harold Hickling after which we inspected the harbour. It has made most impressive progress and Hickling has done very well. Went on to Gold and Juno beaches meeting Dolphin* [Captain George Dolphin, RN, NOIC Gold Beach] *and Maud* [Captain Colin Maud, RN, NOIC Juno Beach]. *Nearly all stranded craft had been got off and the beaches were looking more businesslike. Together with Arromanches and Port-en-Bessin, about 18,000 tons of stores a day are going ashore. Went on to tea with Jim R.C. and discussed affairs with him. He is doing fairly well but is not concerned enough with taking a firm control, reducing extraneous personnel and ships, and coming down to a semi-permanent footing. Am a bit anxious about him and it. Grant* [Captain John Grant, RN, Chief Staff Officer to Admiral Rivett-Carnac] *is running him I'm afraid. Took the air at 1830 and arrived 1930 at Thorney.*

DIARY OF ADMIRAL SIR BERTRAM RAMSAY

Left: **Admiral Ramsay, right, appears pleased with Captain Hickling (left) who managed to achieve the impossible and, within four weeks of the catastrophic damage, increase output to 50 per cent above that originally planned. This level was sustained for the next two months, during which period the daily rate averaged 9,100 tons — the record day exceeding 11,000 tons. In addition, return stores were loaded for outward passage, including personnel, prisoners and casualties.** *Right:* **Navy House — Villa d'Arromanches —still stands on the corner of Rue Enseigne de Vaisseau Jacques Carpentier.**

The Prime Minister spent July 20-23 in Normandy and one of the highlights must have been to see the efficient working of his brainchild — now bearing the unofficial title 'Port Winston'. Next to him, with binoculars, our author Captain Hickling. On the left, Flag Lieutenant Thompson and General Ismay, with John Martin, Churchill's Principal Private Secretary, in civvies.

DUKW. I made a signal to the commander of the Royal Army Service Corps:

'I am aware of the many and varied duties which your DUKWs so efficiently perform but until this morning I did not realise that minesweeping was one of them. If the crew of DUKW 17268 will report at Navy House at your convenience they will receive the customary award which the Admiralty make to anyone who sweeps a mine.'

The soldiers scratched their heads a bit over this, thinking it was another leg-pull. However, they thought they would take a chance on it, and two days later two soldiers shuffled into my office a bit nervously; they were the captain and the crew of the DUKW.

'Come in and sit down and tell me all about it. What's your name?' I addressed the captain.

'My name's Blagden', he replied in broad Lancashire, 'but in Wigan they calls me Sam, this 'ere is Prince — me crew.'

'Now, Sam, let's have the story.'

'Ee — Cap — it was like this 'ere — me and me choom was goin' off in our Dook to the Liberties — and we 'eard tell of this 'ere mine — so I sez to me choom I sez — "Choom, we must keep clear of that there mine" — when all of a sooden there was a nasty bang at the back.'

That concluded Sam's narrative. I pulled out of my drawer a bottle of Scotch. 'Sam', I said, 'this is the reward from Their Lordships — the Lords Commissioners of the Admiralty to you and your crew — Prince, for sweeping a mine.' Their eyes lit up, for they had not so much as a smell of a cork on the beaches in those days, and away they went as pleased as Punch, clasping their bottle to their bosoms. Of course, that story was all over the bridgehead in no time and it had the unfortunate repercussion that, after that, the three or four hundred DUKWs, instead of going straight off to their Liberty ships, went swanning round the harbour looking for another mine!

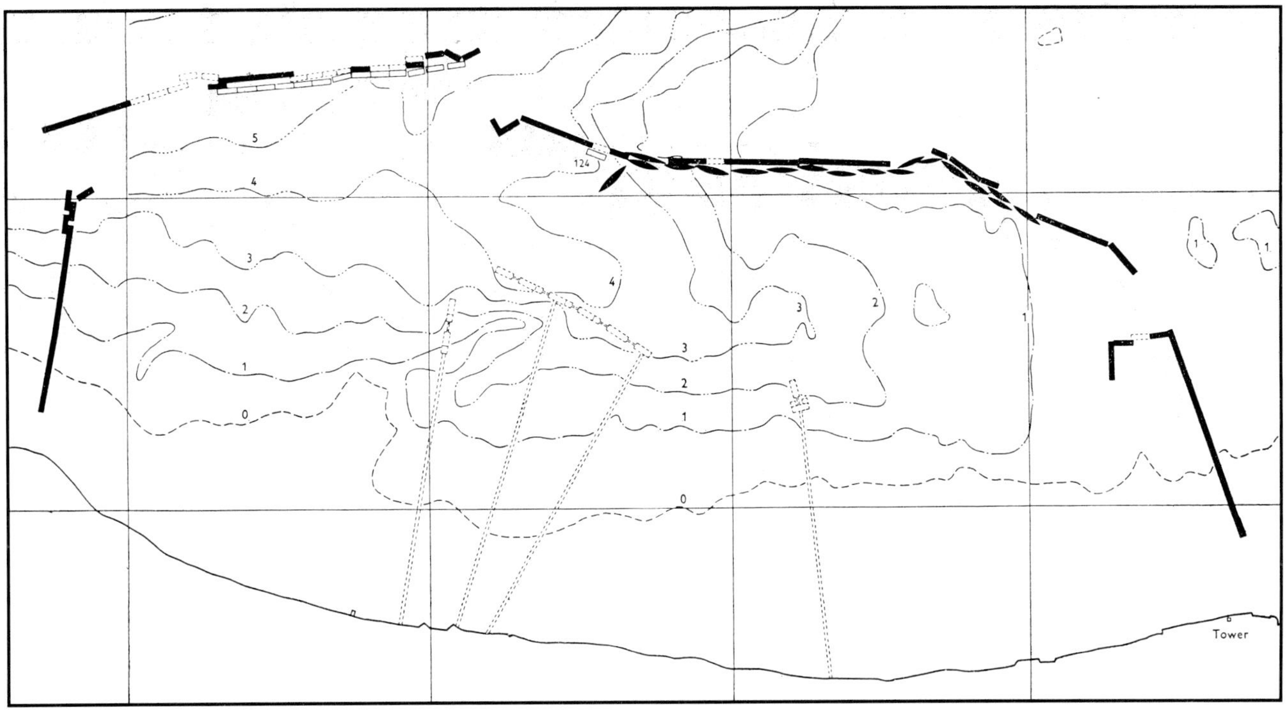

Work to improve 'Port Winston' went on throughout the summer months to try to prepare it for the coming winter. Although the Phoenixes had been designed to withstand the external battering of the sea, it had been found that when the waves began breaking over the open tops, the caissons soon filled with water. This increased the internal pressure beyond that which the valves could cope, and resulted in many of the units breaking apart, so roofs were installed. To try to stop the caissons shifting, additional weight was added by pumping in sand (which had to be brought in from Omaha) but care had to be taken not to fill the units beyond a certain level as this would split the concrete just as the water pressure had done. Double banking was carried out with spare caissons diverted from Mulberry A and by using additional units built in Britain. Some Phoenixes were even refloated and moved to better positions. The Western Shore Arm was lengthened shorewards with surplus units from Mulberry A, while a rubble causeway was pushed out from a quarry started in the cliff at this point with the intention of creating a pier from which rubble could be loaded into barges to be dumped around the breakwaters as an anti-scour protection. The final measure was to protect the whole of the Blockship Breakwater with a line of caissons. The dotted units indicate those destroyed by further gales in September and October.

CONCLUSION

Up to the end of August 1944, a million tons of stores were landed over the British sector; of that, half a million came through Mulberry and it came every day no matter what the weather, and even when discharge over the open beaches was reduced almost to nothing. At the height of the gale, we were still able to get 800 tons of vital ammunition ashore to our artillery when things on the bridgehead were not looking too good.

Was it justified? Could we justify superimposing this additional burden on the manufacturers of this country after five years of war, when the whole of our industrial effort was out to a clinch? I think the answer is 'Yes', because had we not provided this administrative insurance that at least a trickle of stores would get to our armies every day no matter what the weather, the invasion of the Continent would not have been undertaken.

Mr Winston Churchill, who came and spent four days with us at Arromanches, just about summed it up in his signal to me when he left. He referred amongst other things to 'this miraculous Port which has made possible the liberation of Europe'.

Left: **Port Winston in its heyday. We shall see its crumbling remains again later on; meanwhile, compare this with the aerial picture on page 427.**

Airfield Construction

By Air Chief Marshal Sir Trafford Leigh-Mallory

COMMANDER-IN-CHIEF, ALLIED EXPEDITIONARY AIR FORCE

On November 16, 1943, the British forces, Second Tactical Air Force and Nos. 38 and 85 Groups had been built up to about 35 per cent only of their final strength. The United States Ninth Air Force at this time was only approximately 25 per cent of its final strength. To develop these forces in the winter and following spring, and to have them suitably deployed in readiness for the opening of the campaign was a race against time which involved, inter alia:

(i) A comprehensive plan whereby aerodromes and landing grounds in the south of England were progressively evacuated by units not participating directly in 'Overlord', and occupied by 'Overlord' forces as the USAAF arrived from overseas and by the British forces as they were augmented.

(ii) Providing Second Tactical Air Force with a fully mobile organisation for repair, and for the supply of Royal Air Force equipment, in substitution for the service normally provided by the Royal Air Force Maintenance Command in the United Kingdom.

(iii) Integrating the USAAF and RAF administrative services where necessary.

(iv) Re-equipping 110 Royal Air Force squadrons with the most up-to-date types of aircraft.

(v) Changing Second Tactical Air Force from the home system of personnel administration and accounting, to the overseas systems, including the establishment of a Base Personnel Staff Office and a Base Accounts Office.

(vi) On D-Day, the British totalled approximately 232,000 personnel and the Americans 181,000. The organisation of the British part of the force alone involved the formulation and issue of some 250 new type establishments.

Over 90 airfields were deemed necessary in France to sustain 'Overlord' during the first three months, of which 27 were to be constructed in the Normandy countryside by the end of June. There were to be 12 in the US sector and 15 in the British where the more open landscape lent itself to better sites. In the event, only 17 had been completed by June 30: 10 British and 7 American, of which St Laurent, built on the bluffs behind Omaha by the 834th Aviation Engineer Battalion, was the first.

Initially, the 'airfield' was simply an Emergency Landing Strip (ELS) comprising an untracked surface, 3,400ft long and 120ft-wide, and, although suitable for small observation aircraft by 1800 hours on D+2, it could not handle larger machines until 1845 hours on June 9. It was also used for transport aircraft and we saw it as the departure point for General Arnold after his day trip to Normandy on June 12 (page 408).

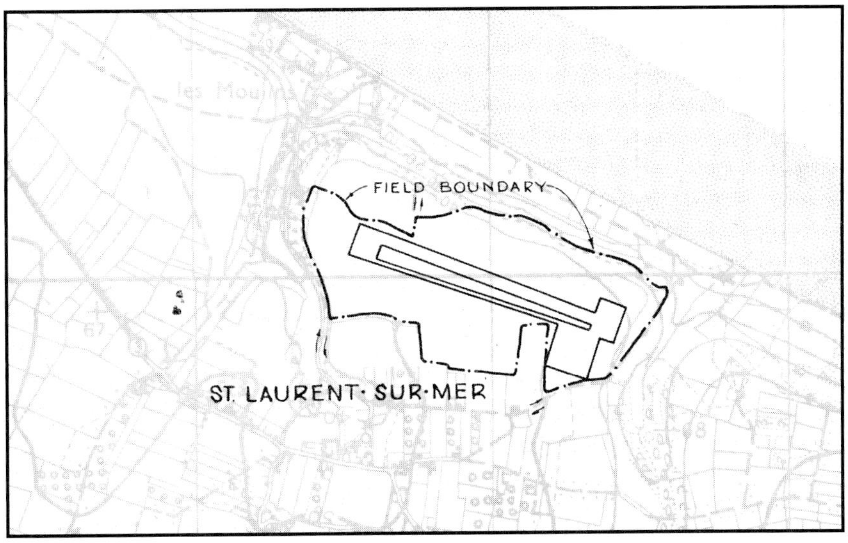

After D-Day, the principal administrative tasks to be executed were:

(i) By means of the inter-Allied and inter-Service machinery known as BUCO (Build-up Control Organisation) and MOVCO (Movement Control Organisation) to control the transfer of air forces to the Continent, together with the stores for immediate use, and to build up reserves.

This Signal Corps picture, showing Corporal Paul Stock on air traffic control duties, is dated June 11, but the one *opposite* taken by the US Navy, which appears to show the same P-38 (268071) at the same time, is dated June 14. A similar discrepancy concerns the numbering of St Laurent. A report by the US IX Engineer Command to 21st Army Group, also dated June 14, gives it as A-1 ('A' standing for American, 'B' for British), but at some later stage it was renumbered A-21.

(ii) Special arrangements to ensure that squadrons could operate at full effort, whether from the United Kingdom or the Continent, even though their normal maintenance organisation was in process of transfer.

(iii) Arrangements by which United States air forces could rearm and refuel at British air strips and vice versa.

(iv) Rapid replacement of personnel casualties, aircraft and equipment.

(v) The institution, quite early in the operations, of arrangements for salvaging aircraft carcasses and certain other equipment, and for returning this material quickly to the United Kingdom.

(vi) Finally, maintaining a high state of mobility for the tactical air forces which were taxed to the limit to keep up with the advance.

Like all the Normandy airfields, St Laurent, be it A-1 or A-21, soon returned to cultivation once the war had passed it by. In a subsequent listing, the number A-1 was given instead to the Refuelling and Re-arming Strip (RRS) constructed at St Pierre-du-Mont.

As far back as December 1942, soon after the US 660th Engineer Topographical Battalion arrived in the UK, the selection of airfield sites in France was begun. At that time, there was only the 1:50,000 GSGS map series available (the 1:25,000 maps *(centre)* had not yet been produced) but from these, possible locations were selected. Meanwhile, a test was carried out to determine the best height to photograph the chosen areas by taking pictures of a specially selected location at 6,000, 9,000 and 12,000 feet, where the photogrammetric data could be compared with a known ground survey. From this, it was determined that photography from 12,000 feet would produce the best result for compilation on the Multiplex apparatus at a scale of 1:10,000, overlaid on the 1:50,000 map series *(right)*. The American unit worked in close liaison with the Director of Survey, Home Forces, and upwards of 120 sites were pre-surveyed in this fashion before D-Day.

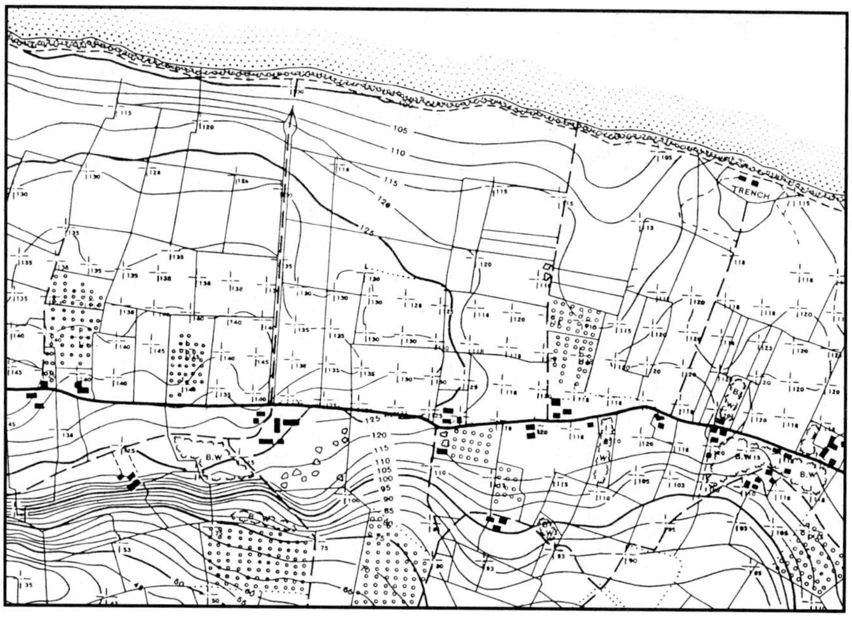

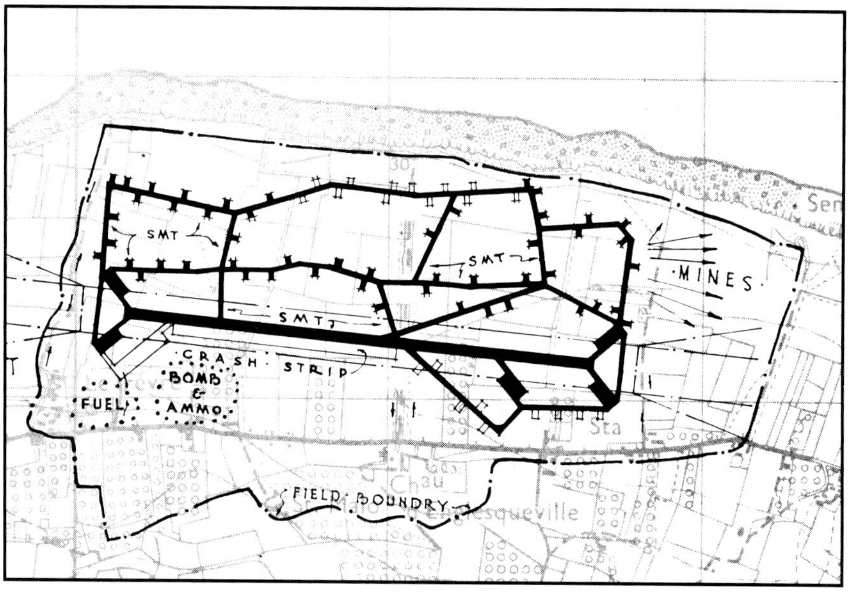

AIRFIELD CONSTRUCTION

In combined operations, it is obviously advantageous that fighters, fighter-bombers and reconnaissance aircraft of the tactical air forces should be able to work from bases in the operational theatre as early as possible, and therefore airfield accommodation was of paramount importance.

The extent to which airfield requirements could be met in this operation depended, in the main, on the ability of the field engineers to locate and develop suitable sites. These sites had been previously chosen by experts after a detailed study of the coverage provided by photographic reconnaissance aircraft and available maps. It also depended upon having a sufficiently high priority within the available shipping space for the movement of equipment and material. Naturally, these claims must be balanced with others of operational urgency.

Thus, the necessary arrangements could be made for the construction work to begin as soon as each site became available. This is St Pierre-du-Mont where the 366th Fighter Group arrived with their P-47s on June 17 from their UK base at Thruxton (see *Airfields of the Ninth Then and Now*). The 390th Fighter Squadron was the last to move on in June 20.

After any tree felling and ditch filling, the site was graded and surfaced with a patent form of tracking; usually Square Mesh Track (SMT) *above*, or Pierced Steel Plank (PSP) *below*. The precise location is not given for this picture, but, as it was taken on June 17, it could show any one of the fields A-3 to A-8 (see page 615) which were being worked on at that time.

In the initial stages, the terrain in the British sector was generally more favourable than that in the American. However, the airfield engineers achieved very fine results in both sectors. The position in the British sector deteriorated because the good area to the east and south-east around Caen was not secured as rapidly as had been planned. Neither did the situation in the American sector greatly improve until the advance had progressed to Le Mans and beyond.

Definitions of the different types of airfields to be provided were as follows:

Emergency Landing Strip (ELS). A strip having sufficient length of level surface to enable pilots in distress to make a landing. These strips had a minimum length of 1,800 feet and were not fit for the operation of aircraft, but were of inestimable value when operations were conducted a long way from bases, especially when a long sea crossing on the way home was involved.

Refuelling and Re-arming Strip (RRS). A strip possessing sufficient length of level compact surface for landing and taking off, adequate marshalling areas for the rapid turn-round of aircraft and adequate tracking to ensure operation under all normal summer and autumn conditions. These strips had a minimum length of 3,600 feet with the marshalling areas of 100 yards × 50 yards at each end.

Advanced Landing Ground (ALG). A landing ground possessing the same facilities as an R and R to be brought up to ALG standard by the addition of dispersal facilities and capable of use to capacity by adopting the 'Roulement' system. (The 'Roulement' system was a means of using landing ground facilities to the maximum capacity by flying in squadrons to replace others as they complete their scale of effort appropriate to the period.)

Airfield. A field with the same facilities as an ALG but with improved dispersal facilities and on which squadrons were established and not operated on the 'Roulement' system as on an ALG. The minimum lengths for both ALGs and airfields were 3,600 feet for fighters, with dispersal facilities for 54 aircraft, and 5,000 feet for fighter-bombers, with the same dispersal facilities.

All-Weather Airfield. The same requirements as for an airfield, but possessing hard-surfaced runways and fit for operation throughout all seasons and all conditions of weather for the appropriate type of aircraft. Within the limits of operational requirements, it was planned that all enemy airfields with hard-surfaced runways would be reinstated, as and when they were captured, if reinstatement could be effected without excessive labour and/or material.

This special PSP hardstanding is 'at an advanced fighter base near the front line to accommodate the personal planes of four-star generals'. The C-47 bears both the 21st Army Group and British Second Army insignia on its nose. The picture is dated July 19 when General Montgomery's TAC HQ was at Blay, close to strip A-9 at Le Molay (just north of Le Molay-Littry) which had been completed on July 8, although work still appears to be continuing in the background.

General Eisenhower moved his own Advanced Command Post to Normandy exactly two months after D-Day to a site on the far side of Le Molay near the village of Tournières (see *After the Battle* No. 84). *Above:* **Inspecting the construction of airstrips in the Cotentin peninsula, Eisenhower gets the details from Sergeant Clide W. Smith, possibly at A-10 at Carentan. Picture taken on July 4 by Lieutenant Lee Moore who took the pictures at Greenham Common (see page 292) just a month before.**

Because we failed in the initial phases to gain the ground in the vicinity of Caen, the development of all of the pre-selected sites could not be started. This caused some delay and made necessary a re-allotment of sites in the beach-head but, as a very high proportion of potential sites proved to be suitable for rapid construction, the intensive preparation of the beach-head area permitted the leeway to be made up.

Later, when the Allied advance became rapid, the problem of finding space to prepare airfields was eased. It became more a problem of getting the airfields constructed rapidly in the now adequate space available. The system adopted for constructing airfields near the front line was to prepare dirt strips 15-20 miles to the rear of the ground forces. These strips were then visited by transport aircraft, which dumped stores and tools there. As a general rule, fighter strips were 50-70 miles behind the front line, and bomber strips 100-120 miles behind. As the ground forces moved forward, so the dirt strips previously prepared were constructed as airfields and became bases for fighters and later for bombers.

The minimum programme for airfields to accommodate the forces allocated was as follows:

3 ELS (2 American and 1 British) by D-Day.
4 RRSs (2 American and 2 British) by the evening of D+3 and not later than D+4.
10 ALG. (5 American and 5 British) by D+8 (these ALGs included 4 of the RRSs).
18 Airfields (8 American and 10 British) by D+14.
27 Airfields (12 American and 15 British) by D+24.
43 Airfields (18 American and 25 British) by D+40.
93 Airfields (48 American and 45 British) by D+90.

The priorities fixed for the construction of these airfields were as follows:

Priority I — ELSs for emergency landing of aircraft.
Priority II — RRS strips for re-fuelling and re-arming fighter aircraft.
Priority III — ALGs to become airfields later.

The following construction units were available for allocation as required in the beach-head:

American — 16 aviation engineering battalions; 2 airborne aviation engineering battalions.
British — 5 airfield construction groups; 1 field force basis construction wing.

The men of the American aviation engineer battalions of the IX Engineer Command and of the British airfield construction units worked exceptionally well, as was proved by the setting-up of the first three Emergency Landing Strips at Pouppeville (LS-1), St Laurent-sur-Mer (A-21) and Asnelles (B-1) by D+1. These men worked right in the battle area and, as well as constructing the airfields, often had to lay down their tools to deal with stray snipers.

July 26 (the day after the Americans bombed their own troops — see page 64) and another Lieutenant Moore picture of Eisenhower talking with the officer who led his escort to France. Unfortunately, he is unnamed as is the airstrip.

In the British sector, the ELS at Asnelles (B-1) was to be completed on D-Day itself with the first RRS at Ste Croix-sur-Mer (B-3) by last light on D+2 and the one at Bazenville (B-2) by midday on D+4, by which time Ste Croix was to have been upgraded to an ALG. No. 16 Airfield Construction Group had completed B-1 by D+1 and B-2 by D+3 which was subsequently upgraded to an ALG by D+7. Ste Croix had been built by No. 24 Airfield Construction Group as an RRS by D+4 whereupon a parallel strip was laid down to upgrade it to ALG standard (completed on D+10). The next ALG to be completed should have been B-4 at Villons-les-Buissons but, as this area was still in German hands, No. 23 Airfield Construction Group moved instead to Bény-sur-Mer *(right)*. This is another case of a switch of airfield numbers, for when it was completed on D+9, Bény became B-4 and Villons, delayed until later in June, was allocated the number B-16.

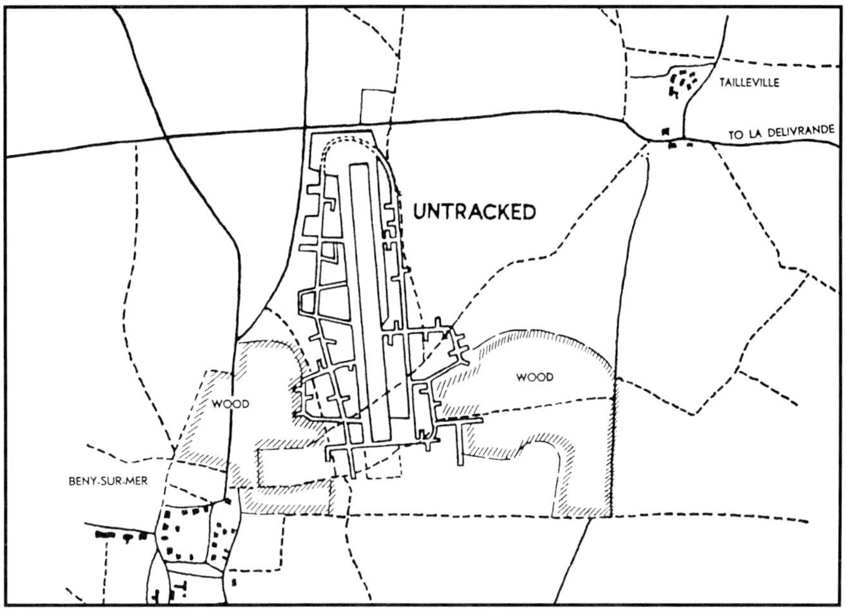

The position at the end of June (D+24) was as follows:

(i) In the British sector, ten airfields completed: at Bazenville (B-2), Ste Croix-sur-Mer (B-3), Bény-sur-Mer (B-4), Camilly (B-5), Coulombs (B-6), Martragny (B-7), Sommervieu (B-8), Lantheuil (B-9), Plumetot (B-10), Longues (B-11). One airfield was under construction at Ellon (B-12).

(ii) In the American sector, seven airfields completed: at St Pierre-du-Mont (A-1), Cricqueville (A-2), Cardonville (A-3), Deux-Jumeaux (A-4), Beuzeville (A-6), Azeville (A-7) and Carentan (A-10). Four were under construction and 75 per cent completed at Chippelle (A-5), Picauville (A-8), Le Molay (A-9) and Cretteville (A-14).

By D+90, in addition to the 81 airfields which were then in use, five fields in the American sector and three in the British sector had been abandoned, as being too far from the scene of ground operations. These make the number of airfields actually completed by D+90, 55 in the American sector and 34 in the British sector, a total of 89, as against the planned total of 93.

Although, as Air Chief Marshal Leigh-Mallory describes overleaf, there were some ten different types of aircraft operating in the Allied Expeditionary Air Force, it is undoubtedly the rocket-firing Hawker Typhoon which so typifies operations on the ALGs in Normandy. *Above:* These aircraft of No. 198 Squadron are taking off from B-7 at Martragny which, even though tracked, still created clouds of dust.

The fact that airfield construction was still a little behind schedule at the end of the planned period, was due mainly to tactical reasons in the assault phase and to the consequent lack of adequate and suitable ground area, and partly to some delay in shipping sufficient material.

***Left:* Landing at B-7 over an Army convoy. *Right:* Today, like all the Normandy ALGs, Martragny has reverted to agriculture, but a memorial was erected on the site in June 1990. L–R: Former Typhoon pilots, George Hardy, George Lane and Denis Sweeting. However, the stone was removed from the airfield site and re-erected in Martragny village in June 1994.**

Supreme Headquarters Allied Expeditionary Force Operational Memoranda called for special markings on aircraft in order that they might be clearly distinguished on D-Day. To achieve success, the markings had to be applied on D–1 so that all aircraft should have broad black and white bands painted on them on D-Day, but not before. The total requirements of distemper for this purpose to mark approximately 10,000 aircraft and gliders was 100,000 gallons or 1,500 tons. There was no such amount immediately available in the United Kingdom. Supply action on a high priority was necessary. Supply to civilians was stopped, overtime was worked in pits and factories, Whitsun weekend holidays were forgotten and by Y-Day all was ready; the distemper and 20,000 brushes to apply it were on hand.

There were over 6,600 operational aircraft in Allied Expeditionary Air Force (AEAF) on D-Day. These aircraft were composed of ten basic types with a large number of varying marks, each with its own problems in servicing. That the maintenance personnel managed to keep the operational serviceability to the high levels stated below is a remarkable achievement. When it is remembered that throughout June and July most of the squadrons operated from new-made landing strips only a few miles from the front line, and that the dust on these Normandy airfields was, in the opinion of many experienced campaigners, worse than that in the North African desert campaigns, then the efforts of the maintenance personnel become even more outstanding.

The maintenance of operational strength was also the result of a carefully-prepared plan for replacement of

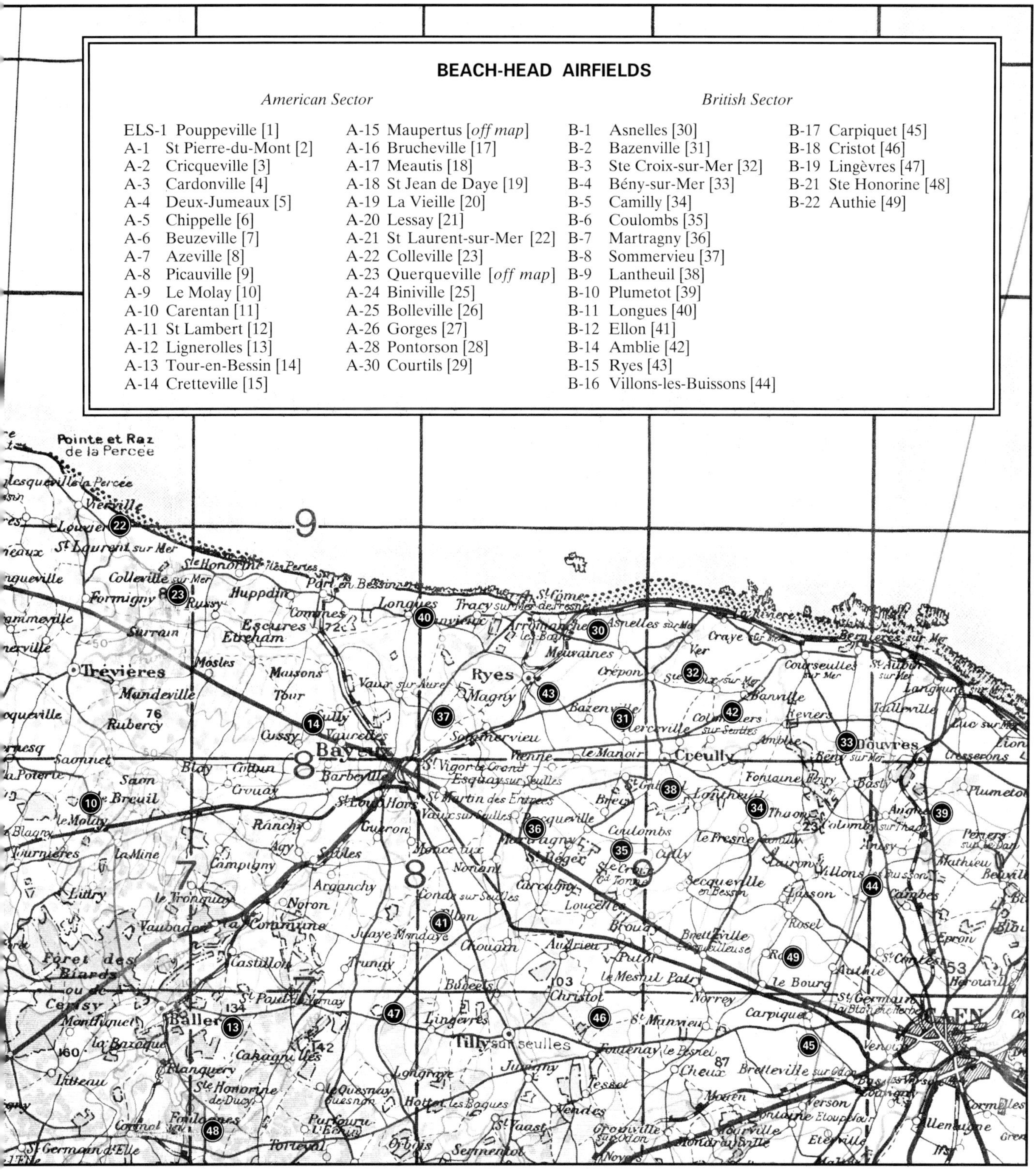

BEACH-HEAD AIRFIELDS

American Sector		*British Sector*	
ELS-1 Pouppeville [1]	A-15 Maupertus [*off map*]	B-1 Asnelles [30]	B-17 Carpiquet [45]
A-1 St Pierre-du-Mont [2]	A-16 Brucheville [17]	B-2 Bazenville [31]	B-18 Cristot [46]
A-2 Cricqueville [3]	A-17 Meautis [18]	B-3 Ste Croix-sur-Mer [32]	B-19 Lingèvres [47]
A-3 Cardonville [4]	A-18 St Jean de Daye [19]	B-4 Bény-sur-Mer [33]	B-21 Ste Honorine [48]
A-4 Deux-Jumeaux [5]	A-19 La Vieille [20]	B-5 Camilly [34]	B-22 Authie [49]
A-5 Chippelle [6]	A-20 Lessay [21]	B-6 Coulombs [35]	
A-6 Beuzeville [7]	A-21 St Laurent-sur-Mer [22]	B-7 Martragny [36]	
A-7 Azeville [8]	A-22 Colleville [23]	B-8 Sommervieu [37]	
A-8 Picauville [9]	A-23 Querqueville [*off map*]	B-9 Lantheuil [38]	
A-9 Le Molay [10]	A-24 Biniville [25]	B-10 Plumetot [39]	
A-10 Carentan [11]	A-25 Bolleville [26]	B-11 Longues [40]	
A-11 St Lambert [12]	A-26 Gorges [27]	B-12 Ellon [41]	
A-12 Lignerolles [13]	A-28 Pontorson [28]	B-14 Amblie [42]	
A-13 Tour-en-Bessin [14]	A-30 Courtils [29]	B-15 Ryes [43]	
A-14 Cretteville [15]		B-16 Villons-les-Buissons [44]	

aircraft. In this connection, it is interesting to note that the forecasting of wastage and casualties by the planning staff was sound and, since the losses were somewhat below those planned, there were never any serious difficulties of supply. The replacement pool and recovery organisation both worked extremely well.

The statistics of the average daily consumption and wastage of POL [petrol, oil and lubricants] and ammunition also reveal something of the achievement of the supply organisation. During July, AEAF expended daily 750 tons of bombs and more than 200,000 rounds of ammunition. The fuel consumption of AEAF in July reached approximately 30,000,000 gallons of petrol, almost 1,000,000 gallons per day. A large part of this fuel and ammunition had to be transported into the beach-head and up to forward airfields. In this connection, the work of air force beach squadrons deserves special mention. These parties went in with the follow-up troops on D-Day and, due in no small measure to their efforts, the first airfields were stocked ready for operations in the beach-head on D+3.

Credit for being the first British squadron to land in France since 1940 is claimed equally by Nos. 130 and 303 Squadrons which came in to B-3 at 1200 on D+4. Soon after, No. 144 (RCAF) Fighter Wing (consisting of Nos. 441, 442 and 443 Squadrons) arrived, being the first aircraft to operate from French soil since Dunkirk. By D+14, eight Spitfire, three Typhoon and three Auster squadrons were operating from British beach-head airfields. In the US sector, the first arrivals were the 397th Fighter Squadron at A-3 on the 16th and the 366th Fighter Squadron the following day on A-1.

An Appreciation

By Generalfeldmarschall Gerd von Rundstedt
GERMAN OBERBEFEHLSHABER WEST

The following most important combat experiences are to be utilised for instruction and exercises on all fronts which have not as yet been attacked; they are to be circulated for the attention of the troops and higher headquarters in the combat area and for the instruction of all headquarters and defence forces all over France.

Four facts must be emphasised:

(1) Complete air superiority of the enemy.

(2) Skilful and overwhelming employment of airborne troops.

(3) Flexible and well-directed support of the ground troops by artillery fire from strong English naval units ranging from battleships to gunboats.

(4) Previous practice manoeuvres by the enemy landing troops, exact knowledge of the coasts, its obstacles and defensive positions, quick establishment of the superiority in men and material at the beach-head after the first days of landing.

All this is matched by the quality of the German soldier, his steadfastness, his uncompromising resolve to hold out to the last man whether in the Heer, Kriegsmarine or Luftwaffe.

All three branches of the Wehrmacht have given their best and will continue to do so.

Said to be the first batch of German prisoners from Normandy, those men have been landed at the Gosport Hard G.H. (we saw it on page 181) and are pictured on June 7 marching to the transit camp at Forton a mile away. No figures appear to have been recorded for German losses on D-Day, but casualties in Heeresgruppe B up to June 30 were given as 1,830 officers (including 9 generals, 109 commanders, and 7 General Staff officers), 75,166 NCOs and other ranks, and 3,787 Russians: total 80,783.

ENEMY LANDING METHODS IN BROAD OUTLINE

The enemy hoped to take us by surprise! In that attempt he failed. Airborne landings began at the western end of the Seine Bay and in Cotentin on June 6 at approximately 0100 in the morning during cloudy, overcast weather with strong wind, partly showers, and rough sea up to Force 4. Simultaneously, flights by strong formations of bombers were made over various sectors of the front and on rear areas. The enemy aimed at initiating air warnings to cause the troops to seek shelter while he could drop his parachutists without being detected. At various places, parachutists turned out to be straw dummies (with wooden boxes filled with explosives). The purpose of this manoeuvre was to force local reserves to disperse and troops to withdraw from crucial points, thereby causing the defender to lose time. Numerous gliders of varying sizes, carrying airborne troops, were uncoupled from their aircraft far out over the sea and at quite different places over land, according to plans that had been worked out in every detail prior to the invasion. The gliders in general reached their points of destination safely and accurately.

Yet, these airborne landings failed to achieve surprise because officers and men had expected them for weeks and had made appropriate preparations. As a result, enemy parachute and airborne troops suffered heavy, even extremely heavy, casualties, and at most places were destroyed in battle. They did not succeed in breaking up the coastal defences from the rear. Only those airborne troops which had been landed in the American bridgehead north of Carentan were pressed against the coastal defences — by our own attacks coming from three sides, in fact — and were able to establish contact with American troops that had been set ashore and had effected a breakthrough. Thus they received reinforcements and relief. Technique and tactics of enemy airborne troops are highly developed. Also, combat training has reached a high degree of efficiency. The men are tough fighters and well trained to adapt themselves to any type of terrain.

It is to be expected that, in addition to paratroopers for regular combat, there will also be specialised parachutists with special missions such as seeking out and reporting the location of command posts, ammunition dumps, rearward communications, etc., carrying out demolitions, erection of obstacles, surprise attacks. These specialists either may be dropped individually or may emerge from troops already landed. These men will keep absolutely quiet in order not to attract attention or to become involved in combat. They must be expected to be well acquainted with the country and to know resources of every description.

The real landings from the sea started four to five hours after the airborne landings. We had thought it probable that the enemy would land during high tide; but he had recognised the strong beach defences and had changed his methods accordingly, by carrying out the landings at a period of low tide. This was found out by our own intelligence from exercises on the English coast a few weeks before the landings. The new method made it possible for the enemy to spot gaps in the beach obstacles, to drive tanks around them, and to have them partially removed by special troops who cleared paths through them.

At points where obstacles were not spotted in time or were still covered by water, the enemy suffered severe losses in ships and men. But even in dry places it was observed that the landings were slowed down and the losses caused by our fire were increased by the obstacles.

The landings started at 0600 in full daylight. The landings were preceded by a bombardment lasting a half-hour and carried out from the air and from the sea with weapons of all calibres. The effect was that field works were more or less covered and 'ploughed up' so that not much more than the permanently-fortified installations were left. Through the gaps between them, the enemy started infiltrating without dealing — during the first phase — with the permanently-fortified installations and the large strong points. These fortified installations in many cases carried on for more than a week and diverted enemy forces. By their stand to the last man, they greatly contributed to the possibility of gaining time for the new measures undertaken by our command and preventing the enemy from breaking out of the bridgehead.

The Hardway lies down the turning on the right at the top of Grove Road.

Above: **More prisoners were brought ashore in Southampton on the two-berth LST Hard S.2, just east of the Royal Pier.** *Below:* **By the 1980s, the pier was unsafe, and two fires finaly caused it to be closed in 1992.**

ENEMY AIR FORCE

The enemy air force dominates, by the number of aircraft as well as by their range, not only the main combat area but also the approach routes and supply to a depth of 150 to 200 kilometres. In addition to this, the enemy with his operational air force carries the battle even into the zone of the interior, aiming at the destruction of the network of rear communications, particularly rail centres, shunting stations, engine-repair shops, bridges, plants which are important for the war effort, etc.

In spite of the fact that the railway network is highly developed in the West and that innumerable highways and secondary roads exist, the enemy has succeeded, by concentrated and cease-

less attacks from the air, in disorganising our supply to such an extent and to cause such losses of railway rolling stocks and vehicles that supply has become a serious problem.

The closer an area is to the combat zone, the more frequently appear fighters and fighter-bombers employed in 'road-hunting'. By attacking in good weather during daytime and with the help of flares at night, they impede any large-scale movement. In the beginning, the main effort of enemy air attacks over the rear of the combat area was directed against the highways; by now, it is directed, in a zone of about 20 kilometres behind the main line of resistance, against any kind of movement, be it on secondary roads or even across country. Wherever assembly areas are detected, an attack by bomber formations is launched without delay. It is therefore necessary to keep a large distance between vehicles moving in convoys.

The location of headquarters is given away by their wireless stations. Wireless stations must therefore be installed at such a distance away from headquarters that bomb carpets or sticks of bombs do not cover them. Where there are no fortified installations for the housing of headquarters, their location must be changed frequently. This requires careful reconnoitering and timely reporting to higher echelons, so that the command posts can be found at any time.

In 2½-days, 29,000 aircraft sorties were counted along a bridgehead about 100 kilometres wide; of these, about 2,300 sorties per day are by low-flying aircraft attacking with bombs and weapons any movement on the ground, even that of single soldiers.

Involved in the attacks on German headquarters, complained about by Generalfeldmarschall von Rundstedt, was No. 198 Squadron which was sent against the LXXXIV. Armeekorps HQ early on the morning of June 6. No. 609 Squadron was to follow up the attack on the Château de la Meauffe *(above)* ten minutes later. The squadron claimed the target destroyed — confirmed in the official British history — yet something seemed wrong for General Marcks was on the telephone repeatedly throughout the morning and no mention is made in his war diary of Typhoons knocking at his front door.

We went to the operations tent in the Commer and were briefed to attack the headquarters of the German 84 Corps at the Château de la Meauffe near St Lo. The attack was to be made at 0800 hours.

At 0715, the 12 Typhoons started up and commenced taxying to the runway. The sky was overcast with cloud at about 5,000ft and it looked as if rain could follow. The CO and I took off side-by-side, followed rapidly by the other ten aircraft. I was flying in JR366.

Soon after we were airborne, there was a tremendous sight. As far as we could see out to sea, there were lines of ships of all shapes and sizes, moving steadily and purposely towards France. The lines continued without a break for the hundred miles to the Normandy coast. The sight was inspiring and comforting; for years we had flown across a deserted Channel where the necessity of a crash landing or baling out, through flak or engine failure, could be a very lonely business. Now, we knew that help would always be on hand.

We flew to one side of the stream of ships, keeping below the clouds which became heavier and lower as we approached France. When a few miles from the coast, we could see the battleships and cruisers of the Royal Navy with constant flashes coming from their guns as they bombarded German strong points inland. Closer in, rocket-launching ships were sending up their shoals of projectiles. We could see assault boats and LCTs making their way to the beaches, with black smoke and flashes of either exploding German shells or German guns firing. Soldiers could be seen moving up the beach and then we were over them and flying inland.

The cloud became lower, forcing us down to 2,000ft, making an easy target for any light flak. However, everything appeared quiet as we sped towards the target; the CO was map-reading while the rest of us kept a sharp lookout for the hordes of German fighters which we expected to encounter. Nothing happened — no flak, no fighters — and nothing appeared to be moving on the ground. Suddenly, Dave Davies' voice came on the radio, 'Baltic aircraft. Target coming up eleven o'clock. Echelon starboard for low-level attack'. I looked down and there, about three miles away, was the large château surrounded by trees with a long circular drive leading up to it with a spacious lawn in the middle. It made a splendid target, large enough for all of us to hit.

I veered my aircraft further away from the leader to give more room for aiming, selected the eight-rocket salvo on the firing switch, checking that the gun button was on 'fire'. The rest of the squadron had now spread out behind in echelon and we were all set. 'Going down Baltic squadron', called the CO, dipping his port wing to commence a shallow dive, with me about 100 yards behind. We came over the tops of the trees and I saw the flash from underneath his port wing as he fired his rockets and then pulled his aircraft up and to port. I started firing my cannon and saw his rockets explode on the front of the building. Now less than 300 yards away, travelling at over 400 mph, I fired my rocket salvo and heaved the aircraft into a steep left-hand climbing turn to avoid any flying debris and to follow the CO. By the time I had pulled around and could see the château again, our fourth aircraft was just firing his rockets. They hit the drive just in front of the building which by then had flames and smoke pouring out of it. With the rest of our aircraft on their way in, more and more rockets exploded on the walls and the smoke and flames rose higher. One could not imagine that any 84 Corps staff inside could have survived.

DENIS SWEETING, No. 198 SQUADRON

Further investigation reveals that the Typhoons had been directed to attack the wrong château as General Marcks's HQ was located over six kilometres away at St Georges-Montcocq. At La Meauffe, a much smaller house *(above)* was built on the site of the old château after the war.

Allied losses suffered on D-Day are difficult to quantify with absolute accuracy. Even establishing who was the first casualty (pages 256-259) threw up a glaring anomaly, so analysing the records of the three nations involved would be fraught with difficulties. Colonel Stacey is probably the one man who has examined the problem in the greatest detail, and even he says that 'the task of compiling accurate casualty figures for the landing in Normandy ought to be easy; but it is, in fact, impossible. Of the three countries involved in the operation, only Canada, it appears, has prepared post-war casualty statistics on the basis of the records of individual soldiers of the units concerned. The only figures available for the UK and US forces are the rough and necessarily approximate ones set down at the time, and in some sectors there are really no figures at all. In these circumstances, it might seem useless to attempt a compilation but Operation "Neptune" was so significant an enterprise that an account of it without casualty figures would be an historical absurdity.'

'Accordingly, the attempt has been made, with the following results: US AIRBORNE SECTOR (82nd and 101st Airborne Divisions). Here specific contemporary figures are available. On the basis of the divisions' reports, Gordon A. Harrison, *Cross-Channel Attack* (Washington, Department of the Army, 1951), gives casualties of 1,259 for the 82nd Division and 1,240 for the 101st, or a total of 2,499. UTAH (4th Infantry Division). Casualties here were extremely low and an official publication (*Utah Beach to Cherbourg*, Washington, Department of the Army, 1947), gives them as 197. OMAHA (1st Infantry Division, with a regiment of 29th Infantry Division attached). Casualties here were extremely heavy, and there appears to be no really reliable figures. Harrison gives "about 2,000" as "frankly a guess", and this official estimate has been accepted. GOLD (50th (Northumbrian) Infantry Division). The only figure found for this division is a compilation in a report by the (British) Army Operational Research Group, which concludes on the basis of examination of war diaries that there were 413 casualties *on the beaches*. The figure for the day as a whole would of course be somewhat higher. It is relevant that this compilation gives the casualties on the beaches for the Canadian 3rd Infantry Division's area as 805, but we know that Canadian casualties here for the day as whole were 961. Another Army Operational Research Group report calculates those of British units on the beaches in the Canadian sector (including No. 48 Royal Marine Commando) as 243. JUNO (Canadian 3rd Infantry Division). Canadian official figures for this sector are 961 casualties; it is impossible to distinguish between beach and inland casualties. Adding 243 on the beaches for the British units, the total for the day is 1,204 but it should be somewhat higher to allow for British casualties inland. SWORD (British 3rd Infantry Division). The only figure found is that of the Army Operational Research Group: 630 casualties on the beaches. The remarks above, under Gold, also apply here. BRITISH AIRBORNE SECTOR (6th Airborne Division). The division's undated report states that the first *two days'* fighting "cost the division over 800 casualties in battle", while in addition "the missing from the drop still numbered approx. 1,000". A War Office analysis gives the final figures of missing for the two parachute brigades in the initial airborne operations as 658 all ranks. The glider units would presumably raise it to at least 800; in addition, glider pilot casualties are given as 95. Since the fighting on June 7 was considerably less heavy than that on D-Day, perhaps 600 of the 800 "battle" casualties might be assigned to June 6. This would give a roughly estimated total of 1,500 D-Day casualties for the sector; a figure comparable with those for the US airborne divisions.' Illustrated, we see some of the wounded arriving at Southampton. *Above left:* American casualties are carried ashore from an LST which has drawn up on Hard S.3. Located just to the east of the Town Quay, we saw the comparison of this view on page 205 when Force 'J' were embarking.

Left: British casualties who have arrived on Hard S.1 (see page 204) are entrained at the Town and Dock Station — now closed and demolished *(right)*. Colonel Stacey concludes that 'the figures above give a grand total of 8,443 casualties, but this is probably low, because the figures for the British 50th and 3rd Divisions cover losses on the beaches only, and there are higher figures for Omaha than Harrison's conservative 2,000. The unsatisfactory nature of the statistics is reflected in the fact that United Kingdom official historians make a considerably higher estimate — 10,865. On the basis of the foregoing Canadian calculation, the total casualties of the Allied armies on June 6, 1944 might be somewhat more than 9,000 men. If we use the Canadian experience as a criterion, roughly one-third of these men must have lost their lives.'

Above: **Having been transferred from Southampton to London, the first train-load of prisoners (364 to be precise) arrives at Kempton Park Station on June 8 for processing at No. 9 PoW Reception Camp which had been established on the nearby race course (see *After the Battle* No. 17). Having been batched in groups of 50, prisoners would then be taken back to the station for onward shipment to a permanent camp in Britain, Canada or the USA.** *Below:* **The station is now only opened for the exclusive use of visitors to Kempton Park Race Course.**

EFFECT ON MOVEMENT

Rail transport which has been cut down to a certain minimum by the general situation anyway can hardly be brought up nearer to the front than 150 to 200 kilometres; even this must be done without definite schedule. The routes must be changed hourly, the trains must follow each other very closely if the weather permits, or they must run exclusively at night. Even so, violent attacks must be reckoned with if the transport has been recognised, and the blocking of transport within certain sectors must be expected.

Peaks of traffic and consequently the detraining of troops or the creation of supply centres are subject to ceaseless changes and require an extremely flexible leadership and mobile labour forces for quick unloading based on the fastest possible transmission of messages.

MISCELLANEOUS

Strict control of the population is imperative, particularly 'loiterers' in the battle zone and in rear areas. When any alarm unit is properly employed, the road situation very quickly assumes another appearance. Suspicious persons, particularly young men with 'attaché cases', may have been secretly inducted. Anybody who does not belong to the actual district or cannot give clear proof of the aim and object of his wandering should be apprehended and conscripted for labour.

It is inevitable that during the first days of large-scale combat, units will have to be mixed according to the situation or split up for separate commitment according to requirements. This is simply a temporary expedient. Immediately the situation permits, logical formations and as a result a straightforward chain of command must be re-established.

I have purposely had these experiences drawn up in a very detailed report, because many units in the West and also newly-arrived forces are still ignorant of the practical aspects of combat proper, despite all the orders and instructions they have received.

Generalfeldmarschall von Rundstedt ended up in South Wales (see *After the Battle* No. 67) where No. 11 (Special) PoW Camp (known locally as Island Farm) for holding high-ranking prisoners had been set up. Britain had over 100 German officers of general or equivalent rank in custody, and von Rundstedt arrived at Bridgend station *(above)* **in January 1946 following interrogation at the Combined Services Interrogation Centre at Wilton Park (see *After the Battle* No. 70). Island Farm Camp was demolished in April 1994 and the site levelled just before the 50th anniversary of D-Day.**

Postscript

By The Editor

The Supreme Commander returns. In August 1963, having served two terms as the 34th President of the United States, Eisenhower went back to Normandy to take part in a Walter Cronkite documentary *D-Day Plus Twenty Years* scheduled for broadcasting the following June. Here, the General boards HMS *Gurkha* at Portsmouth, in a nice parallel to his voyage to the beach-head on June 7, 1944 (see page 404).

'The moment has come for the great captains to recede from the stage of this narrative into the wings of history.'

Well-chosen words — not mine — but John North's, the author of HM Government's popular account of the achievements of 21st Army Group in *North-West Europe, 1944-45*, published in 1953, to conclude this account of D-Day as seen through the eyes of the 'great captains'.

Over 20 years ago, when I launched *After the Battle*, it was as a result of a visit to Normandy on which I wanted to see if it was possible to match up wartime photographs, using a wartime Jeep as a central 'prop'. In the first issue of the magazine, published in August 1973, I managed to squeeze the D-Day story into 40 pages; in 1993, when I sat down to plan this book, I knew I would be lucky to tell it in 400 pages! And although I have sat at my desk for over a year putting these two volumes together — running as they do now to over 700 pages — I still feel that we have only just scratched the surface. Especially when one considers that Admiral Ramsay's operational orders for 'Neptune' — and D-Day is really concerned with that operation, not the wider 'Overlord' — run to over 3,000 pages, and his post-action report, produced after his death, runs to three volumes. And this covers just the naval side!

First, I had to decide how to present — and illustrate — one of the world's greatest military operations; in complexity, certainly *the* greatest. For the latter, there was no problem as our 'then and now' format is well known, yet it was with the text that I had to make a much more difficult decision. Inevitably, any author or editor looks at what has gone before, but one principle that I try to follow is always to tell the story as it was, not as it is perceived by armchair critics today. That is why the first volume opens with General Morgan's own words; it is too easy to look back on things done rather than calculate the unknown.

And so I decided to let the various commanders give their own accounts as they saw it at the time. Most were written in the 1950s when the events were fresh in their minds and untarnished by the passage of time, but no one has previously brought them all together before. This I have done with only the minimum of editing, for example, to standardise on the style and format for units and formations, and to

Pointe du Hoc — General Eisenhower: 'Well, this was a sort isolated but very dramatic phase of the operation. Right on back of where we are now there had been spotted five large guns . . .'

In spite of its banal style, typical of the documentaries of the period, and even though the General makes several mistakes (like the touch-down time being 7.30 a.m.), *D-Day Plus Twenty Years* remains an interesting landmark in the post-war history of D-Day.

It is a pity that some authors and historians delight in debunking the characters of history without always knowing the reasons why. For example, although it does not concern D-Day, Martin Gilbert, Churchill's biographer, discovered that the real reason that the British Prime Minister Herbert Asquith lost his nerve in May 1915 over the Dardanelles, was that he had just had his heart broken by his confidante and cherished love. Eisenhower commented after the last war that 'later curiosity so often concerns itself with responsibility for thought and idea, rather than events and results, that possibly even the most painstaking amanuensis could not leave any clear and unchallengeable account of all the occurrences that go to make up a campaign.'

Cronkite: 'Omaha Beach, on the main coast of Normandy, directly fronting on the English Channel; the centre of the Allied attack . . . General Eisenhower stopped to inspect a German observation post overlooking the beach.'

correct the occasional errors of fact. (Perhaps I ought to explain at this point that I have adopted the original terminology used in 1944 to describe the landings: Sword, Juno, Gold, Omaha and Utah were called 'areas'; the lettered sub-divisions like Jig and King 'sectors', and the sub-sectors 'beaches', like Red Beach.)

I was also very fortunate in that Admiral Ramsay's diary for 1944, *The Year of D-Day*, was published by the University of Hull Press early in 1994, and his son, Major-General Charles Ramsay, kindly gave me permission to include pertinent extracts. It is a marvellous account of events as the Admiral experienced them, including the clashes of personality so often sanitised in later accounts.

Ten years later, the years had taken their toll of the wartime commanders, and, of our authors, only General Sir Richard Gale (in beret) and General Bradley (second right) travelled to France to commemorate the 30th anniversary.

Montgomery and Eisenhower have come in for criticism, in spite of the fact that they achieved an enormous victory in less than a year (not, of course, forgetting the Russians, as Patton *did* say in his oration on page 63). To those of us who remember the wartime leaders, they were heroes, and people at war — and peace — need leaders to look up to. Now they have all faded away: Ramsay and Leigh-Mallory before the war had ended (see *After the Battle* Nos. 39 and 87); General Marshall in October 1959 and General Smith in August 1961; Tedder in June 1967; Eisenhower in March 1969, and Montgomery in March 1976. General Bradley died in April 1981 and General Gale in July 1982; Gerd von Rundstedt in February 1953 and Bodo Zimmermann in April 1963. Captain Hickling of Mulberry fame died a Vice-Admiral in November 1969; General Pyman in October 1971; General McLeod in December 1980; General Belchem in July 1981; Maxwell Taylor in April 1987; Colonel Stacey in November 1989 and Matthew Ridgway in July 1993.

None of the D-Day commanders were able to write about Ultra in their post-war memoirs which form the core of this work, so I was particularly pleased when Ralph Bennett, who worked during the war at the Government Communications Headquarters, gave me permission to include a lengthy extract from his book *Ultra in the West*. A Cambridge historian and Fellow of Magdalene College, he was commissioned and drafted to GCHQ in February 1941 and, as Duty Officer Hut 3, was responsible for all Ultra outgoings on his shift. He began work on *Ultra in the West* — the first campaign narrative based on Ultra — as soon as the Ultra decodes were released in 1977 and it was published two years later.

It is surprising how, even now, over 50 years later, there are still discoveries to be made, and it was only in the latter stages of production that we realised that the US official history, *Cross-Channel Attack*, is incorrect over one very vital point. A footnote on page 275 of that book clearly states that there was one hour difference between Double British Summer Time, used by the Allies in June 1944, and German time, and I, along with other authors, including Cornelius Ryan, have accepted that as gospel. However, it is wrong — Allied and German time was exactly the same, a fact we have now triple checked and it is borne out in the correlation of the times given in German reports as to the various landings.

I have been able to correct or clarify many other points, for example, the over-emphasis on the special ability of the DD Shermans to swim ashore for very few actually did so, and, instead of spearheading the assault, many came in after the troops. The majority of the captioning is mine and I accept responsibility should any errors have crept in, although in some cases the official record is at variance. I have relied on contemporary documents wherever possible and these often do not correspond with later published works so, in some cases, one had to make a balanced judgement.

I have also been dismayed to discover that the failings of military commanders, if they are relieved of their commands, are invariably covered up with euphemisms such as ' . . . was replaced on . . . '. Readers will find examples on pages 46, 312, 330 and 577. For instance, not only is the dismissal of the XXX Corps commander completely omitted from the semi-official *Club Route — 30 Corps in Europe*, published in 1946, but he is not even mentioned by name! Also, two unit associations refused me the names of two officers relieved of their commands even though the events occurred 50 years previously, as if the reputation of the regiment was still at stake.

Another unsavoury aspect I have alluded to is the summary execution of prisoners, but one has the feeling that the Allied nations are still not ready to come to terms with the fact that British, American and Canadian soldiers shot Germans who had surrendered out of hand. Jean Paul Pallud came across numerous French witnesses of the execution of prisoners during the early days, particularly by paratroopers. Not

Field-Marshal Montgomery retired from the Army in 1958 after 50 years service — a record not equalled since that of the Duke of Wellington. That June he returned, not to Normandy, but to the scene of his greatest personal triumph — Victory Hill on Lüneburg Heath — where he had accepted the German surrender 13 years previously (see *After the Battle* No. 48).

far from Collins' future HQ, at la Herguerie, just west of Audouville-la-Hubert, American paratroopers shot about 25 German and Georgian prisoners, many of them wounded, by the side of the D67 (Exit 3 from Utah), on the afternoon of D-Day. They had been held in front of the farm since the early morning of June 6 and were suddenly executed at about 3 p.m. by their guards, seemingly members of the 502nd Parachute Infantry.

Jean Paul goes on to explain that in the context of Normandy, the 'Luxenburger' incident is of special importance as it was most probably the trigger for the increasing spiral of violence which occured over the following days.

'On the morning of June 8, armoured cars from C Squadron, Inns of Court, advanced southwards through the not-really-established German lines (see page 514). On a hill south of Cristot, they came across a group of German artillery officers, about ten in all, from the Panzer-Artillerie-Lehr-Regiment who were to set up their batteries in the sector on the morrow. The surprised Germans were captured and were ordered, as the survivors testified later, to walk in front of the armoured cars to act as a human shield. When they refused to do so, the senior officer, Oberst Luxenburger (a one-armed veteran of World War I) was beaten until he fell unconscious. Bleeding, he was strapped on the front of one of the armoured cars. Having exchanged a radio message with their command (possibly about what to do with the prisoners), the crew of the armoured cars then cut the other men down with their machine guns (although the unit war diary is silent on these events).

'With Luxenburger strapped on a vehicle, the patrol tried to return, but anti-tank guns of the 12. SS-Panzer-Division disabled all the armoured cars. Two British soldiers were killed, two went missing, and four returned on foot. Badly wounded, Oberst Luxenburger was taken to hospital where he died of his wounds on June 18.

One-armed Oberst Luxenburger victim of the war crime incident of June 8, pictured, left, with officers of the Panzer-Lehr-Division in Hungary in 1944. On his left is the divisional CO, Generalmajor Fritz Bayerlein, talking to a Hungarian general, while General Walter Kruger, commander of LVIII. Panzerkorps, looks on.

In the confusion, one of the artillery officers, Major Zeisler, had escaped capture. He had observed what had happened and was in a state of shock when he reached a field command post of the 'Hitlerjugend' some time later. It appears that his story affected many of those who heard him. French civilians later confirmed that the Germans in Audrieu (elements of SS-Panzer-Aufklärungs-Abteilung 12), had learned on June 8 of the Luxenburger incident and that it convinced them that the British were routinely shooting their prisoners. Later in the evening, when the Germans had withdrawn from the château sector, a wounded man left behind even asked French civilians dressing his wounds to take him outside for "if the British find me in the château, they will shoot all of you as well". Over 20 prisoners were shot by the Hitlerjugend at Audrieu on the afternoon of June 8, most likely as a direct response.

'One of the German artillery officers shot on the hill escaped death. Hauptmann von Clary-Aldringen had been badly wounded, shielded as he had been by the bodies of his comrades. He crawled to Le Mesnil-Patry where men of SS-Panzergrenadier-Regiment 26 recovered him. He reported to the CP of the regiment's II. Bataillon near Putot and, next day, three Canadian prisoners were shot in reprisal.'

After the war, the battalion commander, SS-Sturmbannführer Bernhard Siebken, and one of his officers, SS-Untersturmführer Dieter Schnable, were tried for the execution of these three men and hanged in January 1949. 'Therefore', says Jean Paul, 'it is possible that the staff of the Hitlerjugend at the Abbaye d'Ardenne, some distance to the east, heard of the Luxenburger incident on June 8, which resulted in the execution of the Canadian prisoners there as recounted on pages 500-501.'

Of the incident, the Inns of Court war diary simply records that '[Troops] 2 and 6a captured 3 German officers [and] on way back were ambushed and lost all vehicles'. This advance through enemy lines towards the Orne south of Caen also illustrated yet another aspect: attacks by friendly aircraft. The Inns of Court mission was to demolish bridge crossings over the Rivers Orne and Odon to prevent any interference from

21. Panzer. Royal Engineers with half-tracks full of explosives accompanied the armoured cars, but on June 7, at the cross-roads *(above)* at Jerusalem (on the D6 south-east of Bayeux), Thunderbolts submitted two troops to a devastating low-level attack, completely disintegrating one half-track and setting fire to three Dingos and a Daimler. Two officers and five other ranks were killed, with six men wounded.

The fighting qualities of the troops in Normandy is another facet to which one could devote much space. This letter was received in 1951 by the Historical Section of the Cabinet Office in London — the body responsible for producing Britain's official war histories — from their opposite number in New Zealand. The accompanying observations by Brigadier Hargest, whose experiences as a fighting soldier can hardly be questioned, make very interesting reading, of which the following is a brief extract: '50 Div fights well and has gained a lot of ground. Its casualties have been heavy, two brigade commanders, eight COs, officers and over 3,000 men. The casualties among officers is high in percentage. I believe this is due to the closeness of the country permitting snipers to get in close and to the fact that men lie down in such country and are only urged forward by the personal example of their officers. Also that officers carry map boards with talc coverings that flash in the sun. I witnessed one attack by the 8th DLI where from about 600/800 yards I could pick out almost every officer by his map board shining. (The answer is for the officers to carry a small paper map in their map pocket and not stop in the open to refer to it.) In the 9th DLI on 14 June, all four company commanders were hit. The Div is tired and whenever men get into shelter they want to sleep. They cannot be alert while in this condition. The English soldier, i.e. from the UK, differs from the soldier from the Dominions. He demands leadership by officers. I notice that, as soon as men lose their officers, they lose heart. Today (16th) I met several Bren gun sections coming back and, in reply to my enquiries, they said the fire was heavy and they had got out of touch. It did not occur to them to go on. Result great loss of fire power. This is not suggesting that they lack courage, they don't. This lack of independence leads to another fault — bunching together. This morning at a German road-block, which the enemy had obviously registered, eight men were killed or wounded by one mortar — half a mile to the rear, eight more despatch riders were casualties.'

Telegraphic and Cable Address: "Warstory, Wellington."

...ondence to be addressed— "War History Branch, Department of Internal Affairs, P.O. Box 7, Government Buildings, Wellington C.1."

In replying, please quote these numbers. I.A. P/O

AL.1213.

DEPARTMENT OF INTERNAL AFFAIRS.
WAR HISTORY BRANCH,
P.O. BOX 7, GOVERNMENT BUILDINGS,
WELLINGTON C.1.

NEW ZEALAND

9 May 1951.

Brigadier H.B. Latham,
Cabinet Office,
Historical Section,
8 Barton Street,
LONDON SW1.

Dear Harry,

For a change I am writing to you on a matter that may concern the Normandy Campaign, or may interest the historians dealing with it.

Brigadier James Hargest, whose name you will have come across as Commander of 5 New Zealand Infantry Brigade in Greece, Crete and the first stages of the Libya Campaign, was taken prisoner in Libya on 25 November 1941. He was held in a senior officers' camp in Italy, among his fellow prisoners being General O'Connor. All these senior officers escaped in a rather remarkable fashion, digging a tunnel through the floor of the chapel in an ancient castle in which they were confined. Hargest and Miles, whom you will remember as CRA 2 NZ Div, escaped to Switzerland, the others were recaptured.

Hargest and Miles then made their way across France to Spain. They were separated just before crossing the Pyrenees, and when Miles got into Spain afterwards he died under very mysterious circumstances in a Spanish military prison. There is little doubt that he committed suicide under the impression that he had made a mistake while crossing France, which would be fatal to some of the people who helped him. Hargest got to England and immediately applied for re-employment in the field. There was no vacant place in N.Z. Div at the time, but he was given an appointment as N.Z. observer attached to 50 Div. for the landing in Normandy and the Normandy Campaign.

He duly accompanied 50 Div at the landing & until late in Aug 44, having sustained a slight wound in the meantime. The end of the war was thought to be in sight and he was appointed Officer in charge of the reception of N.Z. prisoners of war. He returned to England to make the preliminary arrangements, had lunch with me at the Army and Navy Club, flew back to France to say goodbye to Graham and some of the officers of 50 Div, and was killed that same afternoon by a stray shell while he was on his way to visit one of the forward battalions.

Hargest had a brilliant career in the First World War, going from Second Lieutenant to Lieutenant Colonel, and as an infantryman taking part in more than twenty general actions from Gallipoli to the Sambre in November 1918. He was wounded twice, but at the end of that war was regarded as one of the best officers New Zealand had produced. In between the wars he was a successful farmer and a leading politician on the Conservative side. If he had survived the war he would probably have been the present Prime Minister.

In the Second World War he had sufficient experience to maintain his reputation and perhaps increase it. Just before he returned to France for the last time he left a bundle of notes with the New Zealand Liaison officer in London, Brigadier Park, and these recently came into my possession. He collected many papers which are of no interest to you or your historians, copies of Operations Instructions, Intelligence Summaries, etc, but the notes which he made may be of interest to you, and I enclose copy. I will not make any comment on them other than to say that Hargest was a fair-minded man, and you can judge the value of the notes by perusal, and perhaps on this background information on the writer.

Yours sincerely,

H K Kippenberger

I have tried to avoid bringing in any personal observations as I always like readers to form their own opinions. But everyone is biased to some degree, and the 'over-memorialisation' of the coastline is one aspect that, I feel, 'waters down' their value. Many memorials will not stand the test of time; some are sited on territory rightfully captured by others; and the rush to add yet more for the 50th anniversary may lead, I fear, to the 'Oh-it's-just-another-memorial' syndrome. And the respect for monuments and their meaning changes over the years — perhaps inevitably the further one gets from the event remembered. Paul Griffith of Hitchin, Hertfordshire, wrote in this vein to the Editor of *The Times* on the 10th anniversary of D-Day: 'Sir, Might I put in a plea for a more universal observance of the custom which grew up between the two World Wars for all men and boys to raise their hats as they passed the Cenotaph in Whitehall. Never should this memorial be allowed to deteriorate into a mere testimonial to a forgotten past.'

There are many facets that I have not been able to cover in the detail they deserve. For example, one of the most important, without which 'Neptune' would never have taken place, was the production of the necessary maps. The so-called British 'rearmament' series was begun in 1936 by the Geographical Survey General Staff (GSGS). These maps basically copied the most recent French and Belgian surveys, and were initially available only in 1:250,000 or 1:50,000 scales. When America entered the war, the US became responsible for mapping North and South America, Australia, New Zealand, the Pacific, Dutch East Indies, Japan, the West Indies, Iceland, Greenland and Bermuda, while the British War Office was responsible for all the other areas, including Europe. The 1:50,000 series (GSGS 4040) was revised several times between 1941 and 1944, but, when it was realised that the whole of Normandy and Brittany were the likely operational areas of the invasion, sheets were produced for those areas by enlarging the French 1:80,000 map, the new series (GSGS 4250) just being ready for D-Day. However, the continued development of artillery, radar and other weaponry made it essential that accurate large-scale mapping was available for use on the battlefield at 1:25,000 scale. Special air photography was therefore undertaken at the accuracy necessary for map making, the resulting maps being known as the 'Benson' series after the name of the airfield in the UK most closely associated with aerial survey photography.

Then different maps had to be produced for the airborne forces, naval units, air forces, etc. Special defence overprints were produced for the individual beaches at 1:12,500 scale and included in appendices to the operational orders. To reproduce these in *D-Day Then and Now* would have resulted in inordinate reduction, making the detail almost impossible to read (like the extract from the Utah map on page 392), but fortunately the Department of Printed Books at the Imperial War Museum in London can supply same-size photocopies which are essential for anyone wanting to study in detail the defences and terrain as it was in 1944.

In this work, I have included contemporary mapping from various sources as a guide to the defences and landing points on each beach, and have overlaid these with the military grid in use at the time. I have also included contemporary and modern aerial photography which I hope will be useful to show the changes over the last 50 years.

Extracts from the 1:12,500 series (GSGS 4490), reproduced here at same scale, covered fixed defences, road widths, bridge classifications, obstacles, etc. The May 1944 edition *(above)* was superseded by a stop press overprint *(below)* with late additions in orange.

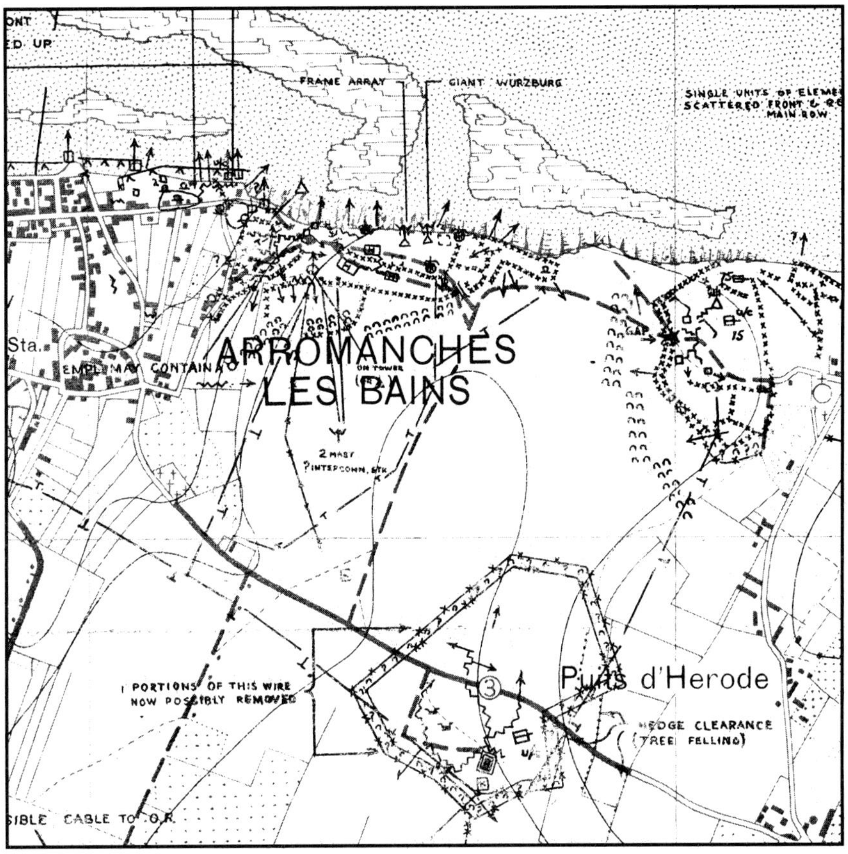

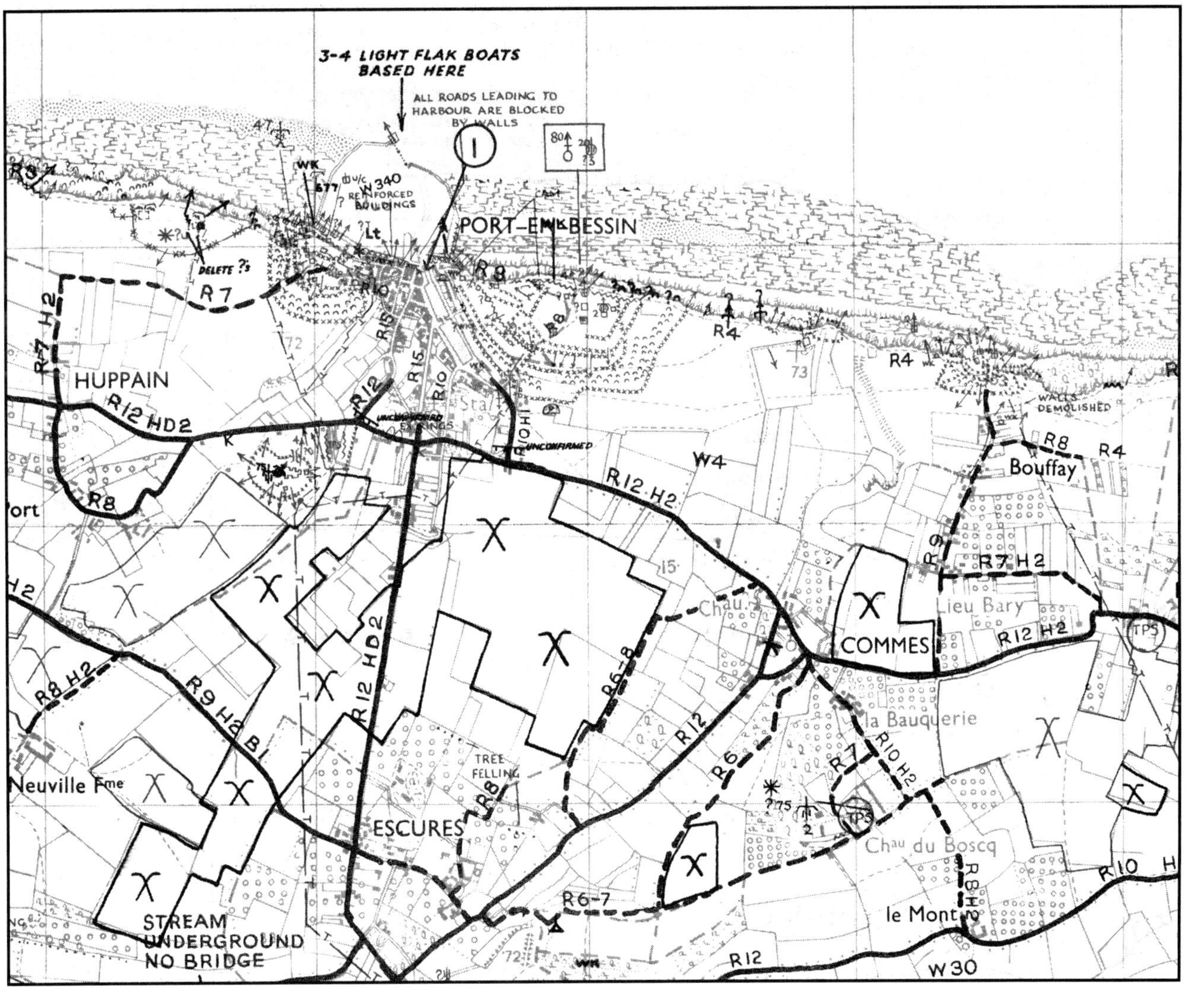

The *After the Battle* Normandy photo team pose for a symbolic comparison exactly 50 years later. L–R: Karel Margry, Steve Casely, and Robert Voskuil. For the location, see page 447.

In this project, I have been ably assisted by my European Editor, Karel Margry, and my long-time technical advisor, Jean Paul Pallud. On them fell the brunt of the comparison photography in Normandy while I covered the UK side. Steve Casely, Brana Radovic and Robert Voskuil filled in around the edges. We were also assisted by many other individuals, particularly David List, who carried out much research at the Public Record Office; Hans Sakkers who has made a detailed study of the coastal inspection tours of Rommel in 1944; and Laurent Mari, the leading French specialist on Omaha. Sadly, he was killed on August 31, 1994, on the very battlefield he knew so well, when the car in which he was driving left the road between Vierville-sur-Mer and Formigny and overturned.

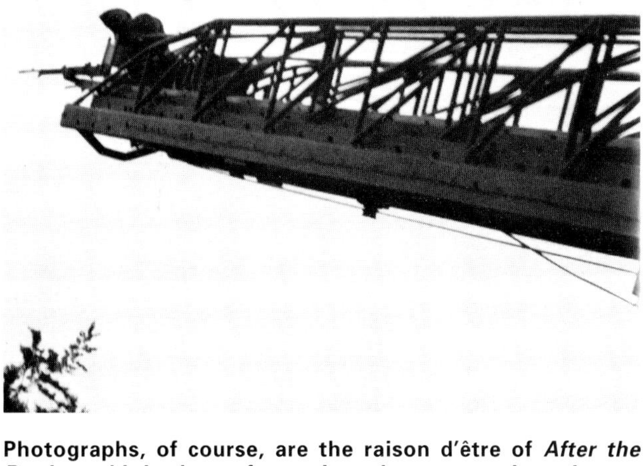

Photographs, of course, are the raison d'être of *After the Battle*, and it is always frustrating when one receives pictures too late. These shots are a good illustration as they were found by Doug McCabe amongst the papers of the late Cornelius Ryan at Ohio University long after I had completed the layout for the Pointe du Hoc pages. I explained on page 330 how extending fire brigade ladders were mounted on DUKWs; now pictures have surfaced of the installations fitted with the twin Lewis machine guns. Although they were never used for their intended purpose of providing easy access up the cliff face, it makes Staff Sergeant Stivison's exploit (page 331) all the more unbelievable.

We owe a huge debt to the work of the combat cameramen, because without their images we would only have our memories — or our imagination — to recall the events of yesterday. I always try where possible to give due credit to the individual cameraman concerned, but so that they are no longer just names, let me introduce some of them from the US Signal Corps. (L–R): Private Louis Weintraub, Pfc Francis Lee, 1st Lieutenant George Stock, T/Sgt Val Pope and Pfc Walter Rosenblum.

'Operation "Overlord", in all its complexity', says David, 'probably stands unique in memory because of the extent and breadth of its pre-planned photographic coverage, whether this was for military intelligence, training or public information purposes.

'The patchwork of photographic imagery that yet remains to us of this great event, and certainly the greatest bulk of it, in the shape of photography from the air, was produced for intelligence analysis. A small proportion of the total, although the one most often remembered and used extensively throughout this book, was taken by men who remain largely anonymous and unsung in their own lifetimes; namely the Services photographers of the public information units of all the nations involved.

'On the Allied side, SHAEF, via its Public Relations Division, was responsible for the co-ordination of film and photography of Allied operations "to be presented to the public with the minimum of delay". The Division's remit took in the official naval photographers of the Royal Navy, Royal Canadian Navy, US Navy and US Coast Guard, all predominantly based aboard the major naval units and concentrating on covering sea power in action. British, Canadian and US Army units provided film and photographic teams landing either with the first waves of assault troops or later in the day with the follow-up units. RAF, RCAF and USAAF photographers flying with day-light missions over the beach-head or also landing over the beaches, depicted the effects of close air support. Then there was the SHAEF Special Coverage Unit concentrating on capturing "history in the making"; accredited civilian cine cameramen and still photographers of the British, Canadian and US news pools; authorised photography by personnel of all the Services involved in operations on an opportunity basis.

Initially, I was intending just to include photographs taken on D-Day itself, but so few were taken on June 6 that it would have been impossible to do justice to all the landing beaches and airborne areas equitably. I have tried to give a varied coverage to the different beaches so that one is not just repeating the same detail. Also, the cut-off point varies but is roughly at the stage where the five landing areas were linked up. David List unearthed many valuable files of pictures at the PRO for us, having made it his personal project to study all the D-Day photography.

Right: **From Canada, Sergeant E. R. Bonter, Lieutenant C. C. McDougall, Sergeant L. E. Weekes, Lieutenant F. L. Dubervill, Sergeants C. E. Roos, W. G. Grant and D. A. Reynolds. (Remote control picture by Frank Dubervill.)**

And from Britain (back row), George Laws, Bill Leeson, Norman Clague (George cannot recall the names of the last two men); (front row) Albert Wilkes, Bob Turner and Freddie Wood.

Of all the American combat photographers, Captain Herman Wall, commanding the US 165th Photographic Company, probably took the highest number of pictures on D-Day. Because his job was organisational rather than photographic, he carried only a 35mm Leica as a backup rather than the heavyweight Speed Graphic used by his photographers (Weintraub is holding one in the group picture on page 629). Wall also took 14 carrier pigeons with him, although one released as he was about to land headed off over German lines! Anyway, Captain Wall arranged to be first off his LCVP which came ashore on Easy Red around 1130, as we saw in his pictures on page 356. He then shot this sequence as men of the beach brigade arrived in LCT 538 but, as he started down the beach, he was hit and badly wounded. He lay on the beach with a bullet in his arm, and shrapnel in his thigh for nearly three hours with other injured men until rescued and evacuated to England. All the time, he held on to his camera with its precious undeveloped film, calling for it before the operation to amputate part of his leg so that he could give instructions as to where the film had to be sent.

'In Normandy, picturing the activities of the German forces was the responsibility of the Wehrmacht's Propaganda-Kompanie 649 of the SS-Standarte "Kurt Eggers", and of other personnel who had been given the appropriate authorisation, or had strong nerves! Caught in the middle of these great events, many French people who had managed to retain cameras and film through the long years of occupation also managed to document the day of their liberation.

'For the historian, assessing the extent and provenance of the photographic coverage of D-Day is of vital importance because it is the only reporting medium where there is the guarantee that the events recorded actually took place in the way shown. Photography also has another uniquely valuable feature; the automatic facility of capturing enormous detail which can be subjected to objectively verifiable and repeatable interpretation, evaluation and analysis at any time by anyone regardless of the language they speak, their experience of life, or their mode of thought.

'As an information scientist concerned with image interpretation for over twenty years, I have become fascinated by the misinterpretation of wartime photography and the exploitation of this priceless resource to gain new insights and improved understanding of the past in what has become an *After the Battle* trade mark style: establishing the "ground truth" of events depicted in the photographic record by going back to its origins and providing modern comparison check photography.

When developed, the roll was found to contain 35 excellent exposures which were wired to the States by radio. Early newspaper reports said that the cameraman (unnamed at the time) who had taken the shots — the first of the actual landings — had been killed. Months after D-Day, in the coffee shop of the Percy Jones Army Hospital in Battle Creek, Missouri, Wall was talking to a patient who had lost a foot — also on Easy Red. Pfc Harold Wordeman said he had landed on D-Day with the beach brigade, whereupon Wall told him that he had photographed the Brigade that morning. Sending for copies of his pictures, Wall asked Wordeman if he could identify anyone. 'Yes', he said, 'myself [arrowed], front and center!'

The identification of particular individuals in photographs is fraught with problems, yet it is understandable that people try to put names to those who appear in well-known pictures. We slipped up ourselves 20 years ago when we accepted a pencilled addition to the caption sheet in the Imperial War Museum for the picture on the dust-jacket of this volume, naming the man in the right foreground as Corporal David Dutton. Joel Tranter in *Caen Une Ville Trop Loin* claimed it was a Peter Lucas, a name repeated by Editions Heimdal in their *Album Memorial Overlord*. Then, ignoring my advice that positive identification of the two soldiers was contentious, the Jersey Post Office stated that the chap in the left foreground of their 23p anniversary stamp *(left)*, released in 1994, was Jersey-man George Catelinet. George *(right)* had always claimed that he was the man in the picture, and it certainly does look like him. George's moment of glory — albeit misplaced — came too late for him to enjoy as he died in May 1993. Then, the following year, as I explained on page 525, Fred Sadler surfaced; David List verified his and the other two names against the No. 84 Field Company nominal roll and they checked out.

'It is possible to show that some 23 military still or cine public information photographers actually landed on the beaches, or with the airborne troops in the course of D-Day itself in the British and Canadian sectors. A far greater number, not all of whom have been identified, landed with the Americans, together with the civilian accredited photographers Bert Brandt, Bob Capa and Jack Leib (who, in addition to his official job of filming in black and white shot his own 16mm colour footage as a private diary for his family, just as did film director George Stevens (see page 473) who commanded SPECOU; the Special Coverage Unit of the United States Army Signal Corps, also known as the SHAEF Special Coverage Unit). Unlike the American sectors, no civilian Press photographers were permitted with 6th Airborne Division or to go in with the assault on Gold, Juno or Sword, although it is true to say that a majority of the Services' photographers on these beaches were originally from the Press.

David goes on to explain that 'in the American (and Canadian by a bit of inspired scrounging) sectors fixed-focus, automatic cine cameras were fitted to some landing craft in an effort to film the assault for both training and public information purposes whilst reducing the risks to the cameramen. One, more often two, cameras were fitted bow and stern, pointing fore and aft, on LCTs with filming under the control of the skipper on the bridge. The majority of these cameras failed, either malfunctioning, becoming waterlogged, or damaged by incoming fire. Some footage shot aboard an LCA landing Canadian infantry did survive the worst excesses of man and nature and gives some of the most dramatic footage of the day (see pages 504-505).

Above left: **This commando or signaller, who also features on the Overlord Embroidery** *(left)* **in the D-Day Museum at Portsmouth (albeit minus his glasses), has been said to be William Sendall. However, Major Sendall's involvement was merely to write to the *Sunday Times* (in 1975) stating that he was present when the picture was taken.** *Above:* **Inevitably, Robert Capa's 10 surviving frames receive much publicity (see page 343). Their poor quality was the result of too much heat in drying the negatives after development which caused the emulsion to run, but nevertheless, the blurred images are still held up to be something extraordinary. The mother of Edward K. Regan was sure the photo on the cover above was of her son, yet *Focus* magazine still claimed when they published the picture in their May 1994 issue that the soldier's identity had only recently been discovered!**

It is these stories behind the pictures which make them so much more interesting. Take another example. For over 40 years this picture has been credited as being taken by Captain Leslie Evans, the original caption stating: 'Troops dig positions ahead of the field in which they were landed. A glider can be seen in the background.' One might guess that the bereted 'troops' are most probably commandos which would then disprove the statement that they landed by glider. However, beyond that there are few clues — except that we now know it is one of the seven frames which survive out of the roll of 35mm film taken, not by Captain Evans, but by George Laws. These are men of No. 4 Commando digging slit trenches in the garden of Lord Lovat's HQ — we saw the reverse angle on page 234, and explained how George had to resort to taking still pictures after his cine camera broke (page 545). The shot on page 560 was also taken nearby. Jean Paul says that the present-day view makes for a poor comparison as conifers now obscure the wall.

'A combination of the photographers' own preserved "dope sheets" together with surviving British and Canadian records, has enabled not only an accurate re-creation of the photographers' order of battle and movements, but has also helped, in the compiling of this work, in resolving many of the problems of misinterpreted photographic evidence that have accrued over 50 years.

'On Gold were Bill Ginger, Norman Midgley and Harry Parkinson. Canadians Ken Bell, Frank Dubervill, Don Grant, W. G. Grant, A. W. Grayston, Gilbert Milne and C. E. Roos, together with Peter Handford, Ernie Walter and Dick Leatherbarrow from the British, all landed on Juno. Norman Clague, Leslie Evans, Ian Grant, Billy Greenhalgh, Derrick Knight, George Laws, Jimmy Mapham and Des O'Neill went in on Sword. Greenhalgh was hit in the arm by mortar fire and O'Neill shot in the left elbow, but both managed to hand over their exposed film before being evacuated. Dave Reynolds for Canada and Jimmy Christie for Britain both came in by glider on the evening of June 6 just in time to complete coverage of the day's events whilst enough photographic light yet remained.

'For obvious reasons, night photography, whilst taken for intelligence purposes on all the predicted approach routes to the lodgement areas by the specially-equipped Wellington XIIIs of No. 69 Squadron, RAF (which could cover a strip 1½ miles long by a quarter of a mile wide in a single sortie), was not an option of choice that night for any of the Allied public information units. However, it is worth noting that, prior to D-Day, men of Hilt Force on Operation 'Tarbrush' appear to have taken a limited amount of infra-red flash photography on their special beach surveys, and later in the campaign some spectacular imagery of anti-aircraft fire over the beach-head was secured.

'Each British or Canadian cine photographer usually landed with ten rolls of film — enough for about ten minutes shooting. They also usually carried a still camera with a couple of rolls of film as a back-up in case of mechanical failure (as happened to George Laws). The stills photographers carried as many rolls of film as they could and it was customary for a cine and a stills photographer to act together as a team. On D-Day in the British and

Comparison photography is, of course, for *After the Battle* the central theme, and it was my intention to make *D-Day Then and Now* something special by taking many of the matching shots exactly 50 years later. I began by arranging a visit to No. 20 Grosvenor Square on the very day — January 18 (a Tuesday both in 1994 and 1944) — when the newly-appointed Supreme Commander was introduced to the press. However, the passage of 50 years had resulted in many alterations to the internal layout of the rooms although the corridor system — which is included *left* in the wartime documentary *D-Day Minus One* — still remains with the stairwell at the end *(right)*. In the film, Eisenhower's office is purportedly shown just beside the guard in the background although it would appear that this is film-makers' licence, for Eisenhower's office is confirmed as being at the opposite end of the building overlooking the square (see pages 9 and 642). Most probably, the film crew were given this rear corridor to use so the real conduct of the war would not be interrupted by their filming.

Canadian sectors, the photographers were spread out amongst the naval task force to limit the effects of casualties and improve the breadth of coverage and it was only after landing that the teams were re-formed.

'The maximum number of photographs taken in these sectors by any one photographer appears to be the eight rolls exposed by Jimmy Mapham. Thus, the number of photographs from Gold, Juno and Sword is not as copious as it would be for a similar mission nowadays when advances in camera and film technology, as well as our thinking about photographic coverage of newsworthy events, is so markedly different from the 1940s.

'Other mishaps befell cine-cameraman C. E. Roos who landed with D Company of The Regina Rifle Regiment and had to jump into the sea when his LCA was mined, and waded ashore under machine gun fire; Don Grant with B Company of The Royal Winnipeg Rifles who pushed the doors of his LCA open, fell into the water, damaged his first camera and then saw ten of the men in the LCA mown down by machine gun fire; and Derrick Knight who narrowly missed death when Brigadier J. C. Cunningham commanding 9th Brigade was severely wounded in an "O Group" on the beach. Jimmy Mapham also spent 12 hours hiding under a knocked-out British tank surrounded by German tanks.

'Having taken their film at considerable personal risk and surmounted the problems of lousy weather and immersion in the sea, all the photographers had the problem of getting their film back to the UK for processing and publication. Bert Brandt and Bob Capa, being civilians, were able to evacuate themselves with their own film in their efforts to gain a "scoop", but the Services' photographers were all under orders to stay put until relieved and to send back their film in marked bags via the navy. On the American beaches, film was lost when a dispatch bag was

The anniversary of the important inspection tour to Newbury and Salisbury Plain (see pages 18-19) fell on March 23-24 and once again we planned to be at the locations on the exact day. For the 101st Airborne demonstration (pages 285-287), with the assistance of Bill King and the members of the Ridgeway Military and Aviation Research Group, we even intended to match the exact time. Some of the group's own comparison set-ups are superb — look at the detail in these two pairs taken at Skeats Corner near Chilton Foliat (near Hungerford) of the 2nd Battalion, 503rd Parachute Infantry training in 1942. Redesignated the 509th, it fought in North Africa and Italy but missed D-Day. The group members re-staged the action in October 1992.

The following month, Lieutenant-Colonel Chris Sexton of 33 Engineer Regiment, RE, based at Carver Barracks at the former RAF airfield at Debden, allowed me to take photographs in the officers' mess at the exact time shown in the picture on page 143. ***Left:*** **By way of showing our appreciation, I later presented Colonel Sexton with a framed enlargement of the original photograph which had kindly been supplied to me by Keith Braybrooke from his extensive archive of historical material on Debden. My visit was particularly fortuitous for I was given a picture showing one of the unit's current tasks: that of clearing the Culbin Forest, on the shore of the Moray Firth in Scotland, which had been used as an impact area for testing the LCT(R) equipment (see pages 472-473). Several fired, yet unexploded, rockets had been unearthed** ***(right).***

dropped in the sea and the British unfortunately lost all track of their film for a week after it had safely crossed the Channel. (As can be imagined, this provoked a major row between Fleet Street and the Service authorities, leading to improved facilities later in the Normandy campaign.) It therefore fell to Frank Dubervill (page 486), Bert Brandt (page 346) and Herman Wall (page 630). to share the enduring, if uncredited, glory of picture splashes in newspapers all over the world next morning.

'Then followed processing only by MI5 approved and inspected film laboratories for the civilian photographers' material and the constraints of censorship, plus a general lack of in-depth knowledge about what was being photographed by both photographer and picture editor. Coupled with a deliberate policy of self-effacement on the part of the British authorities, this meant that the full identification of individuals, let alone military units, pictured by British and Commonwealth Services photographers is poor by comparison with some of the American photography where names of men (and women) and their home towns and states were essential caption material.

'The Germans showed a similar rectitude. For all the thousands of images taken by the Kriegsbildberichter, most of the original captions were lost at the end of the war, so it is rare indeed to find personnel identified unless they are the recipients of an award, are of general officer rank, or are a "personality" deliberately fostered by the German authorities. Similarly, place names and unit identifications, except in the most general terms, were omitted from the situation report which accompanied film despatched to the Abteilung für Wehrmacht-Propaganda in Berlin.

'Finally,' writes David, 'the "then and now" photographs and captions throughout these volumes demonstrate how often and how poorly we have been served over the years by our writers of history who so consistently fail to see the information presented to their senses by the incomparable evidence of photography. Chief amongst these must be the example of Jimmy Mapham's famous photograph of Sword Queen Red (page 525) and the mystery of when, where and who is shown in it.'

Also in April 1944, after a long search, I finally established the location of 'Sharpener' — Eisenhower's Advance CP (see page 33) — where I was interviewed by both American and British television.

And so it went on . . . taking the comparisons as each 50th anniversary came up . . . at Bushy Park . . . St Paul's School . . . Greenham Common . . . until my team took over and positioned themselves on the beaches of Normandy at the precise time of touchdown on June 6. Surprisingly, they met only the odd veteran who had made the effort to get up early and walk the sand they had once trod on D-Day, 50 years before.

Although we are now separated from D-Day by half a century, it is surprising what still remains to be seen. We talk of turning swords into ploughshares, yet it is often only after the plough has done its work that the tell-tale signs of battle show through. These two photographs graphically illustrate the point. *Above:* Bill King took this picture in the winter of 1994-95 from the top of Walbury Hill overlooking the training area for the assault on Merville Battery. Compare with the aerial picture on page 237. *Right:* The memorial stone at Inkpen was unveiled on May 22, 1993, by the Lord Lieutenant of the Royal County of Berkshire, John Henderson. *Below:* Then, Lieutenant-Colonel Michael Chilcott, who is closely associated with the museum at Merville, took this picture from the top of the casemate after a period of prolonged rain. Although the surrounding fields have been tilled for several decades, the impressions of the bomb craters show up clearly in the waterlogged ground.

My personal interest in Normandy and D-Day was aroused way back in the 1950s. In 1954, I was given a copy of the *Daily Express* 10th anniversary picture book *Invasion*. Then, there was little other literature available and its illustrations held a special fascination. I distinctly recall wanting to see the 'Hindenburg' bastion (page 568) for myself, and to stand where Sergeant Savage once stood. But then there were no guide books, and on my first visit in June 1961 there was no hope of finding one particular bunker out of hundreds spread out along 50 miles of coastline.

In those days, the annual commemoration of D-Day was fairly low-key although one was usually treated to a showing of *The True Glory* on television and I still have a sound recording made on an old reel-to-reel Grundig when Granada put it out in June 1957: 'And so tonight, 13 years after the invasion of Normandy . . . '

And now, 50 years after the invasion, as the wheel turns full circle, Sergeant Savage's bunker at Douvres has been identified and may well be dug out in 1996.

The half-century anniversary was an important landmark for all those who participated in the operation, and I am very pleased that Brigadier Tom Longland, who had the unenviable task of organising the national commemorative events in Britain, agreed to contribute the penultimate chapter which follows. His World War II Commemorative Team may have been minute when compared to the vast command structure set up for 'Neptune', yet it was still an inter-Allied effort which mirrored operations in 1944 — a fitting conclusion to our story — after the battle.

And even more impressive are the remains of the Mulberry harbour. *Above:* **Fifty years on, looking as fresh as the day they were made, these Phoenix caissons stand as sentinels off Castletown Pier at Portland where they were sunk to form an additional breakwater. (See also page 202.)** *Below:* **The harbour itself at Arromanches, abandoned in the autumn of 1944; a far cry from the scene described by Frank Gillard that June.**

I'm looking towards the bay now, it is really an almost unbelievable sight. it's stiff with shipping. Warships, landing-craft, merchant vessels — everything right down to motor-launches and small boats. There they are, their signal lights winking in the late evening sun, an occasional siren hooting. Overhead, the sky — there's hardly a cloud to be seen anywhere; but the sky's picked out with silver barrage balloons, as thick as currants in a pre-war Christmas cake. And of course we've got our air cover; they're up there now, as they are every moment of the day. And so, on this ground where a fortnight ago the Germans were masters, tonight the Allies are in complete control. I stood by the roadside yesterday and watched the men and machines and supplies rolling in. And a soldier beside me — I don't know who he was — just turned and said: 'Once you've seen all this, you know we just can't help winning this war.' That's just how we all feel here.

FRANK GILLARD, BBC BROADCAST, JUNE 18, 1944

The 'After the Battle' TV series of the late '50s ran to half a dozen programmes. In each one a war correspondent returned to the scene of WW2 action; for example, Ed Murrow came over to do a film about the London Blitz, and Richard Dimbleby went back to Belsen. In my case, I wanted very much to do the Tunis-to-Naples story, which would have included Lampedusa, Pantelleria, Sicily and Salerno, and enjoyed marvellous territory, pictorially, as well as recalling a largely forgotten campaign. However, the budget would not run to that and I reluctantly had to agree to return to Normandy, though the Normandy story had already been dealt with often enough on television. (It was gratifying that in the end Normandy, nevertheless, drew a larger audience and a higher appreciation index than any of the other five.)

Even in the short span of 15 years since the end of the war, the traces of conflict had disappeared to such a large extent in Normandy. In fact, the recovery was quite astonishing and we had to hunt for relics of the fighting. When we found them, they were trivial — a hanging flower bowl by a cottage doorway, adapted from an upside-down steel helmet; polished and burnished shell cases being used as household ornaments.

The city of Caen, in itself, amazed me. In July 1944, it stood in ruins but by 1959, it was a large new metropolis. As a result of a huge programme of re-landscaping, I could not recognise or find my way around the place. The web of narrow, devastated alleyways along which we had fought to gain entry from the north had totally vanished. They were replaced by well-designed modern clusters of elegant

Frank Gillard, then the BBC's West Region Controller, gives viewers of *After the Battle* his impressions of Normandy in 1959.

buildings set along wide, handsome roadways. The scars of war had healed not only in the physical environment but also in the hearts and minds of the citizens. Interviewing them, the comment was always: 'Look at Caen today; the war made our home town the most modern city in all Europe'. The same sentiment came even from villages and country folk in places like Tilly-sur-Seulles and Villers-Bocage which were obliterated by the tide of war but were now reconstituted in fine, modern style. When one asked 'but what about the sufferings of your parents and friends in 1944?', the answer was always: 'Ah! C'est la guerre'. The bitter, costly battle of Normandy had, in the end, bequeathed new life and vigour to the communities mutilated in the time of calamity. The past had, of course, to be respected, but it would have been hypocritical to grieve over it 15 years later.

But the friends we had made during our brief wartime passage were still there, and still remembered us with the warmest of welcomes. They took part in our film and showered us with hospitality. In the little town of Creully, so close to the beaches, we established in 1944 a lash-up broadcasting studio in the turret room of the famous Creully Château. For the weeks of the Normandy battle, Creully became a major, but secret, broadcasting centre of the Allied world. A bronze plaque in the banqueting hall of the château commemorates this fact, and for the last 50 years the turret room has been preserved as a kind of museum by the people of Creully. Year by year, it has attracted swarms of visitors as they come in coach-loads to tour the ancient châteaux of the region. In 1994, with BBC help, the turret room was refurbished with new but identical exhibits, to carry it forward for decades to come. Here is a small but very sincere Franco-British association which is not going to fade away.

FRANK GILLARD,
LETTER TO THE EDITOR, MARCH 1995

The 50th Anniversary Commemorations of D-Day

By Brigadier Tom Longland

TEAM LEADER, WORLD WAR II COMMEMORATION TEAM

Normandy is preparing elaborate celebrations for the first anniversary of D-Day. The French Ministers of War, Marine, and Air will attend the ceremonies, the first of which, a Canadian one, is scheduled to begin at Bernières at 7 a.m. After an official luncheon given by the town of Bayeux, there will be a march-past at the foot of the Arromanches cliffs, followed by a religious service, in commemoration of the British landing. Later, the official party will attend a Franco-American military ceremony at Ste Marie-du-Mont before going to Ste Mère-Eglise, the scene of some of the bitterest fighting after D-Day, for an official dinner.

THE TIMES, JUNE 6, 1945

Early in January 1993, I found myself staring at a blank sheet of paper which I had carefully entitled the 'Commemorations of D-Day'. Racing through my mind was the succinct brief I had just received that morning from the Adjutant-General, General Sir David Ramsbotham. There can rarely have been a shorter briefing for 18 months' work and it was striking in its brevity: 'I want you to organise the commemoration of the D-Day landings. Let me know what you want'. Armed with this instruction, I began the first tentative steps in planning the largest public event of 1994.

The beach at Arromanches — chosen by Brigadier Longland's World War II Commemoration Team for the finale of the British commemorative events of June 6, 1994 — just as it had been for the first anniversary of D-Day in June 1945.

By order of the Supreme Commander, the Allied forces in Europe so far as possible have made a holiday of this, the first anniversary of D-Day, but the few line of communication troops remaining in Normandy joined in a series of more intimate ceremonies, some of them held on the beaches where the first assault waves came in.

From all accounts, they are little changed. As no doubt happened in the early hours a year ago, when British and American airborne troops struck on the flanks of the landing area, sirens, joined by the ringing of church bells, were sounded during the night throughout the departments of Calvados and the Manche, and throughout the day there have been various military parades and other ceremonies to mark the beginning of the campaign of liberation and retribution, gloriously completed within the year. The British, American, and Canadian Ambassadors, together with the French Ministers of War, Air, and Marine, went down to Normandy from Paris for celebrations in which contingents of French troops joined.

For the British, the main ceremony was naturally under the cliffs at Arromanches, where out to sea the remains of the prefabricated harbour, that amazing achievement which confounded the enemy, are still to be seen. Here a religious service was held, attended by detachments from the three fighting forces

The Canadian act of remembrance was at Bernières, and an official luncheon was given at Bayeux, a little town of memory for the thousands of British troops who whiled away their few leisure hours in its narrow streets during the bitter weeks of fighting in the Bocage.

THE TIMES, JUNE 7, 1945

D-Day+10. René Coty, Président of France, lays his wreath at the newly-completed cemetery at Bayeux.

Official representatives of eight Allied nations, headed by M. Coty, President of the French Republic, have been spending two days commemorating, at different points in Normandy, the 10th anniversary of the Allied landings in 1944.

The Allied delegations were headed by Sir Gladwyn Jebb, for Britain, Senator Cabot Lodge, for the United States, Mr Jean Desy, for Canada, M. Spaak, for Belgium, Hr Antword, for Norway, M. Als, for Luxembourg, and Mr Staf, for Holland. The British Service representatives accompanying Sir Gladwyn Jebb included Marshal of the Royal Air Force Sir John Slessor, General Sir John Crocker, Air Chief Marshal Sir James Robb, Admiral Sir Geoffrey Oliver, Air Chief Marshal Sir Francis Fogarty, and Air Chief Marshal Sir Basil Embry.

The President of the Republic arrived at Bayeux by train from Paris with M. Laniel, the Prime Minister, early on Saturday afternoon, and attended a solemn Te Deum at the Cathedral.

The long column of cars then took the road to Arromanches, where the President passed in review troops of eight nations before cutting the symbolic ribbon and inaugurating the new Musée du Débarquement which has been formed there to commemorate the landings.

Sir Gladwyn Jebb read a message from Sir Winston Churchill, in which he sent greetings to the French people, and paid a special tribute to 'the vital help contributed by those brave and devoted men, those units and groups of the Resistance working secretly, at the peril of their lives, with skill and daring to prepare the way for their compatriots and their allies. The British Government', Sir Winston Churchill said, 'had taken keen pleasure in contributing to the creation of the museum; and he expressed the hope that it would also 'symbolise the lasting friendship which unites, in peacetime as in time of war, the French and British peoples'.

President Eisenhower's message on the 10th anniversary said: 'That combined land-sea-air operation was made possible by the joint labours of co-operating nations. It depended for its success upon the skill, determination, and self-sacrifice of men from several lands. It set in motion a chain of events which affected the history of the entire world. In spite of the losses and suffering involved in that human effort, and in the epic conflict of which it was a part, we, today, find in those experiences reasons for hope and inspiration. They remind us particularly of the accomplishments attainable through close co-operation and friendship among free peoples striving toward a common goal.

'Some of my most cherished memories of that campaign are those of friendly co-operation with such distinguished military leaders of foreign lands as Field-Marshal Lord Montgomery, Admiral Ramsay, Marshal of the Royal Air Force Lord Tedder, Marshal de Lattre de Tassigny, Marshal Juin, and Marshal Leclerc. I recall my pleasant association with the outstanding Soviet soldier Marshal Zhukov and the victorious meeting at the Elbe of the armies of the west and of the east.

'These lessons of unity and co-operation have by no means been lost in the trying period of reconstruction since the fighting stopped; rather, the free peoples, once bitter enemies, burying their antagonisms and joining together to meet the problems of the post-war world.

'If all those nations which were members of the grand alliance have not maintained in time of peace the spirit of that wartime union; if some of the people who were our comrades in arms have been kept apart, that is cause for profound regret but not for despair. The courage, devotion and faith which brought us through the perils of war will inevitably bring us success in our unremitting search for peace, security, and freedom.'

THE TIMES, JUNE 7, 1954

The American D-Day commemoration ceremonies were held this afternoon at Omaha and Utah beaches, where the American forces landed 25 years ago tomorrow under command of General Omar Bradley. Now aged 78, General Bradley made a point of attending today, both on the beaches and at the cemetery at Colleville, where more than 9,000 American dead lie buried on a bluff, facing the open sea. The Normandy weather, which had been characteristically inclement all day, relented for the occasion, and the sun broke out towards the evening, when officials and troops were gathered to commemorate the landings at Utah.

The weather had matched the restored climate in relations between France and the United States, so that these ceremonies could be held in the pure spirit of comradeship in arms, without afterthought or misgiving on either side.

Along the coast road linking up the landing beaches, many houses and village war memorials were touchingly decorated with small French and American flags — a proof that the Normans have not forgotten, although it is hard to believe now that this peaceful, verdant countryside, which resembles parts of southern England, saw some of the fiercest fighting in the Second World War.

Nature and time have healed the wounds inflicted by men, but the memorials and cemeteries are there to remind them of the great armada which was the prelude to the liberation of Europe.

At Vierville, by the memorial to the dead of the American National Guard, M. Triboulet, Général de Gaulle's first commissioner for the liberated territories, declared in a speech that the flags of all the 50 States of the Union flying there today represented the huge cohorts which had come to deliver France and Europe 25 years ago. The people of Normandy, massed on the bluff overlooking the memorial, had come to tell the National Guard veterans: 'Your names are engraved in Normandy in something more durable than stone — in the hearts of the Normans. The Norman people will remember and will be grateful through the centuries.'

Among the other official guests were the Ambassadors of the United States, the Netherlands, Belgium and Norway, senior French and Allied military officers, including General Sir Richard Gale, and representatives of local French authorities.

THE TIMES, JUNE 6, 1969

Another British invasion of Normandy came to a peak today with ceremonies marking the 25th anniversary of the D-Day landings. More than 1,000 men of the three armed Services are here for official commemorations along the invasion beaches. Thousands of old soldiers have converged on the area for more-intimate regimental reunions, mingling, as ever, with the unforgetful inhabitants. For there is magic in a 25th anniversary. After this one, we shall have to wait for the 50th and far fewer will then be left who landed on D-Day.

It was on just such a day as this 25 years ago — not so sunny, perhaps, but a day of high wind — that elements of the 29 British D-Day regiments carried the beaches and pushed inland a few miles along winding Normandy lanes.

Odd fragments of memory come back as one drives past these once murderous hedgerows, though today there is curiously little familiar, save the memorials and war graves, in these gay, spick and span villages where the Allied flags once more stand out in the sea breeze.

Here in Ouistreham there was an immaculate parade of British and French troops, attended by Mr Christopher Soames, the British Ambassador in Paris, and a large group of Allied civil and military officials.

The 1st Battalion, The Royal Hampshire Regiment, whose predecessors were among the first ashore in Normandy, has been under canvas here all the week, to the delight of the people of the district; and kindly hosts they were for many of today's visitors.

And what a place of memory was Pegasus Bridge, across the Caen canal, taken intact by men of 6th Airborne Division as part of their night mission to secure the Allied left flank. It was in these innocent-looking meadows that their gliders crash-landed.

General Sir Richard Gale, who commanded the division and who himself landed by glider, was there for today's brief commemoration.

THE TIMES, JUNE 7, 1969

Left: **Headquarters for the 50th anniversary World War II Commemoration Team was at Empress State Building on Earls Court Road.** *Right:* **The team was led by Brigadier Tom Longland (third from left, front row), former battalion commander in the Royal Anglian Regiment and more recently CO of 3 Brigade in Northern Ireland. Wing Commander Malcolm Carlyle was the RAF representative co-ordinating tri-service planning, marketing, sponsorship, and the fly-pasts, while Commander David Alexander was the Royal Navy planning officer for the Portsmouth end and the flotilla. The Army was represented by Major Helen Merrington-Rust, covering events in Normandy. The team was also tasked with planning appropriate celebrations to mark the 50th anniversary of the end of the war in Europe to be held in May 1995 and the Far East in August 1995.**

It rapidly became apparent that our major partners in the D-Day operation were also at the very beginning of their planning, and visits to the French, American and Canadian authorities quickly revealed that, while we were all agreed that something had to be done, there was no outline plan for us all to work to.

The Americans had already appointed Lieutenant General Claude M. Kicklighter as head of their World War II Commemoration Committee in July 1991, a month after he had retired from the US Army's Pacific Command. His 35-man staff, working from a small office in Crystal City in Arlington, Virginia, was essentially military inasmuch as it had been the intention of President Bush to place the commemorative ceremonies under military control. This allowed the committee to stage relatively low-cost events across America by involving local military commands to underwrite the costs.

General Kicklighter's budget was $2.8 million (£1.3 million), and he described his work as 'a labour of love'. The purpose of his committee was, he said, 'to thank and honor the veterans of World War II, their families, especially families who lost loved ones, and remember those who served on the home front, who turned America into the "Arsenal of Democracy".'

In Canada, my opposite number was Colonel John Gardam who was acting under a similar briefing, while the French commemorations were under the guidance of Philippe Mestre, the Ministre de Anciens Combattants et Victimes de Guerre.

Headquarters for US Navy participation was established in the HQ of the US Navy in Europe at No. 20 Grosvenor Square, London. When we were having difficulty pinpointing General Eisenhower's office (see page 632), we contacted Dick James who had worked in the building from 1942-44. Dick married an English girl and made his home in the UK after the war, and was only too pleased to accompany us on a return visit. Having worked in the G-2 section, just down the corridor from Eisenhower, he was able to go straight to the spot ***(left)*** **on the first (US second) floor where, by an amazing coincidence and completely unbeknown to the present staff, the conference room** ***(right)*** **for D-Day 1994 had been set up! Lieutenant Patrick Holub (left) describes coming events to your Editor (right), watched by Dick James and DMI (SW) Mark Hopkins.**

HMS *Dryad* had already planned to open the Map Room in Southwick House to the public in the anniversary year but, because it is an active base, visitors were to be bussed in through the main gate. *Left:* June 6, 1944. General Eisenhower leaves in his Cadillac for his command post 'Sharpener (see page 33) via the rear entrance (see also page 168). *Right:* Although they do not realise it, 50 years later members of the public are ushered along the same back road to the house.

Very quickly, the nucleus of the British planning team was drawn together and, after considering and discarding a vast range of ideas, it was decided that the focus for the events for commemorating the D-Day landings had to be the south coast of England, the Channel and Normandy. It also became clear that to give some structure to the events, we would have to relate them to the actual phases of the operation itself. After much discussion, we hit upon the device of commemorating the planning of the operation with a garden party at Southwick House, just outside Portsmouth, as a parallel to the time when it had been Admiral Ramsay's headquarters and the venue for the pre-invasion meetings between the commanders. This would then be followed by a Beating of Retreat at Whale Island in Portsmouth harbour to commemorate the embarkation of the forces, with a State Dinner in Portsmouth itself to mark the full range of forces committed to Operation 'Overlord'.

After the Battle reader Peter Thompson was one of those visitors and he took this picture of crew members from the American Liberty Ship *Jeremiah O'Brien* being given a guided tour of the Map Room after the ship arrived at Portsmouth late on the evening of Saturday, May 21.

The *Jeremiah O'Brien* was one of three ex-WWII Liberty Ships preserved in the United States which were due to sail to Europe, but *John W. Brown* never left US waters and the *Lane Victory* had to abort her voyage at Panama due to engine problems. Having left San Francisco on April 18, 1994, to an enthusiastic send-off, her arrival in Portsmouth *(left)*, after a month at sea, was pretty low-key. Part of the problem was that the South Railway Jetty lies within the Naval Dockyard with its tight security, so few visitors were on hand to greet her and her amazing veteran crew, whose average age was not far short of that of her 78-year-old skipper, Captain George Jahn. *Right:* First man ashore: Bill Conannon of Portland, Oregon, one of the 450 — 50 per cent of whom were World War II veterans — who had volunteered to bring the ship to Britain.

Of the many special exhibitions arranged to commemorate D-Day, one of the most significant was that organised at the Airborne Forces Museum at Aldershot where a mock-up of Pegasus Bridge had been constructed in the gymnasium. *Left:* On April 27, Richard Todd, who portrayed Major Howard in ***The Longest Day*** (see page 228), cut the ribbon in the presence of the real John Howard. *Right:* The press then pictured both men in front of the museum's Dakota.

Finally, those who lost their lives in the operation would be remembered in a large Drumhead Service on Southsea Common attended by all the Heads of State of those nations that took part.

Having completed the events within the UK, we would then sail a massive flotilla of ships across the Channel while the aircraft of all those involved carried out the largest multi-national fly-past seen in recent years.

A mass parachute drop in France by British and American airborne forces would follow. Then, once off the shores of Normandy, we would land the flags of the participating nations, which had earlier been used at the Drumhead Service, on the beach at Arromanches as a symbolic re-enactment of the actual assault.

The remainder of June 6 would be given over to a series of Services of Remembrance in the various military cemeteries in Normandy, culminating with the veterans marching past Her Majesty The Queen on the beach at Arromanches.

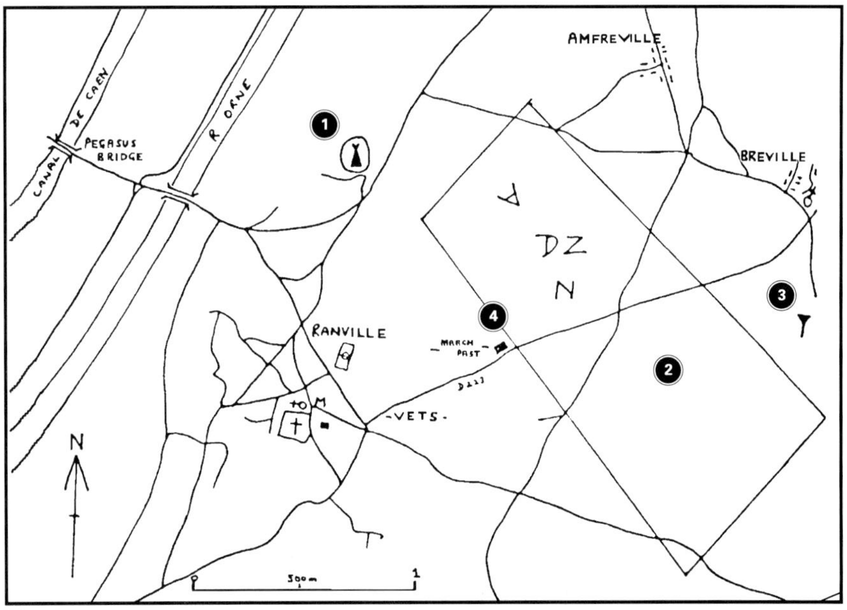

The press briefing which followed the opening ceremony, was conducted by Major Simon Barry, the Regimental Adjutant of the Parachute Regiment, with all the wit and humour that the British officer calls upon for such occasions. 'Our job is not invading Europe', Major Barry began, 'it's been done before. It is to commemorate in a fitting manner the achievements of the Parachute Regiment.' Displaying this sketch map *(right)* of the area — and alluding to the problems which some veterans were then experiencing over pre-booked hotel accommodation in France not being honoured — he pointed out various features: 'These [1] are our bivouac areas and no one is gazumping on these bookings at the moment!' The drop-zone [2], appropriately labelled as DZ 'N', also lay across the northern part of the LZ 'N' of June 1944 (see page 215), and Major Barry explained that power lines nearby would be turned off and that cameramen would be allowed on top of the nearby water tower [3] although he advised them that they would be shooting into the sun. The drop-zone reviewing stand [4] for the Prince of Wales to inspect the regiment was also indicated on the map. He warned that if too many people strayed onto the DZ, the RAF would abort the drop and that minimum weather requirements were 13 knots. 'The drop will take place from 800 feet with the aircraft flying NW-SE, and 150 Canadians, 700 Brits and a few Poles are expected — 800 parachutists in all. They will load 50 per aircraft and exit 25 from each door. Finally', quipped Major Barry, 'the regiment was only responsible for the Ranville area and anything west of the Caen Canal was "a box of Frogs"!'

Arriving at the concept was relatively easy; turning it into reality was considerably more difficult. Meetings in Paris quickly made it obvious that we would have to co-ordinate the whole programme in Normandy very closely with the French authorities but their plans at that stage were somewhat fluid. Negotiations with the American team revealed that although their planning was now moving on apace, it was, sadly, not always in the same direction as ours! Fortunately, French élan and American attention to detail gave us a happy combination of what had to be achieved and how it might be done. The British and Canadian approach remained strictly practical and, throughout a frantic 18 months, the national plans, the forces required, and the veterans slowly came together.

On January 6, 1994, the Prime Minister, John Major, outlined details of HM Government's support for the 50th anniversary during a launch ceremony held at the Imperial War Museum. Representatives of the various veterans' organisations were present, but first the scene was set by showing the assembled guests and members of the press a short film produced by John Symons of the Services Sound Vision Corporation titled *This Great Adventure*. Then Mr Major read the statement which we had prepared on his behalf:

'Ladies and gentlemen, the film could not have put it more clearly: D-Day — 50 years ago — began the deciding battle for the future of Europe.

'The veterans present today were among the over 130,000 who took part in the invasion: the largest amphibious attack in history and the greatest combined land, sea and air operation of the war. They did so in dreadful conditions, with extraordinary determination and courage. If they had lost, our world would be different. But they did not. And their success turned the D-Day landings into one of the great events of history.

'To mark their achievement, this country, together with France and the other countries which took part in the D-Day landings, intends to hold a massive programme of commemorative events both here and in Normandy between 4 and 6 June. These events will involve Heads of State or Government from most of the Allied nations plus many thousands of veterans of the D-Day landings together with service widows.

'Our commemorations will remember the sacrifice made by some 10,000 British, Canadian and American troops who were either killed or wounded on D-Day. By September, Allied casualties were to rise to 210,000 with 37,000 dead. But, by then, most of France had been liberated and Operation "Overlord" was well on its way towards the restoration of peace in Europe.

'These events we are planning will give pride of place to the men who suffered the fire and fear of that remarkable day. The final order to launch the invasion was issued by

Prime Minister John Major pictured at the Imperial War Museum on January 6, 1994 at the official announcement of the British government's plans for commemorating D-Day. Four months later, the Armed Forces Minister, Jeremy Hanley, confirmed that the Ministry of Defence expenditure on the anniversary events was expected to reach £4 million.

Meanwhile, the debate continued over whether or not to invite an official German representative. Normandy estimated that it might receive up to six million visitors over the coming months, including 100,000 veterans including ex-members of the Wehrmacht, and the Mayor of Caen, Jean-Marie Girault, was in favour of inviting the German Chancellor. Helmut Kohl had not been invited to the 40th anniversary in 1984, and the French government, with the consent of Britain and the United States, once again decided against extending an invitation, French officials explaining that it would provoke a strong protest from veterans. The resulting argument between France and Germany resulted in the Chancellor cancelling a planned parade to mark the departure of Allied troops from Berlin in September. The Russians also wanted to attend (and with some justification as a meaningful proportion of the Axis forces in Normandy were from the Soviet Union) but they, too, were excluded. ***Above:*** **In the event, Major Michael Heim brought his Bundeswehr platoon to Normandy to attend an act of remembrance on June 4 at La Cambe (see page 695), claiming: 'We are here on our holidays. We are not official.'**

On April 13, at the first public event, Mr Major dedicated Grosvenor Square as a permanent D-Day Garden of Remembrance. ***Left:*** **Dame Vera Lynn was on hand to sing her wartime songs *The White Cliffs of Dover* and *We'll Meet Again*, much enjoyed by US veterans *(right)* including again, on the right, Dick James.**

General Eisenhower at Southwick House, outside Portsmouth. On 4 June therefore, we will entertain there 1,000 veterans of the D-Day landings. We hope the guest of honour will be Her Majesty the Queen Mother.

'Also on 4 June, Her Majesty The Queen will hold a dinner in the Portsmouth Guildhall for 500 people including the Heads of State or Government of those countries that took part in the operation. Other guests will include members of the armed services, the civilian services, voluntary organisations and those who designed and built the specialised equipment such as the Mulberry harbours.

'On the morning of 5 June, there will be an open air commemorative service in Portsmouth which will be open to all. That afternoon, a flotilla of ships will cross the Channel. It will be led by Her Majesty The Queen and Heads of State or Government from participating nations on board the Royal Yacht, escorted by an armada of small craft. During the crossing, the flotilla will be overflown by an International Fly-past including aircraft which took part in the Battle of Britain or supported the D-Day landings from the air. Also that afternoon, approximately 1,000 paratroops, including servicemen from

With its long association with the USA, the square was already the setting for the Franklin D. Roosevelt Memorial, financed by public subscription in 1946. Now it was the intention to remodel the surround, and this artist's impression was released to show how it might look when completed.

Two months later, on the afternoon of June 3, the memorial was the setting for a reunion of SHAEF veterans sponsored by the US Navy. ***Left:*** **The colour party rehearses under the eagle eyes of two Marine security officers.** ***Right:*** **The veterans are addressed by General George A. Joulwan, Supreme Allied Commander Europe, Eisenhower's present-day counterpart.**

Apart from the events being planned by Brigadier Longland's team, which were firmly centred on the veterans, the Department of National Heritage proposed widening their appeal to encompass civilian 'celebrations', and these were announced by the Prime Minister in Grosvenor Square in March. A public relations firm had been brought in to suggest ideas which were based on nation-wide street parties and a 'family day' to be held in Hyde Park in July. When a report of the announcement was broadcast that evening on BBC *Newsnight*, it created a furore amongst ex-servicemen who viewed it as trivialising a day when their thoughts would be on remembrance, not frivolity. The mood of the Normandy veterans had been completely misjudged, and vehement pressure and a vigorous press campaign *(right)* led to the postponement of plans for civilian events to their more rightful place in concert with celebrations for the 50th anniversary of VE-Day in May 1995.

Veterans win a victory over D-Day revels

By Philip Johnston and Ben Fenton

D FOR DECORATION

Vera Lynn threatens to join boycott

Ministers in retreat over D-Day plans

By Arthur Leathley and Philip Webster

Lord Bramall

...niversary of the liberation of Normandy should be celebrated

Disgruntled veterans blame Tories for D-Day 'muddle'

Drop party, say D-Day veterans

By Philip Johnston, Political Correspondent

Veterans agree on D-Day compromise

By Philip Johnston

Celebrations that struck the wrong note

By Philip Johnston
Richard Spencer

Canada, France and Poland, will parachute into the area of the Pegasus Bridge in Normandy.

'On 6 June there will be a national service of commemoration in the British cemeteries in Normandy. This will be followed by a march-past of veterans in Arromanches. These events have been co-ordinated with the French Government who are organising an international ceremony at Omaha Beach on 6 June. As in 1944, co-operation and joint planning will be the key to success. We have therefore established close links and co-ordination with all the nations intending to commemorate D-Day in Normandy.

'Although it is too early for us to have a full list of those participating, we are expecting President Clinton, Prime Minister Chrétien and of course President Mitterand — who will be hosting the events of French soil — to take part in many of the events; and other Heads of State or Government, including President Walesa and King Harald of Norway, will also be present.

'I must emphasise that these events are merely illustrative of many others that are being organised to commemorate the D-Day landings. During them we will not forget the effort and sacrifice of men and women throughout the Forces, throughout industry, and throughout our nation who combined towards the military success.

'So the 50th anniversary of D-Day is a huge national event and I intend it to be celebrated on a national scale. Many towns and villages across the United Kingdom are already organising their own commemorative events. We expect many more to do so. Events are already planned in all parts of the Kingdom. We will be announcing further events in the months to come.

'All under 50 will have no direct memory of these great events. But it is to the success of D-Day that they owe the peace, security and freedom we have enjoyed since 1945 and which we all take for granted. So we hope and intend to stir the imagination of everyone to what was done.

'Ladies and gentlemen, in our film you heard General Montgomery say, "In the better days that lie ahead men will speak with pride of our doings". Next June, 50 years on, we will redeem that promise and do just that.'

On April 13, with our plans for the national commemorations firmed up, the Prime Minister made a further announcement in Grosvenor Square, London. Owned by the Duke of Westminster, His Grace had kindly agreed to make it available not only for the launch of our programme but also that the square should be refurbished as a permanent memorial to the 50th anniversary of D-Day.

Two days later, Viscount Cranborne, the Government Minister with responsibility for the D-Day commemorative programme, launched the D-Day 'roadshow'. This was part of the Government's plan to raise public awareness of the anniversary, and the mobile trailer display was scheduled to visit ten cities over the following three months. A similar touring exhibit was put together by General Kicklighter's team in the US where three 20-foot trailers, each manned by a World War II committee member having an understanding of the Second World War, were available on request for attendance at events in America.

One of the first unofficial anniversary commemorations took place on April 28 at Slapton Sands where 12 American survivors of the German S-Boat attack (see pages 188-190) met around the Sherman tank memorial established there by a local hotelier, Ken Small. Ken felt so strongly that the hundreds of US servicemen who lost their lives on Exercise 'Tiger' should be remembered by a specific memorial that, back in the 1970s, he purchased a DD Sherman which had once belonged to the 70th Tank Battalion, but then lay submerged three-quarters of a mile offshore, having gone down during exercises in 1944. Just before the 40th anniversary of D-Day, it was raised and brought ashore (see *After the Battle* No. 45) and preserved on a suitable spot facing the sea. It was dedicated on November 9, 1984.

'As the world prepared to commemorate the 50th anniversary of D-Day, a small group of Brits and Americans gathered in a tiny village in southern England to dedicate a memorial to American airmen.' So wrote Major Dan Piper of the Ground Liaison Office of the 437th Airlift Wing, present-day successor to the wartime 437th Troop Carrier Group of the Ninth Air Force. 'The airmen honored were from the 437th TCG, participants in campaigns leading to the defeat of Nazi Germany. As the Allies prepared for the Normandy landings in 1944, the 437th TCG, based in Ramsbury, was busy practising airdrop and glider-towing operations for its eventual rôle carrying paratroopers into France. On March 11, 1944, during a training mission, a Horsa glider prematurely broke free from the tow plane and landed in a field near the sleepy village of Axford in Wiltshire. Major Donald Bradley, 83rd Troop Carrier Squadron commander and his co-pilot, 1st Lieutenant Gaylord Strong, flew one of the unit's C-47s to recover the glider and return to the training base. Accompanying Bradley was flight surgeon Captain Lee Gillette acting as observer. Tragically, while pulling the glider from the field, the C-47 struck telephone wires and crashed into the River Kennet, killing both pilots and severely injuring Gillette. Neil Stevens, a local historian interested in the American forces based in the area during World War II, began searching for the crash site in 1990. After three months of investigation, a metal detector revealed a small piece of aircraft wreckage. Stevens then tracked down the sole survivor, Dr Gillette, and suggested a memorial be erected at the site. On May 28, a special marker was officially dedicated.' *Left:* Grouped around the memorial are Robert F. Maycan, 85th Troop Carrier Squadron radio operator; Neil Stevens; Charles Waltman, 84th TCS pilot; Max Demuth, 85th TCS navigator, and Dr Lee Gillette, the 83rd TCS surgeon and survivor of the crash. A fly-past was provided by a 437th Airllift Wing C-141, specially flown over from the States, an RAF C-130, a C-47 from the Battle of Britain Memorial Flight, and *(right)* Ken Wakefield's L4, seen here refuelling at the small grass strip which remains at Ramsbury (see *Airfields of the Ninth Then and Now*). As Neil commented, 'it was probably the first time the stars and bars had been seen at Ramsbury on a genuine wartime aircraft since the departure of the 437th TCG in 1945.'

Jim Stockdale's L4 (480752) featured in another nostalgic re-enactment which took place after all the D-Day commemorative events were over. Henry Wills took the photograph: 'On June 25-26, Jim Stockdale flew his Piper L4 into Butcher's Field at Breamore House, Hampshire, to mark its use by General Patton as the HQ of the "phantom" US First Army held in England to bluff the Germans that another landing would take place in the Pas-de-Calais area. This actual field was used by US Army L4s for some weeks during the D-Day operations and the re-enactment brought out the older villagers who remembered the L4s buzzing low over the village. As I left the field and turned to look back, it brought a wonderful nostalgic feeling to see the L4 in an English meadow in high summer: thinking that this was exactly how it could have been 50 years ago!'

Another troop carrier memorial was unveiled on June 2 at the service station (westbound) on the M4 motorway which now scythes across the north-eastern corner of Membury airfield, occupied in 1944 by the 436th Troop Carrier Group. A nice touch with ceremonial involving present-day American forces is that the color parties parade with the wartime M-1 Garand rifle.

The 'other events' to which the Prime Minister alluded were outlined in our own press release and included a wide range of activities heralded by a special exhibition which was to open at the Imperial War Museum on February 18. Local events, centred mainly in the southern counties, included an Army Air Corps display at Middle Wallop (in June 1944 the headquarters of the US IX Fighter Command); D-Day Rallies at Plymouth (May 22), Netley (May 27-29), Portsmouth (May 28-30), Torbay (May 29), and Salisbury, Bushy Park and Dartmouth on May 30.

In June, events had been planned locally at Poole (June 1-3), Shepton Mallet (June 1-4), Salcombe (June 2), Weymouth (June 2-4), the Isle of Wight (June 2-4), Plymouth (June 2-6), Gosport (June 3-5), Portsmouth (June 3-6), Milford Haven (June 4-6), to list but a few of those whose timetables had already been notified to us although we would not be involved in the actual organisation of local events.

Left: Later the same day, a commemoration was held around the memorial at Welford, the departure point for Major-General Maxwell Taylor, attended by many 101st Airborne veterans (see also page 296). *Right:* One unexpected 'veteran' was none other than Winston Churchill in the guise of local impresario Joe Mahoney from Swindon.

Harwell (see pages 220-223) hosted its annual service at the memorial stone which marks the end of the runway from which aircraft of No. 38 Group, RAF, took off carrying troops of the 6th Airborne Division. The weather was atrocious on June 4, virtually mirroring conditions 50 years previously. Nevertheless, some 600 persons braved the elements, including Trevor Hancock who took us this picture but, although the Hercules managed a low pass, a planned parachute drop had to be cancelled.

Other colourful veterans of the battle included Thomas J. Nongueskwa *(left)*, a native American. Together with other US vets, he attended at the D-Day Dinner Dance at Sopley, the former RAF camp at Bransgrove near Christchurch, now preserved *(right)*, before travelling to France where he was much-photographed at the official Omaha Beach ceremony.

One of the most interesting veteran reunions had taken place on April 28 when Carolyn Grace flew her restored Spitfire ML407 over the Normandy beaches, her aircraft being credited with shooting down the first German aircraft on D-Day. The Spitfire had been originally built in 1944 as a single-seat LF.IXC and had been delivered to No. 485 Squadron, Royal New Zealand Air Force, on April 29 by Air Transport Auxiliary ferry pilot, Jackie Sorour. Now Mrs Jackie Moggridge, she was able to accompany Carolyn on the historic flight back to France as the Spitfire was later converted to a T9 two-seat trainer. The following day, on the actual anniversary of the delivery flight, Carolyn picked up Jackie from North Weald en route for Duxford. *Right:* Then, at the Great Warbirds D-Day Air Display at Wroughton, Wiltshire, on June 11-12, Henry Wills pictured Jackie, left, and Carolyn together with Johnnie Houlton who had shot down the Ju 88 on D-Day.

Equally veterans of the 'Overlord' operation were the ex-Southern railway locos Class S15 No. 828 *(left)* together with the King Arthur Class No. 777 *Sir Lamiel (right)*, both of which had been based at Salisbury in 1944. On June 4 and 5, 1994, the engines operated a shuttle D-Day Invasion Express from Salisbury to the Ocean Terminal at Southampton where the *Jeremiah O'Brien* and the aircraft carrier USS *Guam* were on view.

A very significant commemorations was organised by the Royal Parks Agency, custodians of Bushy Park. As has been recounted earlier (pages 23-29), this was the location of SHAEF's main headquarters in 1944, yet the only memorial which existed in the park was to the US air forces which had also been based in the long-demolished camp. Therefore, a tribute to its use by Supreme Allied Headquarters was long overdue, and it was an event which Brigadier Longland's team gave their full support. *Above left:* On May 30, representative bands from the United States, Canada and Great Britain led the parade along Chestnut Avenue, which in 1944 was lined with huts (see plan pages 24-25), and into the park where the plaque marking the position of General Eisenhower's office was unveiled *(above right)* by the American Ambassador, Admiral William J. Crowe, Jr. It was fortunate that the admiral was available as he had served in the 1950s as an assistant naval aide to President Eisenhower, and had been with the General on the 10th anniversary of D-Day. He gave his speech standing on the very spot where Commander Butcher must have stood in 1944. 'As we review the surroundings today', he said, 'it is difficult to imagine the park as it was during those hectic days. Most importantly, it was a graphic example of the personnel of different countries, who had different perspectives and backgrounds, overcoming their cultural differences and solving their problems in the name of a common cause . . . the nerve centre of the D-Day team was right here on this spot.'

A moving ceremony was held beside the Commando Monument which stands in an elevated position in Inverness-shire above Spean Bridge, overlooking a vast expanse of windswept Scottish moorland. Commando training was carried out in the region during the war with a headquarters established at nearby Achnacarry Castle by courtesy of Sir Donald Cameron of Locheil, Chief of the Clan Cameron, whose residence it remains to this day. The memorial was unveiled by Queen Elizabeth The Queen Mother in September 1952, six months after the death of King George VI.

Even further afield, Australians commemorated D-Day in a ceremony held at the Shrine of Remembrance in Melbourne with appropriately-attired members of the Victoria Police Force on parade with Lee-Enfields. Most Australians who took part in June 1944 were serving in bombing and strafing operations. Others helped ferry men ashore, and a handful were junior officers attached to the British Army. In all, it is estimated that one in every hundred men who took part in D-Day were Australians. David Green took the photos.

Canadians, on the other hand, made up 20 per cent of the forces operating on D-Day. This display of military vehicles, pictured by Ken Johnson near the Parliament building in Ottawa, added to the events there on D-Day weekend.

By now, our main Operation Order for the events for which we were responsible had grown to over 750 pages. Its formal introduction was by Admiral Sir Michael Layard, the Second Sea Lord and Commander-in-Chief, Naval Home Command, who had 'the responsibility for co-ordinating — with Commander-in-Chief Fleet, Commander-in-Chief United Kingdom Land Forces and the Air Officer Commanding-in-Chief Strike Command — the operations of naval, land and air forces of all nations participating in the programme of government-sponsored events which are to take place within or above the land area of the UK (excluding events in London), French and British territorial waters and international sea and air space'.

The contents of the order mirrored many of the facets in Admiral Ramsay's 'Neptune' operation; the 'enemy' now being the perceived threat from terrorist organisations which might seek to take advantage to strike in the spotlight of the world's media. However, it was believed that the attractiveness of the events to the prime threat to UK forces — the Provisional Irish Republican Army — would be mitigated by the presence of foreign nationals and the adverse effect of the possibility of large-scale civilian casualties. With the main UK event centred on Portsmouth, overall security would rest with the Hampshire Constabulary although the Flag Officer Portsmouth's Area Security Officer would be responsible for security within HMS *Dryad* (Southwick) and HMS *Excellent* (Whale Island). Protection of the Heads of State (designated VVIPs) rested with the Metropolitan Police and officers of the visiting nations involved.

The Map Room at Southwick House was scheduled to be opened to the public for several weeks during the summer of 1994, although all private vehicles were to be excluded, visitors leaving their cars in a car park outside the entrance and being brought inside by coach. The actual library in which the 1944 'go/no go' meetings took place (see page 165), now the wardroom of HMS *Dryad*, was closed to the public who only saw a display centred on the Map Room. Security sweeps of HMS *Excellent* began on May 31 and at HMS *Dryad* the following day.

An illustration of the hectic sequence of events at Portsmouth during the days preceding events is illustrated in the following summary from our orders. All times were given in 'Z' (Zulu) time (GMT) with local times added in parenthesis for events which were to take place across different time zones for clarity. During the course of the operation, Britain would be on British Summer Time or 'A' (Alpha) time and

Above: **Preserved military vehicles were the centrepiece of many events. Back in the UK, an impressive street parade was held in Weymouth on June 4. Bovington Tank Museum provided the leading Sherman, an M4A2 (76mm) with American crew. Behind, a Canadian Grizzly, masquerading as an M4A1, owned and driven by Margaret Gillatt and her all-girl crew.** *Below:* **Not quite an exact comparison but, nevertheless, a nice matching shot of the Normandy veterans' marching past in the footsteps of the Rangers we saw on the same stretch of road on page 328.**

First on parade in Normandy: the 'Hackney Gurkhas' who returned to Bernières a month before anyone else. 'We were always the first ones there', said one veteran with an almighty wink. Unable to find accommodation in Normandy in June, Major Eric Gibbard organised the pilgrimage of the 5th Battalion of the Royal Berkshire Regiment for the beginning of May. The battalion — formerly the 10th City of London (TA) — was attached to the Berkshires between the wars, yet it retained its old nickname when the men formed the core of No. 8 Beach Group, landing with the Canadian 3rd Division. Previously, the men had received no permanent recognition as for a long time the French were under the impression that the Royal Berkshire Regiment was part of the Canadian Army and so were covered by existing memorials. Now their senior officer, Major Michael Pardoe, unveiled a plaque on the casemate on the beach (the one on page 485). The 26 veterans on parade came to attention . . . a moment's reflection before the command: 'By the left, quick march!'

France on Continental Summer Time which would be 'B' (Bravo) time. Thus 1200Z was 1300A in England and 1400B in France.

Wed 1 June
0800 SOUTHSEA COMMON Commence military compound/press compound construction inc. tents/barriers/signposts etc.
EXCELLENT Erect tents on main areas. Helo landing site prepared. PA system rigged and tested
DRYAD Implement security on VIP routes and begin security close down of HMS DRYAD
SOUTHSEA COMMON PA System to be rigged and tested
DRYAD Mark out Helo landing sites and routes to Southwick House. Signs put up for all routes
DRYAD Access for normal route contractors to cease
1300 DRYAD Briefing for guides and service hosts
1400 DRYAD Rehearsal

Thu 2 June
0700 to 1200 DRYAD CBS Broadcasting from the lawns of Southwick House
Media OBVs arrive am
0800 SOUTHSEA COMMON Portsmouth City Council to erect barriers/toilets etc.
0800 EXCELLENT Mast Manning mast to be rigged
AM EXCELLENT Full rehearsal
1000 EXCELLENT All manpower areas briefing on TORs [Time of Review] ready for rehearsal
1500 DRYAD Full rehearsal with bands

Fri 3 June
All Day GUILDHALL Security searches
EXCELLENT Ceremonial training for car door openers and teams
0800 EXCELLENT Commence skirmish
0800 EXCELLENT Signs put up for all routes — arena, assembly area etc.
AM GUILDHALL Dress rehearsal
0900 DRYAD Security sweep of Southwick House and Gardens
DRYAD Ceremonial training for car door openers and teams
DRYAD Position plants and flowers
Site WC at IBM car park
EXCELLENT Set up field kitchens
GUILDHALL Restricted parking in force

Sat 4 June
0800 EXCELLENT Set up litter bins on main arena area
0800 IBM car park facilities set up
0800 DRYAD Security sweep of Southwick House and Gardens
All Day GUILDHALL Security checks
EXCELLENT Install floral decoration
0800 EXCELLENT Fod Plod [Foreign Object Damage Police] prepare helicopter landing site
0800 EXCELLENT Final security sweep of all areas
0800 EXCELLENT Band final rehearsal
1400 Shuttle buses from BR Hilsea Halt and veterans centre to IBM car park commence
By 1200 DRYAD Decision on wet weather routine
1200 DRYAD Team prepare for arrival of veterans
1200 DRYAD Security clearance at IBM for veterans commences at IBM car park, Cosham. Shuttle bus commences
1230 HMS EXCELLENT Car parking marshals and route markers muster for final brief and preps
1240 First shuttle bus arrives DRYAD
1245 DRYAD Hosts talk to veterans
1300 EXCELLENT Lay out red carpet
1310 EXCELLENT Security clearance at IBM for veterans commencing at IBM car park, Cosham. Shuttle bus commences

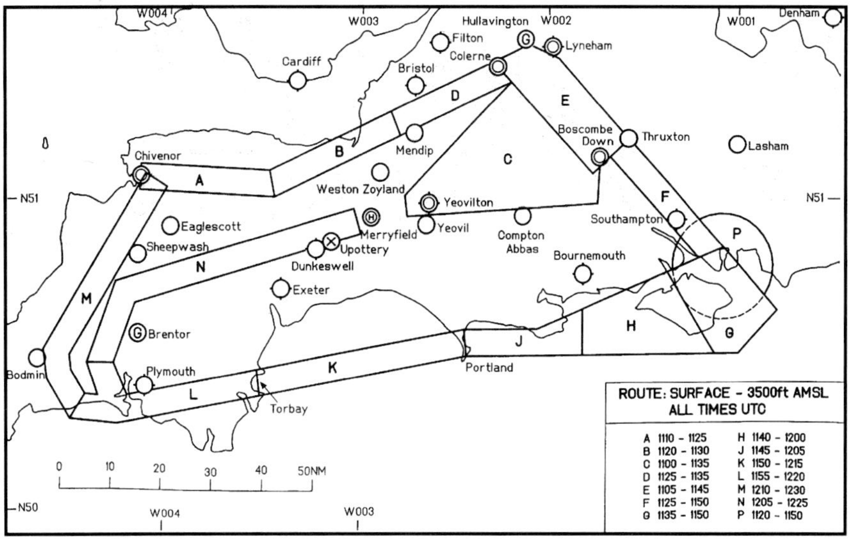

'For reasons of security and to protect four major fly-pasts by large formations of aircraft to commemorate the 50th Anniversary of D-Day in the Portsmouth area during the period 3–6 June 1994, the Secretary of State has introduced Restriction of Flying Regulations under Article 74 of the Air Navigation Order 1989.' So began the preamble to the Aeronautical Information Circular AIC60/1994 issued on May 20. The accompanying maps looked every inch like the operational charts of 1944 . . .

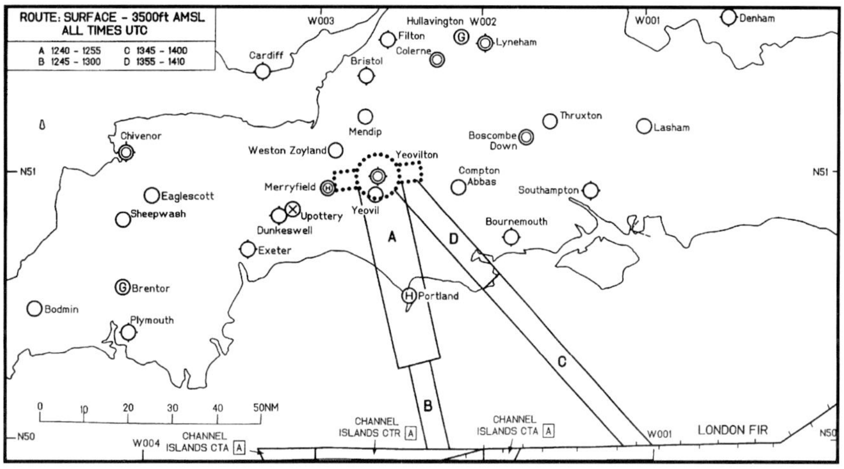

. . . with almost the same approach routes to the drop-zones . . .

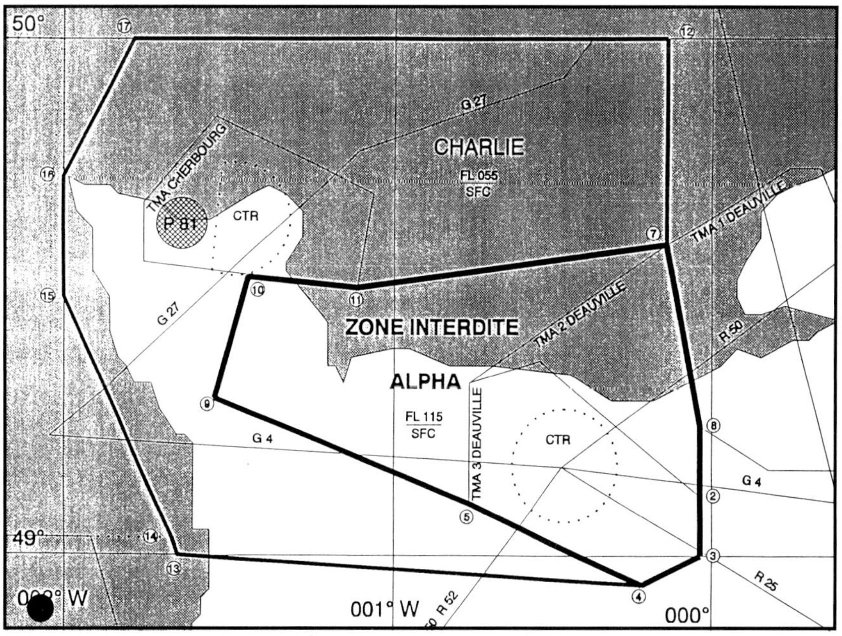

. . . and area of interdiction over the battlefield.

1320 EXCELLENT Hosts muster
1320 EXCELLENT Veterans begin to arrive
1330 EXCELLENT Light refreshment counter opens
1400 DRYAD Incidental music commences
1400 EXCELLENT RMLI Band — Static musical entertainment at the veterans Reception Area
1400 DRYAD Security clearance and processing of veterans and guests ends at IBM car park
1410 DRYAD Last veterans and guests enter
By 1430 DRYAD VIPs arrive
By 1435 DRYAD Secretary of State for Defence arrives
By 1440 DRYAD Foreign Secretary arrives
By 1442 DRYAD Prime Minister arrives
1444 to 1500 DRYAD Heads of State arrive (UK last)
1455 EXCELLENT Band music at reception area finishes.
1455 to 1500 EXCELLENT Narrator gives brief commentary in veteran Reception Area
1500 EXCELLENT Veterans move to main arena
1500 EXCELLENT Helicopter landing site team close up
1500 DRYAD CO accompanies Heads of State into Southwick House
1503 DRYAD The S of S accompanies H of S into Wallmap Room
1505 DRYAD Media move into Wallmap Room via Blue Room doors
1505 EXCELLENT Field kitchens commence serving hot meals
1510 EXCELLENT Narrator commences commentary in main arena
1515 EXCELLENT Skirmish veterans Reception Area/close doors
1515 EXCELLENT Entertainment commences main arena:
RAF Police Dogs — 20 mins
Army Gymnastic Team — 18 mins
VCC Field Gun Teams — 25 mins
1515 DRYAD Garden Party commences
1516 DRYAD H of S meet veterans
1600 DRYAD H of S refreshment
By 1610 DRYAD Prime Minister departs for HMS EXCELLENT
By 1615 EXCELLENT Army Gymnastics Team depart
1615 EXCELLENT Last shuttle bus leaves from Hilsea Halt and veterans Centre
1615 EXCELLENT IBM car park security checks complete. Last shuttle bus departs
1620 EXCELLENT closes to shuttle buses
By 1621 DRYAD H of S depart
By 1623 DRYAD Foreign Sec and S of S depart
1625 DRYAD VIPs depart for EXCELLENT
By 1625 EXCELLENT Prime Minister arrives
By 1630 EXCELLENT Prime Minister prepares to receive H of S in Wardroom
By 1630 EXCELLENT Lord Lieutenant prepares to receive H of S at Wardroom main entrance (ex UK)

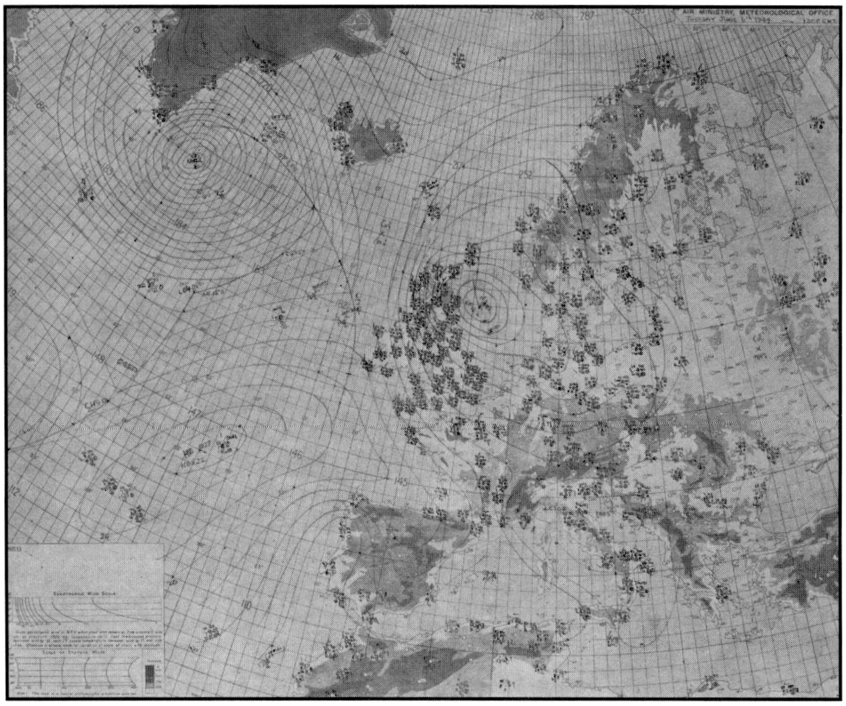

The weather pattern in the days before June 6, 1994, was also very similar to that during the same period in 1944; so much so that one British television forecaster actually put up the wartime chart and read the current weather from it! ***Above:*** **This is the 1944 picture for 1300 hours on June 6 with the 1994 chart** ***below.***

Throughout the planning, one of our main pre-occupations had been with the weather. Foul weather would have left us with rain-sodden ceremonies in England, sea-sick travellers in the Channel and the march past at Arromanches taking place on a flooded beach. In the week preceding the events, the Meteorological Office issued dire warnings that the weather pattern was identical to that of 1944, periods of clear weather interspersed with rain and high winds. Unlike General Eisenhower, however, we were not able to change the date and could only trust to luck.

Lacking the supremo who existed in 1944, a chain of command had to be established for responsibility for the various events, delegated to a single Service two-star HQ. The Portsmouth events were designated the responsibility of the Flag Officer Portsmouth; the Fly-past that of the Senior Air Staff Officer (SASO) Strike Command; the Flotilla that of Flag Officer Surface Flotilla (FOSF), and the events in Normandy to the GOC 3 Division. I was to accompany the Under Secretary of State, Viscount Cranborne, who would make the final 'go/no go' decision if any particular event had to be curtailed or cancelled. During the bulk of the Portsmouth events, my headquarters was at Southampton (Eastleigh) Airport.

Medical facilities had been established to deal with any emergency and, in view of the anticipated 20,000 veterans attending, medical staff were instructed to maintain a strong watching brief and to provide a quick response from First Aid teams. Accident and emergency cover was to be provided at Queen Alexandra Hospital, Cosham, with paramedic-crewed ambulances from the Hampshire Ambulance Service.

Airspace over Portsmouth had already been declared a Temporary Restricted Airspace (TRA) up to 3,500 feet for the period of the commemorations. Known as 'The Portsmouth Zone', it was controlled from the Royal Naval Air Station, Lee-on-Solent (HMS *Daedalus*) for the period of activation: 0800Z May 27 to 1700Z June 6 under the Operation Neptune Display Director, Captain W. K. Benbow, RN.

Helicopter landing sites had been established at HMS *Dryad*, HMS *Excellent*, HMS *Temaraire* (sports field), and HMS *Nelson* (Gunwharf), with the Police Air Support Unit active throughout the TRA period.

The Operational Orders set out anticipated the composition of the aircraft comprising the multi-national fly-past as far as it was then known:

Formation 1. The two Swordfish of the RN Historic Flight are to fly in line abreast. This formation is planned at 90kt groundspeed.

Formation 2. The second formation is to be led by a box comprising the Battle of Britain Memorial Flight Lancaster with an Avenger on the right, the BBMF Hurricane on the left and the RNHF Firefly in the box. One hundred yards astern of the Firefly will be the B-17, with the B-25 a further 100 yards astern, followed by a C-41 a further 100 yards astern. This formation is planned at 150kt groundspeed.

Formation 3. Fighters of the WWII period make up the third formation. The lead element will comprise three Spitfires, followed by [_], flying in low-level battle formation with approximately 75yds between aircraft, the exact spacing to be decided by the formation leader. This formation is planned to transit and hold at 180kt, but to flypast at 210kt groundspeed.

Formation 4. The fourth formation will be 20 Hawk T1s from Nos. 19 and 92 Squadrons, flying in a '50' formation and is planned at 300kt groundspeed.

Formation 5. The fifth formation will be made up, in the main, of box fours of present military fighters, totalling 61 aircraft at 360kt. The lead element will be the Tornado GR1s of No. 13 Squadron flanked by Sea Harriers of No. 899 Squadron, FAA.

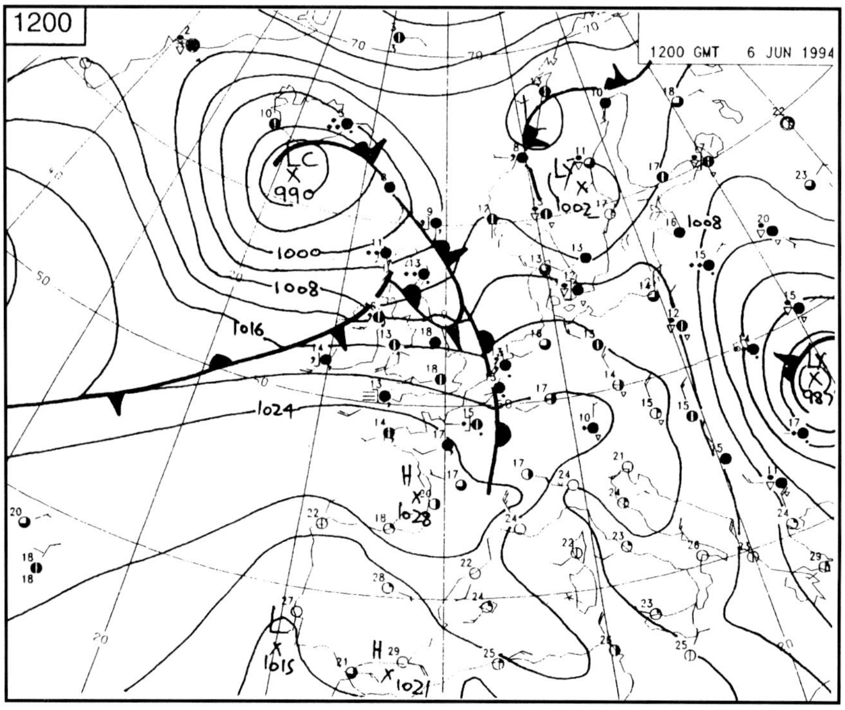

When Brigadier Longland was asked at one top-level briefing as to what would happen if it rained during the Whale Island Beating Retreat display, his reply was brief and to the point: 'People will get wet!'

The first major event in the anniversary calendar — although not specific to D-Day — was the unveiling of the Canadian Memorial in Green Park, London, by the Queen on June 3. The fact that more than one million Canadians came to Britain during two world wars, and that 100,000 of them paid the ultimate price, had tended in years past to be largely overshadowed by the American contribution; now, the record was to be publicly acknowledged and cast in stone. Canadian architect Pierre Granche conceived the idea of marrying granite from Canada with bronze castings and running water to present the illusion of maple leaves floating on the surface of a stream, a concept described by the Canadian High Commissioner as 'quintessentially Canadian'. Sited just inside the Canada Gates close to Buckingham Palace, the memorial is aligned on Halifax, Nova Scotia, from where the majority of Canadian servicemen embarked for Britain.

Formation 6. The sixth formation will be made up of 12 RAF and three Royal Canadian Air Force C-130s, flying at 210kt en route to the para drop at Ranville. The lead aircraft will be operated by No. 47 Squadron.

Formation 7. The seventh formation, of various helicopters, will comprise [_] helicopters from [_] nations, led by No. 706 Squadron. The aircraft will fly at 90kt.

Formation 8. The final formation will be a Concorde of British Airways, flying at 300kt.

Apart from the RAF/RN aircraft, Australia was to provide an F-IIIC; Belgium four F-16s; Canada eight F-18s and three C-130s; France four Mirage 2000 and four Super Etendard; Norway four F-16s; the Slovak Republic four MiG-29s; and the United States four F-14s and four F-15s.

Several options for reduced fly-pasts had to be built into the plans in case of inclement weather. 'Reduced Fly-past 1' would eliminate the Hawk '50', and 'Reduced Fly-past 2' all the fast jets save for the lead Tornado/Sea Harrier formation. 'Reduced Fly-past 3' was unspecified but was at the discretion of the SASO, Strike Command.

The first major event, the unveiling of the Canadian Memorial in Green Park, London, on June 3, passed off well although it was not one for which we were directly responsible. At the time, I was totally involved in the build-up for the events at Portsmouth, with increasing worries about the ominous weather forecasts we were getting, and the disruption which might yet be caused to the tight timetable.

On the morning of June 4, President Clinton flew to Britain from Italy where he had attended ceremonies on the eve of the liberation of Rome anniversary. A team from the USAF airbase at Alconbury (where some 800 American paratroops were already assembled to re-enact the drop over Ste Mère-Eglise the following day) was responsible for organising the first US-British event which took place at the American Cemetery outside Cambridge before an invited audience of 5,000. *Left:* Raymond Shaw, assistant superintendent at the cemetery, sponges the marker on the grave of Sergeant Zee Dunkerson, killed on December 14, 1943 while serving with the 925th Engineer Regiment (Aviation). All the 3,800 graves were decorated with American and British flags. *Right: Air Force One* landed at RAF Mildenhall from where the President flew by helicopter to a private airstrip just beside the cemetery. Other speakers who addressed the assembly were the Prime Minister; the Lord Lieutenant of Cambridge; the US Treasury Secretary, Lloyd Bentsen, who was a B-24 pilot in Italy during the war, and Ed MacLean, president of the Ninth Air Force Association. Plus, of course, the 'voice' of American news broadcasting, Walter Cronkite.

However, on the following day (Saturday), the heavens opened and the Garden Party and the Beating of Retreat were conducted with great spirit in the wind and rain. Fortunately, the State Dinner in Portsmouth, attended by the Heads of State of all those nations involved, took place without a hitch and provided a splendid setting for the first gathering of all the wartime Allies. Despite the poor weather, thousands of people gathered to watch the Son et Lumière display on Southsea Common as the first full day of events came to a dramatic close.

The Garden Party, to be held along traditional British lines on Saturday afternoon at HMS *Dryad,* was meant to symbolise the planning phase of Operation 'Neptune'. A total of 1,000 veterans and guests had been invited, including sons or close relatives of several of the wartime commanders including John Eisenhower, The Viscount Montgomery of Alamein, Trafford Leigh-Mallory Doherty, and Major-General Charles Ramsay. Due to commence at 3.15 p.m., a decision had to be made at 12 noon by the Flag Officer Portsmouth whether or not to invoke the wet-weather routine which, in the event, proved necessary. Although the guests may not have appreciated the rain, it was a symbolic reminder of the weather 50 years earlier (see page 166). The change involved splitting the two bands — the RAF Western Band and the US Atlantic Band — into four combos, one for the Frewin Hall and the others for the marquees; moving tables and chairs, and providing umbrellas for Heads of State.

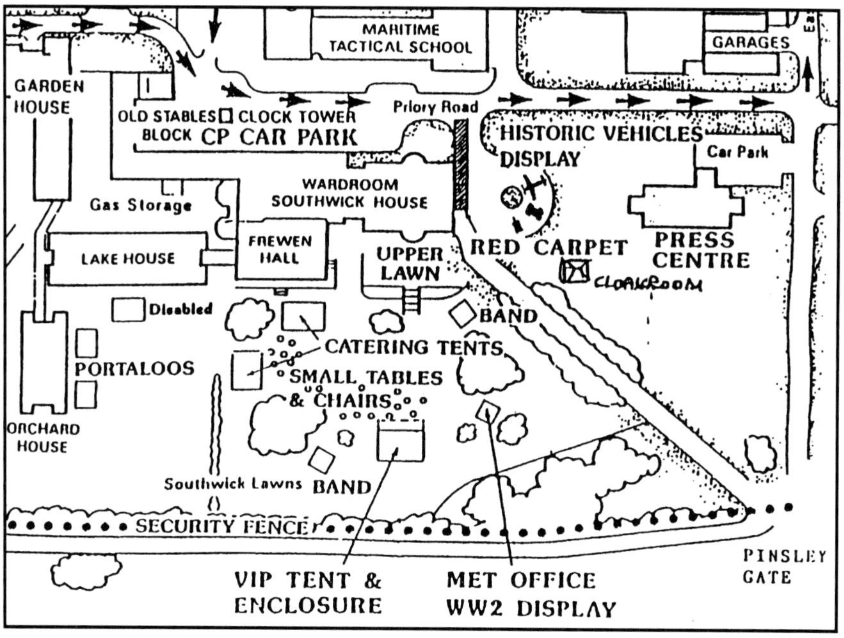

'A Beat Retreat Ceremony will be held at HMS *Excellent* on 4 June 1994 to symbolise the "Embarkation Phase" of the D-Day 94 anniversary commemorations. The ceremony will commence at 1706 and complete at 1800. The Heads of State or Government of Canada, France, the United States of America, Luxembourg and the United Kingdom or their representatives will attend. It will be hosted by the Prime Minister. A maximum of 5,000 veterans will be invited from the four nations attending. Senior Service and Government Officials will be represented. Dress will be jacket and tie for civilians and Ceremonial Day Uniform (negative swords) for service personnel. The Beat Retreat will follow a format that has been designed to include bands from France, Canada, USA and the UK with the Guard of the Queens Colour Squadron, RAF. The Royal Naval Mast Manning Team will take part in the musical finale to the programme. The event will be run on a semi-formal basis to give veterans freedom to mingle throughout the afternoon. Seating will be arranged so that 50 per cent is contained in tiered stands and the remainder at ground level. Veterans will be free to sit wherever they wish or to stand if they prefer.' Annex to Operation Orders, April 12, 1994.

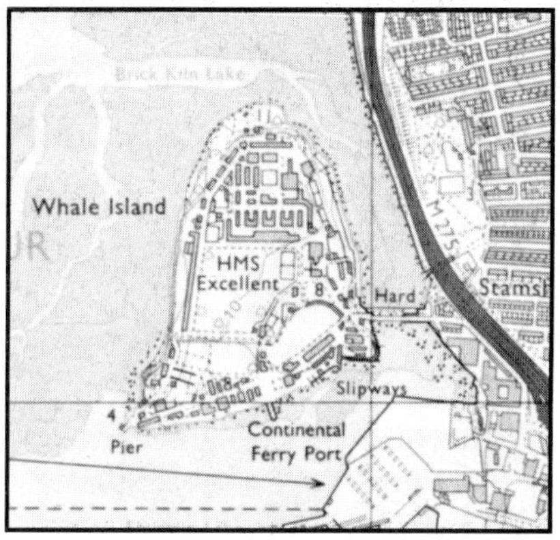

From a security point of view, HMS *Excellent* on Whale Island in Portsmouth Harbour was an ideal choice, but it did mean that while VIP guests could arrive by car and Heads of State by helicopter, veterans had to travel in by coach from the IBM car park at Cosham where security checks would be carried out by 160 Provost Company, Royal Military Police. After the playing of the National Anthems, the Beat Retreat began with the Musique de la Gendarmerie Mobile *(top)*. They were followed by the Royal Canadian Artillery Band *(left)*, and then the United States Air Force in Europe Band 'Ambassadors' *(below)*. Each band was allowed a six-minute programme, the whole display timed to run exactly 60 minutes.

Above: The Queen's Colour Squadron of the RAF — note the modern SA80 rifles — gave a demonstration of their silent drill routine and were followed by the Royal Marines Band *(bottom)*. The photographs belie the awful conditions of driving rain under which the bandsmen had to march and play, but at least they were performing at ground level.

High above, ratings from HMS *Daedalus* braved the elements to carry out a dramatic rigging display on a 100-foot mast specially erected at the end of the arena. The greatest applause was reserved for the courage of the 'Button Boy' at the very top. Sliding down the 120-foot guide rope to end the display, Able Seaman Dougie Gorman — celebrating his 18th birthday — was congratulated by the Queen Mother who then awarded him the traditional Royal Shilling — today a 10p piece!

There then followed a State Banquet hosted by Her Majesty The Queen and HM Government for the leaders of those nations (or their representatives) which participated in Operation 'Neptune'. It was also the first critical test of Operation 'Gleam' mounted by the Hampshire Police who had the overall responsibility for the security operation surrounding the Heads of State of 14 overseas countries. All told, there were 46 VVIPs in attendance, five members of the Royal Family, six senior Government ministers and seven overseas ministers, 13 Ambassadors and High Commissioners, and over 60 other VIPs. Security sweeps of the Guildhall at Portsmouth began on Friday June 3 and continued throughout the day. Parking restrictions were in force and constant patrols were mounted over the following 24 hours. At 5.30 p.m. on Saturday, all security teams were in place ready for the arrival of the guests at 6.15 p.m. Unique passes had been issued to all attending, including over 400 veterans. Each Head of State was allocated a police motor-cycle escort and the drivers provided with individual route cards, with a precise timetable. This example from the operational order shows the movements of the American party.

USA CONFIDENTIAL

APPENDIX 16 TO
ANNEX A TO
PART V TO
OP ORDER A5900/5/4/9
DATED 22 APR 94

Road Transport Programme for President and Mrs Clintonand their Representative(s)
For the Government Sponsored Events in Portsmouth

The Presidential Representative(s)
4th June 1994

SER	**TIME**	**EVENT**	**LOCATION**	**SIZE OF PARTY**	**REMARKS**
1	14	Depart for Garden Party	From Solent Hotel to Southwick House	Representative and Cabinet Party	2Cars + Minibus + Coach. Police Motorcycle Escort (PME). Route Card 1U. Arrive at **1450** hrs.
2	**1612**	Depart for Beating of Retreat	To HMS Excellent	As above	1 USA Car. PME. Route Card 2U. Arrive at **1630** hrs. **With and behind the Canadian cavalcade. Cavalcades to change position on M275 so that USA arrives at HMS EXCELLENT first.** Remaining vehicles travel at 1615 hrs with GB VIP coach.
3	**1810**	Changing Facility	HMS EXCELLENT	As above	Then to Dinner via East Gate (See SER 2 and President's programme).

End of Representative Duty. For the Guildhall Dinner the Ambassador & SofS for Def is to RV with the Presidential cavalcade at Unicorn Gate and follow it to the Guildhall, entering and leaving the Guildhall by the lower door, and on 5th June is to travel to the Drumhead Service at Southsea in the USA coach which departs from HM Naval Base at 0930 hrs (latest).

4	**1933**	Depart for Dinner	To Guildhall From HMY BRITANNIA via Unicorn Gate **(1937)**	President +	USA Car. PME. Route Card 4U. Arrive at **1940 hrs.** Joined at Unicorn Gate by the Representatives in 3 cars. Presidential Group only to enter Guildhall by Upper Stairs, the remainder of the dinner guests in the cavalcade are to enter the Guildhall by the lower door.
5	**2242**	Depart for Residence	To RY BRITANNIA via Unicorn Gate.	As above	Cars as above. PME. Route Card 5U. Arrive at 2248 hrs.

V-A-16-1
16 MAY 94 CONFIDENTIAL

Sunday, June 5. The Naval War Memorial on Southsea Common was the perfect setting for the Drumhead Ceremony which was to commemorate the maritime phase of 'Neptune'. As this was the first event which the general public could attend, a crowd of up to 100,000 was expected. Seating was provided for 12,000 veterans but many were held up when traffic on roads leading to Portsmouth came to a standstill. Road closures for the Heads of State added to the delays which vexed many ex-servicemen. In the background, the guided missile cruiser USS *Normandy* (CG 60).

The Drumhead Service dates back to at least 1790 and derives from the use of drums as a makeshift altar in services on the battlefield. Specially made to ensure uniformity, the National Flags of the 14 Allied nations — Great Britain, Greece, the Czech Republic, Canada, Australia, New Zealand, Slovakia, the USA, Poland, France, Netherlands, Luxembourg, Belgium and Norway — are brought forward for draping on the drumpile. Officiating is the Archbishop of Canterbury, Dr George Carey.

'Greater love hath no man than this, that a man lay down his life for his friends.'

Those words, spoken by Jesus on the night before his own death, come with special poignancy as, 50 years on, we commemorate the glory and the sacrifices of the D-Day invasion.

Many of you are only too well aware of what these words mean. It was your friends who gave their lives in the Normandy campaign. They fought alongside you. Their deaths could have been your own.

Today, from all over the world, we gather here to remember with pride and thanksgiving — yes, and with tears — those who gave everything for freedom 50 years ago, and whom, in our hearts, we have never forgotten.

Much has been written and broadcast recently about the scale and complexity of Operation 'Overlord'. It remains the greatest seaborne invasion in history. One sailor on HMS Orion, recalling the day for me, described the numbers of ships and landing craft as 'simply unbelievable'. By the end of that 6th of June, over a 150,000 troops had landed on the French coast. Over the next ten weeks, more than one million men and women had made the same crossing. By the end of that campaign, almost one-fifth of them were either dead or injured.

But, as always, it is the little details which stay in the memory, and have made the story unique and personal for each one of you. The ship which got separated from one convoy, and latched on to another, not knowing where it was going. The pungent smell of the self-heating soup, doing nothing for seasickness! The separation from loved ones as England fell astern, and the fear in the pit of the stomach as the beaches loomed up ahead. The devastated orchards of Normandy and the stench of dead cattle. The individual acts of great bravery and brilliance — of courage and compassion.

And yet deep inside, submerged perhaps by the storm of war but never lost, was the conviction that the cause to be served and the evil to be destroyed, warranted all the hardship and danger you had to endure.

These words of Montgomery, in the message he sent to his troops, just before the invasion began, are still inspiring: 'To us is given the honour of striking a blow for freedom which will live in history; and in the better days that lie ahead men will speak with pride of our doings. We have a great and righteous cause.' And he ended with these high-hearted lines of Montrose:

> *'He either fears his fate too much*
> *Or his deserts are small,*
> *That puts it not unto the touch*
> *To win or lose it all.'*

Eisenhower, Montgomery and the other commanders, knew just how vast a team effort had been involved. A team from many nations, both of front-line soldiers, sailors, aircrew and their support units. A team of a thousand skills, devising special equipment, gathering crucial intelligence, creating disinformation, building the giant Mulberry harbours, maintaining the supply network by rail and road and sea. Across the Channel, too, were the hidden members of that team — the members of the French Resistance, whose heroism became legendary.

And the Normandy campaign was itself part of a concerted world-wide effort: in the mountains of Italy, in the jungles of Burma, on the vast, heroic Russian Front, in the islands of the Pacific. Everywhere, the peoples of the world were making immense sacrifices in the common cause of freedom and justice.

Fifty years on, we thank God for them all; and today especially for the heroes of Utah, Omaha, Gold, Juno and Sword, for those who sustained the bloody slog around Caen, or rode the tanks that swept round to the Falaise pocket. We thank God for each one of you who played your own special part in that victory.

That spirit of national and international co-operation has its challenge for our own time. Even in those dark days, some caught sight of a better future. Churchill himself frequently quoted these words: 'In war, resolution; in defeat, defiance; in victory, magnanimity; in peace, goodwill.' The vision of the Four Freedoms — freedom of speech, freedom of religion, freedom from want and freedom from fear — also captured the imagination of many. But such fine expressions have to be matched by actions. A future in which those visions can became a reality cannot be achieved by governments alone or by one nation alone. Each one of us must work in harmony with others for evil to be defeated and the fruits of peace to be enjoyed by all.

Fifty years on, we have much for which to give thanks, especially here in Europe. But many more struggles lie ahead; nor can victory in them be won without sacrifice. Peace has its martyrs too, whether in the service of the United Nations or other agencies, whether in the cause of human rights or in the fight against suffering and want worldwide.

Jesus's words speak of gallant souls in every generation who have given their lives; and given them as he did, not just for their friends but also for those who persecute and hate. Only the love that knows no limits can liberate those enslaved by evil and those we remember today gave their lives not only for the liberation of Occupied Europe but also for the German nation itself — to free it from the dark tyranny that was destroying its soul.

I am told that throughout the war Eleanor Roosevelt, wife of the American President, kept by her the following prayer:

> *'Dear Lord, lest I continue on my complacent way*
> *help me to remember, somewhere out there,*
> *a man died for me today.*
> *As long as there be war,*
> *I then must ask and answer*
> *"Am I worth dying for?"'*

In the unending war against evil, that's a question each one of us still needs to ask.

Let all of us, and especially those who on D-Day were not yet born, make our own the words of Abraham Lincoln spoken after another great battle fought in a noble cause. Let us here 'highly resolve that these dead shall not have died in vain', and that all nations 'under God, shall have a new birth of freedom'.

This freedom was what those whom we remember today gave their lives to preserve. We honour them by pressing forward to maintain it in our own day. It is by our actions now that we honour their deaths then. That is the centre of true remembrance; a remembrance we pledge ourselves afresh this day.

'At the going down of the sun, and in the morning, we will remember them.'

ARCHBISHOP OF CANTERBURY, JUNE 5, 1994

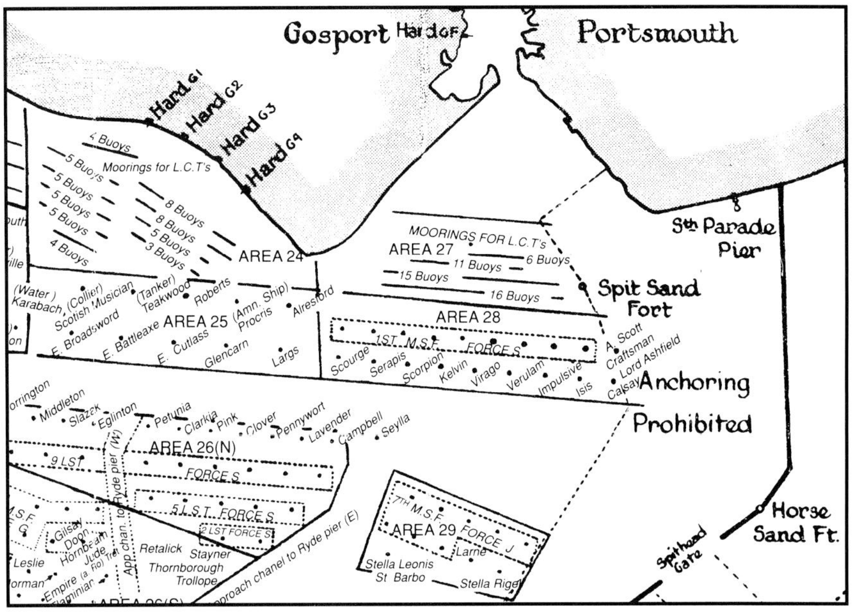

1944. An enlarged section from 'Neptune Plan 2' of the final assembly area for Operation 'Neptune'. Spithead Gate controlled the eastern entrance through the boom which stretched from Portsmouth to the Isle of Wight (out of the plan).

Fortunately Sunday, June 5, dawned bright and clear, ideal flying weather, and in the bright sunshine there was a most impressive service on Southsea Common attended by all the Heads of State with the Naval Memorial and the fleet putting to sea providing a moving backdrop to the enormous crowd.

Over the previous days, ships from all the Allied nations had assembled at Portsmouth. The anticipated list totalled nearly 70 vessels (for which specific abbreviations had been allocated) included (in alphabetical order): HNLMS *Abraham van der Hulst* (ABR), HMS *Active* (ACT), HS *Adrias* (ADR), HMAV *Arakan* (ARA), HMAV *Ardennes* (ARD), HMAV *Arromanches* (AMH), USS *Austin* (AUST), HMS *Avenger* (AVE), *Balmoral* (BAL), USS *Barry* (BAR), HNOMS *Bergen* (BER), *Black Prince* (BLK), HMY *Britannia* (HMY), HMS *Bulldog* (BUL), *Canberra* (CAN), FS *Circé* (CIR), FS *Clio* (CLI), FS *Commandant Blaison* (BLA), FS *Commandant Bouan* (BOU), HMS *Cottesmore* (COT), FS *Croix du Sud* (SUD), USCG *Dallas* (DAL), HMS *Dasher* (DSH), USS *Deyo* (DEY), USS *Doyle* (DOY), FS *Durance* (DUR), FS *Duguay Trouin* (DUG), HMS *Edinburgh* (EDI), FS *Éridan* (ERI), HMS *Fearless*

Then, anti-submarine netting protected the anchorage; now, Ministry of Defence police vessels mounted constant patrols of the same stretch of water.

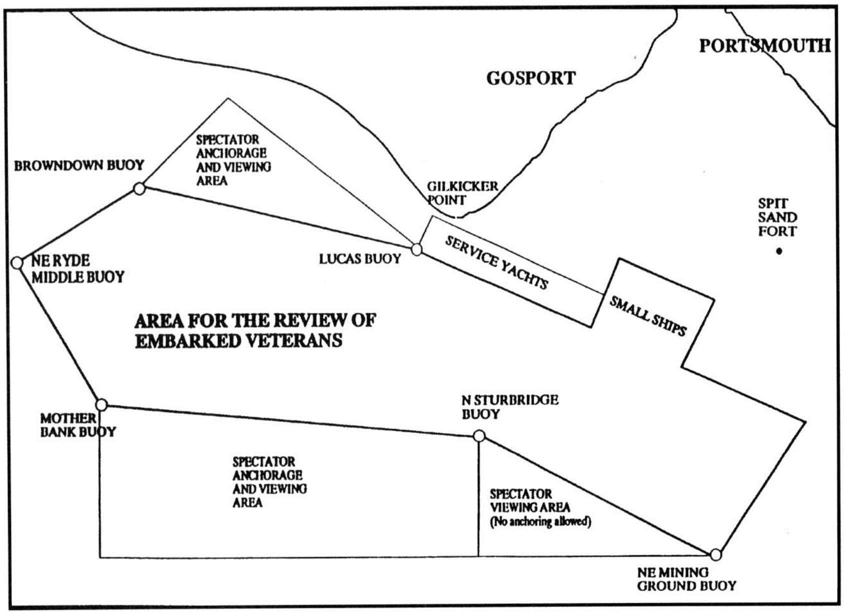

1994. Table 2 to Appendix 2 to Annex F to D-Day Operation Orders Part II. Very appropriately, the reviewing area covered the old Areas 25 and 28 of the 1st Minesweeping Flotilla for Force 'S'.

(FEA), USS *George Washington* (GW), FS *Germinal* (GER), USS *Guam* (GUA), USS *Harlan County* (HAR), HMS *Hurworth* (HUR), HMS *Illustrious* (ILL), *Jeremiah O'Brien* (JER), *John W. Brown* (JWB), USS *Kalamazoo* (KAL), ORP *Krakow* (KRA), *Kristina Regina* (KRR), FS *Loire* (LOI), FS *Ouistreham* (OUI), *Lane Victory* (LAN), USS *Normandy* (NOR), THV *Patricia* (PAT), HMCS *Preserver* (PRE), *Pride of Bilbao* (POB), *Queen Elizabeth 2* (QE2), HMS *Sandown* (SAN), USS *Santa Barbara* (SBA), USS *San Jacinto* (JAC), *Silver Cloud* (SIL), RFA *Sir Bedivere* (BED), RFA *Sir Galahad* (GAL), RFA *Sir Percivale* (PER), *Seabourn Pride* (SEA), FS *Second Maître le Bihan* (BIH), HMS *Spey* (SPY), USTV *State of Maine* (MAN), *Statendam* (STA), FS *Styx* (STX), USS *Thomas S. Gates* (TSG), HMCS *Toronto* (TOR), USS *Tortuga* (TUG), HMS *Ursula* (URS), *Vistafjord* (VIS), *Waverley* (WAV), BNS *Westdiep* (WES).

Six anchor berths (Line A–F) were laid out at Portsmouth with additional berths provided at the various jetties within the Naval Dockyard proper. HMY *Britannia* was to berth alongside the South Railway Jetty where the Liberty ship *Jeremiah O'Brien* had arrived on May 23.

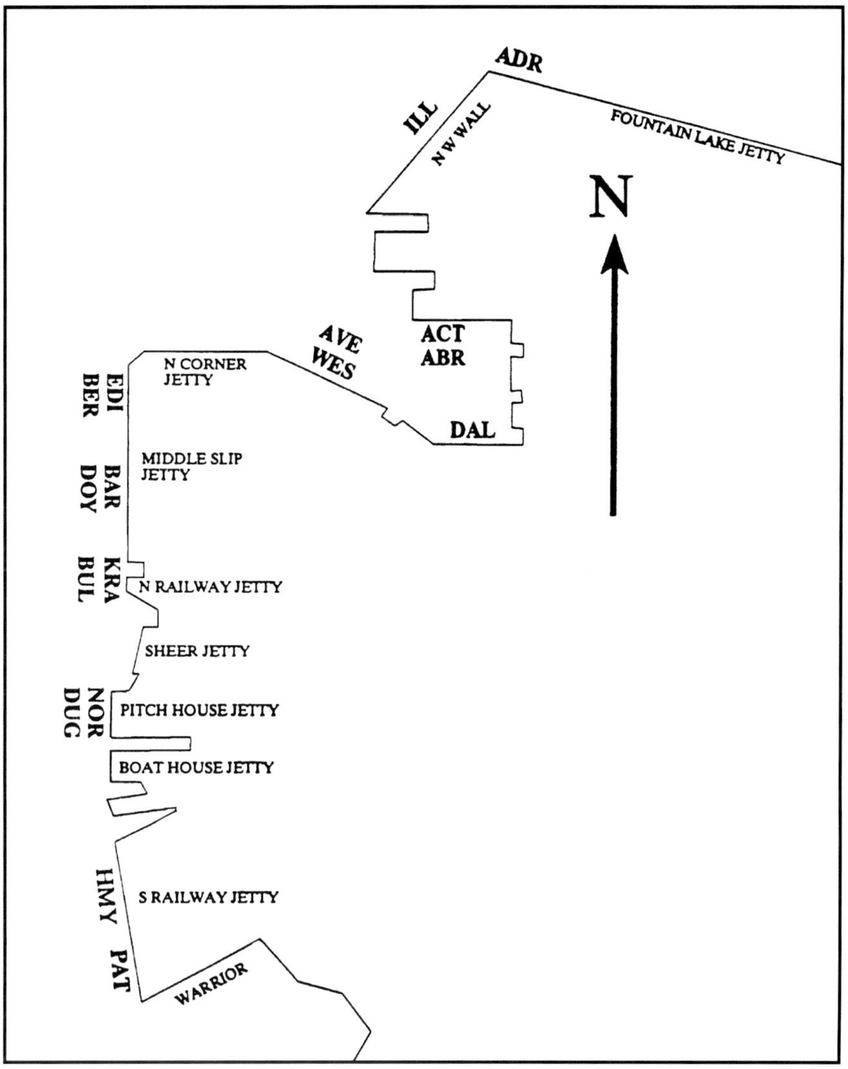

The planned anchorage drawn up before the non-arrival of the two Liberty ships. The USS *George Washington*, flagship of Rear Admiral Alexander J. Krekich, headed the six lines: Line A *Sir Percivale* to *Lane Victory*; Line B *Seabourn Pride* to *Illustrious* (Commander-in-Chief Fleet Admiral Sir Hugo White); Line C *State of Maine* to *Ursula*; Line D *Kristina Regina* to *Arakan*; Line E *Royalist* to *Ernest Brown*; Line F *Balmoral* to *Shieldhall*.

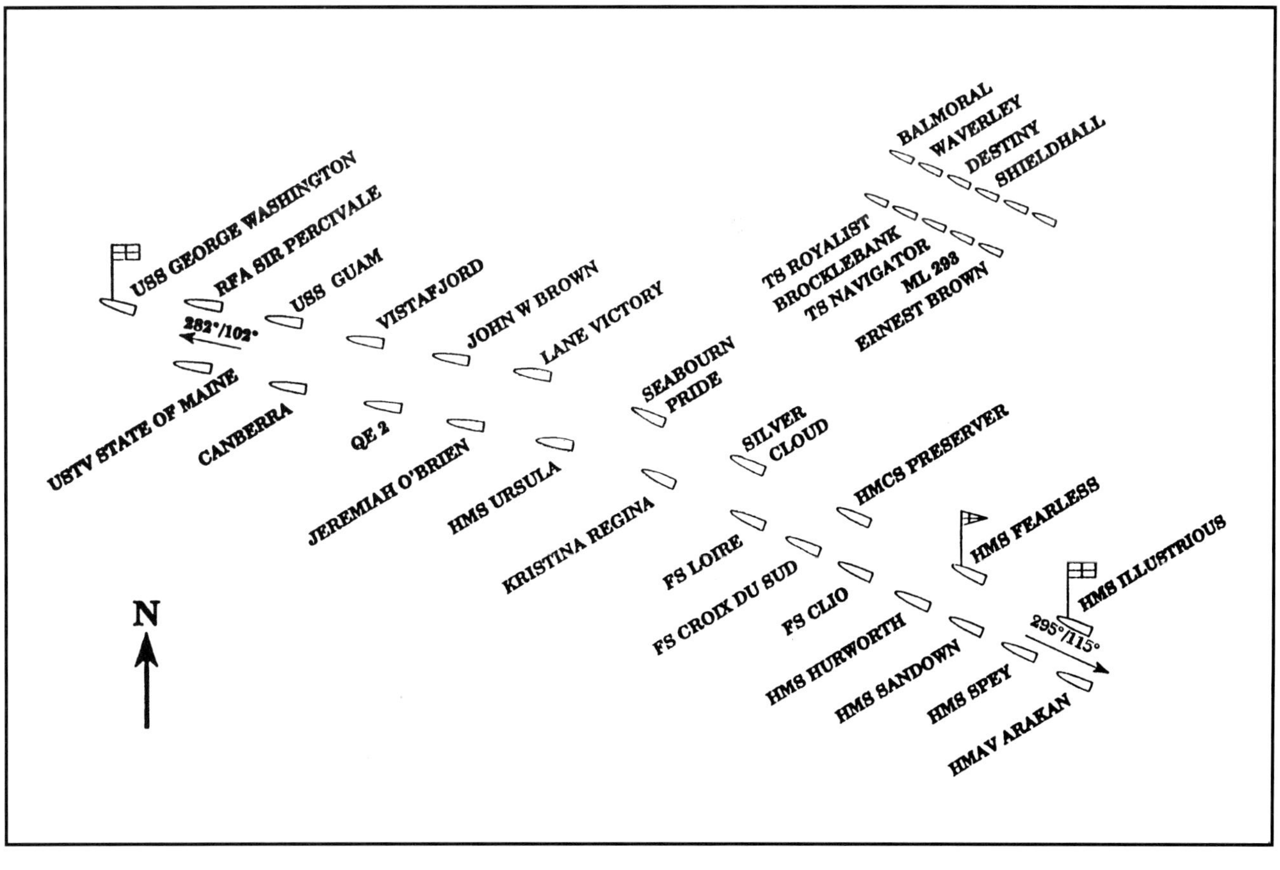

'All ships are to sail with upperdecks lined to port. On passing the Amusement Park, those lining the upperdeck are to be brought to attention and the Memorial saluted. Men are to be fallen in before the ship passes the harbour entrance and may be fallen out as the ship steadies on the 183° leg. All ships sailing from Portsmouth are to be dressed with masthead ensigns.' An extract from the operational orders covering the departure from Portsmouth. The Flag Officer Surface Flotilla (FOSF), Vice-Admiral Michael Boyce, was flying his flag aboard HMS *Edinburgh*, a Type 42 destroyer.

At 1600 hours on June 5, command of the flotilla would transfer to the Amiral Commandant le Groupe d'Action Sous-Marine (ALGASM), Contre-Amiral Maurice Girard aboard the French destroyer *Duguay Trouin*.

Visiting warships were to remain under national command throughout, but commanding officers were requested to comply with the prepared orders 'so far as their facilities, national customs and practice permit'. Tactical command was delegated to FOSF from 0600 hours to 1600 hours on June 5, whereupon it would transfer to the Amiral Commandant le Groupe d'Action Sous-Marine (ALGASM) from 1600 hours on June 5 to 1700 hours on June 6.

The synchronisation of Morning and Evening Colours for all ships at anchor in Portsmouth was controlled from HMY *Britannia* (by radio and the hoisting of a preparative pennant) and in Normandy by the USS *George Washington*.

Embarked aboard HMY *Britannia* were the Queen and the Duke of Edinburgh, the Queen Mother, Princess Royal and Princess Margaret, President and Mrs Bill Clinton, King Harald of Norway, Prince Bernhard of the Netherlands, President Vaclav Havel of the Czech Republic, President Michal Kovac of Slovakia and President Lech Walesa of Poland, Prime Ministers John Major, Paul Keating of Australia, Jean Chrétien of Canada and Jim Bolger of New Zealand.

As the *Britannia* began her voyage down to the Solent, aircraft from the Australian, Belgian, Canadian, Czech, French, Greek, Dutch, Norwegian, Slovakian, US Navy, USAF, RNAS and RAF were approaching for a massed fly-past, simulating the air armada of 50 years previously. (An unfortunate gap in the aircraft stream was caused when the Polish Air Force failed to put in an appearance.) Formation 4 was specially conceived by the RAF for Operation 'Overlord 50'. Here, at RAF Chivenor, the pilots who were to perform it line up in their formation positions in front of a Hawk trainer. From No. 92 Squadron (reading down the '5'): Flight Lieutenant S. Noujaim, Squadron Leader A. Wyatt (OC 92 Squadron), Wing Commander A. Crockatt (OC Flying Wing and formation commander), Flight Lieutenant S. Easton, Flight Lieutenant N. Milne (an exchange instructor from the Royal New Zealand Air Force), Lieutenant I. Reid (Royal Navy), Flight Lieutenant S. Burgess, Squadron Leader P. Adams, Flight Lieutenant N. Batey and Flight Lieutenant A. Gent. No. 19 Squadron formed the '0' (clockwise from the twelve o'clock position): Squadron Leader G. Flack (OC 19 Squadron), Captain P. Masse (on exchange from the French Air Force), Flight Lieutenant P. Underwood, Flight Lieutenant B. Blair, Flight Lieutenant P. McGilvray, Flight Lieutenant T. Couston, Flight Lieutenant G. Thompson, Flight Lieutenant W. Haigh and Flight Lieutenant N. Collins.

Many hours had to be spent practising one of the trickiest formations in the RAF's history. Wing Commander Crockatt explained that the difficulty was perfecting the curve on the bottom of the '5' and making sure that the '0' remained round and did not become a square. Although when viewed from the ground, all the aircraft appeared to be flying at the same height, in actual fact they were in six different layers to avoid the turbulence from the exhaust of other aircraft. Planned height of the formation over Portsmouth was 1,000 feet with a TOT (Time on Target — in this case *Britannia*) of 1143.30 hours.

'Men are to be fallen in on deck in their stations preparatory to manning ship by 1145. No more officers than necessary are to be in charge of the men manning ship. They are to fall in three paces in the rear of their men. The Officer-in-Charge is to be in the centre with his Junior Officers, Chief Petty Officers and Petty Officers equalising the spaces on either side of him. Officers and men are to be called to attention. Men manning the side are to take one pace forward and grasp the guard rail underneath with both hands, palms upwards, right arm over the left arm of the next man to them (except aircraft carriers and other ships without guard rails). Officers' swords are not to be drawn. HMY *Britannia*, led by THV *Patricia*, and followed by HM ships *Bulldog* and *Active* will enter the review lines at 1200 between B and E, reviewing lines in the order B/E/F, A, C and D. On the approach of HMY *Britannia*, the alert (bugle or pipe) is to be sounded. Heads of State and Government will review the Fleet from the Verandah Deck abaft the Mizzen of HMY *Britannia*. No marks of respect are to be paid between other ships of the Review Column and ships of the Fleet. Order to be given: *"Stand by to give 3 cheers. Off Caps"*: Drop the left hand to the side and seize the cap with the right hand, fingers on top and together, thumb underneath the rim. *"Up"*: Remove the cap and hold up at the full extent of the arm at an angle of 45° directly to the front, crown vertical and outboard. *"Three cheers for Her Majesty The Queen. Hip, hip, hip, hooray"*: On the command "Hooray" men cheer "Hooray" synchronising with the command order, at the same time rotating the arm clockwise viewed from the rear around a diameter extending no lower than the shoulder and returning to the original position after each cheer.'

Advance notices to mariners were issued to warn other shipping and fishermen of the movements of the fleet, 'cuttlefish pots off Arromanches' being one particular hazard! CINCFLEET-WOC at Northwood broadcast special D-Day weather forecasts from 0700 hours on June 4 to 1100 hours on June 7. Should the weather prevent the beaching of landing craft, the Embarkation of the Standards was to be undertaken by helicopter.

The international flotilla was split into ten Commemorative Task Groups (CTGs) or Units (TUs) under Vice-Admiral Boyce who was nominally CTG 610.01. The FOSF on HMS *Edinburgh* (CTG 610.01.02) inspected the review lines at 1030 hours at which point ships could rehearse 'Man and Cheer Ship'. The wind speed was also to be checked to determine if chinstays would be necessary on headgear.

Crew members of the USS *George Washington* 'give a rousing cheer to the Queen of England'.

The *Britannia* leading HMS *Hecate* and HMS *Active* (out of picture) past the flotilla, including the *Queen Elizabeth 2*, USS *George Washington*, *Vistafjord*, *Jeremiah O'Brien*, USS *Guam*, *Seabourn Pride*, *Silver Cloud*, HMCS *Preserver and* HMS *Fearless* (flagship of Commodore Amphibious Warfare, Commodore Richard Bridges).

Shortly after midday, the flotilla, made up of both warships and merchant vessels, set sail for Normandy. The Royal Yacht with all the Heads of State embarked led the way surrounded by a swarm of sailing boats. As they drew away from the shore, the size of the naval effort became clear and the vast array of shipping, ranging in size from the massive USS *George Washington* down to the smallest sailing craft, made an impressive setting for the fly-past led by the Battle of Britain Memorial Flight and the Swordfish of the RN Historic Flight.

Alan Hamilton of *The Times* aboard HMS *Active* wrote: 'No marine artist commissioned to decorate a wardroom bulkhead could have painted a more stirring scene. Under diamond-sharp blue skies, the sea was churned to glistening white by foaming wave crests and the wake of many dozens of small boats weaving among the anchored giants.

'As the royal flotilla edged out of harbour, a Swordfish biplane headed a fly-past of 120 aircraft old and new, including a venerable Dakota and one of the only two Lancaster bombers still flying. But the noise that tingled many an elderly spine was the piston-engined growl of four Spitfires, a somehow more comforting sound than the unholy scream of Jaguars, Tornados, Harriers and other modern war machines that followed, ripping the sky apart.'

'CINCFLEET will fire a 42-gun salute from HMS *Illustrious* to the Heads of State and Government embarked in *Britannia*. The salute will be from CINCFLEET on behalf of all ships, nations and Flag Officers afloat and will not be returned.' *Left:* While an estimated 2,000 vessels of all sizes churned the Solent into a huge flotilla to rival the Allied armada of June 1944, one of the real veterans of D-Day, HMS *Belfast* was firing her own salute at her mooring near London's Tower Bridge. *Right:* Len Ellis, 68, and Fred Winstanley, 74, who manned her 6-inch guns during the original naval bombardment of the Juno area.

The symbolic Embarkation of the Flags took place from the beach adjacent to the Naval War Memorial. The Royal Marines and United States Marine Corps had been tasked with providing an Escort for the National Standards of the 14 nations. Commanded by Major Rayson Pritchard, RM, of the Commando Logistic Regiment, the escort comprised two captains, four senior NCOs and 100 corporals/marines split equally between the RM and USMC. After the three-man colour parties from the individual nations had collected their flags at the end of the Drumhead Ceremony, they were embarked in an LCVP at midday, directly following the fly-past. Large ship movements were temporarily halted to avoid their wake causing a hazard to the beached landing craft which then returned to their mother ship, HMS *Fearless*.

During the afternoon, these were followed by 28 C-130s carrying over 1,500 paratroopers from America, Canada, France, Poland and the United Kingdom who were to drop on Ste Mère-Eglise and Ranville to commemorate the initial airborne operation.

Meanwhile the 1,500-strong paratroop element was emplaning at Alconbury and Lyneham. The scenes were so reminiscent of 1944 but even better was the fact that the American contingent *(right)* comprised men from the present-day 82nd and 101st Airborne Divisions from the USA, and the 325th Airborne Infantry Regiment based in Italy. A total of 12 C-130 Hercules were flown in from the 23rd Wing at Pope Air Force Base, North Carolina, and the 435th Airlift Wing at Rhein-Main, Germany.

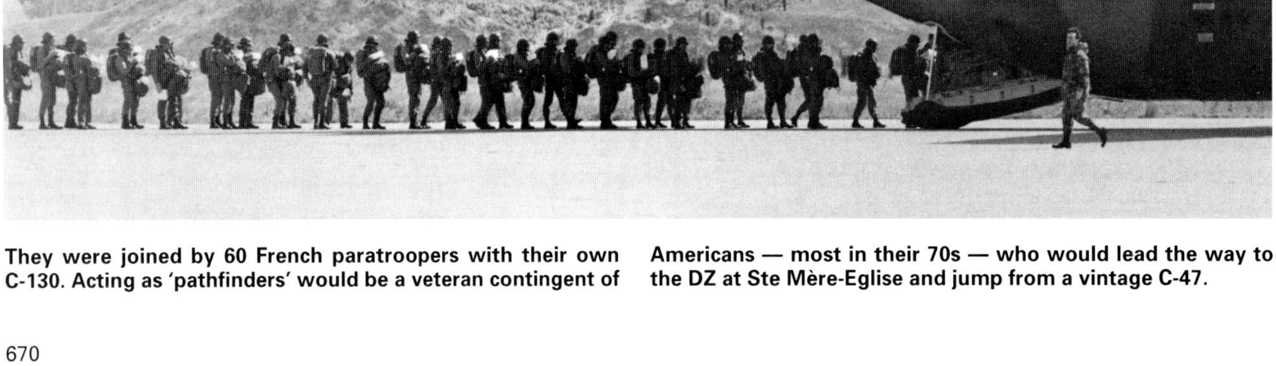

They were joined by 60 French paratroopers with their own C-130. Acting as 'pathfinders' would be a veteran contingent of Americans — most in their 70s — who would lead the way to the DZ at Ste Mère-Eglise and jump from a vintage C-47.

The British/Canadian force of 15 C-130s departed from Lyneham in Wiltshire, the aircraft carrying 750 paratroops from 5 Airborne Brigade and 150 Canadians in what was code-named Exercise 'Normandy Salute'. Formation 6 reached Portsmouth at 1400 hours, overflying the flotilla on its way to Ranville.

The route of the flotilla to Normandy followed the approach through the mine-cleared 'Spout' of June 1944 and, at a point some distance south of the old Area Z (see page 520), the Commemorative Act of the International Maritime Forces began.

Formation 'Ramsay' comprised the *Edinburgh*, *Doyle*, *Toronto*, *Dallas*, *Avenger*, *Duguay Trouin*, *Abraham van der Hulst*, *Westdiep*, *Bergen*, *Adrias*, *Britannia*, *Active*, *QE2*, *Canberra*, *Seabourn Pride* and *Vistafjord*. On the issuing of the code-word 'Kirk' by FOSF, the ships were to form up in two lines at 500-yard intervals on the guideship *Edinburgh*. At this point, *Britannia* would be one mile astern of the *Doyle* and *Adrias*. Each warship was lined with its crew with Church Pennants hoisted. Then, as the Royal Yacht drew abeam each pair of ships, wreaths were cast onto the water 'in memory of all the sailors, both naval and merchant, who gave their lives during Operation 'Neptune'. The USCG *Dallas* laid a wreath on behalf of the US Coast Guard, and the Grand Duke of Luxembourg and President Walesa of Poland cast their own wreaths from the *Britannia*. Then, while a service was held on the largest passenger liner, the SS *Canberra*, a Lancaster flew overhead and scattered half a million poppies over the flotilla in remembrance.

At 1500, the Commemorate Act of Remembrance began. Veterans aboard the *Canberra* (*above*) were led in prayers by the Reverend Henry Lovegrave of the Green Howards and the last serving minister from the Normandy campaign. In one of the most moving events of the day, the Lancaster then returned and flew low overhead to drop hundreds of thousands of linen 'poppy' petals on the assembly as a tribute to fallen comrades. Each vessel in Formation 'Ramsay' then cast its wreath upon the waters of the Channel on behalf of the Royal British Legion and American veteran associations.

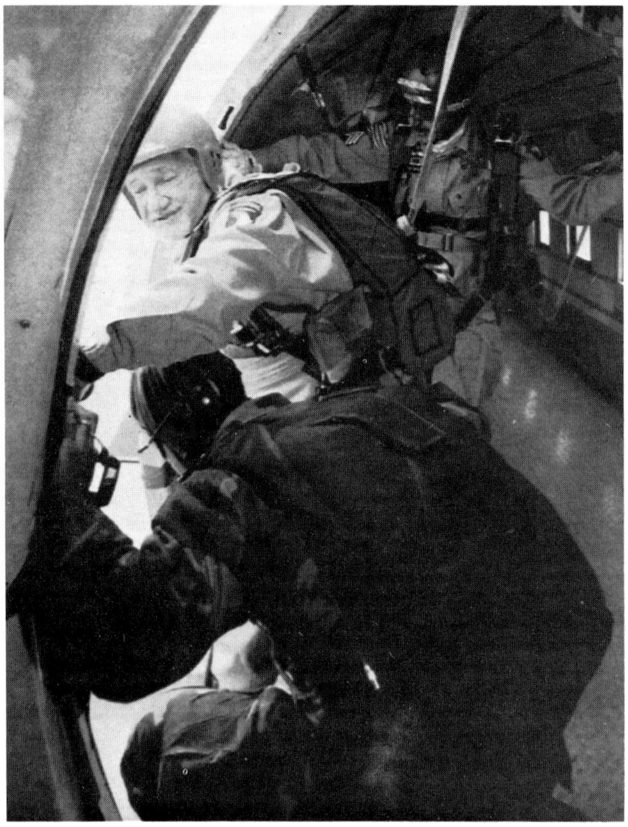

In — or rather out — go the pathfinders. *Left:* Robert C. Dunning, 73-year-old veteran of the 3rd Battalion, 506th Parachute Infantry, 101st Airborne, about to jump again into Normandy.

Right: Earl W. Draper, aged 70, nearly came a cropper when his parachute tangled as he left the aircraft and he had to deploy his back-up 'chute. He was injured in the rough landing.

The Parachute Regiment, on the other hand, wanted to take no chances with its veterans and three Lynx helicopters (*above*) from the Army Air Corps (the descendants of the old Glider Pilot Regiment) brought Major John Howard back to Bénouville to touch down on the very spot where his coup de main glider party landed 50 years (all but eight hours) before. *Right:* Helped by his former glider pilot, Jim Wallwork, Major Howard heads the parade across the 'new' Pegasus Bridge.

The memories come flooding back as the khaki silk blossoms once again over LZ 'N'.

The Prince of Wales, Colonel-in-Chief of the Parachute Regiment, takes the salute from the reviewing stand set up on the actual DZ (see plan page 644). His brother, the Duke of York, wears the uniform of Colonel-in-Chief of the Canadian Airborne Regiment, ignominiously disbanded in March 1995.

That night, with the fleet anchored off the Normandy coast and the paratroopers safely dropped, the stage was set for the events of Monday, June 6.

Three-quarters of an hour later, the focus of attention switched to the veterans of 6th Airborne who held their own parade in Ranville. Once again, the Prince of Wales took the salute before unveiling a bust of Major-General Richard Gale of the 6th Airborne at the local Mairie. It had been a marvellous day of sheer pageantry and moving ceremonial; a day which closely followed the scenario it was seeking to remember, and which perfectly set the scene for that which was to follow.

'A landing was made this morning on the coast of France . . .' June 6, 1994, 0620. The LCVP from HMS *Fearless* grounds on the sands of Normandy as the Allied flags, led by Great Britain and the United States, are brought ashore at Arromanches.

On Monday, the first event at 0630 hours was the landing of the flags of all the participating nations at Arromanches. These colours were brought ashore in a landing craft from HMS *Fearless*. Once landed, they were taken to Omaha in preparation for the main international event later in the day. Immediately afterwards, the American Rangers re-enacted their historic assault on Pointe du Hoc. Shortly after that, President Clinton and Président Mitterand attended the first service in the American Cemetery.

In general, once in France, while responsibility for the Royal Family and British VVIPs and VIPs remained that of the World War II Commemoration Team, that for the foreign heads of state and government became the province of the French government. The only exception was when a foreign personage was within the confines of one of the Commonwealth War Graves Commission cemeteries attending the National Service of Remembrance.

British participation in Normandy was covered under separate orders under Operation 'Iron Tribute', drawn up by HQ 3 Division. The division's participation was an apt choice as their forebears, then commanded by Major-General Tom Rennie, landed on Sword on D-Day.

The Main HQ (where I was stationed for much of June 5 and 6) had been established in the grounds of a sports complex — the Stade Henry Jeanne — in Bayeux. However, because of the spread of the events in Normandy, a second divisional HQ was set up on the bridge of the RFA *Sir Galahad* (of Falklands War fame) berthed in Caen, under the Chief-of-Staff of 3 Division, Colonel Tresham Gregg, to cover the eastern part of Normandy.

The former was responsible for the National Services at Bayeux and Ryes;

Aboard the USS *George Washington*, at dawn, President Clinton addressed the crew and assembled veterans from elevator No. 2 and then watched as a wreath was cast from the side to remember those who died at sea during the invasion. Rear Admiral Krekich is seated to the President's right.

'The longest day is not yet over.' Having flown to Pointe du Hoc by helicopter, the President paid tribute to the Rangers before a wreath — carried here by present-day Rangers of the 2nd Battalion, 75th Ranger Regiment — was laid at the memorial by Colonel Rudder's daughters. The Supreme Allied Commander Europe, General Joulwan, sits next to ex-Sergeant Leonard G. Lomell, a veteran of the 2nd Ranger Battalion, who was wounded shortly after he had come ashore at the base of the cliff in LCA 668. ***Right:*** **Once again, the colour guard parades with rifles of the period, in this case the Springfield Model 1903 rifle.**

the UK participation in the international ceremony at Omaha, and the Veterans' March Past at Arromanches, while the latter would cover the paratroop drop and Veterans' Parade at Ranville; the family service at Hermanville; the French veterans' event at Ver-sur-Mer, and the National Services at Ranville, Hermanville, Douvres-la-Délivrande and the international event in Caen.

Main supplies were brought in aboard the RFA *Sir Galahad* and her sister ship *Sir Bedivere*, with personnel being flown in to Deauville and Carpiquet airports. A helicopter support base was established in a sports complex at Douvres-la-Délivrande to cater for up to five Pumas, with the main Army Air Corps base at the HQ RHQ Para site at another sports field at Franceville/Merville.

It was foreseen that the 50th anniversary would be a major media event. Our public information policy was therefore pro-active, i.e. we provided facilities at each of the events with military or civil PROs at the various sites. However, soldiers were allowed to answer questions within their own area of competence such as: 'What is your task in the preparation for and running of the various events?'

Above: **On November 11, 1944, the memorial to the 1st Engineer Special Brigade was dedicated by its CO, Colonel Eugene M. Caffey.** ***Right:*** **In 1994, it was the setting for the Utah Beach commemoration organised by the 69th Air Defense Artillery Battery stationed in Giebelstadt, Germany. The choir from the 82nd Airborne sang a chorus and Petty Officer 2nd Class Susan Franklin of the Sixth Fleet in Italy played 'Taps'.**

At 1100 hours, Her Majesty The Queen and Président Mitterand led the congregation in a Service of Remembrance in Bayeux British Military Cemetery while concurrent services were held in Ryes, Ranville, Douvres-la-Délivrande and Hermanville at which senior members of the Royal Family represented the Queen.

'Of all the Second World War cemeteries of France, Bayeux is a particularly British shrine, with 3,935 of her dead beneath the scissored turf. The Queen arrived 20 minutes late by helicopter, her least favourite method of transport, to greet Président Mitterrand and conduct him down the long green aisle to the Cross of Remembrance, where they sat with the Duke of Edinburgh on a raised dais in a light drizzle. Rain dripped from the encircling chestnut trees and a leaden sky pressed down on the scene. Here and there, a first aid party struggled into the crowd to stretcher out a veteran cursed by age with the fatigue of standing. The congregation was called to prayer to give thanks for the success of the Normandy landings, to remember those who gave their lives there, and to acknowledge the heritage of freedom they won. Voices, grown tremulous with the years, summoned all their reserves to sing *O God, Our Help in Ages Past*. From a far corner, a Royal Marines bugler sounded the *Last Post*, and two minutes' silence fell on bare and bowed heads, only to be shattered by a wailing police siren on the road outside. Silent prayers before battle must often have been rent asunder by the thunder of shells. With prayers said and duty to the fallen done, the mood lifted. As Queen and Président rose and turned to leave, the band of the Royal Artillery played them out with Händel's *Music for the Royal Fireworks* as the Queen and the Duke inspected two rows of headstones. But then the dam broke, and veterans and their wives almost engulfed the royal couple.' Alan Hamilton *The Times*.

Who better qualified to address the assembled guests than Walter D. Ehlers, awarded the Medal of Honor while serving with the 18th Infantry, 1st Infantry Division, 'for conspicuous gallantry and intrepidity at the risk of his life above and beyond the call of duty on 9-10 June 1944, near Goville, France. Staff Sergeant Ehlers, always acting as the spearhead of the attack, repeatedly led his men against heavily defended enemy strong points exposing himself to deadly hostile fire whenever the situation required heroic and courageous leadership. Without waiting for an order, Staff Sergeant Ehlers, far ahead of his men, led his squad against a strongly defended enemy strong point, personally killing four of an enemy patrol who attacked him en route. Then crawling forward under withering machine gun fire, he pounced upon the guncrew and put it out of action. Turning his attention to two mortars, Staff Sergeant Ehlers led his men through this hail of bullets . . . ' His citation says it all.

The strand which once was Omaha. In the shadow of WN 66 and 68, a VVIP grandstand, fresh tarmac, immaculate paving, and waving flags: can this really be D-3 draw? To the veterans it was all so unreal. How could this be the same place where the 116th RCT landed . . . the 336th Engineers passed by on their epic march (page 364) . . . and Major Bingham and his squad fought around the long-lost house on the seafront (page 371)? Here, too, the first casualties had been laid to rest in the makeshift cemetery just along the beach . . . where landing craft lay rusting and broken . . .

The first major event of the afternoon was the international ceremony held on Omaha and hosted by the Président of France. A reviewing stand had been set up at D-3 draw at Les Moulins at the junction of Dog and Easy sectors. Watched by the Heads of State and thousands of veterans, the combined forces of the D-Day Allies formed up on the beach and then marched past, having heard moving recollections from some of those who had landed 50 years previously.

Then Walt Ehlers stepped up to the microphone: 'I was not new to battle, having survived the North African and Sicily invasions where my brother and I had fought side by side . . . A final battalion briefing readied us for the invasion. My brother and I had been assigned to different companies and, as the briefing ended, we waved to each other [he was killed on D-Day]. We found men pinned down on the beach; many wounded or killed and many terrified, all surrounded by ruined and swamped landing craft. The dead and wounded soldiers; the wreckage; the ability of the enemy to cause so much damage, made us realise that this war was far from over with its noise of mines, detonating bombs, airplanes, continuous roar of mortar and artillery shells bursting on the beach; rifle and machine gun-fire ripping holes in the sand and splashing in the water . . . Sadly it was the end of the war for a great many brave men.'

In 1994, the landing craft, each bearing the name of one of the invasion areas, were modern LARC-XVs. Five touched down and disembarked standard bearers carrying 50 flags representing formations which took part in operations on June 6, 1944.

The march past comprised forces from the United States, Britain, Canada, Poland, the Netherlands, Norway, Belgium, Luxembourg and France, the salute being taken in turn by the particular Head of State concerned.

J. Robert Slaughter (D Company, 116th Infantry, 29th Infantry Division): 'Someone at the White House selected me to accompany two 1st Division veterans who were to escort President Clinton down the hill from the American Cemetery to Omaha Beach. They were Captain Joseph T. Dawson who led G Company, 16th Infantry, 1st Division, ashore in the first wave and Staff Sergeant Walter Ehlers, 18th Infantry, 1st Division, who came in a short time later. The "walk-talk" with Clinton was to follow the conclusion of the main ceremony at the cemetery. At 5.30 p.m., Master of Ceremonies Walter Cronkite opened the ceremony with remarks about his rôle aboard an American bomber flying over the huge armada early D-Day. The President's message was a tribute to the sacrifice of the D-Day warriors: ". . . On these beaches, the forces of freedom turned the tide of the 20th century . . . Let us not forget when they were young, these men saved the world. . . . ". After the conclusion of speeches, the President's handlers whisked Dawson, Ehlers and me to the path leading to the beach. White House staffer Brad Blakely reminded me that I was to walk on the President's right, Dawson on the left and Ehlers to the left of Dawson. When the path narrowed at the steps, I was to step back and let Ehlers move to the President's right. While walking, we were to talk about our respective rôles on D-Day. Brad introduced each of us to the President. While shaking hands, he looked straight into my eyes and said, "Thank you for what you did." I replied, "Thank you, sir." He moved to the others, shaking hands and thanking them as well. Dawson said, "Mr President, shall we walk to the beach?" Each of us assumed our assigned positions, walking slowly down the path. TV cameras were hidden along the pathway and every blind bend was covered by Secret Service agents. After descending the steps, I resumed my original position to Mr Clinton's right. He grabbed me by the elbow to steady me along the uneven path to the sand. At the edge of the sand, there were beach shingles laid out to read "Omaha Beach 1994". Major General Matthew A. Zimmerman, Chief of Army Chaplains, concluded the "walk-talk" with a prayer. Arrangements had been made to transport us back to the cemetery in separate military vehicles. Walking across the loose sand to the waiting Hum-Vees, Mr Clinton caught my left shoulder and removed his loafer-type shoe, shaking sand from it, then the other. Captain Dawson pointed up the hill where he and his G Company penetrated enemy defenses. Brad directed us to our respective vehicles. President Clinton countered, "No, we'll all ride together. Bob, you get up front. Walter, you and Joe sit in the middle and I'll ride in back." The President leaped into the back, sitting on the railing of the truck. Plowing through the loose sand and over the rough shingle, the four-wheel drive vehicle was a bumpy ride. We followed the Colleville exit road which was the route the "Big Red One" opened up for traffic 50 years ago.'

President Clinton is escorted from the wreath-laying ceremony at the Normandy American Cemetery by Al Ungerleider (left) of the 29th Division and Walter Ehlers.

A cross in stones — a gesture to the fallen on Omaha.

Apart from the national commemorations, numerous regimental and unit remembrances were taking place all over Normandy. It is really unfair to single out any one particular event but this picture (*right*) was too good to leave out as the Suffolks held their memorial service at Hillman (see pages 554-555) — this shot being taken by Colonel Lummis. Two days later, the regiment unveiled a new memorial at the Château de la Londe captured on June 28, 1944.

Later that afternoon, Prime Minister Chrétien led the Canadian National Service at Bény-sur-Mer at which those who fell during the landings of June were remembered. Services were also held in Ouistreham to commemorate the action there of the French commandos and in Grainville-Langannerie to remember those members of the 1st Polish Armoured Division who died in the follow-up operations.

Memorials unveiled ranged right across the spectrum: from this unusual creation (*above*) at airfield B-3 at Ste Croix (see page 615), to the statue of General Eisenhower (*right*) dedicated at Bayeux on June 5 by his son, General John Eisenhower. *Below:* Denis Sweeting (see page 619) first proposed a memorial in memory of the Typhoon pilots killed during the liberation of Normandy in 1987 and one was erected at Noyers-Bocage, a small village ten miles south-west of Caen, in 1990 (see *After the Battle* No. 69). A memorial wall listing the names of all the 151 pilots was unveiled in June 1994. Denis Sweeting stands in front of the Canadian Air Cadet from 'Typhoon' Squadron in Ontario. All pictures by Squadron Leader A. I. Le Gresley.

And then there was the participation of the preserved military hardware, without which the sense of occasion would have been lost, although the presence of hundreds of military vehicles on the narrow Normandy roads added to the horrendous traffic problems that occurred due to security restrictions during the official events. Enthusiasts came with their vehicles from all corners of the world: from New Zealand and Australia; the USA and Canada; and all parts of Europe with many entries arriving from former Eastern Bloc countries . . . by land . . . sea . . . and air!

One of the most adventurous was Tor Nørstegaard who flew down from Norway in his Piper L-4J 44-80287 with co-pilots Morten Agerup Myhr and Tor's wife, Mari. Tor purchased the aircraft in Sweden in 1988 when a total write-off but, after a 4½-year rebuild, it took to the air again in July 1992. When he decided to give his 'Grasshopper' the '43-E' code of the US 29th Division's 111th Field Artillery Battalion, it followed that a landing on Omaha would fulfil Tor's wildest dreams; achieved on the morning of June 3. Fortunately, Seimon Pugh Jones was on hand to photograph the historic landing for us.

The parade through Bayeux on June 7 was one of the highlights but was this really 1994 . . . or 1944?

'Monty' rides again — an enthusiastic reception for ex-RAF veteran Norman Hampden. All photographs by Seimon Pugh Jones.

The last act. The veterans march onto the beach at Arromanches where L4003 *Arakan* and the two LCVPs form the backdrop.

The final British event took place on Green Beach in Item sector. With a backcloth of Royal Naval ships and before a large crowd crammed onto the seafront at Arromanches, over 10,000 veterans marched past Her Majesty The Queen and on into history.

Right: **The sights look familiar . . . the message was clear. 'This town and this beach must hold a unique place in the memories of those of you, who were here, in June 1944', the Queen told her assembled servicemen. 'D-Day was the beginning of the end . . . veterans of the Normandy campaign, you deserve your nation's thanks . . . '**

Mosquitos in 1945; a Lancaster, Hurricane and Spitfires in 1994. We end as we began . . . the link over 50 years is now complete.

Operation 'Overlord' stands as one of the largest and most complex military operations ever undertaken. Planning the commemorations 50 years later posed many similar problems, albeit in microcosm. Timings, the weather, tides and international co-operation were all major factors and the logistic problems posed by an international force consisting of hundreds of aircraft, ships and vehicles and thousands of troops and veterans were both challenging and deeply satisfying. No one in any of the planning teams had any idea of the emotion that was to be generated at these simple ceremonies, but everyone was convinced at the end of the day that a fitting tribute had been paid to those who wrote a glorious page in military history.

This AVRE at Lion-sur-Mer was dedicated on June 6, 1994 by General Sir Ian Harris, in 1944 CO of the 2nd Battalion, Royal Ulster Rifles.

Normandy Today

Major Tonie Holt

FOUNDER, MAJOR & MRS HOLT'S BATTLEFIELD TOURS

Over two decades of conducting tour groups around the Normandy beaches has led us to believe that there are two main reasons why people come: firstly, to remember those that lost their lives, and remember the friends of youth; and, secondly, to attempt to recapture the comradeship of those past years and to experience once again the heightened senses that the prospect of imminent death inspires. The youngest veterans of those landings of June 6, 1944 are now approaching 70 years of age yet many thousands of them returned to Normandy in 1994.

But most of those who visit the beaches today are not veterans. Many may be relatives of those that took part in Operation 'Overlord', others will vary in interest from the mildly curious to the serious student of military history. What should they look for along the 50 miles of coastline in order to catch a glimpse of what happened half a century before?

During nearly 20 years in the Army, Tonie Holt had been on a number of battlefield tours to Normandy, including one while he was a student at the Command and Staff College at Camberley. In 1977, having left the Army to pursue a career as an author and historian, Tonie, with his wife Valmai, ran their own inaugural battlefield tour to France. Here, in 1995, they are pictured at the Pegasus Bridge Museum, having now sold their tour company to be free to continue their writing activities.

Early post-war visitors to Normandy needed little to remind them that they were bathing on a battlefield. This is the eastern end of Sword with Gooseberry No. 5 in the background.

BEFORE TRAVELLING

It is in this phase that most travellers fail, that is to say that very few people prepare themselves adequately in advance for a visit to the battlefields. However fleeting the visit is to be, a little work beforehand adds immeasurably to the efficiency and effectiveness of what follows.

First, it is sensible to be aware of the basic facts of the invasion, i.e. the layout of the five landing areas, Utah, Omaha, Gold, Juno and Sword, and that the first two, being nearer to America than the others, were chosen for the US landings in order to allow their direct re-supply by sea from the United States. Second, it is essential to have good maps and to mark the places that you wish to visit.

In former days, we used Michelin Sheet 54 (or the expanded Sheet 231) which covers the entire Normandy area from the Cherbourg peninsula to Le Havre. (Michelin also produce a reprint of the old 1947 edition of Sheet 102 which has much information of interest concerning the battle overprinted in magenta.) However, all are at the 1:200 000 scale or 1cm to 2km (very approximately a half-inch to a mile).

A larger scale (1:100 000) is offered by the IGN 'Green' series although Sheet 6 Caen–Cherbourg annoyingly chops off its eastern edge at Caen, meaning that one needs the adjoining Sheet 7, Le Havre–Rouen, to complete the Sword area and 6th Airborne sector.

However, in the absence of a map that showed the precise locations of memorials, museums, bunkers, cemeteries and battle-lines, *Major & Mrs Holt's Battle Map of Normandy* is invaluable. Complete with detailed indexes, it has a scale of approximately 1cm to 1km and is double-sided in four colours.

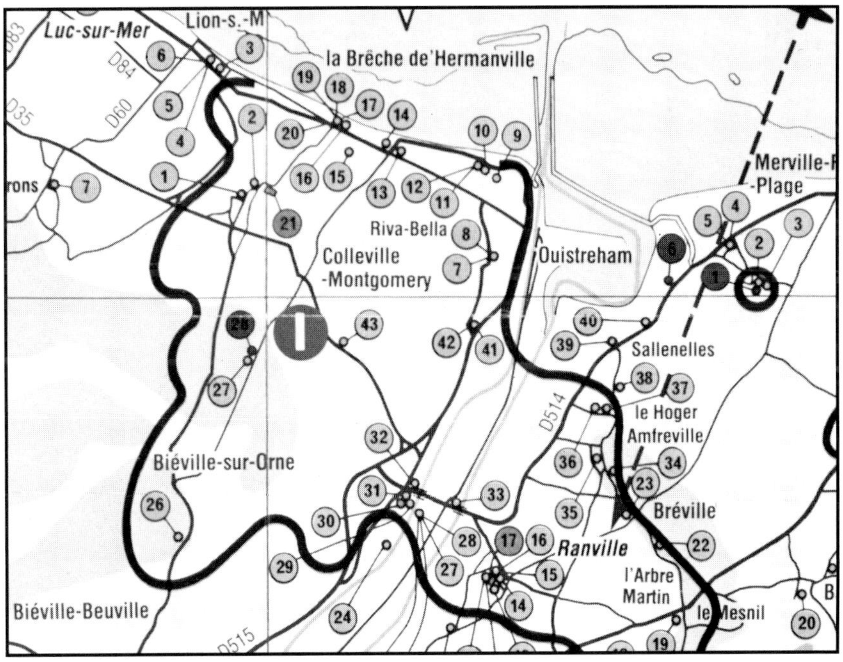

Today, maps and a good guide book are essential tools to get the most out of a visit. *Major & Mrs Holt's Battle Map of Normandy* combines the best of both worlds by listing hundreds of memorials and monuments; the cemeteries; museums; bunkers and other sites of interest.

It is also a good idea to draw in the routes that you propose to follow because, apart from simplifying navigation on the ground, the routes can then be compared with battle sketch maps showing the lines of troop movements, thus adding time and space factors to what otherwise could be just a visit to static features.

If you wish to attempt to see everything, you need a guidebook; either *Major & Mrs Holt's Visitor's Guide to Normandy Landing Beaches* published by Moorland; Patrice Boussel and Eddy Florentin's *Guide to the Landing Beaches* (in French) by Presses de la Cité, or Jean-Pierre Benamou's *Normandy 1944* by Heimdal.

The essential points to be covered during a visit to the D-Day beaches should include some of each of the four elements: the battlefield; the cemeteries, the museums, and the memorials. I deliberately put the museums and memorials last because they are post-battle and most visitors really want to see the actual battlefield itself.

VESTIGES HISTORIQUES

This covers what the French call those things that still remain, i.e., the bunkers and gun positions. In the search to find out what it was like on the day, it is best to concentrate upon those things that have a direct connection with that time and therefore the first element consists of a selection of German defensive sites that featured in the landings and where there are significant remains to be seen. The sites I recommend should not be missed, running from east to west, are the following:

- Merville Battery (pages 235-239). Derelict for many years, the Airborne Assault Normandy Trust sponsored the restoration of No. 1 Casemate in 1982 (see *After the Battle* No. 68) which now displays relics of the battle.
- Pegasus Bridge (pages 224-231). Up until 1993, the original bridge bearing its marks of the battle could still be seen but its removal has destroyed one of the unique 'vestiges' to be seen in the British sector. At the time of writing, the old bridge lies rusting on the river bank, its fate uncertain.
- Hillman Strong point (pages 551-555). Since the Suffolk Regiment Association acquired the plot of land on which the main bunker stands in 1989, an orientation table has been mounted on top, and other blockhouses and bunkers have been progressively unearthed.
- Douvres Radar Station (pages 562-568). This is the remains of the former German radar station. The site covered a large area and, according to the time of year and state of the crops, it is possible to see the remains of the northern blockhouses. A small museum has recently been established in one of the casemates and a Giant Würzburg aerial erected on site, although not on the original position.

All the easily salvageable remnants of 'Neptune' disappeared in the early post-war years. Those gliders that were repairable were recovered for use in later airborne operations; others, like Major Howard's Horsa, wrecked at Pegasus Bridge *(above)*, or those at Les Forges *(below)*, were unceremoniously cut up for scrap.

- The Longues Battery (pages 54 and 419), also called locally Le Chaos Battery, has been well preserved and progressively restored in recent years, although rock falls at the cliff's edge make it essential that visitors take extra care.
- Pointe du Hoc (pages 326-338). The memorial area is 30.5 acres and the site was preserved by the French Comité de la Pointe du Hoc. In 1960, a dramatic granite 'dagger' memorial was raised on top of one of the German bunkers, with inscriptions in English and French that commemorate the Rangers' action. On June 6, 1979, in a ceremony attended by General Omar Bradley, the American Battle Monuments Commission took over responsibility for maintenance of the area.
- The Leclerc Mémorial Area at Les Dunes-de-Varreville (pages 393-394). Utah Beach was the landing place for the US 4th Division and later for General Patton's Third Army and General Leclerc's 2ème Division Blindée. This was where Leclerc's force came ashore and there is a Comité du Débarquement (D-Day Commemorative Committee) memorial to commemorate the fact. There may well also be an armoured car and a half-track vehicle on display, but they seem surprisingly mobile and may not always be there. There are also blockhouses and bunkers hidden in the sands.
- Batterie de Crisbecq (pages 399-401). There are formidable concrete remains here of the control bunkers and gun emplacements of Marinebatterie Marcouf (the discrepancy in the name was explained on page 154). The central bunker has been converted into a small museum and information centre with signs in English, French and German, and it is possible to climb on top of it to get a good view towards Utah Beach. Opening times are very erratic.

Unfortunately, genuine relics of D-Day are very thin on the ground, and even now are getting fewer. *Above:* LCA 1825, which was a centre of attraction at Arromanches for many years, suddenly disappeared in the spring of 1995: destroyed, so we are told, because it was too costly to maintain! *Right:* Without doubt, the best 'veteran' of D-Day must be the AVRE disinterred from behind Mike Red in 1976. Not only was it a proven participant in the assault (see pages 464-465) but when recovered its interior turned out to be a veritable time capsule of D-Day artefacts. It was restored by the French Army in their Caen workshops and returned to the M2 beach exit to be unveiled in the presence of former members of its crew (see page 466) in October 1977. (The AVRE at Hermanville-la-Brèche (page 533) was only brought to Normandy in 1987 and the one at Lion-sur-Mer (page 686) in 1994.)

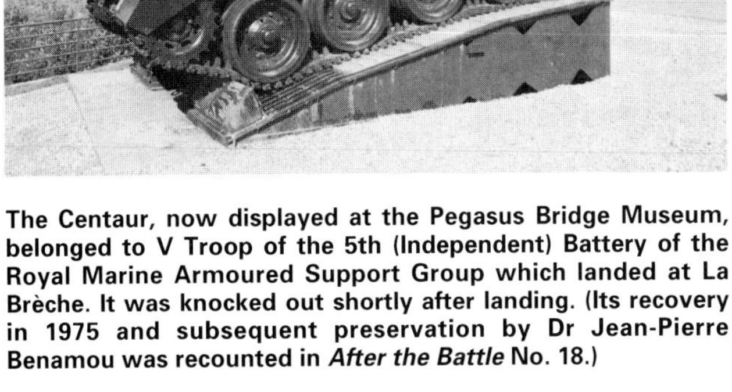

The Centaur, now displayed at the Pegasus Bridge Museum, belonged to V Troop of the 5th (Independent) Battery of the Royal Marine Armoured Support Group which landed at La Brèche. It was knocked out shortly after landing. (Its recovery in 1975 and subsequent preservation by Dr Jean-Pierre Benamou was recounted in *After the Battle* No. 18.)

Although it failed to make dry land, 'Bold', one of the DD Shermans of the Canadian 6th Armoured Regiment, is also a genuine D-Day veteran (see page 475). Having been raised by Jean Demota's salvage company in 1970 (see page 478), Canadian Army engineers took over the restoration and it was set up on Nan Green the following year.

CEMETERIES

The currency of war is death and in the First and Second World Wars, the payment was mostly made with the lives of young men. It is important to remember this otherwise it is too easy to romanticise about deeds of valour and devotion to a cause. Although the cemeteries listed below are military cemeteries, it must not be forgotten that more French civilians died in the fighting that accompanied the Liberation than were killed when the Germans occupied the area.

At the outset, each US division was to be provided with its own cemetery although, as graves registration platoons were pulled back from brigades and divisions and replaced by one company per corps, there was a movement to reduce the number of American cemeteries (see page 305). Company headquarters and all four platoons of the 603rd Graves Registration Company were concentrated at the cemetery at Ste Mère-Eglise *(above)* which was taken over by VII Corps on June 16.

American

Eight battlefield cemeteries had been established by June 10 in the two American beach-heads, or one per division, but during the following week, graves registration companies began to concentrate the dead in five locations: St Laurent, Blosville, La Cambe, Orglandes and St Mère-Eglise. After the war, the US authorities established permanent area cemeteries and the one covering Normandy was developed to replace the wartime No. 1 Cemetery at St Laurent-sur-Mer.

Initially, the collection, evacuation and identification of American dead had to be improvised as pre-combat training of GIs did not include instruction in graves registration procedures. The divisions in Normandy learned only by experience but the system devised by VII Corps was adjudged the best. Details were despatched to operate collecting points as required by each division, each team usually consisting of four men, with one to three teams per division. The teams carried the bodies to a battalion collecting point, from where they were evacuated to the division collecting point by regimental service troops. Here, bodies were identified and transferred to graves registration company vehicles for delivery to the corps cemetery. This identification procedure carried out at the divisional collecting point reduced the number of unknowns which averaged just over 1 per cent in Normandy. The first cemetery at Ste Mère-Eglise was soon filled with some 2,000 burials so a second site, known as Ste Mère-Eglise No. 2, had to be opened on June 25.

The original St Laurent Cemetery No. 1 — now the Normandy American Cemetery — lies in the municipality of Colleville-sur-Mer.

Six years were spent in checking discrepancies and enquiring of next-of-kin as to whether they wanted the remains repatriated to the United States, or buried in a permanent cemetery which would become the responsibility of the American Battle Monuments Commission. In the event, only 41 per cent of the dead were interred in the ten new overseas cemeteries which were approved by Congress in August 1947.

The American Cemetery at St Laurent now contains 9,386 burials of whom 307 are unknown. It is beautifully maintained and there is a memorial chapel, a reflective pool and a visitors' centre at the entrance where the resident supervisor has his office. More than a million people visit here annually.

Padre F. O. Sanders of No. 8 Beach Group officiates at the service held on June 17 at the small battlefield cemetery at Bernières on Nan White.

Jean Paul Pallud found the site on Rue Victor Tesnière near the now-disused station.

British and Canadian

Following the principle laid down in World War I, it was the continuing policy of the Imperial War Graves Commission (the name was changed to Commonwealth in 1960) not to permit the repatriation of British and Commonwealth war dead to the home country of the deceased. Isolated field graves were concentrated into permanent cemeteries and some battlefield burial grounds (like those on pages 446 and 515) were transferred into other locations. Nevertheless, many of the dead remain buried in their original graves established by the wartime graves registration units. Although there are some 20 Commonwealth cemeteries in Normandy, the following contain casualties from D-Day:

Ryes War Cemetery, Bazenville

Situated inland from Arromanches in the area where the 50th Division fought on June 6, this cemetery contains some burials made just two days after the landing. The total of 981 is made up of 630 British, 21 Canadian, 1 Australian, 1 Polish and 328 German dead.

Bény-sur-Mer Canadian War Cemetery, Reviers

The 2,049 buried in this war cemetery are mainly those of the Canadian 3rd Division, who lost their lives either on D-Day, or during the early days of the advance towards Caen. Among those buried here are nine pairs of brothers, and also three British soldiers and an airman, and a French soldier.

The majority of the Canadian dead were subsequently transferred to the permanent cemetery which was begun at Bény-sur-Mer by No. 1 Canadian Cemetery Construction Unit, Royal Canadian Engineers, in November 1944 ***(right).***

Left: **At La Délivrande, M. Pipon, on whose land the cemetery had been established with his agreement, subsequently changed his mind and in September 1944 requested that the bodies be removed.** *Right:* **A new site was found on property belonging to M. Noisette, and exhumation of the original burials was begun on October 11 by the British No. 32 Graves Registration Unit. Exhumation could be a dangerous business and there are frequent reports in the graves unit records of careless original interment with full equipment including grenades and ammunition!** *Below:* **La Délivrande War Cemetery after completion.**

La Délivrande War Cemetery, Douvres

This cemetery contains 1,125 burials, of which 927 are British, 11 Canadian, 3 Australian, 1 Polish, 182 German and 1 unidentified. Most date from June 6; others were brought in later from the battlefields between the coast and Caen.

Hermanville War Cemetery

Many of the 1,005 buried in this cemetery died in the fighting in the surrounding area on June 6, and the first few days of the drive towards Caen. There are 986 British burials, 13 Canadian, 3 Australian and 3 French.

Ranville War Cemetery and Churchyard

The name of Ranville will always be linked with the landing by parachute and glider of the 6th Airborne Division, many of whose dead rest here. The cemetery contains 2,564 burials, of which 2,153 are British, 76 Canadian, 1 Australian, 3 New Zealand, 5 French, 1 Polish, 1 Belgian, 323 German and 1 unidentified. In the adjoining churchyard, 47 British soldiers are buried around the perimeter wall.

Bayeux War Cemetery

There was little fighting in Bayeux itself, and the cemetery, the largest in France from the Second World War, contains 4,648 burials brought in from the surrounding districts and from hospitals that were located nearby. By individual countries they comprise: United Kingdom 3,935, Canada 181, Australia 17, New Zealand 8, South Africa 1, France 3, Czechoslovakia 2, Italy 2, Russia 7, Germany 466, Poland 25, unidentified 1.

Although galvanised pressed-steel crosses had been decided upon in February 1944, they did not reach France until August, and units had to improvise with wooden markers (see page 446). *Left:* **Bayeux was selected in July 1944 by No. 32 Graves Registration Unit as the location for what was to be the largest of the permanent British cemeteries in Normandy with space for 5,661 graves. The first interments took place on July 9; the following month, when the prefabricated crosses arrived, the unit was made responsible for signwriting them for all the permanent cemeteries.** *Right:* **In the event, burials at Bayeux totalled 4,648.**

Bayeux also contains German burials in a separate plot, but it is common practice for the headstones of SS casualties buried in Commonwealth War Graves Commission cemeteries not to bear details of their rank for obvious reasons. SS-Obersturmführer Karl Gotthard was commander of 5. Kompanie, II. Bataillon, of SS-Panzergrenadier-Regiment 26, and he led his company in the dawn attack against the Royal Winnipeg Rifles at Putot-en-Bessin on June 8, (see page 496) being killed the following day. ***Right:*** **Brana Radovic pictured his headstone at Bayeux which, as explained, gives no clue as to his service.**

German

German policy towards the establishment of cemeteries for their war dead varies. Where burials were made in British or Canadian wartime cemeteries, and these cemeteries later became permanent, the graves have been left in situ. In other cases, predominantly in the American sector, the graves have been concentrated into area cemeteries, now maintained by the German War Graves Commission — the Volksbund Deutsche Kriegsgräberfürsorge (VDK). In 1948, British and French graves teams began bringing in German dead from more than 1,400 isolated sites and, in 1956, the VDK began work on concentrating the German burials into six cemeteries (apart from those remaining in CWGC cemeteries). They are:

Champigny-St André, between Evreux and Dreux, 19,809 burials.
Huisnes-sur-Mer, near Mont St Michel, 11,956 burials.
La Cambe, near Isigny, 21,115 burials.
Marigny-la-Chapelle, near St Lô, 11,169 burials.
Orglandes, near Valognes, 10,152 burials.
St Désir-de-Lisieux, 3,735 burials.

The largest is at La Cambe, established on the site of one of the old American cemeteries from which the dead were exhumed in 1947. Inside the cemetery are small groups of black stone crosses. These are symbolic and do not mark graves. The graves are marked by flat stones engraved with the names of those below — often four or more together. The Germans call this 'comradeship in death' though a more practical reason is that the French were unwilling to give up land for the invader to use and the Germans have had to bury all their Normandy dead in the six locations. A mass grave in the centre of the cemetery contains 296 dead. The grassed mound, or ossuary, is ringed at the bottom by stones carrying the names of the dead and surmounted by a huge black cross and two figures representing mourning parents.

American policy towards the burial of German dead varied, the First, Seventh and Ninth Armies using the same cemeteries for their own and enemy dead, segregated in separate plots. However, the Third Army established separate cemeteries for US and German burials, a policy which made the post-war establishment of permanent cemeteries easier. When the American dead were evacuated from the 29th Division Cemetery at La Cambe, which had an adjoining German plot, the whole site was then used to concentrate German casualties from all over Normandy.

After the war, British and French graves registration units carried out further burials at La Cambe so that by the time the German War Graves Commission (the Volksbund Deutsche Kriegsgräberfürsorge) took over in 1956, the cemetery had with some 8,000 graves already become one of the largest provisional German Soldatenfriedhöfe of the Second World War in France. Expansion and improvement of the site was carried out in 1958 under the slogan 'Reconciliation over the Graves' when young volunteers from various countries served in an international youth camp to help the Volksbund lay out the permanent cemetery. This included the building of the large six-metre-high tumulus which was to serve as a mass grave for 207 unknown and 89 named dead. The cemetery was dedicated on September 21, 1961, and today contains 21,115 burials.

The impression here is one of solemnity and of sadness, which is a typical reaction when visiting German cemeteries. Whether this is due to the Teutonic inheritance showing through in the architecture — the use of dark oak trees and granite crosses as symbols of strength — or a deliberate intent to express remorse is impossible to say. It is, however, worthwhile making an effort to contrast the differing styles of the various national cemeteries — German, American and British — and asking the rhetorical question: 'What is their purpose?'

MUSEUMS

The first museum to be opened in Normandy, specific to D-Day, was that at Arromanches inaugurated by M. Coty, Président of the French Republic on the 10th anniversary. Today, there are over 20 museums, varying from those with official funding and support, to commercial ventures and others privately owned.

The Musée du Débarquement (Landing Museum) was established on waste ground behind the beach at Arromanches in 1954 with financial help from the British government.

Situated alongside the Pegasus Bridge café — itself a museum piece — the Musée des Troupes Aéroportées concentrates on the exploits of the 6th Airborne Division. (See also page 231.)

● **Bénouville.** Musée des Troupes Aéroportées. More popularly known as the Pegasus Bridge Museum, it has been remarkably improved in recent years and presents a vivid picture of the British airborne landings via a sand table model and audio-visual display that overlooks the coup de main site at the bridge itself, plus numerous personal effects donated by veterans.

● **Merville.** Battery Museum. The museum is jointly operated with the Pegasus Bridge Museum and is situated in one of the casemates of the Merville battery. Outside, notice boards tell the story of the 9th Parachute Battalion attack on D-Day, while inside are many period photographs, exhibits of parachute equipment, a typical 75mm gun and other British and German pieces of equipment.

Its sister museum is located within No. 1 Casemate at the Merville Battery. ***Left:*** **As it was, having been used as a cattle shelter, and** ***right*** **in 1982 after 10 Field Squadron, RE, had cleared out the muck and mire.**

● **Ste Mère-Eglise.** Airborne Museum. Inaugurated by James Gavin in 1961, this is housed in a parachute-shaped building which is entered through the fuselage of a re-created Waco glider. The story of the American airborne landings is told through donated artefacts and an audio-visual presentation. A C-47 that took part in the operation is displayed in a specially-built hangar.

Left: **American airborne activities are featured at the Airborne Museum at Ste Mère-Eglise.** ***Right:*** **In June 1983, a C-47 Skytrain, 42-00825, was added which was once on the strength of the 439th Troop Carrier Group and carried paratroops of the 101st Airborne Division to Normandy from its base at Upottery in Devon. On the night of June 5/6, it was piloted by 1st Lieutenant Charles H. Imschweiler of the 92nd Troop Carrier Squadron which means that it should bear the code 'J8', not 'D8' of the 94th TCS. (The serial number 43-15159 and name** ***Argonia*** **are also incorrect.) After the war, it was sold off to Scandinavian Airlines, then spent some time back in the USA before being bought by the French Naval Aviation Department. It was painstakingly restored by Yves Tariel, President of the Parachutists' League of Friendship, and his associates.**

- **Utah Beach.** Musée du Débarquement. This museum, built around strong point WN 5, offers dioramas, films and moving models plus the recorded memories of veterans in order to explain the actions here on June 6. Various guns, tanks and landing craft are stationed outside.
- **Quinéville.** Museum of Liberty. A substantial modern building close to the sea, fronted by a Liberty Highway marker stone, the museum concentrates upon telling the D-Day story using photographs, slide shows, dioramas, models and vehicles. It does not show any weapons.
- **Cherbourg.** Musée de la Guerre et de la Libération. Although commemorating later events, the well-intentioned museum, set in the marvellous panoramic viewpoint of Fort du Roule, underwent several serious burglaries in recent years which depleted its exhibits. However, it is now regaining some stature and is well worth a visit for its original maps, posters and photographs, its record of the Free French forces, and its well-documented story of the battle for Cherbourg.

On the Cherbourg peninsula, the Utah Beach Museum was first opened in 1962 in one of the casemates of strong point WN 5. Now, one of the bunkers *(below)* actually lies within the new museum building *(above)*. In front stands the memorial to the US 4th Infantry Division.

It was here that the division's assistant commander earned his Medal of Honor (see page 411) and not far from where the only Ritterkreuz of the land battle was awarded to the commander of the battery at Marcouf (see page 401). We have already covered the exploits surrounding the four D-Day Medals of Honor and the sole Victoria Cross. The only Ritterkreuz awarded for action on D-Day itself would appear to be that of Korvettenkapitän Heinrich Hoffman (see page 570), but we asked Jean Paul Pallud to check his computer database (based on *Die Träger des Ritterkreuzes* by Walther-Peer Fellgiebel) for other possibilities *(right)* although the date of the actual action is not stated. However, with over 9,000 awarded during the Second World War, the Knight's Cross cannot be equated with either the Medal of Honor (431) or the Victoria Cross (182).

RITTERKREUZ

	Date of award	*Unit*
Kriegsmarine		
Korvettenkapitän Heinrich Hoffman	June 7	5. T-Boots-Flottille
Korvettenkapitän Viktor Rall	June 10	15. Vorpost.Flottille
Kapitän zur See Rudolf Petersen	June 13	Führer der Schnellboote
Kapitänleutnant Kurt Johannsen	June 14	5. S-Boots-Flottille
Kapitänleutnant Götz von Mirbach	June 14	9. S-Boots-Flottille
Oberleutnant (MA) Walter Ohmsen	June 14	Mar.Art.Abt. 260
Luftwaffe		
Hauptmann Helmut Bergmann	June 9	8/NJG 4
Oberfeldwebel Rudolf Busch	June 9	1/Aufkl.Gr. 121
Oberleutnant Hans Ehlers	June 9	3/JG 1
Leutnant Hans Grünberg	June 9	5/JG 3
Generalmajor Werner Junck	June 9	II. Jagdkorps
Hauptmann Ludwig Meister	June 9	1/NJG 4
Leutnant Karl Willius	June 9	2/JG 26
Major Kurt Dahlmann	June 11	I/SKG 10
Leutnant Siegfried Lemke	June 14	1/JG 2

Right: **'Exposition Omaha' — a private museum on D-1 Draw at Vierville.**

● **Grandcamp.** Rangers Museum. Facing the sea, the small museum tells the Rangers' story through photographs and minor artefacts. It covers their history from formation to the attack on Pointe du Hoc, and includes a film presentation.

● **Vierville-sur-Mer.** Musée Omaha. This is a private museum housed in a 1944 Nissen hut (used for Allied troop entertainment). It has a good collection of American and German arms, uniforms and insignia.

● **Surrain.** Another privately owned museum on the main N13 between Formigny and Mosles. It contains uniformed Allied and German models, weapons, insignia, World War II ration kits, etc. Outside, a variety of vehicles can be seen.

● **Bayeux.** Musée de la Bataille de Normandie. This is a large museum that tells the story of the landings and the subsequent fighting at Hill 112 and Falaise via a chronological 'walk through' presentation of newspapers, artefacts and film. It also displays a number of British and German vehicles including tanks.

● **Bayeux.** De Gaulle Museum. In the centre of Bayeux, the museum concentrates upon the speech that the Général made during his historic visit to the city on June 14, 1944. It has a small display of personal memorabilia.

Left: **Inland from the beach, another private museum is located on the N13 at Surrain.**

The Musée de la Bataille de Normandie, founded by Dr Jean-Pierre Benamou, was initially based around his personal collection. Housed in a purpose-built museum building opposite the Commonwealth War Graves Commission cemetery, it now encompasses the wider battle for Normandy and displays vehicles of the type used in the campaign.

● **Port-en-Bessin.** Musée des Épaves Sous-Marines du Débarquement. Located near Commes, this private museum is devoted to relics recovered from the sea (like the Sherman DD at Courseulles — see *After the Battle* No. 34), predominantly displaying armour which sank on D-Day off the coast.

● **Arromanches.** Musée du Débarquement. The museum overlooks the remains of the Mulberry harbour and, through models and film, tells its story as well as offering a dioramic presentation of the landings themselves.

● **Creully.** Château Tower. The tower was used as a broadcasting studio by the BBC and a memorial plaque commemorates the fact. The aspect of the room has been preserved and there are a number of photographs on display from the period.

The Musée des Épaves Sous-Marines du Débarquement was created by Jacques Lemonchois just outside Port-en-Bessin. Salvage rights off the Normandy coast were split in 1975 between Jacques and Jean Demota (see page 689) and the museum comprises solely artefacts that he has recovered from the sea. Prime exhibits are *(above)* an M7 Priest, left, and a Sherman M4 with M1 'dozer blade, and DD Shermans *(below)* but there are many other items on display.

● **Douvres.** Radar Museum. This is situated in one of the bunkers of the German radio station. Using photographs, displays and models, it shows the Atlantic Wall and gives an explanation of the radar system. It also presents a picture of everyday life in the complex in 1944.

● **Colleville-Montgomery.** Sword Museum. This is a privately owned collection of invasion artefacts found in the area by the proprietor, M. Chauvin-Doisy, and is located on the corner of the Avenue de Bruxelles.

● **Ouistreham.** No. 4 Commando Museum. Located opposite the Casino, the number of exhibits has grown, despite the setbacks of theft which seems a natural hazard of war museums in Normandy. It concentrates on the commando exploits (including the French under Commandant Kieffer) at Ouistreham.

● **Ouistreham.** Musée du Mur de l'Atlantique. This is the only major German construction left in Ouistreham and is surrounded by new houses. It was designed to control anti-aircraft defence of the harbour and since 1987 has been a museum. Opening times are temperamental.

● **Caen.** Mémorial Musée pour la Paix. Following the latest ideological trend, Caen established its 'Peace' Museum in 1988, inaugurated by Président Mitterand. However, its singular exhibit is a replica Typhoon, the 'museum' itself comprising an audio-visual presentation of the story of the liberation.

The Musée du Mur de l'Atlantique — the Atlantic Wall Museum — is appropriately housed in one of the bunkers which served as the observation post and fire-direction centre for the defence of this sector (see page 547).

The latest museum to open in Normandy is the Douvres Radar Museum. For nearly 50 years, the bunkers of the German position had been largely covered over, but Jean Paul Pallud pictured Casemate 'Anton' being excavated in the autumn of 1993 (see page 567). Now, with the addition of a Würzburg, it is a true 'battlefield' museum.

With more than 300 memorials to choose from, it is almost invidious to single out any one unit, but one of the very first to be erected *(left)* was this plaque at Ranville recording the fact that it was the first village to be liberated at 2.30 a.m. on June 6 by the 13th (Lancashire) Battalion. *Above:* It remains unchanged save for the addition of a plinth.

MEMORIALS

The last aspect of any tour of the battlefields is the memorials erected by the units themselves, or by the French authorities. There are now far too many to list individually and many more were erected in the months prior to and on the 50th anniversary. There are almost 100 unit level memorials and over 200 others spread throughout the battlefield — all shown on *Major & Mrs Holt's Battle Map of Normandy*. (Even journalists and broadcasters are remembered in the Hôtel de Gare at Bernières and at Creully).

Left: **Unveiled on June 6, 1945, the text states that 'This marble plaque was put up in token of gratitude and indebtedness on behalf of the population of Colleville, and also to glorify and immortalise all those who, answering the hopes of one nation, left their families and homeland to drive away the German oppressor. It was to remind future generations of the high deeds of these sublime heroes that Colleville decided to add the name of Marshal Montgomery to their village.' *Right:* One wonders what the Field-Marshal's comments would be about the 1994 monument erected to his memory at Port-en-Bessin!**

The most significant memorials of all are those to the Missing. This one, the Bayeux Memorial, designed by Philip Hepworth, is engraved with the names of 1,805 of the Commonwealth forces (1,534 British, 270 Canadian and 1 South African) who fell in the Battle of Normandy and the subsequent advance to the Seine, and who have no known grave. The connection with William the Conqueror is recalled in the Latin inscription on the frieze of the memorial: 'NOS A GULIELMO VICTI VICTORIS PATRIAM LIBERAVIMUS'. (We, once conquered by William, have now set free the Conqueror's native land.)

And at the Omaha cemetery lies the American Garden of the Missing, comprising five paths dividing the area into four fan-shaped lawn areas. On the surrounding semi-circular wall are engraved 1,557 names commemorating those whose remains were not recovered or, if recovered, could not be identified. Visited by General Eisenhower in August 1963, at the rear of the memorial colonnade is inscribed this extract based on his dedication in the American Roll of Honor in St Paul's Cathedral, London: 'TO THESE WE OWE THE HIGH RESOLVE THAT THE CAUSE FOR WHICH THEY DIED SHALL LIVE.'

FINALLY

Much of the coastline is now vastly different to the way it was in 1944 and, no matter how hard one tries, it is difficult to catch more than a fleeting impression of what it must have been like to have been in Normandy on D-Day. Only those who were there truly know and that is why their memories are so precious if later visitors are to have any hope of sharing the experience. As time marches on, opportunities to meet with veterans will surely fade, so my advice is to get out and talk to them now . . . before it is too late.

'T was on a summer's day — the sixth of June:
I like to be particular in dates,
Not only of the age, and year, but moon;
They are a sort of post-house, where the Fates
Change horses, making History change its tune,
Then spur away o'er empires and o'er states,
Leaving at last not much besides chronology,
Excepting the post-orbits of theology.

'T was on the sixth of June, about the hour
Of half-past six — perhaps still nearer seven . . .

DON JUAN, LORD BYRON, 1788-1824

Bogged tanks and stranded craft have now passed into the pages of history: Hermanville-la-Brèche 1944-1994.

'To these we owe the high resolve that the cause for which they died shall live.'

Complete Index

COMPILED BY PETER B. GUNN

Early post-war photographs by Paul Almasy

Note: page numbers in *italics* refer to illustrations